SAT II
SUBJECT TESTS SUPERCOURSE™

ARCO

SAT* II SUBJECT TESTS SUPERCOURSE™

Thomas H. Martinson
Juliana Fazzone

MACMILLAN
U.S.A.

Previous editions of this book were published under the title
SuperCourse for the College Board Achievement Tests

Second Edition

MACMILLAN
A Prentice Hall/Macmillan Company
15 Columbus Circle
New York, NY 10023

An Arco Book

Library of Congress Cataloging-in-Publication Data

Martinson, Thomas H.
SAT II subject tests SuperCourse / Thomas H. Martinson, Juliana Fazzone.—2nd ed.
p. cm.
Rev. ed. of: SuperCourse for college board achievement tests. c1991.
"An Arco book"—T.p. verso
ISBN 0-671-86403-3
1. College entrance achievement tests—United States—Study guides. I. Fazzone, Juliana. II. Martinson, Thomas H. SuperCourse for college board achievement tests. III. Title. IV. Title: SAT 2 subject tests SuperCourse.
LB2353.6.M37 1994 94-16600
378.1'662—dc20 CIP

Manufactured in the United States of America

10 9 8 7 6 5 4 3 2 1

CONTENTS

Lesson 1

About the SAT II: Subject Tests

What Subjects Are Tested?

Each SAT II Subject Test is designed to measure your mastery of a particular topic. The tests fall into five general categories:

English
- Writing
- Literature

Foreign Languages
- Spanish
- French
- German
- Modern Hebrew
- Latin
- Italian
- Japanese
- Chinese

History and Social Studies
- American History and Social Studies
- World History

Mathematics
- Level I
- Level IIC

Physical Sciences
- Biology
- Chemistry
- Physics

This book provides material that will help you do your best on the subject tests most students take. Each test (except Writing, which includes an essay component) consists entirely of multiple-choice items. The time limit for each test is 60 minutes.

How Are the SAT II Tests Scored?

Scores on SAT II tests (except for the essay component of the Writing Test) are reported on a scale that ranges from 200 (the lowest) to 800 (the highest). This three-digit score is called the scaled score. Your scaled score is a function of your raw score. Your raw score is determined by the number of questions you answer correctly, less an adjustment factor for questions you have answered incorrectly. Questions you omit do not affect your score.

The adjustment factor for wrong answers is a fraction of a point. The fraction depends upon the number of answer choices used in constructing that test. For a test that uses five answer choices, the adjustment for a wrong answer is $-1/4$. For a test that uses four answer choices, the adjustment for a wrong answer is $-1/3$.

How Are SAT II Scores Used?

SAT II scores are used by colleges in two basic ways. First, scores may be used by a college to decide which students to accept. Colleges typically consider a wide range of factors, including grades, SAT scores, teacher recommendations, and extracurricular activities. An SAT II score in a particular subject can give an admissions officer one more measure of an applicant's academic achievements. Second, colleges use scores to guide students in structuring their course of study. For example, a good score on a particular subject test might suggest that a student should be exempted from taking a basic course and proceed directly to a more advanced level.

Which Tests Should You Take?

To decide which tests you should take, consult the catalogs of the colleges to which you are applying. Determine what tests, if any, are required. Additionally, try to determine whether there is any advantage to taking one or another subject test. For example, you may be exempted from taking a freshman English composition course or part of a foreign language requirement if you score well enough on the appropriate test. That would give you more flexibility in structuring your curriculum.

When Should You Take SAT II Tests?

SAT II tests are given five times each year. For test dates and other information, contact your guidance counselor or the College Board:

By mail: College Board SAT Program, Princeton, NJ 08541
By phone: (609) 771-7600 (8:30 A.M.–9:30 P.M. Eastern time)
(415) 849-0959 0950 (8:15 A.M.–4:30 P.M. Pacific time)

You should be aware that not every test is given at each administration. Again, consult the catalogs from the colleges to which you are thinking of applying. A school may have a deadline for receiving scores. In that event, you will have to take the test sufficiently in advance of that deadline to ensure your scores will be received in time.

Multiple-Choice Test-Taking Tips

Work as quickly as possible without sacrificing accuracy. Since your score ultimately depends on the number of questions you answer correctly, you will want to answer as many questions as possible within the time limit. On the other hand, since a fraction of a point is subtracted for each wrong answer, you can't afford to be careless. The practice tests in this book will help you find the right balance between speed and accuracy.

Don't spend too much time on any one item. Each question on the test has the same weight. You don't get any extra credit for a difficult item, so don't waste time on a question that seems too difficult. Skip it! You can come back to it at the end of the test if you have time.

Educated guessing is always a good idea. When your raw score is computed, there is an adjustment for wrong answers, but this adjustment is not intended to be a penalty! The adjustment is designed to make sure that there is no advantage to guessing randomly. Theoretically, if you guessed randomly on every item on a test, your raw score would be zero. (The points subtracted for wrong answers would balance out the lucky guesses.) Therefore, random guessing is probably not a good strategy. On the other hand, if you can eliminate even one answer choice on an item, then statistically it is to your advantage to guess. So random guessing is out; educated guessing is in!

You don't have to answer every question to do well. On an SAT II subject test, you don't have to get 80 percent or more of the items correct to get an A or a B score. For most of the tests, if your raw score (the number of correct answers minus the adjustment for wrong answers) is equal to 80 percent of the maximum raw score, your scaled score will be in the high 600s or the low 700s. And a raw score equal to 50 percent of the maximum is not an F score, but an average or above-average score. Indeed, on the Math Level IIC test, a raw score of 40 out of a possible 50 is a scaled score of about 780!

Code your answers in groups. You will be given a test booklet containing the problems you are to work on and a separate answer sheet for recording your answers. Recording answers is an extra administrative hassle. Be careful! Make sure you code your responses neatly and completely. Don't leave any stray marks on your answer sheet. Finally, code your answers in groups. Work a few items without recording your responses. Just circle the correct choice in your test booklet. Then, as you reach the end of a group of problems or are about to turn the page in your test booklet, take out your answer sheet and tend to the clerical task of transferring choices.

This method of coding in groups is more efficient than entering responses one by one. Additionally, it minimizes the danger of your making a mistake in managing your answer sheet. Of course, as time begins to run out, you should code your responses as you finish each item.

Bring a watch and set it for test time. You don't need a fancy stopwatch to keep track of time on the test. A simple analog watch—one with hands—will be perfect. At the start of the test, just set the minute hand of the watch to "12." This way you can tell at a glance almost exactly how much time you have left.

Familiarize yourself with the directions *before* the test. No additional time is given during the test to read directions. Therefore, it is essential that you know what to expect before you go in. Practicing the materials in this book will help you in this regard. If you are familiar with the layout of the tests you plan to take before you take them, a quick glance at the directions will be sufficient.

Writing Test

Writing Test

The Writing Test includes three different types of multiple-choice questions (Error Recognition, Sentence Correction, and Revision-in-Context) and an essay component. Each of the four question types is discussed below.

The Writing Test is designed to measure your ability to write and to recognize standard written English. It does not presuppose a technical knowledge of English grammar nor require the ability to write prize-winning prose, but it does require the ability to distinguish correct from incorrect usage and the ability to write clearly and correctly. A multiple-choice item, for example, would not ask you to identify the tense of the verb *had sung* as the past perfect form of the verb *to sing,* but you would be expected to recognize that *had sung* is used properly in the sentence "Though she had sung the duet many times before, Natalie was afraid that she might forget the words." And the essay component does not require a lengthy and literate treatment of some esoteric topic, but it does require two to four paragraphs of clear writing on a topic that you will have no trouble discussing.

The Writing Test has the following structure:

Part A	20 minutes	Essay Component
Part B	40 minutes	Multiple-Choice Questions
		1–20 Error Recognition
		21–40 Sentence Correction
		41–50 Revision-in-Context
		51–60 Error Recognition

The multiple-choice part of the Writing Test is scored in the same way as other SAT II tests: your score is a function of the number of questions you answer correctly minus a fraction of the number of questions you answer incorrectly. The Essay Component is graded by two experienced teachers. Each assigns the essay a score from 1 (the lowest) to 6 (the highest), and the essay score is the sum of the two individual scores. The essay score is then combined with the score on the multiple-choice component of the test to produce a single score on the 200-to-800 scale.

Since the Writing Test focuses on standard written English, we will begin by reviewing the important principles that are tested by the Writing Test: grammar, sentence structure, expression, and punctuation. (Punctuation is a matter of obvious concern on the essay component but is not tested by the multiple-choice questions.) After the English review, we will take up each individual question type.

English Review

Grammar

1. Subject-Verb Agreement

As you know, a subject must agree with its verb.

> **EXAMPLE:**
> The professor were traveling in Europe when she received notice of her promotion.

The construction *were traveling* is an error. The subject is *professor,* a singular noun. The verb *were traveling* should be *was traveling.* The sentence should read: "The professor was traveling in Europe. . . ." This example is very simple; the error is easy to spot because the subject and verb are next to each other. Most errors occur when the subject and the verb are separated, when the sentence structure is inverted, or when you cannot recognize whether the subject is singular or plural.

A. When the subject and the verb are separated.

> **EXAMPLES:**
> The professor voted Teacher of the Year by the students were traveling in Europe when she received notice of her promotion.

Professor is singular, yet the verb *were traveling* is plural. This is more difficult to spot in this version of the sentence because of the proximity of the noun *students,* which might be mistaken for the subject of the verb. The sentence sounds correct to the ear: ". . . students were. . . ." The sentence should read: "The professor voted Teacher of the Year by the students was traveling in Europe when she received notice of her promotion."

> Most teachers, unless they have an appointment to a prestigious university, earns relatively less as a teacher than they might in business.

The subject of *earns* is *teachers. Teachers earns* is incorrect. The correct construction is "teachers earn." But it's easy to mistake *university* for the true subject of the sentence. The sentence should read: "Most teachers, unless they have an appointment to a prestigious university, earn relatively less as a teacher than they might in business."

> Many nutritionists now believe that a balanced diet and not large doses of vitamins are the best guarantee of health.

The true subject of the verb *are* is *diet.* The phrase *not large doses* is not part of the subject. The correct construction is: "diet . . . is." The corrected sentence should read: "Many nutritionists now believe that a balanced diet and not large doses of vitamins is the best guarantee of health."

> Television comedies in which there is at least one really detestable character captures the interest of viewers.

The true subject of the verb *captures* is *comedies*. The correct construction is "comedies . . . capture." The correct sentence is: "Television comedies in which there is at least one really detestable character capture the interest of the viewers."

B. When the sentence structure is inverted. An inverted sentence is one in which the verb comes before the subject.

> **EXAMPLES:**
>
> Although this is the wealthiest country in the world, within a few blocks of the White House there is scores of homeless people who live on the streets.

The subject of the verb *is* is not *there* but *scores,* which is plural. The correct construction is: "there are scores." The sentence should read: "Although this is the wealthiest country in the world, within a few blocks of the White House there are scores of homeless people who live on the streets."

> Just a few miles from the factories and skyscrapers stand a medieval castle that looks exactly as it did in the 12th century.

The subject of the verb *stand* is *castle*. The correct construction is: "stands a medieval castle." The sentence should read: "Just a few miles from the factories and skyscrapers stands a medieval castle that looks exactly as it did in the 12th century."

C. When the subject is tricky.

> **EXAMPLES:**
>
> Either the governor or one of his close aides prefer not to have the senator at the head table.

When a subject consists of two or more parts jointed by *or,* the verb must agree with the element that follows the *or.* So for the purpose of agreement, the subject of the sentence is *one.* The correct construction is: "one . . . prefers." The sentence should read: "Either the governor or one of his close aides prefers not to have the senator at the head table."

> Because they were surrounded by layers of excelsior, none of the crystal goblets were broken when the workers dropped the crate.

The subject of the verb were broken is none, and none is singular. The correct construction is: "none . . . was broken." The corrected sentence is: "Because they were surrounded by layers of excelsior, none of the crystal goblets was broken when the workers dropped the crate."

> John, his wife, and the rest of his family plans to attend the awards dinner to be given by the company for the employees with the most seniority.

A subject consisting of two or more elements joined by *and* is plural. The correct construction is: "John, his wife, and the rest of his family plan to attend the awards dinner to be given by the company for the employees with the most seniority."

2. Pronoun Usage

There are three areas of pronoun usage that frequently cause problems and should be reviewed: whether a pronoun has a proper antecedent, agreement between pronoun and antecedent, and choice of pronoun case.

A. A pronoun should have a clear antecedent (also called a referent). The antecedent is the word for which the pronoun substitutes. Setting aside certain idioms—such as *It's raining,* in which the *it* does not have an identifiable antecedent—a pronoun that lacks a clear antecedent is used incorrectly.

EXAMPLES:

During her rise to fame, she betrayed many of her friends; and because of it, very few people trust her.

A pronoun must have an antecedent, but *it* doesn't refer to anything. It "wants" to refer to the woman's *behavior,* but that word doesn't appear in the original sentence. Corrected, the sentence reads: "During her rise to fame, she betrayed many of her friends; and because of her behavior, very few people trust her."

In New York City, they are brusque and even rude but quick to come to one another's assistance in a time of crisis.

This construction might be called the "ubiquitous they." "They" are everywhere: In New York, *they* are rude; in Chicago, *they* like the Cubs; in Atlanta, *they* speak with a southern accent; in California, *they* like parties. "They" do get around! The trouble with this use of "they" is that "they" has no antecedent.

In conversation, the "ubiquitous they" may be acceptable, but not in standard written English. The sentence above is corrected by using the word *people* in place of *they.* So the sentence should read: "In New York City, the people are brusque and even rude but quick to come to one another's assistance in a time of crisis."

Ten years ago, the United States imported ten times as much French wine as Italian wine, but today Americans are drinking more of it.

Here, the antecedent of *it* is unclear. Does the sentence mean to state that Americans are drinking more French wine or more Italian wine? It could be either. The sentence is corrected by specifying which. Corrected, the sentence reads: "Ten years ago, the United States imported ten times as much French wine as Italian wine, but today Americans are drinking more Italian wine."

B. A pronoun must agree with its antecedent, both in number and person.

EXAMPLES:

Although a police officer used to be a symbol of authority, today they receive little respect from most people.

In this sentence the pronoun *they* refers to *police officer*, which is singular. The best way to correct it is to say "he or she." So, the sentence should read: "Although a police officer used to be a symbol of authority, today he or she receives little respect from most people."

> The Abbot was an effective administrator who attempted to assign each monk a task particularly suited to their talents and training.

In this sentence, *their* refers to *each monk*. But *their* is plural and *each monk* is singular. The sentence is corrected by changing *their* to *his*: "The Abbot was an effective administrator who attempted to assign each monk a task particularly suited to his talents and training."

> After three years of college education, a person should be allowed to apply to graduate school, because by that time you are ready to choose a profession.

In the sentence above, *you* refers to *person*. But *you* is a second person pronoun and *person* requires a third-person pronoun. This is called the error of shifting subject. The sentence could be corrected by changing *you are* to *one is* or vice versa: "After three years of college education, a person should be allowed to apply to graduate school, because by that time one is ready to choose a profession."

> If one wishes to apply for a scholarship, you must submit a completed application by March 1.

The error can be corrected by eliminating the incorrect pronoun altogether: "If one wishes to apply for a scholarship, a completed application must be submitted by March 1."

C. Pronouns have case, and a pronoun's function in a sentence determines which case should be used. Subjective case (also called nominative case) pronouns are used as subjects of sentences; objective case pronouns are used as objects (direct objects, indirect objects, and objects of prepositions); and possessive case pronouns are used to show possession.

> **EXAMPLES:**
>
> The judges were unable to make a final decision on a single winner, so they divided first prize between John and he.

In this sentence, *he* cannot serve as the object of a preposition since it is a subject pronoun. The correct pronoun here is the object pronoun *him*. Corrected, the sentence reads: "The judges were unable to make a final decision on a single winner, so they divided first prize between John and him."

> Although Peter had been looking forward to the debate for weeks, a sore throat prevented him taking part.

In this sentence, *him* modifies *taking*, but the correct choice of pronoun is *his*. (When a pronoun modifies a gerund, the *-ing* form of a verb, you must use the possessive case.) The sentence should read: "Although Peter had been looking forward to the debate for weeks, a sore throat prevented his taking part."

3. Adjective versus Adverb

Adjectives are used to modify nouns. Adverbs are used to modify verbs and to modify adjectives.

> **EXAMPLES:**
>
> Some psychologists maintain that a child who has seen violence on television is more likely to react violent in situations of stress.

Violent is intended to modify *to react,* a verb form. So the adverb *violently* is required. The sentence should read: "Some psychologists maintain that a child who has seen violence on television is more likely to react violently in situations of stress."

> The recent created commission has done nothing to address the problem except to approve a new brand of stationery.

In this sentence, *recent* is intended to modify *created,* which is itself an adjective form modifying *commission.* So *recent* should be *recently.* The corrected sentence reads: "The recently created commission has done nothing to address the problem except to approve a new brand of stationery."

4. Double Negatives

Double negatives are not acceptable usage in standard written English.

> **EXAMPLES:**
>
> Not hardly a sound could be heard in the auditorium when the speaker approached the dais to announce the result of the contest.

In this sentence, *not hardly* is a double negative. The sentence must read: "Hardly a sound could be heard in the auditorium when the speaker approached the dais to announce the result of the contest."

> Although she had been hired by the magazine to write book reviews, she knew scarcely nothing about current fiction.

Scarcely nothing is a double negative. The sentence must read: "Although she had been hired by the magazine to write book reviews, she knew scarcely anything about current fiction."

Sentence Structure

1. Parallelism

In a correctly written sentence, similar elements must have a similar form.

> **EXAMPLES:**
>
> To abandon their homes, leave behind their families, and traveling across the ocean required great courage on the part of the immigrants who moved to America.

In this, the three verb forms *abandon, leave,* and *traveling* should be parallel. The sentence is corrected by changing *traveling* to *travel* so that the sentence reads: "To abandon their homes, leave behind their families, and travel across the ocean required great courage on the part of the immigrants who moved to America."

> The review praised the wit, charm, and interpreting of the recitalist but never once mentioned her voice.

In this sentence, *wit* and *charm* are nouns, so *interpreting*, too, should be a noun. The sentence is corrected by changing *interpreting* to *interpretation*. So the corrected sentence reads: "The review praised the wit, charm, and interpretation of the recitalist, but never once mentioned her voice."

> To acknowledge that one has something to learn is taking the first step on the road to true wisdom.

This sentence has a structure similar to a mathematical equation: *This* is the same as *that*. Both parts of the "equation" must have the same form. The sentence is corrected by changing *taking* to *to take*. Corrected, the sentence reads: "To acknowledge that one has something to learn is to take the first step on the road to true wisdom."

2. Split Constructions

A split construction is a sentence structure in which two otherwise separate ideas are joined together by a later element. For example, "The mayor knew or should have known about the corruption." This is a perfectly acceptable split construction in which the ideas *knew* and *should have known* are joined together by the single object *corruption*. In some split constructions, one half or the other never gets completed.

> **EXAMPLES:**
> The students are critical of the dean because he is either unfamiliar or doesn't care about the urgent need for new student housing on campus.

The split construction, *is either unfamiliar or doesn't care*, never gets completed. Leave out the idea following the *or* and the sentence reads: "is unfamiliar the urgent need." Nonsense! The sentence should read: "The students are critical of the dean because he is either unfamiliar with or doesn't care about the urgent need for new student housing on campus."

> Baseball has and probably always will be the sport that symbolizes for people in other countries the American way of life.

The first half of the split verb construction is never completed. Leave out the second idea and the sentence reads "Baseball has the sport." The sentence should read "Baseball has been and probably always will be the sport that symbolizes for people in other countries the American way of life."

3. Verb Tense

The choice of verb tenses in a correctly written sentence reflects the sequence of events described.

EXAMPLES:

The teacher began to discuss the homework assignment when he will be interrupted by the sound of the fire alarm.

The sentence reads: "The teacher began . . . and will be interrupted." One or the other verb tense is wrong. The sentence can be corrected by changing *will be interrupted* to *was interrupted.* Corrected, the sentence reads: "The teacher began to discuss the homework assignment when he was interrupted by the sound of the fire alarm."

The conductor announced that the concert would resume as soon as the soloist replaces the broken string on her violin.

There is a mismatch between the verbs *would resume* and *replaces.* The sentence reads: "the concert would resume as soon as the soloist replaces." Corrected, the sentence might read: "The conductor announced that the concert would resume as soon as the soloist replaced the broken string on her violin."

Many patients begin to show symptoms again after they stopped taking the drug.

This sentence reads: "patients show symptoms after they stopped." The sentence can be corrected by changing *stopped* to *stop.* The sentence would read: "Many patients begin to show symptoms again after they stop taking the drug."

4. Logical Expression

Sometimes a sentence will "want" to say one thing but end up saying something completely illogical.

EXAMPLES:

The great pianist Vladimir Horowitz played the music of the romantic era better than any pianist in history.

As written, the sentence asserts that Vladimir Horowitz was better than anyone—including himself. But that is a logical impossibility. The sentence should read: "The great pianist Vladimir Horowitz played the music of the romantic era better than any other pianist in history."

Educators are now expressing their concern that American schoolchildren prefer watching television to books.

The sentence makes an illogical comparison between *watching television* and *books.* Watching television is an activity; the books are objects. The sentence should read: "Educators are now expressing their concern that American schoolchildren prefer watching television to reading books."

The novels of Nathaniel Hawthorne contain characters that are every bit as sinister and frightening as the master of cinematic suspense, Alfred Hitchcock.

This sentence, too, commits the error just discussed. The sentence literally compares the characters in the novels of Nathaniel Hawthorne to Alfred Hitchcock, the person. The sentence should read: "The novels of Nathaniel Hawthorne contain characters that are every bit as sinister and frightening as those of the master of cinematic suspense, Alfred Hitchcock."

> A Japanese firm has developed a computer so small that users can carry it in their briefcase.

As written, the sentence asserts that all of the users have but a single, jointly owned briefcase. What the sentence means to say is that users can carry the new computer in their briefcases (plural). It should read: "A Japanese firm has developed a computer so small that users can carry it in their briefcases."

Another type of logical error tested is illogical transitions. Words like *therefore, consequently,* and *so* signal logical transitions.

> **EXAMPLE:**
>
> Carlos has a very pleasant personality and he is a talented musician; therefore, he gets good grades in school.

Therefore seems to signal a logical transition from the first two ideas to the third, but there is no logical connection between having a good personality and being a talented musician, on the one hand, and getting good grades, on the other. So the *therefore* is out of place. Substitute *furthermore* for *therefore.* An example of the correct use of *therefore* is: "I see the newspaper is not on the front porch; therefore, my brother must be home already."

Words such as *moreover, further,* and *furthermore* signal the continuation of an idea.

> **EXAMPLE:**
>
> John had already been granted three extensions of the deadline; moreover, the dean refused to grant him another.

The two ideas in this sentence create a contrast, so the *moreover* is out of place. You could correct the sentence by substituting *so* for *moreover.*

However, in spite of, and *instead* are used to contrast ideas.

> **EXAMPLE:**
>
> A poll of students shows that Helen is the top choice for student body president. Helen, however, is likely to win the election.

The *however* seems to signal a contrasting idea, but the logic of the second sentence continues the idea of the first. You can correct the problem by eliminating the *however*: "A poll of students shows that Helen is the top choice for student body president. Consequently, Helen is likely to win the election."

5. Sentence Fragments

A sentence must have a main verb.

> **EXAMPLE:**
>
> Post-modern art, with its vibrant colors and bold shapes, taking its inspiration from artists such as Cézanne but reacting against the pastel indistinctness of the Impressionist canvases.

The original sentence lacks a main verb. This is corrected by changing *taking* and *reacting* (which function as adjectives modifying *art*) to *took* and *reacted.* So, the corrected sentence reads: "Post-modern art, with its vibrant colors and bold shapes, took its inspiration from artists such as Cézanne but reacted against the pastel indistinctness of the Impressionist canvases."

6. Excessive Wordiness

Watch out for excessive wordiness.

> **EXAMPLES:**
>
> After months of separation and being apart, Gauguin finally joined up with Van Gogh in Arles, although Gauguin left a few weeks later.

This sentence is awkward and needlessly wordy. It would be more concise to say: "After months of separation, Gauguin finally joined Van Gogh in Arles but left a few weeks later."

> The nineteenth-century composers of music Wagner and Mahler did more than just write music; as conductors they did their own works.

This sentence is also awkward and needlessly wordy. The very same idea can be expressed more directly: "The nineteenth-century composers Wagner and Mahler did more than just write music; they conducted their own works."

Some expressions are needlessly repetitious.

> **EXAMPLES:**
>
> Since only the ruling party is allowed to vote, its members are able to maintain the existing status quo.
>
> Each year, the geese make their annual migration from Northern Canada to their winter habitats in the United States.
>
> Although the committee met for over two weeks and issued a 50-page report, its findings were of little importance or consequence.

Each of these sentences contains needless repetition. The first can be corrected by eliminating *existing.* The second can be corrected by eliminating either *each year* or *annual.* The third can be corrected by eliminating either *importance* or *consequence.*

7. Misplaced Modifiers

Another common structural error is the misplaced modifier.

> **EXAMPLES:**
>
> Wrapped in several thicknesses of newspaper, packed carefully in a strong cardboard carton, and bound securely with tape, the worker made sure that the fragile figurines would not be broken.

The sentence as originally written suggests that it was the worker who was wrapped, packed, and bound. In general, a modifier should be placed as closely as possible to the part of the sentence it is to modify. The corrected version of this sentence reads: "To make sure that the figurines would not be broken, the worker wrapped them in several thicknesses of newspaper, packed them carefully in a strong cardboard carton, and securely bound the carton with tape."

Riding in a coach and wearing the crown jewels, the crowd cheered the royal couple.

The sentence as originally written suggests that the crowd is wearing the crown jewels and riding in the carriage. This sentence can be made clear by changing it to: "Riding in a coach and wearing the crown jewels, the royal couple was cheered by the crowd."

Correct Expression

Often, sentences are not correct because they are not "idiomatic." An expression that is not idiomatic is one that is not acceptable English for any of several reasons.

1. Wrong Prepositions

In English, as in other languages, only certain prepositions can be used with certain verbs.

EXAMPLES:

In contrast of the prevailing opinion, the editorial places the blame for the strike on the workers and their representatives.

In this sentence, the expression *in contrast of* is not idiomatic. The expression should be *in contrast to*. So the sentence would read: "In contrast to the prevailing opinion, the editorial places the blame for the strike on the workers and their representatives."

Although ballet and modern dance are both concerned in movement in space to musical accompaniment, the training for ballet is more rigorous than that for modern dance.

The expression *concerned in* is not idiomatic. The sentence should read: "Although ballet and modern dance are both concerned with movement in space to musical accompaniment, the training for ballet is more rigorous than that for modern dance."

2. Right Idea, Wrong Word

Make sure you use words that mean what you intend to say. Be careful not to use an incorrect word that sounds like the word you really mean to use.

EXAMPLES:

By midnight the guests still had not been served anything to eat and they were ravishing.

The sentence intends to state that the guests were very hungry, but that is not the meaning of the word *ravishing*. The sentence can be corrected by changing *ravishing* to *ravenous*. Corrected, the sentence reads: "By midnight the guests still had not been served anything to eat and they were ravenous."

> The raise in the number of accidents attributable to drunk drivers has prompted a call for stiffer penalties for driving while intoxicated.

This sentence can be corrected by changing *raise* to *rise*. The corrected sentence reads: "The rise in the number of accidents attributable to drunk drivers has prompted a call for stiffer penalties for driving while intoxicated."

3. Gerund versus Infinitive

The infinitive is the "to" form of a verb, and the gerund is one of the "-ing" forms of a verb. Both are used as nouns. In some circumstances you can use either: "Adding an extra room to the house is the next project," or "To add an extra room to the house is the next project." In some circumstances, however, gerund and infinitive are not interchangeable.

> **EXAMPLES:**
>
> The idea of trying completing the term paper by Friday caused Ken to cancel his plans for the weekend.

Although *completing* can be a noun, here you need the infinitive. The sentence should read: "The idea of trying to complete the term paper by Friday caused Ken to cancel his plans for the weekend."

> Psychologists think that many people eat satisfying a need for affection that is not otherwise fulfilled.

Again you need the infinitive, not the gerund. The sentence should read: "Psychologists think that many people eat to satisfy a need for affection that is not otherwise fulfilled."

4. Unacceptable Expressions

There are a few expressions that are heard frequently in conversation that are regarded as low-level usage and unacceptable in standard written English.

> **EXAMPLES:**
>
> Being that the hour was late, we agreed to adjourn the meeting and reconvene at nine o'clock the following morning.

Being that is not acceptable in standard written English. The sentence is corrected by changing the phrase to *Since*. The sentence should read: "Since the hour was late, we agreed to adjourn the meeting and reconvene at nine o'clock the following morning."

> Why some whales beach themselves in what seems to be a kind of suicide remains a mystery to marine biologists.

Why cannot be the subject of a sentence. The sentence is corrected by changing *Why* to *That*. So, the sentence now reads: "That some whales beach themselves in what seems to be a kind of suicide remains a mystery to marine biologists."

> The reason Harriet fired her secretary is because he was frequently late and spent too much time on personal phone calls.

Because cannot introduce a noun clause. The sentence is corrected by changing *because* to *that.* The corrected sentence reads: "The reason Harriet fired her secretary is that he was frequently late and spent too much time on personal phone calls."

> I read in a magazine where scientists believe that they have discovered a new subatomic particle.

Where cannot introduce a noun clause. The sentence is corrected by changing *where* to *that.* So the corrected sentence reads: "I read in a magazine that scientists believe that they have discovered a new subatomic particle."

Punctuation

1. Commas

Use a comma before *and, but, so, yet, or,* and *nor* when those words are used to join two main clauses.

> **EXAMPLES:**
>
> I think that Doré's illustrations of Dante's *Divine Comedy* are excellent, but my favorite drawing is "Don Quixote in His Library."
>
> Practically all nitrates are crystalline and readily soluble, and they are characterized by marked decrepitation when heated on charcoals by a blowpipe.

The general rule stated above should be qualified in two respects. First, when the two clauses joined by the conjunction are very short, the comma is optional. In the following example, both sentences are correct.

> **EXAMPLE:**
>
> The door was ajar and the house had been ransacked.
> The door was ajar, and the house had been ransacked.

Second, if either clause itself contains commas, you may need to use a semicolon before the conjunction for clarity.

> **EXAMPLE:**
>
> Because many diseases and insects cause serious damage to crops, special national legislation has been passed to provide for the quarantine of imported plants; and under provisions of various acts, inspectors are placed at ports of entry to prevent smugglers from bringing in plants that might be dangerous.

Given the length of the two clauses and the fact that each clause contains a comma, you should use a semicolon following *plants,* rather than a comma.

Use commas to separate the elements of a series.

EXAMPLES:

A full train crew consists of a motorman, a brakeman, a conductor, and two ticket takers.

The procedure requires that you open the outer cover plate, remove the thermostat, replace the broken switch, and then replace the thermostat.

Use a comma to separate a subordinate clause at the beginning of a sentence from the main clause.

EXAMPLES:

After Peter finished painting the bird feeder, he and Jack hung it from a limb of the oak tree.

When Pat explained to his mother that ten was the highest mark given on the entrance test, she breathed a sigh of relief.

If the subordinate clause follows the main clause, you do not need to set it off with a comma.

EXAMPLE:

Tim hopes to score well on the exam because he plans to go to an Ivy League school.

Use a comma after a long introductory phrase.

EXAMPLES:

In this impoverished region with its arid soil, a typical diet may contain only 800 calories per day.

At the height of the moral war against sensational journalism, Horace Greeley moved into the forefront of the journalistic picture.

Regardless of their length, use a comma after introductory gerunds, participles, and infinitives.

EXAMPLES:

Begun in 1981 and completed in 1985, the bridge provided the first link between the island and the mainland.

To slow the bleeding, Van tied a tourniquet around the lower portion of the leg.

Use commas to set off nonrestrictive clauses and phrases and other parenthetical elements.

EXAMPLES:

Niagara Falls, which forms part of the border between the United States and Canada, was the site of a saw mill built by the French in 1725.

The second Nicene Council, the seventh ecumenical council of the Church, was summoned by the Empress Irene and her son Constantine.

The last hope of the French expired when Metz, along with 180,000 soldiers, was surrendered by Bazaine.

Secretary of State Acheson, however, made a reasoned defense of the treaty.

(Nonrestrictive clauses and phrases are ones not essential to the meaning of the main clause. In general, if you can omit the material without changing the meaning of the main clause, then the material is nonrestrictive and should be set off by commas.)

These rules summarize the most important uses of commas. If you use them in just these situations, then you won't make a mistake in their use. In particular, do **NOT** use commas in the following situations.

Do not use a comma to separate a subject from its verb.

EXAMPLE:

Until the end of the 18th century, the only musicians in Norway, were simple, unsophisticated peasants who traveled about.

(The underlined comma is incorrect.)

Do not use commas to set off restrictive or necessary clauses or phrases.

EXAMPLES:

Prizes will be awarded in each event, and the participant, who compiles the greatest overall total, will receive a special prize.

Since learning of the dangers of caffeine, neither my wife nor I have consumed any beverage, containing caffeine.

(The underlined commas are incorrect.)

Do not use a comma in place of a conjunction.

EXAMPLE:

After months of separation, Gauguin finally joined Van Gogh in Arles in October of 1888, Gauguin left a few weeks later.

The sentence is incorrect because clauses cannot be spliced together using only a comma. If you want to join two main clauses, you can use a conjunction (such as *and*) plus a comma or semicolon or even just a semicolon. The sentence above could have been written: "After months of separation, Gauguin finally joined Van Gogh in Arles in October of 1888, but he left a few weeks later."

2. Semicolons

One use of the semicolon has already been mentioned: use a semicolon between main clauses linked by a coordinate conjunction (*and, but,* etc.) when the main clauses are complex; e.g., when they themselves contain commas. (See above.) Another use of semicolons is to separate two main clauses that are not linked by a coordinate conjunction.

> **EXAMPLES:**
>
> He grew up on a farm in Nebraska; he is now the captain of a Navy ship.
> The Smithtown players cheered the referee's decision; the Stonybrook players booed it.

Notice that in these examples, each clause separated by the semicolon could stand alone as an independent sentence:

> He grew up on a farm in Nebraska. He is now the captain of a Navy ship.
> The Smithtown players cheered the referee's decision. The Stonybrook players booed it.

Unless each clause can function as an independent sentence, it probably is wrong to use a semicolon.

> When John entered the room; everyone stood up.
> Clem announced that the prize would be donated to Harbus House; a well-known charity.

The semicolons in the examples above are used incorrectly. Notice that the elements separated by the semicolons cannot stand as independent sentences. These sentences can be corrected by using commas in place of the semicolons.

3. Colons

A colon may be used to introduce or to call attention to elaboration or explanation.

> **EXAMPLES:**
>
> The teacher announced that the course would require three papers: one on Shakespeare, one on Dickens, and one on a contemporary writer.
>
> Will's suggestion was truly democratic: let everyone serve as chair for one meeting.

Be careful not to use a colon to introduce or call attention to material that is already signaled by some other element of the sentence.

> **EXAMPLES:**
>
> The seemingly tranquil lane has been the scene of many crimes including: two assaults, three robberies, and one murder.
>
> In addition to test scores, college admissions officers take into consideration many other factors such as: grades, extracurricular activities, and letters of recommendation.

In each example, the colon is used incorrectly because the special material is already signaled by some other element in the sentence. These sentences are correctly written as follows:

> The seemingly tranquil lane has been the scene of many crimes, including two assaults, three robberies, and one murder.
>
> In addition to test scores, college admissions officers take into consideration many other factors such as grades, extracurricular activities, and letters of recommendation.

4. Periods

The only use you should have for a period on the test is to mark the end of a sentence. Make sure, however, that any underlined material that includes a period does not create a sentence fragment.

> **EXAMPLE:**
>
> Peter notified Elaine. The guidance counselor, that he had been accepted.

The first period creates a sentence fragment out of what follows. The sentence can be corrected as follows:

> Peter notified Elaine, the guidance counselor, that he had been accepted.

5. Dashes

Dashes can be used to set off for emphasis or clarity an explanatory, illustrative, or parenthetical remark.

> **EXAMPLES:**
>
> Careful attention to the details of one's personal appearance—neatly pressed clothing, shined shoes, and well-groomed hair—is an important part of preparing for a job interview.
>
> Many colleges—including the nation's top schools—set aside a certain number of first-year places for students who show academic promise in spite of low test scores.
>
> Peanuts—blanched or lightly roasted—add an interesting texture and taste to garden salads.

The dashes in the sentences above have a function similar to commas when they are used to set off parenthetical remarks. The difference between the two is a matter of emphasis. The dashes mark a more dramatic shift or interruption of thought. Do not, however, mix dashes and commas:

> Peanuts—blanched or lightly roasted, add an interesting texture and taste to garden salads.

The example above is incorrect. You must use either two dashes or two commas.

Question Types

The Essay

The Essay component of the Writing Test is only 20 minutes long, and that is both bad news and good news. The bad news is that you obviously cannot hope to write very much in 20 minutes nor expect that what you write will be highly polished. The good news is that you aren't expected to write very much, nor is it expected that the essay will be highly polished. Instead, the graders will look upon your essay for what it is: a first draft.

You are required to write your essay on an assigned topic, a topic that you will not see until the testing session begins. Because you will not know what your assigned topic is in advance, there is no way to prepare your essay before the test begins. The essay topics do not require any special knowledge, and they do not have right and wrong answers. Instead, these topics are what teachers often call "prompts." For example:

> Human beings are often cruel, but they also have the capacity for kindness and compassion. In my opinion, an example that demonstrates this capacity was ______.

Assignment: Complete the statement above with an example from current affairs, history, literature, or your own personal experience. Then write a well-organized essay explaining *why* you regard that event favorably.

The sample topic is so broad that you can almost certainly think of something to write.

Essay Strategies

1. Write only on the assigned topic. The directions for this part of the Writing Test are very clear on this score: you must write on the assigned topic. On the other hand, that should not be difficult. Given that the assigned topic is "vacuous," you should have no problem coming up with something to write.

2. Let the topic be your prompt. As noted above, the topic is intended to be a prompt, and prompts are designed to encourage students to write. In fact, if you pay careful attention to the language of the prompt, it can actually help you to get started. Consider our example above. The topic explicitly invites you to choose an example of kindness or compassion from history, current events, literature, or even personal experience. Thus, you could write about the end of a war (history), or a mission of humanitarian aid (current events), or the self-sacrifice of a fictional character (literature), or even about the day that your family helped a stranded motorist (personal experience). What you have to say is not as important as how you say it.

3. Do not try to do too much. In twenty minutes, you just are not going to be able to write a great work of literature—so don't try. At the most, you will probably be able to write only three or four paragraphs. It is better to finish what you start than to try to do too much and run out of time before you can finish. Ideally, you want to have the opportunity to proofread your essay before time is called.

4. Organize your essay before you begin to write. Given the twenty-minute time limit, you just are not going to have time to write and then *rewrite* the essay. So before you begin to write, you should take a moment to organize the essay in your mind. (You won't have time to make an elaborate written outline.)

The first step in organizing the essay is to identify the two or three (perhaps four) important points that you want to make. Next, you must decide on the order of presentation for those points. Then, in your writing, as you come to each important point you should pause to organize the details of that part of the discussion.

5. Organize your ideas into paragraphs. Effective use of paragraphs is the hallmark of a good writer. Paragraphs are important because they help the reader to understand the writer's meaning. To illustrate the point with an analogy, imagine a grocery store in which items are not organized into sections. In this store, there is no fresh produce *section*; there is no canned goods *section*; there is no baked goods *section*; there is no frozen foods *section*. Consequently, a single bin might hold bunches of bananas, cans of beans, loaves of bread, and frozen turkeys. And this disorganization characterizes every bin, shelf, rack, and refrigerated case in the store. As you can well imagine, shopping in our imaginary store would be very difficult—if not impossible. So, too, essays without paragraphs are very difficult—if not impossible—to understand.

How do you organize the essay into paragraphs? As was noted in our discussion of the preceding point, your essay should contain two, three, or perhaps four important points. Each important point should be treated in its own paragraph.

6. Write grammatically. The principles of grammar covered above should be used as a checklist as you proofread your essay. At a minimum, your proofreading checklist should include the following:

Does every sentence have a main verb?
Does the main verb agree with its subject?
Does every pronoun have a clear referent and does each pronoun agree with its referent?

If possible, your checklist should also include the other writing principles reviewed above.

7. Strive for clarity of expression. Simple, direct sentences are less likely to get you into trouble than complex, convoluted ones. For an exercise such as this, any sentence more complicated than a sentence with two independent clauses joined by a conjunction such as "and" or "but" or a sentence with one dependent and one independent clause joined by a conjunction such as "while" or "although" is an invitation to error. Unless you are confident in your ability to keep all of the elements of a more complicated sentence under control, you should prefer a simpler method of expression.

8. Punctuate correctly. Again, you can organize the principles of punctuation reviewed above into a checklist for proofreading purposes. Furthermore, since you are in charge of the writing of the essay, you can choose to avoid punctuation errors. If you are unsure how to punctuate a particular construction, choose an alternative.

9. Avoid slang and low-level usage. The Writing Test is a test of standard written English, so you should avoid slang and other low-level usage.

10. Write legibly. While it may not be literally true that neatness counts, it is almost certainly true that an illegible essay will not receive a good grade. Even if you can't do calligraphy, you should be able to write legibly.

Error Recognition

Error recognition questions are the easiest of the three multiple-choice question types. You need only determine whether a sentence contains an error; you do not have to figure out how to correct the error. Here are the directions for error recognition:

Directions: Of the sentences in this part, some are correct and others contain errors of grammar, usage, diction (choice of words), or idiom (correctness of expression). If the sentence contains an error, the error is underlined and lettered. Assume that any part of the sentence that is not underlined is correct and cannot be changed. In analyzing a sentence, keep in mind the requirements of standard written English.

If you find an error in a sentence, select the one underlined part that must be changed in order to make the sentence correct and darken the corresponding space on your answer sheet. If the sentence does not contain an error, darken space (E) on your answer sheet.

EXAMPLES: SAMPLE ANSWERS

I. The principal asked ten of we students
A B
to enter the public speaking contest. No error
C D E

I. Ⓐ ● Ⓒ Ⓓ Ⓔ

II. He saves every penny so that his children
A B C
could someday go to college. No error
D E

II. Ⓐ Ⓑ Ⓒ ● Ⓔ

Error Recognition Strategies

1. Begin by reading the entire sentence through quickly. Often your "ear" for English will turn up an obvious error.

EXAMPLE:

Because she was preparing for an important trial, Mary had
A B
scarcely no time to spend with her family. No error
C D E

A quick read through of this sentence should turn up the error in (C). "Scarcely no" is a double negative.

2. If your first reading doesn't reveal an error, take a closer look at each of the four underlined parts lettered (A) through (D). Ask yourself whether there is an obvious error in any one of those parts.

EXAMPLE:

The college hired Irving to teach sociology because he had wrote
A B C
the standard college text on the subject. No error
D E

The error here appears in (C). Since *wrote* is not the past participle of *to write,* there is no English sentence in which *had wrote* would be correct. Thus, you know that (C) is the correct answer without having to worry about how the various parts of the sentence work together.

EXAMPLE:

In contrasting to the relatively mild weather we enjoyed last
A B C
winter, the weather this winter has included a lot of ice and
D
snow. No error
E

The correct answer to this example is (A), and you don't have to look any farther than the first three words of the sentence to see this. The phrase "in contrasting to" is not idiomatic English.

3. Many times a usage is wrong only because of its connection to something else in the sentence. You have to be alert for this possibility.

EXAMPLE:

After (A) the heavy (B) rains, the construction supervisor, concerned about (C) the moisture content of the soil, ordering (D) new soil samples. No error (E)

The correct answer to this example is (D). The sentence as written is only a fragment—it lacks a main verb. To figure out how to correct the error requires that you pay attention to the entire structure. You can turn the fragment into a complete sentence by changing *ordering* to *ordered.*

4. If you suspect there is an error in the sentence but can't put your finger on it, use the following checklist:

Error Recognition Checklist

Verbs

Does the sentence have a main verb? If not, is there a verb form underlined that could be changed into a main verb?
If any verbs are underlined, do they agree with their subjects?
If any verbs are underlined, are they in the correct tense?

Pronouns

If any pronouns are underlined, do they have referents? (Be specific!)
If any pronouns are underlined, are they in the right case?
If any pronouns are underlined, do they agree with their referents?

Adjectives and Adverbs

If an adjective or adverb is underlined, is it correctly modifying a verb or another adjective?

Prepositions

If a preposition is underlined, is its use idiomatic?

Conjunction

If a conjunction is underlined, is its use consistent with the logic of the sentence?

Introductory Modifiers

If the sentence has an introductory modifier, is the modifier close to what it modifies?

Comparisons

If the sentence makes a comparison, are like things being compared?

Parallelism

If the sentence includes a series of ideas, do the ideas have the same form?

Diction

Do the underlined words mean what the sentence intends for them to mean?

5. Don't find errors where there are none. About one-fifth of the sentences in the error recognition parts are correct! If you can't put your finger on an error, choose answer (E).

Sentence Correction

Sentence correction items not only ask you to find errors, they require that you correct the errors. Here are the directions for the sentence correction parts of the test:

Directions: Each item in this part consists of a sentence, a part or all of which is underlined, followed by five ways of phrasing the underlined material. Answer choice (A) always repeats the original. The other four answer choices are different. If you think that the original is better than any of the alternatives, you should choose answer (A). Otherwise, you should choose the letter of the alternative you consider superior. Then darken the corresponding space on your answer sheet.

This part is a test of correctness and effectiveness of expression. You should pay attention to grammar, choice of words, sentence construction, and punctuation. Choose the answer that best expresses the intended meaning of the original sentence and produces the most effective sentence, one that is clear and precise and is neither awkward nor ambiguous.

EXAMPLE: SAMPLE ANSWER

Allen visiting his cousin in France last summer. Ⓐ Ⓑ Ⓒ Ⓓ ●

(A) visiting
(B) is visiting
(C) does visit
(D) a visit
(E) visited

Sentence Correction Strategies

1. Begin by reading the original sentence to comprehend its overall meaning. As you do this, let your ear alert you to possible errors. If you find an error, decide how you would correct it. Then study the answer choices to find the one that makes your anticipated correction.

2. Do not bother reading answer choice (A). Choice (A) always repeats the underlined part of the original, so there is no point in reading it.

3. If you do not find an error, use the checklist given above for error recognition items. Add to that checklist:

Conciseness

Does the sentence use more words than necessary?

Directness

Can the sentence be worded more directly?

4. Compare answer choices. If you are not sure whether the original contains an error, or if you are not sure how an error should be corrected, look to the answer choices for help. Ask yourself what makes one choice different from the others and whether that difference is good or bad.

5. Do not be afraid to select choice (A). Approximately one-fifth of the correct answers in the sentence correction questions will be (A)s. This means that about one-fifth of the sentences will be correct as originally written. If you can't put your finger on an error, and if you see no good reason for making the changes suggested by choices (B) through (E), select choice (A)!

Revision-in-Context

Revision-in-Context includes a passage that is intended to represent an early draft of a student essay. Since the passage is a draft, it contains errors and is in need of revision. Some questions focus on individual sentences and, like Error Recognition and Sentence Correction items, test grammar, sentence structure, and expression. Other Revision-in-Context questions ask about the development and organization of the passage.

Here is a sample Revision-in-Context passage with questions:

Directions: Questions 1 through 5 are based upon the following passage. You may consider the passage to be an early draft of a student essay. Some of the sentences need to be corrected or revised. Read the passage; then answer the questions.

Some questions require decisions about the structure of individual sentences. Other questions require decisions about the organization and development of the passage or about the appropriateness of particular language in light of the overall tone of the passage. For each question, choose the answer that best expresses the intended meaning clearly and precisely and that follows the conventions of standard written English.

EXAMPLE

(1) In the United States, everyone who drives or rides in a motor vehicle or who even walks the streets is at risk of injury or even death from a motor vehicle accident. (2) This risk is magnified because many motorists drink and drive. (3) In fact, almost one-half of fatally injured drivers have a blood-alcohol concentration of 0.1 percent or higher. (4) (A level of 0.1 percent or higher means the driver is intoxicated.) (5) What can be done about this problem?

(6) It has been suggested that higher taxes on alcoholic beverages would reduce overall consumption and for the reason that overall consumption is

reduced the number of drunk drivers would be reduced. (7) This approach is wrong for two reasons. (8) First, motorists who drink to excess and then drive in all probability will not be deterred by the extra cost of a drink. (9) Second, the tax would penalize everyone who uses alcohol and not just those who abuse it.

(10) It has also been suggested that stricter law enforcement would reduce the problem. (11) It has even been argued that police should be able to stop motorists at random and administer breath tests. (12) This approach, however, violating the rights of innocent individuals. (13) Plus, the National Highway Traffic Safety Administration estimates that even with stricter law enforcement there would still be about 700 drunk drivers for every arrest.

(14) While strict law enforcement must be part of the solution, a real solution must also include education. (15) People must be taught the dangers to themselves and to others of drunk driving.

1. Which of the following would be the best way of combining the underlined portions of sentences (3) and (4)?

   (3) In fact, almost one-half of fatally injured drivers have a blood-alcohol concentration of 0.1 percent or higher. (4) (A level of 0.1 percent or higher means the driver is intoxicated.)

   (A) higher, meaning the driver is intoxicated.
   (B) higher, in that the driver is intoxicated.
   (C) higher, a level indicating the driver is intoxicated.
   (D) higher—the driver is intoxicated.
   (E) higher (intoxicated).

2. Which of the following best describes the writer's purpose in posing a question at the end of the first paragraph?

   (A) To solicit the reader's assistance in solving a problem
   (B) To alert the reader that the essay will discuss one or more options
   (C) To summarize points already made in the essay
   (D) To signal the reader that no solution is possible
   (E) To highlight the hazards of drunk driving

3. Which of the following is the best revision of the underlined portion of sentence (6)?

   (6) It has been suggested that higher taxes on alcoholic beverages would reduce overall consumption and for the reason that overall consumption is reduced the number of drunk drivers would be reduced.

   (A) but the number of drunk drivers would be reduced.
   (B) and thus the number of drunk drivers.
   (C) and therefore reducing the number of drunk drivers.
   (D) and consequently drunk drivers would be reduced.
   (E) and for that reason it would be reduced.

4. Which of the following is the best revision of sentence (12)?

   (A) This approach, furthermore, violating the rights of innocent individuals.
   (B) This approach, however, would be violating the rights of innocent individuals.
   (C) This approach, however, would violate the rights of innocent individuals.
   (D) The rights of innocent individuals, however, would have been violated by this approach.
   (E) Innocent individuals' rights, however, violated by this approach.

5. Which of the following would NOT be an appropriate substitute for the word "Plus" in sentence (13)?

(A) Moreover
(B) Further
(C) Additionally
(D) On the other hand
(E) In addition

Explanations for Questions 1–5

1. (C) (C) combines the two sentences by making the idea in the second sentence an appositive phrase in the first sentence (concentration . . . , a level). Thus, the phrase has a logical connection to the main part of the sentence. The other choices are wrong because they have no such connection to the rest of the sentence. For example, (A) attempts to use a participle to modify something in the main part of the sentence, but it really doesn't have anything to modify. (B), (D), and (E) fail for similar reasons. The phrase added to the main part of the sentence lacks a logical connection to that part of the sentence.

2. (B) This question asks about the overall development of the passage. The writer begins by describing a problem and then asks how to solve the problem. The question at the end of the paragraph one alerts the reader that the writer intends to discuss one or more possible solutions to the problem.

3. (B) The original sentence is awkward and very wordy. (B) states the intended meaning clearly, concisely, and directly.

4. (C) As originally written, (12) is a fragment rather than a sentence: it contains no main (conjugated) verb. (C) makes the needed correction. (B), (D), and (E) are incorrect because the choice of verbs for (12) is inconsistent with the form of the other verbs in the passage. (A) not only fails to correct the error of the original, it introduces another error: "furthermore" signals a continuation of a thought rather than the reversal that is clearly intended by the writer here.

5. (D) In the third paragraph, the writer is arguing against the idea that stricter law enforcement would offer a complete solution to the problem of drunk driving and makes two points: first, stricter enforcement might violate someone's rights; second, stricter enforcement is not completely effective. The second idea, therefore, represents a continuation of the train of thought; but "On the other hand" signals a reversal of thought. Every other choice contains a transitional word or phrase that signals a continuation of thought.

Revision-in-Context Strategies

1. Begin by reading the entire passage. During your initial reading, do not try to identify specific errors in the essay. To be sure, you may identify one or more errors during your first read-through, but the main purpose of the read-through is to become familiar with the structure and development of the essay. The questions that follow will focus your attention on those parts of the passage that the test-writer thinks are in need of correction or revision.

2. Pay careful attention to the relationships between and among sentences. One of the features that distinguishes Revision-in-Context questions from Error Recognition and Sentence Correction is the use of a context, namely, the passage. The use of a passage allows for questions that test your appreciation of the connections between sentences in an essay. (Question 5 is a good example.)

3. Use a checklist of errors. For Revision-in-Context items, you can use the checklist of errors developed for Error Recognition. Add to the checklist the following:

Verbs

Is the tense of the verb in the sentence to be revised consistent with the tense of other verbs in the passage?

Is the form of the verb in the sentence to be revised parallel with that of other verbs in the passage?

Pronouns

If the sentence to be revised contains a pronoun, is its referent in the preceding sentence? Does the pronoun, in fact, have a referent? Does it agree with its referent?

Diction

If a suggested revision includes a choice of specific words, is your choice consistent with the overall tone of the passage?

4. Pay careful attention to the overall development and organization of the passage. Again, the use of a passage for this question type allows for questions about development and organization. (Questions 2 and 5 are examples of such questions.) To your checklist you should also add:

Organization

Does a revision improve the logical development of the passage by presenting ideas in a more coherent way?

If a revised sentence includes a transitional phrase, does the phrase signal the appropriate connection between the first idea and the second?

If a revised sentence includes a paragraphing decision, does the revision ensure that each new paragraph created has one and only one main topic?

Writing Test Answer Sheet

1	A	B	C	D	E	46	A	B	C	D	E
2	A	B	C	D	E	47	A	B	C	D	E
3	A	B	C	D	E	48	A	B	C	D	E
4	A	B	C	D	E	49	A	B	C	D	E
5	A	B	C	D	E	50	A	B	C	D	E
6	A	B	C	D	E	51	A	B	C	D	E
7	A	B	C	D	E	52	A	B	C	D	E
8	A	B	C	D	E	53	A	B	C	D	E
9	A	B	C	D	E	54	A	B	C	D	E
10	A	B	C	D	E	55	A	B	C	D	E
11	A	B	C	D	E	56	A	B	C	D	E
12	A	B	C	D	E	57	A	B	C	D	E
13	A	B	C	D	E	58	A	B	C	D	E
14	A	B	C	D	E	59	A	B	C	D	E
15	A	B	C	D	E	60	A	B	C	D	E
16	A	B	C	D	E	61	A	B	C	D	E
17	A	B	C	D	E	62	A	B	C	D	E
18	A	B	C	D	E	63	A	B	C	D	E
19	A	B	C	D	E	64	A	B	C	D	E
20	A	B	C	D	E	65	A	B	C	D	E
21	A	B	C	D	E	66	A	B	C	D	E
22	A	B	C	D	E	67	A	B	C	D	E
23	A	B	C	D	E	68	A	B	C	D	E
24	A	B	C	D	E	69	A	B	C	D	E
25	A	B	C	D	E	70	A	B	C	D	E
26	A	B	C	D	E	71	A	B	C	D	E
27	A	B	C	D	E	72	A	B	C	D	E
28	A	B	C	D	E	73	A	B	C	D	E
29	A	B	C	D	E	74	A	B	C	D	E
30	A	B	C	D	E	75	A	B	C	D	E
31	A	B	C	D	E	76	A	B	C	D	E
32	A	B	C	D	E	77	A	B	C	D	E
33	A	B	C	D	E	78	A	B	C	D	E
34	A	B	C	D	E	79	A	B	C	D	E
35	A	B	C	D	E	80	A	B	C	D	E
36	A	B	C	D	E	81	A	B	C	D	E
37	A	B	C	D	E	82	A	B	C	D	E
38	A	B	C	D	E	83	A	B	C	D	E
39	A	B	C	D	E	84	A	B	C	D	E
40	A	B	C	D	E	85	A	B	C	D	E
41	A	B	C	D	E	86	A	B	C	D	E
42	A	B	C	D	E	87	A	B	C	D	E
43	A	B	C	D	E	88	A	B	C	D	E
44	A	B	C	D	E	89	A	B	C	D	E
45	A	B	C	D	E	90	A	B	C	D	E

THE WRITING TEST

Part A—20 Minutes

Directions: You have twenty minutes to plan and write an essay on the topic assigned below. DO NOT WRITE ON ANY OTHER TOPIC. AN ESSAY ON ANOTHER TOPIC IS NOT ACCEPTABLE.

"Advances in technology sometimes generate unfavorable consequences, but in general technology benefits humankind."

Assignment: Name one way in which technology benefits humankind using an example taken from history, current affairs, literature, or your own experience. Then write a well-organized essay explaining *why* you regard the benefit you cite as a benefit.

Part B—40 minutes

Directions: Of the sentences in this part, some are correct and others contain errors of grammar, usage, diction (choice of words), or idiom (correctness of expression). If the sentence contains an error, the error is underlined and lettered. Assume that any part of the sentence that is not underlined is correct and cannot be changed. In analyzing a sentence, keep in mind the requirements of standard written English. If you find an error in a sentence, select the one underlined part that must be changed in order to make the sentence correct and darken the corresponding space on your answer sheet. If the sentence does not contain an error, darken space (E) on your answer sheet.

EXAMPLES: SAMPLE ANSWERS

I. The principal asked (A) ten of we (B) students to enter (C) the public speaking (D) contest. No error (E)

I. (A) ● (C) (D) (E)

II. He saves every (A) penny so that (B) his (C) children could (D) someday go to college. No error (E)

II. (A) (B) (C) ● (E)

1. If Mary Outerbridge would not have seen (A) English officers playing (B) tennis in Bermuda where (C) she was vacationing (D) at the time, she would not have introduced the game to America. No error (E)

2. When we consider (A) the miracles of modern science, we find it hard to imagine that (B) in 1349 the Black Death killed (C) one-third of England's (D) population. No error (E)

3. When (A) the critics wrote (B) critical reviews of the Broadway opening (C) of the rock star's new musical, neither the producer nor the director were (D) available for an interview. No error (E)

4. Those who are successful in business (A) often discover that (B) wealth and fame do not guarantee (C) happiness and learning (D) that peace of mind is important. No error (E)

5. About 3500 B.C., ancient Egypt made great progress in agriculture after they (A) adopted several new techniques of cultivation among which (B) were (C) raking, plowing, and manuring. (D) No error (E)

6. In (A) the southwest corner of the cemetery, where the honeysuckle vines have all but (B) covered the grave markers, lays (C) the body of the county's greatest (D) war hero. No error (E)

GO ON TO THE NEXT PAGE

7. The final number of the musical, a duet, was written [A] by Sue and is sung by she [B] and Reginald, the male lead, as [C] the other members of the cast take their [D] bows. No error [E]

8. The owner of the property, who had farmed [A] the land for more than [B] 40 years, listened to [C] the company's offer but said that he could not answer definite [D] without further consideration. No error [E]

9. Immediately after the legislators freezed [A] the level of benefits, citizens groups began contacting [B] their [C] members to encourage them to write letters of protest to [D] their representatives in Congress. No error [E]

10. Since the treasurer and him [A] had already discussed [B] the details of the financial report, Robert felt that it was not necessary for him [C] to attend [D] the budget meeting. No error [E]

11. The history of the ancient Egyptians, as recorded by [A] graphic drawings called [B] hieroglyphics, describe [C] in great detail [D] the burial of King Tutankhamen's body in a sarcophagus of wood and gold. No error [E]

12. The conditions of [A] the subway system having been improved [B] dramatically [C] over the past three years, but [D] much work still remains to be done. No error [E]

13. Introduced at the last moment [A] by the Scholastic Council was [B] a demand that [C] the college allocate funds for a day-care center and a demand that the college hire [D] more minority faculty members. No error [E]

14. Summarily rejecting [A] the demands of the students for a greater voice in determining university [B] policy, the dean now worries that [C] her decision might result [D] in new student demonstrations. No error [E]

15. The dog has been replaced [A] by the cat as the pet of choice for Americans because [B] cats are [C] more independent and require less care than [D] dogs. No error [E]

16. Because many modern actors study [A] method acting, a system devised [B] by Stanislavsky, their [C] interpretations of the role of Hamlet differ from Shakespeare's time [D]. No error [E]

17. During [A] the second half of the nineteenth century, waves of immigration in [B] the United States brought [C] hundreds of thousands of foreigners to America's cities and created [D] the condition termed the "melting pot." No error [E]

18. The governor's oratorical skill, which [A] has helped him to win [B] several elections, comes [C] either from his college debating experience and [D] from an in-depth knowledge of the issues. No error [E]

GO ON TO THE NEXT PAGE

19. The decade of the 1920s was <u>an important one</u> (A) for English literature, for during that time a large <u>amount</u> (B) of works now considered classics were written <u>by</u> (C) great writers <u>such as</u> (D) Ezra Pound, D.H. Lawrence, and T.S. Eliot. <u>No error</u> (E)

20. <u>Although</u> (A) we usually <u>associate</u> (B) the name of Athens with democracy, <u>it</u> (C) is important to remember that slavery <u>was</u> (D) a key element in that city's economy. <u>No error</u> (E)

GO ON TO THE NEXT PAGE

Directions: Each item in this part consists of a sentence, a part or all of which is underlined, followed by five ways of phrasing the underlined material. Answer choice (A) always repeats the original. The other four answer choices are different. If you think that the original is better than any of the alternatives, you should choose answer (A). Otherwise, you should choose the letter of the alternative you consider superior. Then darken the corresponding space on your answer sheet.

This part is a test of correctness and effectiveness of expression. You should pay attention to grammar, choice of words, sentence construction, and punctuation. Choose the answer that best expresses the intended meaning of the original sentence and produces the most effective sentence, one that is clear and precise and is neither awkward nor ambiguous.

EXAMPLE:

Allen visiting his cousin in France last summer.

(A) visiting
(B) is visiting
(C) does visit
(D) a visit
(E) visited

SAMPLE ANSWER

Ⓐ Ⓑ Ⓒ Ⓓ ●

21. Unemployed laborers ignored the picket lines set up by striking workers at the factory's only entrance, and they thereby rendered it ineffective.

(A) entrance, and they thereby rendered it
(B) entrance and therefore rendered it
(C) entrance, by which the strike was rendered
(D) entrance, thereby this rendered the strike
(E) entrance, thereby rendering the strike

22. Ignoring a projected decline in births over the next decade, the school board allocated funds for a new elementary school based upon an increase in the infant population last year.

(A) Ignoring a projected decline in births over the next decade,
(B) By ignoring a projected decline in births over the next decade,
(C) To ignore a projected decline in births over the next decade,
(D) The next decade's projected decline in births having been ignored,
(E) A projected decline in births over the next decade is ignored when

23. The supporters of the volunteer ambulance corps were assured as to the deductibility of their donations on their tax returns.

(A) as to the deductibility of their donations on their tax returns
(B) as to their donations being deductible on their tax returns
(C) that their, the supporters', donations are deductible on their tax returns
(D) that in regards to their tax returns the donations are deductible
(E) that their donations are deductible on their tax returns

24. A million dollars before his twenty-fifth birthday having been made, the young entrepreneur decided to write a book instructing others in the techniques of his success.

(A) A million dollars before his twenty-fifth birthday having been made
(B) A million dollars before his twenty-fifth birthday made
(C) By twenty-five, when he made a million dollars
(D) When he made a million dollars by his twenty-fifth birthday
(E) Having made a million dollars by his twenty-fifth birthday

GO ON TO THE NEXT PAGE

25. The most frequently advanced justifications for rising physicians' fees is they pay increasing malpractice insurance premiums and invest in costly equipment.

(A) is they pay increasing malpractice insurance premiums and invest
(B) are they pay increasing malpractice insurance premiums and invest
(C) are that physicians pay increasing malpractice insurance premiums and that they invest
(D) is increasing malpractice insurance premiums and investing
(E) are increasing malpractice insurance premiums and the need to invest

26. Visiting Europe as a tourist ten years after the end of the war, the rapid pace of the postwar reconstruction amazed the former soldier.

(A) the rapid pace of the postwar reconstruction amazed the former soldier
(B) the postwar reconstruction that had taken place at a rapid pace amazed the former soldier
(C) the former soldier was amazed at the rapid pace of the postwar reconstruction
(D) the former soldier who was amazed at the rapid pace of the postwar reconstruction
(E) the former soldier was amazed at how rapid the postwar reconstruction was

27. Although Janice has expressed a desire to become a couture designer, she lacks the necessary sewing skills and has no interest in detail work.

(A) she lacks the necessary sewing skills and has no
(B) lacking the necessary sewing skills, she has no
(C) she is without the necessary sewing skills and
(D) she does not have the necessary sewing skills nor the
(E) she is lacking in the necessary sewing skills and

28. It is distressing to many would-be teachers that the Board of Examiners in New York City has the sole power to decide about licensing teachers.

(A) about licensing teachers
(B) whether or not a teacher should be licensed
(C) whether or not teachers' licensing
(D) as to whether or not a teacher should be licensed
(E) the licensing of teachers, if they so choose

29. A person's decision to pursue a career in law sometimes results from a lack of any true direction rather than from any commitment to the principles of justice.

(A) from a lack of any true direction rather than from
(B) from a lack of any true direction as from
(C) as a lack of any true direction as much as from
(D) from a lack of any true direction and
(E) from a lack of any true direction but

30. Left to his own devices, a curious four-year-old can learn much from computerized toys, the problem being that the learning experience is devoid of any social element.

(A) toys, the problem being that the learning experience
(B) toys, but the problem is that using computerized toys to learn
(C) toys; in learning from toys, one
(D) toys, but that learning experience
(E) toys; the problem is that in learning from them, it

31. Since some vegetables, such as tomatoes, peppers, and eggplants, are difficult to grow from seed, seedlings will improve your chances of a rich harvest.

(A) seedlings will
(B) seedlings
(C) the use of seedlings will
(D) to use seedlings will
(E) using seedlings to

GO ON TO THE NEXT PAGE

32. Because Ian had been wounded in the European Campaign, so he was asked to serve as Grand Marshal of the Memorial Day Parade.

(A) Campaign, so he was asked

(B) Campaign, he was asked

(C) Campaign, they asked him

(D) Campaign, so they asked him

(E) Campaign, that he was asked

33. The present administration has always and will continue to be committed to a policy of guaranteeing a good education to every child in the district.

(A) has always and will continue to be

(B) has always and continues to be

(C) has always been and will continue

(D) has always been and will continue to be

(E) always has been and continues

34. The gift certificate for a hot-air balloon ride gives the recipient the option that you may exchange the certificate for cash.

(A) that you may exchange the certificate

(B) that the certificate may be exchanged

(C) of exchanging the certificate

(D) of your exchanging the certificate

(E) to exchange the certificate

35. Although heavily damaged by the severe cold, farmers in the south were able to save a substantial portion of the citrus crop.

(A) Although heavily damaged by the severe cold

(B) Although the severe cold caused heavy damage

(C) Though heavy damage by the severe cold

(D) Although the severe cold heavily damaged

(E) Despite being heavily damaged by the severe cold

36. During cross-examination, an attorney's questions are asked as much to discredit the witness as they are for producing facts.

(A) as much to discredit the witness as they are for producing

(B) as much to discredit the witness as for producing

(C) as much to discredit the witness as to produce

(D) to discredit the witness as they are to produce

(E) for discrediting the witness as for producing

37. The degree of dissatisfaction among doctors is astonishingly high for a profession typically regarded as one of the most prestigious and best paid.

(A) typically regarded as one

(B) regarded as typically one

(C) typically regarding as one

(D) typically regarded being one

(E) as one typically regards

38. Because officials feared that the derailed freight train was carrying liquid propane, this caused the evacuation of several hundred residents of the town.

(A) this caused the evacuation of several hundred residents of the town

(B) so several hundred of the town's residents were evacuated

(C) thus evacuating several hundred residents of the town

(D) they evacuated several hundred residents of the town

(E) which evacuated several hundred of the town's residents

39. The E.P.A. plans to build an incinerator that will roast the contaminated dirt, which will break down dioxin molecules into harmless elements.

(A) dirt, which will break

(B) dirt that will break

(C) dirt; the heat will break

(D) dirt; the heat breaking

(E) dirt and will break

GO ON TO THE NEXT PAGE

40. If you concentrate on courses with practical applications only, we risk losing the value of a liberal arts education.

(A) If you concentrate on courses with practical applications only

(B) If you concentrate on courses with only practical applications

(C) If we concentrate on courses with practical applications only

(D) If we concentrate on courses with only practical applications

(E) In order to concentrate on courses with only practical applications

GO ON TO THE NEXT PAGE

Directions: Questions 41 through 45 are based upon Passage I and questions 46 through 50 are based on Passage II. You may consider each passage to be an early draft of a student essay. Some of the sentences in each need to be corrected or revised. Read each passage; then answer the questions.

Some questions require decisions about the structure of individual sentences. Other questions require decisions about organization and development of the passage or about appropriateness of particular language in light of the overall tone of the passage. For each question, choose the answer that best expresses the intended meaning clearly and precisely and that follows the conventions of standard written English.

Questions 41–45 are based on the following passage:

(1) Georgia O'Keeffe, who died in 1986 at the age of ninety-eight, is perhaps best known for her paintings of the American Southwest. (2) Her canvases are filled with desert scenes and images of sun-bleached animal skulls.

(3) O'Keeffe was born in Wisconsin and studied in Wisconsin, Chicago, and New York. (4) Between 1916 and 1918, she taught art in Texas. (5) She gave up teaching in order to devote her energies to painting and joined famed photographer Alfred Stieglitz at his small gallery in New York City. (6) (O'Keeffe and Stieglitz later got married.) (7) O'Keeffe was one of many artists to visit the region that is now called the State of New Mexico during the first half of the twentieth century. (8) Many of these artists had wearied of life in the city and looked to the vast expanse of the American west for new artistic inspiration. (9) Although life and art seemed very separate in New York and Paris, in Taos and Santa Fe they seemed closely related. (10) Most visiting artists were touched by what the writer D.H. Lawrence called the "spirit of the place." (11) Besides the scenic beauty bathed in clear golden light, the traditions of the Indian and Hispanic people who lived there were often chosen as subjects by the artists who visited the region.

(12) Most of these visiting artists stayed only a year or two, and their canvases have all but faded from public view and are usually not mentioned in books on American art history. (13) O'Keeffe, however, stayed a lifetime, and her paintings have made permanent impressions on countless eyeballs.

41. Which of the following additional information would be the LEAST appropriate to include in sentence (4)?

(A) The names of the schools attended by O'Keeffe

(B) The main subject studied by O'Keeffe.

(C) The dates O'Keeffe lived in each area.

(D) Subjects painted by O'Keeffe during the period.

(E) Whether O'Keeffe was married during the period.

42. Which of the following is the most effective way to combine sentences (5) and (6)?

(A) She gave up teaching in order to devote her energies to painting and joined famed photographer Alfred Stieglitz at his small gallery in New York City, and Stieglitz was O'Keeffe's future husband.

(B) She gave it up in order to devote her energies to painting and famed photographer Alfred Stieglitz at his small gallery in New York City, her future husband.

(C) She gave up teaching in order to devote her energies to painting and joined famed photographer Alfred Stieglitz, who later became her husband, at his small gallery in New York City.

(D) She gave it up in order to join Alfred Stieglitz, who was her future husband in addition to being a famed photographer who had a small gallery in New York City, and to devote her energies to painting.

(E) O'Keeffe and Alfred Stieglitz were later married after she gave up teaching in order to devote her energies to painting and joined Stieglitz, a famous photographer, at his small gallery in New York City.

43. Is the inclusion of the quotation from D.H. Lawrence in sentence (10) appropriate?

(A) Yes, because the language of the quotation helps the author of the essay describe the Southwest.

(B) Yes, because an essay should always include at least one quotation from a prominent authority.

(C) Yes, provided that D.H. Lawrence was a personal acquaintance of Georgia O'Keeffe.

(D) No, because D.H. Lawrence was a writer and Georgia O'Keeffe was a painter.

(E) No, because some readers may not be familiar with the works of D.H. Lawrence.

GO ON TO THE NEXT PAGE

44. Which of the following sentences should begin a new paragraph?

(A) (2)

(B) (5)

(C) (6)

(D) (7)

(E) (13)

45. Which of the following changes would most improve the passage?

(A) Deleting teaching in sentence (5)

(B) Deleting the region that is now called in sentence (7)

(C) Substituting felt for touched in sentence (10)

(D) Substituting tourists for visiting artists in sentence (10)

(E) Substituting eyes for eyeballs in sentence (13)

Questions 46–50 are based on the following passage:

(1) Today, planners are looking for renewable energy sources to satisfy the growing demand for energy. (2) One idea that gets much attention in the press is generating electricity from wind power. (3) Articles in newspapers and magazines are often written as though wind power is a new idea, but it is really one of the oldest energy sources used by human beings.

(4) No records of the earliest wind machines survive, but they may have been built in China more than three thousand years ago or perhaps on the windy plains of Afghanistan. (5) Some sources hint that Egyptians during the time of the Pharaohs used wind power for drawing water for agricultural purposes. (6) Around 2,000 B.C., Hammurabi may have taken time out from developing his legal code to sponsor development of some sort of wind machine.

(7) The earliest confirmed wind machines were located in Persia. (8) Persian writers described gardens irrigated by wind-driven water lifts. (9) The Persian machines were horizontal devices, carousel-like contraptions that revolved around a center pole and that caught the wind with bundles of reeds. (10) Indeed, there is a certain engineering advantage to the carousel: it doesn't matter from which direction the wind is blowing.

(11) From the Middle East, wind-machine technology may have been carried to Europe by returning Crusaders, for soon after the Crusades windmills appeared in Northern Europe and on the British Isles. (12) Windmills flourished for a while in Europe but gave way to steam power.

(13) Those engaged in research and development on wind power now face the same problem that caused the shift from wind to steam power: how to handle to extremes of wind velocity. (14) Wind, after all, is real iffy. (15) It can fail to blow just when it is needed, or it can blow a gale right when it isn't needed.

46. Which of the following is the best revision of the underlined portion of sentence (3)?

(3) Articles in newspapers and magazines are often written as though wind power is a new idea, but it is really one of the oldest energy sources used by human beings.

(A) idea, really one of the oldest energy sources

(B) idea, but it was one of the first energy sources

(C) idea, and it is really one of the oldest energy sources

(D) idea, since it is was really one of the first energy sources

(E) idea, but as an energy source, it was one of the first

47. Which of the following best explains why sentence (7) should begin a new paragraph?

(A) The writer begins to discuss wind power in Persia rather than in China, Afghanistan, or Egypt.

(B) The writer shifts to a discussion of historical records rather than speculation.

(C) The Persian wind machines were horizontal wheels rather than vertical ones.

(D) It is not certain that wind-machine technology was brought to Europe from the Middle East.

(E) The Persians were the first to harness successfully the power of the wind.

GO ON TO THE NEXT PAGE

48. Which of the following is the LEAST appropriate revision of the underlined part of sentence (11)?

(11) From the Middle East, wind-machine technology may have been carried to Europe by returning Crusaders, for soon after the Crusades windmills appeared both in Northern Europe and on the British Isles.

(A) since windmills appeared both in Northern Europe and on the British Isles soon after the Crusades

(B) in as much as windmills appeared soon after the Crusades both in Northern Europe and on the British Isles

(C) because windmills appeared both in Northern Europe and on the British Isles soon after the Crusades

(D) given that windmills appeared soon after the Crusades both in Northern Europe and on the British Isles

(E) therefore windmills appeared both in Northern Europe and on the British Isles soon after the Crusades

49. Which of the following revisions is most needed?

(A) Substitute increasing for growing in sentence (1).

(B) Substitute exist for survive in sentence (4).

(C) Substitute built for located in sentence (7).

(D) Substitute yielded for gave way in sentence (12).

(E) Substitute very variable for real iffy in sentence (14).

50. Which of the following is the best order for paragraphs 2, 3, and 4?

(A) 2, 3, 4

(B) 2, 4, 3

(C) 3, 2, 4

(D) 3, 4, 2

(E) 4, 2, 3

Directions: Of the sentences in this part, some are correct and others contain errors of grammar, usage, diction (choice of words), or idiom (correctness of expression). If the sentence contains an error, the error is underlined and lettered. Assume that any part of the sentence that is not underlined is correct and cannot be changed. In analyzing a sentence, keep in mind the requirements of standard written English.

If you find an error in a sentence, select the one underlined part that must be changed in order to make the sentence correct and darken the corresponding space on your answer sheet. If the sentence does not contain an error, darken space (E) on your answer sheet.

EXAMPLES: SAMPLE ANSWERS

I. The principal asked (A) ten of we (B) students to enter (C) the public speaking (D) contest. No error (E)

I. (A) ● (C) (D) (E)

II. He saves every (A) penny so that (B) his (C) children could (D) someday go to college. No error (E)

II. (A) (B) (C) ● (E)

51. Recent (A) medical reports suggest (B) that the consumption of oat bran may not have (C) a significant effect (D) on a person's cholesterol levels. No error (E)

52. The new magazine, which is (A) aimed at the model-airplane enthusiast who spend (B) at least $450 annually (C) on his hobby, will publish its (D) first issue next month. No error (E)

53. It is fairly obvious that the cuisine of Viet Nam was (A) influenced with (B) several other (C) cuisines, including those (D) of France, India, and China. No error (E)

54. When the game finally ended, the home team has (A) one more (B) goal than (C) the visiting team, but the losing coach plans to file (D) a protest. No error (E)

55. Even though few (A) of the metallic fittings survived (B) the salt water, those (C) recovered were especially (D) important to the divers. No error (E)

56. Because (A) he found flaws in (B) the budget's projected revenues, Calvin's criticisms of the plan were different than (C) those (D) of his colleagues. No error (E)

57. The vandals, who (A) were apprehended (B) almost immediately (C) by campus security guards, should of (D) realized that they would probably be caught. No error (E)

58. One of the major domestic manufacturers of passenger vehicles announced that (A) it has developed (B) one (C) with both (D) front and rear steering. No error (E)

GO ON TO THE NEXT PAGE

59. From the outside, the barn appears small and
A
cramped, but the inside has been converted to
B C
living space with ample room for a family of
D
four. No error
E

60. In ancient Rome, where silver was widely
A B
displayed at home in the form of tableware and
C
at the public baths in the form of jewelry,

because it was a status symbol. No error
D E

S T O P

IF YOU FINISH BEFORE TIME IS CALLED, YOU MAY CHECK YOUR WORK ON THIS TEST ONLY. DO NOT WORK ON ANY OTHER TEST IN THIS BOOK.

Explanatory Answers

1. If Mary Outerbridge would not have seen English (A) officers playing (B) tennis in Bermuda where (C) she was vacationing (D) at the time, she would not have introduced the game to America. No error (E)

(A) The verb in an "if" clause cannot be in the conditional aspect. *Would not have introduced* in the main clause requires the past perfect tense in the "if" clause. *Had not seen* would be correct. (In essence, the "if ... not" construction conveys the sense that the statement is about something that might have happened but did not, so the *would,* which can convey the same sense, is superfluous.)

(B) The participle *playing* is used as an adjective to modify the noun *officers.*

(C) *Where* is a subordinate conjunction correctly used to begin a new adverbial clause.

(D) Use of the past progressive tense *was vacationing* is consistent with other verb tenses in the sentence.

2. When we consider (A) the miracles of modern science, we find it hard to imagine that (B) in 1349 the Black Death killed (C) one-third of England's (D) population. No error (E)

(E) The sentence as written is correct.

(A) "When we consider ... science" is a subordinate clause used to modify the main verb of the sentence and explain the circumstances under which we "find" it hard to believe the historical fact described.

(B) *That* is a relative pronoun that introduces the noun clause ("the Black Death killed ...") that functions as the object of the main verb *find.*

(C) *Killed* is the past tense and is correctly used to describe an event that is entirely contained in the past.

(D) The possessive is used correctly to identify the population being discussed.

3. When (A) the critics wrote (B) critical reviews of the Broadway opening (C) of the rock star's new musical, neither the producer nor the director were (D) available for an interview. No error (E)

(D) When *and* is used to join the elements of the subject of the sentence, the elements are "added" together, so the subject is plural (and its verb must be plural). When the elements are joined using *or, either/or,* or *neither/nor,* the elements are not "added." Instead, the verb must agree with the last element of the subject:

. . . neither the producer nor the *director was* . . .

Compare:

. . . neither the producer nor the *actors were* . . .

(A) *When* is the logical conjunction to introduce this subordinate clause.

(B) *Wrote* correctly describes an action completed in the past.

(C) *Opening* is a gerund appropriately used as the object of the preposition *of.*

4. Those who are successful in business (A) often discover that (B) wealth and fame do not guarantee (C) happiness and learning (D) that peace of mind is important. No error (E)

(D) In this sentence we have two ideas that are parallel, that is, that serve similar functions in the sentence: "discover that ..." and "learn that ...". Since the two ideas have similar functions, they must be expressed in parallel or similar grammatical forms, as shown above.

(A) *Who* is a relative pronoun that is used to introduce an adjective clause that identifies the "those" who are the subject of the sentence. Since *who* takes the place of *those,* it must be plural and requires the plural verb *are.*

(B) *That* is a relative pronoun introducing the noun clause that functions as the direct object of *find.* It tells us *what* those who are successful find.

(C) Because "wealth and fame" are two ideas joined by *and,* the subject is plural. The plural form of the verb *do not guarantee* is correct.

5. About 3500 B.C., ancient Egypt made great progress in agriculture after they (A) adopted several new techniques of cultivation among which (B) were (C) raking, plowing, and manuring (D). No error (E)

(A) The antecedent or referent of the pronoun *they* is *Egypt.* (Antecedent or referent is the word the pronoun refers to.) *They* is a plural pronoun, but *Egypt* is singular. The sentence could be corrected by substituting *it* for *they.*

(B) The preposition *among* is the appropriate preposition for referring to a group of three or more items. (*Between* is used for just two, as in "between you and me." *Among* is used for three or more, as in "John divided the money among the three of us.") Additionally, *which* is a relative pronoun that is the subject of the clause that is the object of the preposition *among.*

(C) The clause that is the object of the preposition *among* has an inverted structure, that is, the verb comes before the subject. The subject of the clause is *plowing, raking, and manuring.* Since the elements are joined by *and,* they are "added" and need a plural verb.

(D) The gerund forms *plowing, raking, and manuring,* are used as nouns. They correctly function as the subject of the clause. Notice that they all have the same form, *-ing,* so they have the required parallel structures.

6. In (A) the southwest corner of the cemetery, where the honeysuckle vines have all but (B) covered the grave markers, lays (C) the body of the county's greatest (D) war hero. No error (E)

(C) In English, the verbs *lie* and *lay* are often confused. *To lay* means to place something; *to lie* means to rest. The sentence should say that the body *lies* or *rests* in the specified location.

(A) The preposition *in* has a meaning that is appropriate for this sentence.

(B) The subject of the clause introduced by *where* is *vines,* so *have* agrees with its subject. Additionally, the expression *have all but* is idiomatically correct.

(D) In English, adjectives have three forms: the positive, the comparative, and the superlative. For example:

great, greater, greatest
blue, bluer, bluest
old, older, oldest
good, better, best

The superlative form is used for comparison of three or more items. So here, it is correct to use the superlative form of *great* to describe the war hero.

7. The final number of the musical, a duet, was written (A) by Sue and is sung by she (B) and Reginald, the male lead, as (C) the other members of the cast take their (D) bows. No error (E)

(B) *She* is a nominative case pronoun and cannot be used as the object of the preposition *by*. The correct pronoun is *her.*

(A) *Was written* is a past tense verb that has as its subject *number*. Notice that the verb agrees with its subject and that it correctly puts the action of writing the music (as opposed to performing it) in the past.

(C) *As* functions as a subordinate conjunction to introduce a clause that tells the reader what else goes on as Sue and Reginald sing the final number.

(D) *Their* is a possessive pronoun that serves to identify *bows.* Notice that it is plural and agrees with *members.*

8. The owner of the property, who had farmed (A) the land for more than (B) 40 years, listened to (C) the company's offer but said that he could not answer definite (D) without further consideration. No error (E)

(D) *Definite,* an adjective, is intended here to modify *answer*. Since *answer* is in this context a verb, you must use the adverb *definitely.*

(A) *Had farmed* correctly places the action of farming completely in the past: The owner did that before he heard the company's offer.

(B) *More than* is used here idiomatically.

(C) *Listened* puts this action entirely in the past, but the use of the simple past indicates that the listening occurred after the 40 years of farming. And *to* is correctly used to form an idiomatic phrase.

9. Immediately after the legislators freezed the level
A
of benefits, citizens groups began contacting their
B C
members to encourage them to write letters of
protest to their representatives in Congress.
D
No error
E

(A) The past participle of *to freeze* is *froze,* not *freezed.*

(B) The main verb here is *began,* and the gerund *contacting* functions as its object.

(C) *Their* is a possessive pronoun that identifies the *members.* Notice that it is plural and agrees with its plural referent *groups.*

(D) The preposition *to* is idiomatic here: "write ... to."

10. Since the treasurer and him had already discussed
A B
the details of the financial report, Robert felt that
it was not necessary for him to attend the budget
C D
meeting. No error
E

(A) *Him* is an objective case pronoun and cannot be used as the subject of a sentence. Here you need the nominative case pronoun *he.*

(B) The use of the past perfect *had . . . discussed* correctly places the action in the past and shows that it was completed before another past action, in this case, that it was completed before Robert felt that he did not need to attend the meeting.

(C) Although a pronoun used as the subject of a conjugated verb must be a nominative case pronoun, the subject of an infinitive must be an objective case pronoun. So *him* is correct here.

(D) *To attend* is an infinitive and functions as a noun, here as the objective of the preposition *of. Attending,* the gerund form, can be used as a noun but not here. The construction "necessary of attending" is not idiomatic English.

11. The history of the ancient Egyptians, as recorded
by graphic drawings called hieroglyphics, describe
A B C
in great detail the burial of King Tutankhamen's
D
body in a sarcophagus of wood and gold. No error
E

(C) The subject of the sentence is *history,* not *hieroglyphics.* So the correct verb is *describes,* not *describe.*

(A) The preposition *by* is used here idiomatically.

(B) The past participle *called* is used here as an adjective to modify the noun *drawings.*

(D) *In great detail* is an idiomatic prepositional phrase that is used here to modify *describes.*

12. The conditions of the subway system
A
having been improved dramatically over the past
B C
three years, but much work still remains to be
D
done. No error
E

(B) Standard written English requires the writing of complete sentences; when a sentence contains two or more independent clauses, each must have its own conjugated verb. (Each independent clause must be able to stand alone as a complete sentence.) A complete sentence must have a conjugated verb, for example, *have, has,* or *had.* Neither the participle *having* nor the infinitive *to have* is a conjugated verb. This item, therefore, is a fragment of a sentence—not a complete sentence. You can make it a correct sentence by substituting *have improved.*

(A) *Of* is the correct preposition to use here.

(C) *Dramatically* is used here as an adverb. If the error in (B) is corrected, then *dramatically* will correctly modify the new verb.

(D) *But* is a coordinate conjunction that is used here to join two independent clauses. (Once (B) is corrected, the result will be another independent clause.) Notice that *but* correctly suggests the contrast desired by the speaker.

13. Introduced at the last moment by the Scholastic
A
Council was a demand that the college allocate
B C
funds for a day-care center and a demand that the

college hire (D) more minority faculty members. No error (E)

(B) In English, the subject of a sentence ordinarily comes before the verb, but sometimes the order is reversed. The result of reversing the order is an inverted sentence, such as the one here. The subject is "demand ... and a demand," which is a compound subject (the elements are "added together" by *and*), so a plural verb is needed. Change *was* to *were*.

(A) *At the last moment* is a correct English idiom.

(C) *That* is a relative pronoun that is used here to introduce a relative clause that tells about the demand.

(D) In other languages that you might have studied, the subjunctive mood is very important. In English, the subjunctive has largely disappeared. One of the few vestiges is illustrated here. Ordinarily, you would expect to see *college hires,* not *college hire,* but here the latter construction is correct. Why? The construction *demand that* conveys the idea that the demand might or might not be met. In this "doubt" situation, the subjunctive is still used.

14. Summarily rejecting (A) the demands of the students for a greater voice in determining university (B) policy, the dean now worries that (C) her decision might result (D) in new student demonstrations. No error (E)

(A) The error is *rejecting,* which seems to be an adjective modifying *dean* and implies that the dean is rejecting the demands even as she worries. The sentence means to say, however, that the dean rejected the demands and then later became worried. You can convey this idea and correct the sentence by substituting for (A) the phrase "Having summarily rejected." Notice that this makes it clear that the dean rejected the demands before she began to worry.

(B) Here *policy* is a noun functioning as the object of the gerund *determining,* and *university* is used as an adjective to describe the kind of policy discussed.

(C) *That* is used here idiomatically to introduce a noun clause.

(D) *Might result* is the correct choice of verbs to convey the idea that the renewal of demonstrations is an event that is in doubt.

15. The dog has been replaced (A) by the cat as the pet of choice for Americans because (B) cats are (C) more independent and require less care than (D) dogs. No error (E)

(E) The sentence as written is correct.

(A) The present perfect tense is used to show an action that was begun in the past and can be finished only in the present. Thus, the use of *has been replaced* is the correct choice here. It shows that cats started to become popular in the past and that now they are more popular than dogs.

(B) *Because* is the correct choice of subordinate conjunctions because the speaker is providing a causal explanation.

(C) *Are* correctly agrees with *cats* and describes a current state of affairs.

(D) *Than* is used here to introduce an elliptical clause: Cats require less care than dogs require. Although the second *require* does not appear, the phrase *than dogs* is acceptable English.

16. Because many modern actors study (A) method acting, a system devised (B) by Stanislavsky, their (C) interpretations of the role of Hamlet differ from Shakespeare's time. (D) No error (E)

(D) The error here is one of illogical comparison. The sentence asserts that the interpretations of modern actors are different from Shakespeare's times: Interpretations are different from times. What the sentence is trying to say is that the interpretations of modern actors are different from the interpretations of the actors of Shakespeare's time. The sentence can be corrected by changing (D) to read: "those of Shakespeare's time."

(A) *Study* is an appropriate verb form that agrees with the subject *actors* and is used to describe present actions.

(B) *A system* is an appositive that refers to *method acting,* and *devised* is a past participle that is used to modify and to identify *system.*

(C) *Their* is a possessive pronoun correctly used here because it refers to *actors.*

17. During the second half of the nineteenth
A
century, waves of immigration in the United
B
States brought hundreds of thousands of
C
foreigners to America's cities and created the
D
condition termed the "melting pot." No error
E

(B) *In* is not idiomatic in this context. It suggests movements inside an area, for example, "Once in the house, he moved from room to room." Here we need the idea of going from the outside to the inside, and for that we need *into*, as in "He used the second-story window to get into the house."

(A) *During* is a preposition that correctly modifies *brought*, telling the reader when the people came to the United States.

(C) *Brought* is the past tense of *bring* and is used here correctly to show an action that took place in the second half of the nineteenth century.

(D) *Created*, like *brought*, is in the past tense and correctly describes an action that occurred in the same time frame.

18. The governor's oratorical skill, which has
A
helped him to win several elections, comes
B C
either from his college debating experience

and from an in-depth knowledge of the issues.
D
No error
E

(D) *And* creates an unidiomatic expression. The correct idiom is *either . . . or*, not *either . . . and*.

(A) *Which* is a relative pronoun used here to introduce a clause that provides information about *skill*.

(B) *To win* is used here idiomatically.

(C) *Comes* correctly agrees with its singular subject *skill*. (*Elections* is not the subject of the sentence.)

19. The decade of the 1920s was an important one
A
for English literature, for during that time a

large amount of works now considered classics
B
were written by great writers such as Ezra
C D
Pound, D.H. Lawrence, and T.S. Eliot. No error
E

(B) *Amount* is a word that in English refers to bulk quantities, such as a large amount of sand. When we refer to discrete quantities, we use *number*, as in "a number of grains of sand." *Amount* should be changed to *number*.

(A) *One* is a pronoun that refers to *decade* and is correctly modified.

(C) *By* is used here idiomatically.

(D) *Such as* is an acceptable phrase to introduce examples of a general idea.

20. Although we usually associate the name of
A B
Athens with democracy, it is important to re-
C
member that slavery was a key element in that
D
city's economy. No error
E

(E) The sentence as written is correct.

(A) *Although* is a subordinate conjunction that correctly suggests the contrast intended by the speaker between *democracy* and *slavery*.

(B) *Associate* has the correct form to agree with *we* and has a meaning that is appropriate here.

(C) *It* is used here idiomatically. The phrasing used is similar to other English idioms, such as "It is raining" or "It is well known."

(D) *Was* correctly agrees with its subject, *slavery*, and indicates an action or condition that ended in the past.

21. Unemployed laborers ignored the picket lines set up by striking workers at the factory's only entrance, and they thereby rendered it ineffective.

(A) entrance, and they thereby rendered it
(B) entrance and therefore rendered it
(C) entrance, by which the strike was rendered
(D) entrance, thereby this rendered the strike
(E) entrance, thereby rendering the strike

(E) The underlined portion of this sentence contains an error of grammar. *It* has no referent, that is, there is no other noun (or pronoun) in the sentence for which *it* has been substituted. This can be corrected by using the noun *strike*. Additionally, the original is needlessly wordy. Notice that (E) is more concise, (B) fails to correct the faulty pronoun usage, and (C) and (D) introduce new pronoun errors. *Which* and *this,* like *it,* are pronouns. And just as *it* has nothing to refer to, neither *which* nor *this* has a referent.

22. Ignoring a projected decline in births over the next decade, the school board allocated funds for a new elementary school based upon an increase in the infant population last year.

(A) Ignoring a projected decline in births over the next decade,

(B) By ignoring a projected decline in births over the next decade,

(C) To ignore a projected decline in births over the next decade,

(D) The next decade's projected decline in births having been ignored,

(E) A projected decline in births over the next decade is ignored when

(A) The original is correct as written. The changes suggested by the other choices distort the meaning of the original or result in sentences that are very awkward.

23. The supporters of the volunteer ambulance corps were assured as to the deductibility of their donations on their tax returns.

(A) as to the deductibility of their donations on their tax returns

(B) as to their donations being deductible on their tax returns

(C) that their, the supporters', donations are deductible on their tax returns

(D) that in regards to their tax returns the donations are deductible

(E) that their donations are deductible on their tax returns

(E) The phrase *as to* is low-level usage and is not acceptable in standard written English. What is required is a noun clause: The supporters were assured that something is the case. (B) fails to make this correction. (C) and (D) make the needed correction but introduce new errors. (C) is wrong because the parenthetical expression is unnecessary and disrupts the logical flow of the sentence. (D) is wrong because *in regards* is no better than *as to.*

24. A million dollars before his twenty-fifth birthday having been made, the young entrepreneur decided to write a book instructing others in the techniques of his success.

(A) A million dollars before his twenty-fifth birthday having been made

(B) A million dollars before his twenty-fifth birthday made

(C) By twenty-five, when he made a million dollars

(D) When he made a million dollars by his twenty-fifth birthday

(E) Having made a million dollars by his twenty-fifth birthday

(E) The underlined part of the sentence is an attempt to use a verb form as an adjective to modify the subject of the sentence, that is, to tell us something about the entrepreneur. The original is incorrect for two reasons. First, the use of the passive form *having been made* cuts off the introductory phrase from the rest of the sentence. *Having been made* refers to *dollars* and *before his twenty-fifth birthday* modifies *having been made.* Thus, no element in the underlined part refers to *entrepreneur.* Notice how (E) corrects this problem. *Having made* prompts the question "Who made it?" And that is answered by "the entrepreneur," so *having made* modifies *entrepreneur.* Additionally, the order of the elements in the original is awkward, as you can see by comparing the original to (E). (B) fails to correct either error. The introductory material is still cut off from the rest of the sentence and is, in any event, very awkward. (C) and (D) make similar errors by using the word *when.* Both imply that the events "making a million dollars" and "deciding to write a book" occurred at the same time. But the sentence intends to say that the making of the money came before the decision to write the book.

25. The most frequently advanced justifications for rising physicians' fees is they pay increasing malpractice insurance premiums and invest in costly equipment.

(A) is they pay increasing malpractice insurance premiums and invest

(B) are they pay increasing malpractice insurance premiums and invest

(C) are that physicians pay increasing malpractice insurance premiums and that they invest

(D) is increasing malpractice insurance premiums and investing

(E) are increasing malpractice insurance premiums and the need to invest

(C) The original suffers from three weaknesses. First, the subject of the sentence is the plural noun *justifications*, so the verb should be the plural *are*. Second, the material that follows the *is* must here be a noun or a noun substitute such as a noun clause. But in the original, what follows the *is* is an independent clause. Third, the pronoun *they* has no referent. It could refer to *physicians* if that word appeared in the sentence, but *physicians* does not appear—only *physicians'*. (C) corrects these errors. It uses the plural *are* and creates a noun clause by using *that*, and it uses the noun *physicians* in place of the incorrect pronoun. (B) and (D) fail to correct the errors. While (E) does correct the verb problem, it distorts the intended meaning of the original. For example, (E) says that the justification for high fees is increasing insurance premiums, when in fact the justification is the need to pay those premiums.

26. Visiting Europe as a tourist ten years after the end of the war, the rapid pace of the postwar reconstruction amazed the former soldier.

(A) the rapid pace of the postwar reconstruction amazed the former soldier

(B) the postwar reconstruction that had taken place at a rapid pace amazed the former soldier

(C) the former soldier was amazed at the rapid pace of the postwar reconstruction

(D) the former soldier who was amazed at the rapid pace of the postwar reconstruction

(E) the former soldier was amazed at how rapid the postwar reconstruction was

(C) The original is afflicted with the notorious dangling modifier. In general, a modifier should be placed as close as possible to what it modifies. Here, *visiting* is intended to modify *soldier*, but those two words could not be any farther apart. Consequently, the natural tendency, when reading this sentence, is to hook *visiting* to the first noun in the main clause: *pace*. Thus, the sentence seems to assert "the rapid pace of reconstruction is visiting Europe." (C) corrects this by placing the word modified in its proper position. (B) fails to make the needed correction and seems to assert that the reconstruction is visiting Europe. (D) and (E) do make the needed correction, but the use of *who* in (D) places the verb *was amazed* in a relative clause and turns the entire sentence into a fragment, and (E) is awkward compared to (C).

27. Although Janice has expressed a desire to become a couture designer, she lacks the necessary sewing skills and has no interest in detail work.

(A) she lacks the necessary sewing skills and has no

(B) lacking the necessary sewing skills, she has no

(C) she is without the necessary sewing skills and

(D) she does not have the necessary sewing skills nor the

(E) she is lacking in the necessary sewing skills and

(A) The original is correct as written. Each of the other choices introduces an error. As for (B), this wording implies that Janice's lack of interest is somehow the result of her lack of sewing skills, but that is not the meaning intended by the original sentence. The rendering in (C) is awkward compared to the original. The use of *nor* in (D) is not idiomatic. You would have to say "She has neither the necessary sewing skills nor the interest." Finally, (E) is awkward when compared to the original.

28. It is distressing to many would-be teachers that the Board of Examiners in New York City has the sole power to decide about licensing teachers.

(A) about licensing teachers

(B) whether or not a teacher should be licensed

(C) whether or not teachers' licensing

(D) as to whether or not a teacher should be licensed

(E) the licensing of teachers, if they so choose

(B) The original sentence is ambiguous. It intends to say that the Board can choose not to license a particular teacher, but the sentence as written implies that the Board has the authority to decide whether or not it will implement a licensing scheme in general. (B) eliminates this ambiguity. As for (C), the use of the gerund is not idiomatic. (You might, however, say "whether or not to license a particular teacher.") In (D), the *as* is superfluous and not idiomatic. (E) fails to correct the error of the original, and the words following the comma are not needed.

29. A person's decision to pursue a career in law sometimes results from a lack of any true direction rather than from any commitment to the principles of justice.

(A) from a lack of any true direction rather than from

(B) from a lack of any true direction as from

(C) as a lack of any true direction as much as from

(D) from a lack of any true direction and

(E) from a lack of any true direction but

(A) The original is correct as written. It uses the idiom "from this rather than from that." (B), (C), and (E) each destroy the idiomatic structure:

(B) from this as from that

(C) as this as much as from that

(E) from this but that

These are not acceptable English phrases. (D) drastically changes the meaning of the original, for it asserts that the decision to go to law school is the result of a lack of direction *and* commitment to the principles of justice.

30. Left to his own devices, a curious four-year-old can learn much from computerized toys, the problem being that the learning experience is devoid of any social element.

(A) toys, the problem being that the learning experience

(B) toys, but the problem is that using computerized toys to learn

(C) toys; in learning from toys, one

(D) toys, but that learning experience

(E) toys; the problem is that in learning from them, it

(D) In the original, the part of the sentence that follows the comma is cut off from the rest of the sentence. *Problem* is a noun, and every other word in that part somehow modifies *problem.* But a noun can be added in that fashion only as an appositive, and an appositive must "echo" another noun in the sentence. Here, however, there is no other noun for *problem* to echo. (D) corrects the error by transforming the failed appositive into an independent clause with its own subject and verb and joining that clause to the rest of the sentence with *and.* (B) avoids the error of the original but is needlessly wordy when compared to the correct choice. (C) makes the illogical assertion that a person (*one*) is devoid of any social element. And (E) uses a pronoun, *it,* that has no referent.

31. Since some vegetables, such as tomatoes, peppers, and eggplants, are difficult to grow from seed, seedlings will improve your chances of a rich harvest.

(A) seedlings will

(B) seedlings

(C) the use of seedlings will

(D) to use seedlings will

(E) using seedlings to

(C) The original makes an illogical statement. It states that the seedlings themselves will improve your chances of a rich harvest, but what the speaker means to say is that by using seedlings, you can improve your chances of a rich harvest. (C) eliminates this ambiguity. (B) fails to eliminate the error of the original. (D) uses the infinitive *to use* rather than the gerund *using,* but the infinitive is not idiomatic here. And finally, (E) eliminates the only conjugated verb in the sentence (*improve* becomes *to improve*) and reduces the sentence to a sentence fragment.

32. Because Ian had been wounded in the European Campaign, so he was asked to serve as Grand Marshal of the Memorial Day Parade.

(A) Campaign, so he was asked

(B) Campaign, he was asked

(C) Campaign, they asked him

(D) Campaign, so they asked him

(E) Campaign, that he was asked

(B) The construction *because . . . , so* is not idiomatic English. There is no need for the *so.* (B) solves this problem by eliminating the offending word. (C) does make the needed correction, but uses the pronoun *they,* for which there is no referent. The *that* used in (E) turns the independent clause into a noun clause and reduces the entire construction to a sentence fragment.

33. The present administration has always and will continue to be committed to a policy of guaranteeing a good education to every child in the district.

(A) has always and will continue to be

(B) has always and continues to be

(C) has always been and will continue

(D) has always been and will continue to be

(E) always has been and continues

(D) The original suffers from an incomplete split construction. The auxiliary verb *has* needs the past participle to complete it: has been. But the word *been* doesn't appear in the sentence. As written, the sentence says that the committee *has always . . . to be committed.* (D) corrects this problem by supplying the missing word. (B) fails to supply the needed word. (C) and (E) do include *been*, but they destroy the effectiveness of the second element of the construction. They read *will continue committed* and *continues committed.*

34. The gift certificate for a hot-air balloon ride gives the recipient the option that you may exchange the certificate for cash.

(A) that you may exchange the certificate

(B) that the certificate may be exchanged

(C) of exchanging the certificate

(D) of your exchanging the certificate

(E) to exchange the certificate

(C) The original suffers from two defects. First, it is simply not idiomatic. (C) supplies the correct idiom. Second, *you* seems to refer to *recipient*, but *you* is a second-person pronoun and cannot substitute for *recipient.* (C) also avoids this error. (B) corrects the second error but not the first, whereas (D) corrects the first error but not the second. Finally, (E) is not idiomatic.

35. Although heavily damaged by the severe cold, farmers in the south were able to save a substantial portion of the citrus crop.

(A) Although heavily damaged by the severe cold

(B) Although the severe cold caused heavy damage

(C) Though heavy damage by the severe cold

(D) Although the severe cold heavily damaged

(E) Despite being heavily damaged by the severe cold

(B) This sentence is afflicted with a dangling modifier. The word *damaged* seems to modify *farmers* rather than *crop.* (B) avoids this ambiguity by turning the introductory phrase into a clause. (C) and (E) don't address this problem. As for (D), the switch to active voice requires a direct object, such as "heavily damaged the crops."

36. During cross-examination, an attorney's questions are asked as much to discredit the witness as they are for producing facts.

(A) as much to discredit the witness as they are for producing

(B) as much to discredit the witness as for producing

(C) as much to discredit the witness as to produce

(D) to discredit the witness as they are to produce

(E) for discrediting the witness as for producing

(C) In the original, the parallelism of the idiom "as much to . . . as to . . . " is destroyed in two ways. First, *they* is out of place. Second, the second verb must have the same form as the first. Here, both should be infinitives. The sentence should read "as much to discredit the witness as to produce."

37. The degree of dissatisfaction among doctors is astonishingly high for a profession typically regarded as one of the most prestigious and best paid.

(A) typically regarded as one

(B) regarded as typically one

(C) typically regarding as one

(D) typically regarded being one

(E) as one typically regards

(A) The sentence is correct as written. The changes in the order of the words suggested by the other answer choices result in sentences that are awkward or not idiomatic.

38. Because officials feared that the derailed freight train was carrying liquid propane, this caused the evacuation of several hundred residents of the town.

(A) this caused the evacuation of several hundred residents of the town

(B) so several hundred of the town's residents were evacuated

(C) thus evacuating several hundred residents of the town

(D) they evacuated several hundred residents of the town

(E) which evacuated several hundred of the town's residents

(D) *This* is a pronoun, and a pronoun must have a referent. What noun is *this* replacing? You can't find one, so you must eliminate it. But you must also make sure that the result has a main clause. (D) accomplishes both tasks. (B) and (C) are wrong because *so* and *thus* are superfluous and disrupt the logical flow of the sentence. (*So* and *thus* are usually used as a transition between independent clauses.) With (E), the underlined part is turned into a clause, so the whole is left without a main clause.

39. The E.P.A. plans to build an incinerator that will roast the contaminated dirt, which will break down dioxin molecules into harmless elements.

(A) dirt, which will break

(B) dirt that will break

(C) dirt; the heat will break

(D) dirt; the heat breaking

(E) dirt and will break

(C) The difficulty with the original is that the final relative clause introduced by *which* has no logical connection to the rest of the sentence, because *which* lacks an unambiguous referent. (C) corrects this by starting a new clause with its own noun subject. Simply substituting *that* for *which* does not eliminate the problem, so (B) is wrong. (D) is wrong because the result is a participial phrase with no connection to the rest of the sentence. And (E) is wrong because it changes the intended meaning of the original sentence; it implies that the E.P.A. will break down the dioxin.

40. If you concentrate on courses with practical applications only, we risk losing the value of a liberal arts education.

(A) If you concentrate on courses with practical applications only

(B) If you concentrate on courses with only practical applications

(C) If we concentrate on courses with practical applications only

(D) If we concentrate on courses with only practical applications

(E) In order to concentrate on courses with only practical applications

(D) The original contains two errors. First, the use of *you* is inconsistent with the use of *we* elsewhere in the sentence, so *you* must be changed to *we*. Second, the placement of *only* in the original is illogical. It should be relocated before the phrase *practical applications.*

41. Which of the following additional information would be the LEAST appropriate to include in sentence (4)?

(A) The names of the schools attended by O'Keeffe

(B) The main subject studied by O'Keeffe.

(C) The dates O'Keeffe lived in each area.

(D) Subjects painted by O'Keeffe during the period.

(E) Whether O'Keeffe was married during the period.

(E) Sentences (3) through (6) discuss O'Keeffe's early career. The topics suggested by (A) through (D) would all add detail to that discussion. A discussion of O'Keeffe's marital status, however, would be out of place. In fact, you should notice that the writer implies that O'Keeffe joined Stieglitz in New York City because he was a famous photographer who owned an art gallery and adds as an afterthought that they later married. So the focus of that part of the passage is O'Keeffe's professional not personal life.

42. Which of the following is the most effective way to combine sentences (5) and (6)?

(A) She gave up teaching in order to devote her energies to painting and joined famed photographer Alfred Stieglitz at his small gallery in New York City, and Stieglitz was O'Keeffe's future husband.

(B) She gave it up in order to devote her energies to painting and famed photographer Alfred Stieglitz at his small gallery in New York City, her future husband.

(C) She gave up teaching in order to devote her energies to painting and joined famed photographer Alfred Stieglitz, who later became her husband, at his small gallery in New York City.

(D) She gave it up in order to join Alfred Stieglitz, who was her future husband in addition to being a famed photographer who had a small gallery in New York City, and to devote her energies to painting.

(E) O'Keeffe and Alfred Stieglitz were later married after she gave up teaching in order to devote her energies to painting and joined Stieglitz, a famous photographer, at his small gallery in New York City.

(C) Our analysis of the preceding question will be useful here. Choice (C) incorporates the idea expressed in sentence (6) into sentence (5) as a nonessential dependent clause. Thus, (C) correctly preserves the writer's emphasis on O'Keeffe's professional as opposed to personal life. Choice (A) places the idea into an independent clause, thereby giving it the same weight as the rest of the sentence. (B) avoids the error of (A), but (B) implies that New York City, rather than Stieglitz, was O'Keeffe's future husband. (D) is very awkwardly worded, upsets the balance between professional and personal life, and contains a pronoun ("it") that has no reference either in the revised sentence nor in the sentence that comes before it. Finally, it is natural to describe events in the order in which they occurred, so (E) distorts the chronology of events.

43. Is the inclusion of the quotation from D.H. Lawrence in sentence (10) appropriate?

(A) Yes, because the language of the quotation helps the author of the essay describe the Southwest.

(B) Yes, because an essay should always include at least one quotation from a prominent authority.

(C) Yes, provided that D.H. Lawrence was a personal acquaintance of Georgia O'Keeffe.

(D) No, because D.H. Lawrence was a writer and Georgia O'Keeffe was a painter.

(E) No, because some readers may not be familiar with the works of D.H. Lawrence.

(A) When you are writing an essay or a paper, you may find that someone else has already expressed a point that you wish to make in a very articulate way. It is acceptable to use that language—provided that you place the language in quotation marks and give the original author due credit. That is the technique employed in sentence (10) of this essay.

44. Which of the following sentences should begin a new paragraph?

(A) (2)

(B) (5)

(C) (6)

(D) (7)

(E) (13)

(D) A new paragraph is needed starting at sentence (7). There the writer shifts from the discussion of O'Keeffe's early life to a discussion of artists in the Southwest. Those are two distinct topics and belong in different paragraphs.

45. Which of the following changes would most improve the passage?

(A) Deleting <u>teaching</u> in sentence (5)

(B) Deleting <u>the region that is now called</u> in sentence (7)

(C) Substituting <u>felt</u> for <u>touched</u> in sentence (10)

(D) Substituting <u>tourists</u> for <u>visiting artists</u> in sentence (10)

(E) Substituting <u>eyes</u> for <u>eyeballs</u> in sentence (13)

(E) "Eyeballs" (used to refer to the faculty of sight rather than the organ of sight) is low-level usage that is inconsistent with the tone of the passage. As for (A), deleting the word "teaching" would change the meaning the of sentence. As for (B), the underlined wording is needed to make it clear to the reader that the area visited by the artists had not yet become a state. The changes suggested by (C) and (D) would change the meanings of their respective sentences.

46. Which of the following is the best revision of the underlined portion of sentence (3)?

(3) Articles in newspapers and magazines are often written as though wind power is a new idea, but it is really one of the oldest energy sources used by human beings.

(A) idea, really one of the oldest energy sources

(B) idea, but it was one of the first energy sources

(C) idea, and it is really one of the oldest energy sources

(D) idea, since it is was really one of the first energy sources

(E) idea, but as an energy source, it was one of the first

(B) The difficulty with the original sentence is that it says one thing but means another. The pronoun "it" in the second clause "wants" to refer to a noun such as "technology": wind power technology is very old. But the only possible referent in for "it" is "wind power." And it makes no sense to speak of "wind power" as being older or younger. (B) clarifies this ambiguity.

47. Which of the following best explains why sentence (7) should begin a new paragraph?

(A) The writer begins to discuss wind power in Persia rather than in China, Afghanistan, or Egypt.

(B) The writer shifts to a discussion of historical records rather than speculation.

(C) The Persian wind machines were horizontal wheels rather than vertical ones.

(D) It is not certain that wind-machine technology was brought to Europe from the Middle East.

(E) The Persians were the first to harness successfully the power of the wind.

(B) Sentence (7) must begin a new paragraph because the writer shifts from a discussion that is speculative, that is, not based on actual historical records, to a discussion that is based on historical records. Thus sentences (4) through (6) treat one topic and sentences (7) through (10) another, and they belong in different paragraphs.

48. Which of the following is the LEAST appropriate revision of the underlined part of sentence (11)?

(11) From the Middle East, wind-machine technology may have been carried to Europe by returning Crusaders, for soon after the Crusades windmills appeared both in Northern Europe and on the British Isles.

(A) since windmills appeared both in Northern Europe and on the British Isles soon after the Crusades

(B) in as much as windmills appeared soon after the Crusades both in Northern Europe and on the British Isles

(C) because windmills appeared both in Northern Europe and on the British Isles soon after the Crusades

(D) given that windmills appeared soon after the Crusades both in Northern Europe and on the British Isles

(E) therefore windmills appeared both in Northern Europe and on the British Isles soon after the Crusades

(E) The key to this item is the relationship between the two ideas in sentence (11): Crusaders may have brought wind-power technology to Europe; windmills appeared in Europe soon after the Crusades. The development of the passage makes it clear that the writer believes that the second idea is evidence for the first, and (A) through (D) use structures that preserve this connection. (E), however, implies that the appearance of the windmills was the causal result of the first idea rather than evidence for it.

49. Which of the following revisions is most needed?

(A) Substitute increasing for growing in sentence (1).

(B) Substitute exist for survive in sentence (4).

(C) Substitute built for located in sentence (7).

(D) Substitute yielded for gave way in sentence (12).

(E) Substitute very variable for real iffy in sentence (14).

(E) "Real iffy" is low-level usage that is inconsistent with the tone of the rest of the passage. The changes suggested by the other choices neither strengthen nor weaken the prose of the passage.

50. Which of the following is the best order for paragraphs 2, 3, and 4?

(A) 2, 3, 4

(B) 2, 4, 3

(C) 3, 2, 4

(D) 3, 4, 2

(E) 4, 2, 3

(A) Ideas in an essay should be presented in some logical order; and when the essay describes events that are ordered chronologically, it is natural for the order of the paragraphs to parallel the order of the historical events. Thus, the essay as written is correct.

51. Recent medical reports suggest that the con-
A B
sumption of oat bran may not have a signifi-
C
cant effect on a person's cholesterol levels.
D
No error
E

(E) The sentence as written is correct.

(A) *Recent* is an adjective that modifies *reports* to tell you what kind of reports are discussed.

(B) *Suggest* correctly agrees with the plural subject *reports.*

(C) *May not have* is an acceptable idiom used here to express doubt.

(D) *Effect* is the correct choice of words for this context. Note: *Affect* would not be correct.

52. The new magazine, which is aimed at the
A
model-airplane enthusiast who spend at least
B
$450 annually on his hobby, will publish its
C D
first issue next month. No error
E

(B) *Who* refers to *enthusiast,* which is a singular noun. Therefore, *spend* should be *spends.*

(A) The subject of this clause is *which,* which refers to *magazine.* So the verb *is* does agree with its subject.

(C) *Annually* is an adverb used here to modify *spend.*

(D) *Its* is a pronoun that here substitutes for *the magazine.* Notice that the pronoun agrees with its referent.

53. It is fairly obvious that the cuisine of Viet Nam
was influenced with several other cuisines, in-
A B C
cluding those of France, India, and China.
D
No error
E

(B) *With* is not an appropriate choice of prepositions for use with *influenced.* You should use *by.*

(A) The verb *was* correctly agrees with the subject of the sentence, *cuisine.*

(C) *Other* is used here to avoid the following type of ambiguity: "Abraham Lincoln was greater than any President." The difficulty with this sentence is that it seems to assert that Lincoln, since he falls into the category "President," was greater even than himself. The ambiguity is avoided as follows: "Abraham Lincoln was greater than any other President."

(D) *Those* is a pronoun that here correctly substitutes for *cuisines.*

54. When the game finally ended, the home team
has one more goal than the visiting team, but
A B C
the losing coach plans to file a protest. No error
D E

(A) The use of the present tense here is incorrect. The use of the past tense *ended* in the dependent clause establishes that the action of the game and the scoring belong to the past. So *has* should be *had.*

(B) *More* is correctly used.

(C) *Than* is correctly used to introduce this elliptical clause: "than the visiting team had."

(D) The infinitive *to file* is correctly used here to explain what the losing coach plans to do.

55. Even though few of the metallic fittings
A
survived the salt water, those recovered were
B C
especially important to the divers. No error
D E

(E) The sentence as written is correct.

(A) *Few* is used here idiomatically.

(B) *Survived* is in the past tense and is consistent with the other verbs in the sentence.

(C) *Those* is a pronoun that refers to *fittings.*

(D) *Especially* is an adverb used to modify the adjective *important.*

56. Because he found flaws in the budget's pro-
A B
jected revenues, Calvin's criticisms of the plan
were different than those of his colleagues.
C D
No error
E

(C) *Than* creates an unacceptable phrase: *different than*. The correct idiom is *different from*.

(A) *Because* is an appropriate conjunction to explain why Calvin's criticisms were different.

(B) *In* is the correct preposition to use in this context.

(D) *Those* is a pronoun that correctly substitutes for *criticisms*.

57. The vandals, who were apprehended
A B
almost immediately by campus security
C
guards, should of realized that they would
D
probably be caught. No error
E

(D) *Of* is a preposition that has no place in the middle of a verb. This should read *should have realized*.

(A) *Who* is a relative pronoun that refers to *vandals* and introduces the relative clause that modifies *vandals*.

(B) Since *who* refers to *vandals, were apprehended* is correct.

(C) *Almost immediately* is an adverbial phrase used to modify *were apprehended*.

58. One of the major domestic manufacturers of

passenger vehicles announced that it
A
has developed one with both front and rear
B C D
steering. No error
E

(C) *One* is here used as a pronoun. But what does *one* refer to? It can't refer to *vehicles*, because that is a plural noun. *One* could be changed to *vehicle* or *car*.

(A) *That* correctly introduces a noun clause that here functions as the object of *announced*.

(B) *Has developed* is in the present perfect tense. It correctly conveys the idea that the development, while begun some time in the past, culminated in the present.

(D) *Both* is used here idiomatically.

59. From the outside, the barn appears small and
A
cramped, but the inside has been converted to
B C
living space with ample room for a family of
D
four. No error
E

(E) The sentence as written is correct.

(A) *Appears* correctly agrees with its subject, *barn*.

(B) *But* is an appropriate conjunction to suggest the contrast between the two main ideas of the sentence.

(C) *Has been converted* correctly conveys the idea that the conversion began in the past and that the effects of the conversion are felt even today. And *has* correctly agrees with the noun *inside*.

(D) *Room* is here used correctly.

60. In ancient Rome, where silver was widely dis-
A B
played at home in the form of tableware and at
C
the public baths in the form of jewelry, because

it was a status symbol. No error
D E

(B) The sentence, as written, lacks a main verb. *Where* makes of all that follows a subordinate clause with the result that there is no main clause. You can make sure that the sentence has a main clause by eliminating *where*.

(A) This preposition is used correctly.

(C) *And* is used correctly here to join two similar ideas.

(D) *It* correctly substitutes for *silver*.

Literature Test

Literature Test

The Literature Test uses poems and prose selections to test your skill in reading literature. By "reading," we mean your ability to understand and analyze a literary text. The test does not presuppose that you have read any particular group of authors or poets. Nor does the test require that you be familiar with obscure terms. You are, however, expected to know basic terms such as *tone, alliteration, stanza,* and *blank verse.*

The test uses 60 multiple-choice questions based on different selections. The number of selections per test is usually seven or eight, divided approximately equally between poetry and fiction with an essay or bit of drama thrown in occasionally. Questions may ask about the content of the selection (for example, the writer's meaning) or about the form of the selection (its organization or literary effect).

Here are some sample questions:

The Eagle

He clasps the crag with crooked hands;
Close to the sun in lonely lands,
Ringed with the azure world, he stands.

The wrinkled sea beneath him crawls;
He watches from his mountain walls,
And like a thunderbolt he falls.

EXAMPLE:

1. The phrase "azure world" in line 3 refers to the

(A) mountain
(B) sea
(C) sky
(D) earth
(E) clouds

This question tests your understanding of the meaning of the poem. The poet describes the eagle as perched high on a mountain. The azure world that rings the eagle, therefore, must be the sky. So the correct answer to this question is (C).

EXAMPLE:

2. The poet's attitude toward the eagle can best be described as

(A) admiring
(B) mistrustful
(C) indifferent
(D) fearful
(E) disgusted

This question asks not about what is specifically stated in the poem but about what can be inferred from it. Several clues are available to lead you to the correct answer. First, the eagle is perched on high in a dramatic setting. Next, the poet's diction, or choice of words, is highly suggestive. The eagle is not just sitting on a mountain, he is perched on a "crag" atop "mountain walls." He is not just high on a mountain, he is "close to the sun." Finally, notice that the author uses the word "thunderbolt" in the final line to describe the eagle's descent. Thus, the best response to this question is (A).

Some questions have unusual formats with which you should be familiar:

EXAMPLE:

3. The poet makes use of which of the following?

I. alliteration
II. metaphor
III. blank verse

(A) I only
(B) II only
(C) III only
(D) I and III only
(E) I, II, and III

Notice that the answer choices for this item consist of mixes of the three Roman-numeraled statements. You must examine each statement. First, statement I does belong in the correct answer. In the first two lines, the poet uses the sound of the hard *c* four times. This technique is known as alliteration. Already, we know that neither (B) nor (C) is correct. As for statement II, a metaphor is a comparison using *like* or *as,* as in "my love is like a red, red rose." There is no such explicit comparison in the poem. Since II does not belong in the correct choice, we also eliminate (E). Finally, as for statement III, the poet uses a rhyme scheme, not blank verse. So the correct answer is (A).

EXAMPLE:

4. All of the following statements are true EXCEPT:

(A) In the final line of the poem, the eagle takes flight.
(B) The setting is a sunny day.
(C) The eagle is perched high on a mountain.
(D) The mountain is near the sea.
(E) The eagle is sitting in a nest.

Notice that this question stem includes the word EXCEPT. This word reverses the point of the question. Instead of looking for a statement that is true, we are looking for a statement that is false. The correct answer, therefore, is (E). Nothing in the poem suggests that the eagle is sitting in a nest.

Literature Test Answer Sheet

1	A	B	C	D	E	31	A	B	C	D	E
2	A	B	C	D	E	32	A	B	C	D	E
3	A	B	C	D	E	33	A	B	C	D	E
4	A	B	C	D	E	34	A	B	C	D	E
5	A	B	C	D	E	35	A	B	C	D	E
6	A	B	C	D	E	36	A	B	C	D	E
7	A	B	C	D	E	37	A	B	C	D	E
8	A	B	C	D	E	38	A	B	C	D	E
9	A	B	C	D	E	39	A	B	C	D	E
10	A	B	C	D	E	40	A	B	C	D	E
11	A	B	C	D	E	41	A	B	C	D	E
12	A	B	C	D	E	42	A	B	C	D	E
13	A	B	C	D	E	43	A	B	C	D	E
14	A	B	C	D	E	44	A	B	C	D	E
15	A	B	C	D	E	45	A	B	C	D	E
16	A	B	C	D	E	46	A	B	C	D	E
17	A	B	C	D	E	47	A	B	C	D	E
18	A	B	C	D	E	48	A	B	C	D	E
19	A	B	C	D	E	49	A	B	C	D	E
20	A	B	C	D	E	50	A	B	C	D	E
21	A	B	C	D	E	51	A	B	C	D	E
22	A	B	C	D	E	52	A	B	C	D	E
23	A	B	C	D	E	53	A	B	C	D	E
24	A	B	C	D	E	54	A	B	C	D	E
25	A	B	C	D	E	55	A	B	C	D	E
26	A	B	C	D	E	56	A	B	C	D	E
27	A	B	C	D	E	57	A	B	C	D	E
28	A	B	C	D	E	58	A	B	C	D	E
29	A	B	C	D	E	59	A	B	C	D	E
30	A	B	C	D	E	60	A	B	C	D	E

LITERATURE TEST

Directions: This test contains selections from several literary works followed by questions on their content, form, and style. Read each poem or passage, select the best answer to each question, and darken the corresponding circle on the answer sheet.

Questions 1–8

Not marble, nor the gilded monuments
Of princes, shall outlive this powerful rhyme;
But you shall shine more bright in these conténts
Than unswept stone, besmeared with sluttish time.
When wasteful war shall statues overturn,
And broils root out the work of masonry,
Nor Mars his sword nor war's quick fire shall burn
The living record of your memory.
'Gainst death and all oblivious enmity
Shall you pace forth; your praise shall still find room
Even in the eyes of all posterity
That wear this world out to the ending doom.
So, till the judgment that yourself arise,
You live in this, and dwell in lovers' eyes.

1. The central idea of the poem is the
   (A) inevitability of death
   (B) onset of old age
   (C) power of poetry to preserve a memory
   (D) destructiveness of wars of conquest
   (E) transcendental nature of love

2. According to the poet, all of the following are true of the gilded monuments EXCEPT:
   (A) They are forgotten by future generations.
   (B) They are ruined by natural elements.
   (C) They are destroyed by fire.
   (D) They are destroyed by armies.
   (E) They preserve history.

3. Which of the following best describes the overall structure of the poem?
   (A) Three quatrains and a couplet
   (B) A couplet and three quatrains
   (C) An octet and a sestet
   (D) A sestet and an octet
   (E) Two sestets and a couplet

4. In line 3, the phrase "these conténts" refers to
   (A) history books
   (B) the location of the monuments
   (C) heaven
   (D) a tomb
   (E) the poem itself

5. In the context of the poem, "the ending doom" probably refers to
   (A) Judgment Day
   (B) the destruction of the monuments
   (C) the poet's death
   (D) the destruction of the poem
   (E) a war

6. The tone of the poem is best described as
   (A) angry and resentful
   (B) repentant and contrite
   (C) hopeless and despairing
   (D) assured and confident
   (E) cheerful and lighthearted

7. Which of the following expressions is most nearly synonymous with "oblivious enmity" (line 9)?
   (A) Untold story
   (B) Unsung hero
   (C) Massive retaliation
   (D) Ravages of time
   (E) Unpredictable change

8. The author refers to marble (line 1) because stone
   (A) can be sculpted into human features
   (B) is more durable than other materials
   (C) can be inscribed with words
   (D) has little intrinsic value
   (E) is not an instrument of war

GO ON TO THE NEXT PAGE

Questions 9–14

So far, good. If any man has a right to feel proud of himself, surely it is I. For I have written about the Coliseum, martyrs, and the lions, and have never once used the phrase "butchered to make a Roman holiday." Butchered to make a Roman holiday sounds well for the first seventeen or eighteen hundred thousand times one sees it in print, but after that it begins to grow tiresome.

In this place I may as well jot down a chapter concerning those necessary nuisances, European guides. Many a man has wished he could do without his guide, but knowing he could not, has wished he could get some amusement out of him as a remuneration for the affliction of his society.

Guides know their story by heart—the history of every statue, painting, cathedral, or other wonder they show you—and tell it as a parrot would. If you interrupt and throw them off their track, they have to go back and begin over again. All their lives long they are employed in showing strange things to foreigners and listening to their bursts of admiration. It is human nature to take delight in exciting admiration. Think, then what a passion it becomes with guides whose privilege it is to throw strangers into perfect ecstasies of admiration. He gets so that he could not possibly live in a soberer atmosphere. After we discovered this, we never went into ecstasies any more—we never admired anything—we never showed any but impassible faces and stupid indifference in the presence of the sublimest wonders a guide had to display. We have found their weak point! After they have exhausted their enthusiasm praising the beauties of some broken-legged statue, we look at it stupidly and in silence and then ask: "Is—is he dead?"

9. The tone of the passage can best be described as

(A) humorous
(B) diffident
(C) solemn
(D) didactic
(E) lofty

10. The author accomplishes his purpose in the first paragraph by using

(A) irony
(B) sarcasm
(C) exaggeration
(D) analogy
(E) metaphor

11. The author refuses to show enthusiasm in order to

(A) force the guide to move quickly to the next location
(B) frustrate the guide's expectations
(C) preserve his own sense of superiority
(D) show reverence for the exhibits
(E) avoid paying the guide his fee

12. When the author compares the guide to a parrot, he means that the guide

(A) is difficult to understand
(B) is not very intelligent
(C) doesn't really understand what he is saying
(D) is very considerate of the tourists
(E) knows nothing of history

13. The word "soberer" in line 30 can be taken to mean

(A) less exciting
(B) without alcohol
(C) less pompous
(D) lacking humor
(E) less rigid

14. When the author asks the guide whether the subject of the statue is dead, the author

(A) expects the guide to answer affirmatively
(B) expects the guide to answer negatively
(C) already knows the subject is still living
(D) already knows the subject is dead
(E) believes the guide does not know the answer

GO ON TO THE NEXT PAGE

Questions 15–21

On the Grasshopper and the Cricket

The poetry of earth is never dead:
When all the birds are faint with the hot sun,
And hide in cooling trees, a voice will run
From hedge to hedge about the new-mown mead;
That is the grasshopper's—he takes the lead
In summer luxury—he has never done
With his delights; for when tired out with fun
He rests at ease beneath some pleasant weed.
The poetry of earth is ceasing never:
On a lone winter evening, when the frost
Has wrought a silence, from the stove there shrills
The cricket's song, in warmth increasing ever,
And seems to one in drowsiness half lost,
The grasshopper's among some grassy hills.

15. The poet's primary aim is to
(A) distinguish crickets from grasshoppers
(B) contrast summer and winter
(C) point out the harshness of nature
(D) admire the continuity of nature
(E) criticize the grasshopper and praise the cricket

16. The poet uses the phrase "poetry of earth" to refer to the
(A) changing of the seasons
(B) sounds of animals
(C) vegetation
(D) temperature
(E) poet's role in nature

17. Why in line 9 does the poet use language that is very similar to that used in line 1?
(A) To summarize the content of lines 1 through 8
(B) To suggest that lines 9 through 14 will contradict lines 1 through 8
(C) To emphasize that lines 9 through 14 will help prove the point announced in line 1
(D) To minimize the significance of the ideas developed in lines 1 through 8
(E) To signal the reader that lines 9 through 14 will address a different topic

18. The poem creates a contrast between all of the following pairs of words EXCEPT:
(A) sun and frost
(B) hot and cooling
(C) grasshopper and cricket
(D) summer and winter
(E) drowsiness and hills

19. The last line of the poem refers to the grasshopper's
(A) leaf
(B) mead
(C) voice
(D) delights
(E) weed

20. According to the poem, the effect of the cricket's song is to
(A) create the illusion of summer
(B) remind the listener of a loved one
(C) warm the room
(D) obliterate the memory of the grasshopper
(E) announce the coming of spring

21. In line 6, the word "done" means
(A) finished
(B) enjoyed
(C) known
(D) understood
(E) expected

GO ON TO THE NEXT PAGE

Questions 22–30

He was a tall thin priest, zealous. Everything in nature seemed to him created with an absolute and admirable logic. The "why" and the "because" always balanced. Dawns exist to make arising a pleasure, days for the ripening of crops, rain to water them, evening to prepare for slumber, and the night was dark for sleeping. He never imagined that nature has no intentions at all.

In his opinion, God had made woman only to tempt man and to test him. He was indulgent only of nuns, made inoffensive on account of their vows. Even them he treated severely, because of that eternal yearning which still sought him out, even though he was a priest.

He had a niece who lived nearby with her mother, whom he was determined to make a Sister of Charity. Then it happened one day that he overheard that his niece had taken a lover. All day he was silent, swollen with indignation and rage.

That night he took down his cane and went out. He was surprised at the splendor of moonlight. Why had God done this? Since the night is intended for oblivion, why make it more charming than the day?

On the edge of the fields, under a vault of trees glowing with mist, two shadows appeared, walking side by side. The still country side enfolded the lovers like a setting made divinely for them. And they moved toward the priest like a living answer to his question, flung back by his master.

It certainly was his niece. But was he not on the verge of disobeying God? Must not God permit love since He lavished upon it such visible splendor? And he fled ashamed, as if he had entered a temple where he had no right to be.

22. The idea that nature has no intentions (first paragraph) is most likely held by the

(A) priest

(B) niece

(C) niece's lover

(D) nuns

(E) author

23. Which of the following best describes the priest's attitude toward human sexuality?

(A) Unqualified revulsion

(B) Amused indifference

(C) Uncomfortable ambivalence

(D) Total ignorance

(E) Fiery condemnation

24. It can be inferred that the priest leaves his home at night to

(A) enjoy the beauty of the moonlit countryside

(B) surprise his niece with her lover

(C) avoid sleeping during the period of darkness

(D) visit the mother of his niece

(E) meditate and pray in the fields and woods

25. The priest is tolerant of nuns because they

(A) have foresworn sexual relations

(B) also do the work of God

(C) have agreed to accept his niece

(D) belong to a different temple

(E) are constantly seeking him out

26. In the fifth paragraph, the priest realizes that

(A) God made the night for lovers

(B) the moonlight is beautiful

(C) trees grow to become lumber

(D) his niece has taken a lover

(E) he has sexual desires himself

27. The "oblivion" referred to in paragraph 4 is

(A) death

(B) marriage

(C) sin

(D) sleep

(E) love

GO ON TO THE NEXT PAGE

28. The priest would likely agree with all of the following EXCEPT:

(A) The winter exists because it gives the farmer a rest from his labors.

(B) Sexuality was intended by God to ensure the procreation of the human species.

(C) The earth revolves around the sun so that human beings have a calendar year.

(D) Natural phenomena have no significance independent of human interpretation.

(E) Animals bear their young in the spring because that helps ensure their survival.

29. Which of the following points of information about the niece is LEAST significant?

(A) She has taken a lover.

(B) She and her lover are observed by the priest.

(C) The priest wants her to become a nun.

(D) She lives close to the priest.

(E) She is a woman.

30. The ''vault of trees'' mentioned in paragraph 5 is intended to suggest a

(A) wedding

(B) church

(C) house

(D) convent

(E) cemetery

Questions 31–36

The mountain and the squirrel
Had a quarrel,
And the former called the latter ''Little Prig;''
Bun replied,
''You are doubtless very big;
But all sorts of things and weather
Must be taken in together,
To make up a year
And a sphere.
And I think it no disgrace
To occupy my place.
If I'm not so large as you,
You are not as small as I,
And not half so spry.
I'll not deny you make
A very pretty squirrel track;
Talents differ; all is well and wisely put;
If I cannot carry forests on my back,
Neither can you crack a nut.''

31. Which of the following best summarizes the squirrel's response to the mountain?

(A) A living creature is more important than an inanimate object.

(B) Small creatures are more important than large creatures.

(C) Cracking a nut is more difficult than carrying a forest.

(D) Nature is superior to civilization.

(E) All things great and small have their purpose.

32. The poem is best characterized as

(A) a fable

(B) an elegy

(C) an epic

(D) a sonnet

(E) a ballad

33. In the context of the poem, ''Little Prig'' must be

(A) a nonsense phrase

(B) a compliment

(C) an insult

(D) a literary allusion

(E) a paradoxical phrase

34. In lines 15 and 16, the squirrel implies that the mountain

(A) is not nearly so large as it thinks it is

(B) only exists in the mind of the squirrel

(C) is more attractive than other geographical features in the area

(D) should provide more forestation for animals

(E) exists primarily as a place where squirrels can run

GO ON TO THE NEXT PAGE

35. The poet elaborates the squirrel's viewpoint rather than the mountain's because

(A) the squirrel is more intelligent and clever than the mountain

(B) philosophical ideas are generally associated with animals rather than objects

(C) the argument was initiated by the mountain and not the squirrel

(D) it is often presumed that what is larger is more important than what is smaller

(E) the mountain fails to understand the distinctions drawn by the squirrel

36. Which of the following words, when substituted for "weather" (line 6), would best preserve the meaning of the poem?

(A) Events

(B) Storms

(C) People

(D) Objects

(E) Months

Questions 37–45

The Dream of an Hour

Knowing that Mrs. Mallard was afflicted with a heart trouble, great care was taken to break to her as gently as possible the news of her husband's death. It was her sister Josephine who told her. Her husband's friend Richards had been in the newspaper office when intelligence of the railroad disaster was received, with Brently Mallard's name leading the list of "killed."

She did not hear the story as many women have heard the same, with a paralyzed inability to accept its significance. She wept at once, with sudden, wild abandonment. When the storm of grief had spent itself she went away to her room alone. There she stood, facing the open window. She was young, with a fair calm face, but now there was a dull stare in her eyes, whose gaze was fixed away off yonder on a patch of blue sky.

When she abandoned herself a little whispered word escaped her slightly parted lips: "free!" She knew that she would weep again when she saw the kind, tender hands folded in death; the face that had never looked save with love upon her, fixed and gray and dead. But she saw beyond that bitter moment a long procession of years to come that would belong to her absolutely. And she opened and spread her arms out to welcome them. She would live for herself. There would be no powerful will bending hers in that blind persistence with which men and women believe they have a right to impose a private will upon a fellow-creature. A kind intention or a cruel intention made the act no less a crime. And yet she had loved him—sometimes.

She descended the stairs. Someone was opening the front door with a latchkey. It was Brently Mallard who entered, a little travel-stained. He had been far from the scene of the accident and did not even know there had been one. He stood amazed at his wife's piercing cry. When the doctors came, they were too late. They said she had died of heart disease—of joy that kills.

37. Which of the following best explains the significance of the title of the story?

(A) Mr. Mallard was only an hour late arriving home from his trip.

(B) Mrs. Mallard's hope for freedom lasted for only a short time.

(C) Mrs. Mallard only dreamt that her husband had been killed.

(D) Josephine imagined for a short time that her sister was grieving.

(E) Mrs. Mallard imagined for a brief moment that her husband was still alive.

38. Mrs. Mallard reacts to the news of her husband's death

(A) stoically

(B) indifferently

(C) with mixed emotions

(D) cynically

(E) without emotion

GO ON TO THE NEXT PAGE

39. It can be inferred that Mr. Mallard was

(A) a travelling salesman
(B) a controlling person
(C) an abusive husband
(D) a railway worker
(E) an older man

40. The latchkey turning in the door suggests that the person who will enter is a

(A) family member
(B) doctor
(C) government official
(D) representative of the railroad
(E) newspaper reporter

41. An important characteristic of the story is

(A) allusion
(B) metaphor
(C) simile
(D) skepticism
(E) irony

42. The doctors believed that Mrs. Mallard died because

(A) she was elated to see her husband still alive
(B) she was frightened by her husband's apparition
(C) her grief was too intense for her to bear
(D) the physical exertion of climbing stairs caused a heart attack
(E) a chronic heart condition finally caused her heart to stop beating

43. The author suggests that an attempt to exercise control over the will of another person is

(A) acceptable provided that the person has good intentions
(B) acceptable regardless of the person's intentions
(C) unacceptable only if the person has evil intentions
(D) unacceptable regardless of the person's intentions
(E) morally neutral, that is, neither good nor bad

44. As Mrs. Mallard stands at the window, the fact that her eyes are fixed on a faraway patch of blue sky suggests that she is

(A) thinking of the memory of her late husband
(B) remembering the happy times she shared with her husband
(C) anticipating a future without her husband
(D) planning the funeral arrangements
(E) wondering about the value of her husband's estate

45. The open window (line 16) suggests

(A) Mrs. Mallard's devotion to her husband
(B) Mr. Mallard's open coffin
(C) Mrs. Mallard's new freedom
(D) a window in a railway carriage
(E) the front door of the house

Questions 46–53

War Is Kind

Do not weep, maiden, for war is kind.
Because your lover threw wild hands toward the sky
And the affrighted steed ran on alone,
Do not weep.
War is kind.
Hoarse, booming drums of the regiment,
Little souls who thirst for fight,
These men were born to drill and die.
The unexplained glory flies above them,
Great is the battle god, great, and his kingdom
A field where a thousand corpses lie.
Do not weep, babe, for war is kind.
Because your father tumbled in the yellow trenches,
Raged at his breast, gulped and died,
Do not weep.
War is kind.
Swift blazing flag of the regiment,
Eagle with crest of red and gold,
These men were born to drill and die.
Point for them the virtue of the slaughter,
Make plain to them the excellence of killing
And a field where a thousand corpses lie.
Mother whose heart hung humble as a button
On the bright splendid shroud of your son,
Do not weep.
War is kind.

GO ON TO THE NEXT PAGE

46. The central point of the poem is that

(A) death is sometimes welcome relief
(B) organized battles are glorious
(C) war is not at all kind
(D) fighting is sometimes unavoidable
(E) war is kind because death is oblivion

47. The poem is addressed to which of the following?

I. A soldier's lover
II. A soldier's child
III. A soldier's mother

(A) I only
(B) III only
(C) I and II only
(D) II and III only
(E) I, II, and III

48. The phrase "little souls" (line 8) probably refers to

(A) the enemy
(B) young boys
(C) ordinary soldiers
(D) commanding officers
(E) the corpses

49. The phrase "the unexplained glory" that flies above the men (line 10) probably refers to

(A) the regimental flag
(B) an aircraft
(C) a soldier's hands
(D) clouds
(E) the sound of drums

50. The change in tempo in the second and fourth stanzas is designed to suggest

(A) sporadic gunfire
(B) galloping horses
(C) marching feet
(D) flapping material
(E) falling bodies

51. The poet chose the eagle with a crest of red and gold (line 21) in order to

(A) dramatize the loss of life that occurs in war
(B) highlight the seeming glory of war
(C) emphasize the bravery of the men
(D) echo the sound of the regimental drums
(E) create a contrast between animals and men

52. The "swift blazing flag of the regiment" (line 20) is a parallel to

(A) the "booming drums" (line 7)
(B) "the battle god" (line 11)
(C) "his kingdom" (line 12)
(D) "a field" (line 13)
(E) "father" (line 15)

53. The instructions contained in lines 23 through 26 are issued to

(A) soldiers about to enter a battle
(B) leaders who glorify war
(C) pacifists opposed to war
(D) soldiers who have already died
(E) soldiers dying on the plain of battle

GO ON TO THE NEXT PAGE

Questions 54–60

All mankind is of one author, and is one volume. When one man dies, one chapter is not torn out of the book, but translated into a better language; and every chapter must be so translated. Some pieces are translated by age, some by sickness, some by war, some by justice; but God's hand is in every translation, and his hand shall bind up all our scattered leaves again for that library where every book shall lie open to one another.

No man is an island, entire of itself; every man is a piece of the continent, a part of the main. If a clod be washed away by the sea, Europe is the less, as well as if a promontory were. Any man's death diminishes me. Therefore, never send to know for whom the bell tolls; it tolls for thee.

Neither can we call this a borrowing of misery, as though we were not miserable enough ourselves, but must fetch in more from the next house, in taking upon us the misery of our neighbors. Affliction is a treasure. No man hath affliction enough that is not matured and ripened by it, and made fit for God by that affliction. If a man carry treasure in bullion and have none coined into current money, his treasure will not defray him as he travels. Tribulation is treasure in the nature of it, but it is not current money in the use of it, except we get nearer our home, heaven, by it. Another man may be sick to death, and his affliction may lie in his bowels, as gold in a mine, and be of no use to him. But this bell, that tells me of his affliction, digs out and applies that gold to me: if by this consideration of another's danger I take mine own into contemplation, and so secure myself, by making my recourse to my God, who is our only security.

54. In the context of the passage, the phrase ''translated by justice'' means

(A) death by execution
(B) equitable arrangement
(C) legal contract
(D) state religion
(E) elected judge

55. The author is addressing

(A) only the clergy
(B) only the sick
(C) only Europeans
(D) only scholars
(E) every person

56. In the first paragraph, the author relies upon

(A) metaphor
(B) simile
(C) conceit
(D) allegory
(E) allusion

57. The ''clod'' (line 13) and the ''promontory'' (line 15) represent, respectively,

(A) a criminal and a minister
(B) a sick person and a healthy person
(C) an author and a reader
(D) a single person and a group of persons
(E) a farmer and a sailor

58. The bell in the passage peals to

(A) call worshippers to regular services
(B) announce that someone is near death
(C) signal the birth of a child
(D) alert townspeople of approaching travelers
(E) warn of a natural disaster

59. The distinction drawn by the author in the final paragraph between ''bullion'' and ''current money'' is most likely the distinction between

(A) salt and food
(B) marble and statue
(C) author and book
(D) shepherd and flock
(E) clapper and bell

60. The ''author'' referred to in line 1 is

(A) a minister
(B) God
(C) any writer
(D) a librarian
(E) a traveller

S T O P

IF YOU FINISH BEFORE TIME IS CALLED, YOU MAY CHECK YOUR WORK ON THIS TEST ONLY. DO NOT WORK ON ANY OTHER TEST IN THIS BOOK.

Explanatory Answers

1. The central idea of the poem is the

(A) inevitability of death

(B) onset of old age

(C) power of poetry to preserve a memory

(D) destructiveness of wars of conquest

(E) transcendental nature of love

(C) The poem consists of four sentences. The first three occupy four lines and the last sentence, two lines. If we focus on the main clauses of the sentences, the main points of the poem can be summarized as follows:

Lines 1–4: You will shine more brightly (live on) in this poem.
Lines 5–8: Nothing will destroy the living record of your memory. (Again the poem itself.)
Lines 9–12: This praise (this poem) will last until the end of time.
Lines 13–4: Your memory will endure until Judgment Day.

The best summary of this development is provided by (C).

There is something very interesting about this poem. It seems to be written to a lover, but the subject of the poem is not the lover. Notice that in this poem no characteristic of the lover is ever mentioned. The subject is the poem itself: It speaks of "these conténts" (line 3), "living record of your memory" (line 8), and "in this" (line 14). These are all references not to the lover to whom the poem is addressed but to the poem itself.

As for the other answer choices, the poem includes or suggests elements of these ideas, but they do not constitute the central idea of the poem.

2. According to the poet, all of the following are true of the gilded monuments EXCEPT:

(A) They are forgotten by future generations.

(B) They are ruined by natural elements.

(C) They are destroyed by fire.

(D) They are destroyed by armies.

(E) They preserve history.

(E) In the explanation to question 1, we learned about the main idea of the poem. The poet develops the main idea by contrasting the power of the poem to preserve the memory of the loved one with the inability of monuments and statues to preserve permanently the memory of a historical figure; statues and monuments can be destroyed, but this poem will continue to exist. Thus, an important idea in the poem is that historical monuments do not preserve history.

You will find the ideas referred to in choices (B) through (D) mentioned explicitly in lines 4, 6, and 7, respectively. The idea referred to in choice (A) is strongly suggested throughout the poem.

3. Which of the following best describes the overall structure of the poem?

(A) Three quatrains and a couplet

(B) A couplet and three quatrains

(C) An octet and a sestet

(D) A sestet and an octet

(E) Two sestets and a couplet

(A) In the explanation for question 1, it was noted that the poem consists of four sentences. The first three sentences each occupy four lines, while the last occupies two. Thus, (A) is the best description of the structure of the poem.

Although you would not be expected to know this, the poem was written by Shakespeare, and it has the form of a Shakespearean sonnet: three quatrains and a couplet.

4. In line 3, the phrase "these conténts" refers to

(A) history books

(B) the location of the monuments

(C) heaven

(D) a tomb

(E) the poem itself

(E) In the explanation for question 1, it was observed that the poem is really about itself. Thus, the phrase "these conténts" refers to the poem.

5. In the context of the poem, "the ending doom" probably refers to

(A) Judgment Day

(B) the destruction of the monuments

(C) the poet's death

(D) the destruction of the poem

(E) a war

(A) Several clues in the poem lead to this conclusion. The contrast between the destruction of the monuments and the lasting quality of the poem suggests that the poem is intended to endure until the end of the world. Additionally, line 13 refers to the "judgment that yourself arise," which can only be Judgment Day.

6. The tone of the poem is best described as

(A) angry and resentful

(B) repentant and contrite

(C) hopeless and despairing

(D) assured and confident

(E) cheerful and lighthearted

(D) As was noted above, the poem is really about itself. The 14 lines really amount to the assertion "Other seemingly permanent things will perish, but this poem will live forever." The best description of this sentiment is "assured and confident."

7. Which of the following expressions is most nearly synonymous with "oblivious enmity" (line 9)?

(A) Untold story

(B) Unsung hero

(C) Massive retaliation

(D) Ravages of time

(E) Unpredictable change

(D) The meaning of the phrase "oblivious enmity" is not apparent from the two words themselves. Indeed, *oblivious* and *enmity* seem almost to contradict each other. Oblivious means unaware, and enmity means hate. But how could one hate what one is unaware of? In the context of the poem, however, the idea of enmity is intended to echo the idea of destruction; and when coupled with *oblivious,* the result is the idea of a mindless or uncaring destruction. The best available interpretation of this notion is provided by (D); time has no conscious hatred of statues and monuments, but nonetheless they eventually are destroyed.

8. The author refers to marble (line 1) because stone

(A) can be sculpted into human features

(B) is more durable than other materials

(C) can be inscribed with words

(D) has little intrinsic value

(E) is not an instrument of war

(B) Central to the main idea of the poem is the contrast between the impermanence of what we ordinarily might consider permanent (statues and monuments) and the real permanence of the ideas expressed in the poem. Thus, the poet has selected marble because it suggests a substance of enduring quality (though the poet says it really does not endure).

9. The tone of the passage can best be described as

(A) humorous

(B) diffident

(C) solemn

(D) didactic

(E) lofty

(A) Although you are not expected to recognize the selection, it was written by Mark Twain. And, as you might expect, its main point is humor. At several points the tongue-in-cheek tone is evident: the exaggeration in the first paragraph (has the author really seen this particular phrase in print *several thousand times?*), the comparison of the guide to the parrot in the third paragraph, and the contrast between the sublimity of the exhibits described by the guide and the indifference of the author, also in the third paragraph.

10. The author accomplishes his purpose in the first paragraph by using

(A) irony

(B) sarcasm

(C) exaggeration

(D) analogy

(E) metaphor

(C) As noted in the explanation for question 9, the device used to achieve the humorous effect of the first paragraph is overstatement or exaggeration.

11. The author refuses to show enthusiasm in order to

(A) force the guide to move quickly to the next location

(B) frustrate the guide's expectations

(C) preserve his own sense of superiority

(D) show reverence for the exhibits

(E) avoid paying the guide his fee

(B) In the second paragraph, the author states that he wishes he could get even with his guide for the fact that he really needs his services. In the third paragraph, the author explains how he accomplishes this. The guide, according to the author, expects that his tourist will be suitably impressed by the exhibits he is shown and that the tourist will manifest his approval. By suppressing the natural tendency to show approval, the author frustrates the guide's expectations.

12. When the author compares the guide to a parrot, he means that the guide

(A) is difficult to understand

(B) is not very intelligent

(C) doesn't really understand what he is saying

(D) is very considerate of the tourists

(E) knows nothing of history

(C) Two clues help you here. First is the comparison to a parrot. A parrot merely mimics sounds but has no real understanding of the meaning of the words. Second, the author states that if the guide is interrupted, he finds it necessary to begin again. In other words, the guide has memorized the words but has no understanding of their meanings.

13. The word "soberer" in line 30 can be taken to mean

(A) less exciting

(B) without alcohol

(C) less pompous

(D) lacking humor

(E) less rigid

(A) The idea of *soberer* stands in contrast to the idea of *ecstasies.* Thus, the word does not have its ordinary meaning of "without alcohol" but a related meaning of "less exciting."

14. When the author asks the guide whether the subject of the statue is dead, the author

(A) expects the guide to answer affirmatively

(B) expects the guide to answer negatively

(C) already knows the subject is still living

(D) already knows the subject is dead

(E) believes the guide does not know the answer

(D) As we noted above, the author hopes to frustrate the guide's expectations. That the statue has broken legs and is an exhibit shown by a guide suggests that the statue is an antiquity. The author, therefore, knows full well that the statue is of a subject long dead. But in order to frustrate the guide, the author asks a stupid question.

15. The poet's primary aim is to

(A) distinguish crickets from grasshoppers

(B) contrast summer and winter

(C) point out the harshness of nature

(D) admire the continuity of nature

(E) criticize the grasshopper and praise the cricket

(D) An important structural feature of this poem is the repetition in line 9 of the idea expressed in line 1. The poet in line 1 asserts that the poetry of earth is never dead and then proceeds to prove the point in lines 2 through 8 by describing a summer scene. The poet makes the same assertion in line 9 and proves the point in lines 10 through 14 by talking about a winter scene. The juxtaposition of summer and winter strongly suggests an uninterrupted sequence of events.

16. The poet uses the phrase "poetry of earth" to refer to the

(A) changing of the seasons

(B) sounds of animals

(C) vegetation

(D) temperature

(E) poet's role in nature

(B) As was noted above, the poet begins by announcing in line 1 that the poetry of earth is never dead. He then goes on to talk about the sound made by the grasshopper. The poet reasserts in line 9 the idea announced in line 1 and goes on to talk about the sound made by the cricket. Thus, the best choice is (B).

Further analysis of the poem would suggest that the sounds made by the grasshopper and the cricket are intended to represent some more abstract concept, perhaps life itself. The fact that insects are small and not usually regarded as individuals suggests the notion of an earth "teeming" with life. But that idea of "life" does not appear as an answer choice.

Surely the second-best answer choice here is (A), since it hints at the idea discussed in the preceding paragraph. But (A) must be wrong since the author uses the changing of the seasons as a backdrop against which the continuity of the poetry of earth is measured. More concretely, if the phrase "changing of the seasons" were substituted for "poetry of earth" in line 9, the poet would be asserting that the changing of seasons never stops. But lines 10 through 14 do not help prove that assertion. Lines 10 through 14 go on to show that life continues even in the winter, but they do not prove that the world will never end.

17. Why in line 9 does the poet use language that is very similar to that used in line 1?

(A) To summarize the content of lines 1 through 8

(B) To suggest that lines 9 through 14 will contradict lines 1 through 8

(C) To emphasize that lines 9 through 14 will help prove the point announced in line 1

(D) To minimize the significance of the ideas developed in lines 1 through 8

(E) To signal the reader that lines 9 through 14 will address a different topic

(C) As noted above, the sequence of seasons—summer through winter—is intended to prove the assertion that the poetry of earth is unending. Concretely, this means the sound of life and more abstractly, it refers to life itself. By having line 9 echo line 1, the poet signals that the second part of the poem will be an extension of the idea developed in the first part.

(A) is probably the second-best answer, but it is incorrect because line 9 looks forward and not back. Had the poet intended line 9 to be a summary of the first eight lines of the poem, he would have used a period rather than a colon to punctuate the end of that line. The colon indicates to the reader that what follows in the sentence will further explain or elaborate upon what has come before in that particular sentence.

18. The poem creates a contrast between all of the following pairs of words EXCEPT:

(A) sun and frost

(B) hot and cooling

(C) grasshopper and cricket

(D) summer and winter

(E) drowsiness and hills

(E) The poem uses the juxtaposition of summer and winter to suggest the continuity of nature or life. Thus, (D) contains an important pair of contrasting ideas. Part of that contrast is also given in the juxtaposition between *sun* (line 2) and *frost* (line 10). The juxtaposition of the grasshopper (the summer creature) and the cricket (the winter creature) is also important. Finally, within the first part of the poem, the hot sun is contrasted with the cooling tree. There is no contrast, however, between the idea of drowsiness and the hills.

19. The last line of the poem refers to the grasshopper's

(A) leaf

(B) mead

(C) voice

(D) delights

(E) weed

(C) The last three lines state that the cricket's song is confused with something of the grasshopper's. That can only be the sound made by the grasshopper, which, in the first part of the poem, is referred to as the grasshopper's voice.

20. According to the poem, the effect of the cricket's song is to

(A) create the illusion of summer

(B) remind the listener of a loved one

(C) warm the room

(D) obliterate the memory of the grasshopper

(E) announce the coming of spring

(A) The last five lines describe a warm room during winter. To a person half asleep, the warmth of the room and the chirping of the cricket create the illusion of a summer's day.

21. In line 6, the word "done" means

(A) finished

(B) enjoyed

(C) known

(D) understood

(E) expected

(A) One meaning of the word *done* is over or finished, and that is the meaning intended here.

22. The idea that nature has no intentions (first paragraph) is most likely held by the

(A) priest

(B) niece

(C) niece's lover

(D) nuns

(E) author

(E) The author begins by describing the priest's view of nature: everything has a purpose. Then, in the final sentence of that paragraph, the author says that it never occurred to the priest to think otherwise. Thus, this cannot be an idea held by the priest. Rather, it is a thought of the author inserted to emphasize by contrast the simplicity of the priest's view.

23. Which of the following best describes the priest's attitude toward human sexuality?

(A) Unqualified revulsion

(B) Amused indifference

(C) Uncomfortable ambivalence

(D) Total ignorance

(E) Fiery condemnation

(C) An important feature of the story is the shift in the priest's attitude from absolute certainty about the tidy structure of the world, to the worry that things are not quite so clear, to the realization that his interpretation of the world was wrong. Initially, the priest believes that the dark is for sleeping only, but by the end of the story he realizes that the night is intended also for making love. The word *ashamed* is strongly suggestive of the priest's discomfort. He can only appreciate the validity of the lovers' union because he himself has sexual feelings, but he is forbidden by his vows to enter into such a union. Also, the discussion of the priest's attitude towards nuns in the second paragraph hints that such a shift in attitude is possible.

24. It can be inferred that the priest leaves his home at night to

(A) enjoy the beauty of the moonlit countryside

(B) surprise his niece with her lover

(C) avoid sleeping during the period of darkness

(D) visit the mother of his niece

(E) meditate and pray in the fields and woods

(B) In the first paragraph, we learn that the priest believes that the night is for sleeping—not for taking moonlight strolls. In the third paragraph, we are told that he has learned that the niece has a lover and that he is angry. Thus, we can infer that the priest changes his routine on account of the news about his niece. The best explanation for this change in behavior is that he intends to confront the niece and her lover.

25. The priest is tolerant of nuns because they

(A) have foresworn sexual relations

(B) also do the work of God

(C) have agreed to accept his niece

(D) belong to a different temple

(E) are constantly seeking him out

(A) The first paragraph describes how firmly the priest believes that everything in nature has its purpose. There is a tight fit between the "why" and the "because." According to the priest, the answer to the question "Why are there women?" is "Because God wants to test men with their sexuality." An exception to this rule would be a woman devoid of this sexuality, for example, a nun who had taken a vow of chastity. Notice also in the second paragraph the ambivalence of the priest toward human sexuality, for he treats the nuns harshly because of what he imagines to be his own weakness.

26. In the fifth paragraph, the priest realizes that

(A) God made the night for lovers

(B) the moonlight is beautiful

(C) trees grow to become lumber

(D) his niece has taken a lover

(E) he has sexual desires himself

(A) In the fifth paragraph, the author writes that the countryside enveloped the lovers "like a setting made divinely for them"—that the setting was created by God for the lovers. This disturbs the priest, because it upsets his nice, neat, and tidy view of the world.

Watch out for (B), (D), and (E). These are ideas that come to the priest, but not in the fifth paragraph.

27. The "oblivion" referred to in paragraph four is

(A) death

(B) marriage

(C) sin

(D) sleep

(E) love

(D) In the first paragraph, the author states that the priest believes that the night is dark because God created it for sleeping. In the fourth paragraph, the priest—in the face of rising doubts—reminds himself that the night is intended for "oblivion." In this context, oblivion, or a state of unconsciousness, must mean sleep.

28. The priest would likely agree with all of the following EXCEPT:

(A) The winter exists because it gives the farmer a rest from his labors.

(B) Sexuality was intended by God to ensure the procreation of the human species.

(C) The earth revolves around the sun so that human beings have a calendar year.

(D) Natural phenomena have no significance independent of human interpretation.

(E) Animals bear their young in the spring because that helps ensure their survival.

(D) The first paragraph describes the priest's view of nature: everything has a purpose ordained by God. Choice (D) expresses an idea that is contradictory to this view. It is an idea that is introduced by the author in the last sentence of the first paragraph to show the simplicity of the priest's view by contrasting it with an idea that the priest himself had never had.

29. Which of the following points of information about the niece is LEAST significant?

(A) She has taken a lover.

(B) She and her lover are observed by the priest.

(C) The priest wants her to become a nun.

(D) She lives close to the priest.

(E) She is a woman.

(D) The gender and sexuality of the niece are vital to the development of the story. The fact that the niece lives close by is only incidental. You can prove this to yourself by imagining how the story would read if the niece lived in a faraway town. The priest could still travel to that town, find the lovers—say, walking together along a tree-lined street—and reach the same conclusions.

30. The "vault of trees" mentioned in paragraph five is intended to suggest a

(A) wedding

(B) church

(C) house

(D) convent

(E) cemetery

(B) The use of the word *temple* in the final paragraph is very interesting, because it suggests that the priest has finally realized that the realm of sexuality is equally valid to that of religion—but he has no place there. The "vault of trees" creates an image of a location that is similar to a temple or church but has a different function.

31. Which of the following best summarizes the squirrel's response to the mountain?

(A) A living creature is more important than an inanimate object.

(B) Small creatures are more important than large creatures.

(C) Cracking a nut is more difficult than carrying a forest.

(D) Nature is superior to civilization.

(E) All things great and small have their purpose.

(E) In the heat of a quarrel, the mountain attempts to insult the squirrel by calling him little. The rest of the poem elaborates the squirrel's response to the mountain's attempt to insult him. The burden of the squirrel's response is that the insult has been ineffective: Squirrels are small because that is what they are intended to be. The larger conclusion aimed at by the squirrel is that all things are what they are intended to be. Thus, the mountain is large because that is what it means to be a mountain, and a squirrel cracks nuts because that is what it means to be a squirrel.

32. The poem is best characterized as

(A) a fable

(B) an elegy

(C) an epic

(D) a sonnet

(E) a ballad

(A) A fable is a brief story with a moral that often uses animals as characters.

33. In the context of the poem, ''Little Prig'' must be

(A) a nonsense phrase

(B) a compliment

(C) an insult

(D) a literary allusion

(E) a paradoxical phrase

(C) As noted in the explanation for question 31, the mountain attempts to insult the squirrel because he is small.

34. In lines 15 and 16, the squirrel implies that the mountain

(A) is not nearly so large as it thinks it is

(B) only exists in the mind of the squirrel

(C) is more attractive than other geographical features in the area

(D) should provide more forestation for animals

(E) exists primarily as a place where squirrels can run

(E) In lines 15 and 16, the squirrel manages to invert the usual interpretation of things. Ordinarily, we would think of the squirrel as living on the mountain. But the squirrel suggests that the mountain was created to lie beneath a squirrel. This is somewhat like saying that a river exists for the purpose of flowing beneath a bridge.

35. The poet elaborates the squirrel's viewpoint rather than the mountain's because

(A) the squirrel is more intelligent and clever than the mountain

(B) philosophical ideas are generally associated with animals rather than objects

(C) the argument was initiated by the mountain and not the squirrel

(D) it is often presumed that what is larger is more important than what is smaller

(E) the mountain fails to understand the distinctions drawn by the squirrel

(D) The moral of the fable is that all things, great and small, have a purpose. To understand why the poet takes the point of view of the squirrel, try to rewrite the fable (i.e., with the squirrel insulting the mountain by saying "You're too big").

36. Which of the following words, when substituted for ''weather'' (line 6), would best preserve the meaning of the poem?

(A) Events

(B) Storms

(C) People

(D) Objects

(E) Months

(A) To understand the point of line 6, you must look ahead to lines 8 and 9. *Year* and *sphere* indicate *time* and *space*. Events occur in time, and things occupy space. Thus, in line 6, *things* taken together make up a sphere, and it is the weather, which of course changes, that represents occurrences or events.

37. Which of the following best explains the significance of the title of the story?

(A) Mr. Mallard was only an hour late arriving home from his trip.

(B) Mrs. Mallard's hope for freedom lasted for only a short time.

(C) Mrs. Mallard only dreamt that her husband had been killed.

(D) Josephine imagined for a short time that her sister was grieving.

(E) Mrs. Mallard imagined for a brief moment that her husband was still alive.

(B) The title of the story contains two elements. The first, *dream,* describes Mrs. Mallard's feelings about the future. As is learned in the third paragraph, she is glad as well as sad to learn of her husband's death. She looks forward to the future. The second element of the title is *hour,* a relatively short period of time compared with an entire life. Mrs. Mallard enjoys her dream for only a short time because her husband reappears.

38. Mrs. Mallard reacts to the news of her husband's death

(A) stoically

(B) indifferently

(C) with mixed emotions

(D) cynically

(E) without emotion

(C) We are told in the second paragraph that Mrs. Mallard initially reacts to the news of her husband's death with a "storm of grief." In paragraph three, it is learned that she looks forward to a life without him. This ambivalence is summed up by the final sentence of the third paragraph: "And yet she had loved him—sometimes."

39. It can be inferred that Mr. Mallard was

(A) a traveling salesman

(B) a controlling person

(C) an abusive husband

(D) a railway worker

(E) an older man

(B) In the third paragraph, it is learned that Mrs. Mallard is looking forward to a life without her husband because she wishes to live for herself—without a powerful will trying to control her. Thus, it can be inferred that Mr. Mallard was a controlling person. Watch out for choice (C)! Although Mr. Mallard may have had the objectionable trait of being controlling, there is not sufficient evidence to conclude that he was abusive.

40. The latchkey turning in the door suggests that the person who will enter is a

(A) family member

(B) doctor

(C) government official

(D) representative of the railroad

(E) newspaper reporter

(A) Ask yourself why the author bothered to insert the remark about the latchkey. Why not simply write "Mr. Mallard walked through the door?" What would be lost? The particular effect of the turning of the lock is to prompt the reader to ask "Why is someone coming through the door? Who would have a key to the house?" Thus, it foreshadows, even if only briefly, the arrival of Mrs. Mallard's husband and heightens the dramatic effect of his entrance.

41. An important characteristic of the story is

(A) allusion

(B) metaphor

(C) simile

(D) skepticism

(E) irony

(E) The most important characteristic of the story is its irony. Mrs. Mallard has experienced the grief of losing her husband and the joy of the realization that she will be free to live her own life. She accepts and even welcomes this prospect, only to find out that her husband is not in fact dead.

42. The doctors believed that Mrs. Mallard died because

(A) she was elated to see her husband still alive

(B) she was frightened by her husband's apparition

(C) her grief was too intense for her to bear

(D) the physical exertion of climbing stairs caused a heart attack

(E) a chronic heart condition finally caused her heart to stop beating

(A) The opinion of the doctors reinforces the irony discussed above. The doctors can see only the "outside" of the events: The woman believes she has lost her beloved husband but subsequently learns he is still alive, and the sudden happiness causes heart failure. We as readers, however, are aware of the "inside," so we know that it was not happiness that killed Mrs. Mallard.

43. The author suggests that an attempt to exercise control over the will of another person is

(A) acceptable provided that the person has good intentions

(B) acceptable regardless of the person's intentions

(C) unacceptable only if the person has evil intentions

(D) unacceptable regardless of the person's intentions

(E) morally neutral, that is, neither good nor bad

(D) In the next-to-last sentence in the third paragraph, the author refers to the attempt to control another person's will as a crime and states that it is so regardless of the intentions of the dominant personality. What is interesting about that sentence is that it stands almost outside of the text. Every other thought in the story is clearly a part of the narrative: "great care was taken," "it was Josephine," "she did not hear," "she knew that," "she descended," and "they said." The sentence in question, however, is simply a statement of fact. It is not prefaced by a "she thought" or "she believed." Although the thought must be attributed in the story to Mrs. Mallard, the fact that the idea is almost independent of the narrative indicates that the idea is also shared by the author.

44. As Mrs. Mallard stands at the window, the fact that her eyes are fixed on a faraway patch of blue sky suggests that she is

(A) thinking of the memory of her late husband

(B) remembering the happy times she shared with her husband

(C) anticipating a future without her husband

(D) planning the funeral arrangements

(E) wondering about the value of her husband's estate

(C) Above we noted that Mrs. Mallard reacted to the news of her husband's death with mixed emotions. As she stands at the window in her room, she is in her mind looking far into the future at a "long procession of years to come that would belong to her." This mental gaze is paralleled by her actual vision, which looks to a point a great distance removed and at a patch of open sky.

45. The open window (line 16) suggests

(A) Mrs. Mallard's devotion to her husband

(B) Mr. Mallard's open coffin

(C) Mrs. Mallard's new freedom

(D) a window in a railway carriage

(E) the front door of the house

(C) Why is the window open rather than closed? Or why does the author even mention whether or not the window is open or closed? The fact that Mrs. Mallard is looking out of a window to the freedom of the outdoors is itself suggestive of the freedom she will have in the future, but that idea is reinforced by the fact that the window is open.

46. The central point of the poem is that

(A) death is sometimes welcome relief

(B) organized battles are glorious

(C) war is not at all kind

(D) fighting is sometimes unavoidable

(E) war is kind because death is oblivion

(C) An important feature of this poem is irony. The poet repeatedly asserts that war is kind yet in the very next breath describes events that are inconsistent with this conclusion. For example, in the first sentence of the first stanza the poet says to the maiden that war is kind, yet in the next sentence he says that her lover was killed in battle. In the third stanza, the poet says to the child that war is kind although his father was killed. Thus, the central point is that despite the seeming gallantry of war, war is not in any way kind.

47. The poem is addressed to which of the following?

I. A soldier's lover

II. A soldier's child

III. A soldier's mother

(A) I only

(B) III only

(C) I and II only

(D) II and III only

(E) I, II, and III

(E) Each of three stanzas flush at the left margin addresses a different person: the first, the maiden or soldier's lover; the second, the babe or soldier's child; and the third, the soldier's mother.

48. The phrase "little souls" (line 7) probably refers to

(A) the enemy

(B) young boys

(C) ordinary soldiers

(D) commanding officers

(E) the corpses

(C) Notice that the second and fourth stanzas are parallel: They both have six lines, and each consists of two sentences three lines long. Furthermore, the third line in each is the same. In each, the poet contrasts the seeming or false glory of war (in the first three lines) with the reality of death (in the second three). The contention that some "men were born to drill and die" can only be the cynical rationalization of someone who falsely believes that war is glorious. The phrase "little souls" refers to the ordinary soldiers who are used as cannon fodder.

49. The phrase "the unexplained glory" that flies above the men (line 9) probably refers to

(A) the regimental flag

(B) an aircraft

(C) a soldier's hands

(D) clouds

(E) the sound of drums

(A) We return again to the parallel structure of the second and fourth stanzas. There are two elements to the phrase in question here. First, the "unexplained glory" obviously refers to the false impression that war is glorious. But why is it unexplained? Look to the fourth stanza. Who is the *them* in the fourth line of the fourth stanza? It is the men who were meant to drill and die—the little souls. In the fourth stanza, someone is instructed to explain the virtue or glory of war to these men. Thus, the ordinary soldier does not understand why anyone would regard war as glorious. Second, why is the "unexplained glory" flying above the soldiers? Look again to the fourth stanza. The flag is used there to symbolize the false glory of war. Thus, the "unexplained glory" that flies above the soldiers is the flag, a symbol designed to inspire devotion without regard to rational thought.

50. The change in tempo in the second and fourth stanzas is designed to suggest

(A) sporadic gunfire

(B) galloping horses

(C) marching feet

(D) flapping material

(E) falling bodies

(C) The first, third, and fifth stanzas use a rhythm that is smooth and flowing; the second and fourth stanzas use a rhythm that is staccato—sharp and articulated, and in them the author says that someone believes the men were meant to drill and die. The change in tempo is used to suggest men drilling or marching.

51. The poet chose the eagle with a crest of red and gold (line 18) in order to

(A) dramatize the loss of life that occurs in war

(B) highlight the seeming glory of war

(C) emphasize the bravery of the men

(D) echo the sound of the regimental drums

(E) create a contrast between animals and men

(B) Why not a flag of pastel yellow and blue? Why not a flag with a dove on it? Because those colors do not suggest something heroic or glorious, and the dove is a symbol of peace, not war. The poet here selects a symbol that would inspire devotion and colors that would excite the passions. The choice of symbol and colors heightens the ironic contrast in the fourth stanza.

52. The "swift blazing flag of the regiment" (line 17) is a parallel to

(A) the "booming drums" (line 6)

(B) "the battle god" (line 10)

(C) "his kingdom" (line 10)

(D) "a field" (line 11)

(E) "father" (line 13)

(A) The parallelism between the second and fourth stanzas has already been discussed. The *booming* drums are supposed to inspire the same mindless devotion that the *blazing* flag inspires.

53. The instructions contained in lines 20 through 23 are issued to

(A) soldiers about to enter a battle

(B) leaders who glorify war

(C) pacifists opposed to war

(D) soldiers who have already died

(E) soldiers dying on the plain of battle

(B) Notice the use of the imperative voice in the lines in question: "Point for them the virtue of slaughter,/Make plain to them the excellence of killing." The poet apparently has in mind a particular group of individuals, and they must be the people in authority.

54. In the context of the passage, the phrase "translated by justice" means

(A) death by execution

(B) equitable arrangement

(C) legal contract

(D) state religion

(E) elected judge

(A) In the first paragraph, the author uses the metaphor of a book. All of humanity is like a book with many chapters. A chapter is an individual person. Pursuing the metaphor, the author states than when a person dies, the chapter is not destroyed; rather, it is translated. Thus, translation refers to death. And, according to the author, translation or death can be accomplished in different ways: by age, sickness, war, and justice. What would be death by justice? It must surely refer to death by execution for some crime.

55. The author is addressing

(A) only the clergy

(B) only the sick

(C) only Europeans

(D) only scholars

(E) every person

(E) In the second paragraph, the author emphasizes that all of humanity is bound together, every individual to every other individual. Notice that the last sentence of the second paragraph stands out. While the rest of the essay is written using the third-person point of view, this sentence is written in the imperative. It is directed to "you" as a part of humanity. So the argument of the essay is addressed to every person.

56. In the first paragraph, the author relies upon

(A) metaphor

(B) simile

(C) conceit

(D) allegory

(E) allusion

(A) A metaphor is an implied comparison of two essentially unlike things. In the first paragraph, the author states that humanity is a book, individual people are chapters in the book, and the death of an individual is merely a translation of that chapter into a better language.

57. The "clod" (line 14) and the "promontory" (line 16) represent, respectively,

(A) a criminal and a minister

(B) a sick person and a healthy person

(C) an author and a reader

(D) a single person and a group of persons

(E) a farmer and a sailor

(D) In the second paragraph, humanity is equated with a continent. Since *clod* and *promontory* are parts of the larger land mass, we understand that these are individuals. And remember that the author is arguing that each individual is an important part of humanity: the clod, an individual, is just as important as a promontory, a group of individuals.

58. The bell in the passage peals to

(A) call worshippers to regular services

(B) announce that someone is near death

(C) signal the birth of a child

(D) alert townspeople of approaching travelers

(E) warn of a natural disaster

(B) The significance of the bell was discussed in the second paragraph. The bell is mentioned again in the third paragraph, in which it tells the author of the fact that another person is sick and dying. So we may conclude that the bell tolls to announce that someone is dying or perhaps is already dead.

59. The distinction drawn by the author in the final paragraph between ''bullion'' and ''current money'' is most likely the distinction between

(A) salt and food

(B) marble and statue

(C) author and book

(D) shepherd and flock

(E) clapper and bell

(B) In the third paragraph, the author argues that affliction, or we might say suffering, reminds us of our common bonds to other people. But, the author warns, it is not sufficient just to suffer. It is necessary to convert that suffering into a learning experience. The author illustrates the point with an analogy. Gold itself is valuable, but it can't be spent as money unless it is first converted into a coin. The distinction drawn is nicely paralleled by the distinction between marble and a statue. The marble is potentially a statue as gold is potentially money and suffering potentially a learning experience.

60. The ''author'' referred to in line 1 is

(A) a minister

(B) God

(C) any writer

(D) a librarian

(E) a traveler

(B) In the context of the metaphor in the first paragraph, the author of the book of humanity must surely be its creator, or God.

French Test

French Test

The French Test is available in two formats: one is reading only and one includes a listening component. The French Test with Listening is offered only on selected dates and at specific locations. The reading-only test is the one that is offered on national test dates and is the one discussed here.

The French Test is designed to measure your ability to use French vocabulary correctly, to identify correct grammatical forms, and to read and understand French. The level of difficulty varies, since the test is based on the secondary-school curriculum and is usually taken by students who have had from two to four years of French.

The test consists of 85 multiple-choice questions. Following are examples of the question types, with explanations.

Vocabulary in Context

In this type of question you are given an incomplete sentence and asked to fill in the blank with the word or expression that best completes it.

EXAMPLE:

1. Je voudrais manger tout de suite; j'ai extrêmement ________.

(A) fin
(B) appétit
(C) faim
(D) chaud

The answer is (C) *j'ai extrêmement faim*: I am extremely hungry. (A) is included here because it sounds and looks like the correct answer, *faim*; (B) cannot follow *j'ai* without additional words in between; (D) is structurally correct but meaningless here: "I would like to eat right away; I am extremely hot."

Structure

Here again you are given an incomplete sentence and asked to complete it. In this case, the word or expression that best completes the sentence will be one that makes it grammatically complete.

EXAMPLE:

2. Les hommes que nous avons ________ au match étaient très grands.
   (A) vu
   (B) vues
   (C) vus
   (D) voyant

The answer is (C), *vus,* which is the past participle of *voir.* The past participle of constructions that use *avoir* (*avons* in this example) must agree with the direct object if the direct object precedes the verb in the sentence. This is the case here: *hommes* (masculine plural) precedes *avons vus.*

Structure – One Correct

EXAMPLE:

3. Les étudiants travaillent souvent le samedi.
   (A) tous
   (B) lent
   (C) systématique
   (D) rarement

The answer is (D) *rarement,* which is the only choice that fits grammatically in the sentence; the replacement must be an adverb to qualify the verb *travaillent.*

Structure in Paragraph

EXAMPLES:

Anne a beaucoup d'argent; elle pourrait ________ en

4. (A) ________
   (B) part
   (C) partir
   (D) partie

vacances si elle ________, mais elle est ________

5. (A) voudra
   (B) vouloir
   (C) voulait
   (D) voulu

6. (A) obligé
   (B) obliger
   (C) oblige
   (D) obligée

de rester a Paris avec sa mère qui est malade.

The answer to 4 is (C) *partir,* an infinitive, which is what must be used for the second verb when two verbs follow one another. (B) is a conjugated form of *partir* and (D) is the past participle.

The answer to 5 is (C) *voulait.* In *si* clauses (clauses of condition), when the conditional is used for one verb, it must also be used for the second verb in the sentence.

The answer to 6 is (D) *obligée*, which is the only one of the choices that correctly qualifies the feminine singular subject/noun: *elle/Anne*. (A) is masculine singular; (B) is the infinitive; and (C) is a conjugated form of the verb.

Reading Comprehension

On remonta sur le pont après dîner. Devant nous, la Méditerranée n'avait pas un frisson sur toute sa surface qu'une grande lune calme moirait. Le vaste bateau glissait, jetant sur le ciel, qui semblait ensemencé d'étoiles, un gros serpent de fumée noire; et, derrière nous, l'eau toute blanche, agitée par le passage rapide du lourd bâtiment, battue par l'hélice, moussait, semblait se tordre, remuait tant de clartés qu'on eût dit de la lumière de lune bouillonnant.

Nous étions là, six ou huit, silencieux, admirant, l'oeil tourné vers l'Afrique lointaine où nous allions. Le commandant, qui fumait un cigare au milieu de nous, reprit soudain la conversation du dîner.

« Oui, j'ai eu peur ce jour-là. Mon navire est resté six heures avec ce rocher dans le ventre, battu par la mer. Heureusement que nous avons été recueillis, vers le soir, par un charbonnier anglais qui nous aperçut. »

EXAMPLES:

7. Ce passage nous permet de conclure que

(A) c'est une nuit de tempête

(B) la mer est calme

(C) il y a un incendie

(D) il y a beaucoup de nuages

8. Le bateau dans lequel se trouvent les six ou huit personnages

(A) est un bateau à voiles

(B) a des difficultés mécaniques

(C) n'a pas d'hélice

(D) est un bateau rapide

9. Qu'est-ce que le commandant décide de faire?

(A) D'aller dîner.

(B) De recommencer la conversation.

(C) De parler à un Anglais.

(D) De rester silencieux.

The answer to question 7 is (B). This question requires the reader to arrive at a conclusion based on details given in the passage, although the facts are stated differently in the answer from the way they are in the passage. The passage informs us that there isn't even the slightest ripple (*frisson*) on the sea; the reader can assume that the sea is calm. The other proposed answers are unsupported by information given in the passage; indeed, they are sometimes contradicted by the passage. (A) and (D) are incorrect since we are told that there is a bright moon and stars in the sky. (C), the assumption that there is a fire (*un incendie*) is also incorrect, although one might be misled by the black smoke (*fumée noire*) coming from the ship's smokestack.

The answer to question 8 is (D). The supporting fact is found, although in different form, in the sentence that refers to the *passage rapide du lourd bâtiment* (the ship's rapid course). (A) and (C) are contradicted by other facts mentioned in the passage: there is smoke emerging from the ship's smokestack and there *is* a propeller (*hélice*). (B) is also incorrect because the ship experiencing difficulties is the one the captain tells the passengers about (paragraph 3), not the one they are on.

The answer to question 9 is (B). This question requires the reader to first locate in the passage the person referred to in the question, in this instance, the captain. Once this is done, determining what the character decides to do should be relatively simple. The reader should not be led astray by references to situations or words that are found in the passage but do not fit in the context of a given question; (A) is incorrect because the captain has already had dinner (he is not about to start); (C) is incorrect because the *anglais* the captain mentions refers to a ship in his story; (D) is incorrect because the captain obviously does not remain silent since he takes up, once again, the conversation they were having at dinner.

French Test Answer Sheet

PART A	PART B	PART C	PART D	PART E
1 Ⓐ Ⓑ Ⓒ Ⓓ	24 Ⓐ Ⓑ Ⓒ Ⓓ	38 Ⓐ Ⓑ Ⓒ Ⓓ	53 Ⓐ Ⓑ Ⓒ Ⓓ	65 Ⓐ Ⓑ Ⓒ Ⓓ
2 Ⓐ Ⓑ Ⓒ Ⓓ	25 Ⓐ Ⓑ Ⓒ Ⓓ	39 Ⓐ Ⓑ Ⓒ Ⓓ	54 Ⓐ Ⓑ Ⓒ Ⓓ	66 Ⓐ Ⓑ Ⓒ Ⓓ
3 Ⓐ Ⓑ Ⓒ Ⓓ	26 Ⓐ Ⓑ Ⓒ Ⓓ	40 Ⓐ Ⓑ Ⓒ Ⓓ	55 Ⓐ Ⓑ Ⓒ Ⓓ	67 Ⓐ Ⓑ Ⓒ Ⓓ
4 Ⓐ Ⓑ Ⓒ Ⓓ	27 Ⓐ Ⓑ Ⓒ Ⓓ	41 Ⓐ Ⓑ Ⓒ Ⓓ	56 Ⓐ Ⓑ Ⓒ Ⓓ	68 Ⓐ Ⓑ Ⓒ Ⓓ
5 Ⓐ Ⓑ Ⓒ Ⓓ	28 Ⓐ Ⓑ Ⓒ Ⓓ	42 Ⓐ Ⓑ Ⓒ Ⓓ	57 Ⓐ Ⓑ Ⓒ Ⓓ	69 Ⓐ Ⓑ Ⓒ Ⓓ
6 Ⓐ Ⓑ Ⓒ Ⓓ	29 Ⓐ Ⓑ Ⓒ Ⓓ	43 Ⓐ Ⓑ Ⓒ Ⓓ	58 Ⓐ Ⓑ Ⓒ Ⓓ	70 Ⓐ Ⓑ Ⓒ Ⓓ
7 Ⓐ Ⓑ Ⓒ Ⓓ	30 Ⓐ Ⓑ Ⓒ Ⓓ	44 Ⓐ Ⓑ Ⓒ Ⓓ	59 Ⓐ Ⓑ Ⓒ Ⓓ	71 Ⓐ Ⓑ Ⓒ Ⓓ
8 Ⓐ Ⓑ Ⓒ Ⓓ	31 Ⓐ Ⓑ Ⓒ Ⓓ	45 Ⓐ Ⓑ Ⓒ Ⓓ	60 Ⓐ Ⓑ Ⓒ Ⓓ	72 Ⓐ Ⓑ Ⓒ Ⓓ
9 Ⓐ Ⓑ Ⓒ Ⓓ	32 Ⓐ Ⓑ Ⓒ Ⓓ	46 Ⓐ Ⓑ Ⓒ Ⓓ	61 Ⓐ Ⓑ Ⓒ Ⓓ	73 Ⓐ Ⓑ Ⓒ Ⓓ
10 Ⓐ Ⓑ Ⓒ Ⓓ	33 Ⓐ Ⓑ Ⓒ Ⓓ	47 Ⓐ Ⓑ Ⓒ Ⓓ	62 Ⓐ Ⓑ Ⓒ Ⓓ	74 Ⓐ Ⓑ Ⓒ Ⓓ
11 Ⓐ Ⓑ Ⓒ Ⓓ	34 Ⓐ Ⓑ Ⓒ Ⓓ	48 Ⓐ Ⓑ Ⓒ Ⓓ	63 Ⓐ Ⓑ Ⓒ Ⓓ	75 Ⓐ Ⓑ Ⓒ Ⓓ
12 Ⓐ Ⓑ Ⓒ Ⓓ	35 Ⓐ Ⓑ Ⓒ Ⓓ	49 Ⓐ Ⓑ Ⓒ Ⓓ	64 Ⓐ Ⓑ Ⓒ Ⓓ	76 Ⓐ Ⓑ Ⓒ Ⓓ
13 Ⓐ Ⓑ Ⓒ Ⓓ	36 Ⓐ Ⓑ Ⓒ Ⓓ	50 Ⓐ Ⓑ Ⓒ Ⓓ		77 Ⓐ Ⓑ Ⓒ Ⓓ
14 Ⓐ Ⓑ Ⓒ Ⓓ	37 Ⓐ Ⓑ Ⓒ Ⓓ	51 Ⓐ Ⓑ Ⓒ Ⓓ		78 Ⓐ Ⓑ Ⓒ Ⓓ
15 Ⓐ Ⓑ Ⓒ Ⓓ		52 Ⓐ Ⓑ Ⓒ Ⓓ		79 Ⓐ Ⓑ Ⓒ Ⓓ
16 Ⓐ Ⓑ Ⓒ Ⓓ				80 Ⓐ Ⓑ Ⓒ Ⓓ
17 Ⓐ Ⓑ Ⓒ Ⓓ				81 Ⓐ Ⓑ Ⓒ Ⓓ
18 Ⓐ Ⓑ Ⓒ Ⓓ				82 Ⓐ Ⓑ Ⓒ Ⓓ
19 Ⓐ Ⓑ Ⓒ Ⓓ				83 Ⓐ Ⓑ Ⓒ Ⓓ
20 Ⓐ Ⓑ Ⓒ Ⓓ				84 Ⓐ Ⓑ Ⓒ Ⓓ
21 Ⓐ Ⓑ Ⓒ Ⓓ				85 Ⓐ Ⓑ Ⓒ Ⓓ
22 Ⓐ Ⓑ Ⓒ Ⓓ				
23 Ⓐ Ⓑ Ⓒ Ⓓ				

FRENCH TEST

Part A

Directions: This section contains several incomplete statements, each with four possible completions. Choose the best completion and darken the corresponding circle on your answer sheet.

1. Le ________ à New York, surtout au centre, est énervant et fatigant: il y a trop de taxis, trop de voitures, trop de gens.
   (A) temps
   (B) froid
   (C) bruit
   (D) vent

2. J'ai trop mangé hier soir; j'ai mal au ________.
   (A) bras
   (B) pied
   (C) ventre
   (D) dos

3. Nous n'avons plus de riz et de savon; nous devons aller ________.
   (A) au parking
   (B) à la librairie
   (C) à l'épicerie
   (D) à la boucherie

4. Pour s'amuser, les frères Dupont vont au ________.
   (A) lycée
   (B) cinéma
   (C) cimetière
   (D) bureau

5. Nous devons être chez Robert à huit heures; il est déjà moins cinq. Nous sommes ________.
   (A) rapides
   (B) pressés
   (C) arrêtés
   (D) en avance

6. Quels sont les ________ de l'année?
   (A) jours
   (B) mois
   (C) semaines
   (D) heures

7. Quand ils ont vu le tigre, ils se sont ________.
   (A) enfuis
   (B) embrassés
   (C) rasés
   (D) promenés

8. Dans le réfrigérateur, il n'y a pas assez d'oeufs pour ________ tout le monde.
   (A) couvrir
   (B) nourrir
   (C) ouvrir
   (D) mourir

9. Les spectateurs se sont ________ tout au long de cette pièce compliquée.
   (A) ennuyés
   (B) enveloppés
   (C) eliminés
   (D) assurés

10. Le juge ne savait plus qui a ________ dans cette dispute.
    (A) besoin
    (B) froid
    (C) peur
    (D) raison

GO ON TO THE NEXT PAGE

11. En hiver il faudra faire _________ cette petite pièce.

(A) frire

(B) cuire

(C) chauffer

(D) bouillir

12. Je suis au régime et donc je ne mange pas de _________.

(A) cadeau

(B) bateau

(C) gâteau

(D) radeau

13. Quand j'ai vu la petite fille après tant d'années, je n'arrivais pas à _________ qu'elle avait tellement changé.

(A) devoir

(B) croire

(C) avoir

(D) pouvoir

14. Les ouvriers qui travaillent dans cette _________ japonaise sonts bien payés.

(A) alimentation

(B) plante

(C) colline

(D) usine

15. Nicole n'a plus de timbres; elle doit aller à la _________.

(A) plage

(B) poste

(C) pâtisserie

(D) boulangerie

16. Je dois acheter quelques livres à Paris; les livres français sont trop chers dans les _________ de New York.

(A) bibliothèques

(B) magasins

(C) librairies

(D) marchés

17. Quand je fais la lessive je perds toujours des _________.

(A) chaussettes

(B) chapeaux

(C) chaussures

(D) cendriers

18. Les chauffeurs de taxi font la _________ pour obtenir une augmentation.

(A) fête

(B) grève

(C) cuisine

(D) vaisselle

19. A Paris il y a souvent des _________, surtout le vendredi après-midi.

(A) garages

(B) embouteillages

(C) bagages

(D) emballages

20. J'ai dépensé presque tout mon argent; il ne me _________ plus que dix francs.

(A) faut

(B) reste

(C) donne

(D) réalise

21. Jules est probablement très triste; il ne s'arrête pas de _________.

(A) jouer

(B) pleurer

(C) rire

(D) tousser

22. Les oeuvres des grands _________ se trouvent dans les musées.

(A) pitres

(B) pères

(C) pompiers

(D) peintres

23. A l'agence de voyage on a dit à Humphrey qu'il ne restait plus que deux _________ pour Casablanca.

(A) billets

(B) balais

(C) brosses

(D) bulletins

GO ON TO THE NEXT PAGE

Part B

Directions: Each of the sentences which follow contains a blank. From the four possible answers, choose the one that when inserted will form a grammatically correct sentence and darken the corresponding circle on your answer sheet.

24. Je ne veux ________ aller au cinéma.

(A) toujours
(B) encore
(C) jamais
(D) souvent

25. Roger aime Cassandre; elle est très ________.

(A) passionnément
(B) amoureusement
(C) sincère
(D) aimant

26. Quand Jacques et sa soeur Pauline sont ________, Tom n'était pas chez lui.

(A) arrivant
(B) arrivé
(C) arrivées
(D) arrivés

27. N'importe ________ peut faire ce travail.

(A) quelle
(B) qui
(C) quel
(D) quand

28. Julie est contente. Elle va ________ Europe cet été.

(A) à
(B) en
(C) de
(D) pour

29. Je viens de ________ un rôti de dinde tout seul!

(A) finir
(B) finissant
(C) fini
(D) finirai

30. Je ne veux pas que vous ________ chez moi ce soir!

(A) viendrai
(B) veniez
(C) venez
(D) venir

31. Si Richard est riche il ________ en voyage autour du monde.

(A) partir
(B) partira
(C) est parti
(D) partant

32. Je veux être seul; je ne veux pas voyager avec ________.

(A) il
(B) leurs
(C) ils
(D) elle

33. ________ est le travail des clowns.

(A) Amuser
(B) Amusent
(C) Amusant
(D) Amusés

34. Les gens gagnent ________ de l'argent à Wall Street.

(A) facilement
(B) rares
(C) rapides
(D) volée

35. Quand les enfants ont faim, il faut ________ donner à manger.

(A) les
(B) leurs
(C) leur
(D) ils

GO ON TO THE NEXT PAGE

36. Les femmes que j'ai ________ sont des actrices.

(A) voir

(B) vus

(C) vu

(D) vues

37. Lucien est un très bon tenor; il peut ________ n'importe quoi.

(A) chantez

(B) chanter

(C) chante

(D) chanté

Part C

Directions: Each of the sentences which follow contains one or more underlined words. From the four possible answer choices, choose the one which fits grammatically into the sentence when substituted for the underlined word or words.

38. Le prisonnier ne veut pas manger.

(A) de

(B) tout

(C) beaucoup

(D) jamais

39. Je veux que vous mangiez ce repas.

(A) regardez

(B) vendez

(C) prépariez

(D) digérez

40. Marc a vu cet arbre dans le jardin.

(A) fleur

(B) machine

(C) cottage

(D) homme

41. Nous allons acheter des livres demain.

(A) cherchez

(B) expédions

(C) lire

(D) écrit

42. Les voitures circulent difficilement dans les rues de Rome.

(A) nombreuses

(B) rapidement

(C) facilité

(D) levant

43. Quand j'irai à Paris, j'irai sans Rudolph.

(A) leurs

(B) ses

(C) amies

(D) ton

44. Quand je suis arrivé, il est parti.

(A) reviendra

(B) était déjà revenu

(C) reviendrait

(D) est content

45. Depuis quand êtes-vous marrié? Depuis toujours.

(A) demains

(B) le mois prochaine

(C) de temps le temps

(D) longtemps

46. Elle achète n'importe quoi.

(A) quel

(B) elle

(C) quelle

(D) où

47. Paul lui a parlé de beaucoup des choses.

(A) leur

(B) les

(C) la

(D) elle

GO ON TO THE NEXT PAGE

48. Si nous avons de l'argent, nous partirons.
(A) allions
(B) sommes partis
(C) allons partir
(D) partions

49. Je vais rarement au cinéma.
(A) rien
(B) guère
(C) jamais
(D) tout le temps

50. Qui est passé chez toi ce matin? Lui.
(A) Beaucoup
(B) Plusieurs
(C) Leurs
(D) Les enfants

51. Je suis monté tellement vite que je suis à bout de souffle.
(A) rentrer
(B) envóyé
(C) parlé
(D) parti

52. Les professeurs avec qui je parle sont très vieux.
(A) quelles
(B) lesquels
(C) que
(D) pour qui

Part D

Directions: The paragraphs which follow contain several blank spaces where words have been omitted. For certain blanks, select the completion that is most appropriate to the meaning of the paragraph; for others, select the completion that creates a grammatically correct sentence. For some questions, choice (A) consists of dashes which indicate that no insertion is required in the sentence. For each answer, darken the corresponding circle on your answer sheet. Be certain to read the entire paragraph before answering the questions.

Depuis longtemps ___53___ envie de ___54___ un voyage

53. (A) j'étais
(B) j'avais
(C) je suis
(D) j'aurai

54. (A) faire
(B) prendre
(C) partir
(D) aller

___55___ France. Finalement, je vais ___56___ aller.

55. (A) — — — — —
(B) au
(C) en
(D) Y

56. (A) y
(B) en
(C) par
(D) où

Je n'avais pas ___57___ les voitures devant chez

57. (A) vue
(B) vues
(C) vu
(D) vus

Jacques et je ne ___58___ pas

58. (A) saurai
(B) savais
(C) sait
(D) savoir

qu'il y avait une fête chez ___59___.

59. (A) leur
(B) lui
(C) son
(D) le

GO ON TO THE NEXT PAGE

___60___ décembre, il ___61___ très froid ici

60. **(A)** — — — — —
(B) En
(C) Dans
(D) Le

61. **(A)** est
(B) faire
(C) fait
(D) être

et ___62___ gens portent des manteaux.

62. **(A)** — — — — —
(B) les
(C) le
(D) la

Je voulais que ___63___ mari m'en achète un

63. **(A)** — — — — —
(B) mon
(C) ma
(D) m'

manteau, mais il ne l'a pas ___64___ .

64. **(A)** acheté
(B) achetée
(C) acheter
(D) achète

Part E

Directions: Carefully read the selections which follow. Each selection is followed by several questions or incomplete statements. Choose the answer or completion that, according to the passage, is most appropriate and darken the corresponding circle on your answer sheet.

J'étais dans une chambre qui n'était ni la mienne ni celle d'aucun de mes amis, une chambre où je n'étais jamais venu, et que cependant je connaissais parfaitement bien: les jalousies étais fermées, les rideaux tirés; sur la table de nuit une pâle veilleuse jetait sa lumière agonisante. On ne marchait que sur la pointe du pied, le doigt sur la bouche; des fioles, des tasses encombraient la cheminée. Moi, j'étais au lit comme si j'eusse été malade, et pourtant je ne m'étais jamais mieux porté. Les personnes qui traversaient l'appartement avait une air triste et affairé qui semblait extraordinaire.

65. Qu'est-ce que le narrateur est en train de faire?
(A) Il déjeune.
(B) Il marche.
(C) Il est au lit.
(D) Il ferme les rideaux.

66. Dans la pièce il y a
(A) beaucoup de pluie.
(B) une seule personne.
(C) beaucoup d'animaux.
(D) plusieurs personnes.

67. Que peut voir le narrateur à l'extérieur de la pièce?
(A) Il ne peut rien voir.
(B) Quelqu'un qui le surveille.
(C) Une cheminée.
(D) Ses amis.

Mais ce voyage qu'elle remettait de mois en mois ne se fit point, et le tout se termina par me marquer bien franchement qu'elle ne savait plus quand elle viendrait, mais qu'elle allait prendre des arrangements pour me faire venir à Paris; ce qui n'eut aucun effet non plus, malgré la quantité de lettres dont je la fatiguai depuis, et auxquelles elle ne repondit point; de façon que je me lassai moi-même de lui écrire, et que je restai chez ce fermier, aussi abandonnée que si je n'avais point eu de famille, à quelque argent près qu'on envoyait rarement pour m'habiller, avec une petite pension qu'on payait pour moi, et dont la médiocrité n'empêchait pas mes généreux hôtes de m'aimer de tout leur coeur, et de me respecter en m'aimant.

GO ON TO THE NEXT PAGE

68. La narratrice communique avec quelqu'un

(A) par téléphone.

(B) par la poste.

(C) par messager.

(D) de vive voix.

69. Pourquoi la narratrice s'arrête-t-elle de communiquer avec cette personne?

(A) La personne meurt.

(B) La personne va habiter une autre ville.

(C) La personne ne lui répond pas après un certain temps.

(D) Elle ne sait pas où trouver la personne.

70. Où habite la narratrice?

(A) A Paris.

(B) Dans un hôtel.

(C) A la campagne.

(D) Dans un château.

Je parcourais l'Italie, il y a bien des années. Je fus arrêté dans une auberge de Cerenza, petit village de la Calabre, par un débordement du Neto; il y avait dans la même auberge un étranger qui se trouvait forcé d'y séjourner pour la même cause. Il était fort silencieux et paraissait triste. Il ne témoignait aucune impatience. Je me plaignais quelquefois à lui, comme au seul homme à qui je puisse parler dans ce lieu, du retard que notre marche éprouvait. « Il m'est egal, » me répondit-il, « d'être ici ou ailleurs. » Notre hôte, qui avait causé avec un domestique napolitain, qui servait cet étranger sans savoir son nom, me dit qu'il ne voyageait point par curiosité, car il ne visitait ni les ruines, ni les sites, ni les monuments, ni les hommes. Il lisait beaucoup, mais jamais de manière suivie; il se promenait le soir, toujours seul, et souvent il passait les journées entières assis, immobile, la tête appuyée sur les deux mains. Au moment où les communications, étant rétablies, nous auraient permis de partir, cet étranger tomba très malade. L'humanité me fit un devoir de prolonger mon séjour auprès de lui pour le soigner.

71. Pourquoi le narrateur s'arrête-t-il?

(A) La police l'arrête.

(B) L'eau d'une rivière a envahi les routes.

(C) Un étranger l'oblige à s'arrêter.

(D) Il veut visiter des ruines.

72. De quoi se plaint le narrateur?

(A) Il n'y a personne là où il se trouve.

(B) On mange mal là où il est.

(C) Il n'a pas de domestique.

(D) Il ne peut pas continuer son voyage.

73. Pourquoi le narrateur ne continue-t-il pas son voyage quand cela redevient possible?

(A) Il tombe malade.

(B) Il est mis en prison.

(C) Il veut aider l'étranger.

(D) Il est trop déprimé.

Je passai la nuit sans dormir. Il n'était plus question dans mon âme ni de calculs ni de projets; je me sentais, de la meilleure foi du monde, véritablement amoureux. Ce n'était plus l'espoir du succès qui me faisait agir: le besoin de voir celle que j'aimais, de jouir de sa présence, me dominait exclusivement. Onze heures sonnèrent, je me rendis auprès d'Ellénore; elle m'attendait. Elle voulut parler: je lui demandai de m'écouter. Je m'assis auprès d'elle, car je pouvais à peine me soutenir, et je continuai en ces termes, non sans être obligé de m'interrompre souvent.

« Je ne viens point réclamer contre la sentence que vous avez prononcée; je ne viens point rétracter un aveu qui a pu vous offenser: je le voudrais en vain. Cet amour que vous repoussez est indestructible: l'effort même que je fais en ce moment pour vous parler avec un peu de calme est une preuve de la violence d'un sentiment qui vous blesse. Mais ce n'est plus pour vous en entretenir que je vous ai priée de m'entendre; c'est, au contraire, pour vous demander de l'oublier, de me revoir comme autrefois, d'écarter le souvenir d'un instant de délire, de ne pas me punir de ce que vous savez un secret que j'aurais du renfermer au fond de mon âme. »

GO ON TO THE NEXT PAGE

74. Pourquoi le narrateur se rend-t-il auprès d'Ellénore?

(A) Il veut lui parler de quelqu'un.

(B) Il aime la soeur d'Ellénore.

(C) Il espère un grand succès.

(D) Il veut la voir.

75. Quand le narrateur va-t-il voir Ellénore?

(A) Au milieu de la nuit.

(B) Très tôt le matin.

(C) Dans l'après-midi.

(D) Dans la matinée.

76. Le narrateur admet

(A) qu'il a été en prison.

(B) qu'il est orgueilleux.

(C) qu'il ne peut s'empêcher d'aimer Ellénore.

(D) qu'il a la preuve de l'amour d'Ellénore.

77. Le narrateur voudrait

(A) ne plus voir Ellénore.

(B) continuer à la voir comme avant.

(C) qu'Ellénore parte pour toujours.

(D) partir pour toujours.

Un soir du mois d'août (elle avait alors dix-huit ans), ils l'entraînèrent à l'assemblée de Colleville. Tout de suite elle fut étourdie, stupéfaite par le tapage des ménétriers, les lumières dans les arbres, la bigarrure des costumes, les dentelles, les croix d'or, cette masse de monde sautant à la fois. Elle se tenait à l'écart modestement, quand un jeune homme d'apparence cossue, et qui fumait sa pipe les deux coudes sur le timon d'un banneau, vint l'inviter à la danse. Il lui paya du cidre, du café, de la galette, un foulard, et, s'imaginant qu'elle le devinait, offrit de la reconduire. Au bord d'un champ d'avoine, il la renversa brutalement. Elle eut peur et se mit à crier. Il s'éloigna.

78. Nous pouvons supposer qu' « elle »

(A) a forcé des amis à aller avec elle à Colleville

(B) a été toute seule à Colleville.

(C) a été avec un ami à Colleville.

(D) s'était amenée par des amis à Colleville.

79. A l'assemblée de Colleville il y a

(A) peu de monde.

(B) seulement des femmes.

(C) seulement des hommes.

(D) beaucoup de monde.

80. Que fait-« elle » à l'assemblée tout d'abord?

(A) Elle fait du tapage.

(B) Elle participe pleinement.

(C) Elle reste seule.

(D) Elle danse.

81. En quittant l'assemblée « elle » est

(A) avec sa famille.

(B) toute seule.

(C) avec une personne.

(D) avec ses amis.

Un soir, au milieu d'une joyeuse partie, je reçus un billet tracé par une main faible et qui contenait à peu près ces mots: « Je n'ai plus que quelques moments à vivre; mon ami, je voudrais vous voir pour connaître le sort de mon enfant, savoir s'il sera le vôtre; et aussi pour adoucir les regrets que vous pourriez avoir un jour de ma mort. » Cette lettre me glaça, elle révélait les douleurs secrètes du passé, comme elle renfermait les mystères de l'avenir. Je sortis, à pied, sans attendre ma voiture, et traversai tout Paris, poussé par mes remords, en proie à la violence d'un premier sentiment qui devint durable aussitôt que je vis ma victime. La propreté sous laquelle se cachait la misère de cette femme peignait les angoisses de sa vie; elle m'en épargna la honte en m'en parlant avec une noble réserve, lorsque j'eus solennellement promis d'adopter notre enfant.

82. Nous pouvons conclure dès le début du paragraphe que le narrateur

(A) a remis à quelqu'un une lettre pour une femme.

(B) pensait à quelqu'un qui lui a envoyé une lettre.

(C) avait oublié quelqu'un qui lui envoit une lettre.

(D) habite avec la femme qui lui envoit la lettre.

GO ON TO THE NEXT PAGE

83. La personne qui a envoyé la lettre est

(A) riche.

(B) malade.

(C) malhonnête.

(D) heureuse.

84. Quelle est la réaction du narrateur quand il reçoit le billet?

(A) Il est furieux.

(B) Il ne veut pas se déplacer.

(C) Il est très touché.

(D) Il est joyeux.

85. La personne qui a envoyé la lettre habite

(A) tout près.

(B) de l'autre côté de la ville.

(C) dans une maison luxueuse.

(D) dans une autre ville.

S T O P

IF YOU FINISH BEFORE TIME IS CALLED, YOU MAY CHECK YOUR WORK ON THIS TEST ONLY. DO NOT WORK ON ANY OTHER TEST IN THIS BOOK.

Explanatory Answers

Part A

1. **(C)** The noise in New York, especially in the center, is annoying and tiring: there are too many taxis, too many cars, too many people.
   (A) time
   (B) cold
   (C) noise
   (D) wind

2. **(C)** I ate too much last night; my stomach hurts.
   (A) arm
   (B) foot
   (C) stomach
   (D) back

3. **(C)** We have no more rice and soap; we must go to the grocery store.
   (A) to the parking (lot)
   (B) to the bookstore
   (C) to the grocery store
   (D) to the butcher shop

4. **(B)** To have fun, the Dupont brothers go to the movies.
   (A) high school
   (B) the movies
   (C) the cemetery
   (D) the office

5. **(B)** We have to be at Robert's at eight; it is already five to. We are in a hurry.
   (A) quick
   (B) in a hurry
   (C) stopped
   (D) ahead of time

6. **(B)** What are the months of the year?
   (A) days
   (B) months
   (C) weeks
   (D) hours

7. **(A)** When they saw the tiger, they ran away.
   (A) ran away
   (B) kissed each other
   (C) shaved
   (D) went for a stroll

8. **(B)** In the refrigerator, there are not enough eggs to feed everyone.
   (A) cover
   (B) feed
   (C) open
   (D) die

9. **(A)** The spectators were bored throughout this complicated play.
   (A) bored
   (B) wrapped
   (C) eliminated
   (D) assured

10. **(D)** The judge did not know anymore who was right in this dispute.
    (A) needed
    (B) was cold
    (C) was afraid
    (D) was right

11. **(C)** In the winter it will be necessary to heat this small room.
    (A) fry
    (B) cook
    (C) heat
    (D) boil

12. **(C)** I am on a diet and so I am not eating any cake.
    (A) gift
    (B) boat
    (C) cake
    (D) raft

13. **(B)** When I saw the little girl after so many years, I could not believe that she had changed so much.
(A) to owe, *or* to have to
(B) believe
(C) have
(D) to be able to

14. **(D)** The workers who work in this Japanese factory are well paid.
(A) food business
(B) plant (in French *plante* = [green] plant)
(C) hill
(D) factory

15. **(B)** Nicole has no more stamps; she must go to the post office.
(A) beach
(B) post office
(C) pastry shop
(D) bakery

16. **(C)** I must buy a few books in Paris; French books are too expensive in New York bookstores.
(A) libraries
(B) stores
(C) bookstores
(D) markets

17. **(A)** When I do the laundry I always lose socks.
(A) socks
(B) hats
(C) shoes
(D) ashtrays

18. **(B)** Taxi drivers are on strike in order to obtain a raise.
(A) having a party
(B) on strike
(C) cooking
(D) washing the dishes

19. **(B)** In Paris there are often traffic jams, especially on Friday afternoons.
(A) garages
(B) traffic jams
(C) luggage
(D) cartons

20. **(B)** I have spent almost all of my money; I have left only ten francs.
(A) need
(B) have left
(C) give
(D) realize

21. **(B)** Jules is probably very sad; he does not stop crying.
(A) playing
(B) crying
(C) laughing
(D) coughing

22. **(D)** The works of the great painters are in museums.
(A) fools
(B) fathers (*grands-pères* = grandfathers)
(C) firemen
(D) painters

23. **(A)** At the travel agency they told Humphrey that there were only two tickets left for Casablanca.
(A) tickets
(B) brooms
(C) brushes
(D) bulletins

Part B

24. Je ne veux ________ aller au cinéma.
(A) toujours
(B) encore
(C) jamais
(D) souvent

(C) The blank requires the second part of a negation (*ne* + ________), in this case *jamais* (never). (A), (B), and (D) are positive adverbs.

25. Roger aime Cassandre; elle est très ________.
(A) passionnément
(B) amoureusement
(C) sincère
(D) aimant

(C) The blank requires an adjective to qualify *elle* (Cassandre). (A) and (B) are adverbs; (D) is a present participle.

26. Quand Jacques et sa soeur Pauline sont ________, Tom n'était pas chez lui.

(A) arrivant

(B) arrivé

(C) arrivées

(D) arrivés

(D) The past participle of *arriver* (*arrivé*) must agree with the subject; in this case, Jacques and his sister = a masculine plural subject, thus the ending *-és*.

27. N'importe ________ peut faire ce travail.

(A) quelle

(B) qui

(C) quel

(D) quand

(B) The blank requires a subject pronoun; (A) and (C) are interrogative adjectives (there is no noun here for them to qualify); *quand* is sometimes used with *n'importe* (*n'importe quand* = anytime) but does not make sense here (*Anytime* can do the job).

28. Julie est contente. Elle va ________ Europe cet été.

(A) à

(B) en

(C) de

(D) pour

(B) The prepositions *en* and *de* are used alone with the names of continents (and with countries that are feminine). In the present case, only *en* can be used since Julie is going *to* Europe (*venir de* = coming from).

29. Je viens de ________ un rôti de dinde tout seul!

(A) finir

(B) finissant

(C) fini

(D) finirai

(A) Some verbs followed by *de* are followed by the infinitive, in this case *venir de* (to have just). (B) and (C) are present participles; (D) is the future form of *finir*.

30. Je ne veux pas que vous ________ chez moi ce soir!

(A) viendrai

(B) veniez

(C) venez

(D) venir

(B) The subjunctive is required for the second verb in a construction where the first verb expresses a wish or desire or order (in this case: I do not want) and when the subject of the second verb is different from the subject of the first verb (in this case: you). (B) is the present subjunctive form of *venir* in the first person plural.

31. Si Richard est riche il ________ en voyage autour du monde.

(A) partir

(B) partira

(C) est parti

(D) partant

(B) In *si* (if) clauses, if the first verb is in the present tense, the second verb can only be in either the future, or *futur proche* ("I am going to" as opposed to "I will go"), or in the present. (A) is in the infinitive; (C) is in the *passé composé*; and (D) is a present participle (*-ant* ending).

32. Je veux être seul; je ne veux pas voyager avec ________.

(A) il

(B) leurs

(C) ils

(D) elle

(D) The answer requires an object pronoun. (A) and (C) are subject pronouns; (B) is a possessive adjective. NOTE: *Elle* is used as both a subject pronoun and a direct object pronoun for the feminine singular.

33. ________ est le travail des clowns.

(A) Amuser

(B) Amusent

(C) Amusant

(D) Amusés

(A) The infinitive can be used as a subject in French (as it is in English; for example: To leave is to die a little); conjugated forms cannot (B); present participles cannot (C); and past participles cannot (D).

34. Les gens gagnent ________ de l'argent à Wall Street.

(A) facilement

(B) rares

(C) rapides

(D) volée

(A) An adverb is needed to qualify the verb *gagnent.* (B) and (C) are adjectives; (D) is either an adjective or a past participle.

35. Quand les enfants ont faim, il faut ________ donner à manger.

(A) les

(B) leurs

(C) leur

(D) ils

(C) The blank requires an indirect object pronoun. Watch out for (B) which looks like the answer but is in fact a possessive adjective (their); the indirect object pronoun *leur* (them) *never* takes an *-s*.

36. Les femmes que j'ai ________ sont des actrices.

(A) voir

(B) vus

(C) vu

(D) vues

(D) The past participle (*vues*) must agree with the direct object (*femmes*) when the direct object precedes the verb. (B) and (C) are past participles but they do not agree with *femmes* (feminine plural) and (A) is an infinitive.

37. Lucien est un très bon tenor; il peut ________ n'importe quoi.

(A) chantez

(B) chanter

(C) chante

(D) chanté

(B) When two verbs follow one another in a sentence, the second one is *always* in the infinitive. (A) and (C) are conjugated forms; (D) is the past participle of *chanter*.

Part C

38. Le prisonnier ne veut <u>pas</u> manger.

(A) de

(B) tout

(C) beaucoup

(D) jamais

(D) The question tests negation: The prisoner does *not* want to eat. The answer requires the second element of a negation; only (D) contains such an element, *jamais* (never).

39. Je veux que vous <u>mangiez</u> ce repas.

(A) regardez

(B) vendez

(C) prépariez

(D) digérez

(C) The subjunctive is required since *veux*, a form of *vouloir* (to want) expresses command or wish, and since the subject of the second verb in the construction, *vous*, is different from the subject of the first verb, *je*. Only (C) is in the subjunctive.

40. Marc a vu cet <u>arbre</u> dans le jardin.

(A) fleur

(B) machine

(C) cottage

(D) homme

(D) The demonstrative adjective *cet* can only be followed by a masculine singular noun beginning with a vowel or a mute "h." Only *homme* qualifies.

41. Nous allons <u>acheter</u> des livres demain.

(A) cherchez

(B) expédions

(C) lire

(D) écrit

(C) A verb immediately following another verb is in the infinitive. *Lire* is the only infinitive verb form here. The first verb in this sentence is *allons*.

42. Les voitures circulent difficilement dans les rues de Rome.

(A) nombreuses

(B) rapidement

(C) facilité

(D) levant

(B) An adverb is needed to qualify the verb *circulent*. (A) and (D) are adjectives and (C) is a noun.

43. Quand j'irai à Paris, j'irai sans Rudolph.

(A) leurs

(B) ses

(C) amies

(D) ton

(C) A noun or an object noun is required. (A), (B), and (D) are possessive pronouns.

44. Quand je suis arrivé, il est parti.

(A) reviendra

(B) était déjà revenu

(C) reviendrait

(D) est content

(B) The pluperfect (he had already returned) is the only choice that makes sense here.

45. Depuis quand êtes-vous marrié? Depuis toujours.

(A) demains

(B) le mois prochaine

(C) de temps le temps

(D) longtemps

(D) All the choices are expressions of time, but since the question is "Since when (or "How long") have you been married?", only *longtemps* (for a long time) fits.

46. Elle achète n'importe quoi.

(A) quel

(B) elle

(C) quelle

(D) où

(D) Only *où* correctly completes the expression *n'importe*—(*any* where).

47. Paul lui a parlé de beaucoup des choses.

(A) leur

(B) les

(C) la

(D) elle

(A) The blank requires an indirect object pronoun; *leur* is the only indirect object given.

48. Si nous avons de l'argent, nous partirons.

(A) allions

(B) sommes partis

(C) allons partir

(D) partions

(C) In *si* (if) clauses (clauses of condition), the first verb, when in the present, requires a second verb in either the present, the future, or the *futur proche* (immediate future). (A) and (D) are in the *imparfait* and (B) is in the *passé composé*.

49. Je vais rarement au cinéma.

(A) rien

(B) quère

(C) jamais

(D) tout le temps

(D) The answer requires a positive qualifier/adverb: I go to the movies *all the time*. (A), (B), and (C) are all parts of negative constructions.

50. Qui est passé chez toi ce matin? Lui.

(A) Beaucoup

(B) Plusieurs

(C) Leurs

(D) Les enfants

(D) The answer requires a pronoun or a noun: Who came by your house this morning? *The children* (did) or *the children* (came by). (A) and (B) are adjectives and (C) is a possessive pronoun.

51. Je suis monté tellement vite que je suis à bout de souffle.

(A) rentrer

(B) envóyé

(C) parlé

(D) parti

(D) The required past participle must be that of a verb conjugated with *être* (usually verbs of motion). (A), (B), and (C) are all conjugated with *avoir*.

52. Les professeurs avec qui je parle sont très vieux.

(A) quelles
(B) lesquels
(C) que
(D) pour qui

(D) An object pronoun is required. (A), (B), and (C) are all subject pronouns.

Part D

Depuis longtemps ___53___ envie de ___54___ un voyage

53. (A) j'étais
(B) j'avais
(C) je suis
(D) j'aurai

54. (A) faire
(B) prendre
(C) partir
(D) aller

(B) The expression is *avoir envie de* (to feel like, to desire) which eliminates (A) and (C), both using *être* instead of *avoir*. In addition, the answer must be a conjugated form of *avoir envie de*, and since the expression is preceded by *depuis longtemps* (It has been a long time) the tense of the verb cannot refer to the future, which eliminates (D).

(A) *Faire un voyage* = to take a trip (literally translated: to make a trip). (B), (C), and (D) are all in the infinitive, which is what is needed, but the only correct verb in this expression is *faire*.

___55___ France. Finalement, je vais ___56___ aller.

55. (A) — — — — —
(B) au
(C) en
(D) Y

56. (A) y
(B) en
(C) par
(D) où

(C) In cases of destination (as in: I am going *to*) *en* precedes names of feminine countries (countries whose names usually end with an "e"; a notable exception: *le Mexique*).

(A) *Y* is a pronoun that replaces the names of things (in this case, France); more specifically, *y* replaces a noun preceded by a preposition that indicates position, such as *chez*, *dans*, *sur*, *sous*, *à*, etc. In this particular case *en*, being a contraction of *à la* (or of *à le*) allows *en France* to be replaced by *y*.

Je n'avais pas ___57___ les voitures devant chez

57. (A) vue
(B) vues
(C) vu
(D) vus

(C) A past participle is needed here (I had not *seen*), but no agreement with an object is necessary since there is no direct object preceding the verb (*voitures* is feminine plural and is a direct object but it comes after the verb).

Jacques et je ne ___58___ pas

58. (A) saurai
(B) savais
(C) sait
(D) savoir

(B) Since the entire sentence is in the imperfect, we need an imperfect verb here (the *passé composé* or the *passé simple* are other possibilities but they are not offered here); (A) is in the future, (C) in the present and (D) in the infinitive.

qu'il y avait une fête chez ___59___.

59. (A) leur
(B) lui
(C) son
(D) le

(B) *Chez* is a preposition (= *à la maison de* or *dans la maison de*); after *chez* only a noun or a personal pronoun can be used. *Lui* is the only personal pronoun offered as a choice (*leur* and *son* are possessive adjectives and *le* is a definite article).

___60___ décembre, il ___61___ très froid ici

60. (A) — — — — —
(B) En
(C) Dans
(D) Le

61. (A) est
(B) faire
(C) fait
(D) être

(B) In expressions indicating a time reference (as in: in July, in 1954, etc.) *en* is used directly before the temporal word (month, date, etc.).

(C) The idiomatic expression for "it is cold" is *il fait froid*. (B) is in the infinitive, and (A) and (C) use the wrong verb.

et ___62___ gens portent des manteaux.

62. **(A)** — — — — —

(B) les

(C) le

(D) la

(B) When used by itself *gens* (people) is always preceded by the plural definite article *les*. Exception: when *gens* is qualified, as in "a few people," or "many people" (*peu de gens, beaucoup de gens*), the qualifiers take the place of *les*.

Je voulais que ___63___ mari m'en achète un

63. **(A)** — — — — —

(B) mon

(C) ma

(D) m'

(B) A possessive adjective is needed here (*mon, ton, son, notre, votre, leur,* or the plural counterparts); since the blank precedes *mari* (husband), a masculine singular noun, a masculine singular pronoun is needed: *mon*.

manteau, mais il ne l'a pas ___64___ .

64. **(A)** acheté

(B) achetée

(C) acheter

(D) achète

(A) A past participle is needed. (C) and (D) are in the infinitive and the present tense respectively; in addition, the past participle must agree with any direct object that precedes a verb conjugated with *avoir* in the *passé composé: l' (le)* which refers to *manteau* is located before the verb and is masculine singular, which eliminates (B).

Part E

I was in a bedroom that was neither mine nor that of any of my friends, a room to which I had never come before and which I nevertheless knew perfectly well: the blinds were closed, the curtains pulled; on the night table a night lamp emitted its dying light. People walked only on tiptoe, a finger to their mouths: vials and cups cluttered the mantel. As for me, I was in bed, as if I had been ill, but I had never felt better. The people who passed through the apartment had a sad, bustling air that seemed extraordinary.

65. What is the narrator doing?

(A) He is having lunch.

(B) He is walking.

(C) He is in bed.

(D) He is closing the curtains.

66. In the room there

(A) is a lot of rain.

(B) is one person.

(C) are many animals.

(D) are several people.

67. What can the narrator see outside the room?

(A) He can see nothing.

(B) Someone watching him.

(C) A fireplace.

(D) His friends.

But this trip, which she kept cancelling month after month, did not take place, and, finally, the whole thing showed me quite clearly that she did not know when she would come, but that she was going to make arrangements to have me come to Paris; this did not amount to anything either, in spite of the many letters I pestered her with and to which she did not reply; thus I became tired of writing and remained at the farmer's place as abandoned as if I had no family, the notable exception being the rarely sent money to clothe me and a small fee paid for my food and lodging, a fee whose meagerness did not prevent my generous hosts from loving me with all their heart, and from respecting me while loving me.

68. The narrator communicates with someone

(A) by telephone.

(B) by mail.

(C) by messenger.

(D) by speaking to that person (in person).

69. Why does the narrator stop communicating with this person?

(A) The person dies.

(B) The person goes to live in another city.

(C) The person does not reply after a certain amount of time.

(D) She does not know where to find the person.

70. Where does the narrator live?

(A) In Paris.

(B) In a hotel.

(C) In the country.

(D) In a chateau (castle).

I was traveling through Italy many years ago. I was forced to stop at an inn in Cerenza, a small village in Calabria, by an overflowing of the Neto; in the same inn there was a stranger who was also forced to stay there for the same reason. He was very quiet and seemed sad. He did not show any impatience. I complained to him sometimes, since he was the only person I could speak to in that place, about the delay we were experiencing. "It is the same to me to be here or elsewhere," he replied. Our host, who had spoken to a Neapolitan servant who was waiting on the stranger without knowing his name, told me that he was not traveling to satisfy any sort of curiosity for he was visiting neither ruins, nor sites, nor monuments, nor men. He read quite a bit, but never in any systematic fashion; he took long walks at night, always alone, and, often, he spent entire days sitting still, with his head in his hands.

When the roads were cleared again, making it possible for us to leave, the stranger became very ill. Simple human kindness would not allow me to leave him and I made it my duty to extend my stay in order to take care of him.

71. Why does the narrator stop?

(A) The police arrest him.

(B) A river has (overflowed its banks and) flooded the roads.

(C) A stranger forces him to stop.

(D) He wants to visit the ruins.

72. What does the narrator complain about?

(A) There is no one where he is.

(B) One eats poorly where he is.

(C) He has no servant.

(D) He cannot continue his journey.

73. Why doesn't the narrator continue his journey when that becomes possible?

(A) He becomes ill.

(B) He is put in jail.

(C) He wants to help the stranger.

(D) He is too depressed.

I spent a sleepless night. There was no longer any question in my soul of calculating or of making plans; I earnestly felt truly in love. It was no longer the hope of succeeding that made me act; the need to see the one I loved, to enjoy her presence, completely dominated me. The clock struck eleven, I went to see Ellenore; she was expecting me. She wanted to speak: I asked her to listen to me. I sat next to her, since I could hardly stand up, and I continued speaking, stopping quite often in the process.

"I have not come to appeal the verdict you have given; I have not come to retract an avowal which might have offended you: this would be useless. This love which you refuse is indestructible: even the effort I am making right now to speak calmly to you is proof of the intensity of a feeling that offends you. But I did not ask you to see me to speak about this feeling; on the contrary, I want to ask you to forget it, to put aside the memory of a moment of delirium, not to punish me because you know a secret I should have kept hidden in the depths of my soul."

74. Why does the narrator go to Ellenore?

(A) He wants to speak to her about someone.

(B) He loves Ellenore's sister.

(C) He hopes for a great success.

(D) He wants to see her.

75. When does the narrator go to see Ellenore?

(A) In the middle of the night.

(B) Very early in the morning.

(C) In the afternoon.

(D) In the morning.

76. The narrator admits

(A) that he was in prison.

(B) that he is proud.

(C) that he cannot stop loving Ellenore.

(D) that he has proof of Ellenore's love.

77. The narrator would like

(A) not to see Ellenore again.

(B) to continue to see her as before.

(C) Ellenore to leave forever.

(D) to leave forever.

One evening in August (she was eighteen then), they convinced her to come to the Colleville fair. She was immediately dazed, stupefied by the fiddlers' din, the lights in the trees, the multicolored clothing, the laces, the gold crosses, this mass of people all jumping at once. She was standing aside modestly when an apparently well-off young man, who had been smoking his pipe while leaning with both elbows on a coal-cart, came to ask her to dance. He bought her cider, coffee, cakes, a scarf, and, thinking that she had guessed his intentions, offered to accompany her home. Next to an oatfield, he brutally pushed her down. She became frightened and started to scream. He went away.

78. We can suppose that "she"

(A) forced friends to go with her to Colleville.

(B) went alone to Colleville.

(C) went with a friend to Colleville.

(D) was taken by friends to Colleville.

79. At the Colleville fair there

(A) are very few people.

(B) are only women.

(C) are only men.

(D) are many people.

80. At first, what does "she" do at the fair?

(A) She makes a lot of noise.

(B) She participates fully.

(C) She remains alone.

(D) She dances.

81. When she leaves the fair, "she" is

(A) with her family.

(B) alone.

(C) with someone.

(D) with her friends.

One evening, in the midst of a joyous gathering, I received a note written in a feeble hand, containing close to the following words: "I only have a few moments to live; my friend, I would like to see you in order to know the fate of my child, to know whether he will be yours; and also to allay the regrets you might have someday after my death." This letter froze me; it revealed the secret sorrows of the past just as it contained the mysteries of the future. I left on foot without waiting for my carriage and crossed all of Paris driven by remorse, in the throes of a feeling that became a certainty as soon as I saw my victim. The cleanliness under which the misery of this woman was hidden reflected the anguish of her life; she spared me the shame of it by talking to me with a noble reserve when I solemnly promised to adopt our child.

82. We can conclude from the very beginning of the paragraph that the narrator

(A) has given someone a letter for a woman.

(B) was thinking of someone who has sent him a letter.

(C) had forgotten someone who has sent him a letter.

(D) lives with the woman who sends him the letter.

83. The person who has sent the letter is

(A) rich.

(B) sick.

(C) dishonest.

(D) happy.

84. What is the narrator's reaction when he receives the note?

(A) He is furious.

(B) He does not want to move.

(C) He is very touched.

(D) He is happy.

85. The person who has sent the letter lives

(A) nearby.

(B) on the other side of town.

(C) in a luxurious house.

(D) in another city.

Spanish Test

Lesson 5

Spanish Test

The Spanish Test is available in two formats: one is reading only and one includes a listening component. The Spanish Test with Listening is offered only on selected dates and at specific locations. The reading-only test is the one that is offered on national test dates and is the one discussed here.

The Spanish Test is designed to test your knowledge of Spanish vocabulary and grammar as well as your ability to read and understand the language. It reflects the secondary-school curriculum, and students who take the exam usually have studied Spanish for two to four years.

Vocabulary in Context

In this type of question you are given an incomplete sentence and asked to fill in the blank with the word or expression that best completes it.

EXAMPLE:

1. Esta noche vamos a comer en ________.

(A) el comedor
(B) la servilleta
(C) la cuchara
(D) el cuchillo

The correct answer is (A). The question translates as follows:

This evening let's eat in the ________.

(A) dining room
(B) napkin
(C) spoon
(D) knife

Structure

Here again you are given an incomplete sentence and asked to complete it. In this case, the word or expression that best completes the sentence will be one that makes it a grammatically complete sentence.

EXAMPLE:

2. Es posible que ________ de Madrid mañana.

(A) viene
(B) venir
(C) venga
(D) vino

The correct answer here is (C). The impersonal expression *es posible* always takes the subjunctive. The four choices given are all forms of the verb *venir* which means to come, but only choice (C) is in the present subjunctive necessary to create a grammatically correct sentence. The sentence reads: "It is possible that he is coming from Madrid tomorrow."

Reading Comprehension

In this section you are given short reading passages. You are then asked to answer questions based on your reading of the passage.

Querido tío y venerable maestro: Hace cuatro días que llegué con toda felicidad a este lugar de mi nacimiento, donde he hallado bien de salud a mi padre, al señor vicario y a los amigos y parientes. El contento de verlos y hablar con ellos, después de tantos años de ausencia, me ha embargado el ánimo y me ha robado el tiempo, de suerte que hasta ahora no he podido escribir a usted.

EXAMPLES:

3. ¿Que pasó al narrador?

(A) Fue a una fábrica en la ciudad.
(B) Fue al teatro en Barcelona.
(C) Visitó el campo con su tío.
(D) Volvió a su pueblo natal.

4. ¿Por qué el narrador no pudo escribir a su tío?

(A) No tenía tiempo.
(B) Estaba enfermo.
(C) No tuvo lápiz.
(D) No sabía donde vivía su tío.

The passage is a letter from the narrator to his uncle. It says: "Dear uncle and esteemed teacher. It has been four days since I arrived happily at the place of my birth where I found my father, the vicar, friends, and relatives in good health. The joy of seeing them and speaking with them after so many years of absence has captured my soul and robbed me of time, so that I haven't been able to write to you."

3. What happened to the narrator?

(A) He went to a factory in the city.
(B) He went to the theater in Barcelona.
(C) He visited the country with his uncle.
(D) He returned to his native village.

4. Why wasn't the narrator able to write to his uncle?

(A) He didn't have time.
(B) He was sick.
(C) He didn't have a pen.
(D) He didn't know where his uncle lived.

So the correct choices are (D) and (A).

Spanish Test Answer Sheet

PART A					PART B					PART C				
1	Ⓐ	Ⓑ	Ⓒ	Ⓓ	31	Ⓐ	Ⓑ	Ⓒ	Ⓓ	61	Ⓐ	Ⓑ	Ⓒ	Ⓓ
2	Ⓐ	Ⓑ	Ⓒ	Ⓓ	32	Ⓐ	Ⓑ	Ⓒ	Ⓓ	62	Ⓐ	Ⓑ	Ⓒ	Ⓓ
3	Ⓐ	Ⓑ	Ⓒ	Ⓓ	33	Ⓐ	Ⓑ	Ⓒ	Ⓓ	63	Ⓐ	Ⓑ	Ⓒ	Ⓓ
4	Ⓐ	Ⓑ	Ⓒ	Ⓓ	34	Ⓐ	Ⓑ	Ⓒ	Ⓓ	64	Ⓐ	Ⓑ	Ⓒ	Ⓓ
5	Ⓐ	Ⓑ	Ⓒ	Ⓓ	35	Ⓐ	Ⓑ	Ⓒ	Ⓓ	65	Ⓐ	Ⓑ	Ⓒ	Ⓓ
6	Ⓐ	Ⓑ	Ⓒ	Ⓓ	36	Ⓐ	Ⓑ	Ⓒ	Ⓓ	66	Ⓐ	Ⓑ	Ⓒ	Ⓓ
7	Ⓐ	Ⓑ	Ⓒ	Ⓓ	37	Ⓐ	Ⓑ	Ⓒ	Ⓓ	67	Ⓐ	Ⓑ	Ⓒ	Ⓓ
8	Ⓐ	Ⓑ	Ⓒ	Ⓓ	38	Ⓐ	Ⓑ	Ⓒ	Ⓓ	68	Ⓐ	Ⓑ	Ⓒ	Ⓓ
9	Ⓐ	Ⓑ	Ⓒ	Ⓓ	39	Ⓐ	Ⓑ	Ⓒ	Ⓓ	69	Ⓐ	Ⓑ	Ⓒ	Ⓓ
10	Ⓐ	Ⓑ	Ⓒ	Ⓓ	40	Ⓐ	Ⓑ	Ⓒ	Ⓓ	70	Ⓐ	Ⓑ	Ⓒ	Ⓓ
11	Ⓐ	Ⓑ	Ⓒ	Ⓓ	41	Ⓐ	Ⓑ	Ⓒ	Ⓓ	71	Ⓐ	Ⓑ	Ⓒ	Ⓓ
12	Ⓐ	Ⓑ	Ⓒ	Ⓓ	42	Ⓐ	Ⓑ	Ⓒ	Ⓓ	72	Ⓐ	Ⓑ	Ⓒ	Ⓓ
13	Ⓐ	Ⓑ	Ⓒ	Ⓓ	43	Ⓐ	Ⓑ	Ⓒ	Ⓓ	73	Ⓐ	Ⓑ	Ⓒ	Ⓓ
14	Ⓐ	Ⓑ	Ⓒ	Ⓓ	44	Ⓐ	Ⓑ	Ⓒ	Ⓓ	74	Ⓐ	Ⓑ	Ⓒ	Ⓓ
15	Ⓐ	Ⓑ	Ⓒ	Ⓓ	45	Ⓐ	Ⓑ	Ⓒ	Ⓓ	75	Ⓐ	Ⓑ	Ⓒ	Ⓓ
16	Ⓐ	Ⓑ	Ⓒ	Ⓓ	46	Ⓐ	Ⓑ	Ⓒ	Ⓓ	76	Ⓐ	Ⓑ	Ⓒ	Ⓓ
17	Ⓐ	Ⓑ	Ⓒ	Ⓓ	47	Ⓐ	Ⓑ	Ⓒ	Ⓓ	77	Ⓐ	Ⓑ	Ⓒ	Ⓓ
18	Ⓐ	Ⓑ	Ⓒ	Ⓓ	48	Ⓐ	Ⓑ	Ⓒ	Ⓓ	78	Ⓐ	Ⓑ	Ⓒ	Ⓓ
19	Ⓐ	Ⓑ	Ⓒ	Ⓓ	49	Ⓐ	Ⓑ	Ⓒ	Ⓓ	79	Ⓐ	Ⓑ	Ⓒ	Ⓓ
20	Ⓐ	Ⓑ	Ⓒ	Ⓓ	50	Ⓐ	Ⓑ	Ⓒ	Ⓓ	80	Ⓐ	Ⓑ	Ⓒ	Ⓓ
21	Ⓐ	Ⓑ	Ⓒ	Ⓓ	51	Ⓐ	Ⓑ	Ⓒ	Ⓓ	81	Ⓐ	Ⓑ	Ⓒ	Ⓓ
22	Ⓐ	Ⓑ	Ⓒ	Ⓓ	52	Ⓐ	Ⓑ	Ⓒ	Ⓓ	82	Ⓐ	Ⓑ	Ⓒ	Ⓓ
23	Ⓐ	Ⓑ	Ⓒ	Ⓓ	53	Ⓐ	Ⓑ	Ⓒ	Ⓓ	83	Ⓐ	Ⓑ	Ⓒ	Ⓓ
24	Ⓐ	Ⓑ	Ⓒ	Ⓓ	54	Ⓐ	Ⓑ	Ⓒ	Ⓓ	84	Ⓐ	Ⓑ	Ⓒ	Ⓓ
25	Ⓐ	Ⓑ	Ⓒ	Ⓓ	55	Ⓐ	Ⓑ	Ⓒ	Ⓓ	85	Ⓐ	Ⓑ	Ⓒ	Ⓓ
26	Ⓐ	Ⓑ	Ⓒ	Ⓓ	56	Ⓐ	Ⓑ	Ⓒ	Ⓓ					
27	Ⓐ	Ⓑ	Ⓒ	Ⓓ	57	Ⓐ	Ⓑ	Ⓒ	Ⓓ					
28	Ⓐ	Ⓑ	Ⓒ	Ⓓ	58	Ⓐ	Ⓑ	Ⓒ	Ⓓ					
29	Ⓐ	Ⓑ	Ⓒ	Ⓓ	59	Ⓐ	Ⓑ	Ⓒ	Ⓓ					
30	Ⓐ	Ⓑ	Ⓒ	Ⓓ	60	Ⓐ	Ⓑ	Ⓒ	Ⓓ					

SPANISH TEST

Part A

Directions: This part is made up of a number of incomplete statements. Each statement has four suggested completions. Select the answer choice that BEST completes the statement and mark the corresponding space on your answer sheet.

1. Yo quisiera comprar un billete ________.
   (A) a caballo
   (B) de ida vuelta
   (C) a la izquierda
   (D) dicho y hecho

2. Cuando encontró a Teresa, Juan ________.
   (A) le dio la mano
   (B) dio gritos
   (C) lo echó al correo
   (D) olvidó de ella

3. Estoy enfermo y por eso pienso ________.
   (A) jugar al futbol
   (B) irme a la tienda
   (C) descansar
   (D) dar una vuelta

4. A Marta no le gusta cocinar, y cuando tiene que hacerlo, lo hace________.
   (A) al contrario
   (B) en voz alta
   (C) de mala gana
   (D) al por mayor

5. No comería nunca en este restaurante ________.
   (A) por bueno que sea
   (B) en balde
   (C) hasta no más
   (D) sin aliento

6. Este carro nuevo ________ ir al trabajo.
   (A) se niega a
   (B) insiste en
   (C) trata de
   (D) sirve para

7. Durmió durante la película porque ________.
   (A) tuvo sed
   (B) tuvo hambre
   (C) estuvo cansado
   (D) estuvo de prisa

8. ¡Hace frío! Ponte ________.
   (A) las manos
   (B) los guantes
   (C) los pendientes
   (D) las maletas

9. Mi padre ________ a las ocho para preparar el desayuno.
   (A) se preocupe
   (B) se levanta
   (C) se desarolla
   (D) se casa

10. No vamos a viajar este verano porque nos ________ dinero.
    (A) alegra
    (B) falta
    (C) burla
    (D) acerca

11. El profesor no puede responder a las preguntas ahora porque ________.
    (A) está para salir
    (B) está por salir
    (C) está de vuelta
    (D) está de acuerdo

12. Despues de la canción yo ________.
    (A) di un abrazo
    (B) di la mano
    (C) di unas palmadas
    (D) me di prisa

GO ON TO THE NEXT PAGE

13. Antes de comer pido la _________.

(A) propina

(B) cuenta

(C) carta

(D) cama

14. Mi madre tiene muchos cosas que hacer. Está _________.

(A) lista

(B) ocupada

(C) preparada

(D) triste

15. Esta mañana _________ mi libro y no puedo estudiar para el examen.

(A) encontré

(B) compré

(C) perdí

(D) escribí

16. Llame al médico, mi hijo _________.

(A) se fue a la escuela

(B) se hizo daño

(C) dio un paseo

(D) dio con su abuelo

17. No podemos comer la carne ahora porque _________.

(A) hace calor

(B) no tiene razón

(C) no tengo una taza

(D) está caliente

18. Una persona de cinco años es _________.

(A) vieja

(B) joven

(C) contenta

(D) peligrosa

19. Para saber la hora, necesitamos _________.

(A) un reloj

(B) un paraguas

(C) una camisa

(D) una pelota

20. La calle donde está mi casa no es a la derecha sino a la _________.

(A) izquierda

(B) comida

(C) mancha

(D) duda

21. Cuando vio a la policía, el ladrón _________ correr.

(A) dio gracias

(B) acercó de

(C) estuvo por

(D) empezó a

22. Tengo que pagar la multa porque _________ devolver los libros.

(A) me arrepentí de

(B) me burlé de

(C) me acordé de

(D) me olvidé de

23. Vamos a votar por este hombre porque _________ bajar los impuestos.

(A) está por

(B) se fija en

(C) deja caer

(D) se queja de

24. Yo sé que te gusta esta película pero _________ es aburrida.

(A) hasta después

(B) raras veces

(C) para mi

(D) a lo lejos

25. No puedo hacerlo.¡ _________!

(A) Ayúdame

(B) No hagas nada

(C) Ten prisa

(D) Cállate

26. Prefiero la piscina a la playa porque no me gusta _________.

(A) el campo

(B) el agua

(C) la arena

(D) el prado

GO ON TO THE NEXT PAGE

27. Se puede comprar un añillo en ________.

(A) la carnicería

(B) la joyería

(C) el supermercado

(D) la selva

28. El año que viene ________ comprar una casa.

(A) pienso en

(B) pienso de

(C) pienso

(D) pensar

29. Anoche tú fuiste de compras, ahora me ________ a mí.

(A) toca

(B) carece

(C) hace

(D) da

30. Voy a la cocina porque tengo ganas de ________.

(A) caminar

(B) coser

(C) cocinar

(D) cortar

Part B

Directions: In each of the following sentences there is a blank. Select the choice that, if inserted, would form a grammatically correct sentence. Blacken your choice on your answer sheet.

31. Vas a salir ________ París esta noche.

(A) en

(B) por

(C) para

(D) con

32. Cuando duermo ________ mis vacaciones.

(A) sueño con

(B) soñar de

(C) sueño de

(D) soñar a

33. El maestro quiere que nosotros le ________ atención.

(A) prestar

(B) prestase

(C) preste

(D) prestemos

34. Quisiera cantar. ¿Sabes ________ la guitarra?

(A) jugar

(B) juegas

(C) tocas

(D) tocar

35. Hace buen tiempo, ________ nos agrada mucho.

(A) quien

(B) que

(C) lo que

(D) de que

36. Hacía un año que ________ en México.

(A) vivo

(B) vivir

(C) vivía

(D) viviendo

37. No hay ningún libro que ________ en esta librería.

(A) me gusta

(B) me gustar

(C) gustarse

(D) me guste

38. No conocía a nadie que ________ hacerlo.

(A) sepa

(B) supiera

(C) saber

(D) sabe

GO ON TO THE NEXT PAGE

39. Lo llamo para que _________ temprano.

(A) despertar
(C) se despierte
(C) despierta
(D) despertándose

40. Perdí mis guantes. Dame _________.

(A) la tuya
(B) los tuyos
(C) los suyos
(D) los de usted

41. Los sábados no me gusta estudiar _________ ir de compras.

(A) pero
(B) sino
(C) que
(D) sino que

42. Es dudoso que nos _________ la verdad.

(A) diga
(B) dice
(C) decir
(D) dirá

43. ¿_________ de esos carros es suyo?

(A) Qué
(B) Cuál
(C) Quién
(D) Cómo

44. La mujer sentada delante de _________ es muy alta y no puedo ver el desfile.

(A) yo
(B) mí
(C) me
(D) a mí

45. Jorge está _________.

(A) en la cama
(B) abogado
(C) muy inteligente
(D) con pelo rubio

46. Sabes mejor que _________ que los estudios son difíciles.

(A) nada
(B) quien
(C) nadie
(D) alguien

47. Él es el autor _________ libros son tan interesantes.

(A) cuyo
(B) cuyos
(C) que
(D) quienes

48. Nuestro perro y _________ de la familia Duarte son muy grandes.

(A) lo
(B) el
(C) le
(D) la

49. Mo me gustó el regalo y _________ inmediatamente a mi abuela.

(A) le lo devolví
(B) se la devolvía
(C) devolviéndosela
(D) se lo devolví

50. ¡Es un concierto _________!

(A) flaca
(B) maravilloso
(C) aburrida
(D) fuerte

51. Su casa es _________ como la mía.

(A) más grande
(B) tan pequeño
(C) tan grande
(D) menos grande

52. Es cierto que cuando _________ comer, nos hablará del viaje.

(A) acaba de
(B) acabe de
(C) acabar
(D) acabe

GO ON TO THE NEXT PAGE

53. Yo habría comprado esa casa si ________ bastante dinero.

(A) haya tenido
(B) hubiera tenido
(C) tendría
(D) he tenido

54. Ellos ________ dan la cuenta a nosotros.

(A) la
(B) le
(C) les
(D) nos

55. Por interesante que ________, no quiero visitar este país.

(A) está
(B) es
(C) sea
(D) ser

56. Estaba durmiendo cuando ________ mi hermano.

(A) me llamó
(B) me llamabas
(C) llamarme
(D) llamándome

57. ¡No lo ________! Es peligroso.

(A) hagas
(B) hace
(C) hacer
(D) hizo

58. Tengo dos bicicletas. Ésta es roja y ________ es azul.

(A) aquél
(B) eso
(C) esto
(D) aquélla

59. Podemos sacar al menos ________ dólares del banco.

(A) cien
(B) cientos
(C) cuentos
(D) ciento

60. El alcalde del pueblo ________ por la gente.

(A) eligen
(B) fue elegido
(C) está elegida
(D) se eligían

Part C

Directions: This part contains reading selections followed by questions. Read each selection and then select the BEST answer choice based on your understanding of what you have read. Mark the appropriate space on your answer sheet.

Lo barcos negreros precedentes de África llegaron a Brasil en 1525, llevando los primeros de muchos cargamentos humanos miserables destinados a trabajar en las plantaciones de azúcar, tabaco y café. Los historiadores calculan que a las costas brasileñas llegaron una cantidad extraordinariamente alta en comparación con los Estados Unidos. Alrededor de 10 por ciento de los esclavos morían cada año debido a la comida y la ropa inadecuadas, junto a las largas horas de trabajo y los castigos corporales. El esclavo promedio sobrevivía sólo 10 años. Y debido a que no se alentaba la formación de familias—apenas uno de cada diez esclavos llegaba a casarse—, los terratenientes tenían que importar nuevos trabajadores esclavos.

Mientras la presión internacional forzó a los Estados Unidos a abolir la importación de esclavos en 1808, la sociedad brasileña no prestó atención a las admoniciones de que tendría que reducir su dependencia de la mano de obra esclava. Los historiadores atribuyen esta demora al hecho de que Brasil no tuvo prensa pública hasta 1808 y a que el país no había pasado a través de ningún verdadero movimiento reformista o democrático.

GO ON TO THE NEXT PAGE

61. ¿De qué trata este párrafo?

(A) El colonialismo en África

(B) Las plantaciones de los Estados Unidos

(C) El desarollo de la agricultura en Brasil

(D) La esclavitud en Brasil

62. Según el artículo, la muerte de muchos esclavos fue debido

(A) a la guerra en Norteamérica

(B) a la falta de comida

(C) al calor

(D) al viaje peligroso de África

63. Según el autor,

(A) Brasil tenía más esclavos que los Estados Unidos

(B) los esclavos trabajaban en las fábricas

(C) la mayoría de los esclavos vivían en familia

(D) los esclavos se casaron con los brasileños

64. Según los historiadores, Brasil fue uno de los últimos países en abolir la esclavitud porque

(A) tenía más plantaciones que los otros países

(B) tenía un fuerte movimiento reformista

(C) no tenía prensa pública

(D) los esclavos se rebelaron

65. Según el artículo, Brasil

(A) dependía de la mano de obra esclava

(B) quería abolir la esclavitud más temprano

(C) no podía importar más esclavos después de 1800

(D) prestó atención a la opinión pública

Y un buen día se apareció de nuevo. Cuando oyó que alguien lo llamaba, se dio vuelta y se encontró con ella. Hacía exactamente ocho años que había dejado de verla.

Tenía los ojos castaños y grandes y llevaba el pelo—castaño también—más abajo de los hombros y con flequillo. Sus facciones le recordaban los retratos renacentistas italianos.

—¡Qué bien estás! No has cambiado nada— dijo él. Era el mes de mayo y estaban en una galería de arte en Nueva York.

—Es que mis cambios no se ven.

Se había ido de Manhattan poco después de verla por última vez, porque al marido, prominente crítico literario, le habían ofrecido una cátedra en una universidad del norte del estado.

—¿Estás de visita en la ciudad?—le preguntó.

—Sí. Por unos días—replicó y se le acercó.— ¿Y tú, Mike? ¿Qué es de tu vida?

—Estoy casado, tengo dos hijos y trabajo en un banco—dijo.

—¿Un banco?

Su marido venía de una familia de banqueros.

—Sí. Escribo su boletín mensual.

La última vez que se habían visto, el mayor deseo de Mike era ser dramaturgo. Nunca había querido buscarse un trabajo fijo porque, según él, necesitaba tiempo para escribir.

—¿Te gusta?

—No, claro que no.

Hacía ocho años, cuando los dos eran solteros, habían hablado de cómo sería tener hijos. Él pensaba que sería maravilloso y lo deseaba; pero a ella, la idea la horrorizaba.

66. En este cuento los personajes están en

(A) el parque

(B) una galería

(C) una tienda

(D) un restaurante

67. Según el cuento, la mujer

(A) es italiana

(B) es artista

(C) no está muy cambiada

(D) vive en Nueva York

GO ON TO THE NEXT PAGE

68. ¿Cúal es la relación entre Mike y la mujer?
(A) Son colegas.
(B) Eran novios.
(C) Eran enemigos.
(D) Son turistas del mismo país.

69. ¿Qué hace Mike?
(A) Es dramaturgo.
(B) Es crítico literario.
(C) Es escritor en un banco.
(D) Es economista.

70. ¿Cúal de las declaraciones siguientes NO es verdad?
(A) Mike y la mujer se encuentran acaso.
(B) El marido de la mujer es profesor.
(C) El cuento tiene lugar durante la primavera.
(D) A Mike le gusta su trabajo.

Jorge Amado, autor brasileño cuyas novelas han sido publicadas en 60 países nos declaró: ''No existe una literatura latinoamericana. Ése es un concepto falso y peligroso. La literatura latinoamericana representa diversos países, culturas y pueblos. Hay una gran diferencia entre un mexicano y un brasileño, entre un argentino y un peruano.

''Es muy peligroso rotular los libros de esta manera, porque entonces quedan destinados a un 'ghetto'. Si se publica un autor griego o sueco, no se le denomina literatura europea. Ésa es una actitud colonialista.

''Todos los países latinoamericanos son diferentes. Desafortunadamente, todo lo que nos une es negativo—miseria, opresión, dictadores militares.

''Lo que unifica la posición de los escritores de esos países es que, en general, son fieles a sus pueblos, a la lucha para mitigar sus problemas sociales y procurarles una mejor existencia. Pero la literatura latinoamericana no existe''.

71. Este fragmento es probablemente
(A) una entrevista
(B) un diálogo en una novela
(C) una carta de un autor al otro
(D) una página de un diario

72. Según Amado, ¿por qué no existe una literatura latinoamericana?
(A) Las obras no son escritas todas en español.
(B) Hay dictadores militares en Latinoamérica.
(C) El público no está interesado en la literatura de Latinoamérica.
(D) Los países de Latinoamérica son demasiado diferentes.

73. Según Amado, ¿qué unifica a los países de Latinoamérica?
(A) Todos tienen el español como idioma oficial.
(B) Sus culturas vienen de los indios y los españoles.
(C) Sufren de miseria y opresión.
(D) Son opuestos al colonialismo.

74. ¿Qué tienen en común los escritores latinoamericanos?
(A) Son generalmente educados en Europa.
(B) Son publicados en más de 60 países.
(C) Escriben de problemas sociales.
(D) Son colonialistas.

Pocos saben que a mediados del siglo XVI se trasladó de Europa al Nuevo Mundo un gran número de hombres de extraordinario talento; a México y Perú, las más antiguas y ricas de las colonias españolas y donde los 20.000 monasterios y 70.000 iglesias requirieron el trabajo de pintores y escultores. El arte colonial español se vio afectado por los nuevos estilos que estaban en boga en Europa. La falta de apreciación de este arte fue debida al hecho de que la mayor parte del mismo es religioso y fue creado para las numerosas instituciones religiosas o para los hogares de hombres que regían su vidas por el calendario católico. Y los europeos más cultos no viajaban mucho. Pero eso es parte del problema. El verdadero problema es que nadie parece conocer lo suficiente acerca del arte colonial español como para apreciarlo. En la actualidad, una obra de arte atribuida a una escuela europea secundaria atrae más atención que una obra importante ejecutada por un maestro del Nuevo Mundo. La frecuencia con que esas obras se atribuyeron erróneamente a los grandes maestros europeos representa una prueba de su calidad.

GO ON TO THE NEXT PAGE

75. ¿De qué trata este artículo?

(A) La religión colonial

(B) El arte colonial

(C) La influencia del arte colonial sobre el arte europeo

(D) La importancia de la arquitectura en el Nuevo Mundo

76. Se puede decir que el arte colonial español

(A) es muy popular

(B) es desconocido

(C) no es interesante

(D) es secular en la mayor parte

77. Los artistas hispanoamericanos tenía mucha oportunidad de crear porque

(A) eran ricos y tenían patrones ricos.

(B) había muchas iglesias y monasterios

(C) recibían la ayuda de los artistas europeos

(D) creaban para las instituciones seculares

78. Según el autor, ¿por qué era poco apreciado el arte de las colonias?

(A) Los eruditos no viajaban mucho.

(B) Era inferior al arte de Europa.

(C) No era afectado por los estilos en boga en Europa.

(D) No estaba en los museos importantes.

79. Según el autor, ¿cómo podemos asegurarnos del valor del arte colonial?

(A) Está en todos los museos importantes en este siglo.

(B) Se vende por milliones de dólares.

(C) Algunas veces se confunde con la obra de un maestro europeo.

(D) Imita a los maestros inferiores europeos.

80. Según la selección, México y Perú

(A) tenían más artistas que otros países

(B) fueron las primeras colonias españolas

(C) no tenían bastante dinero para sostener el arte

(D) no tenían ningún contacto con Europa

Hay quienes dicen que el tono suave de la bossa nova fue producto de la necesidad. La historia cuenta que los encuentros musicales tenían lugar durante la noche en los departamentos cercanos a la playa en Rio y se prolongaban hasta el alba, obligando a los intérpretes a bajar la voz para no importunar a los vecinos. En todo caso, lo que nadie sabe es que este estilo de música registra diversas facetas evolutivas.

A finales de la década de los años veinte, cuando aparece la radiodifusión, el tocar la guitarra y cantar samba se consideraba una actitud bohemia para teatros folclóricos populares. Con el advenimiento de la radio se desarrolló una versión más dignificada de la samba y que coincide con el afianzamiento de la industria fonográfica. La radio y los discos comenzaron a regir los destinos de la música popular brasileña.

La avalancha de nuevos talentos surgió en todas las clases sociales, aún en los estratos más altos, con Mario Reis, cuya voz de tonos bajos pudo haber dado origen a la bossa nova. En esta época se introducen variaciones, pero siempre a nivel aficionado. Bando de Lua, el primero en formar un grupo vocal, no aceptó pago por sus presentaciones, diciendo ''No somos profesionales''.

A comienzos de los años treinta, nuevas armonías y composiciones dan al movimiento un verdadero toque profesional y se reconoce especialmente a Radames Ginatelli, creador de un nuevo estilo de orquestación, que adapta los ritmos de la samba a saxófonos e instrumentos metálicos de viento.

81. Se puede decir que el tono suave de la bossa nova es debido

(A) a un esfuerzo por no importunar a la gente

(B) a una actitud bohemia

(C) al nacer de la industria fonográfica

(D) al sonido del saxófono

82. ¿Por qué no aceptó pago el grupo de Bando de Lua?

(A) Se consideraban aficionados.

(B) Sus presentaciones fueron para caridad.

(C) No quería pagar impuestos.

(D) No tocaba bien.

GO ON TO THE NEXT PAGE

83. Según el autor, la bossa nova

(A) fue creada por las clases sociales altas.

(B) no se desarolló en Brasil.

(C) es caracterizada por voces bajas y suaves.

(D) comenzó con un grupo profesional.

84. Según la selección, el desarollo de la industria fonográfica

(A) es importante en la historia de la musica brasileña.

(B) coincide con la popularidad de la música folclórica.

(C) es más importante que el de la radio.

(D) no tiene nada que ver con el desarollo de la Bossa Nova.

85. La bossa nova, según el párrafo es

(A) derivada de la samba

(B) un estilo musical antiguo

(C) basada en ritmos de la música española

(D) semejante al jazz

S T O P

IF YOU FINISH BEFORE TIME IS CALLED, YOU MAY CHECK YOUR WORK ON THIS TEST ONLY. DO NOT WORK ON ANY OTHER TEST IN THIS BOOK.

Explanatory Answers

PART A

1. **(B)** I would like to buy a round trip ticket.
   (A) on horseback
   (B) round trip
   (C) to the left
   (D) said and done

2. **(A)** When he met Teresa, John shook hands.
   (A) shook hands
   (B) shouted
   (C) mailed it
   (D) forgot her

3. **(C)** I am sick and therefore I am thinking about resting.
   (A) playing football
   (B) going to the store
   (C) resting
   (D) taking a walk

4. **(C)** Marta doesn't like to cook and when she has to she does it unwillingly.
   (A) on the contrary
   (B) out loud
   (C) unwillingly
   (D) wholesale

5. **(A)** I will never eat in this restaurant no matter how good it is.
   (A) no matter how good it is
   (B) in vain
   (C) to the utmost
   (D) breathless

6. **(D)** This new car is good for going to work.
   (A) denies
   (B) insists on
   (C) tries to
   (D) is good for

7. **(C)** He slept during the movie because he was tired.
   (A) he was thirsty
   (B) he was hungry
   (C) he was tired
   (D) he was in a hurry

8. **(B)** It's cold. Put on your gloves.
   (A) your hands
   (B) your gloves
   (C) your earrings
   (D) your suitcases

9. **(B)** My father gets up at eight o'clock to make breakfast.
   (A) worries
   (B) gets up
   (C) develops
   (D) gets married

10. **(B)** We are not going to travel this summer because we don't have money. (Money is lacking to us)
    (A) makes us happy
    (B) is lacking to us
    (C) mocks us
    (D) approaches us

11. **(A)** The teacher can't answer the questions right now because he's about to leave.
    (A) he's about to leave
    (B) he's in favor of leaving
    (C) he's returning
    (D) he agrees

12. **(C)** After the song I applauded.
    (A) gave a hug
    (B) shook hands
    (C) applauded
    (D) hurried

13. **(C)** Before eating I ask for the menu.
(A) the tip
(B) the check
(C) the menu
(D) the bed

14. **(B)** My mother has a lot to do. She is busy.
(A) ready
(B) busy
(C) prepared
(D) sad

15. **(C)** This morning I lost my book and now I can't study for the test.
(A) I found
(B) I bought
(C) I lost
(D) I wrote

16. **(B)** Call the doctor, my son hurt himself.
(A) went to school
(B) hurt himself
(C) took a walk
(D) met his grandfather

17. **(D)** We can't eat the meat right now because it's hot.
(A) it's hot (weather)
(B) he's wrong
(C) I don't have a cup
(D) it's hot

18. **(B)** A person who is five years old is young.
(A) old
(B) young
(C) happy
(D) dangerous

19. **(A)** In order to know what time it is we need a clock.
(A) a clock
(B) an umbrella
(C) a shirt
(D) a ball

20. **(A)** The street where I live is not to the right, but to the left.
(A) left
(B) meal
(C) stain
(D) doubt

21. **(D)** When he saw the police, the thief began to run.
(A) gave thanks
(B) approached
(C) was in favor of
(D) began to

22. **(D)** I have to pay the fine because I forgot to return the books.
(A) I repented
(B) I made fun of
(C) I remembered
(D) I forgot

23. **(A)** We are going to vote for this man because he's in favor of lowering taxes.
(A) he's in favor of
(B) he notices
(C) he drops
(D) he complains

24. **(C)** I know you like this movie, but to my mind, it's boring.
(A) until later
(B) rarely
(C) to my mind
(D) from far away

25. **(A)** I can't do it. Help me!
(A) Help me
(B) Don't do anything
(C) Hurry up
(D) Be quiet

26. **(C)** I prefer a pool to the beach because I don't like the sand.
(A) the country
(B) the water
(C) the sand
(D) the meadow

27. **(B)** One can buy a ring in the jewelry store.

(A) the butcher shop

(B) the jewelry store

(C) the supermarket

(D) the forest

28. **(C)** Next year I'm thinking of buying a house.

(A) I think about (ideas)

(B) I think of (opinions)

(C) I'm thinking of (considering or planning)

(D) to think

29. **(A)** Last night you went shopping, now it's my turn.

(A) my turn

(B) lacks

(C) does

(D) gives

30. **(C)** I'm going to the kitchen because I feel like cooking.

(A) walking

(B) sewing

(C) cooking

(D) cutting

Part B

31. Vas a salir ________ París esta noche.

(A) en

(B) por

(C) para

(D) con

(C) The expression "to leave for" in the sense of destination is *salir para.*

32. Cuando duermo ________ mis vacaciones.

(A) sueño con

(B) soñar de

(C) sueño de

(D) soñar a

(A) The expression "to dream about" in Spanish is *sonar con.* Since the subject is *yo,* the correct answer has to be *sueño con.*

33. El maestro quiere que nosotros le ________ atención.

(A) prestar

(B) prestase

(C) preste

(D) prestemos

(D) With expressions of volition such as *quiere que* you must use the subjunctive. (C) and (D) are both in the subjunctive mood but since the subject of the verb *prestar* is *nosotros,* the answer is (D).

34. Quisiera cantar. ¿Sabes ________ la guitarra?

(A) jugar

(B) juegas

(C) tocas

(D) tocar

(D) Although *jugar* does mean "to play," it means to play a game. Only *tocar* means "to play an instrument" so only (C) and (D) are possible. Since the infinitive is needed after *sabes* (D) is the correct choice.

35. Hace buen tiempo, ________ nos agrada mucho.

(A) quien

(B) que

(C) lo que

(D) de que

(C) Here we need an expression that means "which" to refer to the idea of the good weather. *Lo que* is correct because it is a neuter relative pronoun used to refer to complete thoughts or statements such as *hace buen tiempo.*

36. Hacía un año que ________ en México.

(A) vivo

(B) vivir

(C) vivía

(D) viviendo

(C) To complete the thought that begins with "it has been a year" we need the imperfect tense. Only (C) is in the imperfect.

37. No hay ningún libro que ________ en esta librería.

(A) me gusta

(B) me gustar

(C) gustarse

(D) me guste

(D) Since negative expressions like *no hay ningún libro* (there isn't a single book) require the subjunctive, only (D) is a possible choice since it is the only verb form in the subjunctive mood.

38. No conocía a nadie que ________ hacerlo.

(A) sepa

(B) supiera

(C) saber

(D) sabe

(B) This is the same situation we had in the previous example but this time the imperfect subjunctive is required to complete *No conocía,* which is in the imperfect. The only choice in the imperfect subjunctive is (B).

39. Lo llamo para que ________ temprano.

(A) despertar

(C) se despierte

(C) despierta

(D) despertándose

(C) The expression *para que* always takes the subjunctive. Only (C) is in the subjunctive.

40. Perdí mis guantes. Dame ________.

(A) la tuya

(B) los tuyos

(C) los suyos

(D) los de ustedé

(B) Here we need a possessive pronoun. Since the command *dame* is in the second person singular form, the *yours* must be in that form as well and must agree with *los guantes* in number and gender. (B) is the correct choice.

41. Los sábados no me gusta estudiar ________ ir de compras.

(A) pero

(B) sino

(C) que

(D) sino que

(B) Choices (A), (B), and (D) all mean "but." However, (B) is the correct choice here because *sino* is used to mean "but" after negative statements used in contrast to an affirmative statement containing no conjugated verb such as *ir de compras.*

42. Es dudoso que nos ________ la verdad.

(A) diga

(B) dice

(C) decir

(D) dirá

(A) After the impersonal expression *es dudoso* (it is doubtful) you must use the subjunctive. (A) is the only choice in the third person singular subjunctive form.

43. ________ de esos carros es suyo?

(A) Qué

(B) Cúal

(C) Quién

(D) Cómo

(B) Here we need an interrogative pronoun meaning "which." Although the other choices can be interrogative pronouns, only *cuál* means which.

44. La mujer sentada delante de ________ es muy alta y no puedo ver el desfile.

(A) yo

(B) mí

(C) me

(D) a mí

(B) The expression *delante de* must be followed by a prepositional pronoun. Only (B) is a prepositional pronoun. (D) is not a possible choice because this form would only be used to stress an indirect object construction.

45. Jorge está ________.

(A) en la cama

(B) abogado

(C) muy inteligente

(D) con pelo rubio

(A) Since the verb *estar* is used for location and temporary conditions, only (A), "in bed," is a possible choice.

46. Sabes mejor que ________ que los estudios son difíciles.

(A) nada

(B) quien

(C) nadie

(D) alguien

(C) When making a comparison that would use an indefinite pronoun in English, you must use a negative pronoun in Spanish. So you use *nadie* (no one) for "anyone" in the sentence, "you know better than anyone that studies are difficult."

47. És es el autor ________ libros son tan interesantes.

(A) cuyo

(B) cuyos

(C) que

(D) quienes

(B) Here we need something that means "whose." Yet the correct choice *cuyos* is not really a relative pronoun, but a relative adjective that functions as a pronoun, so that even though it refers to the author in one sense, it must agree in number and gender with the thing possessed, in this case *libros.*

48. Nuestro perro y ________ de la familia Duarte son muy grandes.

(A) lo

(B) el

(C) le

(D) la

(B) You can use the definite article *el* to avoid the repetition of the noun *perro.* So the sentence means "Our dog and the one belonging to the Duarte family are large."

49. Mo me gustó el regalo y ________ inmediatamente a mi abuela.

(A) le lo devolví

(B) se la devolvía

(C) devolviéndosela

(D) se lo devolví

(D) (A) and (D) are the only two possible choices since you need a verb in the past tense in the first person singular form. (A) is not a possible construction in Spanish. Instead of *le lo* you must use *se lo* so (D) is the correct choice.

50. ¡Es un concierto ________!

(A) flaca

(B) maravilloso

(C) aburrida

(D) fuerte

(B) Since *concierto* is a masculine singular noun, your only choices are (B) and (D). Since "strong" concert makes no sense, the answer is (B).

51. Su casa es ________ como la mía.

(A) más grande

(B) tan pequeño

(C) tan grande

(D) menos grande

(C) The formula for the "as ________ as" construction is *tan* ________ *como* which leaves you with (B) and (C). Since house is feminine, (B) cannot be the right choice. The comparative construction "more ________ than" is *más* ________ *que.*

52. Es cierto que cuando ________ comer, nos hablará del viaje.

(A) acaba de

(B) acabe de

(C) acabar

(D) acabe

(A) Since this impersonal expression *es cierto* expresses certainty, the present indicative can be used here, so the correct answer is (A).

53. Yo habría comprado esa casa si ________ bastante dinero.

(A) haya tenido

(B) hubiera tenido

(C) tendría

(D) he tenido

(B) The "if" clause must be in the imperfect or pluperfect subjunctive when the main clause is in the conditional or the conditional perfect.

54. Ellos ________ dan la cuenta a nosotros.

(A) la

(B) le

(C) les

(D) nos

(D) Since the *a nosotros* is used to stress the indirect object, the only choice here is the indirect object pronoun *nos.*

55. Por interesante que ________, no quiero visitar este país.

(A) está

(B) es

(C) sea

(D) ser

(C) The expression "no matter how" is *por ________ que* followed by the subjunctive. Here then, you need the third person singular subjunctive of the verb *ser* (to be), not *estar* which also means "to be" but is used to indicate location and temporary condition.

56. Estaba durmiendo cuando ________ mi hermano.

(A) me llamó

(B) me llamabas

(C) llamarme

(D) llamándome

(A) Here, you need the preterite to indicate that the action interrupted something else that was in progress. "I was sleeping when my brother called me."

57. ¡No lo ________! Es peligroso.

(A) hagas

(B) hace

(C) hacer

(D) hizo

(A) This is obviously a command and only (A) is in the negative imperative form (second person singular).

58. Tengo dos bicicletas. Ésta es roja y ________ es azul.

(A) aquél

(B) eso

(C) esto

(D) aquélla

(A) This sentence requires a demonstrative pronoun and since *bicicleta* is feminine, there is only one possible choice.

59. Podemos sacar al menos ________ dólares del banco.

(A) cien

(B) cientos

(C) cuentos

(D) ciento

(A) Before a noun of either gender or before a number larger than one hundred, *ciento* must be contracted to become *cien.*

60. El alcalde del pueblo ________ por la gente.

(A) eligen

(B) fue elegido

(C) está elegida

(D) se eligían

(B) This sentence is in the passive voice and requires *ser* and the past participle.

Part C

The slave ships from Africa arrived in Brazil in 1525, carrying the first of many miserable cargoes of human beings destined to work on the sugar, tobacco, and coffee plantations. Historians calculate that an extraordinarily high number of slaves reached the Brazilian shore, higher than that of the United States. About 10 per cent of the slaves died each year due to the inadequate food and clothing, together with the long hours of work and the corporal punishment. The average slave survived only 10 years. And since the formation of families was not encouraged—hardly one out of every ten slaves succeeded in marrying—the landholders had to import new working slaves.

While international pressure forced the United States to abolish the importation of slaves in 1808, Brazilian society did not pay attention to the admonitions that it would have to reduce its dependence on slave labor. Historians attribute this delay to the fact that Brazil did not have a public press until 1808 and that the country did not have a single true reformist or democratic movement.

61. What is this paragraph about?

(A) Colonialism in Africa

(B) Plantations in the United States

(C) The development of agriculture in Brazil

(D) Slavery in Brazil

62. According to the article, the death of many slaves was due to

(A) the war in North America

(B) the lack of food

(C) the heat

(D) the dangerous trip from Africa

63. According to the author

(A) Brazil had more slaves than the United States

(B) the slaves worked in factories

(C) the majority of slaves lived with their families

(D) the slaves married Brazilians

64. According to historians, Brazil was one of the last countries to abolish slavery because

(A) it had more plantations than other countries

(B) it had a strong reform movement

(C) it didn't have a public press

(D) the slaves revolted

65. According to the article, Brazil

(A) depended on slave labor

(B) wanted to abolish slavery earlier

(C) couldn't import slaves after 1800

(D) paid attention to public opinion

And one day she appeared again. When he heard that someone called him he turned around and encountered her. It was exactly eight years since he had seen her.

She had large brown eyes and wore her hair—brown also—below the shoulders with bangs. Her features reminded him of Italian Renaissance portraits.

—How well you look! You haven't changed a bit—he said. It was the month of May and they were in an art gallery in New York.

—It's just that my changes don't show.

He had left Manhattan a little after having seen her for the last time, because her husband, a prominent literary critic, had been offered a chair in a university in the northern part of the state.

—Are you visiting the city? he asked her.

—Yes. For a few days—she replied and approached him.—And you Mike? How is your life?

—I'm married, I have two children and I work in a bank—he said.

—A bank?

His wife came from a family of bankers.

—Yes. I write their monthly bulletin.

The last time that they had seen each other Mike's greatest desire had been to become a playwright. He had never wanted to look for a steady job because, according to him, he needed time to write.

—Do you like it?

—Of course not.

Eight years ago, when they were both single, they had spoken of how wonderful it would be to have children. He thought about how marvelous it would be and he wanted to; but the idea horrifed her.

66. In this story, the characters are in

(A) the park

(B) a gallery

(C) a store

(D) a restaurant

67. According to the story, the woman
- **(A)** is Italian
- **(B)** is an artist
- **(C)** is not changed much
- **(D)** lives in New York

68. What is the relationship between Mike and the woman?
- **(A)** They are colleagues.
- **(B)** They were lovers.
- **(C)** They were enemies.
- **(D)** They are tourists from the same country.

69. What does Mike do?
- **(A)** He is a playwright.
- **(B)** He is a literary critic.
- **(C)** He is a writer for a bank.
- **(D)** He is an economist.

70. Which of the following statements is NOT true?
- **(A)** Mike and the woman meet by chance.
- **(B)** The husband of the woman is a professor.
- **(C)** The story takes place during the spring.
- **(D)** Mike likes his work.

Jorge Amado, the Brazilian author whose novels have been published in 60 countries, declared to us: "Latin American literature does not exist. It is a false and dangerous concept. Latin American literature represents various diverse countries, cultures and peoples. There is a big difference between Mexican and Brazilian, between Argentine and Peruvian.

"It is very dangerous to label books in this manner, because then they are destined to belong to a 'ghetto.' If a Greek or Swedish author is published, they don't designate it European literature. This is a colonialist attitude.

"All of the the Latin American countries are different. Unfortunately, all that unites us is negative—misery, oppression, and military dictatorships.

"What unifies the positions of the authors of these countries is that, in general, they are loyal to their people, to the fight to mitigate the social problems and secure a better life for them. But Latin American literature does not exist."

71. This passage is probably
- **(A)** an interview
- **(B)** a dialogue in a novel
- **(C)** a letter from one author to another
- **(D)** a page from a diary

72. According to Amado, why doesn't Latin American literature exist?
- **(A)** The works are not all written in Spanish.
- **(B)** There are military dictatorships in Latin America.
- **(C)** The public is not interested in Latin American literature.
- **(D)** The countries of Latin America are too different.

73. According to Amado, what unifies the Latin American countries?
- **(A)** They all have Spanish as an official language.
- **(B)** The cultures come from the Indians and the Spanish.
- **(C)** They suffer misery and oppression.
- **(D)** They are opposed to colonialism.

74. What do Latin American writers have in common?
- **(A)** They are generally educated in Europe.
- **(B)** They are published in more than 60 countries.
- **(C)** They are writing about social problems.
- **(D)** They are colonialists.

Few know that in the middle of the 16th century, a great number of extraordinarily talented men moved from Europe to the New World; to Mexico and Peru, the two oldest and richest Spanish colonies where 20,000 monasteries and 70,000 churches required the work of painters and sculptors. Colonial Spanish art was affected by the new styles in vogue in Europe. The lack of appreciation of this art was due to the fact that the majority of it was religious and created for religious institutions or for the homes of men whose lives were governed by the Catholic calendar. Also, the most cultured Europeans didn't travel much. But this is part of the problem. The true problem is that no one knows enough about colonial Spanish art to appreciate it. In actuality, a work of art attributed to a secondary European school attracts more attention than an important work done by a master of the New World. The frequency with which these works are erroneously attributed to great European masters is a proof of their quality.

75. What is this article about?

(A) Colonial religion

(B) Colonial art

(C) The influence of colonial art on European art

(D) The importance of the architecture of the New World

76. We can say that Spanish colonial art

(A) is very popular

(B) is unknown

(C) is not interesting

(D) is secular for the most part

77. Hispanoamerican artists had a lot of opportunity to create because

(A) they were rich and had rich patrons

(B) there were many churches and monasteries

(C) they received the help of European artists

(D) they created for secular institutions

78. According to the author, why is the art of the colonies so little appreciated?

(A) The scholar didn't travel much.

(B) It was inferior to European art.

(C) It was affected by the styles fashionable in Europe.

(D) It wasn't in important museums.

79. According to the author, how do we know that colonial art is valuable?

(A) It is in all of this century's most important museums.

(B) It is sold for millions of dollars.

(C) Sometimes it is confused with the work of a European master.

(D) It imitates the inferior European work.

80. According to the selection, Mexico and Peru

(A) had more artists than other countries

(B) were the first Spanish colonies

(C) didn't have enough money to support art

(D) didn't have any contact with Europe

There are those who say that the smooth tone of the Bossa Nova was a product of necessity. The story tells that the musical meetings took place at night in the districts near Rio and lasted until dawn, obliging the performers to lower their voices so as not to disturb the neighbors. In any case, what no one knows is that this musical style had various evolutionary phases.

Toward the end of the 1920s, when radio appeared, playing the guitar and singing samba was considered bohemian and for popular folk theater. With the advent of radio a more dignified version of the samba developed and it coincided with the strengthening of the phonograph industry. The radio and records began to direct the fate of popular Brazilian music.

The avalanche of new talent emerged unexpectedly in all social classes, even in the highest strata, with Mario Reis, whose low voice may have given origin to the Bossa Nova. At this time variations were introduced, but always at the amateur level. Bando de Lua, the first to form a vocal group, did not accept payment for its performances, saying "we are not professionals."

In the early 1930s new harmonies and compositions give the movement a true, professional touch, especially by Radames Gnatelli, creator of the new style of orchestration, adapting samba rhythms to the saxophone and brass instruments.

81. We can say that the smooth tone of the Bossa Nova is due to

(A) an effort not to disturb people

(B) a bohemian posture

(C) the birth of the phonograph industry

(D) the sound of the saxophone

82. Why didn't Bando de Lua accept payment?

(A) He considered himself an amateur.

(B) His performances were for charity.

(C) He didn't want to pay taxes.

(D) He didn't play well,

83. According to the author, the Bossa Nova

(A) was created by the upper classes

(B) did not develop in Brazil

(C) is characterized by low, smooth voices

(D) began with a professional group

84. According to the selection, the development of the phonograph industry

(A) is important in the history of the Bossa Nova

(B) coincides with the popularity of folk music

(C) is more important than that of the radio

(D) has nothing to do with the development of Brazilian music

85. The Bossa Nova, according to the paragraph, is

(A) derived from the samba

(B) an old musical style

(C) based on the rhythms of Spanish music

(D) similar to jazz

American History and Social Studies Test

Lesson 6

American History and Social Studies Test

About the Test

The American History and Social Studies Test consists of 95 multiple-choice items. The items mainly test American history from pre-Columbian times to the present. A few items, however, test basic social science concepts used in disciplines such as political science and economics. These *extra* concepts, while they may be taught in courses in government or economics, are almost always included in the typical high school course on American history. In short, to do well on this test, you do not need instruction in a special discipline. A reasonably challenging high school course in American history should be sufficient preparation.

The test writers divide the items into categories according to the type of material covered and the period from which the concept is taken. This ensures that each new test has the proper balance of concepts so that, for example, it doesn't have too many items concerning the colonial period or too few items concerning foreign policy. You don't need to know what these categories are, because that knowledge won't help you do well on the test. You have to answer questions, not put them into categories. You can rest assured, however, that the balance will reflect the treatment given American history by the typical high school text. A test, for example, will probably ask about twice as many questions about the period "1899 to present" as about the colonial period.

Questions Used

The items used are, for the most part, straightforward multiple-choice questions or completions.

EXAMPLE:

Which of the colonies was founded as a refuge for imprisoned debtors?

(A) Connecticut
(B) Delaware
(C) Georgia
(D) New Jersey
(E) North Carolina

This is a typical multiple-choice question. The correct answer is (C). Founder James Oglethorpe viewed his colony primarily as a haven for previously imprisoned debtors, though he also believed it had some significance as a buffer against French and Spanish expansion.

EXAMPLE:

In his 1796 farewell address, George Washington urged the United States to

(A) steer clear of permanent alliances with foreign countries
(B) abolish slavery in every state at the earliest opportunity
(C) organize political parties to nominate candidates for public office
(D) form a long-term military alliance with France against Great Britain
(E) make the government more democratic by providing for universal suffrage

This item differs from the first example only in form. It is phrased as a completion rather than a question. The correct answer is (A). In his farewell address, Washington said, "It is our true policy to steer clear of permanent alliances with any portion of the foreign world."

There are some question forms that have special features.

EXAMPLE:

Amendments to the United States Constitution have dealt with all of the following EXCEPT

(A) manufacture and sale of alcoholic beverages
(B) popular election of senators
(C) separation of church and state
(D) establishment of political parties
(E) the right of women citizens to vote

Notice the wording of the question stem. It informs you that four of the five answer choices refer to topics that are the subject of constitutional amendments. One of the answer choices—the correct one—refers to a topic that is not the subject of a constitutional amendment.

The United States Constitution has been amended to provide for

1. prohibition of the manufacture and sale of alcoholic beverages: 18th (later repealed)
2. popular election of senators: 17th
3. separation of church and state: 1st
4. suffrage for women: 19th

Neither the original document nor any of the amendments provides for the establishment of political parties. So the correct answer to the question is (D).

When addressing a question that uses a word such as EXCEPT, NOT, or LEAST, make sure you know what you are looking for. Be careful, because those words *reverse* the question: what would ordinarily be a wrong answer is the right one, and vice versa.

Occasionally, an item is in a format that makes guessing easier.

EXAMPLE:

Which of the following laws were designed to foster business competition?

I. The Sherman Act
II. The Volstead Act
III. The Clayton Act

(A) I only
(B) III only
(C) I and III only
(D) II and III only
(E) I, II, and III

Notice that the answer choices to this item are various combinations of the numbered statements. Even if you are not certain about the validity of all three statements, you may be able to eliminate one or more answers based on partial information. Suppose, for example, that you know that the Sherman Act is an antitrust act and that the Volstead Act was the prohibition act. And assume further that you do not know the purpose of the Clayton Act. Even given this limited information, you know that the correct answer choice must include I but not II. This narrows your choice to two responses: "(A) I only" and "(C) I and III only." So you should make a guess. (The correct answer is (C). The Clayton Act is also an antitrust act.)

Some questions are based upon maps or charts.

EXAMPLE:

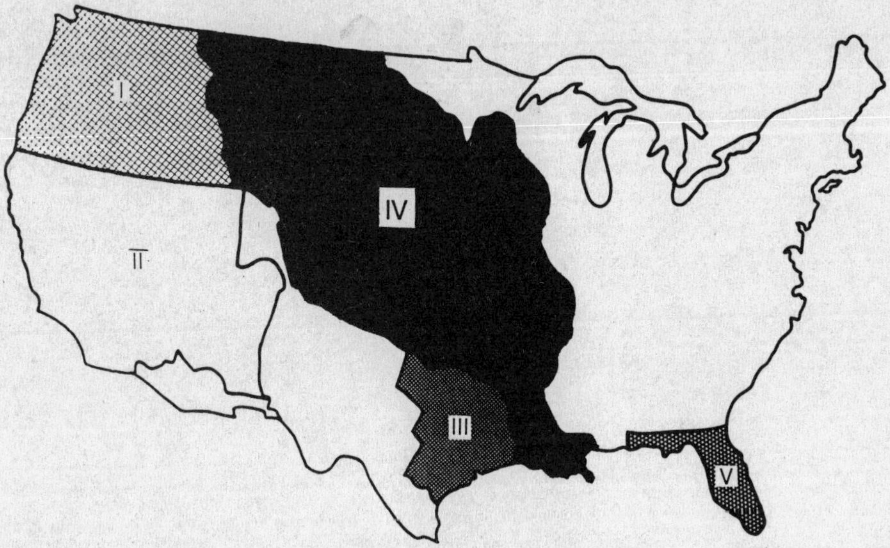

All of the following are true of the map above EXCEPT

(A) I was purchased from Russia.
(B) II was ceded by Mexico following the Mexican War.
(C) III was acquired through the annexation of Texas.
(D) IV was purchased from France.
(E) V was purchased from Spain.

(A) is the correct answer. Alaska was purchased from Russia in 1876, but Alaska is not one of the fifty contiguous states; it is to the north of Area I.

The sample test is followed by complete explanatory answers. These answers are an important part of your preparation for two reasons. First, in most cases, we have tried to explain why the wrong answers are wrong as well as why the right answer is right. Read the entire explanation, because the wrong answer to a question today may be the right answer to a different question tomorrow. Second, where feasible we have given expanded explanations for the correct answer; that is, we have tried to give sufficient background to make the event more memorable. Also, the details provided in the expanded explanation could be tested on your test.

American History and Social Studies Test Answer Sheet

1	Ⓐ	Ⓑ	Ⓒ	Ⓓ	Ⓔ	49	Ⓐ	Ⓑ	Ⓒ	Ⓓ	Ⓔ
2	Ⓐ	Ⓑ	Ⓒ	Ⓓ	Ⓔ	50	Ⓐ	Ⓑ	Ⓒ	Ⓓ	Ⓔ
3	Ⓐ	Ⓑ	Ⓒ	Ⓓ	Ⓔ	51	Ⓐ	Ⓑ	Ⓒ	Ⓓ	Ⓔ
4	Ⓐ	Ⓑ	Ⓒ	Ⓓ	Ⓔ	52	Ⓐ	Ⓑ	Ⓒ	Ⓓ	Ⓔ
5	Ⓐ	Ⓑ	Ⓒ	Ⓓ	Ⓔ	53	Ⓐ	Ⓑ	Ⓒ	Ⓓ	Ⓔ
6	Ⓐ	Ⓑ	Ⓒ	Ⓓ	Ⓔ	54	Ⓐ	Ⓑ	Ⓒ	Ⓓ	Ⓔ
7	Ⓐ	Ⓑ	Ⓒ	Ⓓ	Ⓔ	55	Ⓐ	Ⓑ	Ⓒ	Ⓓ	Ⓔ
8	Ⓐ	Ⓑ	Ⓒ	Ⓓ	Ⓔ	56	Ⓐ	Ⓑ	Ⓒ	Ⓓ	Ⓔ
9	Ⓐ	Ⓑ	Ⓒ	Ⓓ	Ⓔ	57	Ⓐ	Ⓑ	Ⓒ	Ⓓ	Ⓔ
10	Ⓐ	Ⓑ	Ⓒ	Ⓓ	Ⓔ	58	Ⓐ	Ⓑ	Ⓒ	Ⓓ	Ⓔ
11	Ⓐ	Ⓑ	Ⓒ	Ⓓ	Ⓔ	59	Ⓐ	Ⓑ	Ⓒ	Ⓓ	Ⓔ
12	Ⓐ	Ⓑ	Ⓒ	Ⓓ	Ⓔ	60	Ⓐ	Ⓑ	Ⓒ	Ⓓ	Ⓔ
13	Ⓐ	Ⓑ	Ⓒ	Ⓓ	Ⓔ	61	Ⓐ	Ⓑ	Ⓒ	Ⓓ	Ⓔ
14	Ⓐ	Ⓑ	Ⓒ	Ⓓ	Ⓔ	62	Ⓐ	Ⓑ	Ⓒ	Ⓓ	Ⓔ
15	Ⓐ	Ⓑ	Ⓒ	Ⓓ	Ⓔ	63	Ⓐ	Ⓑ	Ⓒ	Ⓓ	Ⓔ
16	Ⓐ	Ⓑ	Ⓒ	Ⓓ	Ⓔ	64	Ⓐ	Ⓑ	Ⓒ	Ⓓ	Ⓔ
17	Ⓐ	Ⓑ	Ⓒ	Ⓓ	Ⓔ	65	Ⓐ	Ⓑ	Ⓒ	Ⓓ	Ⓔ
18	Ⓐ	Ⓑ	Ⓒ	Ⓓ	Ⓔ	66	Ⓐ	Ⓑ	Ⓒ	Ⓓ	Ⓔ
19	Ⓐ	Ⓑ	Ⓒ	Ⓓ	Ⓔ	67	Ⓐ	Ⓑ	Ⓒ	Ⓓ	Ⓔ
20	Ⓐ	Ⓑ	Ⓒ	Ⓓ	Ⓔ	68	Ⓐ	Ⓑ	Ⓒ	Ⓓ	Ⓔ
21	Ⓐ	Ⓑ	Ⓒ	Ⓓ	Ⓔ	69	Ⓐ	Ⓑ	Ⓒ	Ⓓ	Ⓔ
22	Ⓐ	Ⓑ	Ⓒ	Ⓓ	Ⓔ	70	Ⓐ	Ⓑ	Ⓒ	Ⓓ	Ⓔ
23	Ⓐ	Ⓑ	Ⓒ	Ⓓ	Ⓔ	71	Ⓐ	Ⓑ	Ⓒ	Ⓓ	Ⓔ
24	Ⓐ	Ⓑ	Ⓒ	Ⓓ	Ⓔ	72	Ⓐ	Ⓑ	Ⓒ	Ⓓ	Ⓔ
25	Ⓐ	Ⓑ	Ⓒ	Ⓓ	Ⓔ	73	Ⓐ	Ⓑ	Ⓒ	Ⓓ	Ⓔ
26	Ⓐ	Ⓑ	Ⓒ	Ⓓ	Ⓔ	74	Ⓐ	Ⓑ	Ⓒ	Ⓓ	Ⓔ
27	Ⓐ	Ⓑ	Ⓒ	Ⓓ	Ⓔ	75	Ⓐ	Ⓑ	Ⓒ	Ⓓ	Ⓔ
28	Ⓐ	Ⓑ	Ⓒ	Ⓓ	Ⓔ	76	Ⓐ	Ⓑ	Ⓒ	Ⓓ	Ⓔ
29	Ⓐ	Ⓑ	Ⓒ	Ⓓ	Ⓔ	77	Ⓐ	Ⓑ	Ⓒ	Ⓓ	Ⓔ
30	Ⓐ	Ⓑ	Ⓒ	Ⓓ	Ⓔ	78	Ⓐ	Ⓑ	Ⓒ	Ⓓ	Ⓔ
31	Ⓐ	Ⓑ	Ⓒ	Ⓓ	Ⓔ	79	Ⓐ	Ⓑ	Ⓒ	Ⓓ	Ⓔ
32	Ⓐ	Ⓑ	Ⓒ	Ⓓ	Ⓔ	80	Ⓐ	Ⓑ	Ⓒ	Ⓓ	Ⓔ
33	Ⓐ	Ⓑ	Ⓒ	Ⓓ	Ⓔ	81	Ⓐ	Ⓑ	Ⓒ	Ⓓ	Ⓔ
34	Ⓐ	Ⓑ	Ⓒ	Ⓓ	Ⓔ	82	Ⓐ	Ⓑ	Ⓒ	Ⓓ	Ⓔ
35	Ⓐ	Ⓑ	Ⓒ	Ⓓ	Ⓔ	83	Ⓐ	Ⓑ	Ⓒ	Ⓓ	Ⓔ
36	Ⓐ	Ⓑ	Ⓒ	Ⓓ	Ⓔ	84	Ⓐ	Ⓑ	Ⓒ	Ⓓ	Ⓔ
37	Ⓐ	Ⓑ	Ⓒ	Ⓓ	Ⓔ	85	Ⓐ	Ⓑ	Ⓒ	Ⓓ	Ⓔ
38	Ⓐ	Ⓑ	Ⓒ	Ⓓ	Ⓔ	86	Ⓐ	Ⓑ	Ⓒ	Ⓓ	Ⓔ
39	Ⓐ	Ⓑ	Ⓒ	Ⓓ	Ⓔ	87	Ⓐ	Ⓑ	Ⓒ	Ⓓ	Ⓔ
40	Ⓐ	Ⓑ	Ⓒ	Ⓓ	Ⓔ	88	Ⓐ	Ⓑ	Ⓒ	Ⓓ	Ⓔ
41	Ⓐ	Ⓑ	Ⓒ	Ⓓ	Ⓔ	89	Ⓐ	Ⓑ	Ⓒ	Ⓓ	Ⓔ
42	Ⓐ	Ⓑ	Ⓒ	Ⓓ	Ⓔ	90	Ⓐ	Ⓑ	Ⓒ	Ⓓ	Ⓔ
43	Ⓐ	Ⓑ	Ⓒ	Ⓓ	Ⓔ	91	Ⓐ	Ⓑ	Ⓒ	Ⓓ	Ⓔ
44	Ⓐ	Ⓑ	Ⓒ	Ⓓ	Ⓔ	92	Ⓐ	Ⓑ	Ⓒ	Ⓓ	Ⓔ
45	Ⓐ	Ⓑ	Ⓒ	Ⓓ	Ⓔ	93	Ⓐ	Ⓑ	Ⓒ	Ⓓ	Ⓔ
46	Ⓐ	Ⓑ	Ⓒ	Ⓓ	Ⓔ	94	Ⓐ	Ⓑ	Ⓒ	Ⓓ	Ⓔ
47	Ⓐ	Ⓑ	Ⓒ	Ⓓ	Ⓔ	95	Ⓐ	Ⓑ	Ⓒ	Ⓓ	Ⓔ
48	Ⓐ	Ⓑ	Ⓒ	Ⓓ	Ⓔ						

American History and Social Studies Test

Directions: Each of the questions or incomplete statements below is followed by five answer choices or completions. For each item, choose the best answer and darken the corresponding circle on the answer sheet.

1. The Open Door Note of 1899, addressed to England, France, Germany, Russia, and Japan, asked those world powers to

(A) send troops to help the United States put down the Boxer Rebellion

(B) permit the United States to annex the Philippine Islands

(C) allow the United States and each other equal trading rights in China

(D) work together to find a way to end the Russo-Japanese War

(E) form an alliance to block Chinese military expansionism

2. In labor relations, a worker's ''right to work'' is the worker's right to

(A) work at a job that provides a minimally acceptable standard of living

(B) refuse to join the labor union that represents the worker's coworkers

(C) join with other workers in similar jobs to form a labor union

(D) apply for promotions as the worker gains seniority with a company

(E) choose the company by whom the worker will be employed

3. Which of the following was used by President Lyndon B. Johnson in 1964 to step up United States military activities in Vietnam?

(A) The Gulf of Tonkin Resolution

(B) The Platt Amendment

(C) The SEATO Treaty

(D) The Wilmot Proviso

(E) The Zimmerman Note

4. The Treaty of Paris of 1783, which ended the American Revolutionary War, provided for all the following EXCEPT

(A) Fishermen from the United States would have the right to fish off the Coast of Canada.

(B) British creditors could legally attempt to collect debts from American debtors.

(C) The Congress of the United States would recommend that state governments restore the rights of Loyalists.

(D) The United States would have control of most of the area between the Appalachian Mountains and the Mississippi River.

(E) Quotas would be established to limit the number of British citizens allowed to immigrate to the United States each year.

5. W.E.B. DuBois would most likely have agreed with which of the following statements about Booker T. Washington?

(A) The assumptions on which the Tuskegee Institute was found are empirically valid.

(B) Washington is too radical, and his approach is likely to lead to violence.

(C) The theory of the Tuskegee Institute is impractical, but it is not likely to do any harm.

(D) Washington's approach is not only ineffective, it is another form of slavery.

(E) Washington is correct in saying that social and political equality will follow economic advancement.

6. The Congress under the Articles of Confederation had the power to do all of the following EXCEPT

(A) declare war

(B) make treaties

(C) establish post offices

(D) levy direct taxes on people

(E) send diplomatic representatives to foreign countries

GO ON TO THE NEXT PAGE

7. The first author to write in the American vernacular was

(A) Nathaniel Hawthorne

(B) Mark Twain

(C) Ernest Hemingway

(D) John Steinbeck

(E) Edgar Allan Poe

8. The War of 1812 was most vigorously opposed in what region of the United States?

(A) Northeast

(B) Southeast

(C) Southwest

(D) South

(E) Northwest

9. Prior to the ratification of the Twenty-sixth Amendment to the United States Constitution, persons who had not yet reached the age of 21 could vote in

(A) state and local but not federal elections

(B) federal but not state and local elections

(C) neither state nor federal elections

(D) all state and federal elections

(E) elections in states that granted them the right to vote

10. The Teapot Dome (1923) scandal centered on the

(A) questionable billing practices of major defense contractors

(B) improper grants of oil leases in Wyoming and California

(C) illicit campaign contributions made during Harding's presidential campaign

(D) sale of various federal judgeships in southern states

(E) monopolistic pricing policies of large steel companies

11. In his 1961 Farewell Address, President Dwight D. Eisenhower

(A) called for new and more powerful civil rights legislation

(B) warned against the power of the military-industrial complex

(C) proposed that the United States unilaterally reduce its stockpile of nuclear weapons

(D) remonstrated Congress for having undermined the authority of the Presidency

(E) attempted to minimize the threat posed by the Soviet Union

12. In *Schenck* v. *United States* (1919), Supreme Court Justice Oliver Wendell Holmes wrote: "The most stringent protection of free speech would not protect a man in falsely shouting fire in a theater and causing panic." This implies that

(A) freedom of speech is not an absolute right

(B) certain individuals have no constitutional rights

(C) federal legislation takes priority over state laws

(D) the Constitution does not provide for freedom of speech

(E) freedom of speech is unconditionally guaranteed by the Constitution

13. When President Franklin D. Roosevelt explained that the Lend Lease Act of 1941 would make the United States the "arsenal of democracy" he meant that the United States would

(A) send troops to Europe to defend France against the *Blitzkrieg*

(B) provide armaments to Britain but stay out of the war

(C) allow American pilots to fly British war planes

(D) maintain a strict isolationist posture regarding Europe

(E) commit troops to the war only if Japan attacked Pearl Harbor

GO ON TO THE NEXT PAGE

14. Which of the following events directly contributed to passage of the National Defense Education Act, enacted by Congress in 1958 to improve education in mathematics and the sciences?

(A) Soviet Union military intervention in Hungary

(B) The Soviet Union's launching of the satellite Sputnik

(C) Civil rights protests against segregated schools

(D) Eisenhower's election to a second term as President

(E) The Suez Crisis

15. All of the descriptive phrases listed below are correctly associated with the president named EXCEPT

(A) The New Deal—Franklin D. Roosevelt

(B) The Square Deal—Theodore Roosevelt

(C) The Fair Deal—Harry S. Truman

(D) The Great Society—Lyndon B. Johnson

(E) The Return to Normalcy—Calvin Coolidge

16. The National Security Act of 1947 created all of the following EXCEPT

(A) a separate Air Force

(B) the Joint Chiefs of Staff

(C) the National Security Council

(D) the Central Intelligence Agency

(E) the Department of War

17. Which of the following descriptions best defines the concept of a monopoly?

(A) A market dominated by a single buyer

(B) A market dominated by a single seller

(C) A market dominated by a few large buyers

(D) A market with no dominant seller

(E) A market with no dominant buyer

18. The doctrine of judicial review, enunciated in *Marbury* v. *Madison*, is the authority of a court to

(A) invalidate unconstitutional legislative acts and executive actions

(B) punish contempt of court by short-term imprisonment

(C) order the losing party in a civil suit to pay damages

(D) determine what evidence can be excluded in a criminal trial

(E) command public officials to perform their legally required duties

19. The Marshall Plan was adopted in large measure because the United States

(A) wanted to see Germany punished for its aggression during World War II

(B) hoped that Europe could become unified under a single central government

(C) was unsure of the motives of the Soviet Union in Berlin

(D) feared that unstable European countries would succumb to communism

(E) incorrectly believed that the Soviet Union lacked any expansionist plans

20. The Good Neighbor Policy of the United States included which of the following?

I. Economic cooperation with Latin American countries

II. A promise not to intervene in the internal affairs of Latin American countries

III. A military alliance to defend Latin America against foreign invasion

(A) I only

(B) II only

(C) I and II only

(D) I and III only

(E) II and III only

GO ON TO THE NEXT PAGE

21. One of two Italian immigrant radicals executed in 1927 by the Commonwealth of Massachusetts for the crimes of murder and robbery was

(A) Al Capone

(B) Nicola Sacco

(C) Fiorello LaGuardia

(D) Vittorio Orlando

(E) Rocky Marciano

22. Will Rogers' remark that "Mississippi will vote dry and drink wet as long as it can stagger to the polls" refers to the difficulty in

(A) passing the Prohibition amendment

(B) enacting Prohibition legislation

(C) enforcing Prohibition legislation

(D) evading Prohibition legislation

(E) repealing the Prohibition amendment

23. Immigration from which of the following regions was greatest during the period from 1900 to 1920?

(A) The United Kingdom

(B) The Middle East

(C) Southeastern Europe

(D) Asia

(E) Africa

24. Which of the following colonies was founded by an individual persecuted for his political views and religious beliefs?

(A) Virginia

(B) New Jersey

(C) Georgia

(D) New York

(E) Rhode Island

Questions 25 and 26 are based on the following chart.

PRESIDENTIAL ELECTIONS OF 1908 AND 1912

Election	Candidate	Party	Popular Vote	Electoral Vote
1908	William H. Taft	Republican	7,679,006	321
	William J. Bryan	Democrat	6,409,106	162
	Eugene V. Debs	Socialist	420,820	—
1912	Woodrow Wilson	Democrat	6,293,454	435
	Theodore Roosevelt	Progressive	4,119,538	88
	William H. Taft	Republican	3,484,980	8
	Eugene V. Debs	Socialist	897,011	—

25. The chart above suggests which of the following as the primary reason for the Republican defeat in 1912?

(A) The Democrats ran a very unpopular candidate in 1908 and a very popular one in 1912.

(B) In 1912, a substantial number of previously unregistered voters registered and voted for the Democratic candidate.

(C) In 1908, a substantial number of voters belonging to the Socialist Party voted for the Republican candidate.

(D) In 1912, a substantial number of voters deserted the Socialist Party in favor of the Democratic Party.

(E) In 1912, a substantial number of voters deserted the Republican Party in favor of the Progressive Party.

26. The chart most strongly suggests that between 1908 and 1912

(A) the American people lost interest in presidential politics

(B) the Socialist Party lost support among American voters

(C) American voters became disenchanted with the principles of progressivism

(D) the principles of progressivism gained wider support among American voters

(E) the total number of registered voters in the United States declined

GO ON TO THE NEXT PAGE

27. The state of Maine was created from the northeastern counties of Massachusetts in order to

(A) create a buffer between Massachusetts and Canada

(B) provide a sanctuary for religious dissidents

(C) maintain the balance between free and slave states

(D) relieve the pressures of overcrowding in Massachusetts

(E) weaken the power of Massachusetts' Congressional delegation

28. ''Gerrymandering'' is the practice of

(A) imposing high tariffs on imported goods to reduce competition from foreign manufacturers

(B) creating oddly-shaped voting districts to ensure the election of a certain party's nominees

(C) killing a legislative proposal by attaching unacceptable riders to the bill

(D) abstaining from a Congressional vote to protest the content of a piece of legislation

(E) issuing government bonds that are to be redeemed with paper money rather than gold

29. Senator Henry Cabot Lodge's fourteen reservations to the Treaty of Versailles were designed primarily to

(A) reaffirm President Wilson's Fourteen Points for a peace without victory

(B) prevent the United States from becoming a member of the League of Nations

(C) gain popular support for the proposed League of Nations

(D) ensure that reparations assessed on Germany would not be unduly burdensome

(E) isolate the Soviet Union economically and politically from western Europe

30. The Bill of Rights, the first ten amendments to the United States Constitution, guarantees the people of the United States all of the following EXCEPT

(A) freedom from unreasonable search and seizure

(B) freedom from double jeopardy

(C) the right to bear arms

(D) due process of law

(E) equal protection under the law

31. The ''spoils system'' contributed to the development of

(A) modern political parties

(B) antislavery sentiment

(C) isolationism

(D) anti-United States sentiment in Latin America

(E) nuclear proliferation

32. Impeachment is most like which of the following?

(A) Trial

(B) Indictment

(C) Conviction

(D) Sentencing

(E) Imprisonment

33. ''Yellow journalism'' is characterized by

(A) objective reporting of current affairs

(B) scholarly analysis of political trends

(C) sensationalized accounts of news events

(D) lack of a coherent editorial position

(E) descriptions and reports of trivial events

GO ON TO THE NEXT PAGE

PURCHASING POWER OF FARM PRODUCTS 1914–1922

Year	Prices Paid to Farmers	Prices Paid by Farmers
1914*	$1.00	$1.00
1916	1.72	1.42
1918	1.86	1.82
1920	2.03	2.04
1922	1.25	1.54

*In 1914 Prices Paid to Farmers = Prices Paid by Farmers

34. In terms of purchasing power, farmers were best off in which year?

(A) 1914
(B) 1916
(C) 1918
(D) 1920
(E) 1922

35. All of the following acts were New Deal legislation EXCEPT

(A) the Taft-Hartley Act
(B) the National Industrial Recovery Act
(C) the Social Security Act
(D) the Fair Labor Standards Act
(E) the National Labor Relations Act

36. "Redeemers" is a term coined by

(A) white conservatives who succeeded the radical reconstructionists to refer to themselves
(B) radical Republicans who opposed Lincoln's plan of reconstruction to refer to themselves
(C) moderate Republicans who supported Lincoln's plan of reconstruction to refer to Grant's cronies
(D) southern whites who had opposed secession to refer to carpetbaggers
(E) blacks elected to public office during reconstruction to refer to conservative whites

37. A historian who wished to do an analysis of African-Americans who were held in slavery before the Civil War would find which of the following most useful?

(A) Tools, dishes, and other articles excavated from a waste pit on a southern plantation
(B) Treatises written by white authors defending the existence of the slave system
(C) Autobiographies written by African-Americans who were actually held in slavery
(D) Plantation records detailing the economic transactions of the owner
(E) Pamphlets written by abolitionists residing in the northern states

38. The Bank of the United States must not continue. The capitalists of the northeastern states grow richer at the expense of the farmers. Additionally, the Bank is monopolistic and unconstitutional.

The remarks above would most likely have been endorsed by a supporter of

(A) John Marshall
(B) Nicholas Biddle
(C) Daniel Webster
(D) Andrew Jackson
(E) William Duane

GO ON TO THE NEXT PAGE

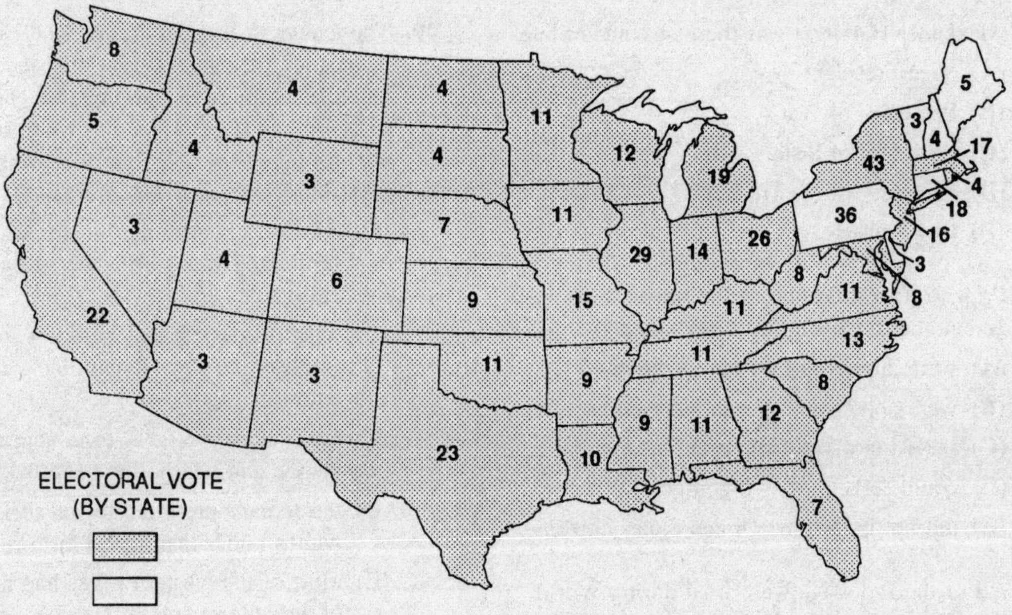

39. Which of the following is an appropriate key for the map above?

	Election	
(A)	Election of 1916 ▩ Wilson	☐ Hughes
(B)	Election of 1924 ▩ Coolidge	☐ Davis
(C)	Election of 1928 ▩ Hoover	☐ Smith
(D)	Election of 1932 ▩ Roosevelt	☐ Hoover
(E)	Election of 1948 ▩ Truman	☐ Dewey

40. All of the following were goals of the Progressive movement in the early twentieth century EXCEPT

(A) elimination of governmental corruption
(B) consumer protection legislation
(C) better conditions for workers
(D) governmental controls over big business
(E) free coinage of silver money

41. The principal author of the Declaration of Independence, Thomas Jefferson, relied heavily on the philosophical writings of

(A) Plato
(B) Aristotle
(C) Aquinas
(D) Machiavelli
(E) Locke

42. The Northwest Ordinance of 1787 set an important precedent for westward expansion because it

(A) established United States military outposts to protect settlers
(B) extinguished the claims of the British to lands north of the Ohio River
(C) transferred disputed western lands from the states to the national government
(D) provided for the creation of additional states rather than for colonies
(E) avoided the problem of high prices caused by land speculators

43. Which of the following peoples were a member of the Iroquois Nation?

(A) Mohawks
(B) Cherokees
(C) Seminoles
(D) Apaches
(E) Pueblos

44. All of the following Supreme Court decisions strengthened the rights of a criminal defendant EXCEPT

(A) *Miranda* v. *Arizona*
(B) *Gideon* v. *Wainwright*
(C) *Roe* v. *Wade*
(D) *Escobedo* v. *Illinois*
(E) *Mapp* v. *Ohio*

GO ON TO THE NEXT PAGE

45. Alexander Hamilton was the first United States

(A) Vice President
(B) Secretary of War
(C) Secretary of State
(D) Secretary of the Treasury
(E) Chief Justice

46. Prior to the ratification of the Seventeenth Amendment, United States senators

(A) were appointed by state governors
(B) were appointed by state legislatures
(C) served terms of four years
(D) could serve only two consecutive terms
(E) did not have to be United States citizens

47. All of the following were used during World War II to control the United States economy EXCEPT

(A) wage and price controls
(B) rent controls
(C) rationing
(D) disbanding of unions
(E) additional taxes

48. The procedure whereby voters can petition to have a special election to determine whether an elected official should be removed from office is termed

(A) an initiative
(B) a referendum
(C) a recall
(D) an arraignment
(E) a mistrial

49. The Dawes Allotment Act of 1887, which distributed parcels of reservation land to Indian heads of families for farming, was an attempt to assimilate the Indians into white society. The attempt failed for all of the following reasons EXCEPT

(A) the land given to the Indians was not very fertile and was particularly difficult to cultivate
(B) most of the Indians could not speak English and were unfamiliar with white culture
(C) the Indians preferred to remain a separate people and had no desire to be assimilated
(D) the Indians preferred to sell their land to whites rather than try to farm it themselves
(E) most of the western tribes had no tradition of agriculture and no knowledge of farming techniques

50. First, Lincoln and the Republicans initially did not aim at abolishing slavery where it already existed. In fact, Lincoln had even promised to enforce the Fugitive Slave Law. Second, most northerners were not abolitionists. Third, four slave states did not secede from the Union. Finally, few southerners owned slaves.

The points raised above could best be used to support the thesis that

(A) the southern economy at the time of the Civil War was not dependent upon slavery
(B) slavery was not the most important cause of the start of the Civil War
(C) slavery was the issue that most clearly divided North from South
(D) the Civil War would not have started had the South agreed to eliminate slavery
(E) Lincoln had already formed his plan to eliminate slavery when he first took office

51. Between 1940 and 1970, all of the following increased EXCEPT

(A) output per farm acre
(B) output per farm worker
(C) farm size
(D) number of farms
(E) farm production

GO ON TO THE NEXT PAGE

52. Rudyard Kipling's poem "The White Man's Burden" was primarily

(A) an apology for imperialism

(B) a condemnation of Southern racism

(C) a justification for United States isolationism

(D) a warning against United States interventionism

(E) a cry against the rising tide of nationalism

53. "The occasion has been judged proper for asserting that the American continents, by the free and independent condition which they have assumed and maintained, are henceforth not to be considered as subjects for future colonization by any European powers."

The statement above articulated what became known as

(A) Seward's Folly

(B) the American System

(C) the Monroe Doctrine

(D) the Policy of Laissez-faire

(E) the XYZ Affair

54. Which of the following is an example of a progressive tax?

(A) Sales tax

(B) Excise tax on liquor and cigarettes

(C) Personal income tax

(D) Property tax

(E) Poll tax

55. Since 1950, all of the following have contributed to the balance of payments deficit EXCEPT

(A) expenditures for foreign military installations

(B) economic assistance to foreign countries

(C) an unfavorable balance of trade

(D) travel by United States tourists in foreign countries

(E) investment by foreign companies in the United States

56. During the twentieth century, labor unions in the United States have been LEAST concerned with which of the following?

(A) Obtaining higher wages

(B) Improving job security

(C) Gaining greater fringe benefits

(D) Increasing union membership

(E) Electing union officials to public office

57. The historian Frederick Jackson Turner theorized that the distinctly American way of life was shaped primarily by

(A) a democratic heritage derived from Britain

(B) the experience of settling the western frontier

(C) industrialism and the factory system

(D) the strength of the seagoing tradition

(E) the religious beliefs of the Puritans

58. All of the following are consequences of the electoral college system of choosing the president EXCEPT

(A) a candidate can win a clear majority of the popular vote but not be elected president

(B) a candidate can win a significant number of popular votes but receive no electoral votes

(C) an elector pledged to a certain candidate can legally break the pledge and vote for another candidate

(D) presidential candidates are encouraged to waste a great deal of time campaigning in less populous states

(E) the system tends to maintain a two-party system by discouraging the growth of third parties

59. Which of the following was NOT a settlement established by the French during the seventeenth century?

(A) Detroit

(B) Montreal

(C) New Orleans

(D) St. Augustine

(E) St. Louis

GO ON TO THE NEXT PAGE

60. The earliest people to reach North America are thought to have arrived from

(A) Siberia via the Bering Strait land bridge
(B) South America via the Central American isthmus
(C) Hawaii via rafts
(D) Scandinavia via boats
(E) Germania via a polar route

61. Which of the following is a felony crime?

(A) Shoplifting
(B) Speeding
(C) Murder
(D) Public drunkenness
(E) Trespassing

62. Which of the following was an important factor in the decision of the United States to enter World War I?

(A) A threatened German invasion of Mexico
(B) German submarine attacks on ships in the Atlantic Ocean
(C) The assassination of the heir to the Austro-Hungarian throne
(D) A Japanese naval blockade of ports on the West Coast of the United States
(E) Formation of a German-Japanese alliance directed against the United States

63. Which of the following black leaders was awarded the Nobel Peace Prize?

(A) Elijah Muhammad
(B) Eldridge Cleaver
(C) Medgar Evers
(D) Martin Luther King, Jr.
(E) Marcus Garvey

64. The War of 1812 is often described as the

(A) "conquest of British Canada"
(B) "American Waterloo"
(C) "dirty little Federalist war"
(D) "war to end all wars"
(E) "second war of independence"

65. In *Brown* v. *Board of Education of Topeka* (1954) the Supreme Court of the United States held that

(A) separate facilities for different races are inherently unequal
(B) segregation is permissible so long as facilities are similar
(C) the federal Constitution makes race relations a matter for the states
(D) there is no constitutional right to a public school education
(E) local school districts may not use busing as a means of desegregating schools

66. The Quartering Act of 1765 was passed to

(A) divide the western lands among various colonies claiming those lands
(B) force the colonies to pay British merchants with silver coins
(C) encourage westward expansion by providing military protection to settlements
(D) deprive colonists of representation in the colonial assemblies
(E) reduce the cost of housing British troops in the American colonies

67. The Constitution of the United States gives the power to make treaties to the

(A) Congress subject to the approval of the president
(B) president subject to the approval of the Senate
(C) president subject to the approval of the House of Representatives
(D) president subject to the approval of the states
(E) states subject to the approval of the Congress

68. The government agency that has the greatest control over interest rates in the United States is the

(A) Federal Trade Commission
(B) Interstate Commerce Commission
(C) Federal Reserve Board
(D) Department of the Interior
(E) Department of Commerce

GO ON TO THE NEXT PAGE

69. Thomas Jefferson theorized that democracy would function best in a society dominated by

(A) merchants and shippers

(B) aristocratic plantation owners

(C) small, independent farmers

(D) unskilled, urban laborers

(E) professionalized government workers

70. In 1962, President John F. Kennedy declared a naval quarantine of Cuba in order to

(A) prevent the Soviet Union from placing offensive missiles in Cuba

(B) ensure that a highly infectious disease did not spread beyond the island

(C) stem the flood of Cubans illegally entering the United States

(D) punish Cuba economically for withdrawing from the Organization of American States

(E) incite a revolution to overthrow the government of Fidel Castro

71. The Chisolm Trail was used by

(A) fur trappers to cross the Appalachian Mountains

(B) cowboys to drive cattle to a rail head in Kansas

(C) prospectors to reach the gold fields of California

(D) settlers to move covered wagons to the West

(E) manufacturers to ship finished goods to the Southwest

72. During the Civil War, the Confederate Army won an important battle at

(A) Little Bighorn

(B) Gettysburg

(C) Vicksburg

(D) Bull Run

(E) Belleau Wood

73. The United States acquired the land to build the Panama Canal by virtue of

(A) a Panamanian revolt against Colombia that was supported by the United States Navy

(B) United States military intervention to resolve a border dispute between Colombia and Panama

(C) an agreement with Colombia under which the United States agreed to a concession fee plus annual payments

(D) a treaty with Nicaragua in which Nicaragua voluntarily relinquished control of the canal zone

(E) an alliance whereby the United States agreed to ensure Colombian neutrality in exchange for the canal route

74. The slogan ''Fifty-four forty or fight'' helped to elect which president?

(A) James Monroe

(B) John Quincy Adams

(C) Andrew Jackson

(D) Martin Van Buren

(E) James K. Polk

75. Which of the following best describes the civil rights policy of President John F. Kennedy?

(A) Very aggressive from the beginning with many new civil rights laws enacted

(B) Very aggressive from the beginning but weakened by resistance from Congress

(C) Initially limited to enforcement of voting rights but later more aggressive

(D) Initially hostile to enforcement of civil rights but later neutral

(E) Hostile toward the enforcement of civil rights throughout the administration

76. The Emancipation Proclamation applied to slaves

(A) throughout the United States

(B) only in border states

(C) only in regions under the control of the Union Army

(D) only in states still in rebellion against the Union

(E) only to escaped slaves who had joined the Union Army

GO ON TO THE NEXT PAGE

77. As applied to Southeast Asia, the "domino theory" held that

(A) a communist takeover of South Vietnam would lead to similar takeovers in other countries in the region

(B) escalating numbers of United States troops would guarantee a military victory in Vietnam

(C) it is impossible to win a guerrilla war using conventional military strategies

(D) only by breaking an enemy's supply lines is it possible to gain victory

(E) a united, communistic but nationalist Vietnam would not be imperialistic

78. The Articles of Confederation, which were never intended to create a strong central government, fostered highly democratic local and state governments. By 1786, the postwar economic depression was all but over, and in general states traded freely among themselves. Even as the Articles were replaced, the states were considering a national tariff, the proceeds of which would be used by the national government.

A historian could use the points made above to support the thesis that

(A) diplomatic negotiations could have avoided the need to fight the Revolutionary War

(B) the Articles of Confederation did not collapse from weakness

(C) the government established by the Constitution is weaker than that of the Articles

(D) the national government ought to have more power than state governments

(E) local government is more likely to be corrupt than a national one

79. In 1824, the House of Representatives was required to choose the president because

(A) the candidate with the largest popular vote died before the electoral college could meet

(B) allegations of widespread vote fraud cast serious doubt on the validity of election results

(C) the Supreme Court had declared unconstitutional certain voting restrictions

(D) each candidate received the same number of votes in the electoral college

(E) sectional voting prevented any of the four candidates from obtaining a majority of the electoral votes

80. Which of the following contributed to the almost ten-year delay in annexing Texas?

I. Sectional opposition to the admission of any more slave states

II. Desire of most Texans to remain a free and independent republic

III. Fear that annexation would alienate France

(A) I only

(B) II only

(C) I and II only

(D) I and III only

(E) II and III only

GO ON TO THE NEXT PAGE

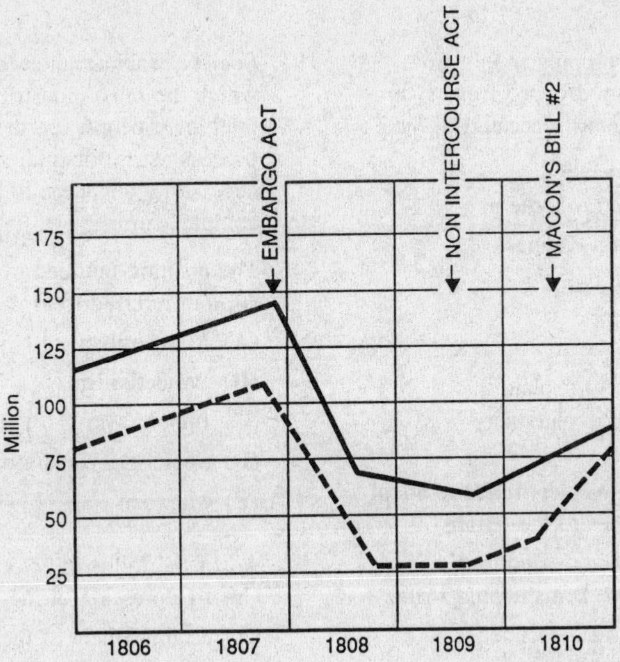

81. The chart above most likely refers to

(A) the strength of the United States army and navy
(B) distribution of population between cities and farms in the United States
(C) the value of United States imports and exports
(D) salaries paid to United States senators and representatives
(E) number of slaves held in Southern versus Northern states

82. All of the following advantages of the North helped to contribute to the Union's victory over the Confederacy EXCEPT

(A) greater industrial base
(B) greater population
(C) easier access to capital
(D) more skillful military leaders
(E) control of the navy

83. A political reactionary would be most likely to favor which of the following?

(A) Higher welfare payments
(B) Higher tax rates
(C) Stricter government regulations on business
(D) National health insurance
(E) Strong military

84. The sharecropping system was predominant in the

(A) North after the Civil War
(B) South after the Civil War
(C) West after the Civil War
(D) Midwest during the depression
(E) Northwest between the world wars

85. Inflation most severely hurts

(A) government workers
(B) retired people
(C) union workers
(D) home owners
(E) white collar workers

86. All of the following presidents were assassinated while in office EXCEPT

(A) William Henry Harrison
(B) Abraham Lincoln
(C) James Garfield
(D) William McKinley
(E) John F. Kennedy

GO ON TO THE NEXT PAGE

87. After 1825, the cost of shipping freight from Buffalo to New York City dropped from $100 per ton to $8 per ton primarily because of the

(A) opening of the Erie Canal

(B) completion of a new rail system

(C) invention of the steam engine

(D) construction of turnpikes

(E) decrease in population

88. All of the following help to explain the American victory in the Revolutionary War EXCEPT

(A) British military commanders failed to adapt their military strategies to the terrain.

(B) There was no one center of political authority at which the British could strike.

(C) The British supply lines extended 3,000 miles across the Atlantic Ocean.

(D) The revolutionary movement had widespread support among the American people.

(E) The revolutionary soldiers were led by well-trained, professional officers.

89. On April 11, 1951, President Harry Truman removed General Douglas MacArthur as commander in chief of United Nation's forces in Korea because

(A) MacArthur was a weak and ineffective military leader

(B) MacArthur was critical of Truman's foreign policy

(C) the United Nations asked for MacArthur's removal

(D) South Korea no longer needed United States military assistance

(E) MacArthur was unpopular with the United States public

90. Which of the following markets would be considered by an economist to be the most competitive?

(A) Steel production

(B) Railroad transportation

(C) Oil refining

(D) Electric utilities

(E) Automobile repair service

91. Society provides an arena for competition in which the most industrious, ingenious, and intelligent people are the most successful. By a process akin to natural selection, civilization necessarily advances to higher and more complex forms.

The position outlined by the statements above is often referred to as

(A) Mercantilism

(B) Protectionism

(C) Imperialism

(D) Social Darwinism

(E) Marxism

92. All of the following were consequences of the Great Depression of the 1930s EXCEPT

(A) establishment of the social security system

(B) enactment of a federally mandated minimum wage

(C) increased unionization of workers

(D) desegregation of public accommodations

(E) creation of a system of federal aid to farmers

93. If Congress passed a law requiring restaurants to set aside a no smoking section, that law would probably be considered

(A) constitutional because it involves the regulation of interstate commerce

(B) unconstitutional because restaurants are private businesses

(C) unconstitutional because the Constitution does not specifically mention use of tobacco

(D) unconstitutional because states have the exclusive authority to regulate tobacco

(E) unconstitutional because states have the exclusive authority to regulate restaurants

GO ON TO THE NEXT PAGE

94. When the United States established formal diplomatic relations with the People's Republic of China in 1979 it also withdrew diplomatic recognition from the government of

(A) Cambodia
(B) Okinawa
(C) Sri Lanka
(D) Sumatra
(E) Taiwan

95. Which of the following groups settled at Great Salt Lake in what is now Utah in search of freedom from religious persecution?

(A) Mennonites
(B) Millerites
(C) Wobblies
(D) Mormons
(E) Quids

S T O P

IF YOU FINISH BEFORE TIME IS CALLED, YOU MAY CHECK YOUR WORK ON THIS TEST ONLY. DO NOT WORK ON ANY OTHER TEST IN THIS BOOK.

Explanatory Answers

1. The Open Door Note of 1899, addressed to England, France, Germany, Russia, and Japan, asked those world powers to

(A) send troops to help the United States put down the Boxer Rebellion

(B) permit the United States to annex the Philippine Islands

(C) allow the United States and each other equal trading rights in China

(D) work together to find a way to end the Russo-Japanese War

(E) form an alliance to block Chinese military expansionism

(C) By the Treaty of Paris (1898), which followed the end of the Spanish-American War, the United States acquired the Philippine Islands from Spain for 20 million dollars. United States businessmen hoped that acquisition of the Philippines would give the United States a strategic and economic base in the Far East. Expansionists worried, however, that this aim might be defeated by Japan and certain European nations that enjoyed spheres of influence in China. In an effort to ensure that the United States would have access to China, John Hay, President McKinley's secretary of state, sent a circular note to several world powers asking that each nation pledge itself to a principle of commercial equality. This note became known as the Open Door Note. A few months after the note was sent, the Boxer Rebellion, an armed uprising by anti-foreign Chinese, had to be put down by a combination of military forces.

2. In labor relations, a worker's "right to work" is the worker's right to

(A) work at a job that provides a minimally acceptable standard of living

(B) refuse to join the labor union that represents the worker's coworkers

(C) join with other workers in similar jobs to form a labor union

(D) apply for promotions as the worker gains seniority with a company

(E) choose the company by whom the worker will be employed

(B) The right to bargain collectively, that is, the right of workers to be represented by a union, is not guaranteed by the Constitution of the United States, but it is recognized by statute. Section 7A of the National Industrial Recovery Act (1933) guaranteed the right of collective bargaining with employers through representatives chosen by employees. When that Act was declared unconstitutional by the Supreme Court, Congress passed the National Labor Relations Act (1935), or Wagner Act. The Wagner Act reaffirmed the rights granted in Section 7A and established the National Labor Relations Board to hear complaints from workers concerning violations of those rights. In the fall of 1945, the country was hit by a wave of strikes, and even more serious labor troubles occurred in 1946, including strikes by coal miners and railroad workers. The Taft-Hartley Act (1947) was intended by its authors to correct the seeming imbalance between labor and management. The Act outlawed the closed shop (under which employers are permitted to hire only members of a union recognized by the collective-bargaining agreement) and restricted the union shop (under which an employer agrees that employees must join a certified union after a period of probation) by allowing states to pass "right-to-work" laws. A "right-to-work" law weakens union power, because a worker doesn't have to join the union even though his co-workers belong to it.

3. Which of the following was used by President Lyndon Johnson in 1964 to step up United States military activities in Vietnam?

(A) The Gulf of Tonkin Resolution

(B) The Platt Amendment

(C) The SEATO Treaty

(D) The Wilmot Proviso

(E) The Zimmerman Note

(A) On August 2, 1964, the United States destroyer *Maddox* reported that it had been attacked by three boats using torpedoes and guns while in international waters in the Gulf of Tonkin off the coast of Vietnam. Two days later there was a report of a similar attack on a different United States vessel. Johnson ordered air strikes against North Vietnam and went before Congress to obtain a resolution empowering the President to "take all necessary measures to repel any armed attack against the forces of the United States and to prevent further aggression." The resolution passed the House unanimously and the Senate with only two dissenting votes. This resolution thereafter was used by the administration as authority for its escalation of the war in Vietnam. Ironically, subsequent research suggests that the attacks may not even have taken place.

The Platt Amendment was a provision attached to a 1901 army appropriations bill that was designed to keep Cuba subservient to the United States even while granting Cuba independence. The terms of the Platt Amendment were later incorporated into the Cuban constitution of 1902 and were reaffirmed in a treaty between the United States and Cuba.

SEATO is an acronym for Southeast Asian Treaty Organization. Formed in 1954, the organization included Australia, Britain, France, Pakistan, the Philippines, Thailand, and New Zealand. Despite the similarity of the acronyms SEATO and NATO, SEATO was not a true military alliance.

The Wilmot Proviso was added to a bill appropriating money to negotiate an end to the war with Mexico. It stipulated that slavery would be forbidden in any territory acquired from Mexico by virtue of any treaty negotiated. The provision failed to pass in the Senate.

4. The Treaty of Paris of 1783, which ended the American Revolutionary War, provided for all the following EXCEPT

(A) Fishermen from the United States would have the right to fish off the coast of Canada.

(B) British creditors could legally attempt to collect debts from American debtors.

(C) The Congress of the United States would recommend that state governments restore the rights of Loyalists.

(D) The United States would have control of most of the area between the Appalachian Mountains and the Mississippi River.

(E) Quotas would be established to limit the number of British citizens allowed to immigrate to the United States each year.

(E) By the terms of the Treaty of Paris (1783), Great Britain acknowledged the independence of the United States. Additionally, Britain acknowledged the claim of the United States to the territory west to the Mississippi River from Florida to Canada. Britain also agreed to allow United States fishermen to fish on and off the coast of Canada and agreed to evacuate the territory of the United States without taking American property. The United States in turn promised that it would not interfere with the attempts of British creditors to collect debts from American debtors and that Congress would recommend to the states that they take steps to restore the rights of Loyalists (this recommendation, however, was largely ignored). So choices (A) through (D) are provisions of the treaty; (E), however, is not.

5. W.E.B. DuBois would most likely have agreed with which of the following statements about Booker T. Washington?

(A) The assumptions on which the Tuskegee Institute was found are empirically valid.

(B) Washington is too radical, and his approach is likely to lead to violence.

(C) The theory of the Tuskegee Institute is impractical, but it is not likely to do any harm.

(D) Washington's approach is not only ineffective, it is another form of slavery.

(E) Washington is correct in saying that social and political equality will follow economic advancement.

(D) In 1881, under the leadership of Booker T. Washington, the Tuskegee Institute for vocational training began providing training for blacks. Until the turn of the century, Washington was widely regarded as the spokesperson for blacks. He argued that black people should resign themselves to social and political segregation because the force of racism was too strong to attack directly. By his theory, if black people were to concentrate on economic advancement, social and political equality would naturally follow. W.E.B. DuBois categorically rejected this philosophy. Such a policy, according to DuBois, was merely a different form of slavery. It would serve only to supply "a voteless herd to run the machines and wash the dishes for the new aristocracy." In *The Souls of Black Folk* (1903), DuBois argued in favor of educating a "talented tenth," a black intellectual elite. In 1909, the National Association for the Advancement of Colored People (NAACP) was formed, and DuBois became its director of research and publications.

6. The Congress under the Articles of Confederation had the power to do all of the following EXCEPT

(A) declare war

(B) make treaties

(C) establish post offices

(D) levy direct taxes on people

(E) send diplomatic representatives to foreign countries

(D) At the beginning of the Revolution, most of the Patriot leaders regarded the war as a struggle against an unjust central authority (read the list of grievances in the Declaration of Independence). The last thing these leaders wanted was another strong central authority. So the Articles of Confederation were designed to keep power in the hands of the state governments. The Confederation Congress consisted of delegates chosen by the states, and the Confederation government had neither a judiciary nor a strong executive (the Articles did provide for a committee of thirteen, consisting of representatives from each state, to act when Congress was not in session). In essence, the government under the Articles was more a league of nations than a national government. Congress could declare war and make peace, send and receive diplomatic representatives, make treaties, provide for an army and a navy, control Indian affairs, establish a postal service, and fix weights and measures. It could not, however, control commerce or banking, and it could not levy direct taxes.

7. The first author to write in the American vernacular was

(A) Nathaniel Hawthorne

(B) Mark Twain

(C) Ernest Hemingway

(D) John Steinbeck

(E) Edgar Allan Poe

(B) *The Adventures of Huckleberry Finn* (1885) is the first book to have been written using the American vernacular. It is the story of a white boy from Missouri who kills his drunkard father and runs away with an escaped slave.

8. The War of 1812 was most vigorously opposed in what region of the United States?

(A) Northeast

(B) Southeast

(C) Southwest

(D) South

(E) Northwest

(A) The post-revolution period was marked by western expansion. During Jefferson's administrations there was sporadic fighting between the American Indians and the settlers in the Northwest. Westerners resented the British presence and even called for a campaign to take over Canada. Southerners were eager to acquire Florida from Spain, but also hated Great Britain. The opposition to the War of 1812 centered in the Northeast and in coastal areas where people had the least to gain from a war and the most to lose economically. There was even talk of secession in New England.

9. Prior to the ratification of the Twenty-sixth Amendment to the United States Constitution, persons who had not yet reached the age of 21 could vote in

(A) state and local but not federal elections

(B) federal but not state and local elections

(C) neither state nor federal elections

(D) all state and federal elections

(E) elections in states that granted them the right to vote

(E) The Twenty-sixth Amendment (1971) made it illegal for any state to deny the right to vote to a person eighteen years or older on the basis of age. Prior to that time, only four states permitted people younger than 21 to vote: Georgia, Kentucky, Hawaii, and Alaska.

10. The Teapot Dome (1923) scandal centered on the

(A) questionable billing practices of major defense contractors

(B) improper grants of oil leases in Wyoming and California

(C) illicit campaign contributions made during Harding's presidential campaign

(D) sale of various federal judgeships in southern states

(E) monopolistic pricing policies of large steel companies

(B) The administration of President Warren G. Harding was the most corrupt since that of President Ulysses S. Grant though Harding himself died two months before the evidence of the Teapot Dome transaction came to light. Presidents Taft and Wilson had set aside certain oil lands in Teapot Dome, Wyoming and Elk Hills, California to ensure that the navy would have an adequate supply of oil. Harding's Secretary of the Interior, Albert B. Fall, persuaded the Secretary of the Navy to transfer those lands to the Department of the Interior. Fall in turn leased the California land to E.L. Doheny and the Wyoming land to Harry F. Sinclair in exchange for bribes. The transaction was uncovered during a Senate investigation in October of 1923.

11. In his 1961 Farewell Address, President Dwight D. Eisenhower

(A) called for new and more powerful civil rights legislation

(B) warned against the power of the military-industrial complex

(C) proposed that the United States unilaterally reduce its stockpile of nuclear weapons

(D) remonstrated Congress for having undermined the authority of the Presidency

(E) attempted to minimize the threat posed by the Soviet Union

(B) In his Farewell Address, President Eisenhower said:

> "Until the latest of our world conflicts, the United States had no armaments industry. American makers of plowshares could, with time and as required, make swords as well. But now we can no longer risk emergency improvisation of national defense; we have been compelled to create a permanent armaments industry of vast proportions. Added to this, three and a half million men and women are directly engaged in the defense establishment. We annually spend on military security more than the net income of all United States corporations.
>
> This conjunction of an immense military establishment and a large arms industry is new in the American experience. The total influence—economic, political, even spiritual—is felt in every city, every state house, every office of the federal government. We recognize the imperative need for this development. Yet we must not fail to comprehend its grave implications. Our toil, resources and livelihood are all involved; so is the very structure of our society.
>
> In the councils of government, we must guard against the acquisition of unwarranted influence, whether sought or unsought, by the military-industrial complex. The potential for the disastrous rise of misplaced power exists and will persist."

As for the other choices, Eisenhower began the Farewell Address by commending Congress. He went on to remark that "We face a hostile ideology—global in scope, atheistic in character, ruthless in purpose, and insidious in method. Unhappily, the danger it poses promises to be of indefinite duration." As for disarmament, he insists that "Disarmament with mutual honor and confidence is a continuing imperative," but he did not propose unilateral disarmament. Finally, Eisenhower did not believe that legislation would solve the nation's racial problems and used the power of the federal government to enforce civil rights only when it could not be avoided.

12. In *Schenck* v. *United States* (1919), Supreme Court Justice Oliver Wendell Holmes wrote: "The most stringent protection of free speech would not protect a man in falsely shouting fire in a theater and causing panic." This implies that

(A) freedom of speech is not an absolute right

(B) certain individuals have no constitutional rights

(C) Federal legislation takes priority over state laws

(D) the Constitution does not provide for freedom of speech

(E) freedom of speech is unconditionally guaranteed by the Constitution

(A) In *Schenck* v. *United States* the Supreme Court unanimously upheld the conviction of a man who had counselled resistance to the draft—a crime under the Espionage Act. Obviously, the man's act was speech. And the First Amendment to the Constitution of the United States specifically states "Congress shall make no law . . . abridging the freedom of speech . . . ." Didn't Congress violate the man's constitutional right of free speech by making his speech (counselling resistance) a crime? According to the Supreme Court, it did not. Justice Holmes explained that the "character of every act depends upon the circumstances in which it is done." He then provided the famous analogy you see above. In other words, freedom of speech is not an absolute right but must yield when the government has a compelling interest, or in Holmes' view, when the government can show that the speech poses a clear and present danger.

13. When President Franklin D. Roosevelt explained that the Lend Lease Act of 1941 would make the United States the "arsenal of democracy" he meant that the United States would

(A) send troops to Europe to defend France against the *Blitzkrieg*

(B) provide armaments to Britain but stay out of the war

(C) allow American pilots to fly British war planes

(D) maintain a strict isolationist posture regarding Europe

(E) commit troops to the war only if Japan attacked Pearl Harbor

(B) American foreign policy between the two world wars can be described as near isolationism. The disillusionment that followed the First World War and the urge toward disarmament created an atmosphere in which involvement in another foreign war seemed to be inconceivable to Americans. After the defeat of the League of Nations, the United States all but washed its hands of Europe and the Far East, though we did continue to play a role in the politics of the Western Hemisphere. This mentality persisted for two decades. Even as hostilities were escalating in Europe, Roosevelt was promising to keep the United States out of the war. As things got worse in Europe, and Britain stood alone, public opinion came to favor providing "all aid short of war." In March 1941, Congress passed the Lend-Lease Act which authorized the President to sell, exchange, or lease any "defense article" to any anti-Axis nation in return for "payment in kind or property, or any other direct or indirect benefit which the President deems satisfactory." Thus, the United States would be the arsenal to supply armaments to the allies without actually committing itself to war.

14. Which of the following events directly contributed to passage of the National Defense Education Act, enacted by Congress in 1958 to improve education in mathematics and the sciences?

(A) Soviet Union military intervention in Hungary

(B) The Soviet Union's launching of the satellite Sputnik

(C) Civil rights protests against segregated schools

(D) Eisenhower's election to a second term as President

(E) The Suez Crisis

(B) In contrast to the 1930s with its depression and the 1940s with the war, the 1950s was a time of relative prosperity for most people. Although there was the ever-present threat of nuclear annihilation, Americans were smugly secure in their knowledge that the capitalistic system was in all respects superior to the communistic system of the cold war enemy. In 1957, Americans were jolted from this complacency. The Soviet Union, supposedly behind the United States in terms of missile technology, orbited the first artificial satellite, called Sputnik or "little moon." The launching of Sputnik suggested that the United States had fallen behind in the arms race. A report by the Federal government on education in the Soviet Union remarked upon the emphasis placed upon studies in mathematics and the sciences. Although the launching of Sputnik did not "cause" the passage of the National Defense Education Act, it certainly contributed to its passage.

15. All of the descriptive phrases listed below are correctly associated with the president named EXCEPT

(A) The New Deal—Franklin D. Roosevelt

(B) The Square Deal—Theodore Roosevelt

(C) The Fair Deal—Harry S. Truman

(D) The Great Society—Lyndon B. Johnson

(E) The Return to Normalcy—Calvin Coolidge

(E) The Return to Normalcy refers to the period following World War I and the administration of President Warren G. Harding.

16. The National Security Act of 1947 created all of the following EXCEPT

(A) a separate Air Force

(B) the Joint Chiefs of Staff

(C) the National Security Council

(D) the Central Intelligence Agency

(E) the Department of War

(E) The National Security Act of 1947 gave the United States military establishment and the intelligence gathering agencies the structures they have today. It created a separate branch of the armed services named the Air Force. It created the Joint Chiefs of Staff to advise the president. It established the National Security Council, consisting of the president, the chairman of the joint chiefs, and certain cabinet officers to provide strategic planning and to advise the president in times of crisis. And it created the Central Intelligence Agency, an intelligence gathering agency. The Act did not, however, create the War Department. Instead, it combined the old War and Navy Departments into the single cabinet-level Department of Defense.

17. Which of the following descriptions best defines the concept of a monopoly?

(A) A market dominated by a single buyer

(B) A market dominated by a single seller

(C) A market dominated by a few large buyers

(D) A market with no dominant seller

(E) A market with no dominant buyer

(B) A true monopoly is the absolute control of a single seller over an entire market. Imagine, for example, that you own the only well in a certain region and that it is impossible to import water into the area. You would have a monopoly on water in that area. What could you charge for water? This is why monopolistic practices are usually outlawed.

Sometimes monopolies are unavoidable, for example, public utilities. Your region is probably serviced by a particular power company. Would it be efficient to have several utilities in your area trying to provide the same service? Probably not. This type of monopoly is tolerated and controlled by the government.

18. The doctrine of judicial review, enunciated in *Marbury* v. *Madison,* is the authority of a court to

(A) invalidate unconstitutional legislative acts and executive actions

(B) punish contempt of court by short-term imprisonment

(C) order the losing party in a civil suit to pay damages

(D) determine what evidence can be excluded in a criminal trial

(E) command public officials to perform their legally required duties

(A) The case of *Marbury* v. *Madison,* decided by the United States Supreme Court in 1803, established the principle of judicial review. The case is as interesting for the details of political intrigue from which it arose as for the masterful judicial reasoning contained in the written opinion of Chief Justice John Marshall.

In 1800, Federalist John Adams lost the presidential election to Republican Thomas Jefferson. One of Adams' last official acts was to fill the posts created by the Judiciary Act of 1801 with loyal members of the Federalist party. Working against the clock on his last night in office, Adams finally signed the commission for the least important posts on the list, the forty-two justices of the peace for the District of Columbia. At that point, then Secretary of State John Marshall should have affixed the Great Seal of the United States to the documents. Because of the time pressure, however, Marshall failed to attend to this final detail.

When President Jefferson later learned how many new federal judges had been appointed at the last moment, he refused to deliver the defective commissions. In 1803, William Marbury, one of the recipients of the last minute but defective commissions, sued the Secretary of State, James Madison, in the Supreme Court of the United States. Marbury asked the Supreme Court to issue a writ of *mandamus* compelling Madison to deliver to him his commission. The Chief Justice of the Supreme Court at that time was former Secretary of State John Marshall.

Chief Justice Marshall found himself in a dilemma. On one side, he could decide in favor of Marbury and order Madison to deliver the commission. He knew, however, that Madison, with the support of a very popular president, would simply ignore the order and that the Supreme Court itself had no way of enforcing the order. On the other side, he could decide for Madison giving the Republicans an important victory. Rather than be impaled on either horn of this dilemma, Marshall slipped between them.

In general, for a court to hear a case it must have jurisdiction over the matter. The jurisdiction of the federal courts is governed both by the Constitution and by legislation. Article III of the Constitution gives the Supreme Court original or trial jurisdiction over only two kinds of cases: those involving ambassadors and public ministers, etc., and those in which a state is a party. For other types of cases, the Supreme Court has jurisdiction only to hear appeals from lower courts. Additionally, Article III gives the Congress the power to create lower federal courts and to define their jurisdiction.

When Marbury brought his suit to compel Madison to deliver his commission, he had to show the Supreme Court that it had jurisdiction to hear the case. Obviously the case was not about ambassadors and didn't involve a state. Instead, Marbury argued that the Supreme Court had jurisdiction over his case based on Section 13 of the Judiciary Act of 1789, which stated that the Court could issue writs of mandamus in cases such as his.

Marshall reasoned that Marbury would be entitled to his writ but that the Supreme Court did not have jurisdiction to give it to him. Section 13, according to Marshall, was in conflict with Article III of the Constitution, which defines the original jurisdiction of the Supreme Court. Congress has the authority to define the original jurisdiction of lower courts and to place restriction on the appellate jurisdiction of the Supreme Court. But the Constitution gave Congress no authority to enlarge the original jurisdiction of the Supreme Court.

Since Congress had exceeded its constitutional authority, Marshall declared Section 13 unconstitutional and therefore void. From this case emerged the doctrine of judicial review under which courts claim the authority to pass on the constitutionality of laws and executive actions. (Marbury never did get his judgeship.)

19. The Marshall Plan was adopted in large measure because the United States

(A) wanted to see Germany punished for its aggression during World War II

(B) hoped that Europe could become unified under a single central government

(C) was unsure of the motives of the Soviet Union in Berlin

(D) feared that unstable European countries would succumb to communism

(E) incorrectly believed that the Soviet Union lacked any expansionist plans

(D) Although the phrase "cold war" was not coined until 1948, the cold war began shortly after the end of World War II. In a speech at Westminster College in Fulton, Missouri, in March of 1946, the former prime minister of Great Britain, Winston Churchill, announced that "an iron curtain" had descended across the European Continent. Churchill proposed that the United States and England form an anti-communist Anglo-American association. Both Greece and Turkey at that time relied heavily on British financial aid, and both countries were in trouble. The Greek monarchy was fighting with communist-supplied rebels, and Turkey was under heavy Soviet pressure. In February 1947, the British admitted that they could no longer supply aid to these two countries. President Truman asked Congress for $400 million in aid for Greece and Turkey. Congress agreed. This was the first time that the United States had even proposed to commit huge sums of financial aid during peacetime. In order to generate popular support for the foreign aid plan, Truman made an address to a joint session of Congress in which he warned that communism was spreading across Europe and immediately threatened Greece and Turkey. It was necessary, he said, for the "United States to support free peoples who are resisting attempted subjugation by armed minorities or by outside pressures." This policy was soon labelled the Truman Doctrine.

In June of 1947, Secretary of State George Marshall called for financial assistance to western Europe in general. At his suggestion, sixteen European countries worked out a plan of economic recovery, a plan that required billions of United States dollars. The United States agreed to provide $17 billion over a four-year period. This European recovery program—or Marshall Plan—encountered little opposition because people were convinced that it was necessary to stop the spread of communism.

20. The Good Neighbor Policy of the United States included which of the following?

I. Economic cooperation with Latin American countries

II. A promise not to intervene in the internal affairs of Latin American countries

III. A military alliance to defend Latin America against foreign invasion

(A) I only

(B) II only

(C) I and II only

(D) I and III only

(E) II and III only

(C) Isolationism in the 1930s aimed at withdrawing the United States from foreign affairs, but, in a sense, "foreign" affairs did not include the affairs of the Western Hemisphere. In fact, the very idea of isolationism required that the nations of the Western Hemisphere close ranks. To that end, the United States during the 1930s was willing to offer Latin American countries economic assistance to combat the worldwide depression and tacitly to disavow the "big stick" policy of President Theodore Roosevelt.

21. One of two Italian immigrant radicals executed in 1927 by the Commonwealth of Massachusetts for the crimes of murder and robbery was

(A) Al Capone

(B) Nicola Sacco

(C) Fiorello LaGuardia

(D) Vittorio Orlando

(E) Rocky Marciano

(B) The "melting-pot" image was both a descriptive and a normative concept. It was intended to describe the process whereby an immigrant was absorbed into the larger American society. The concept was also used as a justification for liberal immigration policies: the defining characteristic of American society is its rich diversity, and diversity requires the continuing addition of new elements. But the idea of a "melting pot" depends on two notions that are in tension with each other. On the one hand, the idea of the "melting pot" seems to imply that the foreign cultures are valid in and of themselves. On the other hand, the idea implies that the American mixture is the ideal culture and insists that the foreign culture be dissolved in to the "melting pot."

The tension between these two ideas is reflected in American immigration policy as the struggle between those who favor liberal immigration policies and those who oppose them. Opposition to liberal immigration was particularly strong during the 1920s. Between 1900 and 1920, a large number of immigrants from southern and southeastern Europe had entered the United States, many of them Catholic or Jewish, which made them targets of bigotry. Additionally, during World War I, many recent immigrants left to fight against the Allies. Opponents of liberal immigration policies argued that the "melting pot" was a mistake. In 1921 Congress passed an immigration quota act restricting the number of persons who could immigrate from a nation to three percent of the number of persons from that nation living in the United States as shown by the 1910 census. The National Origins Act of 1924 was even more restrictive. It lowered the relevant fraction to two percent and used as the basis the 1890 census. This was particularly restrictive of southern and southeastern Europeans since the massive immigration from those areas had begun after the base date.

So the 1920s were characterized by nativism which included irrational hostility toward immigrant groups. Perhaps the most famous example of this hostility was the trial of Nicola Sacco and Bartolomeo Vanzetti, two Italian immigrant radicals, who were charged with a payroll robbery during which a guard was killed. The trial was highly politicized, and both defendants were found guilty on very doubtful evidence. In 1927, both were executed in the state's electric chair.

Al Capone was, of course, a famous gangster, but Capone was convicted only of income tax evasion and was sentenced to prison. Fiorello LaGuardia was mayor of New York City during the 1930s. Vittorio Orlando was Italy's representative at the peace conference at Versailles in 1919. And Rocky Marciano was a professional boxer.

22. Will Rogers' remark that ''Mississippi will vote dry and drink wet as long as it can stagger to the polls'' refers to the difficulty in

(A) passing the Prohibition amendment
(B) enacting Prohibition legislation
(C) enforcing Prohibition legislation
(D) evading Prohibition legislation
(E) repealing the Prohibition amendment

(C) The Eighteenth Amendment to the United States Constitution (1919) provides that "the manufacture, sale, or transportation of intoxicating liquors . . . for beverage purposes is hereby prohibited" and gives "Congress and the several States . . . concurrent power to enforce this article by appropriate legislation." The legislation enacted by Congress to enforce the prohibition was the Volstead Act (1919) which defined "intoxicating liquors" as any beverage containing more than 0.5 percent alcohol.

Two factors made it particularly difficult to enforce this law. One, demand continued. In fact, many people who favored Prohibition were opposed to the consumption of hard liquor but not wine and beer. Yet, the definition of the Volstead Act—more than 0.5 percent—covered those beverages as well. Two, the law made the manufacture but not the consumption of alcoholic beverages illegal. As a consequence, "bootlegging"—the illegal manufacture and distribution of alcoholic beverages—was widespread.

23. Immigration from which of the following regions was greatest during the period from 1900 to 1920?

(A) The United Kingdom
(B) The Middle East
(C) Southeastern Europe
(D) Asia
(E) Africa

(C) Approximately 3.5 million persons immigrated from southeastern Europe during the period cited. Of the regions listed here, the United Kingdom is second with fewer than a million immigrants. Of all regions of the world, Italy was second with more than 3 million immigrants.

24. Which of the following colonies was founded by an individual persecuted for his political views and religious beliefs?

(A) Virginia
(B) New Jersey
(C) Georgia
(D) New York
(E) Rhode Island

(E) Rhode Island was founded in 1635 by Roger Williams, a Puritan minister who was forced out of Massachusetts because of his religious and political views. Virginia was founded by the Virginia Company, a business venture. New Jersey was founded by two men who were interested primarily in land speculation. Georgia was founded by James Oglethorpe who viewed the colony as a refuge for imprisoned debtors. New York was obtained from the Dutch by conquest.

Questions 25 and 26 are based on the following chart.

PRESIDENTIAL ELECTIONS OF 1908 AND 1912

Election	Candidate	Party	Popular Vote	Electoral Vote
1908	William H. Taft	Republican	7,679,006	321
	William J. Bryan	Democrat	6,409,106	162
	Eugene V. Debs	Socialist	420,820	—
1912	Woodrow Wilson	Democrat	6,293,454	435
	Theodore Roosevelt	Progressive	4,119,538	88
	William H. Taft	Republican	3,484,980	8
	Eugene V. Debs	Socialist	897,011	—

25. The chart above suggests which of the following as the primary reason for the Republican defeat in 1912?

(A) The Democrats ran a very unpopular candidate in 1908 and a very popular one in 1912.

(B) In 1912, a substantial number of previously unregistered voters registered and voted for the Democratic candidate.

(C) In 1908, a substantial number of voters belonging to the Socialist party voted for the Republican candidate.

(D) In 1912, a substantial number of voters deserted the Socialist Party in favor of the Democratic Party.

(E) In 1912, a substantial number of voters deserted the Republican Party in favor of the Progressive Party.

(E) In 1901, following the assassination of President McKinley, Vice President Theodore Roosevelt became President Theodore Roosevelt. In 1908, Roosevelt declined to run for a second full term, and the Republican National Convention, acting on Roosevelt's recommendation, nominated Roosevelt's secretary of war and then good friend, William Howard Taft. The Democrats nominated William Jennings Bryan for a third and final try at the presidency. As the chart shows, Taft prevailed. Between 1908 and 1912, Roosevelt became increasingly disenchanted with Taft, and in 1912 Roosevelt made another run for the presidency. Taft, however, was given the Republican nomination and Roosevelt bolted the party to form the Progressive party, nicknamed the Bull Moose party. This split the Republican vote and gave the election to the Democrats.

26. The chart most strongly suggests that between 1908 and 1912

(A) the American people lost interest in presidential politics

(B) the Socialist Party lost support among American voters

(C) American voters became disenchanted with the principles of progressivism

(D) the principles of progressivism gained wider support among American voters

(E) the total number of registered voters in the United States declined

(D) In 1908, the Democratic party, which represented the progressive impulse, tallied 6.4 million votes. In 1912, the platforms of the Democrats and the Progressives were very similar, differing only on the question of how the government should control business to solve the trust problem. Thus, voters in 1912 were able to vote for progressive principles by choosing either the Democrats or the Progressives. Together, those two parties tallied 10.4 million votes. The increase of 4 million votes shows an increased acceptance of principles of the progressive movement.

27. The state of Maine was created from the northeastern counties of Massachusetts in order to

(A) create a buffer between Massachusetts and Canada

(B) provide a sanctuary for religious dissidents

(C) maintain the balance between free and slave states

(D) relieve the pressures of overcrowding in Massachusetts

(E) weaken the power of Massachusetts' Congressional delegation

(C) In 1818, when Missouri applied for statehood, the Union consisted of 20 states, 10 in which slavery was legal and 10 in which it was not. A New York legislator introduced an amendment to the statehood bill that would effectively have banned slavery in the new state and in what remained of the Louisiana Purchase territory. The nation was divided along sectional lines on this issue with the northern states supporting such a restriction and the southern states opposing it. The bill failed to pass, and the issue came up again in the Congress of 1819. The outcome was the Missouri Compromise. With Massachusetts' consent, the northeastern counties of Massachusetts applied for statehood. Both Missouri and Maine were admitted to the Union, and each state was left to decide the status of slavery within its boundaries. As a result, the balance between free and slave states was maintained. Additionally, slavery was prohibited in the remainder of the Louisiana Purchase territory north of the parallel 36° 30′.

28. "Gerrymandering" is the practice of

(A) imposing high tariffs on imported goods to reduce competition from foreign manufacturers

(B) creating oddly-shaped voting districts to ensure the election of a certain party's nominees

(C) killing a legislative proposal by attaching unacceptable riders to the bill

(D) abstaining from a Congressional vote to protest the content of a piece of legislation

(E) issuing government bonds that are to be redeemed with paper money rather than gold

(B) The Constitution did not permanently fix the number of Congressional representatives. The original House met in 1789 with a total of 65 members, and in 1929, Congress fixed the number of representatives at 435. Populations, however, shift; states gain and lose population in relation to one another. This shifting requires adjustments in the distribution of the number of representatives of each of the states. This process, called reapportionment, takes place every ten years and is prepared by the Bureau of Census and submitted for Congressional approval. It is then the state's responsibility to draw the boundaries of the Congressional districts within its borders.

Obviously, there will be a temptation for the party in power to create districts to favor members of its party. The dominant party might, for example, create a district in which it gets a majority of the votes, thereby creating a "safe" Congressional seat for the party. Or, it might sacrifice a seat by creating a district in which opposition voters were highly concentrated. By giving up the one seat, it stands a better chance of success in the other districts in the state.

In 1812, to create a district favoring Governor Elbridge Gerry, the Massachusetts legislature drew a particularly bizarre looking Congressional district. Thus, the practice is called "gerrymandering."

In the first half of the 1960s, the Supreme Court acted to curb the worst of these abuses. It required that "as nearly as is practicable, one man's vote in a congressional election is to be worth as much as another's." This is the doctrine of "one man, one vote."

29. Senator Henry Cabot Lodge's fourteen reservations to the Treaty of Versailles were designed primarily to

(A) reaffirm President Wilson's Fourteen Points for a peace without victory

(B) prevent the United States from becoming a member of the League of Nations

(C) gain popular support for the proposed League of Nations

(D) ensure that reparations assessed on Germany would not be unduly burdensome

(E) isolate the Soviet Union economically and politically from western Europe

(B) On January 8, 1918, President Wilson announced his plan for a "peace without victory" that would avoid the humiliations and bitterness of peace forced upon the losing party. The fourteenth reservation provided:

> "A general association of nations must be formed under specific covenants for the purpose of affording mutual guarantees of political independence and territorial integrity to great and small states alike."

The treaty that was finally negotiated in many respects did not reflect Wilson's concept of "peace without victory," but it did provide for a League of Nations. And this was of prime importance for Wilson, for he believed that the League could eventually correct any imbalances in the rest of the treaty.

The treaty, however, was never ratified by the Senate, and the person generally credited with its defeat is Senator Henry Cabot Lodge. At one point, Lodge himself had favored some sort of world organization, but he was absolutely opposed to Wilson's League of Nations. His opposition was based on his personal distaste for Wilson, his desire to embarrass the Democrats, his insistence that any peace treaty should severely weaken Germany, and his fear that the proposed League would result in United States military involvement around the world.

As head of the Senate Foreign Relations Committee, Lodge was in an excellent position to defeat the League. The committee held lengthy hearings on the treaty; and when it finally emerged from committee, it included fourteen reservations or amendments. Wilson refused to compromise and ordered Democratic senators to vote against it. On the third and final vote, 49 senators voted for the treaty and 35 voted against it. The treaty failed ratification because it lacked the two-thirds majority required by the Constitution.

Ironically, only 14 senators were absolutely opposed to the League. Of the 35 who voted against the amended treaty, 23 were Wilson Democrats. They could have given the president the votes needed to ratify the treaty.

30. The Bill of Rights, the first ten amendments to the United States Constitution, guarantees the people of the United States all of the following EXCEPT

(A) freedom from unreasonable search and seizure

(B) freedom from double jeopardy

(C) the right to bear arms

(D) due process of law

(E) equal protection of the laws

(E) During the push for ratification, several states approved the Constitution on the assumption that it would be amended to include specific guarantees of certain personal freedoms. North Carolina refused to ratify the Constitution until these were added. In June 1789, Madison submitted to Congress seventeen amendments that had been proposed by the states, and ten of these were adopted. The fourth provides that the "right of the people to be secure in their persons, houses, papers, and effects, against unreasonable searches and seizures, shall not be violated." The second provides that "the right of the people to keep and bear arms shall not be infringed." The fifth provides that no person shall "be subject for the same offense to be twice put in jeopardy of life or limb; . . . nor be deprived of life, liberty, or property without due process of law." It is the Fourteenth Amendment, one of the three Reconstruction amendments, that provides that no state shall "deny to any person within its jurisdiction the equal protection of the laws."

31. The spoils system contributed to the development of

(A) modern political parties

(B) antislavery sentiment

(C) isolationism

(D) anti-United States sentiment in Latin America

(E) nuclear proliferation

(A) The spoils system refers to the practice whereby a winning party fills government positions with party loyals, in the process displacing the appointees of the previous winner. The spoils system is often associated with Andrew Jackson. Jackson did not invent the system, but he did institutionalize it. It was Jackson's theory that the changes made the government more responsive to the will of the people. In the final analysis, the promise of a well-paid government position gave people reason to work hard for a candidate's election and made it possible for some people to become professional politicians. Thus, the spoils system was an important factor in the development of modern political parties.

32. Impeachment is most like which of the following?

(A) Trial

(B) Indictment

(C) Conviction

(D) Sentencing

(E) Imprisonment

(B) Article I of the United States Constitution gives the House of Representatives "the sole power of impeachment" and the Senate the "sole power to try all impeachments." An official who has been impeached has only been accused of wrongdoing. Similarly, an indictment is an accusation made by a grand jury based upon evidence presented to it by a prosecutor.

33. "Yellow journalism" is characterized by

(A) objective reporting of current affairs

(B) scholarly analysis of political trends

(C) sensationalized accounts of news events

(D) lack of a coherent editorial position

(E) descriptions and reports of trivial events

(C) Yellow journalism or yellow press refers, usually in a pejorative way, to newspapers that seek to increase circulation by publishing sensationalized accounts of news events. Yellow journalism was first practiced by Joseph Pulitzer in the 1890s. Pulitzer realized that increased rates of literacy and greater urban populations had created a potential market for a new kind of newspaper. Under his management, the *New York World* became famous for its sensational—though essentially accurate—reporting. To increase circulation, the paper employed huge front page cartoons, gave extensive coverage to crime stories, and included a comic strip. Under Pulitzer, the *World* also campaigned on behalf of ordinary people against the rich and powerful. For example, the *World* sought to expose corruption in New York City's government. William Randolph Hearst purchased the *Morning Journal* and proceeded to use similar techniques. Other newspapers, such as the *New York Times*, refused to employ the new techniques. Even today, many cities have two major daily newspapers—one that relies on techniques similar to those used by Pulitzer and Hearst, and one that is more staid. And you sometimes hear the phrase "yellow press" to describe disapprovingly the more sensational paper.

PURCHASING POWER OF FARM PRODUCTS 1914–1922

Year	Prices Paid to Farmers	Prices Paid by Farmers
1914*	$1.00	$1.00
1916	1.72	1.42
1918	1.86	1.82
1920	2.03	2.04
1922	1.25	1.54

*In 1914 Prices Paid to Farmers = Prices Paid by Farmers

34. In terms of purchasing power, farmers were best off in which year?

(A) 1914

(B) 1916

(C) 1918

(D) 1920

(E) 1922

(B) The chart shows the change in prices paid to and by farmers for a certain period. It uses an arbitrary figure of $1.00 for 1914. By 1916, prices paid to farmers had increased by 72 percent while prices paid by farmers increased by only 42 percent. In other words, the value of the farmers' dollar increased during that period. Between 1916 and 1918, the prices paid to farmers again increased, but the prices farmers had to pay increased even more. So farmers were worse off in 1918 than in 1916. In 1920 and 1922, the prices paid by farmers remained higher than prices paid to them, so in those years farmers were worse off than they were in 1914.

35. All of the following acts were New Deal legislation EXCEPT

(A) the Taft-Hartley Act

(B) the National Industrial Recovery Act

(C) the Social Security Act

(D) the Fair Labor Standards Act

(E) the National Labor Relations Act

(A) The Taft-Hartley Act was enacted in 1947 in response to criticisms of labor unions. The law outlawed the closed shop (one in which a worker could not work unless a member of the union) and prohibited certain union practices such as the secondary boycott (an action against a business dealing with a firm involved in a labor dispute) and featherbedding (forcing employers to keep staffed unneeded positions). The other acts listed were passed during the New Deal.

36. "Redeemers" is a term coined by

(A) white conservatives who succeeded the radical reconstructionists to refer to themselves

(B) radical Republicans who opposed Lincoln's plan of reconstruction to refer to themselves

(C) moderate Republicans who supported Lincoln's plan of reconstruction to refer to Grant's cronies

(D) southern whites who had opposed secession to refer to carpetbaggers

(E) blacks elected to public office during reconstruction to refer to conservative whites

(A) The term reconstruction refers to the period following the Civil War during which the states that had formed the Confederacy were reincorporated into the Union. Lincoln had proposed a fairly moderate plan which was opposed by a group of radical Congressional Republicans, lead by Wade, Stevens, and Sumner, who were determined to restructure southern society.

After Lincoln's assassination, Andrew Johnson attempted to carry out Lincoln's plan of moderate reconstruction. The moderate plan failed primarily because of the recalcitrance of southern states: they enacted the "Black Codes" (the effect of which was to impose a new kind of slavery on blacks) and elected to public office many of the same men who had governed the Confederacy. The plan of the radical reconstruction included military occupation and black suffrage.

Eventually, the whole reconstruction scheme just ran out of steam, and white southerners with traditional attitudes about race relationships recaptured the governments. The new white governments ignored the provisions of the Fourteenth and Fifteenth Amendments, and in the end, no wholesale social restructuring ever took place.

The white conservatives who succeeded the radical reconstructionists called themselves "redeemers." Apologists for the redeemer governments pointed to fraud and corruption in the reconstruction administrations and implied that dishonest and incompetent black southerners were largely to blame. The apologists for the redeemer governments used phrases such as the "dreadful decade" to refer to radical reconstruction. Those histories are incorrect on two scores. One, black southerners did not really enjoy the monopoly on political power suggested by the apologists; two, the state governments under reconstruction were not noticeably more corrupt that other governments of the same period.

37. A historian who wished to do an analysis of African-Americans who were held in slavery before the Civil War would find which of the following most useful?

(A) Tools, dishes, and other articles excavated from a waste pit on a southern plantation

(B) Treatises written by white authors defending the existence of the slave system

(C) Autobiographies written by African-Americans who were actually held in slavery

(D) Plantation records detailing the economic transactions of the owner

(E) Pamphlets written by abolitionists residing in the northern states

(C) There are many published autobiographies of African-Americans held in slavery. They indicate that although the white people who physically controlled the African-Americans regarded the African-Americans as slaves, the African-Americans did not regard themselves as such.

38. The Bank of the United States must not continue. The capitalists of the northeastern states grow richer at the expense of the farmers. Additionally, the Bank is monopolistic and unconstitutional.

The remarks above would most likely have been endorsed by a supporter of

(A) John Marshall

(B) Nicholas Biddle

(C) Daniel Webster

(D) Andrew Jackson

(E) William Duane

(D) President Andrew Jackson was bitterly opposed to the Bank of the United States. The South and West, where Jackson enjoyed considerable support, opposed the Bank because the notes issued by the Bank drove from circulation the notes issued by state and other banks. And these other banks were more willing to make riskier loans than the Bank of the United States. Additionally, Jackson considered the Bank monopolistic and that ran counter to his notions of democracy. He also considered the Bank unconstitutional, despite the opinions of the Congress and the Supreme Court.

As for the other answer choices, Chief Justice Marshall was the architect of the Supreme Court decision *McCulloch* v. *Maryland* (1819) holding the Congress did have the authority to charter the Bank; Biddle was the president of the Bank and wanted a renewal of its charter, Webster was on the payroll of the Bank; and Duane was secretary of the treasury under Jackson, who refused to sabotage the Bank at Jackson's request.

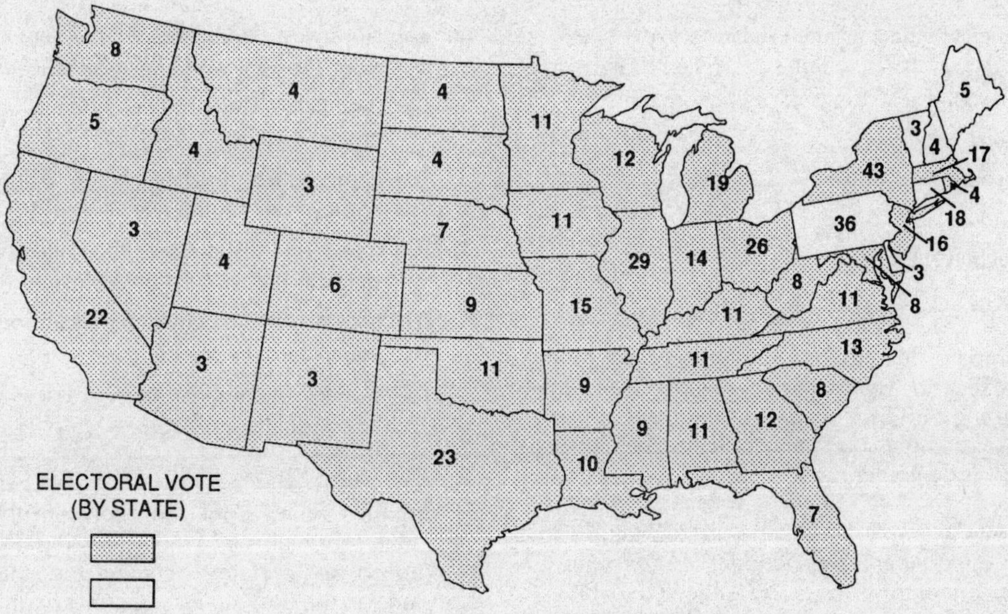

39. Which of the following is an appropriate key for the map above?

	Election of 1916	
(A)	▩ Wilson	☐ Hughes
	Election of 1924	
(B)	▩ Coolidge	☐ Davis
	Election of 1928	
(C)	▩ Hoover	☐ Smith
	Election of 1932	
(D)	▩ Roosevelt	☐ Hoover
	Election of 1948	
(E)	▩ Truman	☐ Dewey

(D) In 1932, the American voters registered their disgust with the Republicans. Hoover carried only Connecticut, Delaware, Maine, New Hampshire, Pennsylvania, and Vermont.

40. All of the following were goals of the Progressive movement in the early twentieth century EXCEPT

(A) elimination of governmental corruption

(B) consumer protection legislation

(C) better conditions for workers

(D) governmental controls over big business

(E) free coinage of silver money

(E) Do not confuse the Populist movement with the Progressive movement. Populism can be traced to the organizations of farmers prominent in the last quarter of the nineteenth century, a particularly difficult time for farmers because farm prices were low and shipping costs were high. The farm organizations secured a few victories for their members, such as the Interstate Commerce Act (1887) which was designed to regulate rates charged by railroads, but lacked the political clout to redress all of their grievances. In the 1890s, farmers allied themselves with other groups whose grievances were not the concern of either the Republican or the Democratic parties to create a new third party called the People's Party. The movement aimed primarily at farmers and workers and attempted to appeal to a class-consciousness. The People's Party advocated government ownership of the railroads, shorter working hours, and free coinage of silver. The last point was based on the theory that unlimited coinage of silver would devalue the dollar to the benefit of farmers. In 1896, William Jennings Bryan used the free silver issue to win the presidential nominations of both the People's Party and the Democratic party. Bryan, however, was soundly defeated by William McKinley, and the People's Party quickly faded. The label "Progressive" was already in use by 1900, but the term was used to describe a movement that was primarily middle-class. To be sure, many of the goals of the Progressive movement, such as antitrust legislation and railroad rate regulation, were similar to those of the earlier Populist movement but they did not include the demand for unlimited coinage of silver.

41. The principal author of the Declaration of Independence, Thomas Jefferson, relied heavily on the philosophical writings of

(A) Plato

(B) Aristotle

(C) Aquinas

(D) Machiavelli

(E) Locke

(E) Compare the following excerpts of John Locke's *Second Treatise of Government: An Essay Concerning the True Origin, Extent, and End of Civil Government* and the language of the Declaration of Independence.

Locke:

Men being, as has been said, by Nature, all free, equal and independent, no one can be put out of this Estate, and subjected to the Political power of another, without his own consent. The only way whereby any one devests himself of his Natural Liberty, and puts on the bonds of Civil Society is by agreeing with other Men to joyn and unite into a Community, for their comfortable, safe, and peaceable living one amongst another, in a secure Enjoyment of their properties . . . .

And 'tis not without reason, that he seeks out, and is willing to joyn in Society with others . . . for the mutual Preservation of their Lives, Liberties and Estates, which I call by the general Name, Property.

[W]hen by the Miscarriages of those in Authority [political power] is forefeited; upon the Forfeiture of their Rules, or at the Determination of the Time set, it reverts to the Society, and the People have a Right to act as Supreme, and continue the Legislative in themselves, or erect a new Form . . . as they think good.

The Declaration of Independence:

We hold these truths to be self-evident, that all men are created equal, that they are endowed by the Creator with certain inalienable rights, that among these are life, liberty and the pursuit of happiness. That to secure these rights, governments are instituted among men, deriving their just powers from the consent of the governed. That whenever any form of government becomes destructive of these ends, it is the right of the people to alter or to abolish it, and to institute new government . . . .

42. The Northwest Ordinance of 1787 set an important precedent for westward expansion because it

(A) established United States military outposts to protect settlers

(B) extinguished the claims of the British to lands north of the Ohio River

(C) transferred disputed western lands from the states to the national government

(D) provided for the creation of additional states rather than for colonies

(E) avoided the problem of high prices caused by land speculators

(D) The Treaty of Paris of 1783 extinguished Britain's claim to the land between the Appalachian Mountains and the Mississippi River, but it did not settle claims between the states. At the start of the Revolution, Connecticut, Georgia, Massachusetts, North and South Carolina, and Virginia claimed lands west to the Mississippi on the ground that these had been conveyed to them during the colonial period. As part of the procedure whereby the Articles of Confederation were adopted, those states claiming lands promised to relinquish their claims in favor of the national government. In 1784 and 1785, the national government negotiated with the Iroquois and other tribes treaties by which those peoples surrendered any claims to the territory. In 1787, Congress adopted the Northwest Ordinance. By its terms, the territory was to be divided into regions that would eventually become states. During the first stage of settlement, the government of a region would be appointed by Congress. In the second stage, the region would have an elected assembly. And in the third and final stage, it could be admitted to the Union as a new and equal state. This arrangement avoided the problems inherent in a colonial status while still allowing the national government to expand its territory.

43. Which of the following peoples were a member of the Iroquois Nation?

(A) Mohawks

(B) Cherokees

(C) Seminoles

(D) Apaches

(E) Pueblos

(A) The Iroquois, a group of tribes living in the northeastern United States and speaking related languages, included the Mohawks, Oneidas, Onondagas, Cayugas, Senecas, and Tuscaroras.

44. All of the following Supreme Court decisions strengthened the rights of a criminal defendant EXCEPT

(A) *Miranda* v. *Arizona*

(B) *Gideon* v. *Wainwright*

(C) *Roe* v. *Wade*

(D) *Escobedo* v. *Illinois*

(E) *Mapp v. Ohio*

(C) *Roe* v. *Wade* is the Supreme Court decision that limits the government's authority to control abortion on the grounds that under certain circumstances the decision to have an abortion is protected by a Constitutional right to privacy.

45. Alexander Hamilton was the first United States

(A) Vice President

(B) Secretary of War

(C) Secretary of State

(D) Secretary of Treasury

(E) Chief Justice

(D) Hamilton was the first Secretary of Treasury. (His picture is on the front of the $10 bill, and on the back is a picture of the Treasury Building.) Hamilton favored a strong national government and used his power as Secretary of Treasury to that end. He proposed that the nation's war debts be paid at full value, that the national government assume the war debts of the states, that the national government establish a mint, charter a national bank, and levy excise taxes, and that the national government impose a protective tariff on imports. Hamilton was successful on all counts save for the last. Congress had already enacted a tariff as a revenue raising device and did agree to raise rates slightly, but the final tariff was not the protective measure Hamilton had sought.

46. Prior to the ratification of the Seventeenth Amendment, United States senators

(A) were appointed by state governors

(B) were appointed by state legislatures

(C) served terms of four years

(D) could serve only two consecutive terms

(E) did not have to be United States citizens

(B) Article I, Section 1, Clause 1 provides that the "Senate of the United States shall be composed of two Senators from each State, chosen by the legislature thereof . . . ." The Seventeenth Amendment (1913) provides that United States senators are to be elected by the people of the state they represent.

47. All of the following were used during World War II to control the United States economy EXCEPT

(A) wage and price controls

(B) rent controls

(C) rationing

(D) disbanding of unions

(E) additional taxes

(D) The enormous governmental expenditures required to prosecute the war were guaranteed to produce inflationary pressures. When there is more money to be spent but fewer things to spend it on, buyers bid up the price of the available goods. The Roosevelt government established an Office of Price Administration and a War Labor Board. The Office of Price Administration fixed prices on everything from food to clothing and rationed essential commodities such as rubber, oil, sugar, and meat. The War Labor Board was created to mediate labor disputes and avoid the interruptions in production that would be caused by strikes. Early in the war, the most powerful labor leaders had given the government a no-strike pledge, a pledge that was for the most part honored, so the War Labor Board's primary function became to hold the line on prices. The unions, therefore, were not disbanded. Finally, the government also used its taxing power to control inflation (when the government raises taxes, people have less money to spend).

48. The procedure whereby voters can petition to have a special election to determine whether an elected official should be removed from office is termed

(A) an initiative

(B) a referendum

(C) a recall

(D) an arraignment

(E) a mistrial

(C) About a third of the states and many cities provide citizens with a method for dismissing from office an elected official even before the next election. It is termed a recall. Voters petition for a special election in which the issue is whether or not the offending official should be permitted to remain in office until the end of that term. If enough signatures are obtained on the petition, a recall vote is held. Initiatives and referendums are related to the recall in that both are procedures that help to make state and local governments more responsive to the people. Several state and many local governments provide for an initiative by which voters can suggest laws that they want considered. Almost all states provide for the referendum, a procedure by which voters can approve or reject proposed legislation. Arraignment and mistrial are judicial procedures. Arraignment is the proceeding at which the defendant appears before the court and is formally charged, and mistrial is a procedure whereby a trial judge determines that a serious error has been made during a trial and discontinues the trial.

49. The Dawes Allotment Act of 1887, which distributed parcels of reservation land to Indian heads of families for farming, was an attempt to assimilate the Indians into white society. The attempt failed for all of the following reasons EXCEPT

(A) the land given to the Indians was not very fertile and was particularly difficult to cultivate

(B) most of the Indians could not speak English and were unfamiliar with white culture

(C) the Indians preferred to remain a separate people and had no desire to be assimilated

(D) the Indians preferred to sell their land to whites rather than try to farm it themselves

(E) most of the western tribes had no tradition of agriculture and no knowledge of farming techniques

(D) As the question stem notes, the Dawes Act was an attempt to superimpose on Indian culture the individualist tradition of white society. The effort failed for the reasons given in (A) through (C) and in (E). As for (D), many Indians did sell their land—after they failed to succeed in farming, for the reasons cited.

50. First, Lincoln and the Republicans initially did not aim at abolishing slavery where it already existed. In fact, Lincoln had even promised to enforce the Fugitive Slave Law. Second, most northerners were not abolitionists. Third, four slave states did not secede from the Union. Finally, few southerners owned slaves.

The points raised above could best be used to support the thesis that

(A) the southern economy at the time of the Civil War was not dependent upon slavery

(B) slavery was not the most important cause of the start of the Civil War

(C) slavery was the issue that most clearly divided North from South

(D) the Civil War would not have started had the South agreed to eliminate slavery

(E) Lincoln had already formed his plan to eliminate slavery when he first took office

(B) One thesis about the start of the Civil War is that the conflict centered on the issue of slavery. The four points raised above, however, undermine that thesis. The first two suggest that the South really had no reason to believe that the North would try to abolish slavery. The third and fourth suggest that the South was not really committed to the preservation of slavery.

51. Between 1940 and 1970, all of the following increased EXCEPT

(A) output per farm acre

(B) output per farm worker

(C) farm size

(D) number of farms

(E) farm production

(D) Technological advances during the period cited, such as new machinery, better fertilizers, and more effective pesticides and herbicides, improved farm productivity; output per acre and per worker hour increased dramatically. Additionally, total production increased. Technological innovation, however, was also responsible for a decline in farm population as farm laborers and migratory workers were replaced by machines and smaller farmers, who lacked sufficient land and capital to take advantage of the advances, were forced out of farming. Moreover, the new techniques were particularly suited to larger operations. As a result, the number of farms has actually declined since 1940 while the number of large commercial farms (agribusinesses) has increased dramatically.

52. Rudyard Kipling's poem "The White Man's Burden " was primarily

(A) an apology for imperialism

(B) a condemnation of Southern racism

(C) a justification for United States isolationism

(D) a warning against United States interventionism

(E) a cry against the rising tide of nationalism

(A) Kipling's poem was written in 1899 to generate support for such acts as the United States' annexation of the Philippines. It calls on developed nations to "take up the White Man's burden." That "burden" is to take charge of people the poem refers to as "half devil and half child."

53. "The occasion has been judged proper for asserting that the American continents, by the free and independent condition which they have assumed and maintained, are henceforth not to be considered as subjects for future colonization by any European powers."

The statement above articulated what became known as

(A) Seward's Folly

(B) The American System

(C) The Monroe Doctrine

(D) The Policy of Laissez-faire

(E) The XYZ Affair

(C) This is one part of the famous Monroe Doctrine announced by President James Monroe in his annual address of 1823. The other part warns European powers against trying to reestablish control over countries that were formerly colonies. Actually, the announcement of the Monroe Doctrine was rather a non-event in Europe. European nations either ignored it or indicated that they would abide by it only if it suited them. It is true that European powers by and large left Latin America alone during the rest of the nineteenth century, but this is because the European nations that might otherwise have decided to intervene in Latin America feared that the British navy would stop them. Certainly, at the time the United States didn't have the naval power to enforce the Monroe Doctrine. Between its initial formulation and the end of the nineteenth century, the Monroe Doctrine languished in obscurity, cited only once or twice. In 1895, Secretary of State Richard Olney cited the Monroe Doctrine as giving the United States priority over Britain in resolving a border dispute between Venezuela and British Guiana. Thereafter, the Monroe Doctrine became an important part of American foreign policy.

Seward's Folly, as you probably remember, refers to the decision of Secretary of State William Seward to purchase Alaska from Russia in 1867 for $7.2 million. It was also referred to as "Seward's Icebox." The American System refers to a plan proposed by Henry Clay in 1824 to make the United States economically self-sufficient. Laissez-faire refers to an economic theory according to which government takes a "hands off" policy toward business. Finally, in 1797, President Adams sent a special mission to Paris to try to reduce hostilities between the United States and France. French agents insulted the delegates by demanding a bribe before they would commence negotiations. Adams reported the incident to Congress, designating the three French agents simply as X, Y, and Z.

54. Which of the following is an example of a progressive tax?

(A) Sales tax

(B) Excise tax on liquor and cigarettes

(C) Personal income tax

(D) Property tax

(E) Poll tax

(C) A progressive tax is one for which the tax rates increase with ability to pay. In a recent year, the federal government taxed the personal income of single persons at the following rates:

Taxable Income	Tax Rate	Tax Liability
$10,000	15.04%	$1,504
$20,000	16.43%	$3,287
$30,000	20.29%	$6,087
$40,000	22.21%	$8,887

Notice that the tax rates increase as income increases. Thus, a person who has taxable income of $40,000 pays a higher percentage of his or her income in taxes (22.21%) than a person who has taxable income of $10,000 (15.04%).

By contrast, a person pays the same sales tax regardless of income. As a consequence, people with lower incomes tend to spend a greater portion of their income in sales tax than people who are wealthier. This type of tax is called a regressive tax. Similarly an excise tax levied on the manufacture, sale, or use of particular products, such as cigarettes or liquor, also taxes without regard to ability to pay. So too property tax rates are fixed without regard to ability to pay. Finally, a poll tax was a fee a voter had to pay before being allowed to cast a ballot. The poll tax is now unconstitutional.

55. Since 1950, all of the following have contributed to the balance of payments deficit EXCEPT

(A) expenditures for foreign military installations

(B) economic assistance to foreign countries

(C) an unfavorable balance of trade

(D) travel by United States tourists in foreign countries

(E) investment by foreign companies in the United States

(E) The balance of payments represents the difference between what a country is owed by all other countries and what it owes. If a country owes more than it is owed, then the country has a negative balance of payments. Any activity that causes money to flow out of a country rather than in would tend to create a negative balance of payments. Notice that the activities described by (A) through (D) do that. The activity mentioned by (E), however, brings money into the country and would tend to improve the balance of payments.

56. During the twentieth century, labor unions in the United States have been LEAST concerned with which of the following?

(A) Obtaining higher wages

(B) Improving job security

(C) Gaining greater fringe benefits

(D) Increasing union membership

(E) Electing union officials to public office

(E) In the nineteenth century, there existed two traditions of labor organization in the United States. One tradition concerned itself with wages and working conditions. It sought benefits such as higher wages and shorter hours. This tradition is sometimes referred to as "bread and butter" unionism. The other tradition cast its nets more widely and sought political and social reform as well. Samuel Gompers directed the American Federation of Labor (1886-1894; 1896-1924) in the first tradition. Essentially a conservative, Gompers was not interested in restructuring the economic pie, he just wanted to make sure that labor got a bigger share. Since then, American unions have been primarily concerned with the bread and butter issues of wages and working conditions.

57. The historian Frederick Jackson Turner theorized that the distinctly American way of life was shaped primarily by

(A) a democratic heritage derived from Great Britain
(B) the experience of settling the western frontier
(C) industrialism and the factory system
(D) the strength of the seagoing tradition
(E) the religious beliefs of the Puritans

(B) In 1893, the historian Frederick Jackson Turner published a paper entitled "The Frontier in American History." The title tells you what Turner thought to be the most important factor in the development of a unique American character.

58. All of the following are consequences of the electoral college system of choosing the president EXCEPT

(A) a candidate can win a clear majority of the popular vote but not be elected president
(B) a candidate can win a significant number of popular votes but receive no electoral votes
(C) an elector pledged to a certain candidate can legally break the pledge and vote for another candidate
(D) presidential candidates are encouraged to waste a great deal of time campaigning in less populous states
(E) the system tends to maintain a two-party system by discouraging the growth of third parties

(D) Under the electoral college system established by the United States Constitution, the system under which we still operate, the president and vice president are not chosen by popular vote. Instead, the popular vote is used to choose electors. These electors in turn cast their votes to elect directly the president and vice president. This peculiar system was designed to ensure that an unqualified candidate, though favored by a majority of the people, would never reach office. It was contemplated that the electors, who would presumably be better educated than the average voter, would ignore the popular vote and choose a better candidate. When a voter casts a ballot in a presidential election, she or he is not actually voting for a candidate. Instead, the vote is cast for a slate of electors who have pledged themselves to cast their electoral votes for a certain candidate. The slate that gets the most votes gets to cast that state's electoral votes. This "winner take all" system can produce some interesting results:

Year	Candidate	Popular Vote	Electoral Vote
1888	Benjamin Harrison	5,444,337	233
	Grover Cleveland	5,540,050	168
1980	Ronald Reagan	43,899,248	489
	Jimmy Carter	35,481,435	49
	John Anderson	5,719,437	0

In 1888, Cleveland received nearly 100,000 more votes than Harrison, but the electoral college made Harrison president by a vote of 233 to 168. In 1980, John Anderson received nearly six million votes, but that fact was not reflected in the electoral college vote.

Critics of the system also point out that electors, while "pledged" to particular candidates, are not legally bound to vote for those candidates. Occasionally, electors ignore their pledges, but this has not occurred very often. Also, say critics, the system discourages the growth of new parties because it is necessary to poll a large number of votes to get any electoral votes.

Finally, analysts say that the system encourages candidates to concentrate on more populous states with their greater electoral votes and to ignore smaller and less populous states. Thus, (D) is the exception and the correct choice.

59. Which of the following was NOT a settlement established by the French during the seventeenth century?

(A) Detroit
(B) Montreal
(C) New Orleans
(D) St. Augustine
(E) St. Louis

(D) The French used the vast system of inland waterways in North America to explore North America:

St. Augustine, the oldest city in the United States, was established in Florida by the Spanish in 1565.

60. The earliest people to reach North America are thought to have arrived from

(A) Siberia via the Bering Strait land bridge

(B) South America via the Central American isthmus

(C) Hawaii via rafts

(D) Scandinavia via boats

(E) Germania via a polar route

(A) By the time Columbus "discovered" the New World, it was already inhabited by 15 million to 20 million people. It is now believed that the first inhabitants of North America came from Siberia and crossed over a land bridge at the site of what is now the Bering Strait.

61. Which of the following is a felony crime?

(A) Shoplifting

(B) Speeding

(C) Murder

(D) Public drunkenness

(E) Trespassing

(C) Criminal codes classify crimes according to their seriousness. The more serious crimes, such as rape, kidnapping, and murder, are called felonies. The less serious crimes, such as petty theft, disorderly conduct, and trespassing, are called misdemeanors. Felonies are, of course, punished more severely than misdemeanors. Conviction of a misdemeanor usually warrants probation, a fine, or a short jail term. Conviction of a felony can result in heavy fines and a long term of imprisonment. Criminal codes also include a third category: offenses or violations. This category covers actions such as smoking in a non-smoking area, violating the public health code, and traffic infractions. Violations are treated as quasi-criminal actions and are tried using some variation of the usual rules of criminal procedure. But conviction of a violation or offense doesn't result in a criminal record.

62. Which of the following was an important factor in the decision of the United States to enter World War I?

(A) A threatened German invasion of Mexico

(B) German submarine attacks on ships in the Atlantic Ocean

(C) The assassination of the heir to the Austro-Hungarian throne

(D) A Japanese naval blockade of ports on the West Coast of the United States

(E) Formation of a German-Japanese alliance directed against the United States

(B) World War I was precipitated by the assassination of the Austrian Archduke at Sarajevo in 1914, but the United States did not immediately enter the war. Although most Americans tended to sympathize with Great Britain and to distrust Germany, the express policy of the United States government was neutrality. Gradually, however, the events of the war, amplified by British propaganda, polarized the Americans, and most favored the British. The immediate cause for U.S. entry into the war was German submarine warfare. In 1915, hoping to stop supplies coming from Britain, Germany announced that it would thenceforth consider the waters surrounding the British Isles a war zone and warned neutral ships to stay clear. The main weapon for enforcing the blockade was the submarine. In 1915, a German U boat (for *unterseeboot*) torpedoed and sank the British passenger liner *Lusitania*. Over a hundred American passengers were lost. After strong protest by the United States, the German government promised that it would sink no more passenger ships. But in March 1916, a German submarine mistakenly sank the ferry *Sussex* in the English Channel. This time the German government responded with the Sussex Pledge promising that it would not attack merchant vessels without warning. This move reduced tensions with the United States but also permitted supplies to reach the Allied forces in Europe. In 1916, Wilson's supporters coined the slogan "He kept us out of war." But in early 1917, Germany decided that it could not win the war without enforcing the blockade and announced the resumption of unrestricted submarine warfare. Several American merchant ships were sunk. In February, the British intercepted a message from the German foreign secretary, Alfred Zimmerman, to the German ambassador in Mexico, instructing the Ambassador to offer Mexico a military alliance against the United States with the promise it would help Mexico recover lost territory. On April 2, President Wilson asked Congress for a declaration of war.

63. Which of the following black leaders was awarded the Nobel Peace Prize?

(A) Elijah Muhammad

(B) Eldridge Cleaver

(C) Medgar Evers

(D) Martin Luther King, Jr.

(E) Marcus Garvey

(D) Dr. King, who advocated a strategy of peaceful mass resistance (used by Gandhi) and civil disobedience (described by Thoreau), was awarded the Nobel Peace Prize in 1964. Elijah Muhammad founded the Black Muslim movement. Eldridge Cleaver was a leader of the Black Panthers. Medgar Evers, who was assassinated in 1963, was secretary of the Mississippi NAACP. And Marcus Garvey, who founded the Universal Negro Improvement Association in 1914, was author of Black Nationalism, a concept that opposed integration and called for the establishment of a black empire on the African continent.

64. The War of 1812 is often described as the

(A) "conquest of British Canada"

(B) "American Waterloo"

(C) "dirty little Federalist war"

(D) "war to end all wars"

(E) "second war of independence"

(E) One important factor leading to the War of 1812 was American resentment toward Great Britain, a resentment aggravated by the British policy of seizing American ships and impressing American sailors. The war itself was a mixed bag. Each side had its victories and defeats, and nothing was really gained or lost in the Treaty of Ghent (1814) which ended hostilities. (Andrew Jackson's famous victory in the Battle of New Orleans actually occurred after the treaty was signed.) The War of 1812 did, however, fire a new feeling of national patriotism. Psychologically, it was a second victory of independence. Additionally, the victory thoroughly discredited the Federalist party, centered in New England, which had so bitterly opposed the war that its leaders, at the Hartford Convention, had actually hinted that New England states might secede from the Union.

65. In *Brown* v. *Board of Education of Topeka* (1954) the Supreme Court of the United States held that

(A) separate facilities for different races are inherently unequal

(B) segregation is permissible so long as facilities are similar

(C) the federal Constitution makes race relations a matter for the states

(D) there is no constitutional right to a public school education

(E) local school districts may not using busing as a means of desegregating schools

(A) In 1896, the Supreme Court ruled that Jim Crow laws (laws that segregated public facilities according to race) were not inherently unconstitutional and that separate facilities were permissible so long as those facilities were equal. This ruling came to be known as the "separate but equal" doctrine. In 1954, in *Brown* v. *Board of Education,* the Supreme Court unanimously decided that racially segregated schools are "inherently unequal."

66. The Quartering Act of 1765 was passed to

(A) divide the western lands among various colonies claiming those lands

(B) force the colonies to pay British merchants with silver coins

(C) encourage westward expansion by providing military protection to settlements

(D) deprive colonists of representation in the colonial assemblies

(E) reduce the cost of housing British troops in the American colonies

(E) Starting in 1763, the British Parliament passed a series of acts designed to raise revenues in the colonies. It made provision for stricter enforcement of existing revenue devices such as the Molasses Act, which was widely circumvented by smugglers, and passed new revenue-raising devices such as the Sugar Act and the Stamp Act. The Quartering Act was not a revenue-raising measure so much as a cost-cutting plan. It provided that where barracks were inadequate to house British troops, the troops were to be quartered in public hostelries or even private buildings and the cost was to be borne by the colonists. Additionally, the colonists were required to provide food and other items to the troops. Since this policy imposed yet another cost on them, what to Great Britain seemed a cost-cutting measure was to the colonists another form of taxation.

67. The Constitution of the United States gives the power to make treaties to the

(A) Congress subject to the approval of the president

(B) president subject to the approval of the Senate

(C) president subject to the approval of the House of Representatives

(D) president subject to the approval of the states

(E) states subject to the approval of the Congress

(B) Article 2, Section 2, Clause 2 of the Constitution provides that the president "shall have power, by and with the advice and consent of the Senate, to make treaties, provided two-thirds of the Senators present concur."

68. The government agency that has the greatest control over interest rates in the United States is the

(A) Federal Trade Commission

(B) Interstate Commerce Commission

(C) Federal Reserve Board

(D) Department of the Interior

(E) Department of Commerce

(C) The Federal Reserve System, established in 1913 and strengthened during the New Deal, is the central banking authority in the United States. It includes twelve Federal Reserve Banks that are often described as "bankers' banks." That is because the customers of the Federal Reserve Banks are not people or businesses but banks. The system is under the control of a Board of Governors, each member of which is appointed for a 14-year term by the President with the consent of the Senate. Thus, the Fed, as it is known, has a good deal of independence, and it has several powers that allow it to exercise control over the economy. One of these powers is the authority to set the *discount rate.* This is the rate at which the Federal Reserve Banks lend money to other banks. If the Fed raises the discount rate, then banks raise the interest rate they charge on loans to customers. And conversely, if the Fed lowers the discount rate, then banks lower the interest rate they charge on loans to customers. In this way, the Fed makes borrowing more difficult or easier and can discourage or encourage economic activity.

69. Thomas Jefferson theorized that democracy would function best in a society dominated by

(A) merchants and shippers

(B) aristocratic plantation owners

(C) small, independent farmers

(D) unskilled, urban laborers

(E) professionalized government workers

(C) Thomas Jefferson envisioned a United States of small and independent farmers with only a limited national government.

70. In 1962, President John F. Kennedy declared a naval quarantine of Cuba in order to

(A) prevent the Soviet Union from placing offensive missiles in Cuba

(B) ensure that a highly infectious disease did not spread beyond the island

(C) stem the flood of Cubans illegally entering the United States

(D) punish Cuba economically for withdrawing from the Organization of American States

(E) incite a revolution to overthrow the government of Fidel Castro

(A) After the Soviet Union's successful Sputnik launch, the United States placed intermediate-range missiles in Italy and Turkey where they could reach the Soviet Union. In 1962, the Soviet Union began building missile bases in Cuba, where they threatened the United States. When the United States learned of the missile bases, President Kennedy went on national television to announce that the U.S. Navy would blockade Cuba to prevent the installation of Soviet missiles there. Shortly thereafter, it was announced that Soviet ships, presumably carrying missiles, were in the Atlantic Ocean and heading for Cuba. Ultimately, in exchange for a U.S. promise to respect Cuba's independence, the Soviet Union abandoned the plan to put missiles in Cuba. Many people believe that the Cuban Missile Crisis brought the world close to a nuclear war.

71. The Chisolm Trail was used by

(A) fur trappers to cross the Appalachian Mountains

(B) cowboys to drive cattle to a rail head in Kansas

(C) prospectors to reach the gold fields of California

(D) settlers to move covered wagons to the West

(E) manufacturers to ship finished goods to the Southwest

(B) The open spaces of South Texas could be used for cattle production, but the markets for beef were geographically too far removed. The Civil War, however, created a tremendous demand for beef, and the railroad provided a means of transportation for getting goods to market. The railroad, however, ended hundreds of miles north of the South Texas cattle-producing region. To reach the market, therefore, cattle were driven across Texas and through Indian territory to the railheads in Missouri and Kansas. One of the routes was known as the Chisolm Trail.

72. During the Civil War, the Confederate Army won an important battle at

(A) Little Bighorn

(B) Gettysburg

(C) Vicksburg

(D) Bull Run

(E) Belleau Wood

(D) The first large battle of the Civil War, fought in Virginia at Bull Run (1861), was won by Confederate forces. The Confederate Army also won the second battle of Bull Run (1862). The battles at Gettysburg (1863) and Vicksburg (1863) were won by the Union Army. At the Battle of the Little Bighorn (1876), a group of Sioux led by Sitting Bull wiped out General George Custer's forces. In one of the first major engagements of World War I in which American forces participated, the American troops drove German forces out of the Belleau Wood (1918).

73. The United States acquired the land to build the Panama Canal by virtue of

(A) a Panamanian revolt against Colombia that was supported by the United States Navy

(B) United States military intervention to resolve a border dispute between Colombia and Panama

(C) an agreement with Colombia under which the United States agreed to a concession fee plus annual payments

(D) a treaty with Nicaragua in which Nicaragua voluntarily relinquished control of the canal zone

(E) an alliance whereby the United States agreed to ensure Colombian neutrality in exchange for the canal route

(A) In 1878, a French company under the direction of Ferdinand de Lesseps, the builder of the Suez Canal, obtained from Colombia a concession to build a canal across its northern province of Panama. After spending about $300 million, the French company ran out of money and had to stop work on the project. In 1903, the United States negotiated a treaty with Colombia for the canal rights, but the treaty was rejected by Colombia, which wanted more money. Phillipe Bunau-Varilla, the former chief engineer of the canal project and a stockholder in the reorganized French company, engineered a revolution to secure Panama's independence from Colombia. The revolution succeeded mainly because the United States Navy prevented Colombia from intervening to suppress the uprising. The United States immediately recognized the new nation, and the Hay-Bunau-Varilla Treaty secured to the United States the canal rights on essentially the same terms that had been offered to Colombia.

74. The slogan "Fifty-four forty or fight" helped to elect which president?

(A) James Monroe

(B) John Quincy Adams

(C) Andrew Jackson

(D) Martin Van Buren

(E) James K. Polk

(E) The United States and Great Britain both claimed the Oregon Country, an area extending from the Pacific Ocean to the Rocky Mountains and from latitude of 42° north to 54°40′ north. In the presidential campaign of 1844, James K. Polk's supporters demanded that the United States be given complete control over the territory or go to war with Britain. In the final analysis, Polk compromised on the Oregon issue by agreeing in 1846 to extend the Line of 1818 that marked the boundary between the United States and Canada all the way to the Pacific. Thus, the territory was split between the United States and Great Britain along the 49th parallel.

75. Which of the following best describes the civil rights policy of President John F. Kennedy?

(A) Very aggressive from the beginning with many new civil rights laws enacted

(B) Very aggressive from the beginning but weakened by resistance from Congress

(C) Initially limited to enforcement of voting rights but later more aggressive

(D) Initially hostile to enforcement of civil rights but later neutral

(E) Hostile toward the enforcement of civil rights throughout the administration

(C) On the issue of civil rights, Kennedy initially continued the policies of Eisenhower, who believed that the real problems of segregation could not be legislated out of existence. President Kennedy and his brother Robert, the Attorney General, concentrated on enforcing voting rights legislation, hoping that once blacks had attained sufficient power at the polls segregation would be dismantled from within. Embarrassed by events in the Deep South in 1963, in which television recorded the violence of white officials against blacks, Kennedy finally proposed a new civil rights act prohibiting racial segregation in all public accommodations.

76. The Emancipation Proclamation applied to slaves

(A) throughout the United States

(B) only in border states

(C) only in regions under the control of the Union Army

(D) only in states still in rebellion against the Union

(E) only to escaped slaves who had joined the Union Army

(D) The Emancipation Proclamation had very little effect on the status of slaves. It freed only those slaves held in states still at war against the Union, but those were areas still under Confederate control.

77. As applied to Southeast Asia, the ''domino theory'' held that

(A) a communist takeover of South Vietnam would lead to similar takeovers in other countries in the region

(B) escalating numbers of United States troops would guarantee a military victory in Vietnam

(C) it is impossible to win a guerrilla war using conventional military strategies

(D) only by breaking an enemy's supply lines is it possible to gain victory

(E) a united, communistic but nationalist Vietnam would not be imperialistic

(A) In a news conference in 1954, President Eisenhower, in addressing the French request for American aid for its military efforts in Vietnam, stated that Southeast Asia was like a row of dominoes and that if one were knocked over the entire row would follow. The "domino theory" was a frequently used justification for the United States' military presence in Vietnam.

78. The Articles of Confederation, which were never intended to create a strong central government, fostered highly democratic local and state governments. By 1786, the postwar economic depression was all but over, and in general states traded freely among themselves. Even as the Articles were replaced, the states were considering a national tariff, the proceeds of which would be used by the national government.

A historian could use the points made above to support the thesis that

(A) diplomatic negotiations could have avoided the need to fight the Revolutionary War

(B) the Articles of Confederation did not collapse from weakness

(C) the government established by the Constitution is weaker than that of the Articles

(D) the national government ought to have more power than state governments

(E) local government is more likely to be corrupt than a national one

(B) The received wisdom regarding the transition from the Articles of Confederation to the Constitution argues that the step was a necessary one given several serious weaknesses in the government established by the Articles.The weaknesses included the lack of any taxing power and the lack of power to control interstate commerce. The statements above can be used to argue that a strong national government was not needed because state and local governments did the job in a more democratic way. Further, interstate commerce didn't need controlling. And finally, the national government did not itself need any taxing authority.

79. In 1824, the House of Representatives was required to choose the president because

(A) the candidate with the largest popular vote died before the electoral college could meet

(B) allegations of widespread vote fraud cast serious doubt on the validity of election results

(C) the Supreme Court had declared unconstitutional certain voting restrictions

(D) each candidate received the same number of votes in the electoral college

(E) sectional voting prevented any of the four candidates from obtaining a majority of the electoral votes

(E) By 1820, the Federalist party was a defunct organization, killed by its opposition to the War of 1812 and by growth in the West where its policies were opposed. In 1820, the Republican party candidate, James Monroe, won all but one electoral vote. This landslide, however, concealed the fact that the Republican party was not a party unified by a common vision but a loose affiliation of different factions. In 1824, the party nominated William Crawford, a southerner, as its presidential candidate. This choice did not meet with the approval of other segments of the party, and three other candidates were nominated: Andrew Jackson from Tennessee, Henry Clay from Kentucky, and John Quincy Adams from Massachusetts. In the electoral college the vote was:

Jackson	99
Adams	84
Crawford	41
Clay	37

Jackson received most of his support from the South and West and Adams from the Northeast. Since no candidate received a majority of the electoral votes, the matter was transferred to the House of Representatives. Although it was expected that Jackson would be chosen, Clay threw his support behind Adams, who finally won the election.

80. Which of the following contributed to the almost ten-year delay in annexing Texas?

I. Sectional opposition to the admission of any more slave states

II. Desire of most Texans to remain a free and independent republic

III. Fear that annexation would alienate France

(A) I only

(B) II only

(C) I and II only

(D) I and III only

(E) II and III only

(A) On March 2, 1836, Texans declared their independence from Mexico, independence which was secured by their victory at San Jacinto on April 21 of that year. Most Texans favored immediate annexation by the United States, but this proposal was opposed by the antislavery elements in the North.

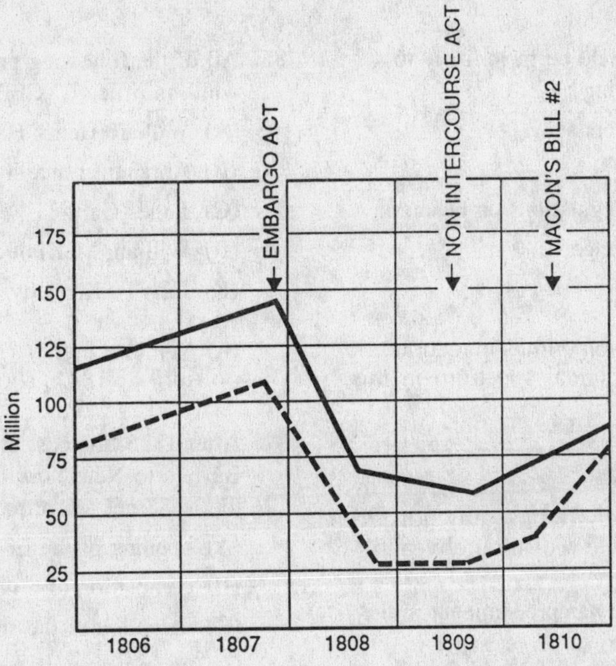

81. The chart above most likely refers to

(A) the strength of the United States army and navy

(B) distribution of population between cities and farms in the United States

(C) the value of United States imports and exports

(D) salaries paid to United States senators and representatives

(E) number of slaves held in southern versus northern states

(C) During the second half of the first decade of the nineteenth century, Great Britain and France were at war. The United States attempted to maintain its neutrality and to continue exporting and importing goods, but both belligerents followed policies whereby they seized American ships and goods. Additionally, the British navy, hard pressed to man its ships, impressed American seaman (forced them into service in the British navy). A particularly egregious example of this policy occurred in June of 1807 when the British frigate *Leopard* fired upon the American frigate *Chesapeake*. In December of 1807, Congress passed the Embargo act prohibiting commerce with any foreign port. The act had three goals: one, to reduce the likelihood of war by preventing seizures of ships and men; two, to punish Britain with economic sanctions; and three, to reduce American dependence on imports. In spite of the economic dislocation caused to the United States, most sections of the nation supported President Jefferson's decision. The exception was the Northeast which was particularly hard hit by the sanctions and even talked of secession. The Embargo Act was replaced by the Non-intercourse Act in 1809 which restricted the prohibition of commerce to Great Britain and France. The chart shows the devastating effect on trade. Finally, even that prohibition was repealed in 1810 by Macon's Bill #2 (so called because Macon's Bill number #1 didn't pass). As you would expect, trade recovered.

82. All of the following advantages of the North helped to contribute to the Union's victory over the Confederacy EXCEPT

(A) greater industrial base

(B) greater population

(C) easier access to capital

(D) more skillful military leaders

(E) control of the navy

(D) (A), (B), (C), and (E) are all advantages that the North enjoyed over the South, and they help explain the course of the war. The South had some initial successes, as the North mobilized for war; but once mobilized, the North with its greater resources wore down the South. Most historians agree, however, that the military leaders of the South, particularly Generals Thomas J. "Stonewall" Jackson and Robert E. Lee, were as able as and perhaps more able than their Union counterparts.

83. A political reactionary would be most likely to favor which of the following?

(A) Higher welfare payments

(B) Higher tax rates

(C) Stricter government regulations on business

(D) National health insurance

(E) Strong military

(E) Although labels are sometimes inaccurate, it is useful to view the political spectrum in this way:

LEFT ←		CENTER		→ RIGHT
Radicals	Liberals	Moderates	Conservatives	Reactionaries

A reactionary would likely oppose any government programs designed to redistribute wealth.

84. The sharecropping system was predominant in the

(A) North after the Civil War

(B) South after the Civil War

(C) West after the Civil War

(D) Midwest during the depression

(E) Northwest between the world wars

(B) After the Civil War, blacks along with whites were free to enter employment contracts, but landowners had no money to pay wages. So there developed the sharecropping system under which a farmer would work land owned by another, often using seeds, mules, and tools provided by the owner, and pay rent in the form of a share of the crop.

85. Inflation most severely hurts

(A) government workers

(B) retired people

(C) union workers

(D) home owners

(E) white collar workers

(B) Inflation, a continual increase in the general price level, erodes the purchasing price of the dollar, that is, it is necessary to pay more for the same goods or services. Retired people often live on fixed incomes; the income from savings or pensions does not increase even though prices do. People still in the work force can usually count on some kind of cost-of-living adjustment: as prices rise so do wages and salaries. Additionally, owning a home is usually a good hedge against inflation. Though property values sometimes decline in a specific area for a short time, nationwide and over the long run, the price of property continues to rise.

86. All of the following presidents were assassinated while in office EXCEPT

(A) William Henry Harrison

(B) Abraham Lincoln

(C) James Garfield

(D) William McKinley

(E) John F. Kennedy

(A) William Henry Harrison died of pneumonia on April 4, 1841, shortly after assuming office.

87. After 1825, the cost of shipping freight from Buffalo to New York City dropped from $100 per ton to $8 per ton primarily because of the

(A) opening of the Erie Canal

(B) completion of a new rail system

(C) invention of the steam engine

(D) construction of turnpikes

(E) decrease in population

(A) Started in 1817 and completed in 1825, the Erie Canal provides a water route from New York City, with its deep water harbor, to Buffalo on Lake Erie. In 1817, it had cost almost 20 cents per ton per mile to ship freight overland, and in 1850 the cost per ton per mile to ship freight via the canal was less than one cent.

88. All of the following help to explain the American victory in the Revolutionary War EXCEPT

(A) British military commanders failed to adapt their military strategies to the terrain

(B) there was no one center of political authority at which the British could strike

(C) the British supply lines extended 3,000 miles across the Atlantic Ocean

(D) the revolutionary movement had widespread support among the American people

(E) the revolutionary soldiers were led by well-trained, professional officers

(E) The revolutionary forces consisted of the Continental Army of about 5,000 troops, supplemented by state militia units. The forces were lead by inexperienced amateur officers. George Washington, for example, the commander in chief, had been only a regimental colonel on the Virginia frontier. The British army consisted of 50,000 professional soldiers and some 30,000 German mercenaries. Yet, partly for the reasons described in choices (A) through (D), the Americans managed to win.

89. On April 11, 1951, President Harry Truman removed General Douglas MacArthur as commander in chief of United Nation's forces in Korea because

(A) MacArthur was a weak and ineffective military leader

(B) MacArthur was critical of Truman's foreign policy

(C) the United Nations asked for MacArthur's removal

(D) South Korea no longer needed United States military assistance

(E) MacArthur was unpopular with the United States public

(B) In 1945, Korea—a colony of Japan since 1910—was divided at the 38th parallel. The southern portion was occupied by American troops, the northern portion by Soviet troops. The Soviet Union created a government in North Korea over which it held considerable influence. On June 25, 1950, North Korean forces crossed the 38th parallel. The United States secured a United Nations resolution condemning the aggression and committed ground troops to defend South Korea. These troops were commanded by General Douglas MacArthur, a highly popular military leader. MacArthur drove the North Korean forces back across the 38th parallel and began to talk about using military force, including nuclear weapons against China, to unify Korea. In November, China committed troops on the side of North Korea, and a battle line eventually stabilized along the 38th parallel. MacArthur still envisioned a total victory, but President Truman and the joint chiefs of staff had settled on the much more limited aim of reestablishing the status quo. When MacArthur publicly sided with Congressional leaders who favored total victory, Truman relieved him of his command.

90. Which of the following markets would be considered by an economist to be the most competitive?

(A) Steel production

(B) Railroad transportation

(C) Oil refining

(D) Electric utilities

(E) Automobile repair service

(E) The more business entities there are in a market to compete against each other, the more competitive the market is. Steel production and oil refining are concentrated in the hands of a few large businesses. As for railroad transportation and electrical service, your own experience should tell you that you don't have much choice in the matter.

91. Society provides an arena for competition in which the most industrious, ingenious, and intelligent people are the most successful. By a process akin to natural selection, civilization necessarily advances to higher and more complex forms.

The position outlined by the statements above is often referred to as

(A) Mercantilism

(B) Protectionism

(C) Imperialism

(D) Social Darwinism

(E) Marxism

(D) The statements describe a philosophy often called Social Darwinism. On this view, a process analogous to natural selection of the fittest members of animal species operates in society to select for social and economic reward those who are the fittest.

92. All of the following were consequences of the Great Depression of the 1930s EXCEPT

(A) establishment of the social security system

(B) enactment of a federally mandated minimum wage

(C) increased unionization of workers

(D) desegregation of public accommodations

(E) creation of a system of federal aid to farmers

(D) (A), (B), (C), and (E) were all consequences of New Deal legislation spurred by the need for economic recovery or by concern for those who suffered economically during the Great Depression. Advancing civil rights, however, was not an important objective of the New Deal.

93. If Congress passed a law requiring restaurants to set aside a no smoking section, that law would probably be considered

(A) constitutional because it involves the regulation of interstate commerce

(B) unconstitutional because restaurants are private businesses

(C) unconstitutional because the Constitution does not specifically mention use of tobacco

(D) unconstitutional because states have the exclusive authority to regulate tobacco

(E) unconstitutional because states have the exclusive authority to regulate restaurants

(A) Article I, Section 8, Clause 3 gives Congress the power to "regulate commerce . . . among the several states." This power has been interpreted very broadly and has been the foundation for legislation such as the minimum wage law and civil rights acts. Here the restaurant would be considered to be engaged in interstate commerce because it feeds customers from out-of-state, buys food which was grown in another state, uses utensils which came from another state, and so on. So if Congress found a legitimate legislative purpose, such as protecting nonsmokers from secondary smoke, the law would probably be constitutional.

94. When the United States established formal diplomatic relations with the People's Republic of China in 1979 it also withdrew diplomatic recognition from the government of

(A) Cambodia

(B) Okinawa

(C) Sri Lanka

(D) Sumatra

(E) Taiwan

(E) With the withdrawal of Japanese troops from China following World War II, Nationalist Chiang Kai-shek and Communist Mao Zedong resumed a civil war. The United States for a time supplied military aid to the corrupt Chiang Kai-shek regime in hopes of preventing the communists from taking control of the country. By 1949, however, the Nationalists were in full retreat, and Chiang Kai-shek's army was evacuated to the island of Taiwan. Although the communists were in control of China, the United States refused to recognize the government and for more than 20 years maintained that the legitimate government was the Nationalist government on Taiwan. This unrealistic view was undermined when President Richard Nixon made a trip to China in 1972; and in 1979, President Jimmy Carter established formal diplomatic relations with the People's Republic, thereby recognizing it as the legitimate government of China.

95. Which of the following groups settled at Great Salt Lake in what is now Utah in search of freedom from religious persecution?

(A) Mennonites

(B) Millerites

(C) Wobblies

(D) Mormons

(E) Quids

(D) In 1830 in upstate New York, Joseph Smith, Jr. published *The Book of Mormon,* a translation, he said, of inscriptions of golden tablets the location of which had been revealed to him by an angel. *The Book of Mormon* became the holy book of Smith's followers, the Church of Christ, later renamed the Church of Jesus Christ of Latter-day Saints. Faced with religious persecution from the very beginning, Smith and his followers moved westward. They founded new cities only to be subjected again to persecution. In 1844, Smith himself was killed by a mob in Illinois. Leadership of the church passed to Brigham Young who in 1847 led the Mormons to the Great Salt Lake Valley in Utah.

World History Test

World History Test

The World History Test consists of 95 multiple-choice questions designed to measure knowledge and understanding of the history and development of both western and nonwestern cultures. About two-thirds of the test will be questions about Europe. The remaining questions cover the Middle East, Africa, Asia, and the Western Hemisphere. Although the test covers events from prehistory to the present, about half of the questions are based upon events after 1750.

The test uses a fairly straightforward multiple-choice format. A few of the questions utilize maps, political cartoons, or other illustrations, but these don't require any special talent to answer. The only question form that is a little tricky utilizes a thought-reverser, a word such as NOT, EXCEPT, BUT, or LEAST. These words turn the question "inside out." What ordinarily would be a wrong answer is the right answer, and vice versa.

EXAMPLE:

All of the following statements about the Fabian Society are true EXCEPT

(A) it originated in Great Britain
(B) it advocated peaceful social reform
(C) it was one root of the Labour party
(D) it did not engage in direct political action
(E) it endorsed all of the teachings of Karl Marx

The correct answer to this item is (E). The Fabians stressed gradual social reform, not the violent overthrow of the existing structure. Thus, the one statement that is not true becomes the correct answer to this question.

EXAMPLE:

In 1954, the Vietminh won the Battle of the Dien Bien Phu over what colonial power?

(A) United States
(B) Soviet Union
(C) China
(D) France
(E) Germany

The correct answer is (D). In the nineteenth century, France annexed Indo-China. After World War II, Indo-Chinese nationalists formed an independence movement called the Vietminh. This movement was controlled by the Moscow-trained Ho Chi Minh and received aid from Communist China. The Vietminh won a decisive battle against the French at Dien Bien Phu.

EXAMPLE:

A cathedral building characterized by massive walls, rounded arches, and strong columns and having few windows would best be described as an example of what kind of architecture?

(A) Romanesque
(B) Gothic
(C) Baroque
(D) Roccoco
(E) Post-Modern

The correct answer is (A). The features described are characteristic of Romanesque architecture used before the twelfth century.

Special Question Formats

Most questions on the test are worded in the affirmative mode, e.g., "What was the most important factor . . .?" Some questions, however, contain "thought-reversers." These are words such as "except," "not," "but," and "least." The effect of such a word is to turn the question in-side-out.

EXAMPLE:

Which of the following conditions is LEAST important for the survival of a democratic form of government?

(A) Decent standard of living for most of the people
(B) History of democratic traditions
(C) High rate of literacy among the population
(D) Willingness by people to debate and to compromise on public issues
(E) A very powerful and politically influential armed forces

The correct answer to this question is (E). Notice the presence of the thought-reverser "LEAST" in the question stem. Ordinarily, we would expect the correct answer to a question about conditions for democracy to be an important factor contributing to the rise of democracy. Here, however, we are looking for the factor that is NOT conducive to democracy. And that factor is (E). A powerful and politically influential military is likely to threaten rather than strengthen democratic institutions.

Another special question form uses a group of three or perhaps four Roman numeral statements. The question then asks you to determine which of the statements is or are correct (or perhaps which are incorrect).

EXAMPLE:

Which of the following accurately characterize Czarist Russia at the beginning of the twentieth century?

I. Rigid class distinctions
II. Religious toleration
III. Political absolutism

(A) I only
(B) II only
(C) I and II only
(D) I and III only
(E) II and III only

The correct answer is (D). Czarist Russia was an absolute monarchy and was characterized by a sharp division into privileged and unprivileged classes. So statements I and III are part of the correct response. Statement II, however, is incorrect. Jews in Russia were severely persecuted, and many left Russia, migrating chiefly to the United States.

As you can see, a question of this type may allow you to answer with only partial knowledge. Assume, for example, that you know that Czarist Russia was characterized by absolute monarch and sharp class divisions but were unsure about religious freedom. You know that both statement I and statement III must appear in the answer choice you select. Now look at the choices and eliminate every choice that does not contain both I and III. You will eliminate every choice but (D). So the correct answer must be (D). Of course, you won't always be able to eliminate four choices on the basis of partial knowledge, but you can often eliminate one or more. And that gives you an additional edge when you make your guess.

World History Test Answer Sheet

1	A	B	C	D	E	49	A	B	C	D	E
2	A	B	C	D	E	50	A	B	C	D	E
3	A	B	C	D	E	51	A	B	C	D	E
4	A	B	C	D	E	52	A	B	C	D	E
5	A	B	C	D	E	53	A	B	C	D	E
6	A	B	C	D	E	54	A	B	C	D	E
7	A	B	C	D	E	55	A	B	C	D	E
8	A	B	C	D	E	56	A	B	C	D	E
9	A	B	C	D	E	57	A	B	C	D	E
10	A	B	C	D	E	58	A	B	C	D	E
11	A	B	C	D	E	59	A	B	C	D	E
12	A	B	C	D	E	60	A	B	C	D	E
13	A	B	C	D	E	61	A	B	C	D	E
14	A	B	C	D	E	62	A	B	C	D	E
15	A	B	C	D	E	63	A	B	C	D	E
16	A	B	C	D	E	64	A	B	C	D	E
17	A	B	C	D	E	65	A	B	C	D	E
18	A	B	C	D	E	66	A	B	C	D	E
19	A	B	C	D	E	67	A	B	C	D	E
20	A	B	C	D	E	68	A	B	C	D	E
21	A	B	C	D	E	69	A	B	C	D	E
22	A	B	C	D	E	70	A	B	C	D	E
23	A	B	C	D	E	71	A	B	C	D	E
24	A	B	C	D	E	72	A	B	C	D	E
25	A	B	C	D	E	73	A	B	C	D	E
26	A	B	C	D	E	74	A	B	C	D	E
27	A	B	C	D	E	75	A	B	C	D	E
28	A	B	C	D	E	76	A	B	C	D	E
29	A	B	C	D	E	77	A	B	C	D	E
30	A	B	C	D	E	78	A	B	C	D	E
31	A	B	C	D	E	79	A	B	C	D	E
32	A	B	C	D	E	80	A	B	C	D	E
33	A	B	C	D	E	81	A	B	C	D	E
34	A	B	C	D	E	82	A	B	C	D	E
35	A	B	C	D	E	83	A	B	C	D	E
36	A	B	C	D	E	84	A	B	C	D	E
37	A	B	C	D	E	85	A	B	C	D	E
38	A	B	C	D	E	86	A	B	C	D	E
39	A	B	C	D	E	87	A	B	C	D	E
40	A	B	C	D	E	88	A	B	C	D	E
41	A	B	C	D	E	89	A	B	C	D	E
42	A	B	C	D	E	90	A	B	C	D	E
43	A	B	C	D	E	91	A	B	C	D	E
44	A	B	C	D	E	92	A	B	C	D	E
45	A	B	C	D	E	93	A	B	C	D	E
46	A	B	C	D	E	94	A	B	C	D	E
47	A	B	C	D	E	95	A	B	C	D	E
48	A	B	C	D	E						

World History Test

Directions: Each question or incomplete statement below is followed by five answer choices or completions. For each item, select the best answer and darken the corresponding circle on the answer sheet.

1. The influence of the classical Mediterranean civilizations (Greece and Rome) on modern western Europe is LEAST evident in

(A) political structures

(B) languages

(C) religion

(D) architecture

(E) philosophy

2. Beginning with the earliest, what is the correct chronological order of the following events in the history of France?

I. The Reign of Terror

II. The coup d'etat of Napoleon Bonaparte

III. The execution of Louis XVI

IV. The transformation of the Estates-General into the National Assembly

V. The destruction of the Bastille

(A) V, IV, III, I, II

(B) V, IV, III, II, I

(C) IV, V, III, I, II

(D) IV, III, V, I, II

(E) IV, V, III, II, I

3. The culture of the Byzantine Empire was based chiefly upon the civilization of

(A) Rome

(B) Greece

(C) India

(D) China

(E) Russia

4. The term "enlightened despotism" has been used by some historians to refer to

(A) a stage of absolutism in which rulers took a deliberate interest in the civil rights and welfare of their citizens

(B) a period of history during which many monarchs abdicated their thrones in favor of republican governments

(C) the tendency of monarchs to pursue their own self-interests to the detriment of their subjects

(D) the theory that power corrupts and that absolute power corrupts absolutely

(E) an attempt by some monarchs to have themselves established as objects of divine worship

5. The religion that has influenced the greatest number of people in East Asia is

(A) Buddhism

(B) Christianity

(C) Hinduism

(D) Islam

(E) Transcendentalism

6. All of the following are tenets of the socialism espoused by Karl Marx EXCEPT

(A) governments must forever remain strong in order to protect workers from exploitation

(B) the course of history is ultimately determined by underlying economic conditions

(C) capitalists exploit workers by retaining the surplus value of goods produced

(D) historical change is the result of a struggle between social classes

(E) the proletariat will eventually overthrow the bourgeoisie

GO ON TO THE NEXT PAGE

7. An underdeveloped region that is under the formal control and government of an imperialist country is referred to as a

(A) concession
(B) sphere of influence
(C) protectorate
(D) colony
(E) satellite

8. By what authority does one monk presume to stand against the common faith of the entire Church and the opinion of all Christendom? He insists that the Word of God revealed in the Bible is alone authoritative. He argues that no Church Father, not even the pope, has the right to teach something that cannot be demonstrated from Scripture. And he even posted his criticisms of indulgences on the very door of the church at Wittenberg.

The speaker above is most likely referring to

(A) St. Augustine
(B) Pope Gregory I
(C) Martin Luther
(D) John Calvin
(E) John Knox

9. The Baroque architecture of the seventeenth century was characterized by

(A) lavish decoration
(B) minarets
(C) simple lines
(D) cantilevers
(E) flying butresses

10. All of the following factors help to explain why the Industrial Revolution began in Great Britain EXCEPT

(A) large landowners were successful in enclosing land that was formerly available to small farmers
(B) England had no strong tradition of exploration and colonization of sparsely inhabited lands
(C) many people displaced from farms sought employment in newly created manufacturing centers
(D) a long-established fleet of merchant vessels ensured ready access to needed raw materials
(E) capital was available for investment in the development of machinery and construction of factories

GO ON TO THE NEXT PAGE

The Americas after the Treaty of Paris (1763)

Question 11 refers to the following map.

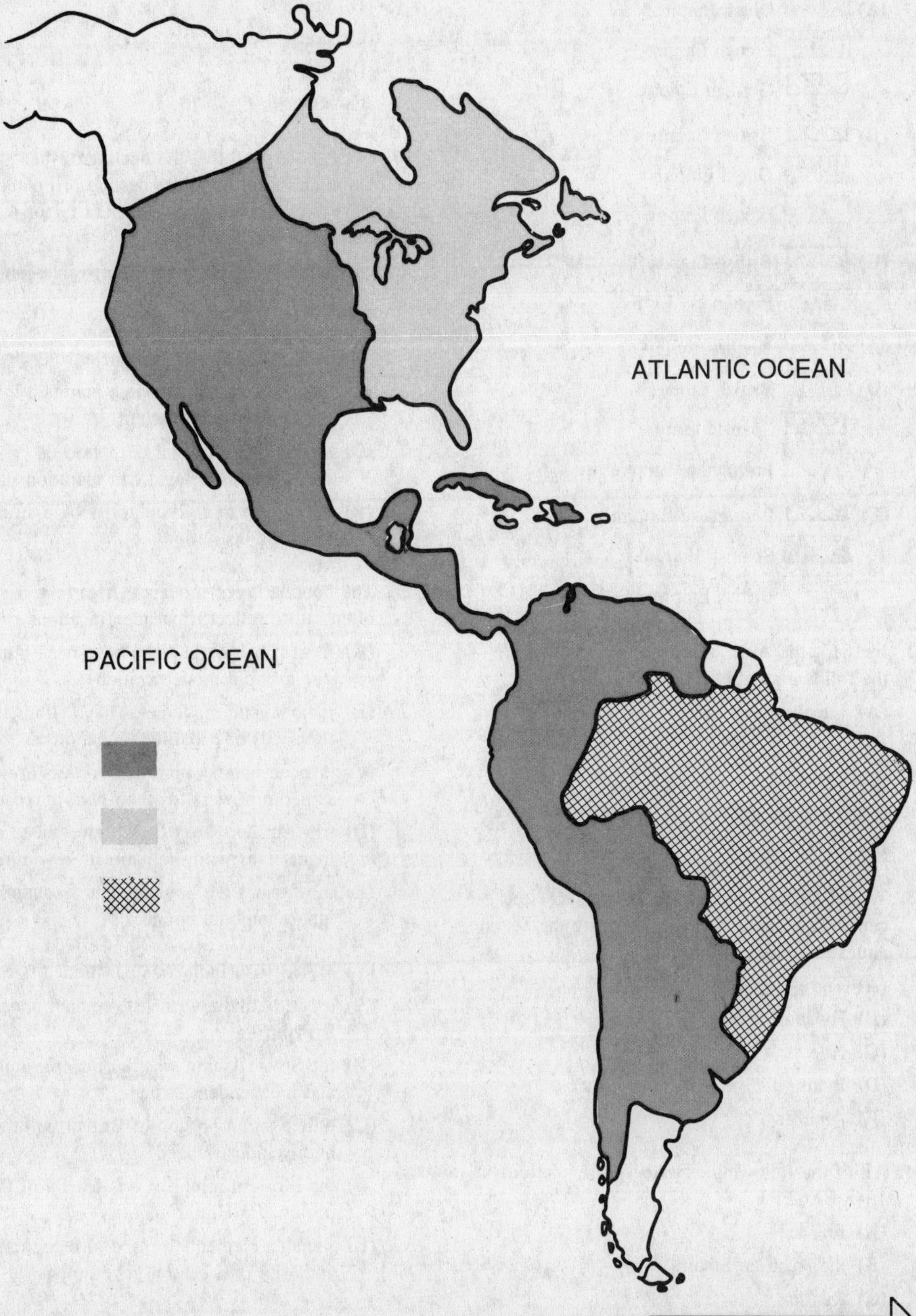

GO ON TO THE NEXT PAGE

11. Which of the following is a correct interpretation of the key to the map on page 207?

(A) 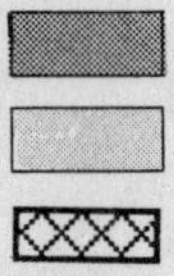
Dutch Empire
French Empire
German Empire

(B) 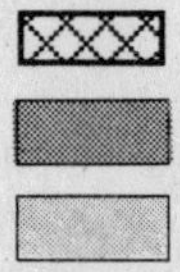
British Empire
Dutch Empire
French Empire

(C) 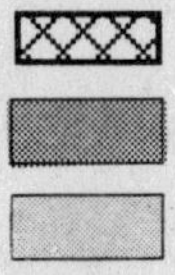
British Empire
Portuguese Empire
Spanish Empire

(D) 
British Empire
Spanish Empire
Portuguese Empire

(E) 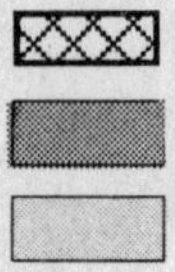
Portuguese Empire
Spanish Empire
British Empire

12. In 1815, the Austrian Empire included all of the following nationalities EXCEPT

(A) Czechs
(B) Slovaks
(C) Germans
(D) Yugoslavs
(E) Greeks

13. Which of the following rivers was NOT the center of a major civilization during the Second and Third Millenia B.C.

(A) Tigris-Euphrates
(B) Hwang (Yellow)
(C) Nile
(D) Indus
(E) Amazon

14. All of the following experienced revolutions in 1848 EXCEPT

(A) France
(B) the Austrian Empire
(C) Russia
(D) Italy
(E) Germany

15. The Phoencians made their most lasting mark on civilization as

(A) builders
(B) farmers
(C) priests
(D) traders
(E) scholars

16. It can be argued that the decline of the Ottoman Empire and the decline of Poland were similar in that an important factor in both cases was the

(A) superimposition of western values on a conservative population
(B) increasing independence and insubordination of provincial rulers
(C) weakness of the monarch hemmed in by constitutional limitation
(D) strength of a central despotic rule unhampered by legal considerations
(E) opposition to civil authority by a strong religious institution

17. The boundaries of modern African nations often fail to reflect tribal identifications because

(A) most tribal distinctions have been blurred due to rapid modernization
(B) nationalistic movements have eliminated the need for tribal identification
(C) African nations inherited borders drawn by imperial powers for their own purposes
(D) tribal leaders are usually reluctant to ally themselves with the national government
(E) most tribes are nomadic and frequently ignore national boundaries

18. In 1947, British India was partitioned because

(A) a part of India wished to remain under British rule
(B) the Soviet Union was fearful of a united and independent India
(C) only a small portion of British India was highly industrialized
(D) the Moslem minority was fearful of the power of a Hindu majority
(E) socialist elements refused to recognize the authority of a central government

GO ON TO THE NEXT PAGE

19. Which of the following statements about the constitution established by Japan during the Meiji restoration is NOT correct?

(A) It was established in response to a popular uprising against the Emperor's power.

(B) It was modeled on the constitutions of western nations.

(C) It was part of the Emperor's plan to modernize Japanese society.

(D) It provides for executive, legislative, and judicial branches of government.

(E) It continues the principle of imperial government developed over 2,500 years.

20. The main effect of the French Revolution (1789) on Great Britain was to

(A) inspire an unsuccessful revolution

(B) generate support for radical reforms

(C) create a backlash against change

(D) prompt the King to dissolve Parliament

(E) encourage reform of the Anglican church

21. The Open Door Note of 1899, sent by the United States to England, France, Germany, Russia, and Japan, asked those world powers to

(A) send troops to help the United States put down the Boxer Rebellion

(B) permit the United States to annex the Philippine Islands

(C) allow the United States and each other equal trading rights in China

(D) work together to find a way to end the Russo-Japanese War

(E) form an alliance to block Chinese military expansionism

22. Which of the following modern nations does NOT include territory that was once part of the Moslem empire?

(A) England

(B) France

(C) Spain

(D) Egypt

(E) India

23. Which of the following contributed significantly to the spread of humanism?

(A) The voyages of Columbus

(B) The invention of printing

(C) Trade with China

(D) The unification of Italy

(E) The Crusades

24. If a historian believes that the events of the Russian Revolution paralleled the events of the French Revolution, then she would probably equate Stalin with

(A) Louis XVI

(B) Marat

(C) Robespierre

(D) Danton

(E) Napoleon

25. During the Berlin Blockade, the Soviet Union attempted to drive western Allies out of West Berlin by blocking access to the city by which of the following methods?

I. Land

II. Air

III. Water

(A) I only

(B) II only

(C) I and III only

(D) II and III only

(E) I, II, and III

26. Which of the following helps to explain why ancient Greece was organized into city-states?

(A) Previous experience with tyrannical emperors

(B) Reluctance to venture outside of a certain locale

(C) Geographical features that isolated regions

(D) Inability to devise effective governments

(E) Lack of a common language

GO ON TO THE NEXT PAGE

27. Robert Owen, Claude Saint-Simon, and Charles Fourier all advocated

(A) overthrow of governments by violent revolution

(B) conquest of foreign territories for financial gain

(C) strict laissez-faire economic policies

(D) cooperative production and distribution of goods

(E) reinstatement of feudal rights and privileges

28. England's Glorious Revolution (1688) helped to establish the

(A) divine right of the English king to rule

(B) Parliament's supremacy over the king

(C) authority of the Roman Catholic Church in England

(D) right of the king to tax feudal lords

(E) principle of a balance of power

29. We returned to the hall to find it closed. Everyone agreed that the Assembly should adjourn to another location. There we all swore not to disband until we had drawn up a constitution limiting the powers of the monarchy.

The location referred to in the statement above was a

(A) cafe

(B) church

(C) tennis court

(D) train station

(E) ship

30. The Good Neighbor Policy of the United States included which of the following?

I. Economic cooperation with Latin American countries

II. A promise not to intervene in the internal affairs of Latin American countries

III. A military alliance to defend Latin America against foreign invasion

(A) I only

(B) II only

(C) I and II only

(D) I and III only

(E) II and III only

31. Which of the following terms associated with western European feudalism is correctly associated with its equivalent term in Japanese feudalism?

I. Chivalry : Bushido

II. Mikado : King

III. Samurai : Knight

(A) I only

(B) III only

(C) I and II only

(D) I and III only

(E) I, II, and III

32. Which of the following helps explain why the Renaissance began in Italy?

I. Italy had been a center of Greco-Roman culture

II. Moslem and Byzantine ideas had reached Italy

III. Wealthy Italian patrons supported the arts

(A) I only

(B) III only

(C) I and III only

(D) II and III only

(E) I, II, and III

33. After 1451, the center of economic power in Europe gradually shifted from

(A) northern Italy to Spain and Portugal to eastern Europe

(B) northern Italy to Spain and Portugal to England and the low countries

(C) northern Italy to England and the low countries to Spain and Portugal

(D) Spain and Portugal to England and the low countries to northern Italy

(E) Spain and Portugal to northern Italy to England and the low countries

GO ON TO THE NEXT PAGE

34. Which of the following statements about Napoleon's Continental System is LEAST accurate?

(A) It was very difficult to administer.

(B) France's allies were forbidden to trade with England.

(C) It eventually led to a war with Portugal.

(D) The United States suspended trading with foreign nations.

(E) England suffered tremendous economic hardship.

Question 35 refers to the following drawing.

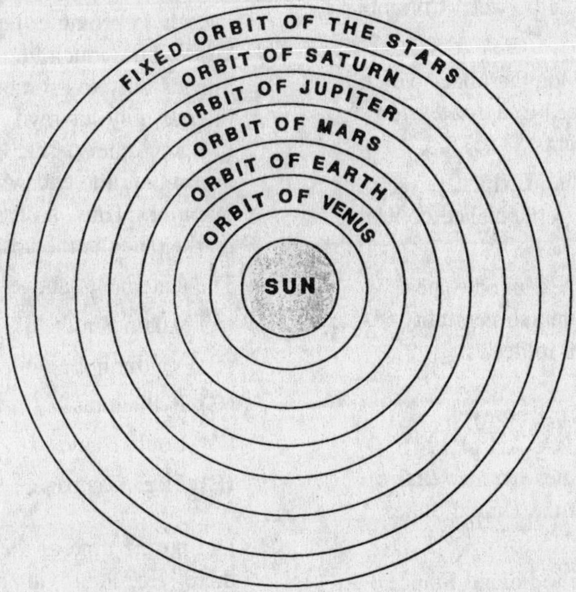

35. The drawing above depicts a model of the universe developed by

(A) Plato

(B) Aristotle

(C) Ptolemy

(D) Copernicus

(E) Einstein

36. Of the following, which country exerted the LEAST influence at the Congress of Vienna (1814–1815)?

(A) Austria

(B) England

(C) France

(D) Prussia

(E) United States

37. All of the following are true of the Romantic movement (1800–1830) EXCEPT

(A) it was a reaction against the Classical movement of the eighteenth century

(B) it emphasized sponteneity and irregularity

(C) it drew inspiration from nature

(D) it appealed to people's emotions and feelings

(E) it was distinctly antireligious

38. Which of the following were used by the Church during the Middle Ages against civil rulers?

I. Indulgences

II. Excommunication

III. Interdict

(A) II only

(B) III only

(C) I and III only

(D) II and III only

(E) I, II, and III

GO ON TO THE NEXT PAGE

39. Which of the following had a great influence on the writings of Thomas Aquinas?

(A) Alexander

(B) Aristotle

(C) Confucius

(D) Mohammed

(E) Zoroaster

40. The United States acquired the land to build the Panama Canal by virtue of

(A) a Panamanian revolt against Colombia that was supported by the United States Navy

(B) United States military intervention to resolve a border dispute between Colombia and Panama

(C) an agreement with Colombia under which the United States agreed to a concession fee plus annual payments

(D) a treaty with Nicaragua in which Nicaragua voluntarily relinquished control of the canal zone

(E) an alliance whereby the United States agreed to ensure Colombian neutrality in exchange for the canal route

41. When President Franklin D. Roosevelt explained that the Lend-Lease Act of 1941 would make the United States the ''arsenal of democracy'' he meant that the United States would

(A) send troops to Europe to defend France against the *Blitzkrieg*

(B) provide armaments to Great Britain but stay out of the war

(C) allow American pilots to fly British war planes

(D) maintain a strict isolationist posture regarding Europe

(E) commit troops to the war only if Japan attacked Pearl Harbor

42. The government of Great Britain differs from that of the United States in all of the following ways EXCEPT

(A) Great Britain does not have a written constitution

(B) Great Britain has a hereditary monarchy

(C) Great Britain's legislature has but one house

(D) Great Britain's true chief executive is not directly elected

(E) the terms of Great Britain's legislators are indeterminate

43. A person who is engaged in business neither intends to promote the public interest nor knows how much he is promoting it. He intends only to promote his own security, intends only his own gain, and he is in this, as in many other cases, led by an invisible hand to promote the end which was no part of his intention. Thus, a laissez-faire approach to the marketplace is the best approach.

The statements above represent the views of

(A) Adam Smith

(B) Vladimir Lenin

(C) Pythagoras

(D) Louis Blanc

(E) Fidel Castro

44. During the time of the Holy Roman Empire, there were approximately how many German states?

(A) 3

(B) 15

(C) 40

(D) 100

(E) 300

45. All of the following statements about Northern Ireland (Ulster) are true EXCEPT

(A) it is no longer a part of Great Britain

(B) it is heavily industrialized

(C) the majority of its population is descended from English and Scottish settlers

(D) a significant minority of its population is Roman Catholic

(E) the majority of its population is Protestant

GO ON TO THE NEXT PAGE

46. When God created the world, he incorporated into the universe the laws of nature. He set the world in motion and He insures that the universe continues to operate according to these laws, but He does not interfere in human affairs. Prayers, therefore, are useless. God does not do miracles.

The ideas expressed in the statements above are characteristic of

(A) an atheist
(B) an agnostic
(C) a deist
(D) a polytheist
(E) a pagan

47. The style of the column capital shown above is

(A) Byzantine
(B) Corinthian
(C) Doric
(D) Ionic
(E) Romanesque

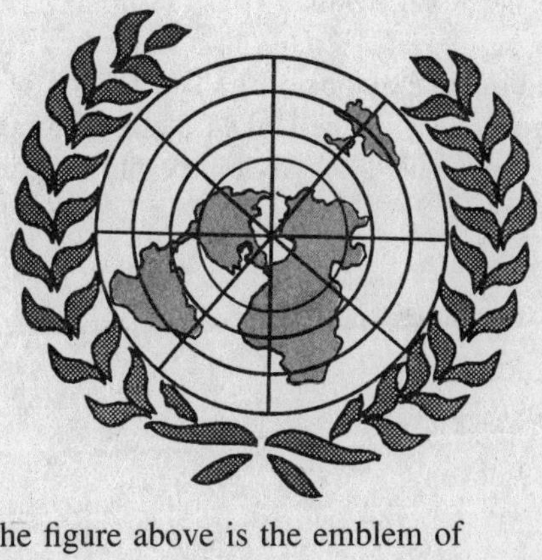

48. The figure above is the emblem of

(A) the Soviet Union
(B) the United Nations
(C) NATO
(D) the British Commonwealth
(E) the European Economic Community

49. All of the following demands of the Chartist movement eventually became law in Great Britain EXCEPT

(A) universal manhood suffrage
(B) annual elections for Parliament
(C) secret ballot
(D) compensation for members of Parliament
(E) equal electoral districts

50. The statement "The sun never sets on the British Empire" was

(A) a boast about the extent of British overseas possessions
(B) an apology for Great Britain's role during the War of 1812
(C) a criticism of Great Britain for its imperialistic policies
(D) an epitaph for the decline of the British Empire
(E) a prediction that Great Britain would one day rule the entire world

51. The immediate cause of the collapse of France's Fourth Republic was

(A) rapid devaluation of the franc
(B) threatened invasion by Germany
(C) governmental corruption
(D) rebellion in Algeria
(E) widespread labor unrest

52. The Crusades of the twelfth and thirteenth centuries had all of the following effects EXCEPT

(A) encouraging trade
(B) stimulating the growth of towns
(C) strengthening central governments
(D) undermining power of the nobles
(E) reinforcing the system of serfdom

53. At the outbreak of World War II, which of the following nations was a member of the League of Nations?

(A) Great Britain
(B) Germany
(C) Japan
(D) United States
(E) Italy

GO ON TO THE NEXT PAGE

54. Which of the following assertions would be the most difficult for a historian to prove?

(A) The development of air travel has changed the way that people view the world.

(B) The annual flooding of the Nile River was an important factor in the development of ancient Egyptian civilization.

(C) Vladimir Lenin suffered the first of a series of strokes in 1922 and died in 1924.

(D) Belgium gained its independence as a result of a revolution in 1830.

(E) Ancient Greece contributed more to the development of Western civilization than did ancient Rome.

55. Mercantilism advocated which of the following?

I. The value of a nation's exports should exceed the value of its imports

II. A nation should export large quantities of precious metals

III. A nation should impose tariffs on imported goods

(A) I only

(B) II only

(C) I and III only

(D) II and III only

(E) I, II, and III

56. In the early twentieth century all of the following had possessions in Africa EXCEPT

(A) Belgium

(B) France

(C) Portugal

(D) Germany

(E) Russia

57. All of the following are characteristics of Gothic architecture EXCEPT

(A) pointed arches

(B) tall spires

(C) gargoyles

(D) many stained glass windows

(E) thick, heavy walls

58. The Quadruple Alliance included all of the following EXCEPT

(A) Austria

(B) Prussia

(C) Spain

(D) Russia

(E) Britain

59. Rudyard Kipling's poem "The White Man's Burden" was primarily

(A) an apology for imperialism

(B) a condemnation of racism

(C) a justification for isolationism

(D) a warning against interventionism

(E) a cry against the rising tide of nationalism

60. The occasion has been judged proper for asserting that the American continents, by the free and independent condition which they have assumed and maintained, are henceforth not to be considered as subjects for future colonization by any European powers.

The statement above articulated what became known as

(A) Seward's Folly

(B) the American System

(C) the Monroe Doctrine

(D) the Policy of Laissez-faire

(E) the XYZ Affair

61. The principal author of the Declaration of Independence of the United States, Thomas Jefferson, relied heavily on the philosophical writings of

(A) Socrates

(B) Descartes

(C) Rousseau

(D) Machiavelli

(E) Locke

GO ON TO THE NEXT PAGE

62. Which of the following was an important factor in the decision of the United States to enter World War I?

(A) A threatened German invasion of Mexico
(B) German submarine attacks on ships in the Atlantic Ocean
(C) The assassination of the heir to the Austro-Hungarian throne
(D) A Japanese naval blockade of ports on the West Coast of the United States
(E) Formation of a German-Japanese alliance directed against the United States

63. A person who had lived his entire life in a feudal society would likely have difficulty understanding which of the following concepts?

(A) Aggression
(B) Loyalty
(C) Nationalism
(D) Marriage
(E) Monasticism

64. A corporation, operating under a government charter, enjoys which of the following advantages over a business operated by a single person?

I. Increased ability to raise capital
II. Limited liability of shareholders
III. Ability to survive the death of individual members

(A) I only
(B) III only
(C) I and II only
(D) II and III only
(E) I, II, and III

65. The first artificial satellite to orbit the earth was launched by

(A) Great Britain
(B) France
(C) Italy
(D) the Soviet Union
(E) the United States

66. Great Britain and France intervened militarily in Egypt in 1956 in response to

(A) Egypt's invasion of Libya
(B) Egypt's nationalization of the Suez Canal
(C) the discovery of oil in Egypt
(D) a coup d'etat by Egypt's military leaders
(E) civil war inspired by religious differences

67. In 1914, one U.S. dollar was equivalent to 4.2 German marks. At the beginning of 1923, one U.S. dollar bought 1,800 marks. By the fall of 1923, one U.S. dollar had the same buying power as 4.2 trillion marks.

The economic phenomenon described above is

(A) depression
(B) recession
(C) boom
(D) creeping inflation
(E) runaway inflation

68. Napoleon never invaded England because

(A) Great Britain was allied with France
(B) the British fleet controlled the English Channel
(C) the French did not support his wars of conquest
(D) the French army was understaffed
(E) England offered little of value to a conqueror

GO ON TO THE NEXT PAGE

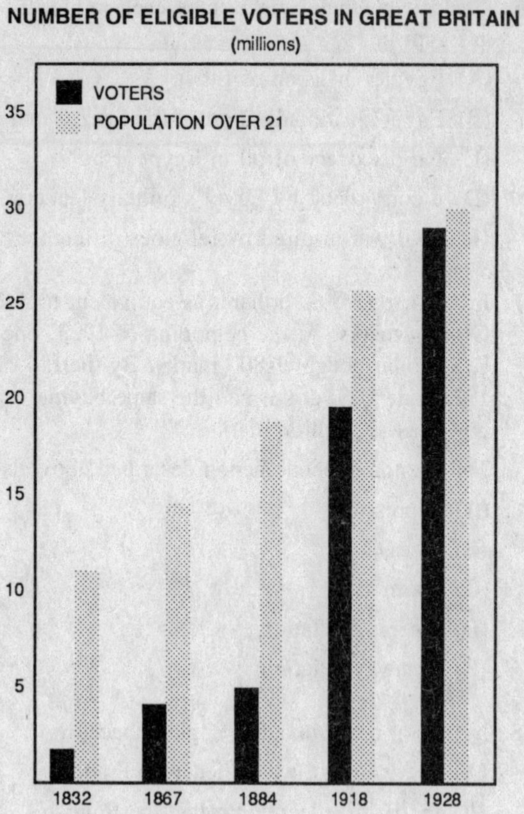

69. Which of the following best explains the trend shown in the chart above?

(A) Acquisition of foreign territories
(B) Increases in population
(C) Lengthening of average life span
(D) Series of election reform bills
(E) Immigration into Great Britain

70. Great Britain did not join the European Economic Community (Common Market) until 1971 because

(A) French President de Gaulle vetoed Britain's applications
(B) Australia and New Zealand feared a loss of trade
(C) British leaders felt the EEC would not survive very long
(D) some members of the EEC were allied with the Soviet Union
(E) British industry refused to export goods to the continent

71. The philosophical movement with which the French philosopher Jean-Paul Sartre was associated is

(A) stoicism
(B) existentialism
(C) idealism
(D) scholasticism
(E) rationalism

72. The artists Claude Monet, Edgar Degas, and Auguste Renoir belonged to a school of painting called

(A) realism
(B) naturalism
(C) impressionism
(D) dadaism
(E) surrealism

73. The requirement that the eldest male child receive his father's title and possessions is called

(A) primogeniture
(B) *droit de seigneur*
(C) *noblesse oblige*
(D) defeasance
(E) subinfeudation

GO ON TO THE NEXT PAGE

74. Between 1880 and 1900 the number of newspapers in northwestern Europe doubled from 6,000 to 12,000. By 1900, several newspapers had daily circulations of more than a million copies, compared with 50,000 for the largest selling newspaper during the 1860s.

The increase in newspaper sales described above resulted from

(A) the invention of movable type

(B) the discovery of electricity

(C) improved sanitation

(D) increased rates of literacy

(E) the invention of the telegraph

75. A student of demographics would be most interested in which of the following?

(A) The Irish potato famine of the 1840s

(B) The sinking of the *Lusitania*

(C) The crowning of Napoleon Bonaparte as emperor

(D) The wording of the Magna Carta

(E) The date of birth of the present British monarch

Questions 76–78 refer to the following:

(A) Poland

(B) England

(C) Spain

(D) Italy

(E) France

76. While the United States was engaged in its Civil War, which country used its army to establish Archduke Maximilian as emperor of Mexico?

77. Which country disappeared from the map of Europe in 1795?

78. Which country was finally unified during the second half of the nineteenth century?

79. Society provides an arena for competition in which the most industrious, ingenious, and intelligent people are the most successful. By a process akin to natural selection, civilization necessarily advances to higher and more complex forms.

The position outlined by the statements above is often referred to as

(A) mercantilism

(B) protectionism

(C) imperialism

(D) Social Darwinism

(E) Marxism

80. When the United States established formal diplomatic relations with the People's Republic of China in 1979 it also withdrew diplomatic recognition from the government of

(A) Cambodia

(B) Okinawa

(C) Sri Lanka

(D) Sumatra

(E) Taiwan

81. The Marshall Plan was adopted in large measure because the United States

(A) wanted to see Germany punished for its aggression during World War II

(B) hoped that Europe could be unified under a single central government

(C) was unsure of the motives of the Soviet Union in Berlin

(D) feared that unstable European countries would succumb to communism

(E) incorrectly believed that the Soviet Union lacked any expansionist plans

82. Which of the following was used by President Lyndon Johnson in 1964 to step up United States military activities in Vietnam?

(A) the Gulf of Tonkin Resolution

(B) the Platt Amendment

(C) the SEATO Treaty

(D) the Wilmot Proviso

(E) the Zimmerman Note

GO ON TO THE NEXT PAGE

83. A historian who wished to do an analysis of African-Americans who were held in slavery would find which of the following most useful?

(A) Tools, dishes, and other articles excavated from a waste pit on a southern plantation

(B) Treatises written by white authors defending the existence of the slave system

(C) Autobiographies written by African-Americans who were actually held in slavery

(D) Plantation records detailing the economic transactions of the owner

(E) Pamphlets written by abolitionists residing in the northern states

84. The earliest people to reach North America are thought to have arrived from

(A) Siberia via the Bering Strait land bridge

(B) South America via the Central American isthmus

(C) Hawaii via rafts

(D) Scandinavia via boats

(E) Germania via a polar route

85. As applied to Southeast Asia, the ''domino'' theory held that

(A) a communist takeover of South Vietnam would lead to similar takeovers in other countries in the region

(B) escalating numbers of United States troops would guarantee a military victory in Vietnam

(C) it is impossible to win a guerilla war using conventional military strategies

(D) only by breaking an enemy's supply lines is it possible to gain victory

(E) a united, communistic but nationalist Vietnam would not be imperialistic

86. A political reactionary would be most likely to favor which of the following?

(A) Higher welfare payments

(B) Higher tax rates

(C) Stricter government regulations on business

(D) National health insurance

(E) Strong military

87. On April 11, 1951, President Harry S. Truman removed General Douglas MacArthur as commander in chief of United Nations forces in Korea because

(A) MacArthur was a weak and ineffective military leader

(B) MacArthur was critical of Truman's foreign policy

(C) the United Nations asked for MacArthur's removal

(D) South Korea no longer needed United States military assistance

(E) MacArthur was unpopular with the United States public

GO ON TO THE NEXT PAGE

Questions 88–91 refer to the following map:

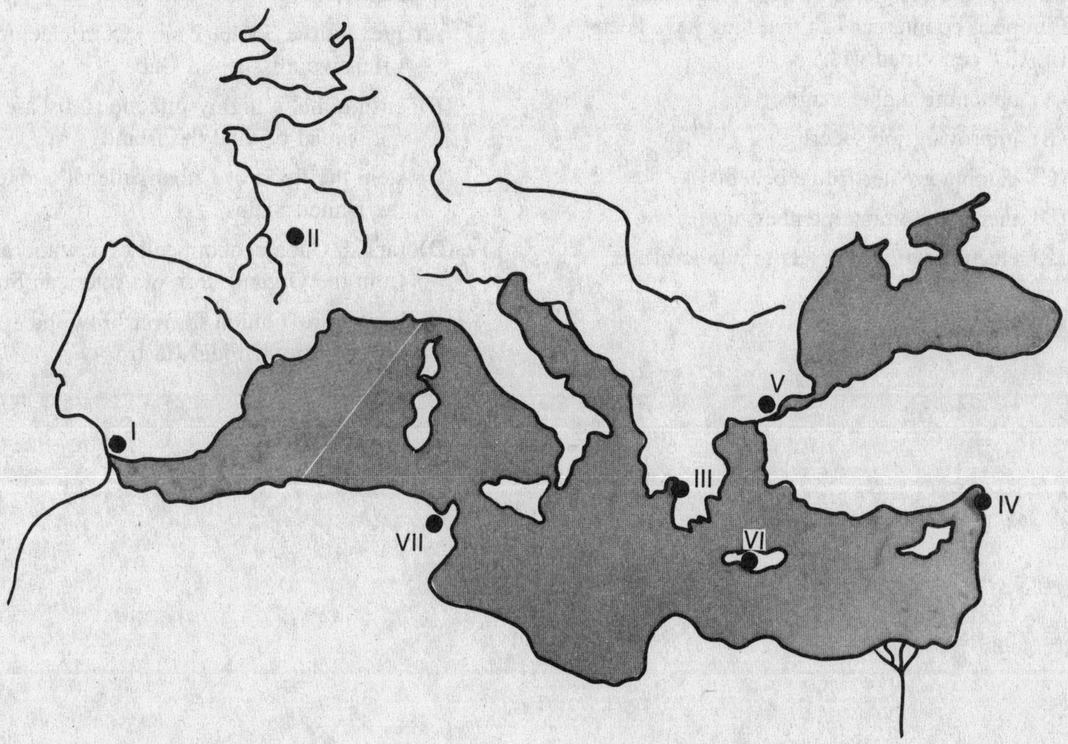

88. The site of the Minoan Civilization (3000–1400 B.C.) was

(A) I
(B) III
(C) V
(D) VI
(E) VII

89. The city whose general attacked Roman forces in Italy during the Second Punic War by leading his army across the Alps was

(A) II
(B) III
(C) IV
(D) V
(E) VIII

90. The capital of the eastern part of the later Roman Empire was

(A) I
(B) II
(C) IV
(D) V
(E) VI

91. The city-state that developed democratic institutions was

(A) II
(B) III
(C) IV
(D) V
(E) VII

Questions 92 and 93 refer to the following:

(A) Hitler
(B) Bismarck
(C) Kaiser William II
(D) Metternich
(E) Hindenburg

92. Dominated the Congress of Vienna

93. Accomplished the unification of Germany

GO ON TO THE NEXT PAGE

94. During the twentieth century, labor unions in the United States have differed from their European counterparts in that they have been LEAST concerned with

(A) obtaining higher wages
(B) improving job security
(C) gaining greater fringe benefits
(D) increasing union membership
(E) electing union officials to public office

95. In 1962, President John F. Kennedy declared a naval quarantine of Cuba in order to

(A) prevent the Soviet Union from placing offensive missiles in Cuba
(B) ensure that a highly infectious disease did not spread beyond the island
(C) stem the flood of Cubans illegally entering the United States
(D) punish Cuba economically for withdrawing from the Organization of American States
(E) incite a revolution to overthrow the government of Fidel Castro

S T O P

IF YOU FINISH BEFORE TIME IS CALLED, YOU MAY CHECK YOUR WORK ON THIS TEST ONLY. DO NOT WORK ON ANY OTHER TEST IN THIS BOOK.

Explanatory Answers

1. The influence of the classical Mediterranean civilizations (Greece and Rome) on modern western Europe is LEAST evident in

(A) political structures

(B) languages

(C) religion

(D) architecture

(E) philosophy

(C) Neither Greece nor Rome produced a lasting religion. Christianity originated in the Mediterranean region during the Roman Empire but was not a product of the Roman Empire. Although Greek and Roman culture influenced Christianity, Christianity did not become an important historical force until after the decline of the Roman Empire. You can easily see the classical influences in the other areas. The concept of democracy originated in Greece. French, Spanish, and Italian are called Romance languages, because they derive from Latin. Many public buildings are erected in the *classical* style. And the philosophical tradition of western Europe can be traced to Socrates.

2. Beginning with the earliest, what is the correct chronological order of the following events in the history of France?

I. The Reign of Terror

II. The coup d'etat of Napoleon Bonaparte

III. The execution of Louis XVI

IV. The transformation of the Estates-General into the National Assembly

V. The destruction of the Bastille

(A) V, IV, III, I, II

(B) V, IV, III, II, I

(C) IV, V, III, I, II

(D) IV, III, V, I, II

(E) IV, V, III, II, I

(C) The financial policies of Louis XVI helped to create one of the most important conditions leading to the French Revolution. The financial excesses of his predecessors left Louis XVI with an already impoverished treasury that the king's policies further depleted. France sent considerable aid to the American colonies to aid them in their fight against Great Britain, and Louis XVI maintained an extravagant court at Versailles. Despite these burdens, Louis XVI refused to tax those best able to pay, the privileged class.

By 1788, France was bankrupt. To address the financial crisis, Louis convened the French legislature, the Estates-General, thereby admitting that the power of the monarchy alone was not enough to solve the problem. The Estates-General was not exactly a democratic institution. The privileged classes were represented by the First and Second Estates, while the unprivileged were represented by the Third Estate. Each Estate, however, had one vote. Thus the privileged Estates were able to outvote the Third Estate.

Leaders of the Third Estate demanded that the voting procedure be changed so that each representative's vote would count. When the king rejected this demand, the representatives of the Third Estate declared themselves to be the National Assembly and in the famous "Tennis Court Oath" pledged themselves to create a new constitution.

On July 14, 1789, incited by rumors that the King had ordered troops to disperse the members of the National Assembly, mobs in Paris stormed and destroyed the Bastille, a prison. At first the National Assembly was controlled by moderates and adopted a number of reforms, and in 1791 it produced a constitution providing for a limited monarchy. The limited monarchy, however, was short-lived. Fearful that foreign powers would crush the revolution and reinstitute an absolute monarchy, radicals seized control of the government. The legislature deposed the king and called for the election of a National Convention to create a new constitution.

The National Convention declared France a republic, tried Louis XVI, and executed him on the guillotine. In the face of the military invasion, the radicals, or Jacobins, concentrated all governmental power in the Committee of Public Safety, initially under the control of Danton and later under Robespierre. The Committee of Public Safety instituted the Reign of Terror, during which many persons suspected of treason were arrested and guillotined on questionable evidence. Eventually, people turned against the radicals, and in 1794 both Danton and Robespierre were guillotined.

The French people had wearied of the upheaval of the revolution by 1799. In that year, Napoleon was able to overthrow the Directory.

3. The culture of the Byzantine Empire was based chiefly upon the civilization of

(A) Rome
(B) Greece
(C) India
(D) China
(E) Russia

(B) With the final division of the Roman Empire in 395 A.D., Constantinople became the capital of the eastern or Greek Empire and the chief center, for centuries, of Christian art and learning, especially of Greek culture as distinguished from Latin.

4. The term "enlightened despotism" has been used by some historians to refer to

(A) a stage of absolutism in which rulers took a deliberate interest in the civil rights and welfare of their citizens
(B) a period of history during which many monarchs abdicated their thrones in favor of republican governments
(C) the tendency of monarchs to pursue their own self-interests to the detriment of their subjects
(D) the theory that power corrupts and that absolute power corrupts absolutely
(E) an attempt by some monarchs to have themselves established as objects of divine worship

(A) The concept of a *philosopher king* originated in ancient Greece. This ideal leader should be virtuous and knowledgeable and should have the power to implement policies that reflect virtue and knowledge. During the eighteenth century, a group of leaders emerged who seemed to their contemporaries to embody this idea by uniting the power of monarchy with the intellectual tendencies of contemporary philosophy. Their monarchial powers made them *absolutes,* and their knowledge made them *enlightened.* The term is generally associated with King Frederick II ("the Great") of Prussia, the Hapsburg Emperor Joseph II, and Empress Catherine II ("the Great") of Russia.

5. The religion that has influenced the greatest number of people in East Asia is

(A) Buddhism
(B) Christianity
(C) Hinduism
(D) Islam
(E) Transcendentalism

(A) Buddhism, one of the great religions of Asia, derives its name from its founder, Gotama the Buddha.

6. All of the following are tenets of the socialism espoused by Karl Marx EXCEPT

(A) governments must forever remain strong in order to protect workers from exploitation
(B) the course of history is ultimately determined by underlying economic conditions
(C) capitalists exploit workers by retaining the surplus value of goods produced
(D) historical change is the result of a struggle between social classes
(E) the proletariat will eventually overthrow the bourgeoisie

(A) Karl Marx (1818–1883) was born in the Prussian Rhineland to middle-class parents and was educated in German universities. At the age of 23, he became an editor of a radical democratic newspaper. When the newspaper was suppressed by the authorities, Marx moved to Paris where he met Friedrich Engels (1820–1895), son of a wealthy German businessman who had an ownership interest in an English textile firm. In 1847, at Engels' request, Marx moved to England, and in 1848 the two published the *Communist Manifesto.* Later Marx published a critical analysis of mid-nineteenth century capitalism. These works contain the basic ideas of Marxism.

Marxism includes the ideas contained in choices (B) through (E). (A), however, is an idea rejected by Marxists. According to Marx, the workers, or proletariat, will eventually become so exploited that they will be conscious of their position and revolt. After overthrowing the government of the capitalists, the workers will set up a state of their own as the remnants of capitalism are dismantled. After private property and the wage and profit system have been removed, the class struggle will have ended and there will be no need for a state. Gradually, therefore, the state will wither away.

7. An underdeveloped region that is under the formal control and government of an imperialist country is referred to as a

(A) concession

(B) sphere of influence

(C) protectorate

(D) colony

(E) satellite

(D) When an imperialist nation exercises formal governing powers over an underdeveloped area, the underdeveloped area is referred to as a colony of the imperialist nation. The other forms of imperialism given as choices are less formal. A concession is granted by an underdeveloped country to a business interest for a specific economic privilege, for example, to build a railroad or to dig a mine. A sphere of influence is created when a powerful nation secures exclusive economic privileges in an underdeveloped region. In a protectorate, the native government nominally retains power but the imperialist nation has the real power. Finally, a satellite is a kind of protectorate that emerged in eastern Europe following World War II.

8. By what authority does one monk presume to stand against the common faith of the entire Church and the opinion of all Christendom? He insists that the Word of God revealed in the Bible is alone authoritative. He argues that no Church Father, not even the pope, has the right to teach something that cannot be demonstrated from Scripture. And he even posted his criticisms of indulgences on the very door of the church at Wittenberg.

The speaker above is most likely referring to

(A) St. Augustine

(B) Pope Gregory I

(C) Martin Luther

(D) John Calvin

(E) John Knox

(C) Martin Luther was born in 1483, the son of a prosperous mining entrepreneur of peasant stock. He was well-educated and became a monk and later a professor of theology. Even though a monk and a professor of Holy Scriptures, Luther was never spiritually satisfied. This dissatisfaction caused him to reexamine the beliefs that had been taught to him by the Roman Catholic Church. Luther's initial protest was against the Church practice of selling indulgences—the practice of selling forgiveness of sins. In 1517, he posted the 95 Theses against indulgences to the door of the Church of Wittenburg. Gradually, his criticism broadened into an all-out attack on the formal structure and authority of the Catholic Church.

9. The Baroque architecture of the seventeenth century was characterized by

(A) lavish decoration

(B) minarets

(C) simple lines

(D) cantilevers

(E) flying buttresses

(A) The baroque movement manifested itself in art, music, and architecture. Its defining characteristic is its lavishness, and Baroque architects incorporated considerable decoration into their plans. The term itself was coined by contemporary critics who considered the style to be in bad taste.

10. All of the following factors help to explain why the Industrial Revolution began in Great Britain EXCEPT

(A) large landowners were successful in enclosing land that was formerly available to small farmers

(B) England had no strong tradition of exploration and colonization of sparsely inhabited lands

(C) many people displaced from farms sought employment in newly created manufacturing centers

(D) a long-established fleet of merchant vessels ensured ready access to needed raw materials

(E) capital was available for investment in the development of machinery and construction of factories

(B) No single factor can explain why the Industrial Revolution began in Great Britain, but several different circumstances helped to create the conditions that fostered the rapid industrial development that marks Great Britain as the cradle of the Industrial Revolution. Innovations in farming and livestock management prompted large landholders to encourage legislation to enclose for their exclusive use lands that had formerly been open for common exploitation. As a result, large numbers of idle farmers migrated to the urban areas. Additionally, Great Britain had access to large supplies of raw materials and had available the surplus of capital to invest in the new undertakings. So the correct answer must be (B). In fact, you can arrive at that conclusion with a little common sense: Great Britain did have colonies at one time, for example, the United States.

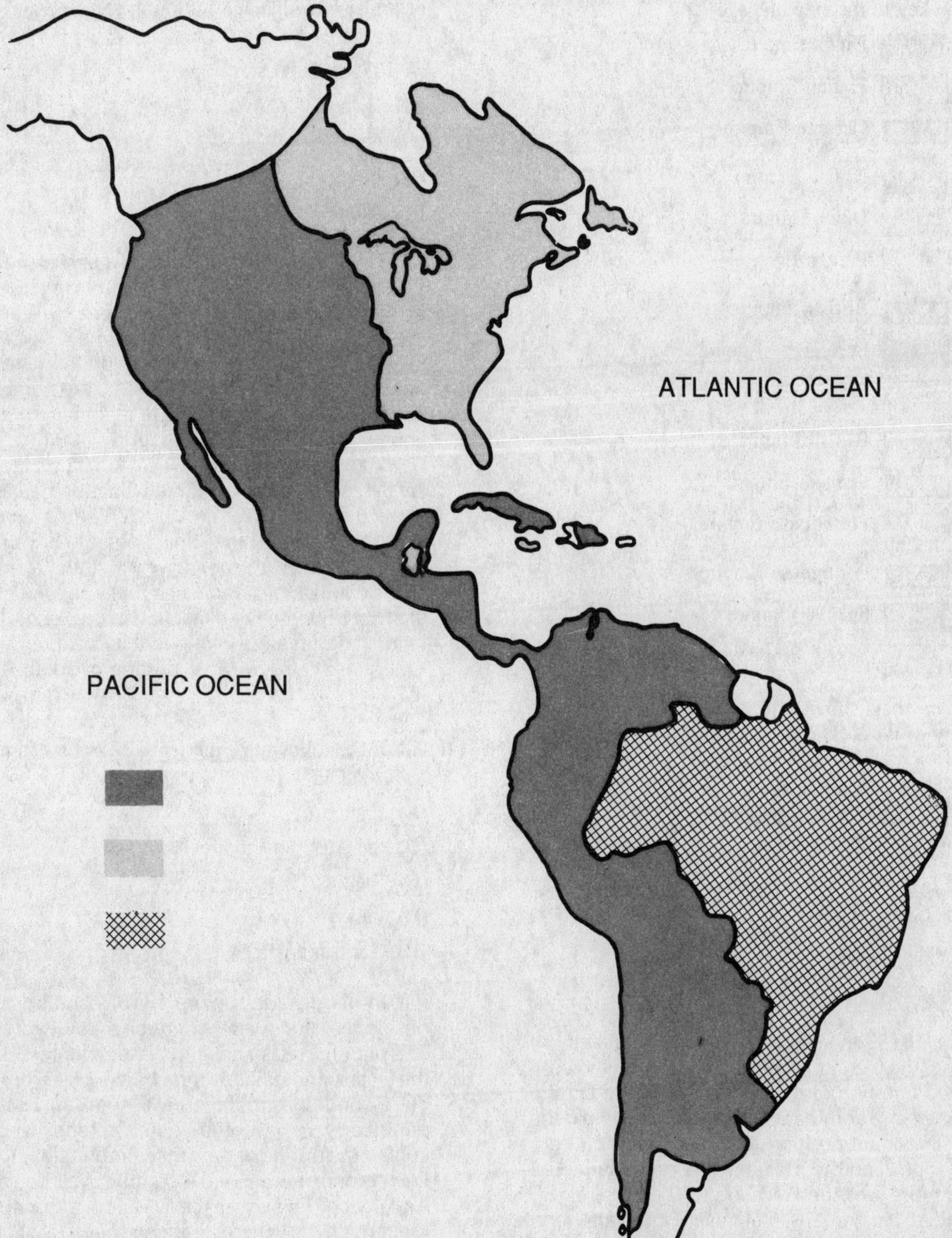
ATLANTIC OCEAN
PACIFIC OCEAN

11. Which of the following is a correct interpretation of the key to the map on page 225?

(A) Dutch Empire
French Empire
German Empire

(B) British Empire
Dutch Empire
French Empire

(C) British Empire
Portuguese Empire
Spanish Empire

(D) British Empire
Spanish Empire
Portuguese Empire

(E) Portuguese Empire
Spanish Empire
British Empire

(E) The map shows the Americas following the Treaty of Paris (1763).

12. In 1815, the Austrian Empire included all of the following nationalities EXCEPT

(A) Czechs

(B) Slovaks

(C) Germans

(D) Yugoslavs

(E) Greeks

(E) In 1815, the Austrian Empire included, of course, the German-speaking Austrians who constituted one-fifth of the population of the Empire and were the dominant nationality. They held the most important positions in government, church, education, and the military. The ruling family of the Empire was the Hapsburgs. The Empire also included Hungarians, Italians, Rumanians, and the Slavic-speaking peoples.

13. Which of the following rivers was NOT the center of a major civilization during the Second and Third Millennia B.C.?

(A) Tigris-Euphrates

(B) Hwang (Yellow)

(C) Nile

(D) Indus

(E) Amazon

(E) The first civilization arose in a part of the Middle East long known as Mesopotamia in the valley of the Tigris and Euphrates Rivers. As early as 4000 B.C., Mesopotamian farmers knew of bronze and copper and were using the wheel for transportation; and by 3500 B.C., the Sumerians had developed a cuneiform alphabet, the first known form of human writing. By 3000 B.C., the Egyptian civilization grew up along the Nile River. By 2500 B.C., an urban civilization had arisen along the Indus River, and by 2000 B.C., an organized state existed in China along the Hwang Ho or Yellow River. As for answer (E), the Mayan and Aztec civilizations flourished in the second half of the First Millennia and first half of the Second Millennia and, in any event, were located in Central America and the western portion of South America.

14. All of the following experienced revolutions in 1848 EXCEPT

(A) France

(B) the Austrian Empire

(C) Russia

(D) Italy

(E) Germany

(C) In the decades before 1848, conditions had developed that were conducive to revolution. The poor harvests and commercial depressions of the years immediately preceding 1848 brought these conditions to the critical point. In 1848, rioting Paris mobs forced Louis Philippe, who occupied the throne of the limited monarchy, to flee France and the Second Republic was declared. And, according to an observation attributed to Metternich, "When France sneezes, Europe catches cold." Before the end of the year, revolts had taken place in many other European countries. Only Russia was immune to the virus.

15. The Phoenicians made their most lasting mark on civilization as

(A) builders

(B) farmers

(C) priests

(D) traders

(E) scholars

(D) Phoenicia was a narrow strip of land, situated between the mountains and the Mediterranean Sea, about 200 miles long and not much more than 20 miles wide. Its chief cities were Tyre and Sydon. The Phoenicians (fl. 1250 B.C.) were highly skilled shipbuilders and navigators and became seafaring traders. As traders and merchants, they developed an alphabet for record keeping that replaced the cumbersome cuneiform alphabet.

16. It can be argued that the decline of the Ottoman Empire and the decline of Poland were similar in that an important factor in both cases was the

(A) superimposition of western values on a conservative population

(B) increasing independence and insubordination of provincial rulers

(C) weakness of the monarch hemmed in by constitutional limitation

(D) strength of a central despotic rule unhampered by legal considerations

(E) opposition to civil authority by a strong religious institution

(B) On one level, the conditions that lead to the decline of the Ottoman empire (1922) and those that lead to the decline of Poland at the end of the eighteenth century were different. The Sultan was a powerful despot who commanded service from the nobles. Thus, the central authority of the government could only be maintained by powerful leadership. With the decline in leadership, provincial leaders became stronger. A similar process took place in Poland. The Polish king, limited by a constitution, lacked the unfettered authority of a Sultan and was therefore unable to exert a strong control of the great nobles who controlled various parts of the kingdom.

17. The boundaries of modern African nations often fail to reflect tribal identifications because

(A) most tribal distinctions have been blurred due to rapid modernization

(B) nationalistic movements have eliminated the need for tribal identification

(C) African nations inherited borders drawn by imperial powers for their own purposes

(D) tribal leaders are usually reluctant to ally themselves with the national government

(E) most tribes are nomadic and frequently ignore national boundaries

(C) The boundaries of modern African nations tend to reflect the colonial boundaries drawn during the era of European imperialism. As a result, a tribe may be divided by a national boundary, and many tribes, some with traditions of rivalry, may be included within the same boundaries.

18. In 1947, British India was partitioned because

(A) a part of India wished to remain under British rule

(B) the Soviet Union was fearful of a united and independent India

(C) only a small portion of British India was highly industrialized

(D) the Moslem minority was fearful of the power of a Hindu majority

(E) socialist elements refused to recognize the authority of a central government

(D) In 1930, a crisis occurred in India. The British government's refusal to make a firm commitment to independence triggered a new round of protest and civil disobedience, led by Gandhi. The British government realized that some sort of accommodation was necessary and agreed to a round-table discussion with the pro-independence Congress party. The conference produced a dramatic split between Hindus and Moslems. The Moslems, fearful of a Hindu majority, demanded a separate electorate. When independence finally came in 1947, British India was partitioned into India (chiefly Hindu) and Pakistan (predominantly Moslem).

19. Which of the following statements about the constitution established by Japan during the Meiji restoration is NOT correct?

(A) It was established in response to a popular uprising against the Emperor's power.

(B) It was modeled on the constitutions of western nations.

(C) It was part of the Emperor's plan to modernize Japanese society.

(D) It provides for executive, legislative, and judicial branches of government.

(E) It continues the principle of imperial government developed over 2,500 years.

(A) In the middle of the seventeenth century, feudal Japan embarked on a 200-year period of isolationism. In the middle of the nineteenth century, Commodore Matthew Perry, leading an American naval squadron, persuaded Japan to open its ports to trade. Soon afterward, European countries obtained similar rights. These contacts with the West created internal dissension that ultimately resulted in the overthrow of the Tokugawa Shogunate and the transfer of governmental power back to the Emperor. This became known as the Meiji restoration. In 1868, the Emperor proclaimed an imperial oath that included the promise to "seek knowledge and wisdom in an outside world and establish the national assembly where the important affairs of state shall be established by public opinion." In 1890, the Emperor established a constitution modeled along those of western nations. Thus, unlike the constitutional governments of most western nations, the Japanese constitution represents an extension of existing authority rather than an attempt to curtail that authority.

20. The main effect of the French Revolution (1789) on Great Britain was to

(A) inspire an unsuccessful revolution

(B) generate support for radical reforms

(C) create a backlash against change

(D) prompt the king to dissolve Parliament

(E) encourage reform of the Anglican church

(C) In Britain, the initial reaction to the French Revolution was mixed. Groups of lower-middle class and working class people formed clubs based on the principles of the French Revolution. Others, however, were alarmed. Following the abolition of the French monarchy, the British passed legislation making it treason to speak or write against the government. Thus, in Great Britain, conservatism and reaction were strengthened for a while.

21. The Open Door Note of 1899, sent by the United States to England, France, Germany, Russia, and Japan, asked those world powers to

(A) send troops to help the United States put down the Boxer Rebellion

(B) permit the United States to annex the Philippine Islands

(C) allow the United States and each other equal trading rights in China

(D) work together to find a way to end the Russo-Japanese War

(E) form an alliance to block Chinese military expansionism

(C) By the Treaty of Paris (1898), which followed the end of the Spanish-American War, the United States acquired the Philippine Islands from Spain for 20 million dollars. United States businessmen hoped that acquisition of the Philippines would give the United States a strategic and economic base in the Far East. Expansionists worried, however, that this aim might be defeated by Japan and certain European nations which enjoyed spheres of influence in China. In an effort to ensure that the United States would have access to China, John Hay, President McKinley's secretary of state, sent a circular note to several world powers asking that each nation pledge itself to a principle of commercial equality. This note became known as the Open Door Note. A few months after the note was sent, the Boxer Rebellion, an armed uprising by anti-foreign Chinese, had to be put down by a combination of military forces.

22. Which of the following modern nations does NOT include territory that was once part of the Moslem empire?

(A) England

(B) France

(C) Spain

(D) Egypt

(E) India

(A) Mohammed advocated the union of religious, civil, and military authority. By the time of his death in 632 A.D., he had established control over the principal cities of Arabia. Following his death, his followers conquered territory with astonishing rapidity. Within a century, they had spread as far east as India. They controlled the northern coast of Africa, most of Spain, and part of Gaul. Their advance in the west was stopped by Charles Martel at the Battle of Tours (732). Consequently, the Moslems never reached England.

23. Which of the following contributed significantly to the spread of humanism?

(A) The voyages of Columbus
(B) The invention of printing
(C) Trade with China
(D) The unification of Italy
(E) The Crusades

(B) Humanism originated in Italy in the fourteenth century and represented, among other things, a rekindled interest in the literature of classical Greece and Rome. Consequently, the spread of humanism was greatly facilitated by the invention of printing.

24. If a historian believes that the events of the Russian Revolution paralleled the events of the French Revolution, then she would probably equate Stalin with

(A) Louis XVI
(B) Marat
(C) Robespierre
(D) Danton
(E) Napoleon

(E) Some historians have argued that both the French and Russian Revolutions can be divided into three stages. The first stage is a moderate phase extending from the beginning of the revolution during which time significant reforms were made. The second stage is the radical stage. Here the historian would compare the Reign of Terror with the Red Terror of the Russian Revolution. Finally, the historian would probably compare the return to stability under Napoleon to the return to stability under Stalin.

25. During the Berlin Blockade, the Soviet Union attempted to drive western Allies out of West Berlin by blocking access to the city by which of the following methods?

I. Land
II. Air
III. Water

(A) I only
(B) II only
(C) I and III only
(D) II and III only
(E) I, II, and III

(C) At the end of World War II, Germany was divided into four zones, with each of the Big Four powers—the Soviet Union, the United States, Great Britain, and France—controlling one zone. Berlin, which happened to fall in the Soviet zone, was likewise divided into four parts, and the three Western Allies were guaranteed access to the city through the Soviet zone. On June 24, 1948, the Soviets cut off all land and water communications with the city. Apparently, the Soviets overlooked or at least discounted the possibility that the city could be supplied by air. And that is what happened. The Soviets, understandably reluctant to shoot down Allied planes, eventually abandoned the blockade.

26. Which of the following helps to explain why ancient Greece was organized into city-states?

(A) Previous experience with tyrannical emperors
(B) Reluctance to venture outside of a certain locale
(C) Geographical features that isolated regions
(D) Inability to devise effective governments
(E) Lack of a common language

(C) The average Greek city-state covered an area equal to that of a small county in the United States. Its boundaries were usually natural features such as a range of hills or the sea.

27. Robert Owen, Claude Saint-Simon, and Charles Fourier all advocated

(A) overthrow of governments by violent revolution

(B) conquest of foreign territories for financial gain

(C) strict laissez-faire economic policies

(D) cooperative production and distribution of goods

(E) reinstatement of feudal rights and privileges

(D) The three persons mentioned are sometimes referred to as Utopian Socialists—socialists because they favored some form of cooperation rather than competition in the production and distribution of goods, and utopian because their plans are considered to be unrealistic.

28. England's Glorious Revolution (1688) helped to establish the

(A) divine right of the English king to rule

(B) Parliament's supremacy over the king

(C) authority of the Roman Catholic Church in England

(D) right of the king to tax feudal lords

(E) principle of a balance of power

(B) James II, who ascended the throne of England in 1685, was a devout Roman Catholic. The English resented his systematic attempts—of dubious legality—to relax the laws against the few Catholics in England and to promote them to positions of authority. A group of members of Parliament secretly invited his Protestant daughter, Mary, and her husband William to assume the throne. They accepted, and when William and Mary arrived, James fled the country, whereupon Parliament declared the throne to be vacant and proclaimed William and Mary to be king and queen of England. This bloodless revolution helped to establish Parliament's supremacy over the crown.

29. We returned to the hall to find it closed. Everyone agreed that the Assembly should adjourn to another location. There we all swore not to disband until we had drawn up a constitution limiting the powers of the monarchy.

The location referred to in the statement above was a

(A) cafe

(B) church

(C) tennis court

(D) train station

(E) ship

(C) The event referred to is the famous "Tennis Court Oath." In 1789, with France facing bankruptcy, Louis XVI convened the Estates-General at Versailles. The Third Estate, consisting mostly of members of the middle class, demanded that the members of the Estates-General be counted individually (rather than allowing each Estate to have a single vote). The effect of such a change would have been to give the Third Estate control of the Estates-General. The government refused to agree to this demand. In response, the Third Estate declared itself to be a National Assembly and the only true representative of the nation. Three days later, they returned to find their assembly room locked. The group adjourned to a nearby tennis court and swore the Tennis Court Oath.

30. The Good Neighbor Policy of the United States included which of the following?

I. Economic cooperation with Latin American countries

II. A promise not to intervene in the internal affairs of Latin American countries

III. A military alliance to defend Latin America against foreign invasion

(A) I only

(B) II only

(C) I and II only

(D) I and III only

(E) II and III only

(C) Isolationism in the 1930s was aimed at withdrawing the United States from foreign affairs, but, in a sense, "foreign" affairs did not include the affairs of the Western Hemisphere. In fact, the very idea of isolationism required that the nations of the Western Hemisphere close ranks. To that end, the United States during the 1930s was willing to offer Latin American countries economic assistance to combat the worldwide depression and tacitly to disavow the "big stick" policy of President Theodore Roosevelt.

31. Which of the following terms associated with western European feudalism is correctly associated with its equivalent term in Japanese feudalism?

I. Chivalry:Bushido

II. Mikado:King

III. Samurai:Knight

(A) I only

(B) III only

(C) I and II only

(D) I and III only

(E) I, II, and III

(E) Each of the pairs provides terms that are roughly equivalent. Of course, the parallels are not exact. For example, the Japanese feudal mikado, or emperor, lacked any real power. The real authority of government was lodged in the shogun, or chief lord. The closest approximation of shogun in European feudalism was the office of "mayor of the palace" under the Merovigian kings from the fifth to the eighth century.

32. Which of the following help explain why the Renaissance began in Italy?

I. Italy had been a center of Greco-Roman culture

II. Moslem and Byzantine ideas had reached Italy

III. Wealthy Italian patrons supported the arts

(A) I only

(B) III only

(C) I and III only

(D) II and III only

(E) I, II, and III

(E) All three statements describe factors that were conducive to the start of the Renaissance in northern Italy.

33. After 1451, the center of economic power in Europe gradually shifted from

(A) northern Italy to Spain and Portugal to eastern Europe

(B) northern Italy to Spain and Portugal to England and the low countries

(C) northern Italy to England and the low countries to Spain and Portugal

(D) Spain and Portugal to England and the low countries to northern Italy

(E) Spain and Portugal to northern Italy to England and the low countries

(B) During the fifteenth century, the cities of northern Italy were the primary centers of economic activity in Europe. During the sixteenth century, Portugal was able to break the Italian spice monopoly, and Spain received large quantities of silver and gold from the Western Hemisphere. The Portuguese, however, did not develop their commercial institutions, preferring to rely instead on the other countries to function as distributors of their goods. And Spain foolishly created a state monopoly over trade in precious metals. Gradually, therefore, economic power shifted to the North, to England and the low countries.

34. Which of the following statements about Napoleon's Continental System is LEAST accurate?

(A) It was very difficult to administer.

(B) France's allies were forbidden to trade with England.

(C) It eventually led to a war with Portugal.

(D) The United States suspended trading with foreign nations.

(E) England suffered tremendous economic hardship.

(E) The Continental System was conceived as a form of economic warfare against Britain. In 1806, Napoleon issued a decree forbidding the importation of British goods into countries controlled by or allied with France. The ban, however, proved very difficult to enforce, so the economic injury inflicted on Great Britain was relatively minor.

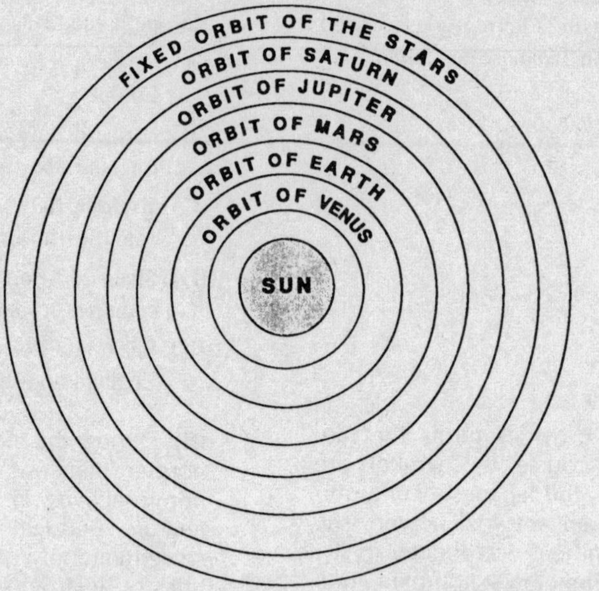

35. The drawing above depicts a model of the universe developed by

(A) Plato
(B) Aristotle
(C) Ptolemy
(D) Copernicus
(E) Einstein

(D) The Polish astronomer Copernicus (1473–1543) rejected the notion that the earth is the center of the universe. In his model, the sun occupies the center, and the planets move in circular orbits about it.

36. Of the following, which country exerted the LEAST influence at the Congress of Vienna (1814–1815)?

(A) Austria
(B) England
(C) France
(D) Prussia
(E) United States

(E) After Napoleon's defeat, representatives of the victorious nations and France met at the Congress of Vienna to reconstruct war-ravaged Europe. The major players were Great Britain, Prussia, France, and Austria. The United States was not yet a world power.

37. All of the following are true of the Romantic movement (1800–1830) EXCEPT

(A) it was a reaction against the Classical movement of the eighteenth century
(B) it emphasized spontaneity and irregularity
(C) it drew inspiration from nature
(D) it appealed to people's emotions and feelings
(E) it was distinctly antireligious

(E) The Romantic movement was a reaction against the classical movement of the eighteenth century. In contrast to the Enlightenment and the French Revolution, which emphasized reason, the Romantic movement emphasized emotions, intuition, nature, and faith.

38. Which of the following were used by the Church during the Middle Ages against civil rulers?

I. Indulgences

II. Excommunication

III. Interdict

(A) II only
(B) III only
(C) I and III only
(D) II and III only
(E) I, II, and III

(D) Excommunication (expelling an individual from the Church) and interdict (forbidding religious services in a geographical region) were powerful weapons of the Church during the Middle Ages. As for I, Church members could purchase indulgences that would relieve them of the burden of some sin.

39. Which of the following had a great influence on the writings of Thomas Aquinas?

(A) Alexander
(B) Aristotle
(C) Confucius
(D) Mohammed
(E) Zoroaster

(B) Aquinas was a great medieval philosopher who was profoundly influenced by Aristotle. In his *Summa Theologica,* Aquinas attempts to reconcile Church doctrine and reason.

40. The United States acquired the land to build the Panama Canal by virtue of

(A) a Panamanian revolt against Colombia that was supported by the United States Navy
(B) United States military intervention to resolve a border dispute between Colombia and Panama
(C) an agreement with Colombia under which the United States agreed to a concession fee plus annual payments
(D) a treaty with Nicaragua in which Nicaragua voluntarily relinquished control of the canal zone
(E) an alliance whereby the United States agreed to ensure Colombian neutrality in exchange for the canal route

(A) In 1878, a French company under the direction of Ferdinand de Lesseps, the builder of the Suez Canal, obtained from Colombia a concession to build a canal across its northern province of Panama. After spending about $300 million, the French company ran out of money and had to stop work on the project. In 1903, the United States negotiated a treaty with Colombia for the canal rights, but the treaty was rejected by Colombia, which wanted more money. Phillipe Bunau-Varilla, the former chief engineer of the canal project and a stockholder in the reorganized French company, engineered a revolution to secure Panama's independence from Colombia. The revolution succeeded mainly because the United States navy prevented Colombia from intervening to suppress the uprising. The United States immediately recognized the new nation, and the Hay-Bunau-Varilla Treaty secured to the United States the canal rights on essentially the same terms that had been offered to Colombia.

41. When President Franklin D. Roosevelt explained that the Lend-Lease Act of 1941 would make the United States the "arsenal of democracy" he meant that the United States would

(A) send troops to Europe to defend France against the *Blitzkrieg*

(B) provide armaments to Great Britain but stay out of the war

(C) allow American pilots to fly British war planes

(D) maintain a strict isolationist posture regarding Europe

(E) commit troops to the war only if Japan attacked Pearl Harbor

(B) American foreign policy between the two world wars can be described as near isolationism. The disillusionment that followed the First World War and the move toward disarmament created an atmosphere in which involvement in another foreign war seemed to Americans to be inconceivable. After the defeat of the League of Nations, the United States all but washed its hands of Europe and the Far East, though it did continue to play a role in the politics of the Western Hemisphere. This mentality persisted for two decades. Even as hostilities were escalating in Europe, Roosevelt was promising to keep the United States out of the war. As the situation worsened in Europe and Great Britain stood alone, public opinion came to favor providing "all aid short of war." In March 1941, Congress passed the Lend-Lease Act which authorized the President to sell, exchange, or lease any "defense article" to any anti-Axis nation in return for "payment in kind or property, or any other direct or indirect benefit which the President deems satisfactory." Thus, the United States would be the arsenal to supply armaments to the Allies without actually committing itself to war.

42. The government of Great Britain differs from that of the United States in all of the following ways EXCEPT

(A) Great Britain does not have a written constitution

(B) Great Britain has a hereditary monarchy

(C) Great Britain's legislature has but one house

(D) Great Britain's true chief executive is not directly elected

(E) the terms of Great Britain's legislators are indeterminate

(C) Great Britain does not have a formal, written constitution. Instead, the principles of government have evolved over centuries. The country still retains its monarch as a figurehead. The real executive power is vested in the prime minister who is not elected directly by the voters but is chosen by the legislature. The legislature consists of two houses: the hereditary House of Lords with only minor powers and the elected House of Commons with unlimited legislative power. Members of the House of Commons are elected for a maximum term of five years but the House may be dissolved at any time by the prime minister's calling for elections.

43. A person who is engaged in business neither intends to promote the public interest nor knows how much he is promoting it. He intends only to promote his own security, intends only his own gain, and he is in this, as in many other cases, led by an invisible hand to promote the end which was no part of his intention. Thus, a laissez-faire approach to the marketplace is the best approach.

The statements above represent the views of

(A) Adam Smith

(B) Vladimir Lenin

(C) Pythagoras

(D) Louis Blanc

(E) Fidel Castro

(A) A key phrase in the selection is "invisible hand." These words clearly connect the selection to Adam Smith who believed that self-interested individuals pursuing their own ends ultimately promote the common good.

44. During the time of the Holy Roman Empire, there were approximately how many German states?

(A) 3

(B) 15

(C) 40

(D) 100

(E) 300

(E) Germany did not become a nation until the second half of the nineteenth century. From the Middle Ages, the Holy Roman Empire encompassed an astonishing 300 German principalities but really exercised little control over them.

45. All of the following statements about Northern Ireland (Ulster) are true EXCEPT

(A) it is no longer a part of Great Britain

(B) it is heavily industrialized

(C) the majority of its population is descended from English and Scottish settlers

(D) a significant minority of its population is Roman Catholic

(E) the majority of its population is Protestant

(A) England conquered Ireland during the Middle Ages and ruled the country, sometimes brutally, for several hundred years. In 1921, Ireland—minus the six northern provinces that make up Northern Ireland—was granted dominion status. Gradually, Ireland severed all political ties to Great Britain. Northern Ireland, however, remains a part of Great Britain.

46. When God created the world, he incorporated into the universe the laws of nature. He set the world in motion and He insures that the universe continues to operate according to these laws, but He does not interfere in human affairs. Prayers, therefore, are useless. God does not do miracles.

The ideas expressed in the statements above are characteristic of

(A) an atheist

(B) an agnostic

(C) a deist

(D) a polytheist

(E) a pagan

(C) The statements are characteristic of Deism, a philosophy of the Enlightenment. It originated in Great Britain as a natural theology and was distinctly antitheological. In France, the *philosophes* mounted caustic attacks on the clergy and church doctrine.

47. The style of the column capital shown above is

(A) Byzantine

(B) Corinthian

(C) Doric

(D) Ionic

(E) Romanesque

(D) The three styles of Greek columns are:

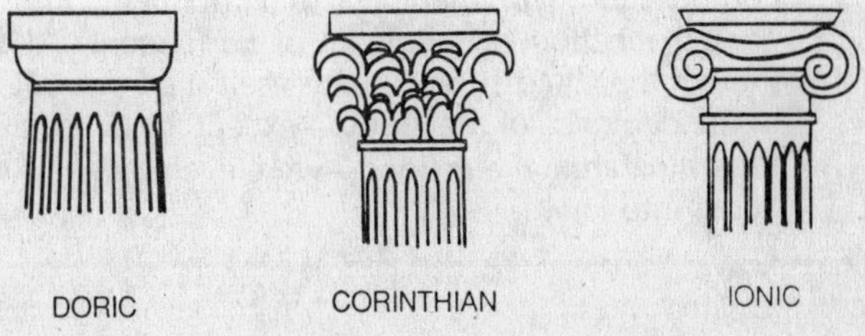

48. The figure above is the emblem of

(A) the Soviet Union

(B) the United Nations

(C) NATO

(D) the British Commonwealth

(E) European Economic Community

(B) The figure is the emblem of the United Nations.

49. All of the following demands of the Chartist movement eventually became law in Great Britain EXCEPT

(A) universal manhood suffrage

(B) annual elections for Parliament

(C) secret ballot

(D) compensation for members of Parliament

(E) equal electoral districts

(B) The Chartist movement was organized in Great Britain in the late 1830s by city workers to attain political reforms and to improve living conditions. Its Charter (the Peoples' Charter) demanded universal manhood suffrage, an end to property qualifications for members of Parliament, equal electoral districts, secret ballots, compensation for members of Parliament, and annual election of members of Parliament. Although the Chartist movement itself died out, all of the demands of the group—except for the one regarding annual elections—were eventually enacted into law.

50. The statement "The sun never sets on the British Empire" was

(A) a boast about the extent of British overseas possessions

(B) an apology for Great Britain's role during the War of 1812

(C) a criticism of Great Britain for its imperialistic policies

(D) an epitaph for the decline of the British Empire

(E) a prediction that Great Britain would one day rule the entire world

(A) Over a period of three hundred years, Great Britain created the largest empire in the history of the world. It included a fourth of the world's land area and population. Because it included possessions all around the world, Britons boasted that the sun never set on the British Empire.

The British Empire in 1920

Europe: Great Britain, Ireland, Gibraltar, Malta

Africa: Egypt, Gambia, Gold Coast, Kenya, Nigeria, Nyasaland, Rhodesia, Sierra Leone, South-West Africa, Sudan, Tanganyika, Uganda, Union of South Africa, Zanzibar

Indian Ocean: Mauritius, Seychelles

Middle East: Aden, Cyprus, Iraq, Kuwait, Palestine

Far East: Burma, Ceylon, Hong Kong, India, Malaya, North Borneo, Singapore

Australasia: Australia, Fiji, New Zealand, Tonga

North America: Bermuda, British Honduras, Canada

South America: Guyana, Falkland Islands

West Indies: Bahamas, Barbados, Grenada, Jamaica, Tobago, Trinidad

51. The immediate cause of the collapse of France's Fourth Republic was

(A) rapid devaluation of the franc

(B) threatened invasion by Germany

(C) governmental corruption

(D) rebellion in Algeria

(E) widespread labor unrest

(D) After the German occupation during World War II, France established the Fourth Republic. The Fourth Republic spanned the difficult period of post-war recovery and was beset with numerous problems. The immediate cause of the demise of the Fourth Republic was the inability of the government to resolve the Algerian crisis. Algeria was inhabited mainly by Moslems but with a significant minority of Europeans called *colons*. In 1954, the Moslem National Liberation Front initiated a guerilla war to win independence from France. The war dragged on for many months, and the inability of the government to solve the problem suggested to many military officers that it could only be solved by changing the government. In 1958, the army in Algeria seized control of the civil government and demanded that General Charles de Gaulle assume the powers of the government.

52. The Crusades of the twelfth and thirteenth centuries had all of the following effects EXCEPT

(A) encouraging trade

(B) stimulating the growth of towns

(C) strengthening central governments

(D) undermining power of the nobles

(E) reinforcing the system of serfdom

(E) The Crusades mark the end of the Middle Ages in western Europe. Those who participated in the Crusades were exposed to Moslem and Byzantine civilizations with their great cities, powerful governments, and prosperous trade. The Crusades, therefore, encouraged trade and stimulated the growth of towns. Additionally, the drain on both the human and economic resources of the nobles weakened that class to the benefit of the central authority. And the increase in economic activity also permitted many serfs to escape from the feudal strictures that had bound them.

53. At the outbreak of World War II, which of the following nations was a member of the League of Nations?

(A) Great Britain

(B) Germany

(C) Japan

(D) United States

(E) Italy

(A) One of the reasons for the failure of the League of Nations was the failure of the United States to join and the subsequent withdrawal of other powerful nations. Germany and Japan withdrew in 1933, and Italy left in 1937. By the time the war began, France and Great Britain were the only powerful nations that remained as members.

54. Which of the following assertions would be the most difficult for a historian to prove?

(A) The development of air travel has changed the way that people view the world.

(B) The annual flooding of the Nile River was an important factor in the development of ancient Egyptian civilization.

(C) Vladimir Lenin suffered the first of a series of strokes in 1922 and died in 1924.

(D) Belgium gained its independence as a result of a revolution in 1830.

(E) Ancient Greece contributed more to the development of Western civilization than did ancient Rome.

(E) The statements lettered (A) through (D) are essentially assertions of fact. Choice (C), for example, can be proved or disproved by the examination of historical records. (E) differs from these statements because (E) makes a value judgment. Whether Greece or Rome was more important in the history of western civilization cannot be settled by reference to any single document or set of statistics.

55. Mercantilism advocated which of the following?

I. The value of a nation's exports should exceed the value of its imports

II. A nation should export large quantities of precious metals

III. A nation should impose tariffs on imported goods

(A) I only

(B) II only

(C) I and III only

(D) II and III only

(E) I, II, and III

(C) One result of the European expansion overseas in the sixteenth, seventeenth, and eighteenth centuries has been called the commercial revolution. It included increased world trade, a shift in the center of economic power away from northern Italy, and the adoption of mercantilism. Interested in increasing the holding of royal treasuries, the mercantilists placed great importance on amassing stocks of precious metals. According to this theory, wealth was accumulated by encouraging exports and discouraging imports. Ideally, a nation would be owed the difference and could collect the difference in the form of precious metals such as gold and silver.

56. In the early twentieth century all of the following had possessions in Africa EXCEPT

(A) Belgium

(B) France

(C) Portugal

(D) Germany

(E) Russia

(E) Russia had no particular interest in Africa. Rather it looked to the Far East, specifically to China, as a possible area of colonial expansion.

57. All of the following are characteristics of Gothic architecture EXCEPT

(A) pointed arches

(B) tall spires

(C) gargoyles

(D) many stained glass windows

(E) thick, heavy walls

(E) When you think of Gothic architecture, think of the cathedral of Notre Dame in Paris with its flying buttresses. The flying buttresses were necessary to support the thin walls of that style of architecture.

58. The Quadruple Alliance included all of the following EXCEPT

(A) Austria

(B) Prussia

(C) Spain

(D) Russia

(E) Great Britain

(C) In 1815, Metternich organized the Quadruple Alliance to enforce the Vienna settlements and to suppress revolution. In 1818, France became a member. This cooperative effort is referred to as the Concert of Europe.

59. Rudyard Kipling's poem "The White Man's Burden" was primarily

(A) an apology for imperialism

(B) a condemnation of racism

(C) a justification for isolationism

(D) a warning against interventionism

(E) a cry against the rising tide of nationalism

(A) Kipling's poem was written in 1899 to generate support for such acts as the United States' annexation of the Philippines. It calls on developed nations to "take up the White Man's burden." That "burden" is to take charge of people the poem refers to as "half devil and half child."

60. The occasion has been judged proper for asserting that the American continents, by the free and independent condition which they have assumed and maintained, are henceforth not to be considered as subjects for future colonization by any European powers.

The statement above articulated what became known as

(A) Seward's Folly

(B) the American System

(C) the Monroe Doctrine

(D) the Policy of Laissez-faire

(E) the XYZ Affair

(C) This is one part of the famous Monroe Doctrine announced by President James Monroe in his annual address of 1823. The other part warns European powers against trying to reestablish control over countries that were formerly colonies. Actually, the announcement of the Monroe Doctrine was rather a non-event in Europe. European nations either ignored it or indicated that they would abide by it only if it suited them. It is true that European powers by and large left Latin America alone during the rest of the nineteenth century, but this is because the European nations that might otherwise have decided to intervene in Latin America feared that the British navy would stop them. Certainly, at the time the United States didn't have the naval power to enforce the Monroe Doctrine. Between its initial formulation and the end of the nineteenth century, the Monroe Doctrine languished in obscurity, cited only once or twice. In 1895, Secretary of State Richard Olney cited the Monroe Doctrine as giving the United States priority over Great Britain in resolving a border dispute between Venezuela and British Guiana. Thereafter, the Monroe Doctrine became an important part of American foreign policy.

Seward's Folly, as you probably remember, refers to the decision of Secretary of State William Seward to purchase Alaska from Russia in 1867 for $7.2 million. It was also referred to as "Seward's Icebox." The American System refers to a plan proposed by Henry Clay in 1824 to make the United States economically self-sufficient. Laissez-faire refers to an economic theory according to which government takes a "hands off" policy toward business. Finally, in 1797, President Adams sent a special mission to Paris to try to reduce hostilities between the United States and France. French agents insulted the delegates by demanding a bribe before they would commence negotiations. Adams reported the incident to Congress, designating the three French agents simply as X, Y, and Z.

61. The principal author of the Declaration of Independence of the United States, Thomas Jefferson, relied heavily on the philosophical writings of

(A) Socrates

(B) Descartes

(C) Rousseau

(D) Machiavelli

(E) Locke

(E) Compare the following excerpts of John Locke's *Second Treatise of Government* and the language of the Declaration of Independence:

Locke:

> Men being, as has been said, by Nature, all free, equal and independent, no one can be put out of this Estate, and subjected to the Political power of another, without his own consent. The only way whereby any one devests himself of his Natural Liberty, and puts on the bonds of Civil Society is by agreeing with other Men to joyn and unite into a Community, for their comfortable, safe, and peaceable living one amongst another, in a secure Enjoyment of their properties . . . .
>
> And 'tis not without reason, that he seeks out, and is willing to joyn in Society with others . . . for the mutual Preservation of their Lives, Liberties and Estates, which I call by the general Name, Property.
>
> [W]hen by the Miscarriages of those in Authority [political power] is forefeited; upon the Forfeiture of their Rules, or at the Determination of the Time set, it reverts to the Society, and the People have a Right to act as Supreme, and continue the Legislative in themselves, or erect a new Form . . . as they think good.
>
> The Declaration of Independence:
>
> We hold these truths to be self-evident, that all men are created equal, that they are endowed by the Creator with certain unalienable rights, that among these are life, liberty and the pursuit of happiness. That to secure these rights, governments are instituted among men, deriving their just powers from the consent of the governed. That whenever any form of government becomes destructive of these ends, it is the right of the people to alter or to abolish it, and to institute new government . . . .

62. Which of the following was an important factor in the decision of the United States to enter World War I?

(A) A threatened German invasion of Mexico

(B) German submarine attacks on ships in the Atlantic Ocean

(C) The assassination of the heir to the Austro-Hungarian throne

(D) A Japanese naval blockade of ports on the West Coast of the United States

(E) Formation of a German-Japanese alliance directed against the United States

(B) World War I was precipitated by the assassination of the Austrian Archduke at Sarajevo in 1914, but the United States did not immediately enter the war. Although most Americans tended to sympathize with Great Britain and to distrust Germany, the express policy of the United States government was neutrality. Gradually, however, the events of the war, amplified by British propaganda, polarized the Americans, and most favored the British. The immediate cause for U.S. entry into the war was German submarine warfare. In 1915, hoping to stop supplies coming from Britain, Germany announced that it would thenceforth consider the waters surrounding the British Isles a war zone and warned neutral ships to stay clear. The main weapon for enforcing the blockade was the submarine. In 1915, a German U boat (for *unterseeboot*) torpedoed and sank the British passenger liner *Lusitania*. Over a hundred American passengers were lost. After strong protest by the United States, the German government promised that it would sink no more passenger ships. But in March 1916, a German submarine mistakenly sank the ferry *Sussex* in the English Channel. This time the German government responded with the Sussex Pledge promising that it would not attack merchant vessels without warning. This move reduced tensions with the United States but also permitted supplies to reach the Allied forces in Europe. In 1916, Wilson's supporters coined the slogan "He kept us out of war." But in early 1917, Germany decided that it could not win the war without enforcing the blockade and announced the resumption of unrestricted submarine warfare. Several American merchant ships were sunk. In February, the British intercepted a message from the German foreign secretary, Alfred Zimmerman, to the German ambassador in Mexico, instructing the ambassador to offer Mexico a military alliance against the United States with the promise it would help Mexico recover lost territory. On April 2, President Wilson asked Congress for a declaration of war.

63. A person who had lived his entire life in a feudal society would likely have difficulty understanding which of the following concepts?

(A) Aggression

(B) Loyalty

(C) Nationalism

(D) Marriage

(E) Monasticism

(C) Nationalism is a feeling of patriotism or strong loyalty to a nation state. Until the fifteenth century, nation states simply did not exist. Instead, individuals gave their greatest loyalty to a local authority or to the church. Therefore, someone who had lived all of his life in a feudal society would have real difficulty in understanding the concept of allegiance to a national government.

64. A corporation, operating under a government charter, enjoys which of the following advantages over a business operated by a single person?

I. Increased ability to raise capital

II. Limited liability of shareholders

III. Ability to survive the death of individual members

(A) I only

(B) III only

(C) I and II only

(D) II and III only

(E) I, II, and III

(E) In the late nineteenth century, the corporation became the most important form of business organization. The corporation is a legal entity created by a government that is, in effect, an artificial person. As an artificial person, it enjoys certain advantages over a real person. First, by selling shares of stock a corporation can raise the money it needs to operate. Second, the individual investors or shareholders of the company are not personally liable for the debts incurred by the company. Third, the company can continue to accumulate wealth even after the death of a shareholder.

65. The first artificial satellite to orbit the earth was launched by

(A) Great Britain

(B) France

(C) Italy

(D) the Soviet Union

(E) the United States

(D) The first artificial satellite to orbit the earth was launched by the Soviet Union in 1957. The United States followed with Explorer I in 1958.

66. Great Britain and France intervened militarily in Egypt in 1956 in response to

(A) Egypt's invasion of Libya

(B) Egypt's nationalization of the Suez Canal

(C) the discovery of oil in Egypt

(D) a coup d'etat by Egypt's military leaders

(E) civil war inspired by religious differences

(B) In the late nineteenth century, in order to protect its "lifeline" to the Far East, Great Britain acquired a controlling interest in the Suez Canal. In 1956, Egyptian leader Gamal Abdel Nasser announced that Egypt would nationalize the canal. This prompted the intervention of French and British troops. Militarily, the operation was successful, but the French and British had miscalculated American reaction. The United States and the Soviet Union, cooperating at the United Nations, forced the British and French to accept a cease fire. The Suez crisis is important because it represents the end of a chapter in the history of British imperialism.

67. In 1914, one U.S. dollar was equivalent to 4.2 German marks. At the beginning of 1923, one U.S. dollar bought 1,800 marks. By the fall of 1923, one U.S. dollar had the same buying power as 4.2 trillion marks.

The economic phenomenon described above is

(A) depression

(B) recession

(C) boom

(D) creeping inflation

(E) runaway inflation

(E) Inflation is a rise in prices that is not the result of some increase in the value of goods purchased. Inflation is said to erode the purchasing power of money. Assume, for example, that a loaf of bread cost $1.00 last year. If a similar loaf of bread costs $1.10 this year, then there has been a 10 percent increase in the price of bread that is not the result of some improvement in the quality of the bread. This is inflation. Most industrialized countries experience some inflation, but the rate of price increases is not intolerable. When prices rise tremendously in a short period of time, as described above, the result is runaway inflation. Runaway inflation has disastrous consequences because wages don't keep pace with prices. People with relatively fixed incomes, for example, pensions, rental income from long-term leases, and government employees, are particularly hurt. The social upheaval that followed the runaway inflation after World War I in Germany was one factor in the rise to power of the Nazis.

68. Napoleon never invaded England because

(A) Great Britain was allied with France

(B) the British fleet controlled the English Channel

(C) the French did not support his wars of conquest

(D) the French army was understaffed

(E) England offered little of value to a conqueror

(B) In 1803, Napoleon amassed a large army on the French coast as a prelude to an invasion of England. For two years, the expeditionary force waited for the French navy to establish control over the English Channel. On October 21, 1805, a British squadron under the command of Admiral Horatio Nelson decisively defeated the French navy in the Battle of Trafalgar. Unable to execute the planned invasion of England, Napoleon concentrated on acquiring territory on the Continent.

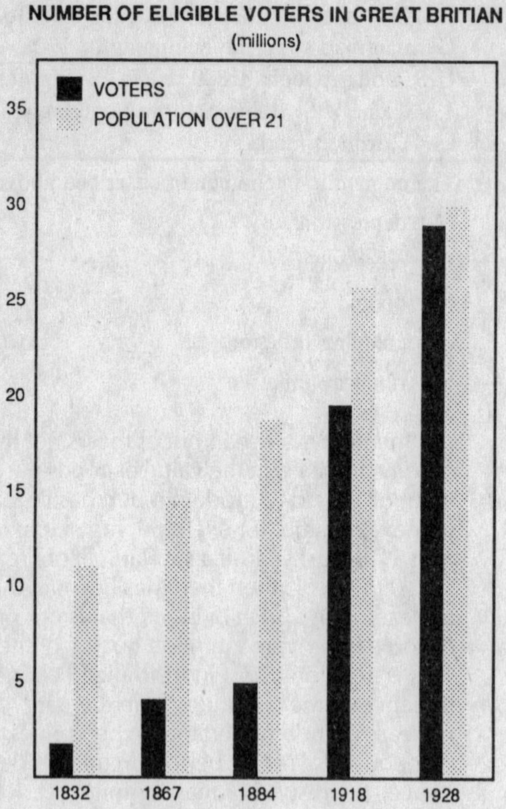

69. Which of the following best explains the trend shown in the chart above?

(A) Acquisition of foreign territories

(B) Increases in population

(C) Lengthening of average life span

(D) Series of election reform bills

(E) Immigration into Great Britain

(D) Between 1832 and 1928 a series of reform bills gradually extended the franchise to provide for universal suffrage for all persons over the age of 21. This explains why the number of people eligible to vote reflects an increasing portion of the population over 21.

70. Great Britain did not join the European Economic Community (Common Market) until 1971 because

(A) French President de Gaulle vetoed Britain's applications

(B) Australia and New Zealand feared a loss of trade

(C) British leaders felt the EEC would not survive very long

(D) some members of the EEC were allied with the Soviet Union

(E) British industry refused to export goods to the continent

(A) Great Britain did not join the EEC until 1971 because her two applications for membership were vetoed by French President Charles de Gaulle who feared that British membership might jeopardize his goal of making France the dominant power in Europe.

71. The philosophical movement with which the French philosopher Jean-Paul Sartre was associated is

(A) stoicism

(B) existentialism

(C) idealism

(D) scholasticism

(E) rationalism

(B) Sartre was born in Paris in 1905 where he would later teach philosophy. During the 1930s, he published *La Nausée,* a philosophical novel, and *Le Mur,* a collection of short stories. During the German occupation of France, Sartre was active in the Resistance movement, and after the war he emerged as the dominant figure in the Existentialist movement. His most famous philosophical work is *L'Etre et le Néant (Being and Nothingness).*

72. The artists Claude Monet, Edgar Degas, and Auguste Renoir belonged to a school of painting called

(A) realism

(B) naturalism

(C) impressionism

(D) dadaism

(E) surrealism

(C) Impressionism originated in France during the second half of the nineteenth century. The name derives from a painting by Claude Monet that is translated into English as "Impression of the Setting Sun." In the painting, Monet attempted to capture the effects of sunlight. Because these artists ignored some of the traditional artistic conventions, their works were at first severely criticized and even ridiculed.

73. The requirement that the eldest male child receive his father's title and possessions is called

(A) primogeniture

(B) *droit de seigneur*

(C) *noblesse oblige*

(D) defeasance

(E) subinfeudation

(A) The requirement that the eldest male child be accorded priority over any siblings is known as primogeniture.

74. Between 1880 and 1900 the number of newspapers in northwestern Europe doubled from 6,000 to 12,000. By 1900, several newspapers had daily circulations of more than a million copies, compared with 50,000 for the largest selling newspaper during the 1860s.

The increase in newspaper sales described above resulted from

(A) the invention of movable type

(B) the discovery of electricity

(C) improved sanitation

(D) increased rates of literacy

(E) the invention of the telegraph

(D) The increased availability of educational opportunities resulted in a tremendous rise in the literacy rates in the countries of northern Europe. During the 1860s, just over half of the population in that region could be classified as literate, but by 1900 about 90 percent could be so classified.

75. A student of demographics would be most interested in which of the following?

(A) the Irish potato famine of the 1840s

(B) the sinking of the *Lusitania*

(C) the crowning of Napoleon Bonaparte as emperor

(D) the wording of the Magna Carta

(E) the date of birth of the present British monarch

(A) Demographics is the study of populations—their characteristics and their movements. The Irish potato famine of the 1840s prompted many Irish to emigrate to the United States.

Questions 76–78 refer to the following:

(A) Poland

(B) England

(C) Spain

(D) Italy

(E) France

76. While the United States was engaged in its Civil War, which country used its army to establish Archduke Maximilian as emperor of Mexico?

(E) Napoleon III of France sought to take advantage of the fact that the United States was engaged in a Civil War. Reasoning that the United States would be unable to intervene, Napoleon sent an army to Mexico to set up Maximilian as its emperor. Once the Civil War concluded, the United States government forced France to withdraw its troops from Mexico and the French-Mexican empire collapsed.

77. Which country disappeared from the map of Europe in 1795?

(A) In 1772, Poland was the third largest state in Europe. By 1795 it had disappeared entirely. Weakened by its lack of a central authority, Poland was unable to protect its territorial integrity. Austria, Prussia, and Russia forced on Poland a series of three partitions that ultimately divided all of Poland's territory among them.

78. Which country was finally unified during the second half of the nineteenth century?

(D) At the Congress of Vienna (1814-1815), the territory that is now Italy was divided into various states and provinces, many of them controlled by Austria. Resentment of Austrian control and memories of earlier Italian glory gave rise to nationalistic feelings. Unification was finally completed in 1870.

79. Society provides an arena for competition in which the most industrious, ingenious, and intelligent people are the most successful. By a process akin to natural selection, civilization necessarily advances to higher and more complex forms.

The position outlined by the statements above is often referred to as

(A) mercantilism

(B) protectionism

(C) imperialism

(D) Social Darwinism

(E) Marxism

(D) The statements describe a philosophy often called Social Darwinism. In this view, a process analogous to natural selection of the fittest members of animal species operates in society to select for social and economic reward those who are the fittest.

80. When the United States established formal diplomatic relations with the People's Republic of China in 1979 it also withdrew diplomatic recognition from the government of

(A) Cambodia

(B) Okinawa

(C) Sri Lanka

(D) Sumatra

(E) Taiwan

(E) With the withdrawal of Japanese troops from China following World War I, Nationalist Chiang Kai-shek and Communist Mao Zedong resumed a civil war. The United States for a time supplied military aid to the corrupt Chiang Kai-shek regime in hopes of preventing the communists from taking control of the country. By 1949, however, the Nationalists were in full retreat, and Chiang Kai-shek's army was evacuated to the island of Taiwan. Although the communists were in control of China, the United States refused to recognize the government and for more than 20 years maintained that the legitimate government was the Nationalist government on Taiwan. This unrealistic view was undermined when President Richard Nixon made a trip to China in 1972; and in 1979, President Jimmy Carter established formal diplomatic relations with the People's Republic, thereby recognizing it as the legitimate government of China.

81. The Marshall Plan was adopted in large measure because the United States

(A) wanted to see Germany punished for its aggression during World War II

(B) hoped that Europe could be unified under a single central government

(C) was unsure of the motives of the Soviet Union in Berlin

(D) feared that unstable European countries would succumb to communism

(E) incorrectly believed that the Soviet Union lacked any expansionist plans

(D) Although the phrase "cold war" was not coined until 1948, the cold war began shortly after the end of World War II. In a speech at Westminster College in Fulton, Missouri, in March of 1946, the former prime minister of Great Britain, Winston Churchill announced that "an iron curtain" had descended across the European continent. Churchill proposed that the United States and England form an anti-communist Anglo-American association. Both Greece and Turkey at that time relied heavily on British financial aid, and both were in trouble. The Greek monarchy was fighting with communist-supplied rebels, and Turkey was under heavy Soviet pressure. In February 1947, the British admitted that they could no longer supply aid to these two countries. President Truman asked Congress for $400 million in aid for Greece and Turkey, and Congress agreed. This was the first time that the United States had even proposed to commit huge sums of financial aid during peacetime. In order to generate popular support for the foreign aid plan, Truman made an address to a joint session of Congress in which he warned that communism was spreading across Europe and immediately threatened Greece and Turkey. It was necessary, he said, for the "United States to support free peoples who are resisting attempted subjugation by armed minorities or by outside pressures." This policy was soon labelled the Truman Doctrine.

In June of 1947, Secretary of State George Marshall called for financial assistance to western Europe in general. At his suggestion, sixteen European countries worked out a plan of economic recovery, a plan that required billions of United States dollars. The United States agreed to provide $17 billion over a four-year period. This European Recovery Program—or Marshall Plan—encountered little opposition because people were convinced that it was necessary to stop the spread of communism.

82. Which of the following was used by President Lyndon Johnson in 1964 to step up United States military activities in Vietnam?

(A) The Gulf of Tonkin Resolution

(B) The Platt Amendment

(C) The SEATO Treaty

(D) The Wilmot Proviso

(E) The Zimmerman Note

(A) On August 2, 1964, the United States destroyer *Maddox* reported that it had been attacked by three boats using torpedoes and guns while in international waters in the Gulf of Tonkin off the coast of Vietnam. Two days later there was a report of a similar attack on a different United States vessel. Johnson ordered air strikes against North Vietnam and went before Congress to obtain a resolution empowering the president to "take all necessary measures to repel any armed attack against the forces of the United States and to prevent further aggression." The resolution passed the House unanimously and the Senate with only two dissenting votes. This resolution was thereafter used by the administration as authority for its escalation of the war in Vietnam. Ironically, subsequent research suggests that the attacks may not even have taken place.

The Platt Amendment was a provision attached to a 1901 army appropriations bill that was designed to keep Cuba subservient to the United States even while granting Cuba independence. The terms of the Platt Amendment were later incorporated into the Cuban constitution of 1902 and were reaffirmed in a treaty between the United States and Cuba.

SEATO is an acronym for Southeast Asian Treaty Organization. Formed in 1954, the organization included Australia, Great Britain, France, Pakistan, the Philippines, Thailand, and New Zealand. Despite the similarity of the acronyms SEATO and NATO, SEATO was not a true military alliance.

The Wilmot Proviso was added to a bill appropriating money to negotiate an end to the war with Mexico. It stipulated that slavery would be forbidden in any territory acquired from Mexico by virtue of any treaty negotiated. The provision failed to pass the Senate.

83. A historian who wished to do an analysis of African-Americans who were held in slavery would find which of the following most useful?

(A) Tools, dishes, and other articles excavated from a waste pit on a southern plantation

(B) Treatises written by white authors defending the existence of the slave system

(C) Autobiographies written by African-Americans who were actually held in slavery

(D) Plantation records detailing the economic transactions of the owner

(E) Pamphlets written by abolitionists residing in the northern states

(C) There are many published autobiographies of African-Americans held in slavery. They indicate that although the white people who physically controlled the African-Americans regarded the African-Americans as slaves, the African-Americans did not regard themselves as such.

84. The earliest people to reach North America are thought to have arrived from

(A) Siberia via the Bering Strait Land Bridge

(B) South America via the Central American isthmus

(C) Hawaii via rafts

(D) Scandinavia via boats

(E) Germania via a polar route

(A) By the time Columbus "discovered" the New World, it was already inhabited by 15 million to 20 million people. It is now believed that the first inhabitants of North America came from Siberia and crossed over a land bridge at the site of what is now the Bering Strait.

85. As applied to Southeast Asia, the "domino theory" held that

(A) a communist takeover of South Vietnam would lead to similar takeovers in other countries in the region

(B) escalating numbers of United States troops would guarantee a military victory in Vietnam

(C) it is impossible to win a guerilla war using conventional military strategies

(D) only by breaking an enemy's supply lines is it possible to gain victory

(E) a united, communistic but nationalist Vietnam would not be imperialistic

(A) In a news conference in 1954, President Dwight D. Eisenhower, in addressing the French request for American aid for its military efforts in Vietnam, stated that Southeast Asia was like a row of dominoes and that if one were knocked over the entire row would follow. The "domino theory" was a frequently used justification for the United States military presence in Vietnam.

86. A political reactionary would be most likely to favor which of the following?

(A) Higher welfare payments

(B) Higher tax rates

(C) Stricter government regulations on business

(D) National health insurance

(E) Strong military

(E) Although labels are sometimes inaccurate, it is useful to think of the political spectrum in this way:

LEFT ←———— CENTER ————→ RIGHT
Radicals   Liberals Moderates Conservatives   Reactionaries

A reactionary would likely oppose any government programs designed to redistribute wealth.

87. On April 11, 1951, President Harry S. Truman removed General Douglas MacArthur as commander in chief of United Nations forces in Korea because

(A) MacArthur was a weak and ineffective military leader

(B) MacArthur was critical of Truman's foreign policy

(C) the United Nations asked for MacArthur's removal

(D) South Korea no longer needed United States military assistance

(E) MacArthur was unpopular with the United States public

(B) In 1945, Korea—a colony of Japan since 1910—was divided at the 38th parallel. The southern portion was occupied by American troops, the northern portion by Soviet troops. The Soviet Union created a government in North Korea over which it held considerable influence. On June 25, 1950, North Korean forces crossed the 38th parallel. The United States secured a United Nation resolution condemning the aggression and committed ground troops to defend South Korea. These troops were commanded by General Douglas MacArthur, a highly popular military leader. MacArthur drove the North Korean forces back across the 38th parallel and began to talk about using military force, including nuclear weapons against China, to unify Korea. In November, China committed troops on the side of North Korea, and a battle line eventually stabilized along the 38th parallel. MacArthur still envisioned a total victory, but President Truman and the joint chiefs of staff had settled on the much more limited aim of reestablishing the status quo. When MacArthur publicly sided with Congressional leaders who favored total victory, Truman relieved him of his command.

Questions 88–91 refer to the following map:

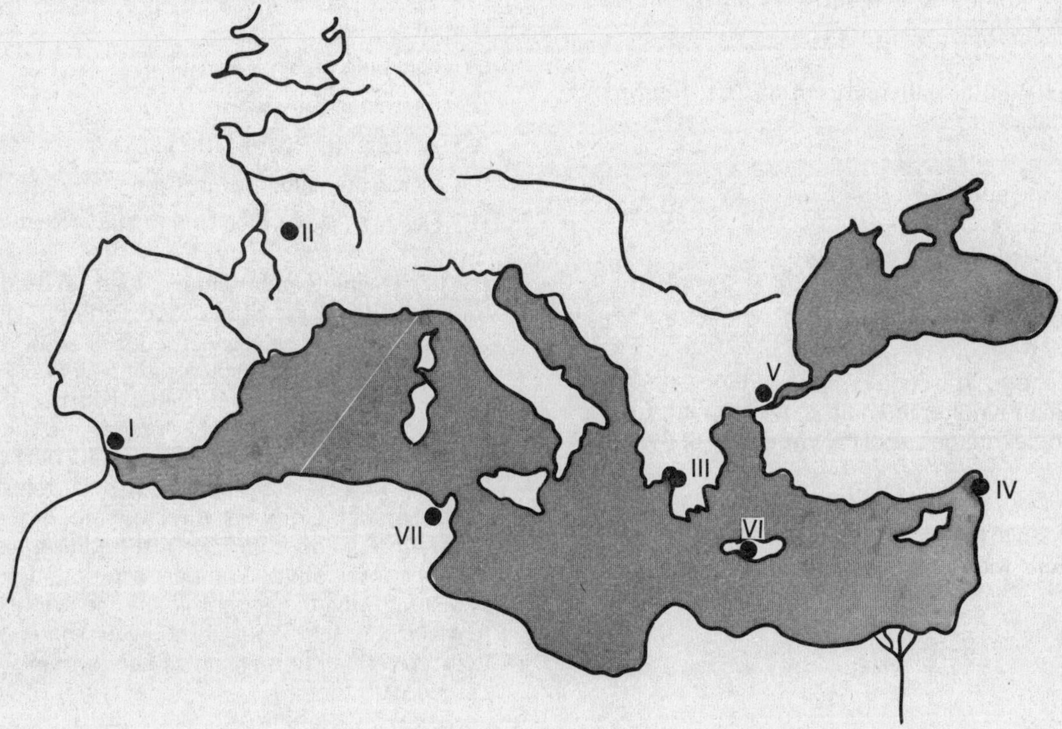

88. The site of the Minoan Civilization (3000–1400 B.C.) was

(A) I
(B) III
(C) V
(D) VI
(E) VII

(D) The Minoan Civilization was located on the island of Crete. Its capital city was Knossos.

89. The city whose general attacked Roman forces in Italy during the Second Punic War by leading his army across the Alps was

(A) II
(B) III
(C) IV
(D) V
(E) VII

(E) The Punic Wars pitted Rome against the powerful commercial empire of Carthage. In the Second Punic War, Hannibal led his troops and elephants from Carthage through Spain and across the Alps. Rome finally destroyed Carthage in the Third Punic War.

90. The capital of the eastern part of the later Roman Empire was

(A) I
(B) II
(C) IV
(D) V
(E) VI

(D) In the fourth century, Constantine reunited the Roman empire and built a new capital, Constantinople, on the site of the Greek city of Byzantium.

91. The city-state that developed democratic institutions was

(A) II
(B) III
(C) IV
(D) V
(E) VII

(B) This is, of course, Athens.

Questions 92 and 93 refer to the following:

(A) Hitler
(B) Bismarck
(C) Kaiser William II
(D) Metternich
(E) Hindenburg

92. Dominated the Congress of Vienna

(D) After Napoleon's defeat, representatives of the victorious nations and France met at the Congress of Vienna to reconstruct Europe. This conference was dominated by the powerful Prince Metternich of Austria.

93. Accomplished the unification of Germany

(B) Otto von Bismarck, a member of the dominant, landowning aristocracy called the Junkers was appointed chief minister of Prussia in 1862. A reactionary who opposed democracy, Bismarck united Germany by military force.

94. During the twentieth century, labor unions in the United States have differed from their European counterparts in that they have been LEAST concerned with

(A) obtaining higher wages
(B) improving job security
(C) gaining greater fringe benefits
(D) increasing union membership
(E) electing union officials to public office

(E) In the nineteenth century, there existed two traditions of labor organization in the United States. One tradition concerned itself with wages and working conditions. It sought benefits such as higher wages and shorter hours. This tradition is sometimes referred to as "bread and butter" unionism. The other tradition cast its nets more widely and sought political and social reform as well. Samuel Gompers directed the American Federation of Labor into the first tradition. Essentially a conservative, Gompers was not interested in restructuring the economic pie, he just wanted to make sure that labor got a bigger share. Since then, American unions have been primarily concerned with the bread and butter issues of wages and working conditions.

95. In 1962, President John F. Kennedy declared a naval quarantine of Cuba in order to

(A) prevent the Soviet Union from placing offensive missiles in Cuba

(B) ensure that a highly infectious disease did not spread beyond the island

(C) stem the flood of Cubans illegally entering the United States

(D) punish Cuba economically for withdrawing from the Organization of American States

(E) incite a revolution to overthrow the government of Fidel Castro

(A) After the Soviet Union's successful Sputnik launch, the United States placed intermediate-range missiles in Italy and Turkey where they could reach the Soviet Union. In 1962, the Soviet Union began building missile bases in Cuba, where they threatened the United States. When the United States learned of the missile bases, President Kennedy went on national television to announce that the U.S. Navy would blockade Cuba to prevent the installation of Soviet missiles there. Shortly thereafter, it was announced that Soviet ships, presumably carrying missiles, were in the Atlantic Ocean and heading for Cuba. Ultimately, in exchange for a U.S. promise to respect Cuba's independence, the Soviet Union abandoned the plan to put missiles in Cuba. Many people believe that the Cuban Missile Crisis brought the world close to a nuclear war.

Mathematics Tests

Mathematics Tests

The College Board offers two Mathematics Subject Tests, Level I and Level IIC. Both Level I and Level IIC consist of 50 multiple-choice questions, and both test algebra, geometry, trigonometry, functions, and some miscellaneous topics.

Level I versus Level IIC

The content of the two tests overlaps somewhat, especially in questions that treat elementary algebra, coordinate geometry, and basic trigonometry. The Level IIC test, however, emphasizes more advanced concepts with a greater concentration on trigonometry, functions, and various pre-calculus topics. Further, Level I emphasizes topics taken from plane geometry, while Level IIC does not test plane geometry per se. The trigonometry problems on the Level I test focus primarily on right triangle trigonometry and fundamental relationships among the trigonometric ratios, while Level IIC problems place more emphasis on the properties and graphs of the trigonometric functions, inverse trigonometric functions, trigonometric equations and identities, and the laws of sines and cosines.

The approximate number of questions in each category is shown in the table below:

Topic	Level I	Level IIC
Algebra	15	9
Geometry		
Plane Geometry	10	0
Solid Geometry	3	4
Coordinate Geometry	6	6
Trigonometry	4	10
Functions	6	12
Statistics	3	6
Miscellaneous	3	3
TOTAL	50	50

A further important difference between the two levels is the calculator requirement of the Level IIC test. (A calculator is not just permitted—it is required!) Candidates can use almost any scientific or graphing calculator on the Mathematics Level IIC test. However, pocket organizers, hand-held minicomputers, laptop and notebook computers, models with typewriter keypads, models that "talk," "clamshells," and models that require an outside power source are *NOT* permitted. You should consult the booklet "Taking the SAT II Subject Tests" published by The College Board for further information about the list of approved models.

Which test should you take?

If you have had a course in trigonometry and elementary functions and have done fairly well, and if you know how to use a scientific or graphing calculator, then you should take Mathematics Level IIC. Otherwise, plan to take Level I. Although Level IIC tends to test more advanced topics, you should not automatically elect to take Level I in the hope of "acing" an easier test. Level I is not necessarily easier than Level IIC because the two forms test different topics. For example, Level I includes approximately 10 questions on plane geometry; and if you have not studied plane geometry for two years, you may find that you will not do as well on Level I as Level IIC even though you have subsequently studied more advanced concepts. You can use the sample Level I and Level IIC tests in this book to determine which version you should take.

Sample Problems

Algebra

EXAMPLE:

If $i = \sqrt{-1}$ and if $x = 3 - 2i$, then $x^2 =$

(A) $3 - 12i$
(B) $5 - 12i$
(C) $9 - 12i$
(D) $13 - 12i$
(E) $13 - 15i$

Solution:

$x^2 = (3 - 2i)^2 = (3 - 2i)(3 - 2i) = 9 - 12i + 4i^2$

Since $i = \sqrt{-1}$, $i^2 = -1$. Therefore:

$9 - 12i + 4i^2 = 9 - 12i + 4(-1) = 5 - 12i$

So the correct answer is (B).

Plane Geometry

EXAMPLE:

In Figure 1, if *PQ* is parallel to *ST*, then $y =$

(A) 20
(B) 40
(C) 50
(D) 60
(E) 80

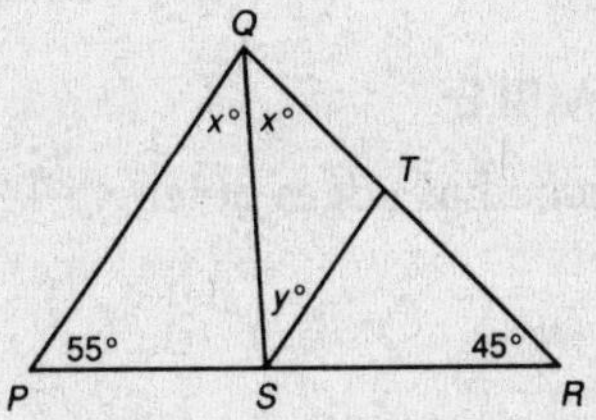

A.1, Figure 1

Solution: Since the sum of the degree measures of the interior angles of a triangle is 180:

$45 + 55 + PQR = 180$

$PQR = 180 - 100 = 80$

Since $PQR = x + x$:

$2x = 80$

$x = 40$

Since *PQ* and *ST* are parallel, $x = y$, and $y = 40$.

So the correct answer is (B).

(NOTE: Level II does not test plane geometry per se, so this is a problem that might appear on Level I, but would not appear on Level II.)

Coordinate Geometry

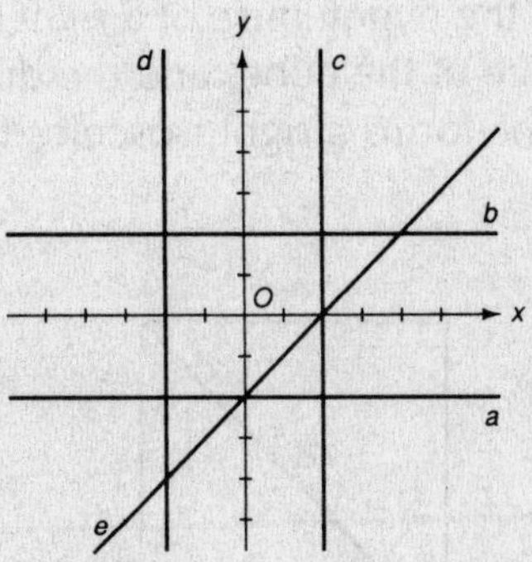

A.2, Figure 2

EXAMPLE:

Which of the lines in Figure 2 is the graph of $y = -2$?

(A) *a*
(B) *b*
(C) *c*
(D) *d*
(E) *e*

Solution: The graph of $y = -2$ is a horizontal line with *y* intercept -2. So the correct answer is (A).

Solid Geometry

EXAMPLE:

If a cube has edges of length 1, what is the distance from any vertex to the center of the cube?

(A) $\frac{\sqrt{2}}{2}$

(B) $\frac{\sqrt{3}}{2}$

(C) 1

(D) $\sqrt{2}$

(E) $\sqrt{3}$

Solution: A figure will make the solution to the problem easier to understand:

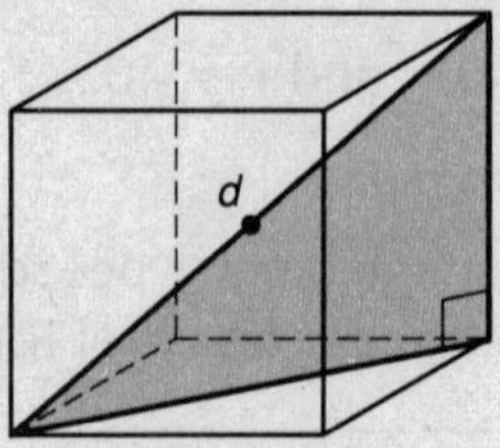

The center of the cube lies on the hypotenuse of a right triangle formed by an edge of the cube, a diagonal of the face of the cube, and the diagonal of the cube itself. The diagonal of the face of the cube forms a right isosceles triangle:

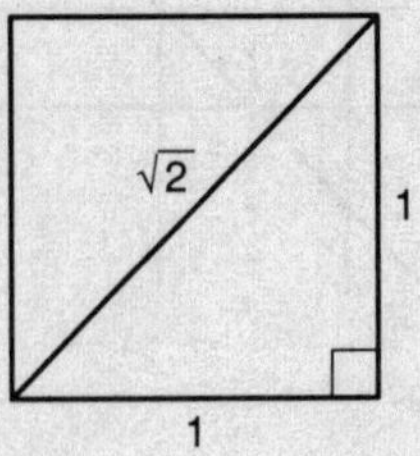

Since the legs of the triangle have length 1, the hypotenuse has length $1 \times \sqrt{2} = \sqrt{2}$. Now we can calculate the length of the diagonal of the cube using the Pythagorean Theorem:

$$d^2 = (1)^2 + (\sqrt{2})^2$$
$$d^2 = 1 + 2$$
$$d = \sqrt{3}$$

Since the center of the cube lies at the midpoint of the diagonal of the cube, the distance from any vertex to the center of the cube is $\frac{\sqrt{3}}{2}$. So the correct answer is (B).

Trigonometry

EXAMPLE:

$\sin^2(2x) + \cos^2(2x) =$

(A) 0
(B) 1
(C) 2
(D) 4
(E) $4 \sin^2 x^2 \cos x^2$

The correct answer to this item is (B): "$\sin^2 A + \cos^2 A = 1$" is one of the Pythagorean Identities.

Elementary Functions

EXAMPLE:

If $f(x) = 2x + 1$ and $g(x) = 3x - 2$, for what real number k does $f(k) = g(k)$?

(A) -3
(B) -1
(C) 0
(D) 3
(E) 5

Solution: $f(k) = g(k)$ when $2x + 1 = 3x - 2$:

$2x + 1 = 3x - 2$

$-x = -3$

$x = 3$

So the correct answer is (D).

Miscellaneous

EXAMPLE:

All *P* are *M*.
No *M* are *S*.

Which of the following conclusions can be logically deduced from the statements above?

(A) No *S* are *P*.
(B) No *M* are *P*.
(C) Some *S* are *P*.
(D) Some *P* are *S*.
(E) some *P* are not *M*.

Solution: A diagram might be useful here. The first statement can be rendered as:

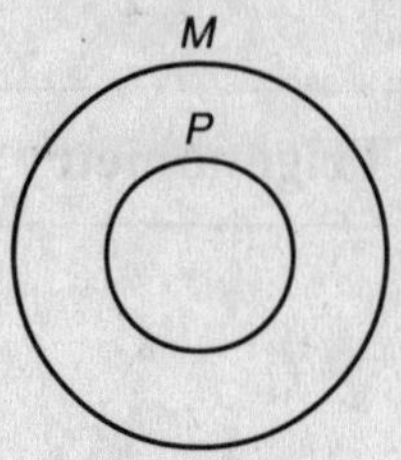

The *P*-circle contains all things that are *P*s, and the *M*-circle contains all things that are *M*. Notice that the *P*-circle is entirely contained within the *M*-circle. Now we add the second statement:

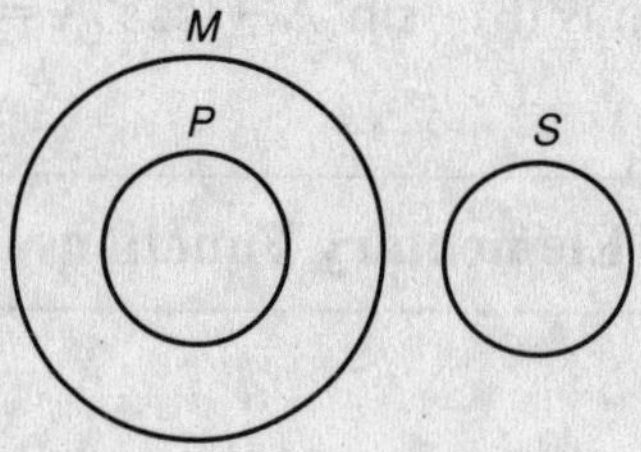

Notice that there is no overlap between the *S*-circle and the *M*-circle. The diagram also shows no overlap between the *P*-circle and the *S*-circle. Thus, answer (A) is deducible.

Unusual Question Structures

Most of the questions that make up the Mathematics Tests have forms similar to those shown above. There are, however, two special cases. First, some question stems contain "reversers." A reverser is a word such as "not" or "except" that turns the question inside-out. For example:

EXAMPLE:

If k is a negative integer, then all of the following must be positive integers EXCEPT

(A) $-k$

(B) $\frac{1}{k^2}$

(C) k^2

(D) $(-k)^2$

(E) $-k^2$

Solution: Notice the presence of the word "EXCEPT." It tells us that four of the five expressions must be positive and that one is negative. We are looking for the EXCEPTION. The correct answer is (E). Since k is negative, k^2 is positive. Thus $-k^2$ must be negative.

When addressing a problem, be sure that you read the question stem carefully. If the question stem contains a reverser, you may want to circle that word so that you make sure you answer the question asked.

Another special form uses combinations of Roman-numeraled statements to form answer choices:

EXAMPLE:

If x is an odd integer, which of the following must be even?

I. $2x$
II. $x + 3$
III. x^2

(A) I only
(B) II only
(C) I and II only
(D) I and III only
(E) I, II, and III

Solution: x is odd, but $2x$ must be even; and statement I must be part of the correct answer choice. On this ground, you can eliminate (B)—it does not include statement I. Next, since an odd number plus an odd number yields an even number, II must be part of the correct choice. And this allows us to eliminate (A) and (D). The only remaining choices are (C) and (E), and we examine statement III. Since an odd number multiplied by an odd number yields an odd number, x^2 must be odd. Therefore, statement III should not be part of the correct choice, and the correct answer is (C).

Special Strategies

There are certain special strategies that are useful only for the Mathematics Tests. These strategies, as you will see, could not be applied to non-math tests. They take advantage of the multiple-choice format of the tests to obtain answers by non-orthodox means.

Our first strategy is called "picking numbers." This strategy can be used when the answer choices are algebraic formulas. Let us return to a problem we just worked and solve it by "picking a number."

EXAMPLE:

If k is a negative integer, then all of the following must be positive integers EXCEPT

(A) $-k$
(B) $\frac{1}{k^2}$
(C) k^2
(D) $(-k)^2$
(E) $-k^2$

A very easy way to solve this problem is to pick a value for k, say $k = -1$. Now substitute -1 for k into the answer choices:

(A) $-(-1) = 1$ Positive

(B) $\frac{1}{(-1)^2} = \frac{1}{1} = 1$ Positive

(C) $(-1)^2 = 1$ Positive

(D) $(-(-1))^2 = (1)^2 = 1$ Positive

(E) $-(-1)^2 = -(1) = -1$ Negative

A second strategy that is uniquely applicable to the Mathematics Tests is "working backwards." Here is an example:

EXAMPLE:

If $2^{2x} = 64$, then $x =$

(A) $\frac{1}{2}$

(B) 1

(C) $\frac{3}{2}$

(D) 2

(E) 3

One of these five numbers is the value of x. Just substitute numbers for x until you find the right one:

(A) $2^{2(1/2)} = 64$

$2 = 64$ Wrong

(B) $2^{2(1)} = 64$

$4 = 64$ Wrong

(C) $2^{2(3/2)} = 64$

$2^3 = 64$

$8 = 64$ Wrong

(D) $2^{2(2)} = 64$

$2^4 = 64$

$16 = 64$ Wrong

(E) $2^{2(3)} = 64$

$2^6 = 64$

$64 = 64$ Correct

The explanations to the questions that make up the practice exams use these and similar strategies when they are available.

Mathematics Level I Answer Sheet

1	Ⓐ	Ⓑ	Ⓒ	Ⓓ	Ⓔ	26	Ⓐ	Ⓑ	Ⓒ	Ⓓ	Ⓔ
2	Ⓐ	Ⓑ	Ⓒ	Ⓓ	Ⓔ	27	Ⓐ	Ⓑ	Ⓒ	Ⓓ	Ⓔ
3	Ⓐ	Ⓑ	Ⓒ	Ⓓ	Ⓔ	28	Ⓐ	Ⓑ	Ⓒ	Ⓓ	Ⓔ
4	Ⓐ	Ⓑ	Ⓒ	Ⓓ	Ⓔ	29	Ⓐ	Ⓑ	Ⓒ	Ⓓ	Ⓔ
5	Ⓐ	Ⓑ	Ⓒ	Ⓓ	Ⓔ	30	Ⓐ	Ⓑ	Ⓒ	Ⓓ	Ⓔ
6	Ⓐ	Ⓑ	Ⓒ	Ⓓ	Ⓔ	31	Ⓐ	Ⓑ	Ⓒ	Ⓓ	Ⓔ
7	Ⓐ	Ⓑ	Ⓒ	Ⓓ	Ⓔ	32	Ⓐ	Ⓑ	Ⓒ	Ⓓ	Ⓔ
8	Ⓐ	Ⓑ	Ⓒ	Ⓓ	Ⓔ	33	Ⓐ	Ⓑ	Ⓒ	Ⓓ	Ⓔ
9	Ⓐ	Ⓑ	Ⓒ	Ⓓ	Ⓔ	34	Ⓐ	Ⓑ	Ⓒ	Ⓓ	Ⓔ
10	Ⓐ	Ⓑ	Ⓒ	Ⓓ	Ⓔ	35	Ⓐ	Ⓑ	Ⓒ	Ⓓ	Ⓔ
11	Ⓐ	Ⓑ	Ⓒ	Ⓓ	Ⓔ	36	Ⓐ	Ⓑ	Ⓒ	Ⓓ	Ⓔ
12	Ⓐ	Ⓑ	Ⓒ	Ⓓ	Ⓔ	37	Ⓐ	Ⓑ	Ⓒ	Ⓓ	Ⓔ
13	Ⓐ	Ⓑ	Ⓒ	Ⓓ	Ⓔ	38	Ⓐ	Ⓑ	Ⓒ	Ⓓ	Ⓔ
14	Ⓐ	Ⓑ	Ⓒ	Ⓓ	Ⓔ	39	Ⓐ	Ⓑ	Ⓒ	Ⓓ	Ⓔ
15	Ⓐ	Ⓑ	Ⓒ	Ⓓ	Ⓔ	40	Ⓐ	Ⓑ	Ⓒ	Ⓓ	Ⓔ
16	Ⓐ	Ⓑ	Ⓒ	Ⓓ	Ⓔ	41	Ⓐ	Ⓑ	Ⓒ	Ⓓ	Ⓔ
17	Ⓐ	Ⓑ	Ⓒ	Ⓓ	Ⓔ	42	Ⓐ	Ⓑ	Ⓒ	Ⓓ	Ⓔ
18	Ⓐ	Ⓑ	Ⓒ	Ⓓ	Ⓔ	43	Ⓐ	Ⓑ	Ⓒ	Ⓓ	Ⓔ
19	Ⓐ	Ⓑ	Ⓒ	Ⓓ	Ⓔ	44	Ⓐ	Ⓑ	Ⓒ	Ⓓ	Ⓔ
20	Ⓐ	Ⓑ	Ⓒ	Ⓓ	Ⓔ	45	Ⓐ	Ⓑ	Ⓒ	Ⓓ	Ⓔ
21	Ⓐ	Ⓑ	Ⓒ	Ⓓ	Ⓔ	46	Ⓐ	Ⓑ	Ⓒ	Ⓓ	Ⓔ
22	Ⓐ	Ⓑ	Ⓒ	Ⓓ	Ⓔ	47	Ⓐ	Ⓑ	Ⓒ	Ⓓ	Ⓔ
23	Ⓐ	Ⓑ	Ⓒ	Ⓓ	Ⓔ	48	Ⓐ	Ⓑ	Ⓒ	Ⓓ	Ⓔ
24	Ⓐ	Ⓑ	Ⓒ	Ⓓ	Ⓔ	49	Ⓐ	Ⓑ	Ⓒ	Ⓓ	Ⓔ
25	Ⓐ	Ⓑ	Ⓒ	Ⓓ	Ⓔ	50	Ⓐ	Ⓑ	Ⓒ	Ⓓ	Ⓔ

MATHEMATICS TEST, LEVEL I

Directions: For each problem in this test, determine which is the best of the five choices given. Then darken the corresponding oval space on the answer sheet.

Notes: (1) Figures that accompany problems in this test are drawn as accurately as possible EXCEPT when accompanied by the words "NOTE: Figure not drawn to scale."

(2) Unless otherwise indicated, all figures lie in a plane.

(3) Unless otherwise specified, the domain of a function is assumed to be the set of all real numbers x such that $f(x)$ is a real number.

1. If $x = (b + 3)^2$ and $b = -4$, then $x =$

(A) -49
(B) -1
(C) 0
(D) 1
(E) 49

2. If $f(x) = 4x - 1$ and $1 < x < 3$, then which of the following defines all and only the possible values of $f(x)$?

(A) $-3 < f(x) < 12$
(B) $3 < f(x) < 11$
(C) $3 < f(x) < 12$
(D) $4 < f(x) < 11$
(E) $5 < f(x) < 11$

3. If $\frac{5}{k+4} = \frac{7}{k+6}$, then $k =$

(A) $\frac{24}{35}$
(B) $\frac{9}{13}$
(C) $\frac{2}{3}$
(D) 1
(E) 2

4. The average cost of 13 items in a display case is \$12. After one of the items is removed, the average cost of the remaining 12 items is \$11. The cost of the item removed is

(A) \$1.00
(B) \$11
(C) \$12
(D) \$13
(E) \$24

5. If $2^{3x} = 2$, then $x =$

(A) $\frac{1}{3}$
(B) 1
(C) $\frac{3}{2}$
(D) 4
(E) 6

6. If $\frac{1}{\frac{2}{x}} = \frac{2}{3}$, then $x =$

(A) $\frac{3}{4}$
(B) 1
(C) $\frac{4}{3}$
(D) $\frac{3}{2}$
(E) $\frac{9}{4}$

7. The distance between the points $(-2,-3)$ and $(-2, 4)$ is

(A) $\sqrt{65}$
(B) 7
(C) 5
(D) $\sqrt{7}$
(E) 1

GO ON TO THE NEXT PAGE

8. In Figure 1, if $RT = 2\frac{1}{4}$, then $RS =$

(A) $\frac{3}{4}$

(B) $\frac{11}{12}$

(C) $\frac{5}{4}$

(D) $\frac{19}{12}$

(E) $\frac{5}{3}$

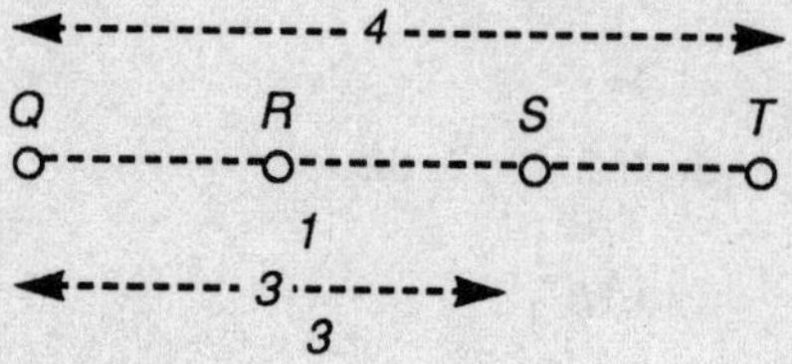

Figure 1

9. In Figure 2, which of the following points falls within the shaded area?

(A) (5,0)

(B) (5,1)

(C) (4,2)

(D) (4,3)

(E) (3,4)

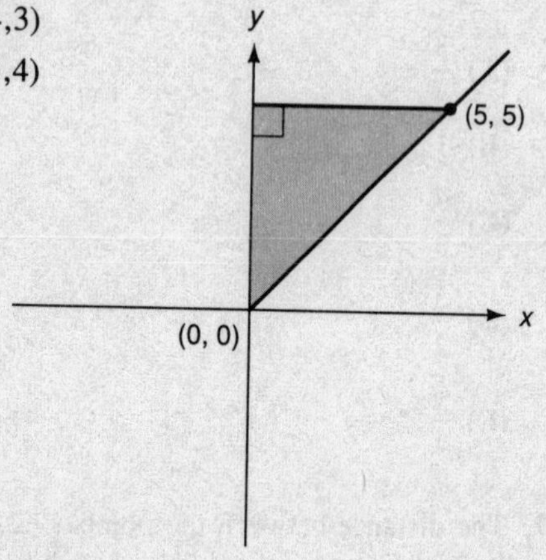

Figure 2

10. If $4 < x < 12$ and $6 < y < 8$, then which of the following must be true?

(A) $\frac{2}{3} < xy < \frac{3}{2}$

(B) $2 < xy < 4$

(C) $6 < xy < 12$

(D) $24 < xy < 96$

(E) $32 < xy < 72$

11. In Figure 3, three equilateral triangles have a common vertex. $x + y + z =$

(A) 270

(B) 180

(C) 120

(D) 90

(E) 60

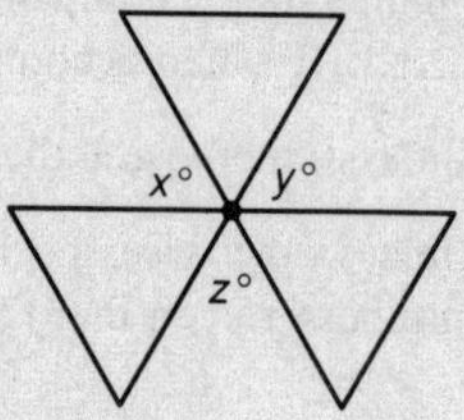

Figure 3

12. If the operation ϕ is defined for all real numbers x and y by the equation $x \phi y = xy - y - x$, then $-2 \phi - 1 =$

(A) -3

(B) -2

(C) 1

(D) 3

(E) 5

13. In Figure 4, if the circle has a radius of 3, what is the length of minor arc PR?

(A) $\frac{\pi}{6}$

(B) $\frac{\pi}{3}$

(C) π

(D) $\frac{3\pi}{2}$

(E) 3π

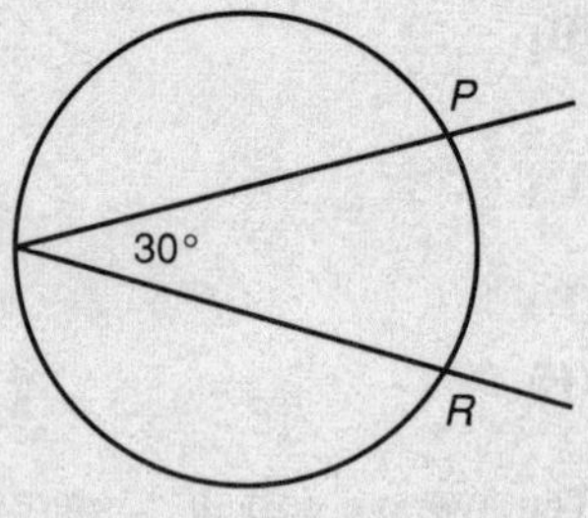

Figure 4

GO ON TO THE NEXT PAGE

14. $\sqrt{45} - \sqrt{20} + \sqrt{5} =$

(A) $2 - \sqrt{5}$

(B) 0

(C) $2 + \sqrt{5}$

(D) $2\sqrt{5}$

(E) 10

15. Which of the following must be true of a square?

I. The intersection of the diagonals forms four equal angles.

II. The area is equal to the square of the diagonal.

III. The number of square units of the area is equal to the number of linear units of the perimeter.

(A) I only

(B) III only

(C) I and II only

(D) I and III only

(E) I, II, and III

16. What is the least positive integer x for which $12 - x$ and $15 - x$ will be non-zero and have opposite signs?

(A) 3

(B) 4

(C) 7

(D) 11

(E) 13

17. The solution set to the pair of equations:

$mx + ny = 15$
$nx + my = 13$

is $x = 3$ and $y = 1$. What are the values of m and n?

(A) $m = 5$
$n = 3$

(B) $m = 4$
$n = 3$

(C) $m = 3$
$n = 4$

(D) $m = 3$
$n = 5$

(E) $m = 2$
$n = 6$

18. The lengths of the sides of quadrilateral Q are all integers. If three of the sides have lengths of 3, 4, and 5, then the maximum length of the fourth side is

(A) 13

(B) 12

(C) 11

(D) 7

(E) 2

19. In Figure 5, if ABD is a right isosceles triangle, then $x =$

(A) 25

(B) 30

(C) $37\frac{1}{2}$

(D) 45

(E) 60

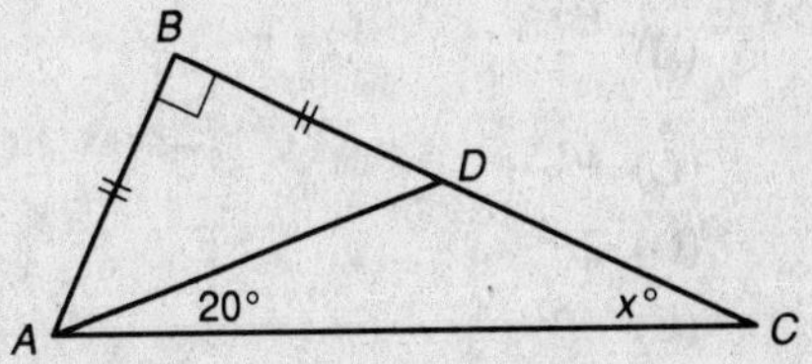

Figure 5

20. If $xyz \neq 0$, then $\dfrac{2x^3y^2z}{8x^2y^3z^2} =$

(A) $4xyz$

(B) $\dfrac{4x}{yz}$

(C) $\dfrac{xyz}{4}$

(D) $\dfrac{xy}{4z}$

(E) $\dfrac{x}{4yz}$

GO ON TO THE NEXT PAGE

21. If $f(x) = \frac{1}{1-x}$ and $g(x) = \frac{1}{x^2}$, then $g(f(3)) =$

(A) -2
(B) $\frac{1}{4}$
(C) $\frac{1}{2}$
(D) 2
(E) 4

22. A polygon Q with a certain perimeter P will have its greatest area when all of its sides have the same length. What is the maximum area of a rectangle with a perimeter of P units?

(A) $\frac{P^2}{16}$
(B) $\frac{P^2}{4}$
(C) P^2
(D) $2P^2$
(E) $4P^2$

23. Which of the following graphs is NOT the graph of a function?

(A)

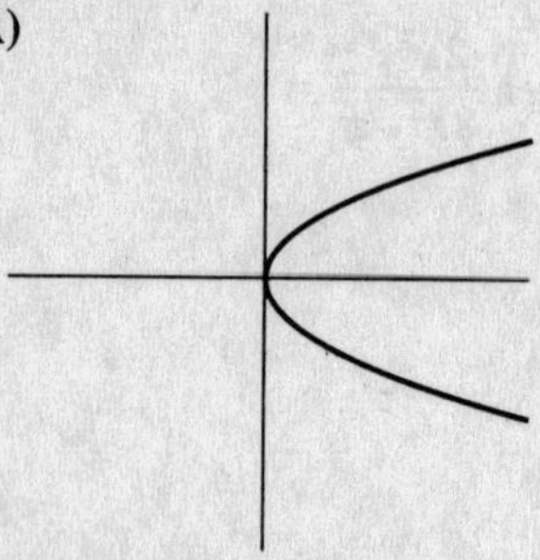

(B)

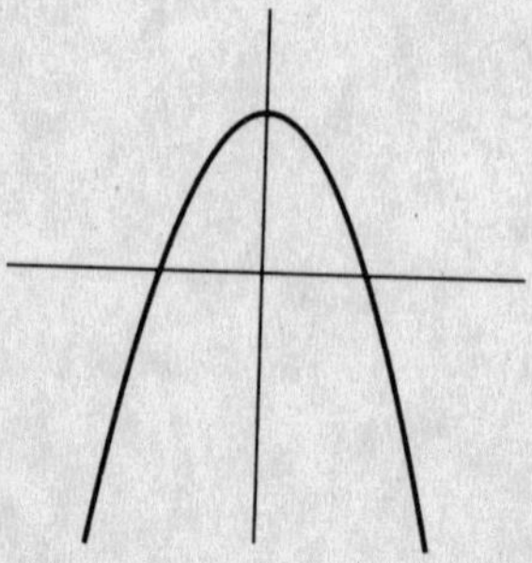

(C)

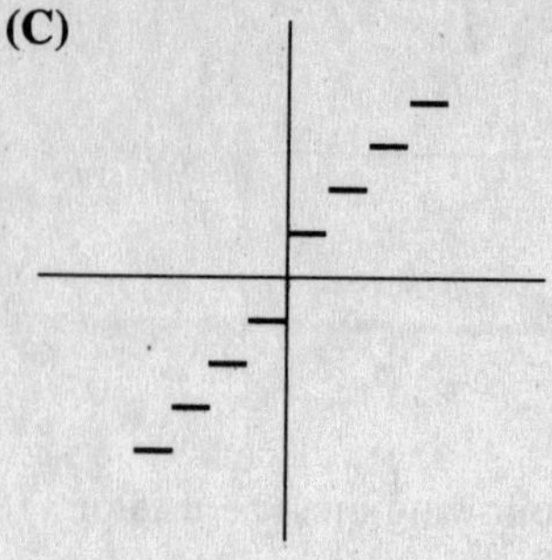

(D)

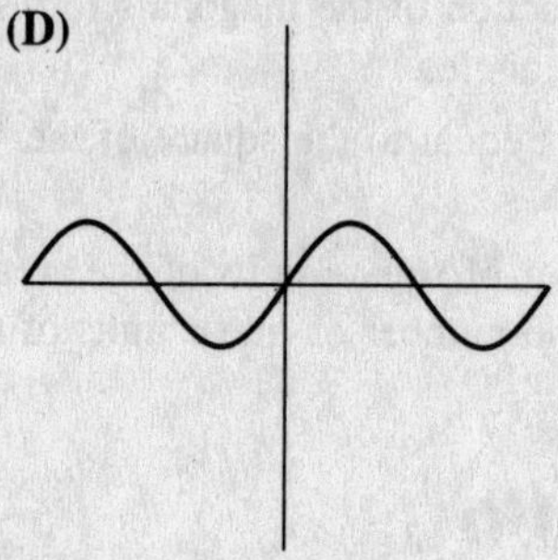

(E)

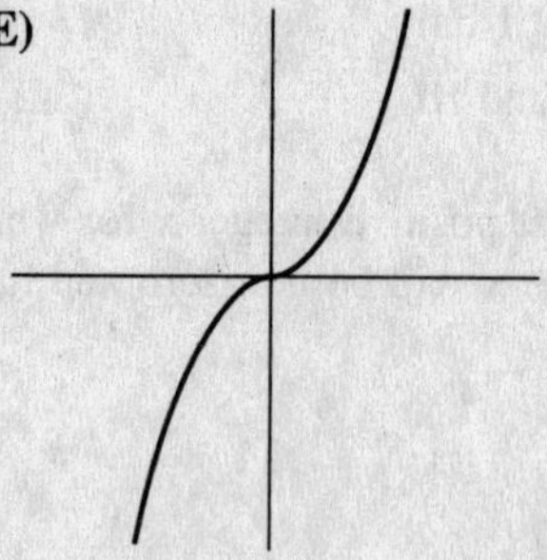

24. In Figure 6, if $\sin A = \frac{2}{3}$, then $BC =$

(A) 18
(B) 8
(C) $3\sqrt{2}$
(D) 4
(E) $2\sqrt{5}$

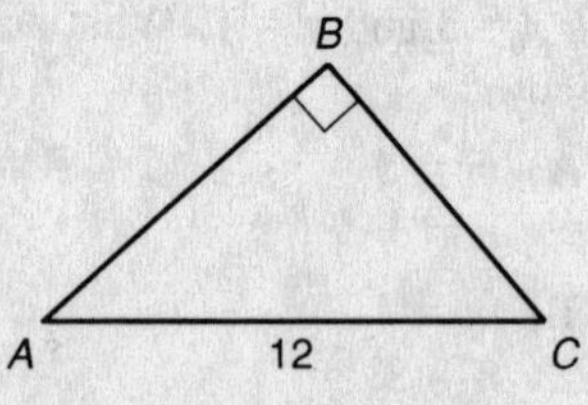

Figure 6

GO ON TO THE NEXT PAGE

25. An equation for the circle with its center at the origin and passing through the point (1,2) is

(A) $x^2 + y^2 = \sqrt{5}$

(B) $x^2 + y^2 = 3$

(C) $x^2 + y^2 = 5$

(D) $x^2 + y^2 = 9$

(E) $x^2 + y^2 = 25$

26. How many integers are in the solution set of $|1 - 3x| < 5$?

(A) None

(B) One

(C) Two

(D) Three

(E) Infinitely many

27. If x, y, and z are positive integers such that

$4x + 6y = z$

then z must be divisible by

(A) 2

(B) 4

(C) 6

(D) 10

(E) 24

28. If the points $(-2,4)$, $(3,4)$, and $(3,-2)$ are connected to form a triangle, the area of the triangle is

(A) $\frac{11}{2}$

(B) 6

(C) 12

(D) 15

(E) 24

29. If $i^2 = -1$ and if $k = 2 + i$, then $k^2 =$

(A) 1

(B) $3 + 4i$

(C) $4 + 3i$

(D) $6 + 7i$

(E) $9 + 12i$

30. If a line contains the points $(-2, 1)$ and $(4,4)$, then the x-intercept is

(A) -4

(B) $-\frac{1}{2}$

(C) 0

(D) $\frac{2}{3}$

(E) $\frac{3}{2}$

31. In Figure 7, if the radius of the circle is r, then the ratio $\frac{\text{area of the larger square}}{\text{area of the smaller square}} =$

(A) $\frac{2\sqrt{2}}{1}$

(B) $\frac{2}{1}$

(C) $\frac{\sqrt{2}}{1}$

(D) $\frac{1}{\sqrt{2}}$

(E) $\frac{1}{2}$

Figure 7

32. If $0° < \theta < 90°$, then $\sin^2\theta + \cos^2\theta - 1 =$

(A) -2

(B) 0

(C) 1

(D) 2

(E) 4

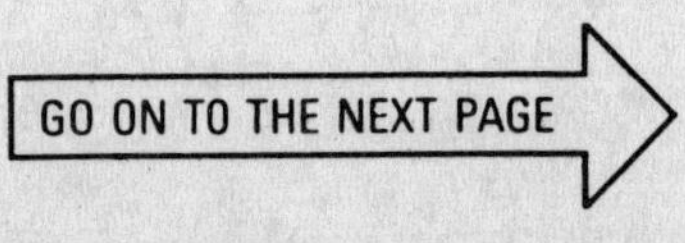

33. If $f(x) = 3x - 2$ and $g(f(x)) = x$, then $g(x) =$

(A) $3x + 2$

(B) $2 - 3x$

(C) $\frac{1}{3x - 2}$

(D) $\frac{x}{3} + 2$

(E) $\frac{x + 2}{3}$

34. In Figure 8, if $AC \,//\, GE$ and $GF = x$ and $FE = y$, then the ratio $\frac{\text{area } \triangle BCD}{\text{area } \triangle BCA} =$

(A) $\frac{x}{y}$

(B) $\frac{y}{x}$

(C) $\frac{x}{x + y}$

(D) $\frac{y}{x + y}$

(E) $\frac{y}{2(x + y)}$

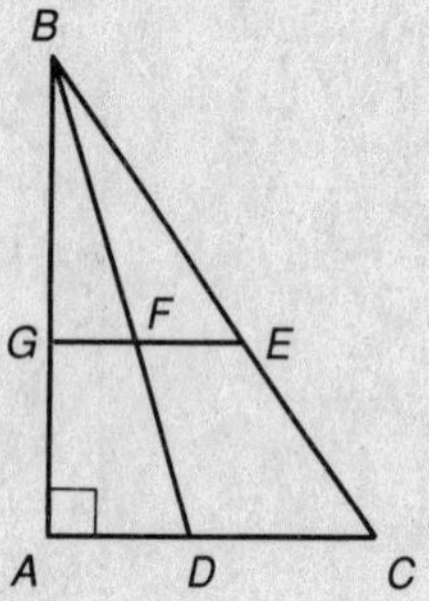

Figure 8

35. If $\frac{1}{a} + \frac{1}{b} = \frac{1}{c}$, then $c =$

(A) $\frac{1}{ab}$

(B) ab

(C) $\frac{a + b}{ab}$

(D) $\frac{ab}{a + b}$

(E) $\frac{2ab}{a + b}$

36. If $x^3y^2z < 0$, then it must be true that

(A) $x^3 < 0$

(B) $z < 0$

(C) $xy < 0$

(D) $xz < 0$

(E) $yz < 0$

37. If the slope of a line is 3 and the y-intercept is 2, then the x-intercept of the line is

(A) $-\frac{3}{2}$

(B) $-\frac{2}{3}$

(C) -1

(D) $\frac{2}{3}$

(E) $\frac{3}{2}$

38. For the right triangle in Figure 9, all of the following statements are true EXCEPT:

(A) $\sin \theta = \frac{b}{c}$

(B) $\tan \sigma = \frac{a}{b}$

(C) $\cos \theta = \frac{c}{a}$

(D) $\sin \theta = \cos \sigma$

(E) $\cot \sigma = \tan \theta$

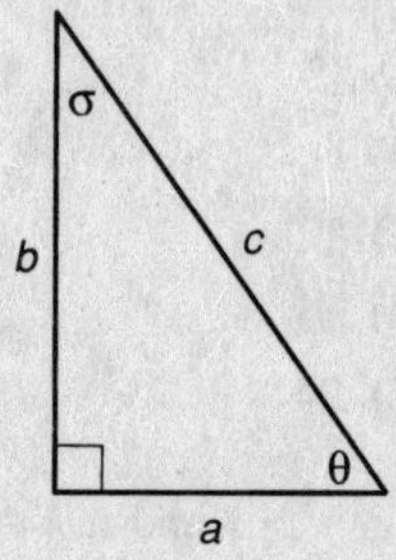

Figure 9

39. Three candidates for president of the Student Council—Ashley, José, and Kim—must each be scheduled for a single 10-minute address to the entire student body. If the order of the presentations is determined randomly, how many different orders are possible?

(A) 3

(B) 6

(C) 9

(D) 12

(E) 27

40. If $x \neq 0$ then $\frac{8^{2x}}{2^{4x}} =$

(A) 2^{2x}

(B) 4^{-x}

(C) 4^{2x}

(D) 4^{1-x}

(E) 8^{-x}

All S are M.
No P are M.

41. Which of the following conclusions can be logically deduced from the two statements above?

(A) All S are P.

(B) All M are S.

(C) Some S are not M.

(D) Some M are P.

(E) No P are S.

42. Cube Q has volume V. In terms of V, a cube with edges only one-fourth the length of those of Q will have a volume of

(A) $\frac{V^3}{64}$

(B) $\frac{V^3}{4}$

(C) $\frac{V}{64}$

(D) $\frac{V}{4}$

(E) $\frac{\sqrt[3]{V}}{8}$

43. If θ is an acute angle and $\cos \theta = \frac{b}{c}$, $b > 0$ and $c > 0$ and $b \neq c$, then $\sin \theta =$

(A) $\frac{b}{\sqrt{b^2 - c^2}}$

(B) $\frac{c}{\sqrt{c^2 - b^2}}$

(C) $\frac{\sqrt{b^2 - c^2}}{b}$

(D) $\frac{\sqrt{b^2 - c^2}}{c}$

(E) $\frac{\sqrt{c^2 - b^2}}{c}$

44. If a cube has an edge of length 2, what is the distance from any vertex to the center of the cube?

(A) $\frac{\sqrt{2}}{2}$

(B) $\sqrt{3}$

(C) $2\sqrt{2}$

(D) $2\sqrt{3}$

(E) $\frac{3}{2}$

45. If $x^2 + ax + bx + ab = 0$, and $x + b = 2$, then $x + a =$

(A) -8

(B) -4

(C) -2

(D) 0

(E) 2

46. Figure 10 shows two right circular cylinders, C and C'. If $r = kr'$ and $h = kh'$, then what is the ratio of:

$$\frac{\text{Volume of } C}{\text{Volume of } C'}?$$

(A) $\frac{1}{\pi}$

(B) π

(C) $k\pi$

(D) $\frac{1}{k^3}$

(E) k^3

GO ON TO THE NEXT PAGE

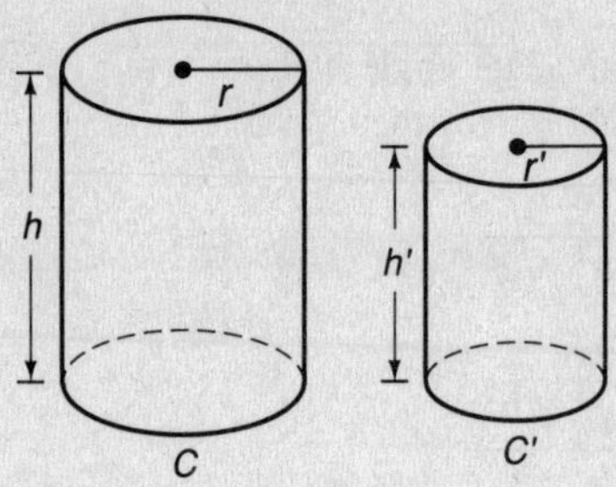

Figure 10

47. In Figure 11, if the triangle has an area of 1, then the area of the circle is

(A) π

(B) 2π

(C) $2\sqrt{3}\pi$

(D) 4π

(E) $4\sqrt{3}\pi$

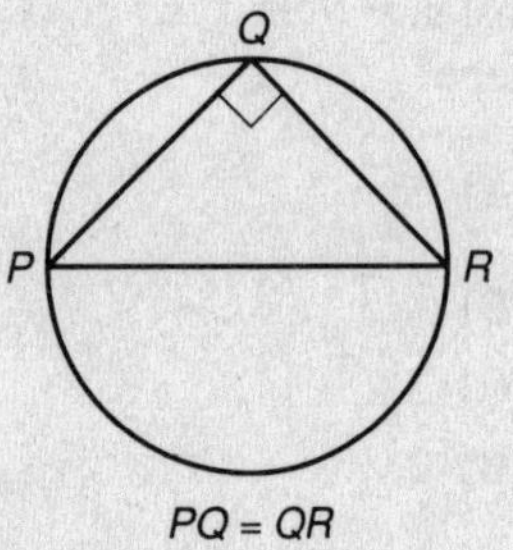

Figure 11

48. What are the coordinates of the point of intersection of the lines having the following equations:

$x - \sqrt{3}y = \sqrt{3}$

$\sqrt{3}x + y = 1$

(A) $\left(-\frac{1}{2}, -\frac{\sqrt{3}}{2}\right)$

(B) $\left(-\frac{2\sqrt{3}}{3}, -\frac{1}{2}\right)$

(C) $\left(\frac{1}{2}, \frac{2}{\sqrt{3}}\right)$

(D) $\left(-\frac{\sqrt{3}}{2}, -\frac{1}{2}\right)$

(E) $\left(\frac{3}{2\sqrt{3}}, -\frac{1}{2}\right)$

49. In Figure 12, the radius of the circles is 1. What is the perimeter of the shaded part of the figure?

(A) $\frac{4\pi}{3}$

(B) π

(C) $\frac{2\pi}{3}$

(D) $\frac{\pi}{3}$

(E) $\frac{\pi}{6}$

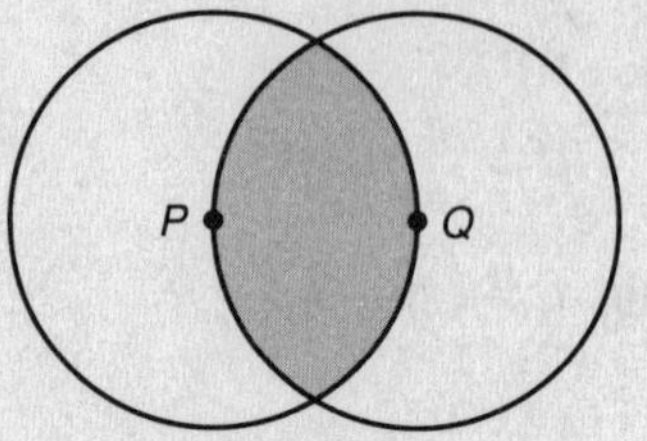

Figure 12

50. If $f(x) = \frac{x-2}{(x-2)(x^2+2)}$, for what value of x is $f(x)$ undefined?

(A) -4

(B) -2

(C) 0

(D) $\frac{1}{2}$

(E) 2

S T O P

IF YOU FINISH BEFORE TIME IS CALLED, YOU MAY CHECK YOUR WORK ON THIS TEST ONLY. DO NOT WORK ON ANY OTHER TEST IN THIS BOOK.

Explanatory Answers

1. If $x = (b + 3)^2$ and $b = -4$, then $x =$

(A) -49

(B) -1

(C) 0

(D) 1

(E) 49

(D) This first problem is, as we would anticipate, an easy one. Simply substitute -4 for b in the equation:

$x = (-4 + 3)^2$

$x = (-1)^2$

$x = 1$

2. If $f(x) = 4x - 1$ and $1 < x < 3$, then which of the following defines all and only the possible values of $f(x)$?

(A) $-3 < f(x) < 12$

(B) $3 < f(x) < 11$

(C) $3 < f(x) < 12$

(D) $4 < f(x) < 11$

(E) $5 < f(x) < 11$

(B) Find the minimum and maximum values of $f(x)$ by testing the limits of x. For $x = 1$:

$f(x) = 4(1) - 1 = 3$

For $x = 3$:

$f(x) = 4(3) - 1 = 12 - 1 = 11$

Therefore, $f(x)$ must be greater than 3 but less than 11.

3. If $\frac{5}{k+4} = \frac{7}{k+6}$, then $k =$

(A) $\frac{24}{35}$

(B) $\frac{9}{13}$

(C) $\frac{2}{3}$

(D) 1

(E) 2

(D) There are at least two ways to approach this problem. One is to solve for k. Begin by cross-multiplying:

$5(k + 6) = 7(k + 4)$

$5k + 30 = 7k + 28$

$2 = 2k$

$k = 1$

You could also solve the problem by substituting the answer values into the equation for k. Obviously, the values provided by (A), (B), and (C) will require more complex calculations than those provided by (D) and (E). So start with (D):

$$\frac{5}{1+4} = \frac{7}{1+6}$$

Since $1 = 1$, this proves that (D) is correct.

4. The average cost of 13 items in a display case is \$12. After one of the items is removed, the average cost of the remaining 12 items is \$11. The cost of the item removed is

(A) \$1.00

(B) \$11

(C) \$12

(D) \$13

(E) \$24

(E) This problem requires you to think about the concept of an average. An average is the sum of the values to be averaged divided by the number of values in the average. Therefore:

$$\frac{\text{Sum}}{13} = \$12$$

Which means the total value of the 13 items is:

Sum = \$12 × 13 = \$156

The sum of the 12 items that remain after the one is removed is:

$$\frac{\text{Sum}}{12} = \$11$$

Sum = \$11 x 12 = \$132

The difference between the two sums is the value of the item removed:

\$156 − \$132 = \$24

5. If $2^{3x} = 2$, then $x =$

(A) $\frac{1}{3}$

(B) 1

(C) $\frac{3}{2}$

(D) 4

(E) 6

(A) One way of attacking this problem would be to reason that the exponent must be one that gives the expression on the left the value 2. Since the base is 2, the exponent must be 1. What number when multiplied by 3 yields the value 1? That number is 1/3. Or you might simply substitute the values provided by the answer choices into the equation. Here you are lucky, for the first substitution is the correct one:

$$2^{3(1/3)} = 2^1 = 2$$

6. If $\frac{1}{\frac{2}{x}} = \frac{2}{3}$, then $x =$

(A) $\frac{3}{4}$

(B) 1

(C) $\frac{4}{3}$

(D) $\frac{3}{2}$

(E) $\frac{9}{4}$

(C) This problem is fairly straightforward. Solve for *x*! Dividing 1 by 2/*x*, we have:

$$\frac{x}{2} = \frac{2}{3}$$

$$3x = 4$$

$$x = \frac{4}{3}$$

The alternative of substituting answer values into the equation would also be available to you, but you have to realize that with simple problems, the direct approach is most often the better one.

7. The distance between the points $(-2,-3)$ and $(-2,4)$ is

(A) $\sqrt{65}$

(B) 7

(C) 5

(D) $\sqrt{7}$

(E) 1

(B) For this problem you might want to sketch the coordinate plane:

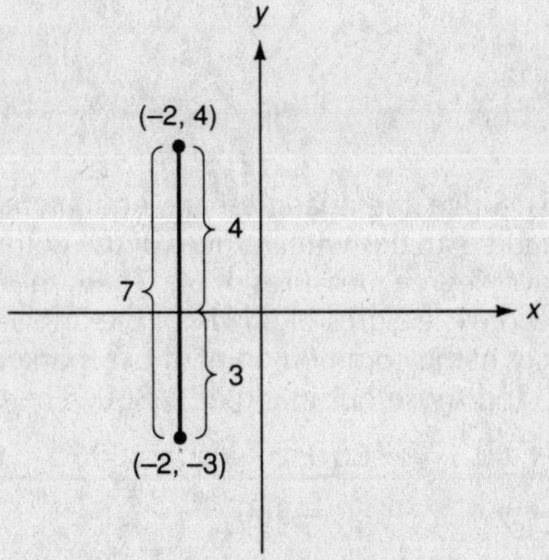

Since the line connecting the points is parallel to the y-axis, the distance is simply the difference between the y coordinates:

Distance $= 4 - (-3) = 4 + 3 = 7$

8. In Figure 1, if $RT = 2\frac{1}{4}$, then $RS =$

(A) $\frac{3}{4}$

(B) $\frac{11}{12}$

(C) $\frac{5}{4}$

(D) $\frac{19}{12}$

(E) $\frac{5}{3}$

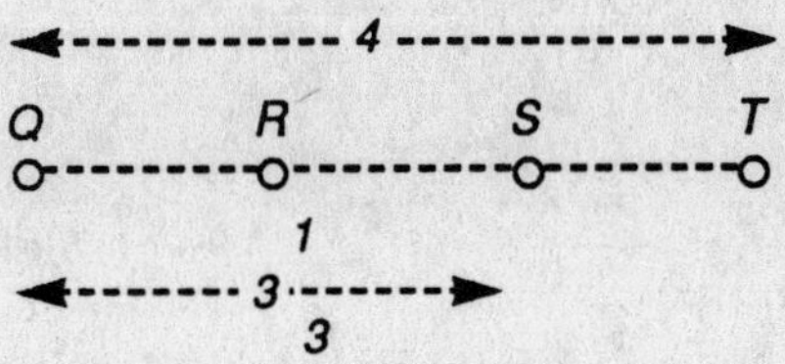

Figure 1

(D) This is a good exercise in problem solving. Since "Cannot be determined" is not an answer choice, we can be certain that we have sufficient information to find RS. We already know:

$$QT = 4 \qquad QS = 3\frac{1}{3} \qquad RT = 2\frac{1}{4}$$

And the figure shows:

$$QS + RT = QR + RS + RS + ST$$

All we have to do is find a way to manipulate these symbols until we isolate RS:

$$(QR + RS) + (RS + ST) = QS + RT$$

$$RS + (QR + RS + ST) = (QS + RT)$$

$$RS = (QS + RT) - (QR + RS + ST)$$

Since $QR + RS + ST = QT$:

$$RS = (QS + RT) - QT$$

And, using the values provided:

$$RS = \left(3\frac{1}{3} + 2\frac{1}{4}\right) - 4$$

$$RS = \left(\frac{10}{3} + \frac{9}{4}\right) - 4$$

$$RS = \left(\frac{40 + 27}{12}\right) - 4$$

$$RS = \frac{67}{12} - \frac{48}{12}$$

$$RS = \frac{19}{12}$$

If you tend to reason spatially, you might just have looked at the figure and seen:

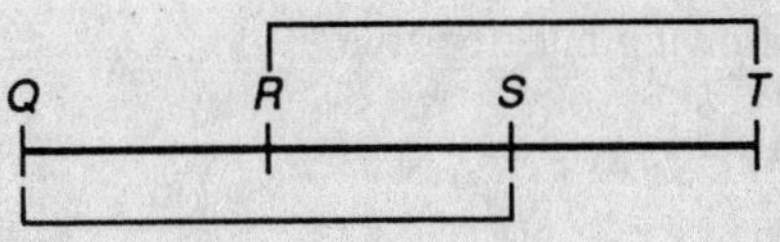

Then you would see that the length of QS and RT together exceeds that of QT by the length of RS. So, just add QS and RT and subtract QT.

9. In Figure 2, which of the following points falls within the shaded area?

(A) (5,0)

(B) (5,1)

(C) (4,2)

(D) (4,3)

(E) (3,4)

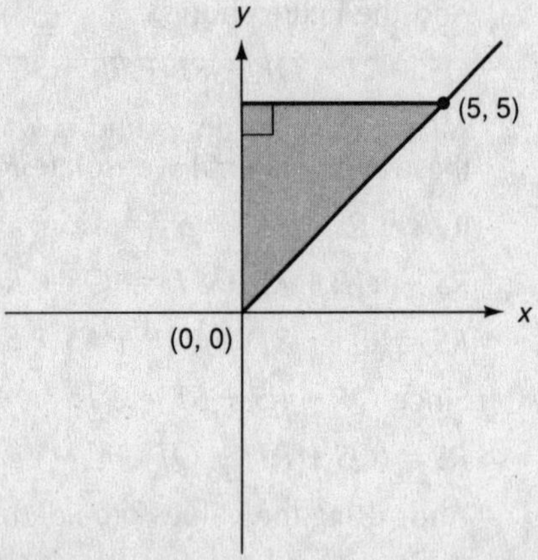

Figure 2

(E) There are several ways of reaching the correct answer here. One, since the line that bounds the lower portion of the shaded area includes the points (0,0) and (5,5), it is the graph of the equation $x = y$. For a point to be in the shaded region, the y coordinate must be greater than the x coordinate. Only (E) meets this requirement. Or, you might reason less formally that the line contains points in which the "rise" is equal to the "run." So you are looking for a point for which the "rise" is greater than the "run." Or you might just choose to plot the points on the diagram.

10. If $4 < x < 12$ and $6 < y < 8$, then which of the following must be true?

(A) $\frac{2}{3} < xy < \frac{3}{2}$

(B) $2 < xy < 4$

(C) $6 < xy < 12$

(D) $24 < xy < 96$

(E) $32 < xy < 72$

(D) To handle this item, just ask yourself how to obtain the minimum and maximum values for xy. Since $x > 4$ and $y > 6$, the lower limit for xy is 24. And since $x < 12$ and $y < 8$, the upper limit for xy is 96.

11. In Figure 3, three equilateral triangles have a common vertex. $x + y + z =$

(A) 270

(B) 180

(C) 120

(D) 90

(E) 60

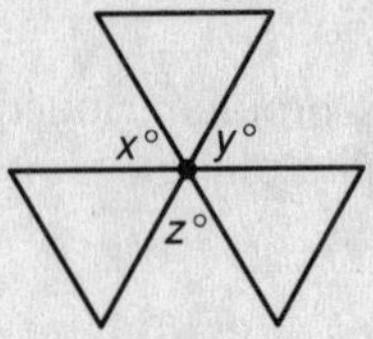

Figure 3

(B) Since the triangles are equilateral, the unmarked angles with vertices at the common point have degree measures of 60. Then, the sum of the degree measures of all six of the angles with vertices at the common point (those marked x, y, and z, and those not marked) is 360. Therefore:

$x + 60 + y + 60 + z + 60 = 360$

$x + y + z + 180 = 360$

$x + y + z = 180$

12. If the operation ϕ is defined for all real numbers x and y by the equation $x \phi y = xy - y - x$, then $(-2) \phi (-1) =$

(A) -3

(B) -2

(C) 1

(D) 3

(E) 5

(E) This is a "defined operation" problem. Don't let the Greek letter throw you. Just substitute -2 for x and -1 for y into the expression $xy - y - x$:

$(-2)(-1) - (-1) - (-2) = 2 + 1 + 2 = 5$

13. In Figure 4, if the circle has a radius of 3, what is the length of minor arc *PR*?

(A) $\frac{\pi}{6}$

(B) $\frac{\pi}{3}$

(C) π

(D) $\frac{3\pi}{2}$

(E) 3π

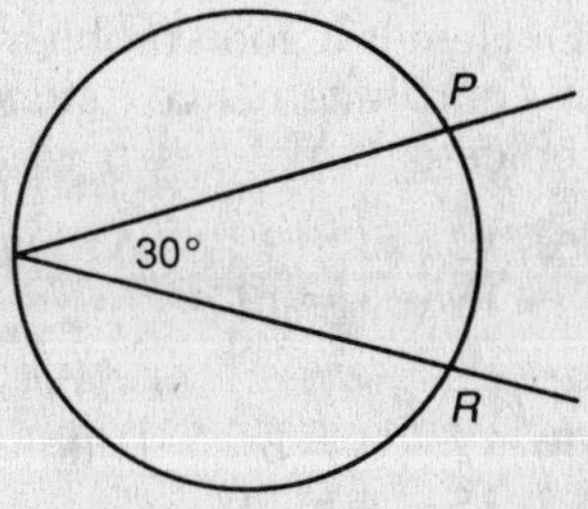

Figure 4

(C) For this problem, you have to know that the degree measure of an inscribed angle is one-half that of the intercepted arc. (Or, an inscribed angle intercepts twice the arc.) Since the inscribed angle has a measure of 30 degrees, the minor arc *PR* has a measure of 60 degrees. And since the total measure of the circle is 360 degrees, minor arc *PR* is 60/360 = 1/6 of the circumference.

$$PR = \frac{C}{6}$$

And since $C = 2\pi r$

$$PR = \frac{2\pi r}{6}$$

And $r = 3$:

$$PR = \frac{2\pi\,(3)}{6} = \frac{6\pi}{6} = \pi$$

14. $\sqrt{45} - \sqrt{20} + \sqrt{5} =$

(A) $2 - \sqrt{5}$

(B) 0

(C) $2 + \sqrt{5}$

(D) $2\sqrt{5}$

(E) 10

(D) Here use common sense about the test. There must be something you can do with these expressions to combine them. And the key is $\sqrt{5}$. 45 and 20 are both multiples of 5:

$$\sqrt{9 \times 5} - \sqrt{4 \times 5} + \sqrt{5} =$$

$$3\sqrt{5} - 2\sqrt{5} + \sqrt{5} = 2\sqrt{5}$$

15. Which of the following must be true of a square?

I. The intersection of the diagonals forms four equal angles.

II. The area is equal to the square of the diagonal.

III. The number of square units of the area is equal to the number of linear units of the perimeter.

(A) I only

(B) III only

(C) I and II only

(D) I and III only

(E) I, II, and III

(A) Test each statement. Statement I must be true and can be demonstrated in a number of ways. For example, just draw a square with its diagonals, and you can see that they are perpendicular to one another. (No need for an elaborate proof.) Statement II, however, is not true:

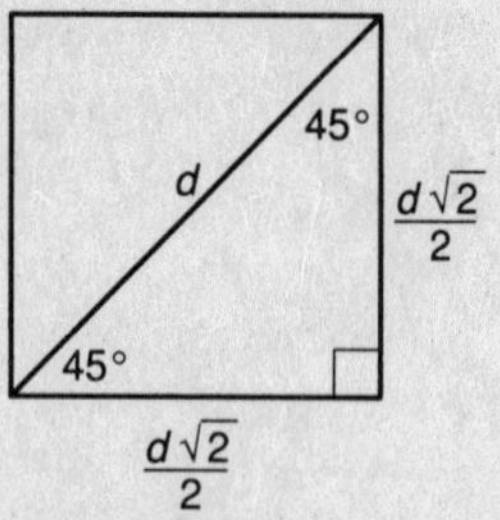

Since the area of a square is found by squaring the length of one of its sides:

$$\text{Area} = \left(\frac{d\sqrt{2}}{2}\right)\left(\frac{d\sqrt{2}}{2}\right) = \frac{2d^2}{4} = \frac{d^2}{2}$$

So the area of a square is actually equal to *half* the square of its diagonal. And III is not necessarily true. If we let s designate the length of the side of a square, then the perimeter is equal to $4s$ and the area to s^2. But $4s$ and s^2 are not necessarily equal. (They will be equal only if $s = 4$.)

16. What is the least positive integer x for which $12 - x$ and $15 - x$ will be non-zero and have opposite signs?

(A) 3

(B) 4

(C) 11

(D) 12

(E) 13

(E) Here is a good problem on which to use one of our alternative strategies. Test answer choices:

(A) $12 - 3 = 9$ $15 - 3 = 12$	Wrong!	Both expressions have the same sign.
(B) $12 - 4 = 8$ $15 - 4 = 11$	Ditto!	
(C) $12 - 11 = 1$ $15 - 11 = 4$	Ditto!	
(D) $12 - 12 = 0$ $15 - 12 = 3$	Wrong!	Both expressions are said to be non-zero.
(E) $12 - 13 = -1$ $15 - 13 = 2$	Bingo!	

But how do we prove mathematically that 13 is correct? We don't have to. We eliminated four of the choices, so the one that remains has to be the correct answer to the test question.

17. The solution set to the pair of equations:

$mx + ny = 15$
$nx + my = 13$

is $x = 3$ and $y = 1$. What are the values of m and n?

(A) $m = 5$
$n = 3$

(B) $m = 4$
$n = 3$

(C) $m = 3$
$n = 4$

(D) $m = 3$
$n = 5$

(E) $m = 2$
$n = 6$

(B) I think here that you could use either of two approaches. First, you can attack the problem by treating the equations as a system of simultaneous equations:

$3m + n = 15$
$3n + m = 13$

Use the first equation to solve for n:

$n = 15 - 3m$

Substitute this expression for n in the second equation:

$3(15 - 3m) + m = 13$

$45 - 9m + m = 13$

$-8m + 45 = 13$

$8m = 32$

$m = 4$

And find the value of n:

$3(4) + n = 15$

$12 + n = 15$

$n = 3$

As an alternative, you could test answer choices. Just substitute the values given for m and n until you find a pair that satisfies both equations.

18. The lengths of the sides of quadrilateral Q are all integers. If three of the sides have lengths of 3, 4, and 5, then the maximum length of the fourth side is

(A) 13

(B) 12

(C) 11

(D) 7

(E) 2

(C) The problems on this test are arranged in ascending order of difficulty. Often, what makes a problem more difficult than another problem is that the insight required to solve the more difficult problem is more subtle. We know from the fact that this problem is situated more than one third of the way through the test that it is not a give-away. Therefore, you should not make the mistake of reasoning "3 plus 4 plus 5 is equal to 12, therefore the answer is (B)." If the problem were that obvious, it would be one of the first few, not number 18. The correct answer is (C). Since the sum of the lengths of the other three sides is 12, the longest side of integral length that could be used to close the figure is 11.

19. In Figure 5, if ABD is a right isosceles triangle, then $x =$

(A) 25

(B) 30

(C) $37\frac{1}{2}$

(D) 45

(E) 60

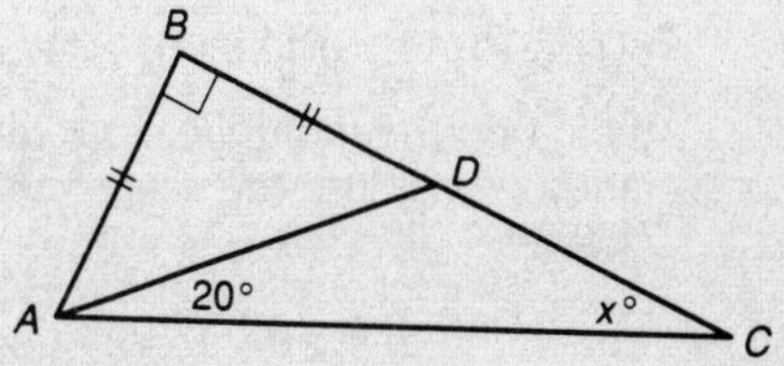

Figure 5

(A) Let y represent the degree measure of angle BAD. Since ABC is isosceles, $y = 45$. And since the sum of the degree measures of the interior angles of a triangle is 180:

$90 + 45 + 20 + x = 180$

$155 + x = 180$

$x = 25$

20. If $xyz \neq 0$, then $\frac{2x^3y^2z}{8x^2y^3z^2} =$

(A) $4xyz$
(B) $\frac{4x}{yz}$
(C) $\frac{xyz}{4}$
(D) $\frac{xy}{4z}$
(E) $\frac{x}{4yz}$

(E) You can solve this problem by applying the rules for manipulating exponents. When dividing terms of the same base, you subtract exponents. Therefore, the x term is x to the $3 - 2 = 1$ power. The y term is y to the $2 - 3 = -1$ power, which is $1/y$. And similarly, the z term is z to the $1 - 2 = -1$ power, which is $1/z$. Since 2/8 is 1/4, the final result is $\frac{x}{4yz}$.

Alternatively, you could assume some values for the variables. Use those values to evaluate the complex expression and derive a value. Then, using the same values, evaluate each answer choice until you find one that generates the same value. You can make it easy on yourself by assuming small values that are easy to work with, such as 1. But watch out! Since $1 \times 1 = 1 \div 1$, you may find that more than one answer choice seems to be correct. (If you use 1 for x, y, and z, in this problem, you will find that the complex expression has the value 1/4 but that (C), (D), and (E) all equal 1/4 as well.) If this happens, or if you anticipate this may happen, use other numbers. Assume, for example, $x = 1$, $y = 2$, and $z = 3$. The complex expression has the value:

$$\frac{2(1)^3(2)^2(3)}{8(1)^2(2)^3(3)^2} = \frac{2(1)(4)(3)}{8(1)(8)(9)} = \frac{1}{24}$$

(Don't do the multiplication. Simplify by cancellation.) Now use the same values in the answer choices:

(A) $4(1)(2)(3) = 24$ Wrong!

(B) $\frac{4(1)}{(2)(3)} = \frac{2}{3}$ Wrong!

(C) $\frac{(1)(2)(3)}{4} = \frac{6}{4} = \frac{3}{2}$ Wrong!

(D) $\frac{(1)(2)}{4(3)} = \frac{2}{12} = \frac{1}{6}$ Wrong!

(E) $\frac{1}{4(2)(3)} = \frac{1}{24}$ Correct!

Yes, substituting numbers is likely to take longer here than using the rules of exponents, but at least you have an alternative available if you can't remember what to do.

21. If $f(x) = \frac{1}{1-x}$ and $g(x) = \frac{1}{x^2}$, then $g(f(3)) =$

(A) -2
(B) $\frac{1}{4}$
(C) $\frac{1}{2}$
(D) 2
(E) 4

(E) Here we have a nested function. (One function is to be done to the result of doing another function. Do the one on the inside first.) Perform $f(x)$ on 3:

$$f(3) = \frac{1}{1-3} = -\frac{1}{2}$$

Now perform $g(x)$ on that value:

$$g\left(-\frac{1}{2}\right) = \frac{1}{(-1/2)^2} = \frac{1}{\frac{1}{4}} = 4$$

22. A polygon Q with a certain perimeter P will have its greatest area when all of its sides have the same length. What is the maximum area of a rectangle with a perimeter of P units?

(A) $\frac{P^2}{16}$
(B) $\frac{P^2}{4}$
(C) P^2
(D) $2P^2$
(E) $4P^2$

(A) The rectangle with four equal sides is the square. And a square with perimeter P will have sides of $P/4$. The area of this figure is:

$$A = \frac{P}{4} \times \frac{P}{4} = \frac{P^2}{16}$$

You can also solve this problem by assuming a value for P. For example, let the perimeter of square P be 4. On that assumption, each side has a length of 1, and the area of the square is 1. Now, substitute 4 for P in the answer choices until you find one that generates the value 1:

(A) $\frac{4^2}{16} = 1$ Correct!

(B) $\frac{4^2}{4} = 4$ Wrong!

(C) $4^2 = 16$ Wrong!

(D) $2(4)^2 = 32$ Wrong!

(E) $4(4)^2 = 64$ Wrong!

23. Which of the following graphs is NOT the graph of a function?

(A)

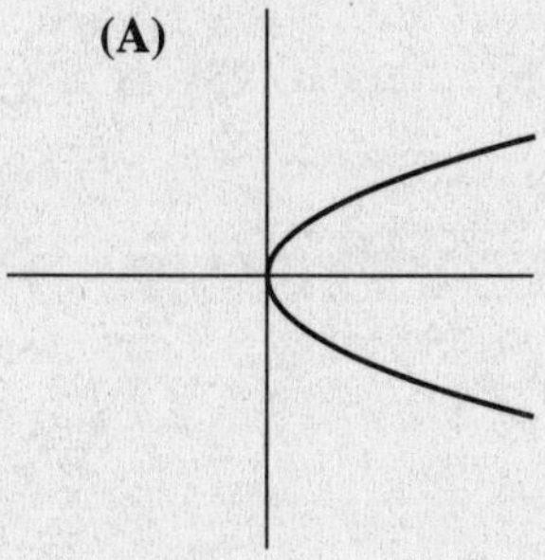

(B)

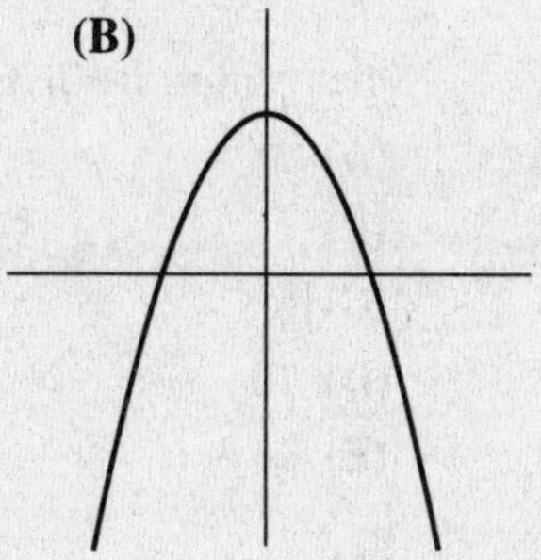

(C)

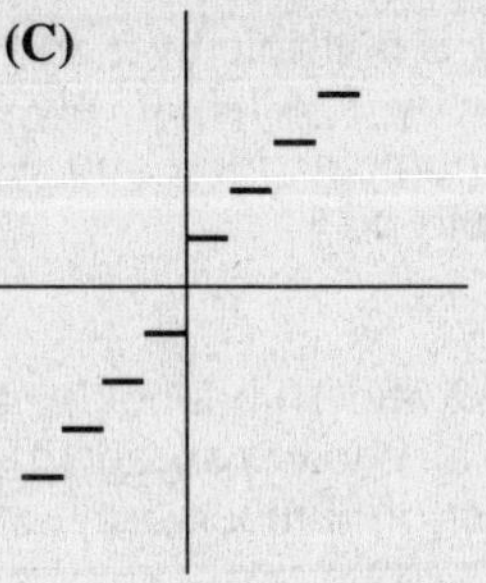

(D)

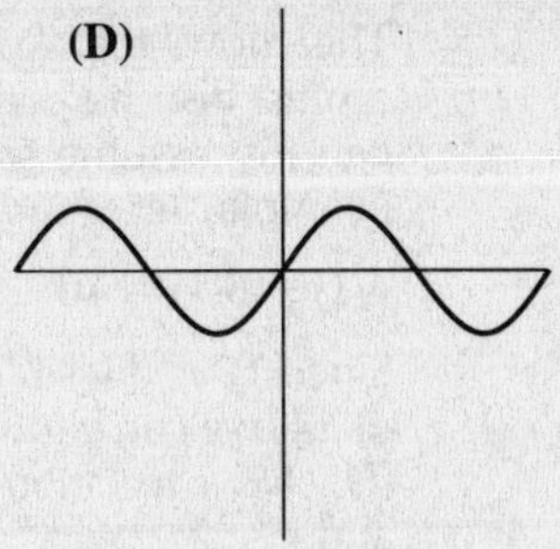

(E)

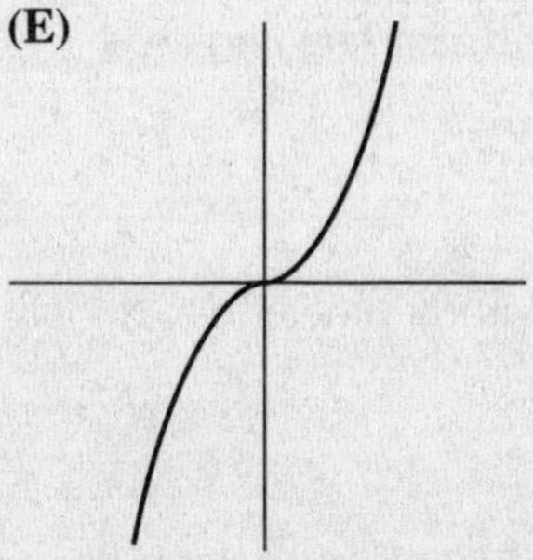

(A) The defining characteristic of a function is "for each element in the domain, there is only one element in the range." Since the x coordinates are the domain, and the y coordinates are the range, for each x coordinate there can be no more than one y coordinate. The graphs of (B), (C), (D), and (E) all fit this description. (A) does not. For the relationship described by (A), every value of x (except for one) has two y values.

24. In Figure 6, if $\sin A = \frac{2}{3}$, then $BC =$

(A) 18
(B) 8
(C) $3\sqrt{2}$
(D) 4
(E) $2\sqrt{5}$

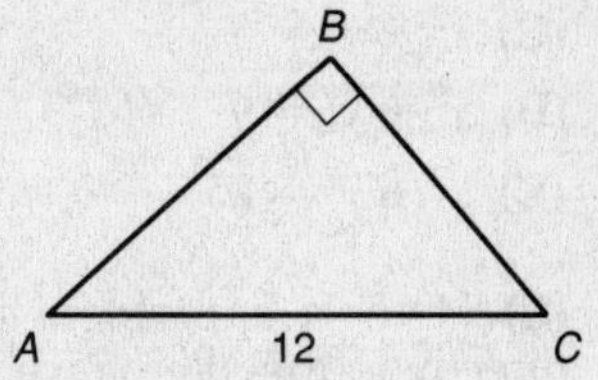

Figure 6

(B) The sine of an angle is defined as $\frac{\text{opposite side}}{\text{hypotenuse}}$. So:

$$\frac{2}{3} = \frac{BC}{12}$$

$$3BC = 24$$

$$BC = 8$$

There is an alternative strategy you can use here. The directions to this test state that the figures, unless specifically stated to be otherwise, are drawn as accurately as possible. You can just measure the length of BC. I know that you are not allowed to take a rule into the exam with you, but you do have a straight-edge: your answer sheet. Measure off a known distance on the edge of the answer sheet. (Make your tics lightly and remember to erase them when you are done.) Here, measure the distance 12. Now, compare that distance with the unknown distance of BC. You should be able to see that BC is about 2/3 of 12, or about 8. It certainly is not as long as 18 (choice (A)), nor as short as $3 \times 1.4 = 4.2$ (choice (C)). And numerical answer choices are always arranged in either ascending or descending order. Since BC is longer than the number given in choice (C), BC is also longer than the numbers given in (D) and (E). This *proves* that the correct answer is (B).

25. An equation for the circle with its center at the origin and passing through the point (1,2) is

(A) $x^2 + y^2 = \sqrt{5}$

(B) $x^2 + y^2 = 3$

(C) $x^2 + y^2 = 5$

(D) $x^2 + y^2 = 9$

(E) $x^2 + y^2 = 25$

(C) Here is a problem for which I would go directly to the alternative attack strategy. Instead of trying to figure out which equation correctly describes the circle in question, I would simply put the pair (1,2) into the equations. The one that works is the right answer:

(A) $1^2 + 2^2 = \sqrt{5}$ Wrong!

(B) $1^2 + 2^2 = 3$ Wrong!

(C) $1^2 + 2^2 = 5$ Correct!

So we know that (C) is the right answer.

26. How many integers are in the solution set of $|1 - 3x| < 5$?

(A) None

(B) One

(C) Two

(D) Three

(E) Infinitely many

(D) They are −1, 0, and 1:

$|1 - 3(-1)| = |1 + 3| = 4$

$|1 - 3(0)| = |1 - 0| = 1$

$|1 - 3(1)| = |1 - 3| = 2$

If, however, you try an integer larger than 1:

$|1 - 3(2)| = |1 - 6| = 5$

which is not less than 5, or one that is less than −1:

$|1 - 3(-2)| = |1 + 6| = 7$

27. If x, y, and z are positive integers such that

$4x + 6y = z$

then z must be divisible by

(A) 2

(B) 4

(C) 6

(D) 10

(E) 24

(A) One way of attacking this problem is to factor the expression $4x + 6y$:

$4x + 6y = 2(2x + 3y)$

This shows that $4x + 6y$ is divisible by 2 and that z must also be divisible by 2. Alternatively, you can just assume some numbers for x and y. For example, let x and y both be 1:

$4(1) + 6(1) = 10$

Since 10 is divisible by 2 and 10 but not by 4, 6, or 24, we can eliminate all choices except (A) and (D). Now try another set of numbers, say, $x = 1$ and $y = 2$:

$4(1) + 6(2) = 16$

16 is divisible by 2 but not by 10, so we eliminate (D). By the process of elimination, we have established that (A) must be the correct choice.

28. If the points (−2,4), (3,4), and (3,−2) are connected to form a triangle, the area of the triangle is

(A) $\frac{11}{2}$

(B) 6

(C) 12

(D) 15

(E) 24

(D) For this problem, you may want to sketch a figure:

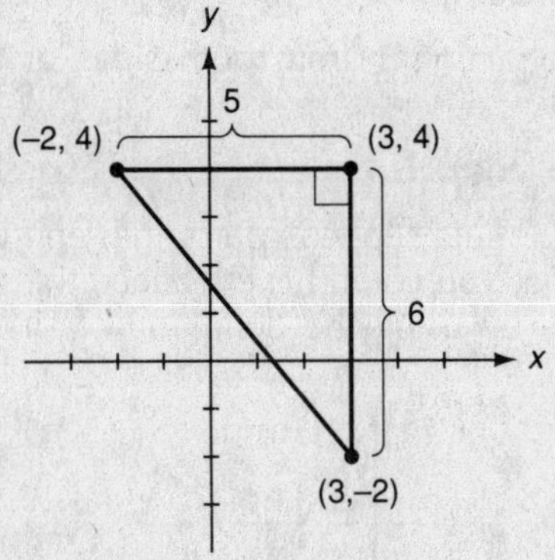

Since the figure is a right triangle, we can use the adjacent sides as altitude and base:

$$\text{Area} = \frac{1}{2}(5)(6) = 15$$

(It makes no difference which you consider the altitude and which you consider the base.)

29. If $i^2 = -1$ and if $k = 2 + i$, then $k^2 =$

(A) 1

(B) $3 + 4i$

(C) $4 + 3i$

(D) $6 + 7i$

(E) $9 + 12i$

(B) First find the value of k^2 in terms of i:

$k^2 = (2 + i)^2 = (2 + i)(2 + i) = 4 + 2i + 2i + i^2 = 4 + 4i + i^2$

Since $i^2 = -1$:

$4 + 4i + i^2 = 4 + 4i + (-1) = 3 + 4i$

30. If a line contains the points (−2, 1) and (4,4), then the x-intercept is

(A) −4

(B) $-\frac{1}{2}$

(C) 0

(D) $\frac{2}{3}$

(E) $\frac{3}{2}$

(A) One way to attack this problem is to try to find the values for the general equation $y = mx + b$, where m is the slope of the line and b the y-intercept. Since the line contains the points (−2,1) and (4,4), the value of m is:

$$\frac{4-1}{4-(-2)} = \frac{3}{6} = \frac{1}{2}$$

Now, to find b, use one of the sets of points already known:

$y = mx + b$

$4 = \frac{1}{2}(4) + b$

$4 = 2 + b$

$b = 2$

The equation of the line is:

$y = \frac{1}{2}x + 2$

The line crosses the x-axis where the value of y is 0:

$0 = \left(\frac{1}{2}\right)x + 2$

$\frac{x}{2} = -2$

$x = -4$

Alternatively, you can quickly sketch the line:

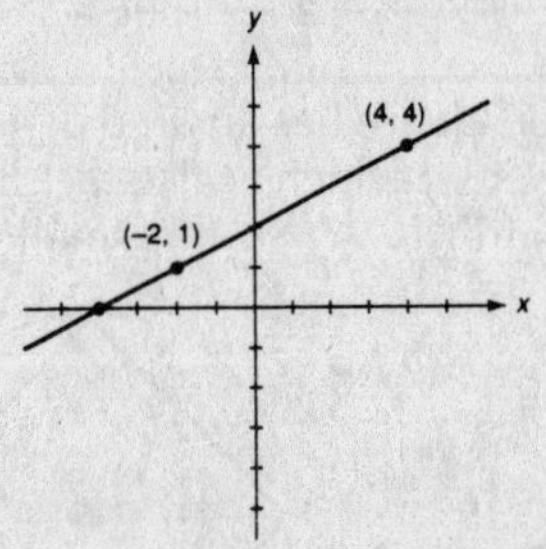

Now look at the choices. There is only once choice available that could be the value for x when $y = 0$. And that is (A).

31. In Figure 7, if the radius of the circle is r, then the ratio $\dfrac{\text{area of the larger square}}{\text{area of the smaller square}} =$

(A) $\dfrac{2\sqrt{2}}{1}$

(B) $\dfrac{2}{1}$

(C) $\dfrac{\sqrt{2}}{1}$

(D) $\dfrac{1}{\sqrt{2}}$

(E) $\dfrac{1}{2}$

Figure 7

(B) Before we do any math on this problem, use common sense to eliminate some choices. The question asks for the ratio of the area of the larger figure to the area of the smaller figure. That means that the numerator of the fraction must be larger than the denominator of the fraction. What about (D) and (E)? They must be wrong. Now for the math. Since r is the radius of the circle, the larger square has a side of length $2r$:

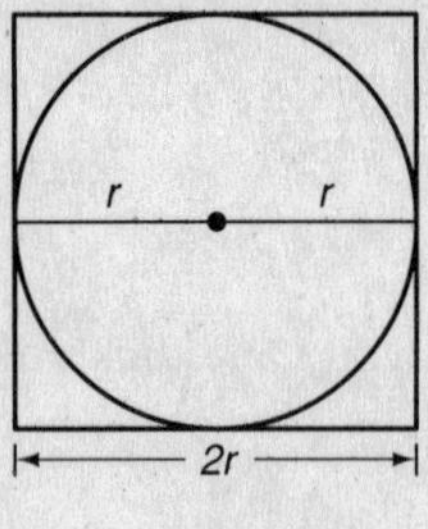

So the larger square has an area of $4r^2$. The diameter of the circle, which is also the diagonal of the smaller square, is $2r$. So the smaller square has sides of $r\sqrt{2}$:

$s = \frac{1}{2}d\sqrt{2}$

$s = \frac{1}{2}(2r)\sqrt{2}$

$s = r\sqrt{2}$

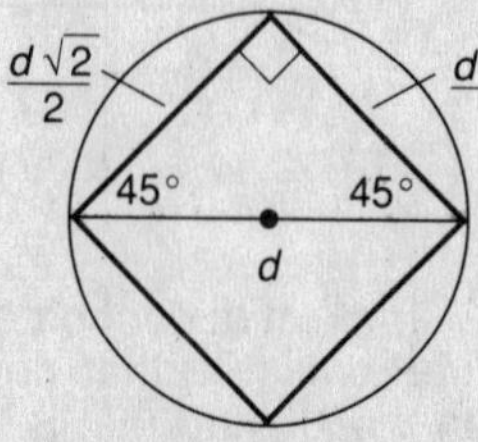

And the area of the smaller square is $2r^2$. So the ratio asked for is:

$\dfrac{4r^2}{2r^2} = \dfrac{2}{1}$

32. If $0° < \theta < 90°$, then $\sin^2\theta + \cos^2\theta - 1 =$

(A) -2

(B) 0

(C) 1

(D) 2

(E) 4

(B) This problem is easily solved if you remember that:

$\sin^2\theta + \cos^2\theta = 1$

By subtracting 1 from both sides of the equation:

$\sin^2\theta + \cos^2\theta - 1 = 0$

If the formula slipped your mind, and if you had the time, you could have reached the same conclusion by using the definition of sine and cosine:

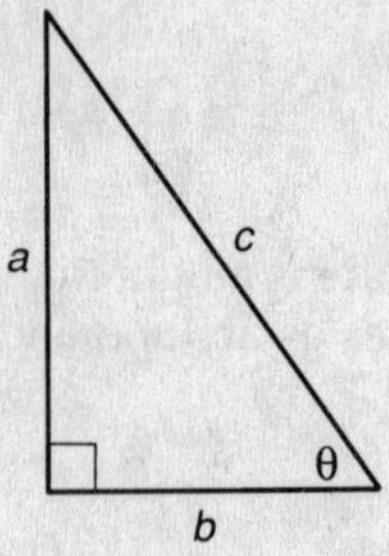

Since this is a right triangle, $a^2 + b^2 = c^2$. And if we divide both sides of the equation by c^2:

$\dfrac{a^2}{c^2} + \dfrac{b^2}{c^2} = 1$

Since:

$\sin\theta = \dfrac{a}{c}$ and $\cos\theta = \dfrac{b}{c}$

it follows that:

$\sin^2\theta = \dfrac{a^2}{c^2}$ and $\cos^2\theta = \dfrac{b^2}{c^2}$

Therefore: $\sin^2\theta + \cos^2\theta = 1$

And: $\sin^2\theta + \cos^2\theta - 1 = 0$

Or you could have worked from the expression given in the problem:

$\sin^2\theta = \dfrac{a^2}{c^2}$ and $\cos^2\theta = \dfrac{b^2}{c^2}$

$\sin^2\theta + \cos^2\theta = \dfrac{a^2}{c^2} + \dfrac{b^2}{c^2} = \dfrac{a^2 + b^2}{c^2}$

Since $c^2 = a^2 + b^2$,

$\sin^2\theta + \cos^2\theta = \dfrac{a^2 + b^2}{a^2 + b^2} = 1$

33. If $f(x) = 3x - 2$ and $g(f(x)) = x$, then $g(x) =$

(A) $3x + 2$

(B) $2 - 3x$

(C) $\frac{1}{3x - 2}$

(D) $\frac{x}{3} + 2$

(E) $\frac{x + 2}{3}$

(E) One way to solve this problem is to figure out what mathematical operations would be needed in $g(x)$ to produce x from $3x - 2$. First, you need x rather than $3x$, so the function would have to include dividing $3x$ by 3. And you don't want -2 in the final result, so it should also include adding 2 to the result of $f(x)$. The expression that describes this procedure is $\frac{x + 2}{3}$

And we confirm that this is correct by performing this on $f(x)$:

$$g(f(x)) = g(3x - 2) = \frac{(3x - 2) + 2}{3} = \frac{3x}{3} = x$$

Alternatively, you could substitute the result of performing $f(x)$ on x into each answer choice until you find one that produces the value x:

(A) $3(3x - 2) + 2 = 9x - 6 + 2 = 9x - 4$ Wrong!

(B) $2 - 3(3x - 2) = 2 - 9x + 6 = 8 - 9x$ Wrong!

(C) $\frac{1}{3(3x - 2) - 2} = \frac{1}{9x - 6 - 2} = \frac{1}{9x - 8}$ Wrong!

(D) $\frac{(3x - 2)}{3} + 2 = \frac{3x}{3} - \frac{2}{3} + 2 = x + \frac{4}{3}$ Wrong!

(E) $\frac{(3x - 2) + 2}{3} = \frac{3x}{3} = x$ Correct!

An even easier approach is to assign a value for x. Let $x = 2$. Then $f(x) = 3(2) - 2 = 4$. Now use the result of $f(x)$, 4, in the choices. The one that generates the value 2 (which is x) is the winner:

(A) $3(4) + 2 = 14$ Wrong!

(B) $2 - 3(4) = -10$ Wrong!

(C) $\frac{1}{3(4) - 2} = \frac{1}{10}$ Wrong!

(D) $\frac{4}{3} + 2 = \frac{10}{3}$ Wrong!

(E) $\frac{4 + 2}{3} = 2$ Correct!

34. In Figure 8, if $AC \parallel GE$ and $GF = x$ and $FE = y$, then the ratio $\frac{\text{area } \triangle BCD}{\text{area } \triangle BCA} =$

(A) $\frac{x}{y}$

(B) $\frac{y}{x}$

(C) $\frac{x}{x + y}$

(D) $\frac{y}{x + y}$

(E) $\frac{y}{2(x + y)}$

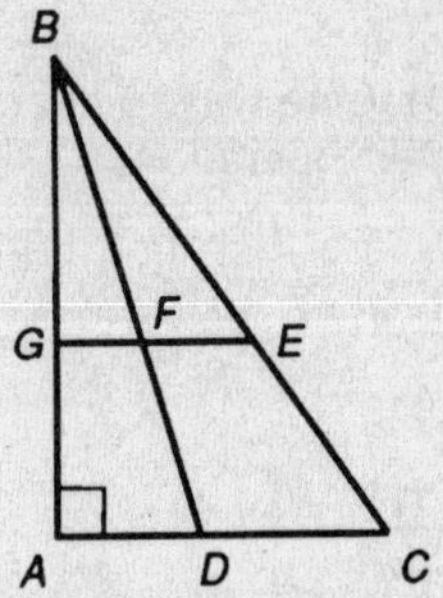

Figure 8

(D) There are two insights required to handle this problem. First, $\triangle BEG$ is similar to $\triangle BCA$, and $\triangle BEF$ is similar to $\triangle BCD$. This means that the ratio area $\triangle BEF$:area $\triangle BEG$ is the same as the ratio area of $\triangle BCD$:area $\triangle BCA$. So if we find the first ratio, we also have the second. Second, side BG, because it is perpendicular to side GE, is an altitude of triangle BEG and of triangle BEF:

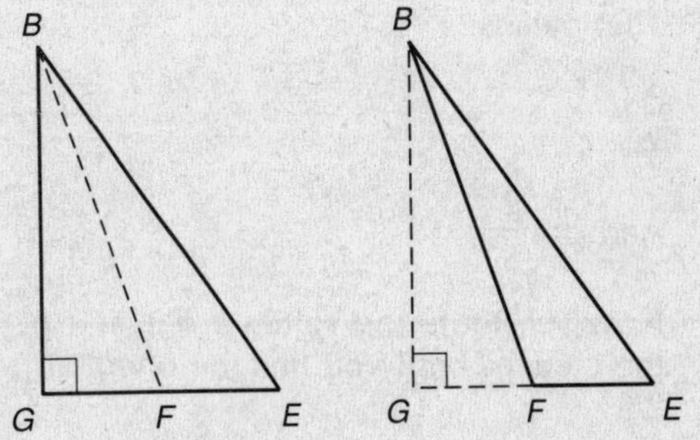

The formula for finding the area of a triangle is 1/2 × altitude × base. So the areas of the triangles are:

$$\text{Area } \triangle BEG = \frac{1}{2}(BG)(x + y)$$

$$\text{Area } \triangle BEF = \frac{1}{2}(BG)(y)$$

Therefore, the ratio is:

$$\frac{\text{Area } \triangle BEF}{\text{Area } \triangle BEG} = \frac{1/2(BG)(y)}{1/2(BG)(x + y)} = \frac{y}{x + y}$$

And that is the ratio of the areas of the two larger triangles as well.

35. If $\frac{1}{a} + \frac{1}{b} = \frac{1}{c}$, then $c =$

(A) $\frac{1}{ab}$

(B) ab

(C) $\frac{a+b}{ab}$

(D) $\frac{ab}{a+b}$

(E) $\frac{2ab}{a+b}$

(D) One way to attack this item is to do the indicated operations:

$$\frac{1}{a} + \frac{1}{b} = \frac{b+a}{ab}$$

So:

$$\frac{b+a}{ab} = \frac{1}{c}$$

Cross multiply:

$$c(b+a) = ab$$

And divide by $(b + a)$

$$c = \frac{ab}{a+b}$$

Alternatively, you could assign some values to a and b. Let $a = 1$ and $b = 2$:

$$\frac{1}{1} + \frac{1}{2} = \frac{3}{2}$$

That means:

$$\frac{3}{2} = \frac{1}{c}$$

And $c = \frac{2}{3}$

Now substitute the values $a = 1$ and $b = 2$ into the choices until you find the one that produces 2/3:

(A) $\frac{1}{(1)(2)} = \frac{1}{2}$ Wrong!

(B) $(1)(2) = 2$ Wrong!

(C) $\frac{1+2}{(1)(2)} = \frac{3}{2}$ Wrong!

(D) $\frac{(1)(2)}{1+2} = \frac{2}{3}$ Right!

(E) $\frac{2(1)(2)}{1+2} = \frac{4}{3}$ Wrong!

36. If $x^3y^2z < 0$, then it must be true that

(A) $x^3 < 0$

(B) $z < 0$

(C) $xy < 0$

(D) $xz < 0$

(E) $yz < 0$

(D) This question tests your understanding of the properties of numbers. First, since the entire expression is less than zero, we know that none of the variables is 0. (Otherwise, the expression would be equal to and not less than 0.) Additionally, we know that y^2 must be positive. And this means that either x or z—but not both—must be negative! This is what (D) means.

Alternatively, you could assign sets of numbers to x, y, and z, until you manage to eliminate all but one choice.

37. If the slope of a line is 3 and the y-intercept is 2, then the x-intercept of the line is

(A) $-\frac{3}{2}$

(B) $-\frac{2}{3}$

(C) -1

(D) $\frac{2}{3}$

(E) $\frac{3}{2}$

(B) You can attack this problem by using the general equation $y = mx + b$, where m is the slope and b is the y-intercept. The line intercepts the x-axis where $y = 0$:

$$0 = 3x + 2$$

$$3x = -2$$

$$x = -\frac{2}{3}$$

38. For the right triangle in Figure 9, all of the following statements are true EXCEPT:

(A) $\sin \theta = \frac{b}{c}$

(B) $\tan \sigma = \frac{a}{b}$

(C) $\cos \theta = \frac{c}{a}$

(D) $\sin \theta = \cos \sigma$

(E) $\cot \sigma = \tan \theta$

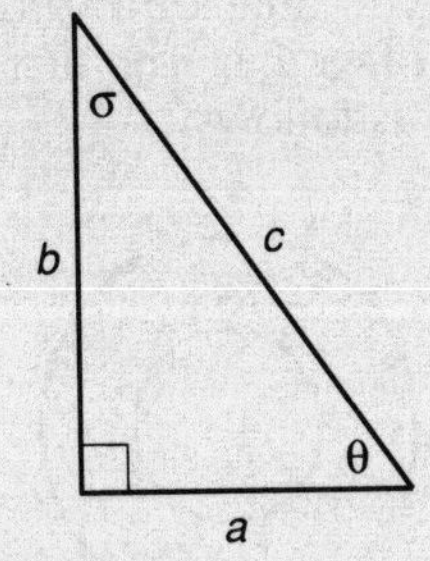

Figure 9

(C) Test each statement:

(A) $\sin = \frac{\text{opp}}{\text{hyp}}$ so $\sin \theta = \frac{b}{c}$ True.

(B) $\tan = \frac{\text{opp}}{\text{adj}}$ so $\tan \sigma = \frac{a}{b}$ True.

(C) $\cos = \frac{\text{adj}}{\text{hyp}}$ so $\cos \theta = \frac{a}{c}$ not $\frac{c}{a}$ False.

(D) $\sin \theta = \frac{b}{c}$ and $\cos \sigma = \frac{b}{c}$, $\sin \theta = \cos \sigma$ True.

(E) $\cot \sigma = \frac{b}{a}$ and $\tan \theta = \frac{b}{a}$, so $\cot \sigma = \tan \theta$ True.

39. Three candidates for president of the Student Council—Ashley, José, and Kim—must each be scheduled for a single 10-minute address to the entire student body. If the order of the presentations is determined randomly, how many different orders are possible?

(A) 3

(B) 6

(C) 9

(D) 12

(E) 27

(B) One solution to this problem is to recognize that since the question asks about different orders, this is an appropriate problem for the formula used to calculate permutations: $3! = 3 \times 2 \times 1 = 6$. Even if you didn't recall the formula, don't panic. You should be able to count the number of possibilities on your fingers:

1. AJK
2. AKJ
3. KAJ
4. KJA
5. JAK
6. JKA

And that's all there is to it.

40. If $x \neq 0$ then $\frac{8^{2x}}{2^{4x}} =$

(A) 2^{2x}

(B) 4^{-x}

(C) 4^{2x}

(D) 4^{1-x}

(E) 8^{-x}

(A) Remember that the rules of exponents can be applied only to terms of like bases. Here, the numerator has a base of 8, and the denominator a base of 2. Before we can manipulate the expression, it will be necessary to change one or the other term. There are several different routes available to us. For example:

$8^{2x} = (8)^{2x} = (2 \times 2 \times 2)^{2x} = (2^{2x})(2^{2x})(2^{2x}) = 2^{2x + 2x + 2x} = 2^{6x}$

Now we can complete our division:

$2^{6x} \div 2^{4x} = 2^{6x - 4x} = 2^{2x}$

Or:

$(8)^{2x} = (2^3)^{2x} = (2)^{(3)(2x)} = 2^{6x}$

And complete the division as shown above. Or you could choose to work with the denominator. I think, however, that the best approach to this problem is just to assume a value for x. Say $x = 1$:

$$\frac{8^{2(1)}}{2^{4(1)}} = \frac{8^2}{2^4} = \frac{64}{16} = 4$$

If we substitute 1 for x into the answer choices, the correct choice will generate the value 4:

(A) $2^{2(1)} = 4$ Correct!

(B) $4^{-1} = \frac{1}{4}$ Wrong!

(C) $4^{2(1)} = 16$ Wrong!

(D) $4^{1-1} = 4^0 = 1$ Wrong!

(E) $8^{-1} = \frac{1}{8}$ Wrong!

All S are M.
No P are M.

41. Which of the following conclusions can be logically deduced from the two statements above?

(A) All S are P.

(B) All M are S.

(C) Some S are not M.

(D) Some M are P.

(E) No P are S.

(E) A good way to attack this problem is to use Venn or circle diagrams. The first statement can be represented as follows:

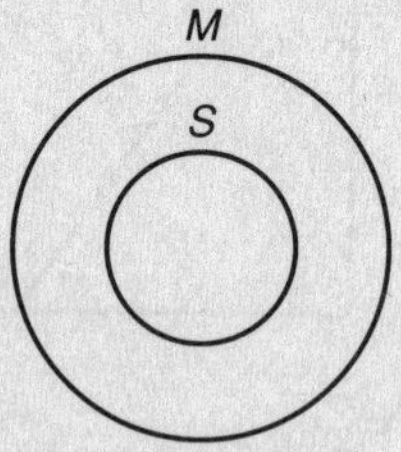

The S circle contains all items that are S's, and the M circle all those that are M's. Notice that the S circle is entirely contained within the M circle. The second statement can be added to the diagram as follows:

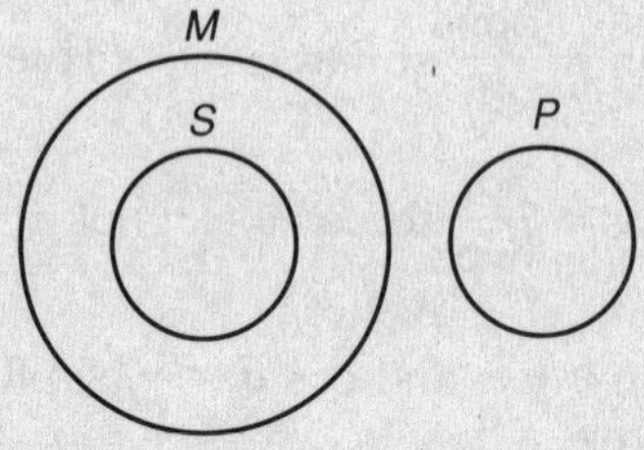

The fact that there is no overlap between the P and M circles shows that "No P are M." Now we examine the answer choices. The correct answer is (E). There is no overlap between the P and S circles.

42. Cube Q has volume V. In terms of V, a cube with edges only one-fourth the length of those of Q will have a volume of

(A) $\frac{V^3}{64}$

(B) $\frac{V^3}{4}$

(C) $\frac{V}{64}$

(D) $\frac{V}{4}$

(E) $\frac{\sqrt[3]{V}}{8}$

(C) One way of attacking this problem is to use letters. The formula for finding the volume of a cube is simply "edge cubed." Therefore:

$V = e^3$

And:

$e = \sqrt[3]{V}$

And a cube with an edge one-fourth of that has an edge of:

$\frac{\sqrt[3]{V}}{4}$. And a volume of:

$$V = \left(\frac{\sqrt[3]{V}}{4}\right)^3 = \frac{V}{64}$$

As an alternative strategy, you could assume some numbers. Assume that the larger cube has an edge of 4. (Why 4? Because that means the smaller cube has an edge of 1!) The larger cube has a volume of $4 \times 4 \times 4 = 64$, and the smaller cube a volume of $1 \times 1 \times 1 = 1$. Now, just substitute 64 for V into the answer choices, and the one that generates the value 1 is the correct choice.

43. If θ is an acute angle and $\cos\theta = \frac{b}{c}$, $b > 0$ and $c > 0$ and $b \neq c$, then $\sin\theta =$

(A) $\frac{b}{\sqrt{b^2 - c^2}}$

(B) $\frac{c}{\sqrt{c^2 - b^2}}$

(C) $\frac{\sqrt{b^2 - c^2}}{b}$

(D) $\frac{\sqrt{b^2 - c^2}}{c}$

(E) $\frac{\sqrt{c^2 - b^2}}{c}$

(E) A sketch will make it easier to keep track of the relationships:

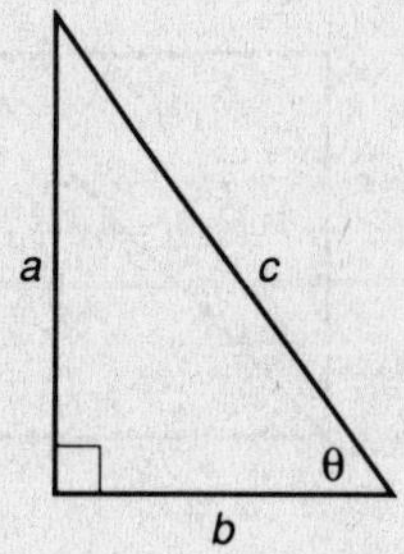

Notice that I have placed side b in relation to θ to reflect the cosine relation specified in the problem. I have also designated the third side as a. The $\sin\theta$, therefore, is equal to a/c. And we can use the relationships between the sides of the right triangle to find a in terms of b and c:

$a^2 + b^2 = c^2$

And:

$a^2 = c^2 - b^2$

Therefore:

$a = \sqrt{c^2 - b^2}$

Substituting this for a:

$$\sin\theta = \frac{\sqrt{c^2 - b^2}}{c}$$

44. If a cube has an edge of length 2, what is the distance from any vertex to the center of the cube?

(A) $\frac{\sqrt{2}}{2}$

(B) $\sqrt{3}$

(C) $2\sqrt{2}$

(D) $2\sqrt{3}$

(E) $\frac{3}{2}$

(B) The neat thing about a cube is that if you have any one feature, e.g., volume, edge, diagonal of a face, diagonal of the cube, surface area, you can calculate every other feature. It is for this reason that cubes are often the focus of test problems. Given that the edge has a length of 2, we can use the Pythagorean Theorem to find the length of the diagonal of a face:

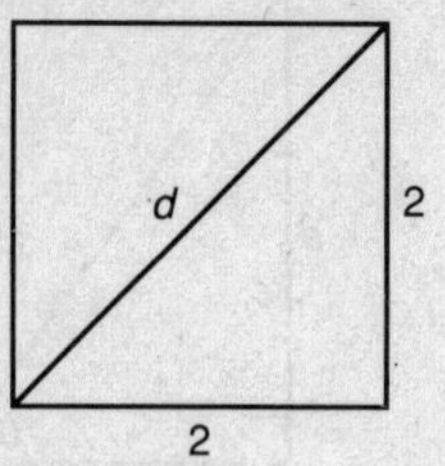

$d^2 = 2^2 + 2^2$

$d^2 = 4 + 4 = 8$

$d = 2\sqrt{2}$

Now we can find the length of the diagonal of the cube:

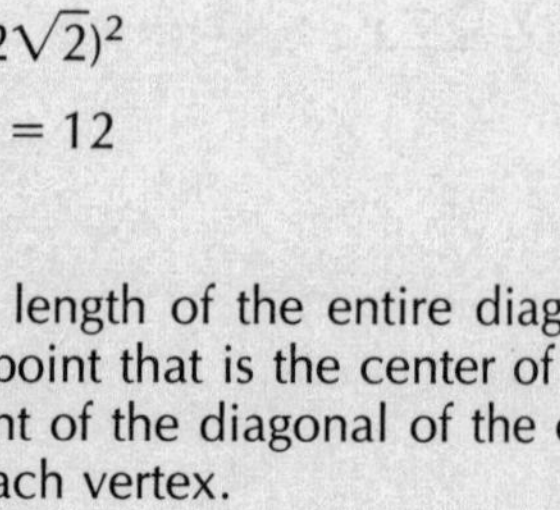

$D = 2^2 + (2\sqrt{2})^2$

$D^2 = 4 + 8 = 12$

$D = 2\sqrt{3}$

That is the length of the entire diagonal of the cube. The point that is the center of the cube is the midpoint of the diagonal of the cube and is $\sqrt{3}$ from each vertex.

45. If $x^2 + ax + bx + ab = 0$, and $x + b = 2$, then $x + a =$

(A) −8

(B) −4

(C) −2

(D) 0

(E) 2

(D) The trick to this problem is to recognize that:

$x^2 + ax + bx + ab = (x + a)(x + b)$

Since $(x + a)(x + b) = 0$, one or the other factor must be 0. Since $x + b = 2$, $x + a = 0$.

46. Figure 10 shows two right circular cylinders, C and C'. If $r = kr'$ and $h = kh'$, then what is the ratio of:

$$\frac{\text{Volume of } C}{\text{Volume of } C'}?$$

(A) $\frac{1}{\pi}$

(B) π

(C) $k\pi$

(D) $\frac{1}{k^3}$

(E) k^3

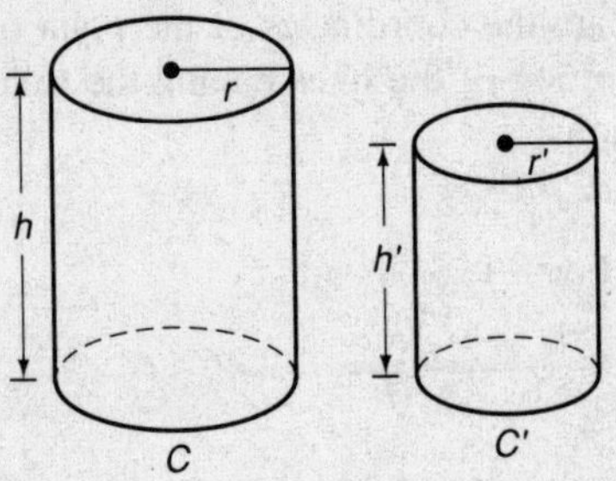

Figure 10

(E) The formula for calculating the volume of a cylinder is: $V = \pi r^2 h$

So the volume of the larger cylinder is just that. Now we redefine the dimensions of the smaller cylinder in terms of r and h:

$r = kr'$ so $r' = r/k$

$h = kh'$ so $h' = h/k$

And the volume of the smaller cylinder is:

$$V = \pi\left(\frac{r}{k}\right)^2\left(\frac{h}{k}\right) = \frac{\pi r^2 h}{k^3}$$

And the ratio is:

$$\frac{\pi r^2 h}{\frac{\pi r^2 h}{k^3}} = k^3$$

As an alternative, you could assume some numbers. Let the radius and height of the larger cylinder be 4 and 4, respectively, and those of the smaller cylinder 2 and 2. Since $r = kr'$ and $h = kh'$, k must be 2. Now the larger cylinder has a volume of:

$V = \pi(4)^2 4 = 64\pi$

And the smaller cylinder a volume of:

$V = \pi(2)^2 2 = 8\pi$

And the ratio of 64π to 8π is 8 to 1 or simply 8. Now, using $k = 2$, find an answer choice that has the value of 8:

(A) $1/\pi$ Wrong.
(B) π Wrong.
(C) 8π Wrong.
(D) 1/8 Wrong.
(E) 8 Correct.

47. In Figure 11, if the triangle has an area of 1, then the area of the circle is

(A) π
(B) 2π
(C) $2\sqrt{3}\pi$
(D) 4π
(E) $4\sqrt{3}\pi$

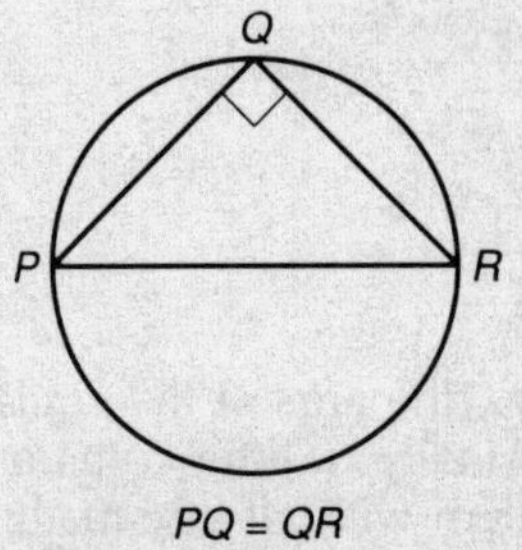

Figure 11

(A) Since this is a right triangle, the adjacent sides intercept an arc of 180 degrees. (An inscribed angle intercepts twice the arc.) So the hypotenuse of the triangle is also the diameter of the circle. And given any bit of information about a right isosceles triangle, e.g., either side, the hypotenuse, or the area, we can find the other information. If we designate the two adjacent sides as s and use them as altitude and base:

$$\text{Area} = \frac{1}{2}(s)(s)$$

$$1 = \frac{1}{2}s^2$$

$$s^2 = 2$$

$$s = \sqrt{2}$$

And the length of the hypotenuse is equal to the length of the side multiplied by $\sqrt{2}$. So the hypotenuse/diameter is equal to 2. Thus, the radius of the circle is 1, and the area of the circle:

$$\text{Area} = \pi(1)^2 = \pi$$

You can arrive at this same conclusion in a slightly different manner:

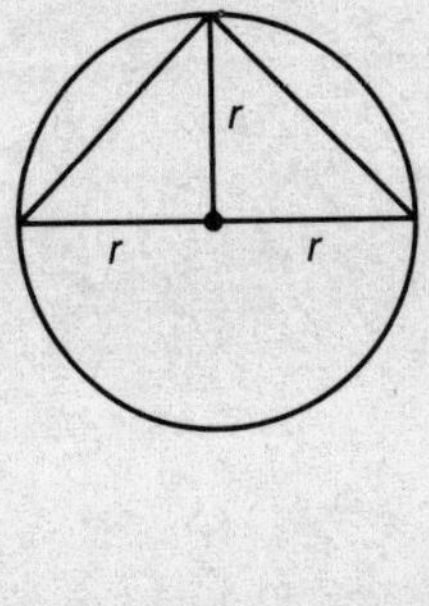

r is now the length of the altitude of the triangle, and $2r$ the length of the base:

$$\text{Area} = \frac{1}{2}(r)(2r)$$

$$1 = \frac{1}{2}(r)(2r)$$

$$2 = 2r^2$$

$$r^2 = 1$$

$$r = 1$$

Again, the area of the circle is just π.

Finally, a little common sense gets you this problem without any math. The triangle, which has an area of 1, takes up slightly less than half of the circle:

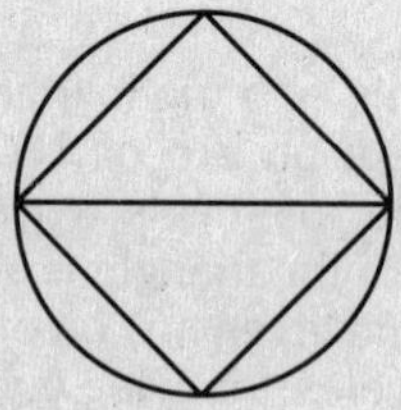

So the correct answer choice must be something that's a bit larger than 2. Only one of the answer choices qualifies. (B) says, for example, that the triangle is less than 1/6 of the circle. So (B), and with it the other choices that are larger, have to be incorrect.

48. What are the coordinates of the point of intersection of the lines having the following equations:

$x - \sqrt{3}y = \sqrt{3}$

$\sqrt{3}x + y = 1$

(A) $\left(-\frac{1}{2}, -\frac{\sqrt{3}}{2}\right)$

(B) $\left(-\frac{2\sqrt{3}}{3}, -\frac{1}{2}\right)$

(C) $\left(\frac{1}{2}, \frac{2}{\sqrt{3}}\right)$

(D) $\left(-\frac{\sqrt{3}}{2}, -\frac{1}{2}\right)$

(E) $\left(\frac{3}{2\sqrt{3}}, -\frac{1}{2}\right)$

(E) The point of intersection will have the coordinates that satisfy both of the equations. So treat the equations as a system of simultaneous equations. Using the first equation, solve for x:

$$x = \sqrt{3} + \sqrt{3}y$$

Substitute this into the second equation:

$$\sqrt{3}(\sqrt{3} + \sqrt{3}y) + y = 1$$

And solve for y:

$$3 + 3y + y = 1$$

$$4y = -2$$

$$y = -\frac{1}{2}$$

(This allows you to eliminate (A) and (C). And that would be important if you were about to run out of time.) Now use this value to find x:

$$\sqrt{3}x + \left(-\frac{1}{2}\right) = 1$$

$$\sqrt{3}x = \frac{3}{2}$$

$$x = \frac{3}{2\sqrt{3}}$$

49. In Figure 12, the radius of the circles is 1. What is the perimeter of the shaded part of the figure?

(A) $\frac{4\pi}{3}$

(B) π

(C) $\frac{2\pi}{3}$

(D) $\frac{\pi}{3}$

(E) $\frac{\pi}{6}$

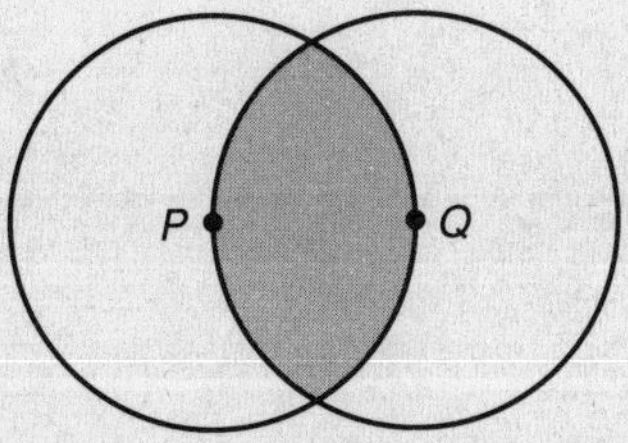

Figure 12

(A) This is a good exercise in organized problem solving. Look at the figure and ask yourself what you already know. You know the radius of the circle. Additionally, you know that the perimeter of the shaded area consists of two arcs. There must be some way to use the information about the radius to find the length of the arcs. Arcs can be measured in terms of length or in terms of degrees. Is it possible to find the degree measures of those arcs? Yes:

Since the sides of the triangles are all radii, the triangles must be equilateral. This means that the degree measure of each arc is 120. Since the circles have a radius of 1, they have circumferences of $2\pi(1) = 2\pi$. And since each arc is a third that long: $2\pi/3$. And since there are two such arcs, the perimeter of the shaded area is $2 \times 2\pi/3 = 4\pi/3$.

50. If $f(x) = \frac{x-2}{(x-2)(x^2+2)}$, for what value of x is $f(x)$ undefined?

(A) -4

(B) -2

(C) 0

(D) $\frac{1}{2}$

(E) 2

(E) The function will be undefined when one of the terms in the denominator is 0. (Division by 0 yields an undefined term.) Using 2 will cause $(x - 2)$ to be 0, and the entire expression will be undefined.

Mathematics Level IIC Answer Sheet

1	Ⓐ	Ⓑ	Ⓒ	Ⓓ	Ⓔ	26	Ⓐ	Ⓑ	Ⓒ	Ⓓ	Ⓔ
2	Ⓐ	Ⓑ	Ⓒ	Ⓓ	Ⓔ	27	Ⓐ	Ⓑ	Ⓒ	Ⓓ	Ⓔ
3	Ⓐ	Ⓑ	Ⓒ	Ⓓ	Ⓔ	28	Ⓐ	Ⓑ	Ⓒ	Ⓓ	Ⓔ
4	Ⓐ	Ⓑ	Ⓒ	Ⓓ	Ⓔ	29	Ⓐ	Ⓑ	Ⓒ	Ⓓ	Ⓔ
5	Ⓐ	Ⓑ	Ⓒ	Ⓓ	Ⓔ	30	Ⓐ	Ⓑ	Ⓒ	Ⓓ	Ⓔ
6	Ⓐ	Ⓑ	Ⓒ	Ⓓ	Ⓔ	31	Ⓐ	Ⓑ	Ⓒ	Ⓓ	Ⓔ
7	Ⓐ	Ⓑ	Ⓒ	Ⓓ	Ⓔ	32	Ⓐ	Ⓑ	Ⓒ	Ⓓ	Ⓔ
8	Ⓐ	Ⓑ	Ⓒ	Ⓓ	Ⓔ	33	Ⓐ	Ⓑ	Ⓒ	Ⓓ	Ⓔ
9	Ⓐ	Ⓑ	Ⓒ	Ⓓ	Ⓔ	34	Ⓐ	Ⓑ	Ⓒ	Ⓓ	Ⓔ
10	Ⓐ	Ⓑ	Ⓒ	Ⓓ	Ⓔ	35	Ⓐ	Ⓑ	Ⓒ	Ⓓ	Ⓔ
11	Ⓐ	Ⓑ	Ⓒ	Ⓓ	Ⓔ	36	Ⓐ	Ⓑ	Ⓒ	Ⓓ	Ⓔ
12	Ⓐ	Ⓑ	Ⓒ	Ⓓ	Ⓔ	37	Ⓐ	Ⓑ	Ⓒ	Ⓓ	Ⓔ
13	Ⓐ	Ⓑ	Ⓒ	Ⓓ	Ⓔ	38	Ⓐ	Ⓑ	Ⓒ	Ⓓ	Ⓔ
14	Ⓐ	Ⓑ	Ⓒ	Ⓓ	Ⓔ	39	Ⓐ	Ⓑ	Ⓒ	Ⓓ	Ⓔ
15	Ⓐ	Ⓑ	Ⓒ	Ⓓ	Ⓔ	40	Ⓐ	Ⓑ	Ⓒ	Ⓓ	Ⓔ
16	Ⓐ	Ⓑ	Ⓒ	Ⓓ	Ⓔ	41	Ⓐ	Ⓑ	Ⓒ	Ⓓ	Ⓔ
17	Ⓐ	Ⓑ	Ⓒ	Ⓓ	Ⓔ	42	Ⓐ	Ⓑ	Ⓒ	Ⓓ	Ⓔ
18	Ⓐ	Ⓑ	Ⓒ	Ⓓ	Ⓔ	43	Ⓐ	Ⓑ	Ⓒ	Ⓓ	Ⓔ
19	Ⓐ	Ⓑ	Ⓒ	Ⓓ	Ⓔ	44	Ⓐ	Ⓑ	Ⓒ	Ⓓ	Ⓔ
20	Ⓐ	Ⓑ	Ⓒ	Ⓓ	Ⓔ	45	Ⓐ	Ⓑ	Ⓒ	Ⓓ	Ⓔ
21	Ⓐ	Ⓑ	Ⓒ	Ⓓ	Ⓔ	46	Ⓐ	Ⓑ	Ⓒ	Ⓓ	Ⓔ
22	Ⓐ	Ⓑ	Ⓒ	Ⓓ	Ⓔ	47	Ⓐ	Ⓑ	Ⓒ	Ⓓ	Ⓔ
23	Ⓐ	Ⓑ	Ⓒ	Ⓓ	Ⓔ	48	Ⓐ	Ⓑ	Ⓒ	Ⓓ	Ⓔ
24	Ⓐ	Ⓑ	Ⓒ	Ⓓ	Ⓔ	49	Ⓐ	Ⓑ	Ⓒ	Ⓓ	Ⓔ
25	Ⓐ	Ⓑ	Ⓒ	Ⓓ	Ⓔ	50	Ⓐ	Ⓑ	Ⓒ	Ⓓ	Ⓔ

MATHEMATICS TEST, LEVEL IIC

Directions: For each problem in this test, determine which is the best of the five choices given. Then darken the corresponding oval space on the answer sheet.

Notes: (1) Figures that accompany problems in this test are drawn as accurately as possible EXCEPT when accompanied by the words "NOTE: Figure not drawn to scale."

(2) Unless otherwise indicated, all figures lie in a plane.

(3) Unless otherwise specified, the domain of a function is assumed to be the set of all real numbers x such that $f(x)$ is a real number.

(4) A calculator is necessary for answering some—but not all—of the questions in this test. In each case, you must decide whether or not to use a calculator. For some items, you will need to determine whether the calculator should be in the degree mode or the radian mode.

1. If x and y are positive integers such that x divided by 7 leaves a remainder of 4, and y divided by 7 leaves a remainder of 3, then what is the remainder when xy is divided by 7?

(A) 0 **(D)** 5
(B) 1 **(E)** 6
(C) 3

2. The radius of a sphere with volume 35 is how much greater than the radius of a sphere with volume 24?

(A) 0.58 **(D)** 0.24
(B) 0.49 **(E)** 0.12
(C) 0.37

3. If S is the set of all integers that can be written in the form $n^2 + 1$, then which of the following is a member of S?

(A) 8 **(D)** 52
(B) 16 **(E)** 65
(C) 24

4. A group of students consisting of 4 seniors, 5 juniors, and 6 sophomores plans to nominate a slate of 3 officers—president, vice-president, and treasurer—for the student government election. If the presidential candidate must be a senior and the vice-presidential candidate must be a junior, how many different slates are possible?

(A) 3,375 **(D)** 260
(B) 840 **(E)** 120
(C) 300

5. If $f(x) = x^2 + bx + 1$, and if $f(1) = 4$, then $b =$

(A) 4
(B) 2
(C) 1
(D) 0
(E) -2

6. Points P and Q lie in the coordinate plane. If the coordinates of P are (5,3) and Q are $(-2,-6)$, what is the distance between point P and point Q?

(A) 11.4
(B) 13.2
(C) 15.8
(D) 17.5
(E) 21.2

7. During the last 4 hours of a 400-kilometer trip, a passenger train traveled at an average speed of t kilometers per hour. If the train completed the entire trip in 6 hours, at what speed, in kilometers per hour, did the train travel during the first 2 hours?

(A) $\dfrac{200 + t}{2}$
(B) $\dfrac{200 - t}{2}$
(C) $200 + t$
(D) $200 - 2t$
(E) $2t - 100$

GO ON TO THE NEXT PAGE

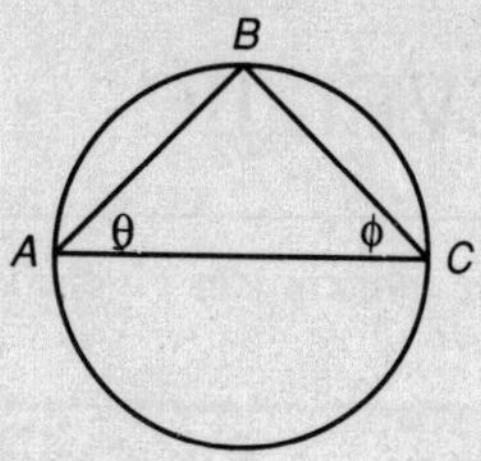

Figure 1

8. In Figure 1, if AC is a diameter of the circle, B is a point on the circle, and $\sin\theta = 1/2$, then $\sin\phi =$

(A) $\frac{\sqrt{2}}{3}$

(B) $\frac{\sqrt{3}}{3}$

(C) $\frac{\sqrt{3}}{2}$

(D) $\frac{2\sqrt{2}}{3}$

(E) $\frac{2\sqrt{3}}{3}$

9. If an equilateral triangle is rotated 360° around one of its altitudes, the resulting solid is a

(A) cone

(B) cube

(C) cylinder

(D) sphere

(E) right prism

10. How many integers are in the solution set of $|3x - 2| < 1$?

(A) None

(B) One

(C) Two

(D) Three

(E) Infinitely many

11. If $f(x,y) = x^2 - xy + y^2$, for all real numbers, then which of the following must be true?

(A) $f(x,y) = f(x,-y)$

(B) $f(x,y) = f(-x,y)$

(C) $f(x,y) = f(-x,-y)$

(D) $f(x,y) = f(x,1/y)$

(E) $f(x,y) = f(x,-1/y)$

12. If $f(x)\ \frac{x-2}{(x+2)(4+x^2)}$, for what value of x is $f(x)$ undefined?

(A) -4

(B) -2

(C) 0

(D) 2

(E) 4

13. An angle measure of 45° is equivalent to an angle measure of

(A) 1/4 radians

(B) $1/\pi$ radians

(C) $\pi/4$ radians

(D) $\pi/2$ radians

(E) radians

14. If $\cos x = 0.2586$ and $0 < x < \pi/2$, what is the value of x?

(A) 8.254

(B) 1.309

(C) 0.999

(D) 0.688

(E) 0.005

15. If $\log_3 2 = x$, then $x =$

(A) 0.27

(B) 0.63

(C) 0.89

(D) 1.2

(E) 1.7

16. If $f(x) = 3x - 6$, and if $g(f(x)) = x$, then $g(x) =$

(A) $\frac{1}{3x-6}$

(B) $\frac{1}{6x-3}$

(C) $6 - 3x$

(D) $\frac{x}{3} + 2$

(E) $-\frac{x}{3} + 2$

17. Where defined, $\frac{\cot x}{\csc x} =$

(A) $\sin x$

(B) $\cos x$

(C) $\tan x$

(D) $\sin x \csc x$

(E) $\frac{1}{\sin x}$

18. What is the area of a right triangle with an angle of 58° and with a shorter leg of 5?

(A) 8

(B) 15

(C) 20

(D) 27

(E) 33

19. The diameter and the height of a right circular cylinder are equal. If the volume of the cylinder is 6, what is the height of the cylinder?

(A) 1.5

(B) 2.0

(C) 2.2

(D) 2.5

(E) 2.8

20. If $x^{1/4} = 20$, then $x =$

(A) $\sqrt[4]{20}$

(B) 5

(C) 80

(D) 2,000

(E) 160,000

21. In the coordinate plane, the graph of which of the following lines is perpendicular to the graph of line $y = \frac{3}{2}x + 1$?

(A) $y = \frac{3}{2}x - 1$

(B) $y = \frac{3}{4}x + 1$

(C) $y = \frac{3}{4}x - 1$

(D) $y = -\frac{2}{3}x + 2$

(E) $y = -\frac{3}{2} - 1$

22. If $x = \sum_{k=1}^{3} (2k - 1)$, then $x =$

(A) 6

(B) 9

(C) 12

(D) 15

(E) 16

23. If the probability that an event, e, will occur is represented by the expression $\frac{x}{x-1}$, then which of the following expressions represents the probability that event e will not occur?

(A) $\frac{x-1}{x}$

(B) $\frac{x+1}{x}$

(C) $\frac{1}{1-x}$

(D) $x + 1$

(E) $x - 1$

24. A student's final grade in a certain course is the average of his scores on ten tests graded on a scale of 0 to 100, inclusive. For the first six tests, the student's scores averaged 83. If x is the student's final grade for the course, then which of the following is true?

(A) $8.3 \leq x \leq 83.0$

(B) $49.8 \leq x \leq 83.0$

(C) $49.8 \leq x \leq 89.8$

(D) $54.7 \leq x \leq 89.8$

(E) $83.0 \leq x \leq 89.8$

GO ON TO THE NEXT PAGE

25. Which of the following represents the multiplicative inverse of the complex number $2 - i$?

(A) $2 + i$

(B) $i - 2$

(C) $\frac{2 + i}{3}$

(D) $\frac{2 - i}{3}$

(E) $\frac{2 + i}{5}$

26. $\log_3 \sqrt{3} =$

(A) -1

(B) $\frac{1}{3}$

(C) $\frac{1}{2}$

(D) $\frac{2}{3}$

(E) 2

27. If $f(x) = \sqrt[3]{x^3 - 2}$, what is $f^{-1}(2.5)$?

(A) 0.4

(B) 0.9

(C) 1.3

(D) 1.7

(E) 2.3

28. If $0 < x < \frac{\pi}{2}$, then which of the following must be true?

I. $\sin x < \cos x$

II. $\tan x < \cot x$

III. $\sec x < \cos x$

(A) I only

(B) II only

(C) III only

(D) I, II, and III

(E) None

Figure 3

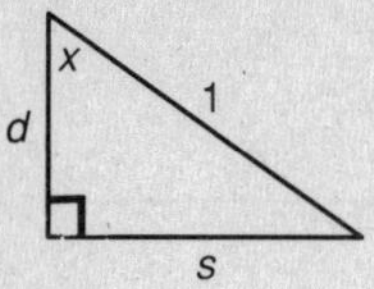

29. In Figure 3, if Arcsin $s = 2$ Arcsin d, then $x =$

(A) 15°

(B) 30°

(C) 45°

(D) 60°

(E) 75°

30. If, for all n, $2^n + 2^n + 2^n + 2^n = x(2^{n+1})$, then $x =$

(A) 2

(B) 4

(C) 2^n

(D) 2^{2n}

(E) 2^{n+1}

31. If $i^x = 1$, then x could equal

(A) 13

(B) 14

(C) 15

(D) 16

(E) 17

32. The formula for the area enclosed by an ellipse is $A = \pi ab$, where a and b are one-half the lengths of the major and minor axes, respectively. In the figure above, the equation of the circle is $x^2 + y^2 = 12$, then what is the area enclosed by the ellipse?

(A) 62

(B) 87

(C) 103

(D) 117

(E) 131

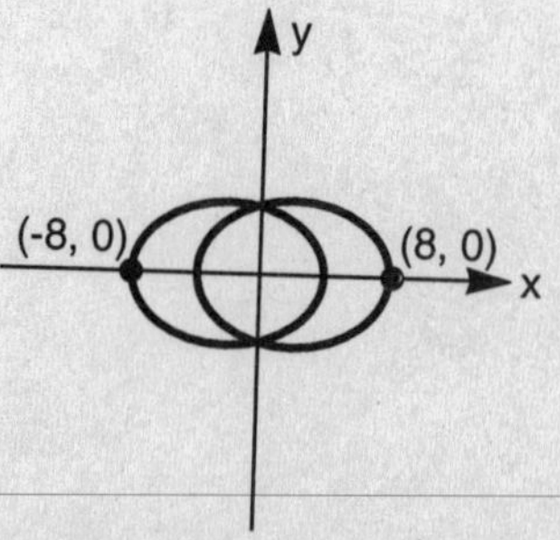

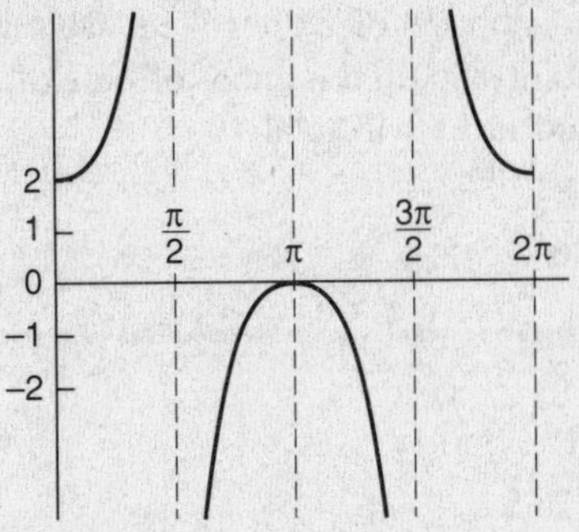

Figure 4

33. Figure 4 is a possible graph for which of the following equations?

(A) $y = 2 \sin x$

(B) $y = \sin x + 2$

(C) $y = \csc x + 1$

(D) $y = \csc x - 1$

(E) $y = \sec x + 1$

34. What is $\lim\limits_{x \to 1} \dfrac{x^2 - 1}{x - 1}$?

(A) -1

(B) 0

(C) 1

(D) 2

(E) The limit does not exist.

35. If $0 \leq x \leq \pi$ and $\cos x = -1$, then $\cos \dfrac{x}{2} =$

(A) $-\dfrac{\sqrt{3}}{2}$

(B) $-\dfrac{1}{2}$

(C) 0

(D) $\dfrac{1}{2}$

(E) $\dfrac{\sqrt{3}}{2}$

36. Which of the following defines the range of the function $f(x) = \dfrac{1 - x}{x}$?

(A) All real numbers

(B) All real numbers except -1

(C) All real numbers except 0

(D) All real numbers except 1

(E) All real numbers greater than -1

37. Which of the following figures represents the graph of

$x = 3 \sin \theta$
$y = 2 \cos \theta$

(A)

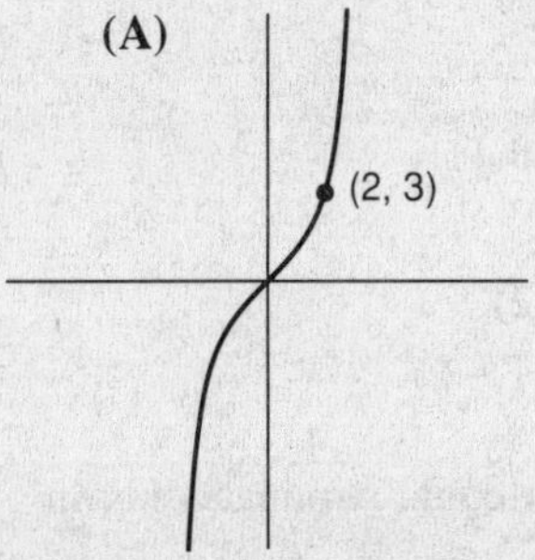

(B)

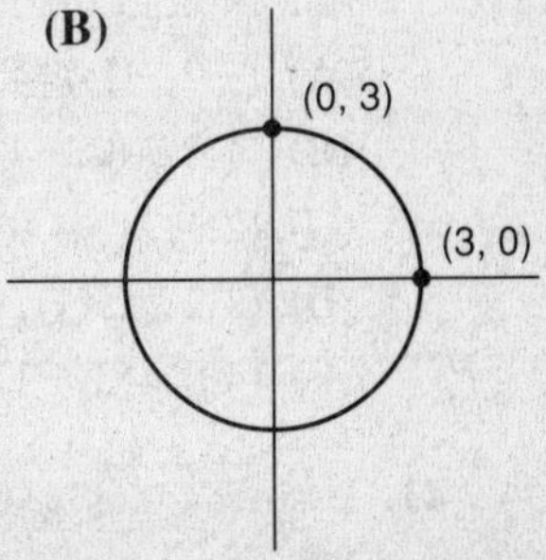

(C)

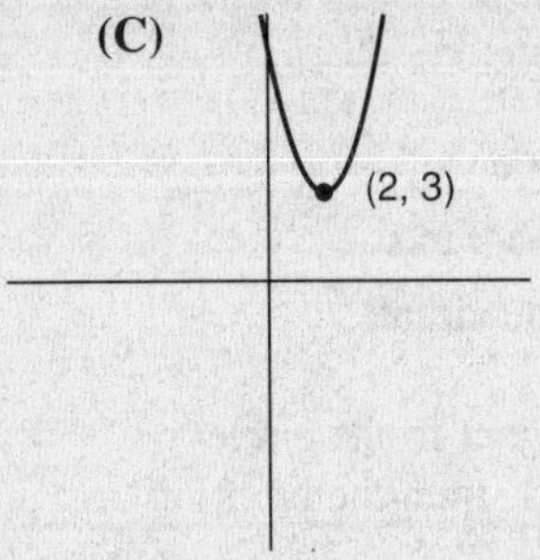

(D)

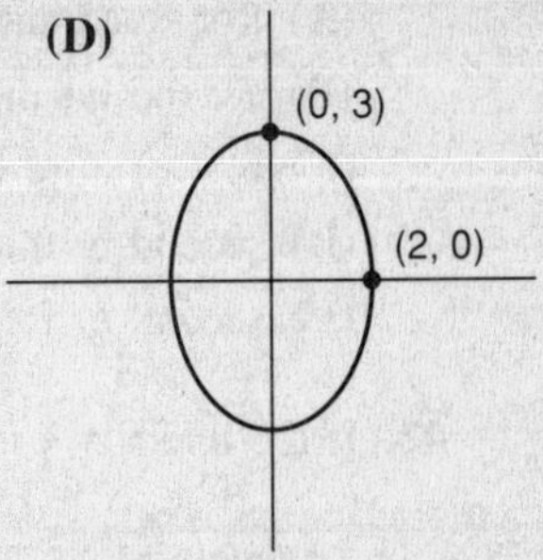

(E)

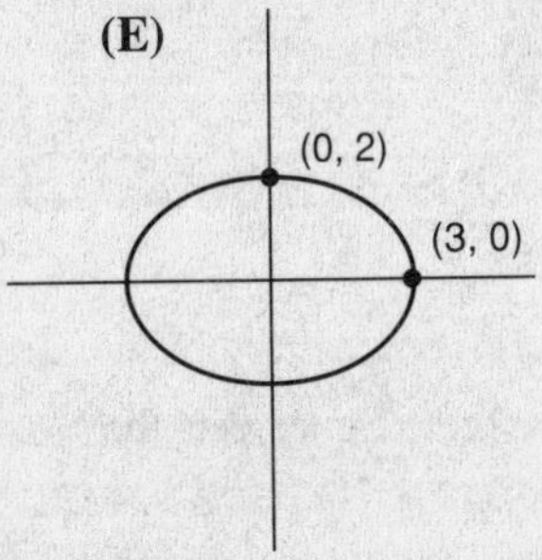

38. If $5^x = 2$, what does 3^x equal?

(A) 2.8

(B) 2.3

(C) 2.1

(D) 1.9

(E) 1.6

39. If $4 \cos x = \sin x$ and if x is in radian measure, what is the least positive value of x?

(A) 6.452

(B) 2.133

(C) 1.326

(D) 1.021

(E) 0.933

GO ON TO THE NEXT PAGE

40. Triangle ABC has coordinates $A(-1,-2)$, $B(0,4)$, and $C(3,-1)$. Which of the following provides the coordinates of triangle $A'B'C'$, respectively, the image of triangle ABC after a reflection in the line $y = -x$?

(A) $(-2,-1)$, $(4,0)$, $(-3,-1)$

(B) $(1,2)$, $(0,-4)$, $(-3,1)$

(C) $(2,1)$, $(-4,0)$, $(1,-3)$

(D) $(3,2)$, $(5,1)$, $(2,-2)$

(E) $(4,0)$, $(3,-1)$, $(-1,-2)$

41. If $\sin x = \cos x$, then x could terminate only in the

(A) first quadrant

(B) second quadrant

(C) first or third quadrants

(D) second or third quadrants

(E) second or fourth quadrants

42. If the line $x = k$ is tangent to the circle $(x-2)^2 + (y+1)^2 = 4$, then the point of tangency is

(A) $(-6,-1)$ or $(2,-1)$

(B) $(-2,-1)$ or $(6,-1)$

(C) $(0,-1)$ or $(4,-1)$

(D) $(0,1)$ or $(4,1)$

(E) $(2,1)$ or $(6,1)$

43. The graph of $y = 2\cos 2x + 2$ intersects the y-axis where $y =$

(A) 0

(B) 2

(C) 3

(D) 4

(E) 5

44. What is the last term in the expansion $(2x + 3y)^4$?

(A) y^4

(B) $9y^4$

(C) $27y^4$

(D) $81y^4$

(E) $(xy)^4$

45. If two unbiased dice are rolled, what is the probability that the number of dots on the two exposed faces will total 4?

(A) $\frac{1}{36}$

(B) $\frac{1}{18}$

(C) $\frac{1}{12}$

(D) $\frac{1}{9}$

(E) $\frac{1}{6}$

46. Which of the following could be a graph of the equation $y = ax^2 + bx + c$, where $b^2 - 4ac = 0$?

(A)

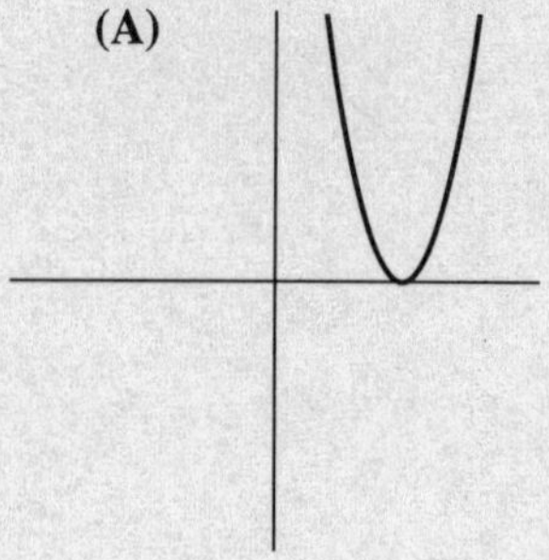

(B)

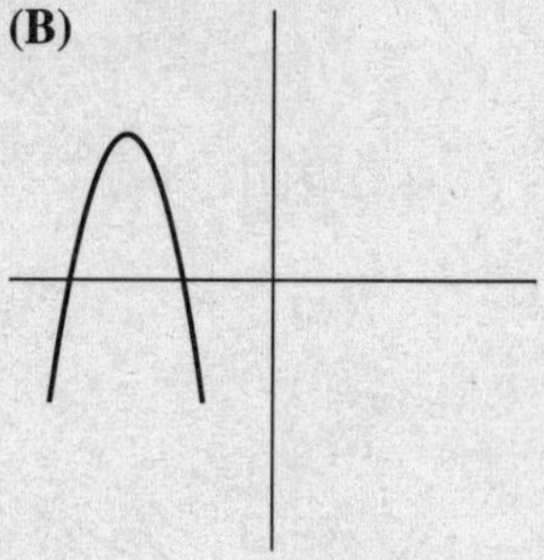

(C)

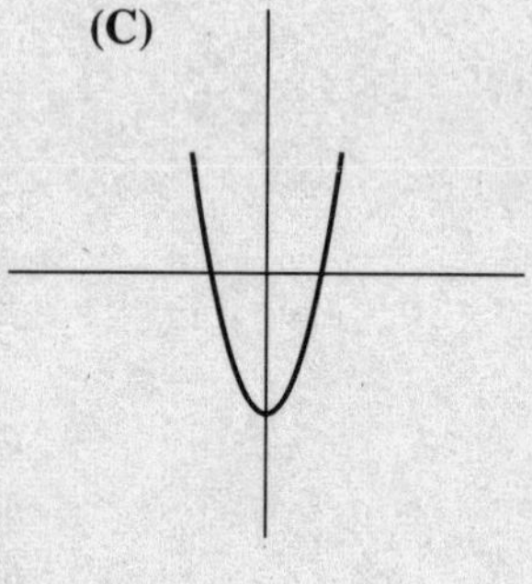

(D)

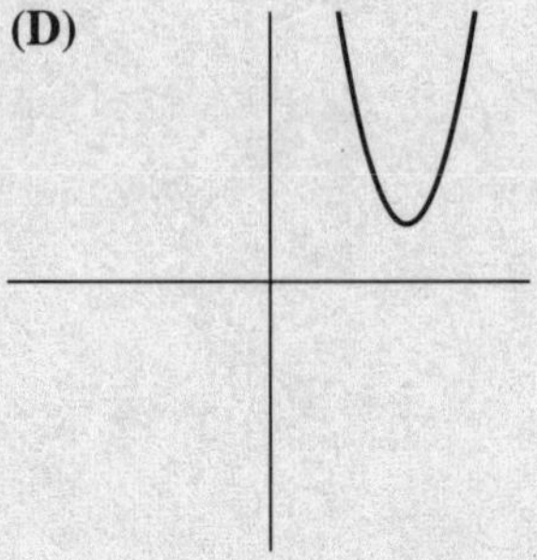

(E)

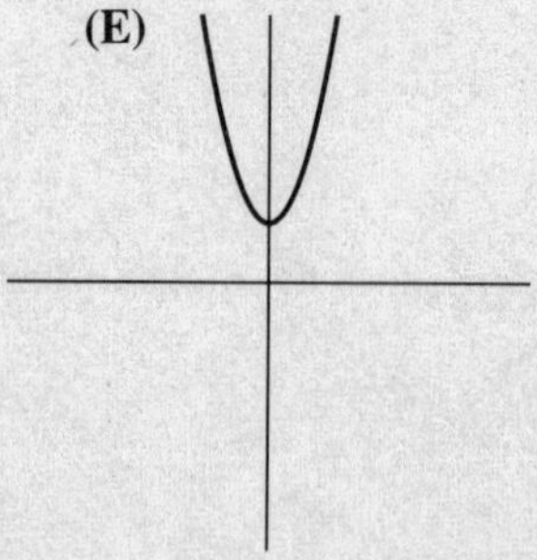

47. A plane cuts through a cube in such a way that the plane passes through three of the cube's vertices, no two of which lie on the same edge. If the edge of the cube has a length of 1, what is the surface area of the smaller fragment of the cube?

(A) 2.4

(B) 2.7

(C) 3.1

(D) 3.7

(E) 4.3

48. Which of the following equations describes a parabola with focus (2,3) and directrix $y = 0$?

(A) $(x + 2)^2 + (y + 3)^2 = 2$

(B) $(x - 2)^2 + (y - 3)^2 = 4$

(C) $(x - 2)^2 = -(y - 3)^2$

(D) $(x - 2)^2 = 2(y + 3)$

(E) $(x - 2)^2 = 3(2y - 3)$

49. A student taking a true-false test guesses randomly on three items. What is the probability that exactly two of the guesses will be correct?

(A) 1/16

(B) 1/8

(C) 1/4

(D) 3/8

(E) 1/2

50. (1) Given any individual x, if x is a C, then x is also a Q.

(2) There exists at least one individual x such that x is not a Q.

Which of the following conclusions can be logically deduced from the two statements above?

(A) There exists at least one x such that x is not a C.

(B) There exists at least one x such that x is a C.

(C) There exists at least one x such that x is a Q.

(D) There are no x's that are C's.

(E) There are no x's that are Q's.

S T O P

IF YOU FINISH BEFORE TIME IS CALLED, YOU MAY CHECK YOUR WORK ON THIS TEST ONLY. DO NOT WORK ON ANY OTHER TEST IN THIS BOOK.

Explanatory Answers

Each of the following explanations contains a "Calculator Status Report":

[+] Calculator is necessary for this problem.
[0] Calculator is not necessary for this problem but might be useful.
[−] Calculator is probably not useful for this problem.

1. If x and y are positive integers such that x divided by 7 leaves a remainder of 4, and y divided by 7 leaves a remainder of 3, then what is the remainder when xy is divided by 7?

   (A) 0 (D) 5
   (B) 1 (E) 6
   (C) 3

   (D) [0] Since x divided by 7 leaves a remainder of 4, x has the form $7m + 4$, where m is an integer. And since y divided by 7 leaves a remainder of 3, y has the form $7n + 3$, again where n is an integer. So xy has the form:

   $(7m + 4)(7n + 3) = 49mn + 21m + 28n + 12$

   The sum of the first three terms of that expression—$49mn + 21m + 28n$—is evenly divisible by 7. So the remainder is determined by the last term. And 12 divided by 7 leaves a remainder of 5.

   Alternatively, you can just use some numbers. Let x be 4 (4 divided by 7 leaves a remainder of 4), and let y be 3 (3 divided by 7 leaves a remainder of 3). On those assumptions, $xy =$ 12. And 12 divided by 7 leaves a remainder of 5.

2. The radius of a sphere with volume 35 is how much greater than the radius of a sphere with volume 24?

   (A) 0.58 (D) 0.24
   (B) 0.49 (E) 0.12
   (C) 0.37

   (D) [+] First calculate the radius of each sphere:

$35 = 4/3\ \pi r^3$	$24 = 4/3\ \pi r^3$
$r^3 = 35(3/4)/\pi$	$r^3 = 24(3/4)/\pi$
$r^3 = 8.3556$	$r^3 = 5.7295$
$r = 2.0292$	$r = 1.7894$

   So the difference between the length of the radius of the larger sphere and that of the smaller is:

   $2.0292 - 1.78940 = 0.2398$

3. If S is the set of all integers that can be written in the form $n^2 + 1$, then which of the following is a member of S?

   (A) 8 (D) 52
   (B) 16 (E) 65
   (C) 24

   (E) [−] If x is a member of S, then $x - 1$ is a perfect square:

   (A) $8 - 1 = 7$ Not a perfect square.
   (B) $16 - 1 = 15$ Not a perfect square.
   (C) $24 - 1 = 23$ Not a perfect square.
   (D) $52 - 1 = 51$ Not a perfect square.
   (E) $65 - 1 = 64$ and $8 \times 8 = 64$

4. A group of students consisting of 4 seniors, 5 juniors, and 6 sophomores plans to nominate a slate of 3 officers—president, vice-president, and treasurer—for the student government election. If the presidential candidate must be a senior and the vice-presidential candidate must be a junior, how many different slates are possible?

   (A) 3,375 (D) 260
   (B) 840 (E) 120
   (C) 300

   (D) [0] One of 4 seniors must be selected as the presidential candidate, and one of 5 juniors must be selected as the vice-presidential candidate. So 13 people remain for the position of treasurer:

   $4 \times 5 \times 13 = 260$

5. If $f(x) = x^2 + bx + 1$, and if $f(1) = 4$, then $b =$

(A) 4

(B) 2

(C) 1

(D) 0

(E) -2

(B) [−] Since $f(1) = 4$:

$(1)^2 + b(1) + 1 = 4$

$1 + b + 1 = 4$

$b + 2 = 4$

$b = 2$

Alternatively, you could test the answer choices:

(A) $(1)^2 + 4(1) + 1 = 4$
$6 = 4$ · False.

(B) $(1)^2 + 2(1) + 1 = 4$
$4 = 4$ True.

(C) $(1)^2 + 1(1) + 1 = 4$
$3 = 4$ False.

(D) $(1)^2 + 0(1) + 1 = 4$
$2 = 4$ False.

(E) $(1)^2 + -2(1) + 1 = 4$
$0 = 4$ False.

6. Points P and Q lie in the coordinate plane. If the coordinates of P are (5,3) and Q are (−2,−6), what is the distance between point P and point Q?

(A) 11.4

(B) 13.2

(C) 15.8

(D) 17.5

(E) 21.2

(A) [+] Use the distance formula:

$d = \sqrt{(x_2 - x_1)^2 + (y_2 - y_1)^2}$

$d = \sqrt{(-2 - 5)^2 + (-6 - 3)^2}$

$d = \sqrt{(-7)^2 + (-9)^2}$

$d = \sqrt{49 + 81} = \sqrt{130} = 11.401$

7. During the last 4 hours of a 400-kilometer trip, a passenger train traveled at an average speed of t kilometers per hour. If the train completed the entire trip in 6 hours, at what speed, in kilometers per hour, did the train travel during the first 2 hours?

(A) $\frac{200 + t}{2}$

(B) $\frac{200 - t}{2}$

(C) $200 + t$

(D) $200 - 2t$

(E) $2t - 100$

(D) [−] To find the train's average speed for the first two hours, you need to find how many kilometers is traveled during that time. You can do that by subtracting the kilometers covered during the last four hours from 400:

$400 - 4(t) = 400 - 4t$

The train covered that many kilometers during the first two hours:

$$\text{Average Speed} = \frac{400 - 4t}{2} = 200 - 2t$$

Alternatively, you can just assume a value for t. Let us assume that the train traveled 100 kilometers per hour for the last four hours, that is, $t = 100$. On that assumption, the train covered all 400 kilometers during the last four hours of the trip and didn't move at all during the first two hours. So if we substitute 100 for t into the formulas given as answer choices, the correct choice will generate the value 0:

(A) $\frac{200 + 100}{2} = 150$ Wrong

(B) $\frac{200 - 100}{2} = 50$ Wrong

(C) $200 + 100 = 300$ Wrong

(D) $200 - 200 = 0$ Correct!

(E) $2(100) - 100 = 100$ Wrong

8. In Figure 1, if AC is a diameter of the circle, B is a point on the circle, and $\sin \theta = 1/2$, then $\sin \phi =$

(A) $\frac{\sqrt{2}}{3}$

(B) $\frac{\sqrt{3}}{3}$

(C) $\frac{\sqrt{3}}{2}$

(D) $\frac{2\sqrt{2}}{3}$

(E) $\frac{2\sqrt{3}}{3}$

(C) [0] Since $\sin \theta = 1/2$:

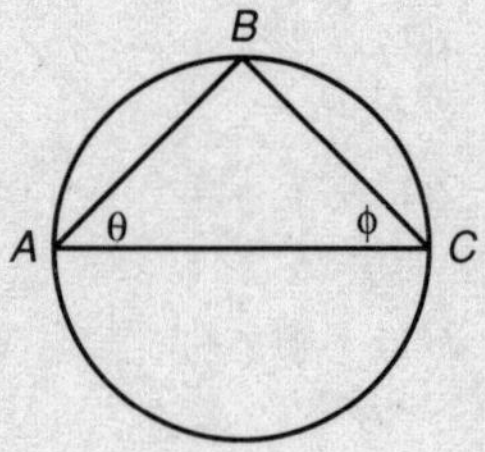

$\frac{BC}{AC} = \frac{1}{2}$

And:

$BC = \frac{AC}{2}$

Since ABC is a right triangle:

$AC^2 = AB^2 + BC^2$

Substituting $AC/2$ for BC:

$AC^2 = AB^2 + (AC/2)^2$

$AC^2 = AB^2 + AC^2/4$

$AC^2 - AC^2/4 = AB^2$

$3AC^2/4 = AB^2$

$\sqrt{3}AC/2 = AB$

$\frac{AB}{AC} = \frac{\sqrt{3}}{2}$

Since AB/AC is $\sin \phi$, $\sin \phi = \frac{\sqrt{3}}{2}$

9. If an equilateral triangle is rotated 360° around one of its altitudes, the resulting solid is a

(A) cone

(B) cube

(C) cylinder

(D) sphere

(E) right prism

(A) [−] Sometimes, one picture truly is worth a thousand words:

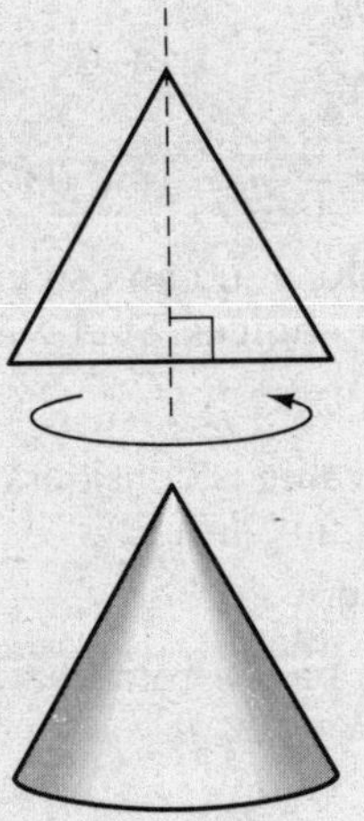

10. How many integers are in the solution set of $|3x - 2| < 1$?

(A) None

(B) One

(C) Two

(D) Three

(E) Infinitely many

(A) [−] If x is an integer, then the expression $|3x - 2|$ will have its minimum value when $x = 1$:

$|3(1) - 2| = |3 - 2| = |1| = 1$

But 1 = 1. Therefore, there are no integral solutions to the inequality given.

11. If $f(x,y) = x^2 - xy + y^2$, for all real numbers, then which of the following must be true?

(A) $f(x,y) = f(x,-y)$

(B) $f(x,y) = f(-x,y)$

(C) $f(x,y) = f(-x,-y)$

(D) $f(x,y) = f(x,1/y)$

(E) $f(x,y) = f(x,-1/y)$

(C) [0] One way of attacking this problem is to substitute the suggested equivalences into the function. For choice (C), the result is:

$x^2 - xy^2 + y^2 = (-x)^2 - (-x)(-y) + (-y)^2 =$
$x^2 - xy + y^2$

You can reach the same conclusion by examining the structure of the function in light of the answer choices. Since the first and third terms have variables of the second power, the sign before the substituted variable is irrelevant. The only question is whether the middle term—the xy term—will have the same sign. Since $(-x)(-y) = xy$, (C) is necessarily true.

Finally, you can solve this problem very easily just by assuming some values for x and y—say 2 and 2. On that assumption, the function yields:

$(2)^2 - (2)(2) + (2)^2 = 4$

The correct answer choice, therefore, will also generate the value 4:

(A) $(2)^2 - (2)(-2) + (-2)^2 = 12$ Wrong.

(B) $(-2)^2 - (-2)(2) + (2)^2 = 12$ Wrong.

(C) $(-2)^2 - (-2)(-2) + (-2)^2 = 4$ Correct!

(D) $(2)^2 - (2)(1/2) + (1/2)^2 = 13/4$ Wrong.

(E) $(2)^2 - (2)(-1/2) + (-1/2)^2 = 21/4$ Wrong.

12. If $f(x) = \dfrac{x-2}{(x+2)(4+x^2)}$, for what value of x is $f(x)$ undefined?

(A) −4

(B) −2

(C) 0

(D) 2

(E) 4

(B) [0] When $x = -2$, $(x + 2) = 0$, and $f(x)$ is undefined.

13. An angle measure of 45° is equivalent to an angle measure of

(A) 1/4 radians

(B) $1/\pi$ radians

(C) $\pi/4$ radians

(D) $\pi/2$ radians

(E) π radians

(C) [0] An angle has a measure of one radian if, when its vertex is placed at the center of a circle, it intercepts an arc equal to the radius of a circle.

The full circumference of a circle has a radian measure of $2\pi r/r = 2\pi$. Now a simple proportion will solve our problem:

$$\frac{360}{45} = \frac{2\pi}{x}$$

$$360x = 90\pi$$

$$x = \frac{\pi}{4}$$

14. If $\cos x = 0.2586$ and $0 < x < \pi/2$, what is the value of x?

(A) 8.254

(B) 1.309

(C) 0.999

(D) 0.688

(E) 0.005

(B) [+] Since angle x is measured in radians, set your calculator to the radian mode. The value of x is the inverse cosine of 0.2586:

$$\cos^{-1} 0.2586 = 1.3092$$

15. If $\log_3 2 = x$, then $x =$

(A) 0.27

(B) 0.63

(C) 0.89

(D) 1.2

(E) 1.7

(B) [+] By definition, $\log_3 2 = x$ can be rewritten as $3^x = 2$. Solve for x by taking the log of both sides of the equation:

$$\log 3^x = \log 2$$

$$x\log 3 = \log 2$$

$$x = \frac{\log 2}{\log 3} = \frac{0.3010}{0.4771} = 0.6309$$

Alternatively, you can use your calculator to test answer choices. Start with (C):

$$3^{0.89} = 2.6585$$

Since that value is considerably more than 2, you should next test (B):

$$3^{0.63} = 1.9979$$

So (B) must be the correct answer.

16. If $f(x) = 3x - 6$, and if $g(f(x)) = x$, then $g(x) =$

(A) $\frac{1}{3x-6}$

(B) $\frac{1}{6x-3}$

(C) $6 - 3x$

(D) $\frac{x}{3} + 2$

(E) $\frac{x}{3} - 2$

(D) [0] One way of attacking this problem is to examine the structure of the two functions in light of the answer choices, but for most people that will probably be a matter of trial and error. Alternatively, you could subsitute $3x - 6$ into the answer choices until you find the formula that generates the value x. But an even easier solution is to assign a value to x. Let $x = 1$. On that assumption, $f(1) = 3(1) - 6 = -3$. Now, if you substitute -3 into the answer choices, the correct choice will generate the value 1:

(A) $\frac{1}{3(-3)-6} = -\frac{1}{15}$ Wrong

(B) $\frac{1}{6(-3)-3} = -\frac{1}{21}$ Wrong

(C) $6 - 3(3) = -3$ Wrong

(D) $\frac{-3}{3} + 2 = 1$ Correct!

(E) $\frac{-3}{3} + 2 = -3$ Wrong

17. Where defined, $\frac{\cot x}{\csc x} =$

(A) $\sin x$

(B) $\cos x$

(C) $\tan x$

(D) $\sin x \csc x$

(E) $\frac{1}{\sin x}$

(B) [0] Use an acute right triangle:

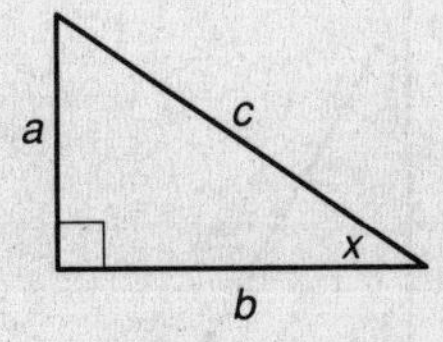

$\cot x = \frac{b}{a}$ and $\csc x = \frac{c}{a}$

And:

$$\frac{\cot x}{\csc x} = \frac{\frac{b}{a}}{\frac{c}{a}} = \frac{b}{a} \times \frac{a}{c} = \frac{b}{c}$$

And $\frac{b}{c} = \cos x$

As for choices (A) and (C), $\sin x = \frac{a}{c}$ and $\tan x = \frac{a}{b}$.

As for (D) and (E), sine and cosecant are reciprocal functions, so $\sin x \cdot \csc x = 1$ and $1/\sin x = \csc x$.

18. What is the area of a right triangle with an angle of 58° and with a shorter leg of 5?

(A) 8 **(D)** 27
(B) 15 **(E)** 33
(C) 20

(C) [+] Since the triangle is a right triangle, the shorter side and the longer side can be used to find the area of the figure:

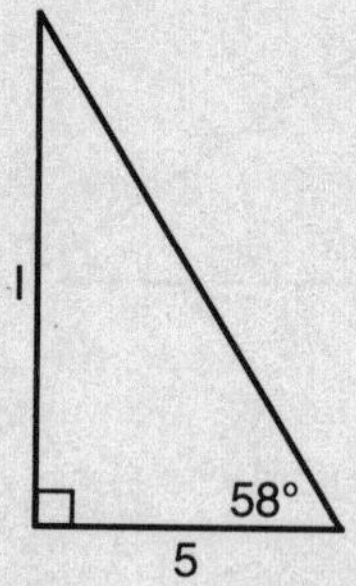

One way of finding the length of the longer side is:

$$\tan 58^\circ = \frac{s}{5}$$

$$s = \tan 58^\circ \times 5 = 1.6003 \times 5 = 8.0015$$

Using the value 8 as the length of the longer side, we calculated the area of the triangle:

$$A = \frac{1}{2}(8)(5) = 20$$

This problem is assigned a "+" for calculator usage, because using the trig function of the calculator seems the most natural approach. Given that the answer choices are fairly far apart, however, the problem can actually be solved without using a calculator. The 32°–58–90° triangle of the problem is very similar in shape to a 30°–60°–90° triangle. And in a 30°–60°–90° triangle, the two sides are related in the following way:

$$s = \frac{1}{2}h \text{ and } l = \frac{1}{2}h \times \sqrt{3}$$

where s and l represent the shorter and longer sides, respectively. Therefore:

$$h = 2s \text{ and } h = \frac{2l}{\sqrt{3}}$$

And:

$$2s = \frac{2l}{\sqrt{3}}$$

$$s = \frac{l}{\sqrt{3}}$$

Since $s = 5$:

$$5 = \frac{l}{\sqrt{3}}$$

$$l = 5\sqrt{3} \approx 5 \times 1.7 = 8.5$$

And the area of a right triangle with sides of 5 and 8.5 would be:

$$A = \frac{1}{2}(8.5)(5) = 21.25$$

The closest answer is (C).

19. The diameter and the height of a right circular cylinder are equal. If the volume of the cylinder is 6, what is the height of the cylinder?

(A) 1.5 **(D)** 2.5
(B) 2.0 **(E)** 2.8
(C) 2.2

(B) [+] Since the diameter and the height of the cylinder are equal:

$$6 = \pi r^2 h = \pi\left(\frac{h}{2}\right)^2 h = \frac{\pi h^3}{4}$$

$$h^3 = \frac{(6 \times 4)}{\pi} = \frac{24}{\pi} = 6.6394$$

$$h = 1.9694$$

So (B) is the best response.

20. If $x^{1/4} = 20$, then $x =$

(A) $\sqrt[4]{20}$ **(D)** 2,000
(B) 5 **(E)** 160,000
(C) 80

(E) [0] Raise both sides of the equation to the fourth power:

$$(x^{1/4})^4 = 20^4$$

$$x = 20^4 = (2 \times 10)^4 = 2^4 \times 10^4 = 16 \times 10{,}000 = 160{,}000$$

21. In the coordinate plane, the graph of which of the following lines is perpendicular to the graph of line $y = \frac{3}{2}x + 1$?

(A) $y = \frac{3}{2}x - 1$ (D) $y = -\frac{2}{3}x + 2$
(B) $y = \frac{3}{4}x + 1$ (E) $y = -\frac{3}{2} - 1$
(C) $y = \frac{3}{4}x - 1$

(D) [−] This problem can be easily solved if you recall that two lines are perpendicular just in case the product of their slopes is −1. Alternatively, you could sketch the graph of each of the lines.

22. If $x = \sum_{k=1}^{3} (2k - 1)$, then $x =$

(A) 6

(B) 9

(C) 12

(D) 15

(E) 16

(B) [0] $\sum_{k=1}^{3} (2k - 1)$ stands for the summation of all the values of $2k - 1$ for the integers 1 through 3, inclusive:

$$\sum_{k=1}^{3} (2k - 1) = (2(1) - 1) + (2(2) - 1) + (2(3) - 1) =$$

23. If the probability that an event, e, will occur is represented by the expression $\frac{x}{x - 1}$, then which of the following expressions represents the probability that event e will not occur?

(A) $\frac{x - 1}{x}$

(B) $\frac{x + 1}{x}$

(C) $\frac{1}{1 - x}$

(D) $x + 1$

(E) $x - 1$

(C) [−] Event e either occurs or does not occur—that is certain. Thus the probability of (e or not−e) is a certainty or 1. If we let y represent the probability that e does not occur, then:

$$\frac{x}{x - 1} + y = 1$$

$$(x - 1)\left(\frac{x}{x - 1} + y\right) = (1)(x - 1)$$

$$x + y(x - 1) = x - 1$$

$$y(x - 1) = -1$$

$$y = \frac{-1}{x - 1}$$

$$y = \frac{1}{1 - x}$$

24. A student's final grade in a certain course is the average of his scores on ten tests graded on a scale of 0 to 100, inclusive. For the first six tests, the student's scores averaged 83. If x is the student's final grade for the course, then which of the following is true?

(A) $8.3 \leq x \leq 83.0$

(B) $49.8 \leq x \leq 83.0$

(C) $49.8 \leq x \leq 89.8$

(D) $54.7 \leq x \leq 89.8$

(E) $83.0 \leq x \leq 89.8$

(C) [0] For the first six tests, the student has accumulated a total point count of $6 \times 83 = 498$. If the student scores zero on each of the remaining four tests, the total point count will remain 498 and the average will be 498/10 = 49.8. If the student scores 100 on each of the four remaining tests, the total point count will be 898 and the average will be 898/10 = 89.8.

25. Which of the following represents the multiplicative inverse of the complex number $2 - i$?

(A) $2 + i$

(B) $i - 2$

(C) $\frac{2 + i}{3}$

(D) $\frac{2 - i}{3}$

(E) $\frac{2 + i}{5}$

(E) [−] Let x be the multiplicative inverse of $2 - i$: $(x)(2 - i) = 1$

$$x = \frac{1}{2 - i}$$

And rationalize the right side of the equation:

$$x = \left(\frac{1}{2 - i}\right)\left(\frac{2 + i}{2 + i}\right)$$

$$x = \frac{2 - i}{4 - i^2}$$

Since $i = \sqrt{-1}$, $i^2 = -1$, so:

$$x = \frac{2 + i}{4 - (-1)} = \frac{2 + i}{5}$$

26. $\log_3\sqrt{3} =$

(A) -1

(B) $\frac{1}{3}$

(C) $\frac{1}{2}$

(D) $\frac{2}{3}$

(E) 2

(C) [0] By definition, the logarithm of a number, to a given base, is the exponent that is used with the base to obtain that number:

$b^e = n \leftrightarrow e = \log_b n$

Here the base, b, is 3, and the number, n, is $\sqrt{3}$. So all you need to do is rewrite the statement in its equivalent exponential form:

3 to what power equals $\sqrt{3}$

Since the fractional exponent 1/2 indicates "square root," the statement should read:

3 to the 1/2 power equals $\sqrt{3}$

27. If $f(x) = \sqrt[3]{x^3 - 2}$, what is $f^{-1}(2.5)$?

(A) 0.4

(B) 0.9

(C) 1.3

(D) 1.7

(E) 2.3

(A) [+] The best approach to this problem is to use your calculator to find the value of $f^{-1}(2.5)$:

$f(2.5) = \sqrt[3]{(2.5)^3 - 2} = \sqrt[3]{15.625 - 2}$

$= \sqrt[3]{13.625} = 2.3884$

So $f^{-1}(2.5) = 1/2.3884 = 0.4186$. And (A) is the best answer.

28. If $0 < x < \frac{\pi}{2}$, then which of the following must be true?

I. $\sin x < \cos x$

II. $\tan x < \cot x$

III. $\sec x < \cos x$

(A) I only

(B) II only

(C) III only

(D) I, II, and III

(E) None

(E) [0] The following table summarizes the behavior of the trigonometric functions in the first quadrant:

$y = \sin x$	increases from 0 to 1
$y = \cos x$	decreases from 1 to 0
$y = \tan x$	increases from 0 to ∞
$y = \cot x$	decreases from ∞ to 0
$y = \sec x$	increases from 1 to ∞
$y = \csc x$	decreases from ∞ to 1

You could also solve this problem by sketching a graph of the functions.

Figure 3

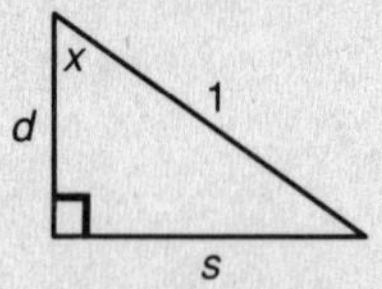

29. In Figure 3, if Arcsin s = 2 Arcsin d, then $x =$

(A) 15°

(B) 30°

(C) 45°

(D) 60°

(E) 75°

(D) [0] Arcsin s indicates the angle for which the sine is s, and Arcsin d indicates the angle for which the sine is d. Since Arcsin s is twice Arcsin d, angle x must be twice the unmarked angle. Since those two angles are complementary, x must be 60.

30. If, for all n, $2^n + 2^n + 2^n + 2^n = x(2^{n+1})$, then $x =$

(A) 2

(B) 4

(C) 2^n

(D) 2^{2n}

(E) 2^{n+1}

(A) [−] $2^n + 2^n + 2^n = x(2^{n+1})$

$2^2(2^n) = x(2^{n+1})$

$2^{n+2} = x(2^{n+1})$

$x = 2^{n+2} \div 2^{n+1} = 2^{(n+2)-(n+1)} = 2^1 = 2$

31. If $i^x = 1$, then x could equal

(A) 13

(B) 14

(C) 15

(D) 16

(E) 17

(D) [−] $i^1 = i$ $\quad i^5 = i$ $\quad i^9 = i$

$i^2 = -1$ $\quad i^6 = -1$ $\quad i^{10} = -1$

$i^3 = -i$ $\quad i^7 = -i$ $\quad i^{11} = -i$

$i^4 = 1$ $\quad i^8 = 1$ $\quad i^{12} = 1$

And the pattern repeats itself. Therefore, i raised to any power which is a multiple of 4 is equal to 1.

32. The formula for the area enclosed by an ellipse is A = πab, where a and b are one-half the lengths of the major and minor axes, respectively. In the figure above, the equation of the circle is $x^2 + y^2 = 12$, then what is the area enclosed by the ellipse?

(A) 62

(B) 87

(C) 103

(D) 117

(E) 131

(B) [+] The general equation for a circle is $x^2 + y^2 = r^2$, where r is the radius. So the length of the radius of the circle above, which is also the length of the minor axis of the ellipse, is 12. So the area of the ellipse is:

$A = \pi(8)(\sqrt{12}) = 87.0623$

And (B) is the best response.

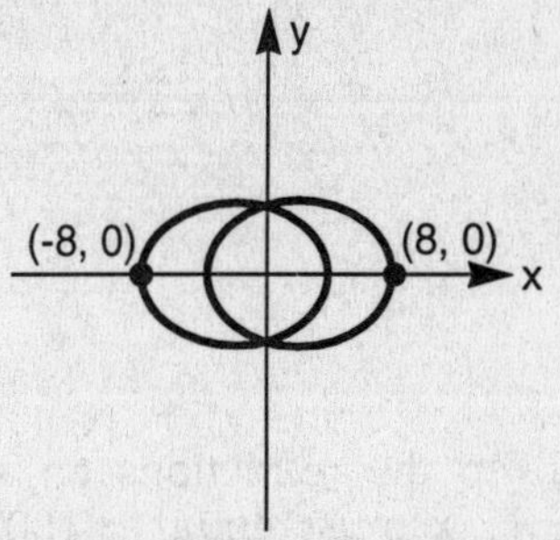

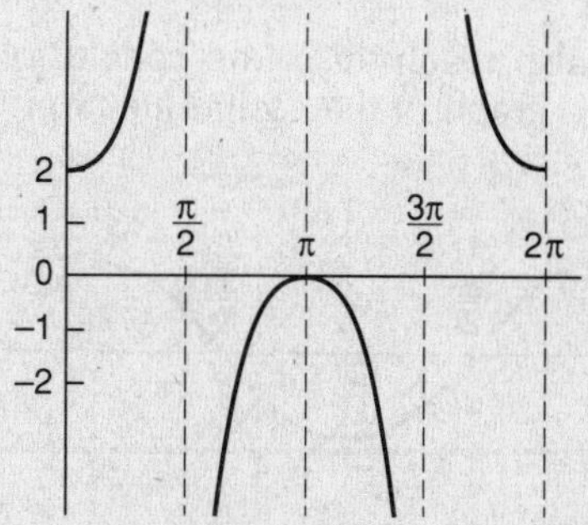

Figure 4

33. Figure 4 is a possible graph for which of the following equations?

(A) $y = 2 \sin x$

(B) $y = \sin x + 2$

(C) $y = \csc x + 1$

(D) $y = \csc x - 1$

(E) $y = \sec x + 1$

(E) [0] You should recognize the figure as the graph of the secant function displaced one unit up on the coordinate axis.

34. What is $\lim_{x \to 1} \dfrac{x^2 - 1}{x - 1}$?

(A) -1

(B) 0

(C) 1

(D) 2

(E) The limit does not exist.

(D) [0] $\dfrac{x^2 - 1}{x - 1} = \dfrac{(x + 1)(x - 1)}{x - 1} = x + 1$

As x approaches 1, $x + 1$ approaches 2. (Note: Although the expression is not defined at $x = 1$, we are not concerned with what happens at that point.)

35. If $0 \le x \le \pi$ and $\cos x = -1$, then $\cos \dfrac{x}{2} =$

(A) $-\dfrac{\sqrt{3}}{2}$

(B) $-\dfrac{1}{2}$

(C) 0

(D) $\dfrac{1}{2}$

(E) $\dfrac{\sqrt{3}}{2}$

(C) [0] Given the restrictions on x, since $\cos x = -1$, x must equal π(180°). And $\cos \pi/2 = 0$.

You can also reach this same conclusion if you visualize a graph of the cosine function:

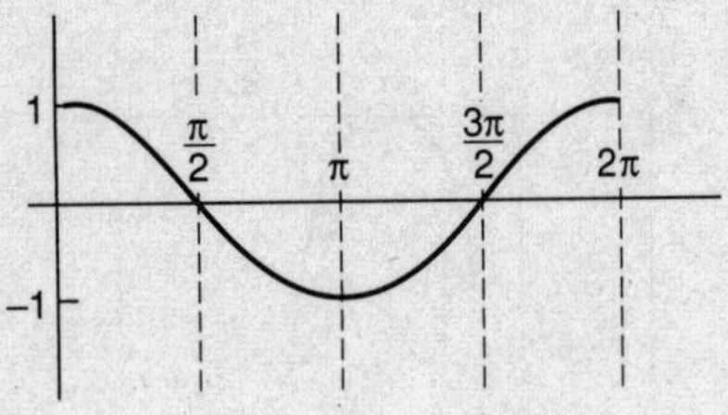

36. Which of the following defines the range of the function $f(x) = \dfrac{1 - x}{x}$?

(A) All real numbers

(B) All real numbers except -1

(C) All real numbers except 0

(D) All real numbers except 1

(E) All real numbers greater than -1

(B) [−] Sketch a graph of the function:

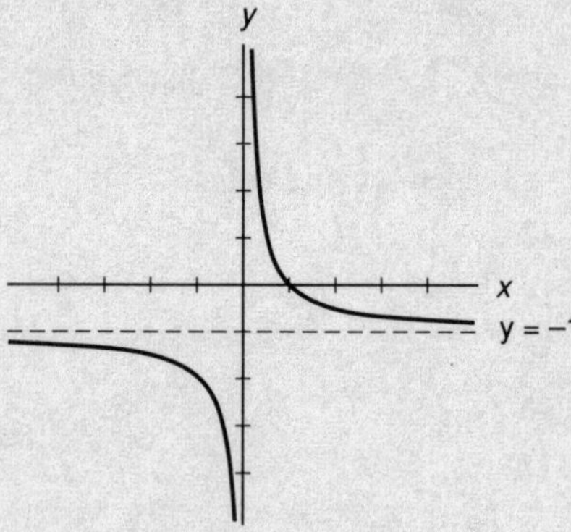

The function cannot generate the value -1 because $1/x$ cannot have the value 0.

37. Which of the following figures represents the graph of

$x = 3 \sin \theta$
$y = 2 \cos \theta$

(A)

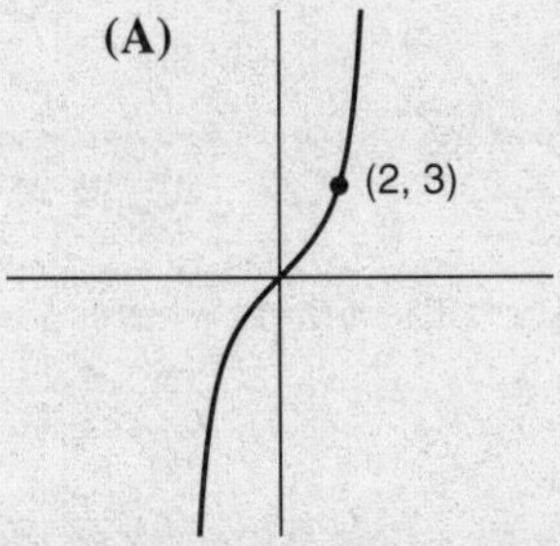

(B)

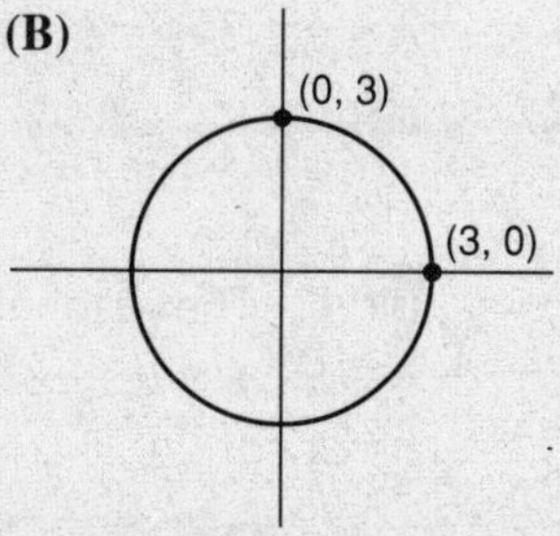

(C)

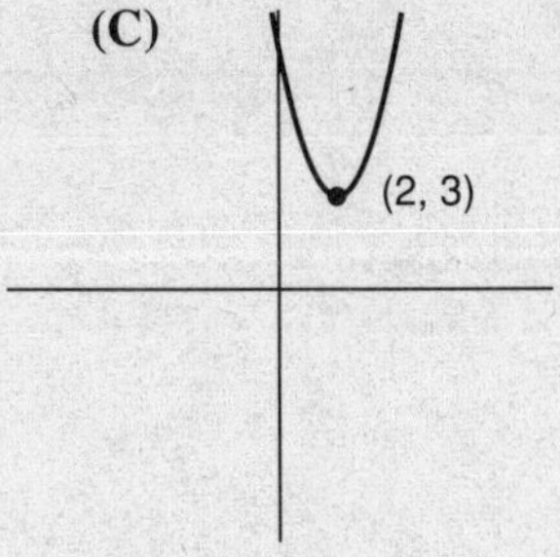

(D)

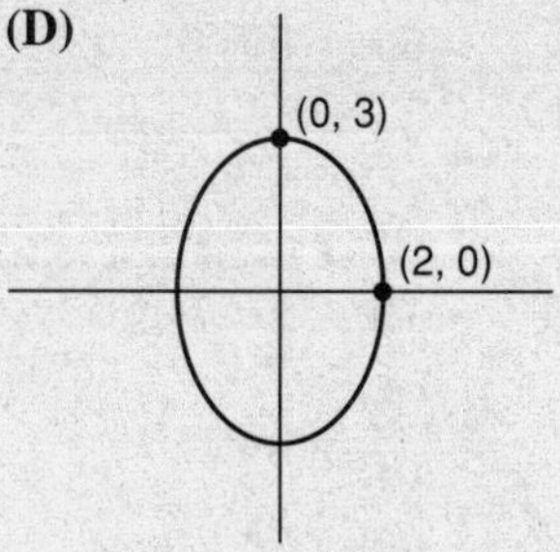

(E)

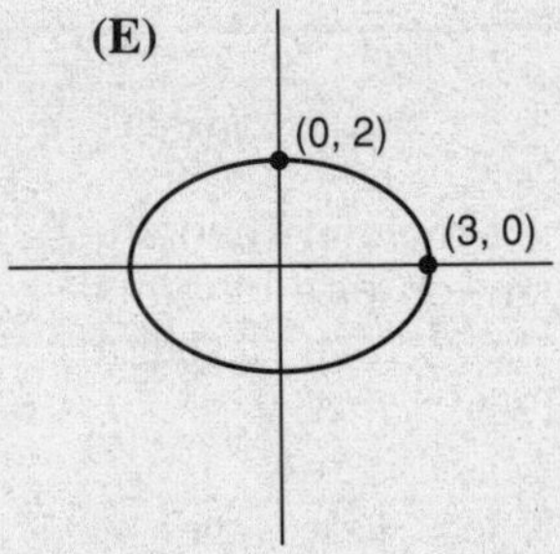

(E) [0] Since $x = 3 \sin \theta$ and $y = 2 \cos \theta$, $\sin \theta = x/3$ and $\cos \theta y/2$. Since $\sin^2\theta + \cos^2\theta = 1$:

$$\left(\frac{x}{3}\right)^2 + \left(\frac{y}{2}\right)^2 = 1$$

And the equation:

$$\frac{x^2}{9} + \frac{y^2}{4} = 1$$

is the equation of an ellipse with center (0,0) that passes through the points (3,0) and (0,2)

Alternatively, you could try some values for θ:

$\theta = 0$

$x = 3 \sin 0 = 3(0) = 0$
$y = 2 \cos 0 = 2(1) = 2$

$\theta = \pi/2$

$x = 3 \sin \pi/2 = 3(1) = 3$
$y = 2 \cos \pi/2 = 2(0) = 0$

So the graph must include the points (3,0) and (0,2). The only graph given that contains both of those points is (E).

38. If $5^x = 2$, what does $3x$ equal?

(A) 2.8
(B) 2.3
(C) 2.1
(D) 1.9
(E) 1.6

(E) [+] To find x, take the log of both sides of the equation:

$\log 5^x = \log 2$

$x \log 5 = \log 2$

$$x = \frac{\log 2}{\log 5} = \frac{0.3010}{0.6989} = 0.4307$$

and $3^{0.4307} = 1.6050$. So (E) is the best answer.

39. If $4 \cos x = \sin x$ and if x is in radian measure, what is the least positive value of x?

(A) 6.452
(B) 2.133
(C) 1.326
(D) 1.021
(E) 0.933

(C) [+] Put your calculator in the radian mode. Since $4 \cos x = \sin x$, $\sin x/\cos x = 4$. But since $\sin x/\cos x = \tan x$ (by Quotient Identity), $\tan x = 4$. The value of x is the inverse tangent of 4:

$x = \tan^{-1} 4 = 1.3258$ or 1.326.

40. Triangle ABC has coordinates $A(-1,-2)$, $B(0,4)$, and $C(3,-1)$. Which of the following provides the coordinates of triangle $A'B'C'$, respectively, the image of triangle ABC after a reflection in the line $y = -x$?

(A) $(-2,-1)$, $(4,0)$, $(-3,-1)$
(B) $(1,2)$, $(0,-4)$, $(-3,1)$
(C) $(2,1)$, $(-4,0)$, $(1,-3)$
(D) $(3,2)$, $(5,1)$, $(2,-2)$
(E) $(4,0)$, $(3,-1)$, $(-1,-2)$

(C) [0] A reflection in the line $x = -y$ maps a point P with coordinates (x,y) onto point P' with coordinates $(-y,-x)$.

$(x,y) \qquad (-y,-x)$

$A(-1,-2) \rightarrow A'(2,1)$
$B(0,4) \rightarrow B'(-4,0)$
$C(3,-1) \rightarrow C'(1,-3)$

41. If $\sin x = \cos x$, then x could terminate only in the

(A) first quadrant

(B) second quadrant

(C) first or third quadrants

(D) second or third quadrants

(E) second or fourth quadrants

(C)[0] You can answer this question either by applying the information provided in the explanation for question 28, above, or by visualizing the graph of the sine and cosine functions:

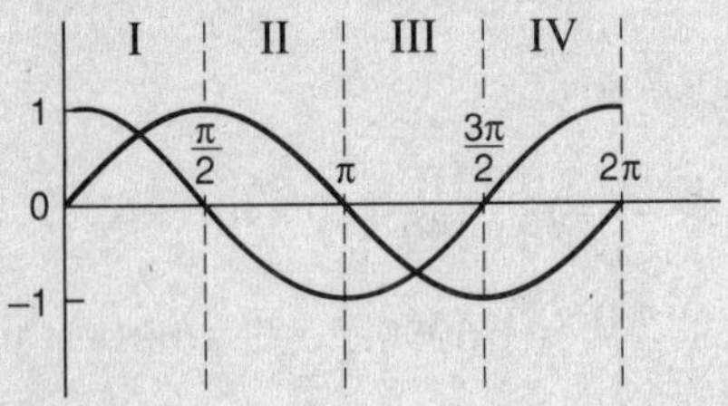

42. If the line $x = k$ is tangent to the circle $(x-2)^2 + (y+1)^2 = 4$, then the point of tangency is

(A) $(-6,-1)$ or $(2,-1)$

(B) $(-2,-1)$ or $(6,-1)$

(C) $(0,-1)$ or $(4,-1)$

(D) $(0,1)$ or $(4,1)$

(E) $(2,1)$ or $(6,1)$

(C) [−] The general form of the equation of a circle is:

$(x-h)^2 + (y-k)^2 = r^2$

where (h,k) is the center of the circle and r its radius. The circle described in the question stem has a radius of 2 and its center at $(2,-1)$:

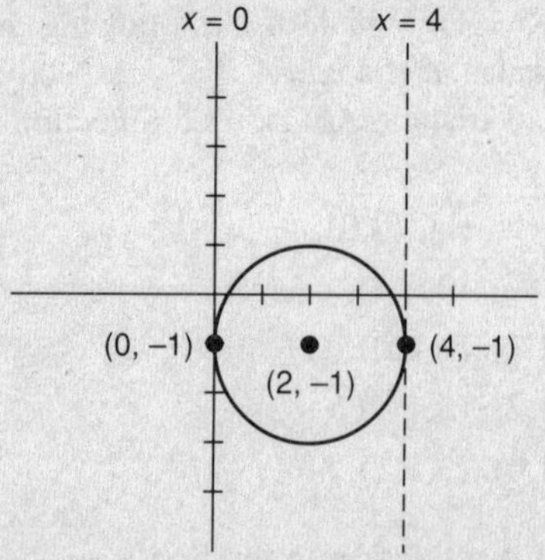

If a line of the form $x = k$ (a vertical line) is tangent to this circle, it passes through point $(0,-1)$ or $(4,-1)$.

43. The graph of $y = 2\cos 2x + 2$ intersects the y-axis where $y =$

(A) 0

(B) 2

(C) 3

(D) 4

(E) 5

(D) [0] The graph intersects the y-axis where $x = 0$:

$y = 2\cos 2(0) + 2$

$y = 2\cos 0 + 2$

Since $\cos 0 = 1$:

$y = 2(1) + 2 = 4$

44. What is the last term in the expansion $(2x + 3y)^4$?

(A) y^4

(B) $9y^4$

(C) $27y^4$

(D) $81y^4$

(E) $(xy)^4$

(D) [−] According to the Binomial Theorem, the last term in the expansion of a binomial having the form $(a+b)^n$ is b^n. So the last term of this expansion will be $(3y)^4 = 81y^4$.

45. If two unbiased dice are rolled, what is the probability that the number of dots on the two exposed faces will total 4?

(A) $\frac{1}{36}$

(B) $\frac{1}{18}$

(C) $\frac{1}{12}$

(D) $\frac{1}{9}$

(E) $\frac{1}{6}$

(C) [−] Since a die has six faces, the chance that any one of those faces will be exposed is 1 out of 6. With two dice, the chance that any two faces will both be exposed is $1/6 \times 1/6 = 1/36$. There are, however, three combinations that total 4: $1+3$, $2+2$, and $3+1$. Thus the chance that a 4 will appear is $3/36 = 1/12$.

46. Which of the following could be a graph of the equation $y = ax^2 + bx + c$, where $b^2 - 4ac = 0$?

(A)

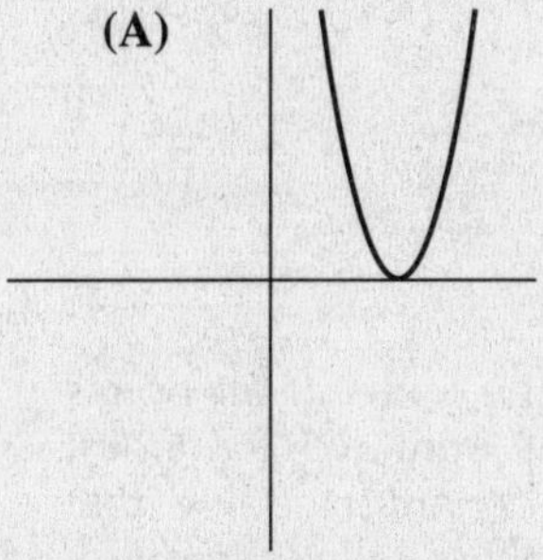

(B)

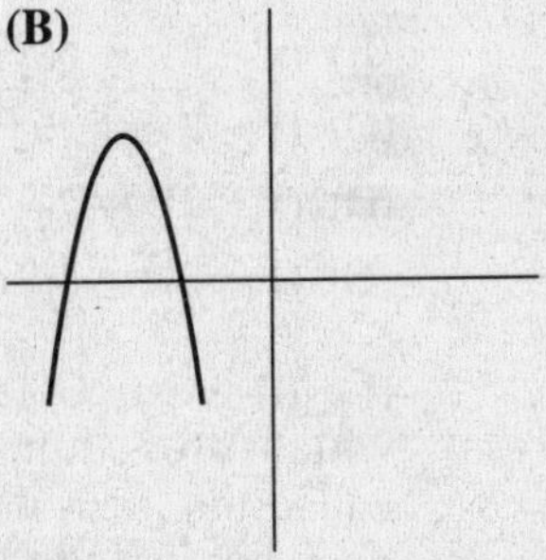

(C)

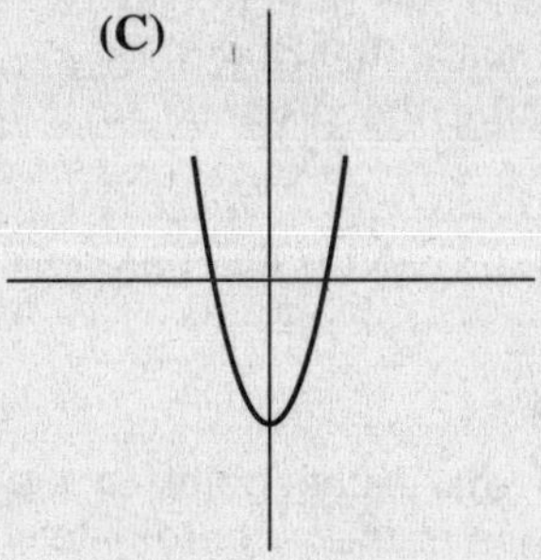

(D)

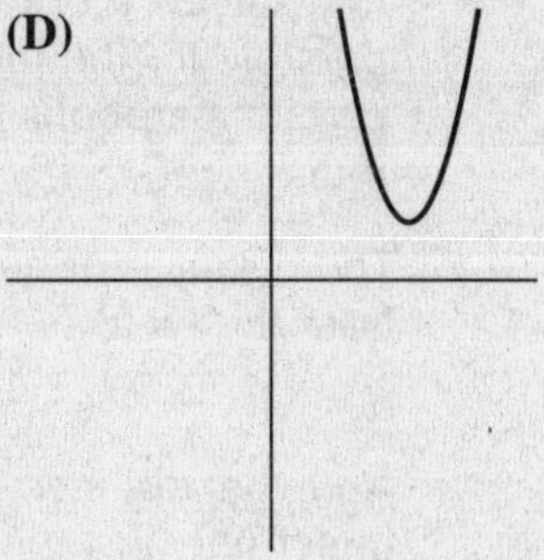

(E)

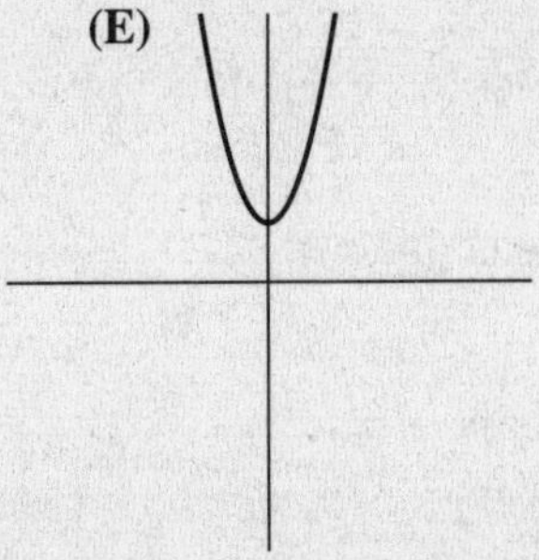

(A) [0] The Quadratic Formula:

$$x = \frac{-b \pm \sqrt{b^2 - 4ac}}{2a}$$

is used to find the roots of a quadratic equation having the form $ax^2 + bx + c$. $b^2 - 4ac$ is called the discriminant because it discriminates among three possibilities:

(1) When $b^2 - 4ac = 0$, the equation has two equal real roots.

(2) When $b^2 - 4ac > 0$, the equation has two unequal real roots.

(3) When $b^2 - 4ac < 0$, the equation has no real roots.

Therefore, for the equation given in the question stem, $ax^2 + bx + c = 0$ has only one solution. The graph given in choice (A) is the only one that has only one point on the x axis (where $y = 0$).

47. A plane cuts through a cube in such a way that the plane passes through three of the cube's vertices, no two of which lie on the same edge. If the edge of the cube has a length of 1, what is the surface area of the smaller fragment of the cube?

(A) 2.4

(B) 2.7

(C) 3.1

(D) 3.7

(E) 4.3

(B) The plane cuts the cube in this way:

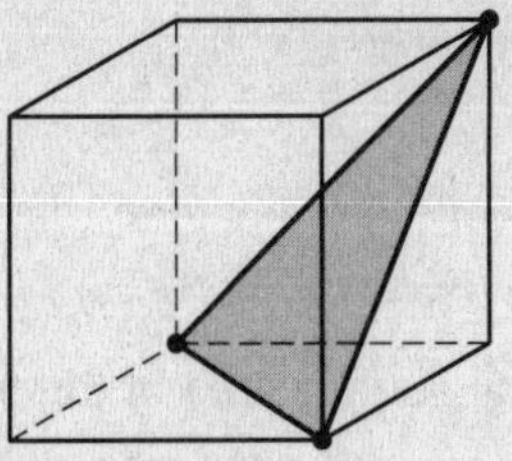

The smaller fragment has four sides: three right isosceles triangles with sides of 1, and an equilateral triangle with sides equal to the diagonal of the face of the cube. So we need only find the areas of those triangles and add in order to find the surface area of the smaller fragment.

The area of the three right isosceles triangles is:

$$\frac{1}{2}(1)(1) = \frac{1}{2}$$

(Or you might just see that their area is half that of the face of the cube, and 1/2 of 1 = 1/2.) And since there are three of them:

$$3 \times \frac{1}{2} = \frac{3}{2}$$

The sides of the equilateral triangle are diagonals of faces of the cube.

$$d^2 = (1) + (1)$$

$$d^2 = 2$$

$$d = \sqrt{2}$$

To find the area of the equilateral triangle, we need an altitude:

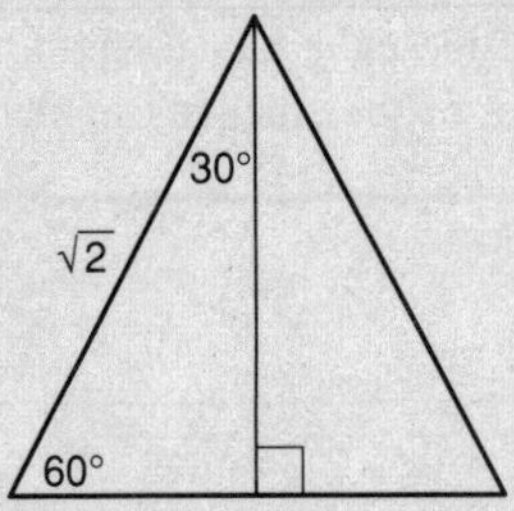

Using the properties of the 30-60-90 triangle, we determine the length of the altitude:

Side opposite 60° angle = 1/2 × hypotenuse × $\sqrt{3}$

$$\text{Alt} = 1/2 \times \sqrt{2} \times \sqrt{3} = \frac{\sqrt{6}}{2}$$

So the area of the equilateral triangle is:

$$\text{Area} = 1/2(\sqrt{6}/2)(\sqrt{2}) = \sqrt{12}/4 = \sqrt{3}/2$$

And the total surface area of the fragment is:

$$\text{Area} = 3/2 + \sqrt{3}/2 = \frac{3 + \sqrt{3}}{2}$$

$$= \frac{3 + 1.73}{2} = 2.36$$

48. Which of the following equations describes a parabola with focus (2,3) and directrix $y = 0$?

(A) $(x + 2)^2 + (y + 3)^2 = 2$

(B) $(x - 2)^2 + (y - 3)^2 = 4$

(C) $(x - 2)^2 = -(y - 3)^2$

(D) $(x - 2)^2 = 2(y + 3)$

(E) $(x - 2)^2 = 3(2y - 3)$

(E) [0] A parabola is the locus of all points which are equidistant from a fixed point called the focus and a certain fixed line (that does not include the focus) called the directrix. Given the focus and the directrix, it is possible to find the equation that describes a certain parabola by using the distance formula.

The distance of any point (x,y) on this parabola from the focus is:

$$d = \sqrt{(x - 2)^2 + (y - 3)^2}$$

And the distance from that same point to the directrix is just the change in the y-coordinate:

$$d = y - 0$$

So the equation that describes the parabola is:

$$\sqrt{(x - 2)^2 + (y - 3)^2} = y$$

Square both sides of the equation:

$$(x - 2)^2 + (y - 3)^2 = y^2$$

And:

$$(x - 2)^2 + (y^2 - 6y + 9) = y^2$$

$$(x - 2)^2 - 6y + 9 = 0$$

$$(x - 2)^2 = 6y - 9$$

$$(x - 2)^2 = 3(2y - 3)$$

49. A student taking a true-false test guesses randomly on three items. What is the probability that exactly two of the guesses will be correct?

(A) 1/16

(B) 1/8

(C) 1/4

(D) 3/8

(E) 1/2

(D) [0] The probability of exactly *x* results out of *n* events is given by the formula:

$_nC_x\ [P(A)]^x[P(B)]^{n-x}$

Where $_nC_x$ is the number of combinations of n things taken x at a time, *P*(*A*) is the probability of the occurrence of the event, and *P*(*B*) is the probability of the non-occurrence of the event. Here the probability of the student's getting a correct or an incorrect answer on any given item is 1/2 and there are 3 such items:

$$_3C_2\left[P\left(\frac{1}{2}\right)\right]^2\left[P\left(\frac{1}{2}\right)\right]^{3-2}=\frac{(3)(2)}{(2)(1)}\left(\frac{1}{4}\right)\left(\frac{1}{2}\right)=\frac{3}{8}$$

50. (1) Given any individual *x*, if *x* is a *C*, then *x* is also a *Q*.

(2) There exists at least one individual *x* such that *x* is not a *Q*.

Which of the following conclusions can be logically deduced from the two statements above?

(A) There exists at least one *x* such that *x* is not a *C*.

(B) There exists at least one *x* such that *x* is a *C*.

(C) There exists at least one *x* such that *x* is a *Q*.

(D) There are no *x*'s that are *C*'s.

(E) There are no *x*'s that are *Q*'s.

(A) [−] The first statement says that any *x* that is a *C* must also be a *Q*. The second statement states that there is an *x* that is not a *Q*. Since an *x* cannot be a *C* without also being a *Q*, this means that the *x* that is not a *Q* cannot be a *C*.

Biology Test

Lesson 9

Biology Test

The Biology Test consists of 95 multiple-choice questions. In terms of its overall level of difficulty, the test is intended for students who have had a one-year introductory course in biology of the sort that is included in a college preparatory curriculum.

The following table summarizes the topics tested and the approximate number of questions for each:

Topics Tested	Approximate Number of Questions
Behavior	4–5
Cellular and Molecular Biology	23–24
Classical Genetics	9–10
Ecology	14–15
Evolution and Systematics	14–15
Organismal Structure and Function	28–29
TOTAL	95

Although 95 questions is a lot to answer in an hour, this is not a large number of questions when compared with the amount of information that is conveyed in a full-year course in biology. For this reason, everything you learned in biology cannot be the basis for a test question. Therefore, you may encounter some questions that test areas not emphasized in your course.

The following are samples of the types of questions you will encounter on your exam:

EXAMPLE:

Ribosomes' function in a cell is controlled by the

(A) endoplasmic reticulum
(B) mitochondria
(C) golgi bodies
(D) ribosomal RNA
(E) gamete

(D) The RNA is the immediate determinant of the characteristic function of an organism.

EXAMPLE:

Which of the following are secretions of the pituitary gland?

I. Somatotropic hormone
II. Pitocin
III. Adrenalin

(A) I only
(B) II only
(C) I and II only
(D) I and III only
(E) I, II, and III

(C) Adrenalin is secreted by the adrenal cortex.

EXAMPLE:

The nutrients that supply an animal with its main source of energy are

(A) proteins
(B) carbohydrates
(C) lipids
(D) nucleic acids
(E) peptides

(B) Carbohydrates are the main source of energy for animals.

EXAMPLE:

How might echolocation enable insect-eating bats to avoid competing with birds for food?

(A) The bats can cover a greater territory than birds can.
(B) The bats can find more insects that birds can.
(C) The bats can fly faster than birds can.
(D) The bats can hunt at night while the birds are asleep.
(E) The bats roost in areas usually avoided by birds.

(D) Echolocation allows the bats to hunt insects at night, while birds are asleep. None of the other choices relate to echolocation.

EXAMPLE:

A biologist viewing a cell under a microscope could tell that the cell was from a plant rather than an animal if the cell had

(A) a cell membrane and a nucleus
(B) a cell wall and chloroplasts
(C) a contractile vacuole and mitochondria
(D) a cell membrane and cilia
(E) a nucleus and cilia

(B) Only plant cells have a cell wall and chloroplasts.

EXAMPLE:

A leaf from a green-and-white variegated colleus that was placed in the sun for several hours was treated in the following manner: 1) placed in hot alcohol until colorless, 2) placed in a clean Petri dish and flooded with Lugol's iodine, 3) washed in distilled water, 4) spread out on clean white paper. The same procedure was followed with the leaf from a green-and-white variegated plant that was stored without light for twelve hours. The following chart shows the results:

Treatment	White Area of Leaf		Green Area of Leaf	
	without light	with light	without light	with light
alcohol	white	white	white	white
Lugol's	brown	brown	brown	blue-black
water	no change	no change	no change	no change

EXAMPLE:

Which of the following statements best explains the observed results of the experiments?

(A) In green plants, light plus the green pigment chlorophyll results in the presence of starch.
(B) Plants must have chlorophyll in order to synthesize organic nutrients.
(C) Plants cannot grow without light.
(D) The green chlorophyll molecule uses light energy to split one molecule of water.
(E) In green plants, light plus starch produces water.

(A) During photosynthesis, glucose sugar is produced from carbon dioxide and water. Some of the sugar may be stored as starch, the presence of which can be tested. This experiment tests the effects of both the presence and absence of light and the presence and absence of chlorophyll. Only choice (A) relates all of these factors.

Biology Test Answer Sheet

1	Ⓐ	Ⓑ	Ⓒ	Ⓓ	Ⓔ	49	Ⓐ	Ⓑ	Ⓒ	Ⓓ	Ⓔ
2	Ⓐ	Ⓑ	Ⓒ	Ⓓ	Ⓔ	50	Ⓐ	Ⓑ	Ⓒ	Ⓓ	Ⓔ
3	Ⓐ	Ⓑ	Ⓒ	Ⓓ	Ⓔ	51	Ⓐ	Ⓑ	Ⓒ	Ⓓ	Ⓔ
4	Ⓐ	Ⓑ	Ⓒ	Ⓓ	Ⓔ	52	Ⓐ	Ⓑ	Ⓒ	Ⓓ	Ⓔ
5	Ⓐ	Ⓑ	Ⓒ	Ⓓ	Ⓔ	53	Ⓐ	Ⓑ	Ⓒ	Ⓓ	Ⓔ
6	Ⓐ	Ⓑ	Ⓒ	Ⓓ	Ⓔ	54	Ⓐ	Ⓑ	Ⓒ	Ⓓ	Ⓔ
7	Ⓐ	Ⓑ	Ⓒ	Ⓓ	Ⓔ	55	Ⓐ	Ⓑ	Ⓒ	Ⓓ	Ⓔ
8	Ⓐ	Ⓑ	Ⓒ	Ⓓ	Ⓔ	56	Ⓐ	Ⓑ	Ⓒ	Ⓓ	Ⓔ
9	Ⓐ	Ⓑ	Ⓒ	Ⓓ	Ⓔ	57	Ⓐ	Ⓑ	Ⓒ	Ⓓ	Ⓔ
10	Ⓐ	Ⓑ	Ⓒ	Ⓓ	Ⓔ	58	Ⓐ	Ⓑ	Ⓒ	Ⓓ	Ⓔ
11	Ⓐ	Ⓑ	Ⓒ	Ⓓ	Ⓔ	59	Ⓐ	Ⓑ	Ⓒ	Ⓓ	Ⓔ
12	Ⓐ	Ⓑ	Ⓒ	Ⓓ	Ⓔ	60	Ⓐ	Ⓑ	Ⓒ	Ⓓ	Ⓔ
13	Ⓐ	Ⓑ	Ⓒ	Ⓓ	Ⓔ	61	Ⓐ	Ⓑ	Ⓒ	Ⓓ	Ⓔ
14	Ⓐ	Ⓑ	Ⓒ	Ⓓ	Ⓔ	62	Ⓐ	Ⓑ	Ⓒ	Ⓓ	Ⓔ
15	Ⓐ	Ⓑ	Ⓒ	Ⓓ	Ⓔ	63	Ⓐ	Ⓑ	Ⓒ	Ⓓ	Ⓔ
16	Ⓐ	Ⓑ	Ⓒ	Ⓓ	Ⓔ	64	Ⓐ	Ⓑ	Ⓒ	Ⓓ	Ⓔ
17	Ⓐ	Ⓑ	Ⓒ	Ⓓ	Ⓔ	65	Ⓐ	Ⓑ	Ⓒ	Ⓓ	Ⓔ
18	Ⓐ	Ⓑ	Ⓒ	Ⓓ	Ⓔ	66	Ⓐ	Ⓑ	Ⓒ	Ⓓ	Ⓔ
19	Ⓐ	Ⓑ	Ⓒ	Ⓓ	Ⓔ	67	Ⓐ	Ⓑ	Ⓒ	Ⓓ	Ⓔ
20	Ⓐ	Ⓑ	Ⓒ	Ⓓ	Ⓔ	68	Ⓐ	Ⓑ	Ⓒ	Ⓓ	Ⓔ
21	Ⓐ	Ⓑ	Ⓒ	Ⓓ	Ⓔ	69	Ⓐ	Ⓑ	Ⓒ	Ⓓ	Ⓔ
22	Ⓐ	Ⓑ	Ⓒ	Ⓓ	Ⓔ	70	Ⓐ	Ⓑ	Ⓒ	Ⓓ	Ⓔ
23	Ⓐ	Ⓑ	Ⓒ	Ⓓ	Ⓔ	71	Ⓐ	Ⓑ	Ⓒ	Ⓓ	Ⓔ
24	Ⓐ	Ⓑ	Ⓒ	Ⓓ	Ⓔ	72	Ⓐ	Ⓑ	Ⓒ	Ⓓ	Ⓔ
25	Ⓐ	Ⓑ	Ⓒ	Ⓓ	Ⓔ	73	Ⓐ	Ⓑ	Ⓒ	Ⓓ	Ⓔ
26	Ⓐ	Ⓑ	Ⓒ	Ⓓ	Ⓔ	74	Ⓐ	Ⓑ	Ⓒ	Ⓓ	Ⓔ
27	Ⓐ	Ⓑ	Ⓒ	Ⓓ	Ⓔ	75	Ⓐ	Ⓑ	Ⓒ	Ⓓ	Ⓔ
28	Ⓐ	Ⓑ	Ⓒ	Ⓓ	Ⓔ	76	Ⓐ	Ⓑ	Ⓒ	Ⓓ	Ⓔ
29	Ⓐ	Ⓑ	Ⓒ	Ⓓ	Ⓔ	77	Ⓐ	Ⓑ	Ⓒ	Ⓓ	Ⓔ
30	Ⓐ	Ⓑ	Ⓒ	Ⓓ	Ⓔ	78	Ⓐ	Ⓑ	Ⓒ	Ⓓ	Ⓔ
31	Ⓐ	Ⓑ	Ⓒ	Ⓓ	Ⓔ	79	Ⓐ	Ⓑ	Ⓒ	Ⓓ	Ⓔ
32	Ⓐ	Ⓑ	Ⓒ	Ⓓ	Ⓔ	80	Ⓐ	Ⓑ	Ⓒ	Ⓓ	Ⓔ
33	Ⓐ	Ⓑ	Ⓒ	Ⓓ	Ⓔ	81	Ⓐ	Ⓑ	Ⓒ	Ⓓ	Ⓔ
34	Ⓐ	Ⓑ	Ⓒ	Ⓓ	Ⓔ	82	Ⓐ	Ⓑ	Ⓒ	Ⓓ	Ⓔ
35	Ⓐ	Ⓑ	Ⓒ	Ⓓ	Ⓔ	83	Ⓐ	Ⓑ	Ⓒ	Ⓓ	Ⓔ
36	Ⓐ	Ⓑ	Ⓒ	Ⓓ	Ⓔ	84	Ⓐ	Ⓑ	Ⓒ	Ⓓ	Ⓔ
37	Ⓐ	Ⓑ	Ⓒ	Ⓓ	Ⓔ	85	Ⓐ	Ⓑ	Ⓒ	Ⓓ	Ⓔ
38	Ⓐ	Ⓑ	Ⓒ	Ⓓ	Ⓔ	86	Ⓐ	Ⓑ	Ⓒ	Ⓓ	Ⓔ
39	Ⓐ	Ⓑ	Ⓒ	Ⓓ	Ⓔ	87	Ⓐ	Ⓑ	Ⓒ	Ⓓ	Ⓔ
40	Ⓐ	Ⓑ	Ⓒ	Ⓓ	Ⓔ	88	Ⓐ	Ⓑ	Ⓒ	Ⓓ	Ⓔ
41	Ⓐ	Ⓑ	Ⓒ	Ⓓ	Ⓔ	89	Ⓐ	Ⓑ	Ⓒ	Ⓓ	Ⓔ
42	Ⓐ	Ⓑ	Ⓒ	Ⓓ	Ⓔ	90	Ⓐ	Ⓑ	Ⓒ	Ⓓ	Ⓔ
43	Ⓐ	Ⓑ	Ⓒ	Ⓓ	Ⓔ	91	Ⓐ	Ⓑ	Ⓒ	Ⓓ	Ⓔ
44	Ⓐ	Ⓑ	Ⓒ	Ⓓ	Ⓔ	92	Ⓐ	Ⓑ	Ⓒ	Ⓓ	Ⓔ
45	Ⓐ	Ⓑ	Ⓒ	Ⓓ	Ⓔ	93	Ⓐ	Ⓑ	Ⓒ	Ⓓ	Ⓔ
46	Ⓐ	Ⓑ	Ⓒ	Ⓓ	Ⓔ	94	Ⓐ	Ⓑ	Ⓒ	Ⓓ	Ⓔ
47	Ⓐ	Ⓑ	Ⓒ	Ⓓ	Ⓔ	95	Ⓐ	Ⓑ	Ⓒ	Ⓓ	Ⓔ
48	Ⓐ	Ⓑ	Ⓒ	Ⓓ	Ⓔ						

BIOLOGY TEST

Part A

Directions: Each of the following questions or incomplete statements is followed by five possible answers or completions. Select the one choice that is best in each case and then darken the corresponding circle on the answer sheet.

1. In the normal human circulatory system, the mean blood pressure is lowest in the
   (A) aorta
   (B) arteries
   (C) arterioles
   (D) capillaries
   (E) inferior vena cava

2. Structural components common to plant cell walls but not part of bacterial cell walls include which of the following?
   I. Peptidoglycan
   II. Cellulose
   III. Lignin
   (A) I only
   (B) II only
   (C) I and III only
   (D) II and III only
   (E) I, II, and III

3. In the bird egg, which of the following functions as a reservoir for wastes produced during development?
   (A) Allantois
   (B) Amnion
   (C) Chorion
   (D) Yolk sac
   (E) Placenta

4. Food chains end with
   (A) producers
   (B) autotrophs
   (C) decomposers
   (D) primary consumers
   (E) tertiary consumers

5. What would be the sequence of bases for the two anticodons that correspond to the codon base sequence of 5′—UGC—GGA—3′?
   (A) 5′—TCC—GCA—3′
   (B) TCG—CCT
   (C) 5′—UCC—GCA—3′
   (D) TGG—CCU
   (E) ACC—GGU

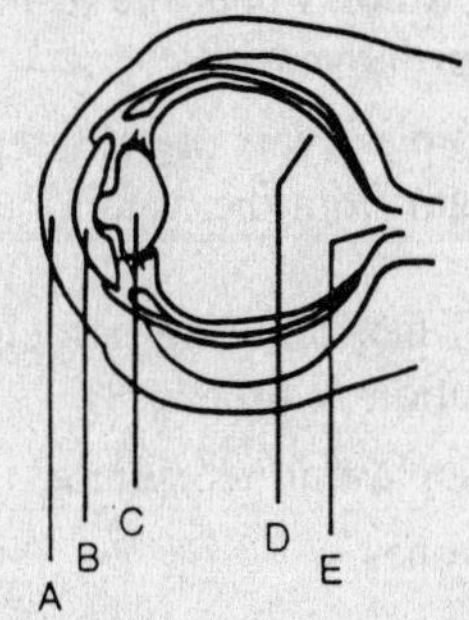

6. In the diagram above, which part of the eye causes the blind spot?
   (A) A
   (B) B
   (C) C
   (D) D
   (E) E

7. Which of the following occurs during anaphase I of meiosis?
   (A) Formation of tetrads
   (B) Separation of homologous chromosomes
   (C) Crossing over
   (D) Separation of sister chromatids, with one chromatid pulled toward each pole
   (E) Assembly of chromosomes along the equatorial plane

GO ON TO THE NEXT PAGE

8. The wings of sparrows and flies are said to represent
(A) homologous structures
(B) analogous structures
(C) vestigial structures
(D) mutualism
(E) mimicry

9. Oxygen transport from the water to the bloodstream in the gills of fish occurs by diffusion. However, the efficiency of oxygen extraction by the blood is higher than would be predicted. This is because
(A) water flow and blood flow are parallel
(B) diffusion of oxygen is much greater in water than in air
(C) oxygen has a very high solubility in water
(D) blood flows opposite to the direction of water movement
(E) multiple layers of cells separate the bloodstream from the water

10. Which of the following participates in the glycosylation of proteins?
I. Endoplasmic reticulum
II. Histones
III. Golgi apparatus
(A) I only
(B) II only
(C) I and III only
(D) II and III only
(E) I, II, and III

11. Each of the following statements about cellular bioenergetics is true EXCEPT
(A) fermentation may yield lactic acid
(B) fermentation may yield ethyl alcohol
(C) glycolysis occurs within the mitochondria
(D) oxidative phosphorylation (electron transport chain) occurs within the mitochondria
(E) the Krebs cycle occurs within the mitochondria

12. Each of the following is a characteristic of imprinting EXCEPT
(A) it is a conditioned response
(B) it is a learned behavior
(C) it typically occurs very early in an animal's life
(D) it occurs only during the critical, or sensitive, phase
(E) once imprinting occurs, the young animal cannot be imprinted on another animal or object

13. Stimulation of the parasympathetic nervous system causes each of the following EXCEPT
(A) release of bile
(B) acceleration of the heart rate
(C) constriction of bronchi
(D) pupillary constriction
(E) increased peristalsis in the gastrointestinal tract

14. The euglena possesses an organelle that synthesizes a polysaccharide for storage. This organelle is the
(A) stigma
(B) pyrenoid
(C) eyespot
(D) cytopharynx
(E) oral groove

15. The structure of a flowering plant that produces pollen is which of the following?
(A) Stigma
(B) Style
(C) Filament
(D) Anther
(E) Sepal

16. Severe vitamin K deficiency may cause
(A) scurvy
(B) pernicious anemia
(C) pellagra
(D) bleeding
(E) rickets

GO ON TO THE NEXT PAGE

17. Which of the following best describes the sapwood of a woody dicot?

(A) Cork cambium
(B) Peripheral, more recent rings of xylem
(C) Central area of pith
(D) Area filled with pigments, gums, and resins
(E) Inner, older rings of xylem

18. Impulses carried from the central nervous system to the effector organs are conducted via the

(A) Schwann cells
(B) dendrites
(C) axon
(D) cerebrospinal fluid
(E) myelin sheath

19. The biome dominated by conifers, such as spruces and firs, is the

(A) chaparral
(B) deciduous forest
(C) tropical rain forest
(D) tundra
(E) taiga

20. Inheritance of color in a certain plant is known to follow simple Mendelian rules. Green leaf color is dominant and yellow leaf color is recessive to green. If a homozygous green-leafed plant is mated with a homozygous yellow-leafed plant, what proportion of offspring (F_1 generation) would be expected to possess yellow leaves?

(A) 0%
(B) 25%
(C) 50%
(D) 75%
(E) 100%

21. Archaeopteryx is important to the study of evolution because

(A) it is believed to represent the evolutionary link between the kingdom Plantae and the kingdom Fungi
(B) it is believed to represent the evolutionary link between the class Reptilia and the class Aves
(C) it is believed to represent the evolutionary link between the sponges and the molluscs
(D) it represents the last known evidence of the dinosaurs
(E) it represents the first known terrestrial animal

22. Enzymes accomplish each of the following EXCEPT

(A) increase the rate of the forward reaction
(B) increase the rate of the reverse reaction
(C) decrease the activation energy of the reaction
(D) increase the activation energy of the reaction
(E) allow reactions to occur more readily

23. High energy molecules involved in the dark reactions of photosynthesis include which of the following?

I. ATP
II. NADH
III. NADPH

(A) I only
(B) II only
(C) I and III only
(D) II and III only
(E) I, II, and III

24. The "all-or-none response" refers to which of the following?

(A) Flocking defense scheme utilized by various birds
(B) Nondisjunction
(C) Fitness of an animal
(D) Expressivity of a phenotype
(E) Transmission of neural impulses

GO ON TO THE NEXT PAGE

25. Bile, a complex fluid that assists in the digestion of fatty substances, is produced by the

(A) gallbladder
(B) small intestine
(C) pancreas
(D) stomach
(E) liver

26. A dominant gene that shows X-linked inheritance is being studied by a biologist. If an affected male is mated with an unaffected female, which of the following most likely represents an accurate description of their immediate offspring?

(A) 100% affected males, 0% affected females
(B) 0% affected males, 100% affected females
(C) 50% affected males, 25% affected females, 100% carrier females
(D) 50% affected males, 50% affected females, 100% carrier females
(E) 25% affected males, 25% affected females, 25% carrier females

27. The diagram below depicts the cell cycle for an asynchronously growing cell population (cells at each stage are present at any given time). If the cell population is briefly exposed to $_3$H-thymidine, cells at which phase would immediately demonstrate incorporation of the radiolabeled thymidine?

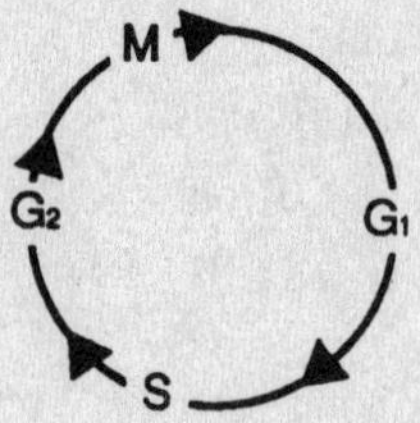

(A) M
(B) G_1
(C) S
(D) G_2
(E) S and M

28. Energy dependent processes for cellular transport include each of the following EXCEPT

(A) cytoplasmic streaming in algae
(B) $Na^+ - K^+$ ATPase
(C) osmosis
(D) axonal transport
(E) active transport

29. Which of the following is not a direct function of the vertebrate liver?

(A) Synthesis of plasma proteins
(B) Carbohydrate metabolism
(C) Deamination
(D) Reabsorption of water
(E) Detoxification

30. Which of the following pairs of organisms are the least related?

(A) Squid - Octopus
(B) Crayfish - Shrimp
(C) Shark - Ray
(D) Sea lily - Iris
(E) Lemur - Monkey

31. Which of the following would be expected to have the most stable ecosystem?

(A) Ocean floor beneath Antartic polar ice
(B) Pacific shore along California
(C) Subtropical forests of Africa
(D) Coniferous forest of North America
(E) Grasslands of Southwestern United States

32. Sperm stored in the epididymis flow into what immediate structure during copulation?

(A) Ureter
(B) Urethra
(C) Seminal vesicle
(D) Vas deferens
(E) Prostate

GO ON TO THE NEXT PAGE

33. Carolus Linnaeus classified organisms according to their

(A) evolutionary trends

(B) morphologic similarities

(C) ability to mate

(D) ability to produce viable offspring

(E) ecological interrelationships

34. Which of the following represents the most likely succession of man?

(A) Homo erectus → Australopithecus → Homo habilis → Homo sapiens

(B) Australopithecus → Homo erectus → Homo habilis → Homo sapiens

(C) Homo sapiens → Australopithecus → Homo erectus → Homo habilis

(D) Australopithecus → Homo habilis → Homo erectus → Homo sapiens

(E) Homo habilis → Homo erectus → Australopithecus → Homo sapiens

35. Hemoglobin is a protein that functions in the transport of oxygen contained within red blood cells. Hemoglobin has been shown to consist of four independent polypeptide chains. The manner in which these four chains interact to form functional molecules is a characteristic of hemoglobin's

(A) secondary structure

(B) tertiary structure

(C) quaternary structure

(D) denaturation

(E) melting point

36. In humans, which of the following allow efficient absorption of digested foodstuffs to occur?

I. Microvilli

II. Large surface area

III. Presence of certain viruses

(A) I only

(B) II only

(C) I and II only

(D) I and III only

(E) I, II, and III

37. Each of the following methods of reproduction occurs without genetic recombination EXCEPT

(A) binary fission

(B) conjugation

(C) budding

(D) production of gemmae

(E) cloning

38. The ruminants—animals such as deer and cows—are able to digest cellulose. Each of the following contributes to the special digestive abilities of the ruminant EXCEPT

(A) multichambered gastrointestinal tract

(B) bacteria within digestive tract

(C) protozoa within digestive tract

(D) ability to convert β-glucose to α-glucose

(E) mutualism

39. A cell is removed from its normal environment and placed into another medium. It is then noted that the cell appears to shrink. Which term best describes the *medium* relative to the cell?

(A) Hypertonic

(B) Hypotonic

(C) Isotonic

(D) Osmotic

(E) Pinocytosis

40. Organic molecules, such as vitamin C and vitamin B_{12}, are required for specific enzymes to function. Such organic molecules are called

(A) substrates

(B) coenzymes

(C) allosteric modulators

(D) active sites

(E) competitive inhibitors

41. The corpus luteum secretes a hormone that prepares the uterus for implantation. This hormone is most likely

(A) a luteinizing hormone

(B) a follicle-stimulating hormone

(C) estrogen

(D) progesterone

(E) chorionic gonadotropin

GO ON TO THE NEXT PAGE

42. The graph below depicts the population trend in a predator-prey system. Assuming this is a stable system (free from outside influences), which of the following statements is most likely true?

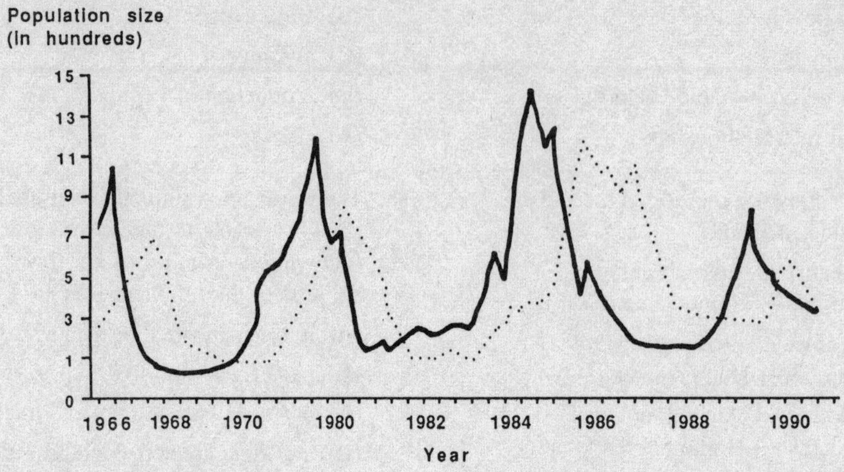

(A) The solid line most likely represents the predator population trend.

(B) The populations of predator and prey reach peak levels concomitantly.

(C) Four years after the population of predator begins to decrease, there is a dramatic decrease in the population of prey.

(D) One year after the population of prey increases, there is a parallel rise in the population of predator.

(E) No correlation between predator and prey populations is observed.

43. According to the Hardy-Weinberg law, genetic equilibrium within a gene pool is contingent upon several factors. Which of the following is one of the requirements?

(A) Population size must be small.

(B) Genetic drift occurs.

(C) There is an absence of gene flow.

(D) Mutations are frequent and not balanced.

(E) There is an absence of random reproduction.

44. Several general characteristics of the angiosperms allow for the separation of this class of plants into two subclasses. Properties that differentiate these subclasses include each of the following EXCEPT

(A) the number of seed leaves

(B) arrangement of vascular tissue in the stem

(C) petal arrangement

(D) color scheme of petals

(E) vein structure of leaves

45. Which of the following hormones is NOT correctly matched with a known function of that hormone?

(A) Insulin - Glucose metabolism

(B) Calcitonin - Calcium metabolism

(C) Parathyroid hormone - Calcium metabolism

(D) Aldosterone - Electrolyte balance

(E) Erythropoietin - White blood cell regulation

GO ON TO THE NEXT PAGE

46. The diagram below illustrates the growth curve of a certain bacteria in a controlled environment. Which time period represents the maximal growth acceleration of the bacterial population?

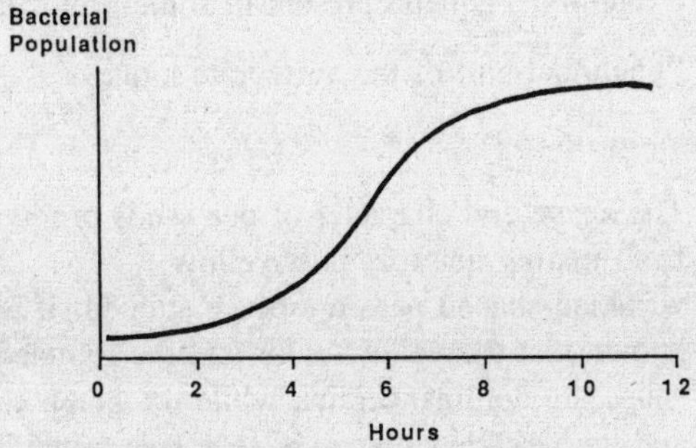

(A) Between hours 2 and 4
(B) Between hours 4 and 6
(C) Between hours 6 and 8
(D) Between hours 8 and 10
(E) Between hours 10 and 12

47. In the early stages of certain diseases, pooled immunoglobulin may be administered. Often, the disease process will be significantly less severe as a result of this treatment. The pooled immunoglobulin contains antibodies that are specific for the infectious agent. This treatment is an example of

(A) active immunity
(B) passive immunity
(C) colostrum
(D) vaccination
(E) autoimmunity

48. Which of the following is derived from the ectodermal germ layer?

(A) Mammary glands
(B) Thyroid gland
(C) Liver
(D) Eustachian tube
(E) Adrenal cortex

49. The first dinosaurs probably inhabited the earth during which era?

(A) Cenozoic
(B) Paleozoic
(C) Mesozoic
(D) Precambrian
(E) Silurian

50. The main reservoir of carbon for the carbon cycle is which of the following?

(A) Hydrocarbons contained in coal and oil
(B) Calcium carbonate contained in limestone
(C) Carbon contained in diamonds
(D) Carbon dioxide contained in air and dissolved in water
(E) Carbon contained in living organisms

51. Each of the following is a characteristic of mammals EXCEPT

(A) four-chambered heart
(B) homothermy
(C) only one bone in the middle ear
(D) ventral orientation of the limbs
(E) only one bone comprising the lower jaw

52. Which of the following is NOT a characteristic of procaryotes?

(A) Few, if any, organelles
(B) Synthesis of protein and RNA occurs within the same compartment
(C) Contain DNA within the cytoplasm
(D) Transcription and translation are closely coupled events
(E) Occurrence of introns within the primary RNA transcript

GO ON TO THE NEXT PAGE

Part B

Directions: Each set of lettered answer choices below refers to the numbered statements following it. Select the one lettered answer choice that best fits each statement and then darken the corresponding circle on the answer sheet. An answer choice may be used once, more than once, or not at all in a given set.

Questions 53–57

(A) Stomata
(B) Guard cells
(C) Mesophyll
(D) Companion cells
(E) Petiole

53. Regulate the exchange of gases between the leaf and the environment

54. Stalk of a leaf

55. Region between the upper and lower epidermis of a leaf

56. Openings in the epidermis that allow transpiration to occur

57. Adjacent to sieve tube

Questions 58–61

(A) Ribosome
(B) Mitochondrion
(C) Centriole
(D) Nucleolus
(E) Peroxisome

58. Membrane-bound vesicle that contains the enzyme catalase

59. Possesses its own genetic material and self-replicates

60. Interacts with the endoplasmic reticulum during protein synthesis

61. Composed of microtubules and functions in cytoskeletal organization

Questions 62–65

(A) Contractile vacuole
(B) Flame-cell
(C) Nephridial system
(D) Malpighian tubules
(E) Nephron

62. Excretory system of insects

63. Excretory system of the earthworm

64. Excretory organelle present in some protozoans

65. Functional unit of the vertebrate kidney

Questions 66–69

The shape and character of pea seeds produced from mating heterozygous yellow, wrinkled-shaped peas are being studied. It is known that the yellow color and the rounded shape are dominant traits, while the green color and the wrinkled shape are recessive traits. The parent seeds are dihybrids. Furthermore, it has been determined that the genes for these traits are inherited independently. The lettered answer choices below represent the expected proportions of the various first-generation offspring from this mating experiment (dihybrid cross).

(A) 1/16
(B) 3/16
(C) 4/16
(D) 9/16
(E) 12/16

66. Yellow, rounded

67. Green, wrinkled

68. Green, rounded

69. Wrinkled

Questions 70–72

(A) Cerebellum
(B) Olfactory bulb
(C) Medulla
(D) Hypothalamus
(E) Thalamus

70. Involved in processing odors

71. Integrates sensory information from somatic receptors

72. Contains centers responsible for control of blood pressure and respiration

GO ON TO THE NEXT PAGE

Part C

Directions: The following questions refer to the diagram containing specific parts labeled with numbers. Each question is followed by five suggested labels as possible answers. For each question, select the one best answer and then darken the corresponding circle on the answer sheet.

Questions 73–77

Female Reproductive System

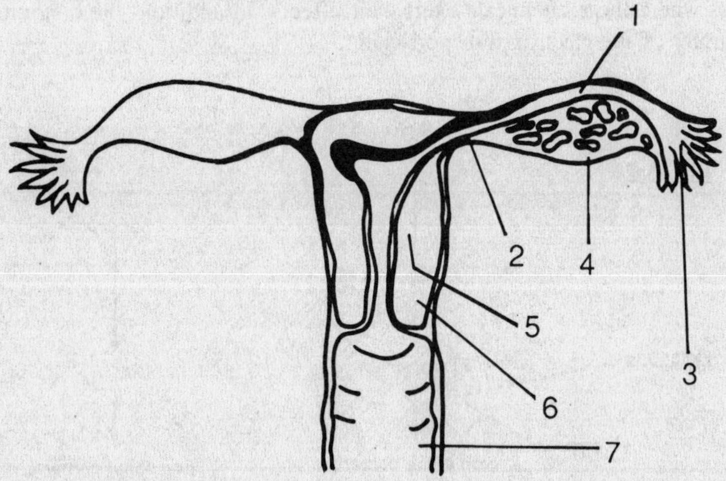

73. Fertilization normally occurs in

(A) 1
(B) 2
(C) 3
(D) 6
(E) 7

74. Implantation normally occurs in

(A) 1
(B) 4
(C) 5
(D) 6
(E) 7

75. Gametes are produced in

(A) 1
(B) 2
(C) 3
(D) 4
(E) 5

76. Synthesis of sex hormones occurs in

(A) 3
(B) 4
(C) 5
(D) 6
(E) 7

77. The diaphragm, a birth control device, covers

(A) 1
(B) 2
(C) 5
(D) 6
(E) 7

GO ON TO THE NEXT PAGE

Part D

Directions: Each group of questions below concerns a laboratory or experimental situation. In each case, study the description of the situation. Then, for each question following it select the one best answer and darken the corresponding circle on the answer sheet.

Questions 78–80 pertain to the electron transport chain. The reaction sequence below illustrates some of the components of the electron transport chain and the sites where ATP is generated. Also shown are various inhibitors and the steps where these chemicals exert their effects. In addition, the diagram depicts the sites of entry for several substrates of the electron transport chain.

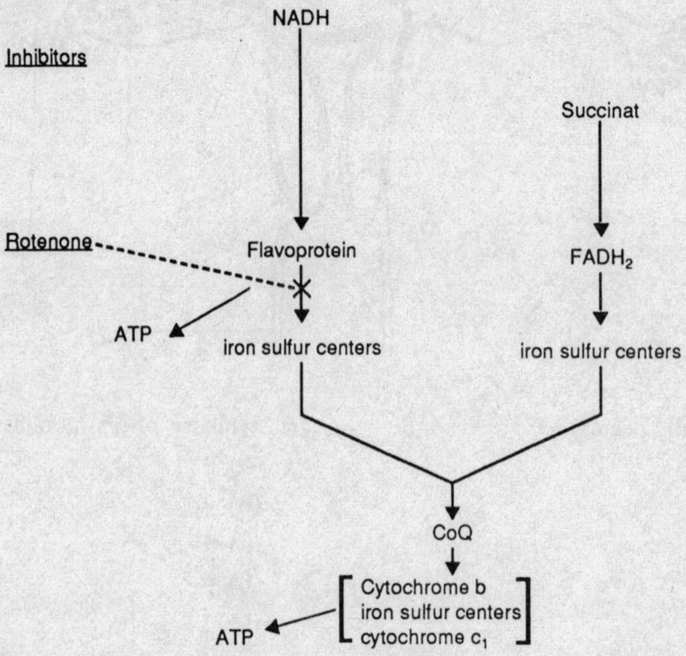

78. According to the diagram, how many ATP would succinate be expected to yield under normal circumstances?

(A) 0
(B) 1
(C) 2
(D) 3
(E) 4

79. If the inhibitor rotenone is present, how many ATP would succinate be expected to yield?

(A) 0
(B) 1
(C) 2
(D) 3
(E) 4

80. Antimycin A blocks the transfer of electrons at the site shown in the diagram. Which of the following occurs if Antimycin A is present?

(A) Electron transfer proceeds normally.
(B) Electron carriers before the inhibition site become more oxidized.
(C) Oxidation of succinate occurs completely.
(D) Electron carriers after the inhibition site become more oxidized.
(E) Succinate would yield only 1 ATP while ascorbate would yield 2 ATP.

GO ON TO THE NEXT PAGE

Questions 81–84 refer to the action potential of a nerve fiber. The diagram below demonstrates the effect of several stimuli on the membrane potential of a neuron. Each triangle indicates the time at which a stimulus is applied to the nerve.

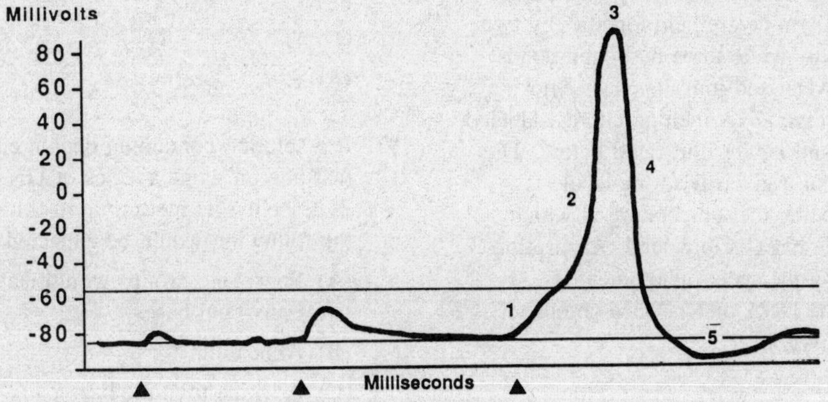

81. The interrupted line at −90 millivolts most likely represents the

(A) resting membrane potential
(B) threshold potential
(C) inhibitory potential
(D) refractory period
(E) hyperpolarization potential

82. The threshold potential for this nerve is most likely

(A) +80 millivolts
(B) +20 millivolts
(C) −56 millivolts
(D) −70 millivolts
(E) −90 millivolts

83. Rapid depolarization of the membrane, as occurs in the area labeled 2, is due to which of the following?

(A) Influx of K^+ ions
(B) Efflux of Ca^{2+} ions
(C) Influx of SO_4^{2-}
(D) Efflux of ATP
(E) Influx of Na^+ ions

84. Which of the following most likely explains repolarization?

(A) $Na^+ - K^+ -$ ATPase ceases to function
(B) Rapid influx of Na^+ ions
(C) Rapid efflux of K^+ ions
(D) Rapid influx of Cl^- ions
(E) Rapid efflux of Cl^- ions

GO ON TO THE NEXT PAGE

Questions 85–87

Experiments have demonstrated that DNA is a very well organized, cooperative structure. The two strands of the DNA double helix are joined by hydrogen bonds between the paired bases. Adenine and thymine are held together by two hydrogen bonds, while three hydrogen bonds will form between and join the bases cytosine and guanine. Five DNA melting curves, labeled A, B, C, D, and E, are illustrated below. The melting point of a given DNA molecule is described as being the temperature at which half the double helix is unwound. Absorption, as measured by the spectrophotometer, increases as the DNA melts. Once completely melted, the curve levels.

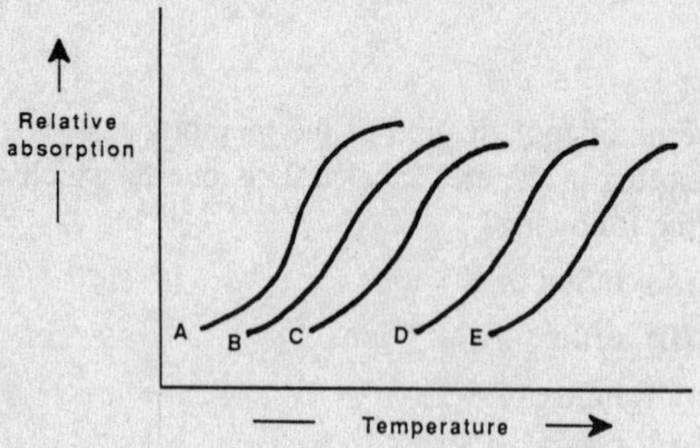

85. Which species of DNA melts at the lowest temperature?

(A) A

(B) B

(C) C

(D) D

(E) E

86. Which species of DNA possesses the greatest content of adenine-thymine base pairs?

(A) A

(B) B

(C) C

(D) D

(E) E

87. If a solution containing denatured DNA (assume only one species of DNA) is cooled to 25°C below its melting temperature, which of the following would be expected to occur?

(A) Phosphate groups would leave the individual bases.

(B) Annealing.

(C) Adenine-thymine base pairs would again form three intermolecular hydrogen bonds.

(D) The individual strands composing the double helices will remain isolated and irreversibly altered.

(E) Adenine will reliably base pair with guanine and with thymine.

GO ON TO THE NEXT PAGE

Questions 88–90 concern the physiology of muscle contraction. The diagram below represents a tracing from a kymograph. The contraction pattern of a frog's leg muscle is being studied. Under appropriate experimental conditions, the muscle is repeatedly stimulated. Note the frequency of stimulation varies throughout the first portion of the tracing.

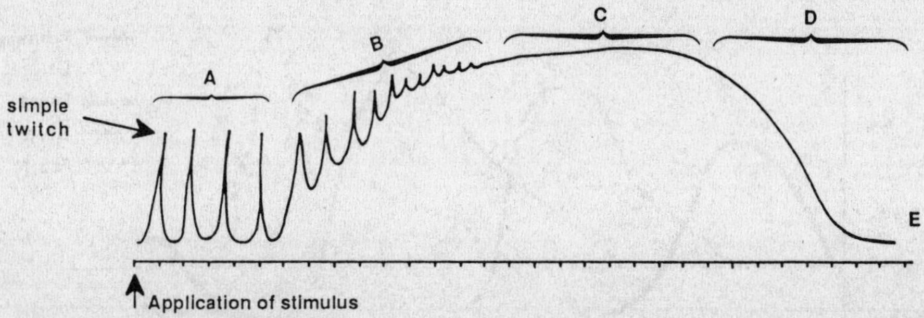

88. The portion of the kymograph labeled D probably represents which of the following?

(A) Simple twitch
(B) Tetanus
(C) Latent period
(D) Relaxation period
(E) Fatigue

89. In part A of the kymograph, it is noted that muscle movement does not occur immediately with the application of the stimulus. Rather, there exists a finite time period between the application of the stimulus and the resultant muscle contraction. This time period is known as the

(A) simple twitch period
(B) latent period
(C) contraction period
(D) relative refractory period
(E) absolute refractory period

90. The energy for muscular contraction may come from each of the following EXCEPT

(A) ATP
(B) creatine phosphate
(C) glycolysis
(D) complete oxidation of glucose
(E) urea

GO ON TO THE NEXT PAGE

Questions 91–92

It has been demonstrated that hormones within plants can exert influences on plant growth. The chart below depicts the differential sensitivity of various parts of a certain plant to changing levels of plant growth regulators. These results are based on laboratory studies and have not been confirmed on plants growing freely in nature.

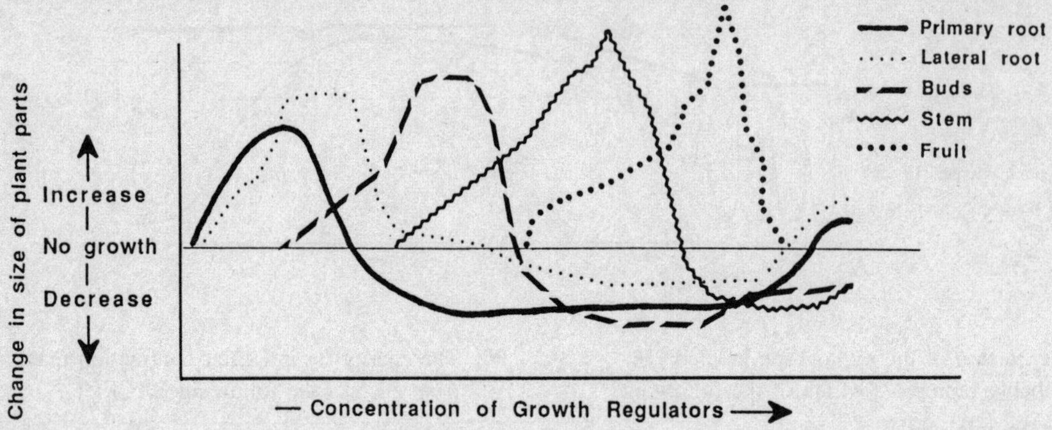

91. Which of the following will grow with the least amount of plant growth regulators relative to the other plant parts?

(A) primary root

(B) lateral root

(C) buds

(D) stem

(E) fruit

92. The terminal bud of a stem is known to produce apical dominance in this plant. Which of the following best describes this condition?

(A) As the fruit of the plant grows larger, stem elongation occurs.

(B) As the fruit of the plant stops growing, stem elongation occurs.

(C) Primary root growth precedes lateral root growth.

(D) As stem elongation occurs, lateral bud growth is inhibited.

(E) As stem growth decreases, terminal bud growth increases.

Questions 93–94

Interactions between mesoderm and its overlying epidermis can have profound effects. Several experiments using the embryonic chicken demonstrate the results of such interactions. In the first experiment, mesoderm from a feathered region of the chick is combined with ectoderm from a nonfeathered region. As a result, the ectoderm produces feathers. In a second experiment, mesoderm from a scaled area is combined with ectoderm from a feather-producing area. The result is ectoderm which produces scales.

93. Differentiation of cells as a result of location is best termed

(A) integration

(B) ingression

(C) restriction

(D) induction

(E) morphogenesis

GO ON TO THE NEXT PAGE

94. If ectoderm from the wing area is supplanted for the ectoderm covering leg mesoderm, which of the following is most likely to occur? Use the above experiments as a guide.

(A) Ectoderm will produce scales.

(B) Ectoderm will produce wing feathers.

(C) Ectoderm will produce leg feathers.

(D) Ectoderm will produce no feathers.

(E) Ectoderm will produce both scales and wing feathers.

Question 95

The curves below illustrate the early development of a young mammal. The normal fully developed adult of this species weighs 8 kilograms and maintains a core temperature of 99°F.

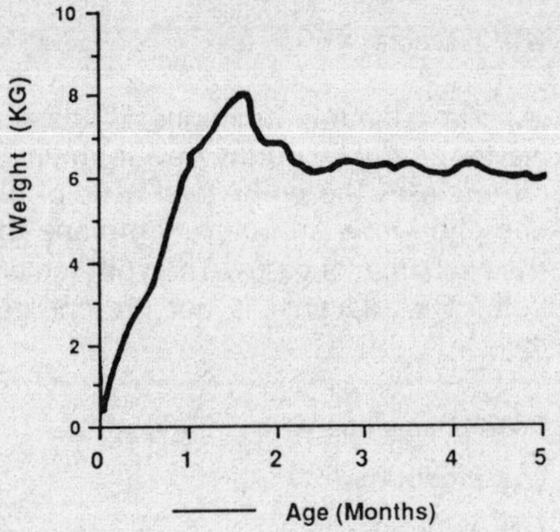

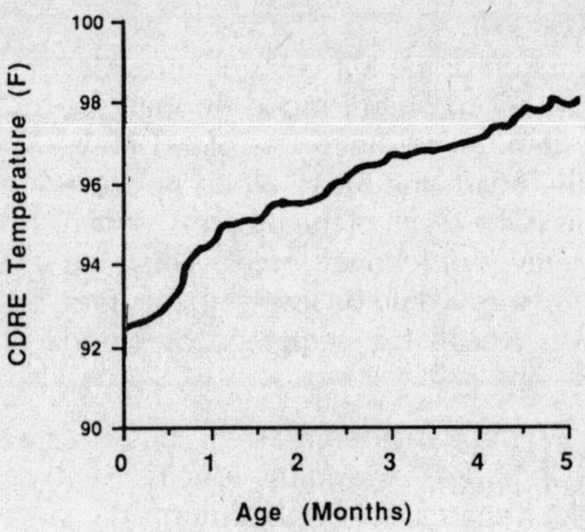

95. Based on the data presented for this animal, which of the following is a reasonable conclusion?

(A) Temperature regulation occurs as the animal's activity level increases.

(B) Weight increases linearly over the first three months of development.

(C) Maximum weight is attained after adult temperature regulation is achieved.

(D) Adult weight is attained prior to adult temperature regulation.

(E) Core temperature and body weight are inversely related over the first three months of development.

S T O P

IF YOU FINISH BEFORE TIME IS CALLED, YOU MAY CHECK YOUR WORK ON THIS TEST ONLY.
DO NOT WORK ON ANY OTHER TEST IN THIS BOOK.

Explanatory Answers

1. In the normal human circulatory system, the mean blood pressure is lowest in the

(A) aorta

(B) arteries

(C) arterioles

(D) capillaries

(E) inferior vena cava

(E) The contraction of the left ventricle provides the force necessary to propel blood through the circulatory system. Accordingly, as blood flows further from the heart, the mean blood pressure decreases. This is the result of the progressive dissipation of energy by frictional forces. Thus, the mean blood pressure would be lowest in the inferior vena cava. Recall the sequence of blood flow:

Left ventricle → aorta → arteries → arterioles → capillaries → venules → veins → inferior/superior vena cava → right atrium

2. Structural components common to plant cell walls but not part of bacterial cell walls include which of the following?

I. Peptidoglycan

II. Cellulose

III. Lignin

(A) I only

(B) II only

(C) I and III only

(D) II and III only

(E) I, II, and III

(D) Cellulose and lignin are structural components unique to plant cells. These materials serve supportive functions. Peptidoglycan, also called murein, is a complex structure consisting of polysaccharide chains connected by short sequences of amino acids. This substance composes part of the bacterial cell wall, but it is not present in plant cells.

3. In the bird egg, which of the following functions as a reservoir for wastes produced during development?

(A) Allantois

(B) Amnion

(C) Chorion

(D) Yolk sac

(E) Placenta

(A) The allantois functions as the reservoir for wastes produced during development. The amnion encloses the embryo in a fluid-filled cavity. The chorion is an outer membrane that permits the exchange of gases. The yolk sac encloses the yolk. The placenta is not present in the chick egg.

4. Food chains end with

(A) producers

(B) autotrophs

(C) decomposers

(D) primary consumers

(E) tertiary consumers

(C) Food chains begin with the producers (autotrophs) and end with the decomposers. The pathway between the beginning and the end of a food chain is variable, and may involve primary consumers, secondary consumers, tertiary consumers, etc.

5. What would be the sequence of bases for the anticodon that corresponds to the codon base sequence of UGC—GGA?

(A) ACG—CCT

(B) TCG—CCT

(C) ACG—CCU

(D) TGG—CCU

(E) ACC—GGU

(C) The anticodon base sequence is complementary to the codon base sequence. The codon is a triplet of bases on messenger RNA that specifies for a single amino acid. The anticodon is a triplet of bases on transfer RNA that is complementary to the codon sequence. Transfer RNA is responsible for the transport of a specific amino acid during the process of protein synthesis. In this question, since the codon and anticodon are parts of RNA molecules, the bases present will be A, C, G, and U. Recall that T is present in DNA and not RNA. Remembering the base pairing rules (A:U, C:G) then, the correct anticodon sequence is determined.

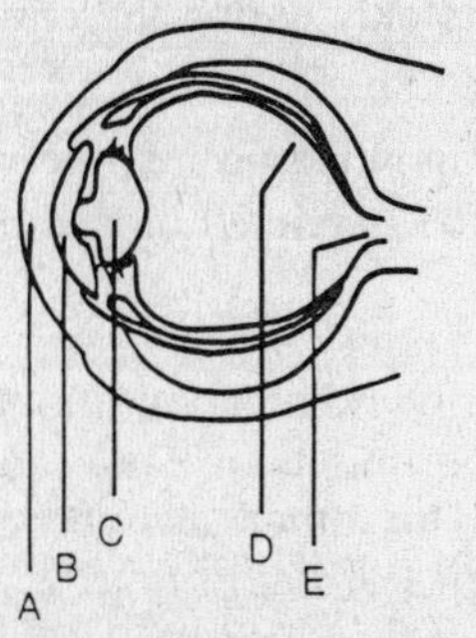

6. In the diagram above, which part of the eye causes the blind spot?

(A) A

(B) B

(C) C

(D) D

(E) E

(E) The blind spot is the point on the retina where the nerve fibers converge to form the optic nerve. At this location, the retina is devoid of visual receptors. The other labelled parts of the diagram are the cornea (A), pupil (B), lens (C), and the fovea (D).

7. Which of the following occurs during anaphase I of meiosis?

(A) Formation of tetrads

(B) Separation of homologous chromosomes

(C) Crossing over

(D) Separation of sister chromatids, with one chromatid pulled toward each pole

(E) Assembly of chromosomes along the equatorial plane

(B) During anaphase I, homologous chromosomes separate. This is in contrast to the separation of sister chromatids, which occurs during anaphase II (and in anaphase of mitosis). Answer choices (A) and (C) occur during prophase I, and answer choice (E) describes metaphase.

8. The wings of sparrows and flies are said to represent

(A) homologous structures

(B) analogous structures

(C) vestigial structures

(D) mutualism

(E) mimicry

(B) Structures that serve similar functions but arose along different evolutionary lines are referred to as analogous. Similarities between species that are the result of common ancestry represent homologous structures. Vestigial structures are homologous organs that have no known function in some species. Mutualism refers to a type of symbiotic relationship, and mimicry is a type of protective adaptation.

9. Oxygen transport from the water to the bloodstream in the gills of fish occurs by diffusion. However, the extraction of oxygen by the blood is higher than would be predicted. This is because

(A) water flow and blood flow are parallel

(B) diffusion of oxygen is much greater in water than in air

(C) oxygen has a very high solubility in water

(D) blood flows opposite to the direction of water movement

(E) multiple layers of cells separate the bloodstream from the water

(D) The gills of fish are able to efficiently extract oxygen from water by utilizing a countercurrent exchange mechanism. In this system, the flow of blood is in the opposite direction to the flow of water. Such an arrangement allows for a continuous oxygen gradient between water and blood, which favors the passive flow of oxygen to the bloodstream.

10. Which of the following participates in the glycosylation of proteins?

I. Endoplasmic reticulum

II. Histones

III. Golgi apparatus

(A) I only

(B) II only

(C) I and III only

(D) II and III only

(E) I, II, and III

(C) Glycosylation (the addition of oligosaccharides) is initiated in the endoplasmic reticulum. The Golgi apparatus then modifies the oligosaccharide structures. Histones are proteins involved in the organization of DNA into chromosomes.

11. Each of the following statements about cellular bioenergetics is true EXCEPT

(A) fermentation may yield lactic acid

(B) fermentation may yield ethyl alcohol

(C) glycolysis occurs within the mitochondria

(D) oxidative phosphorylation (electron transport chain) occurs within the mitochondria

(E) the Krebs cycle occurs within the mitochondria

(C) Glycolysis is the initial reaction sequence involved in the breakdown of glucose. The set of reactions occurs in the cytoplasm of the cell and not within the mitochondria.

12. Each of the following is a characteristic of imprinting EXCEPT

(A) it is a conditioned response

(B) it is a learned behavior

(C) it typically occurs very early in an animal's life

(D) it occurs only during the critical, or sensitive, phase

(E) once imprinting occurs, the young animal cannot be imprinted on another animal or object

(A) Imprinting is not a conditioned response. The famous experiments of Pavlov demonstrate conditioning. The other answer choices describe characteristics of imprinting.

13. Stimulation of the parasympathetic nervous system causes each of the following EXCEPT

(A) release of bile

(B) acceleration of the heart rate

(C) constriction of bronchi

(D) pupillary constriction

(E) increased peristalsis in the gastrointestinal tract

(B) The parasympathetic nervous system would slow the heart rate. The sympathetic nervous system, which readies the body for emergencies ("fight-or-flight"), would cause acceleration of the heart rate.

14. The euglena possesses an organelle that synthesizes a polysaccharide for storage. This organelle is the

(A) stigma

(B) pyrenoid

(C) eyespot

(D) cytopharynx

(E) oral groove

(B) The pyrenoid is the organelle described in this question. The stigma—or eyespot—functions as a light detector for the euglenoids. The cytopharynx and the oral groove are structures of the paramecium.

15. The structure of a flowering plant that produces pollen is which of the following?

(A) Stigma

(B) Style

(C) Filament

(D) Anther

(E) Sepal

(D) The anther is at the distal end of a filament, and is responsible for producing pollen. The filament and its terminal anther comprise the structure known as the stamen. The style is part of the pistil. Sepals are specialized leaves of the flowering plant and serve a protective function.

16. Severe vitamin K deficiency may cause

(A) scurvy

(B) pernicious anemia

(C) pellagra

(D) bleeding

(E) rickets

(D) Vitamin K is necessary for the proper synthesis of some clotting factors. Thus, with a severe deficiency, spontaneous hemorrhage may occur. The other answer choices represent the results of other vitamin deficiencies: scurvy (vitamin C), pernicious anemia (vitamin B_{12}), pellagra (nicotinamide), and rickets (vitamin D).

17. Which of the following best describes the sapwood of a woody dicot?

(A) Cork cambium

(B) Peripheral, more recent rings of xylem

(C) Central area of pith

(D) Area filled with pigments, gums, and resins

(E) Inner, older rings of xylem

(B) The outer rings of xylem in trees provide support as well as assist in transport. Such outer, more recent rings compose the sapwood. The older, innermost rings no longer serve transport functions and are called the heartwood. Vessels of the inner xylem become clogged with various pigments, resins, and gums.

18. Impulses carried from the central nervous system to the effector organs are conducted via the

(A) Schwann cells

(B) dendrites

(C) axon

(D) cerebrospinal fluid

(E) myelin sheath

(C) The axon is responsible for impulse transmission to the effector organ. Dendrites typically receive some sort of stimulation and conduct such information to the cell body. The Schwann cell and its myelin sheath serve to envelop the peripheral nerve and thereby act as an insulator.

19. The biome dominated by conifers, such as spruces and firs, is the

(A) chaparral

(B) deciduous forest

(C) tropical rain forest

(D) tundra

(E) taiga

(E) Dominated by the presence of conifers is the taiga. This biome is south of the tundra. Moose, bears, and birds are a few of the characteristic animals in the taiga.

20. Inheritance of color in a certain plant is known to follow simple Mendelian rules. Green leaf color is dominant and yellow leaf color is recessive to green. If a homozygous green-leafed plant is mated with a homozygous yellow-leafed plant, what proportion of offspring (F_1 generation) would be expected to possess yellow leaves?

(A) 0%

(B) 25%

(C) 50%

(D) 75%

(E) 100%

(A) The offspring of a homozygous dominant-homozygous recessive cross will demonstrate the dominant phenotype. This result can quickly be ascertained from a Punnett square:

G = dominant, green leaf color
g = recessive, yellow leaf color
GG × gg

	g	g
G	Gg	Gg
G	Gg	Gg

Thus, it is observed that 100% of the offspring will be heterozygous for leaf color. However, since green leaf color is dominant, the phenotype will accordingly be green.

21. Archaeopteryx is important to the study of evolution because

(A) it is believed to represent the evolutionary link between the kingdom Plantae and the kingdom Fungi

(B) it is believed to represent the evolutionary link between the class Reptilia and the class Aves

(C) it is believed to represent the evolutionary link between the sponges and the molluscs

(D) it represents the last known evidence of the dinosaurs

(E) it represents the first known terrestrial animal

(B) Archaeopteryx is the oldest known fossil of the class Aves (birds). This animal possessed characteristics of both reptiles and birds. Hence, it is believed to represent the evolutionary link between the classes Reptilia and Aves. Although Archeopteryx had a long tail and teeth, it also had wings, leading systematists to classify this animal as a bird.

22. Enzymes accomplish each of the following EXCEPT

(A) increase the rate of the forward reaction

(B) increase the rate of the reverse reaction

(C) decrease the activation energy of the reaction

(D) increase the activation energy of the reaction

(E) allow reactions to occur more readily

(D) Enzymes do not affect the equilibrium constant for a given reaction. Instead, enzymatic catalysis simply allows equilibrium to be reached more quickly than would occur in the non-catalyzed reaction. Enzymes accomplish such a task by allowing reactions to occur more readily; reactive portions of substrates are brought into close approximation. Consequently the activation energy is lowered, and the forward and reverse reactions will occur more readily.

23. High energy molecules involved in the dark reactions of photosynthesis include which of the following?

I. ATP

II. NADH

III. NADPH

(A) I only

(B) II only

(C) I and III only

(D) II and III only

(E) I, II, and III

(C) Carbon fixation occurs in the dark reactions. In these reactions, CO_2 is used to synthesize carbohydrates. The energy sources for this set of reactions are ATP and NADPH. The ATP and NADPH are products of the light-dependent reactions.

24. The "all-or-none response" refers to which of the following?

(A) Flocking defense scheme utilized by various birds

(B) Nondisjunction

(C) Fitness of an animal

(D) Expressivity of a phenotype

(E) Transmission of neural impulses

(E) The all-or-none response is a property of neurons. This concept refers to the response of a neuron to a given stimulus. If a stimulus is of threshold intensity (or greater), then the neuron will "fire." However, if the stimulus is of sub-threshold intensity, the neuron will not propogate a signal.

25. Bile, a complex fluid that assists in the digestion of fatty substances, is produced by the

(A) gallbladder

(B) small intestine

(C) pancreas

(D) stomach

(E) liver

(E) Bile is produced by the liver. The gallbladder functions as a reservoir for bile and also concentrates this complex fluid by absorbing water. In response to hormonal stimulation the walls of the gallbladder contract, and bile is released into the small intestine. In the gastrointestinal tract, bile emulsifies fats and allows for more efficient digestion of these substances.

26. A dominant gene that shows X-linked inheritance is being studied by a biologist. If an affected male is mated with an unaffected female, which of the following most likely represents an accurate description of their immediate offspring?

(A) 100% affected males, 0% affected females

(B) 0% affected males, 100% affected females

(C) 50% affected males, 25% affected females, 100% carrier females

(D) 50% affected males, 50% affected females, 100% carrier females

(E) 25% affected males, 25% affected females, 25% carrier females

(B) An X-linked gene signifies that such a gene is sex-linked and occupies a locus on the X sex chromosome. Furthermore, since the gene in question is dominant, one "dose" of this gene will allow its full expression. (This is in contrast to a recessive gene, which requires the absence of the dominant gene in order for it to be expressed.) If X* is allowed to represent the particular dominant, X-linked gene in question, the mating can be described as

XX	×	X*Y
unaffected female		affected male

Note that the female has to be XX and cannot be X*X or X*X*. Why? Realize that X*X or X*X* would signify an affected female—the X* is dominant! Hence, an unaffected female could not possess this gene. In addition, if it is assumed that the carrier state represents an individual who possesses the gene in question but is not affected, there can be no carriers for this gene. That is, each offspring who possesses the X* gene will be affected. Arranging a Punnett square for the cross that occurs in this problem, then:

	x*	y
x	xx*	xy
x	xx*	xy

So, 100% of the female offspring will inherit the X* chromosome. However, the X chromosome of the male offspring will be one of the unaffected X chromosomes from the unaffected female parent. Hence, none of the males will be affected.

27. The diagram below depicts the cell cycle for an asynchronously growing cell population (cells at each stage are present at any given time). If the cell population is briefly exposed to $_3$H-thymidine, cells at which phase would immediately demonstrate incorporation of the radiolabeled thymidine?

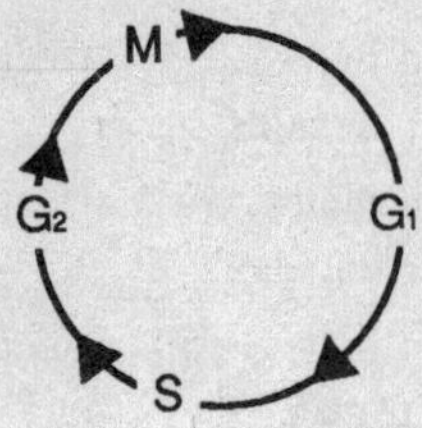

(A) M

(B) G_1

(C) S

(D) G_1

(E) S and M

(C) Thymidine is one of the nucleotides found in DNA. The various phases of the cell cycle are mitosis (M), gap 1 (G_1), replication or synthesis of DNA (S), and gap 2 (G_2).During the gap phases, the cell synthesizes the various cellular products that are necessary. Note that only during the S phase is DNA being synthesized. Thus, thymidine will be utilized during this phase, and radiolabeled thymidine will be incorporated.

28. Energy dependent processes for cellular transport include each of the following EXCEPT

(A) cytoplasmic streaming in algae

(B) $Na^+ - K^+$ ATPase

(C) osmosis

(D) axonal transport

(E) active transport

(C) Active transport is an energy-dependent process for cellular transport. Specific types of active transport include the $Na^+ - K^+$ ATPase and axonal transport. Active transport allows for the movement of a particle against its concentration gradient. This is in contrast to diffusion and osmosis, which are passive processes: movement of a particle occurs down its concentration gradient (from higher to lower concentrations). Cytoplasmic streaming has been well-characterized in algae. This process involves the movement of cellular contents by microfilaments and utilizes energy.

29. Which of the following is not a direct function of the vertebrate liver?

(A) Synthesis of plasma proteins

(B) Carbohydrate metabolism

(C) Deamination

(D) Reabsorption of water

(E) Detoxification

(D) Reabsorption of water is not a direct function of the vertebrate liver. The vertebrate digestive tract (intestines) absorbs water and the kidney functions to maintain salt and water balance. The other answer choices represent several of the functions served by the liver.

30. Which of the following pairs of organisms are the least related?

(A) Squid - Octopus

(B) Crayfish - Shrimp

(C) Shark - Ray

(D) Sea lily - Iris

(E) Lemur - Monkey

(D) Recall the classification hierarchy employed by taxonomists:

Kingdom, Phylum, Class, Order, Family, Genus, Species

The more closely related two organisms are, the more common is their classification (i.e., same kingdom, phylum, class, order, etc.) In examining the answer choices, one choice clearly depicts disparate organisms. The sea lily is a member of the kingdom Animalia, while the iris belongs to the kingdom Plantae. Do not be misled by their names. The iris is a monocot *flower,* while the sea lily is a primitive marine *animal.* The other answer choices are related as follows: squid-octopus, same class; crayfish-shrimp, same class; shark-ray, same class; and lemur-monkey, same order. Note that it necessarily follows that organisms of the same class belong to the same phylum and kingdom.

31. Which of the following would be expected to have the most stable ecosystem?

(A) Ocean floor beneath Antarctic polar ice

(B) Pacific shore along California

(C) Subtropical forests of Africa

(D) Coniferous forest of North America

(E) Grasslands of Southwestern United States

(A) The term ecosystem describes a community of living organisms, the surrounding environment, and the interactions between the members of the community. The most stable ecosystem would have the least amount of change among its living organisms and physical environment. The ocean floor beneath the Antarctic is the most stable of the ecosystems listed. Meteorological factors are negligible. A very cold, dark state exists. Tides do not have much effect. The living population, though not static, is relatively unchanging in comparison to the other ecosystems given.

32. Sperm stored in the epididymis flow into what immediate structure during copulation?

(A) Ureter

(B) Urethra

(C) Seminal vesicle

(D) Vas deferens

(E) Prostate

(D) Sperm are produced within the seminiferous tubules of the testis. The epididymis serves as the reservoir for sperm until they are released. Upon ejaculation, sperm in the epididymis enter the vas deferens. The vas deferens is connected to the urethra, and it is though the urethra that the sperm reach the outside.

33. Carolus Linnaeus classified organisms according to their

(A) evolutionary trends

(B) morphologic similarities

(C) ability to mate

(D) ability to produce viable offspring

(E) ecological interrelationships

(B) Carolus Linnaeus devised a classification scheme based upon the morphologic similarities of organisms.

34. Which of the following represents the most likely succession of man?

(A) Homo erectus → Australopithecus → Homo habilis → Homo sapiens

(B) Australopithecus → Homo erectus → Homo habilis → Homo sapiens

(C) Homo sapiens → Australopithecus → Homo erectus → Homo habilis

(D) Australopithecus → Homo habilis → Homo erectus → Homo sapiens

(E) Homo habilis → Homo erectus → Australopithecus → Homo sapiens

(D) The first, primitive human is said to belong to the genus Australopithecus. A species within this genus is believed to have given rise to the genus Homo. Homo habilis may represent one of the earliest members of Homo. Homo erectus, also called Java man, is recognized as a later representative of this genus and probably is the precursor of modern man, Homo sapiens.

35. Hemoglobin is a protein that functions in the transport of oxygen contained within red blood cells. Hemoglobin has been shown to consist of four independent polypeptide chains. The manner in which these four chains interact to form functional molecules is a characteristic of hemoglobin's

(A) secondary structure

(B) tertiary structure

(C) quaternary structure

(D) denaturation

(E) melting point

(C) The interaction of the four distinct polypeptide chains that compose hemoglobin is referred to as its quaternary structure. Primary structure refers to the amino acid sequence of a protein. Secondary structure refers to the interactions of amino acids with their nearest neighbors. Examples of secondary structure include the alpha helix, the β-turn, and the pleated sheet. Tertiary structure refers to the three-dimensional shape of the protein.

36. In humans, which of the following allow efficient absorption of digested foodstuffs to occur?

I. Microvilli

II. Large surface area

III. Presence of certain viruses

(A) I only

(B) II only

(C) I and II only

(D) I and III only

(E) I, II, and III

(C) In humans, the bulk of digestion and absorption occurs within the small intestine. The intestines are quite long and present a large surface area for digestion. To enhance the surface available for digestion and absorption, small projections called villi protrude from the lumen wall. Furthermore, the entire surface of the lumen is lined with microvilli. Although colonic bacteria can form vitamin K, vitamin B_{12}, and various gases, viruses play no known role in absorption of digested foodstuffs.

37. Each of the following methods of reproduction occurs without genetic recombination EXCEPT

(A) binary fission

(B) conjugation

(C) budding

(D) production of gemmae

(E) cloning

(B) Conjugation is a reproductive process used by some bacteria. During conjugation, two bacteria are connected by a cytoplasmic bridge. Via this connection, genetic material may be passed from one bacterial cell to the other. The other answer choices represent asexual methods of reproduction that occur without genetic recombination.

38. The ruminants—animals such as deer and cows—are able to digest cellulose. Each of the following contributes to the special digestive abilities of the ruminant EXCEPT

(A) multichambered gastrointestinal tract

(B) bacteria within digestive tract

(C) protozoa within digestive tract

(D) ability to convert β-glucose to α-glucose

(E) mutualism

(D) Glucose occurs as both α-glucose and β-glucose. β-glucose is the form found in cellulose and composes the majority of the plant cell wall. Humans and ruminants do not possess the ability to directly digest β-glucose. However, the ruminants do have bacteria and protozoa within their digestive tracts that are able to digest β-glucose. β-glucose is not converted to α-glucose. Since the microorganisms and the ruminants each benefit, this situation is an example of mutualism. Ruminants also have a multichambered gastrointestinal tract to aid in digestion.

39. A cell is removed from its normal environment and placed into another medium. It is then noted that the cell appears to shrink. Which term best describes the *medium* relative to the cell?

(A) Hypertonic

(B) Hypotonic

(C) Isotonic

(D) Osmotic

(E) Pinocytosis

(A) Osmosis is the diffusion of a solvent through a semipermeable membrane. The solvent involved is usually water. In this question, the cell is placed in a medium and the cell shrinks. This occurs because the medium contains more osmotically active particles than the cell (hypertonic). Thus, water will flow down its concentration gradient: water moves from the cell interior to the external medium.

40. Organic molecules, such as vitamin C and vitamin B_{12}, are required for specific enzymes to function. Such organic molecules are called

(A) substrates

(B) coenzymes

(C) allosteric modulators

(D) active sites

(E) competitive inhibitors

(B) A coenzyme is an organic molecule that is required for an enzyme to accomplish its function.

41. The corpus luteum secretes a hormone that prepares the uterus for implantation. This hormone is most likely

(A) a luteinizing hormone

(B) a follicle-stimulating hormone

(C) estrogen

(D) progesterone

(E) chorionic gonadotropin

(D) The hormone mainly responsible for preparing the uterus for implantation is progesterone. The corpus luteum does secrete this hormone for a period.

42. The graph below depicts the population trend in a predator-prey system. Assuming this is a stable system (free from outside influences), which of the following statements is most likely true?

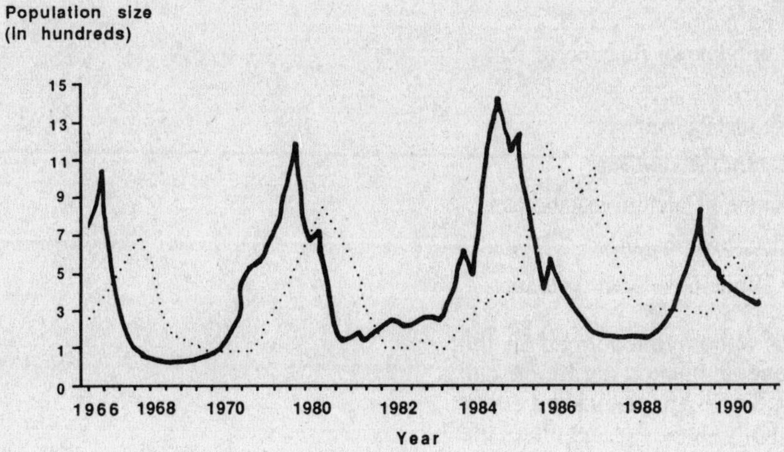

(A) The solid line most likely represents the predator population trend.

(B) The populations of predator and prey reach peak levels concomitantly.

(C) Four years after the population of predator begins to decrease, there is a dramatic decrease in the population of prey.

(D) One year after the population of prey increases, there is a parallel rise in the population of predator.

(E) No correlation between predator and prey populations is observed.

(D) The graph depicts the classic relationship between predator and prey. The solid line represents the prey population, while the interrupted line represents the predator population. Note that the population curves are approximately parallel, but that there exists a time lag between the two. In the stable predator-prey system, as the population of prey increases, there will be more food for the predator. Hence, the predator population will increase. However, as more and more of the prey are killed, there will be less food for the growing predator population. Consequently, the predator population will not have an appropriate food supply and the population will decrease. Once fewer predators exist, the prey population will again increase as fewer of their members are being killed.

43. According to the Hardy-Weinberg law, genetic equilibrium within a gene pool is contingent upon several factors. Which of the following is one of the requirements?

(A) Population size must be small.

(B) Genetic drift occurs.

(C) There is an absence of gene flow.

(D) Mutations are frequent and not balanced.

(E) There is an absence of random reproduction.

(C) According to the Hardy-Weinberg law, genetic equilibrium may exist if the following occur: (1) the population is sufficiently large, (2) there is a net absence of mutations, (3) no gene migration occurs, and (4) reproduction is random within the species. Gene migration may also be referred to as gene flow, so answer choice (C) is the only requirement listed.

44. Several general characteristics of the angiosperms allow for the separation of this class of plants into two subclasses. Properties that differentiate these subclasses include each of the following EXCEPT

(A) the number of seed leaves

(B) arrangement of vascular tissue in the stem

(C) petal arrangement

(D) color scheme of petals

(E) vein structure of leaves

(D) The two subclasses of the angiosperms are the Monocotyledoneae (monocots) and the Dicotyledoneae (dicots). Distinguishing characteristics include each of the answer choices given, except (D) petal color.

45. Which of the following hormones is NOT correctly matched with a known function of that hormone?

(A) Insulin - Glucose metabolism

(B) Calcitonin - Calcium metabolism

(C) Parathyroid hormone - Calcium metabolism

(D) Aldosterone - Electrolyte balance

(E) Erythropoietin - White blood cell regulation

(E) Erythropoietin is a hormone formed in the kidney. This hormone stimulates red blood cell production (red blood cells are also called erythrocytes). Erythropoietin does not regulate the white blood cell population.

46. The diagram below illustrates the growth curve of a certain bacteria in a controlled environment. Which time period represents the maximal growth acceleration of the bacterial population?

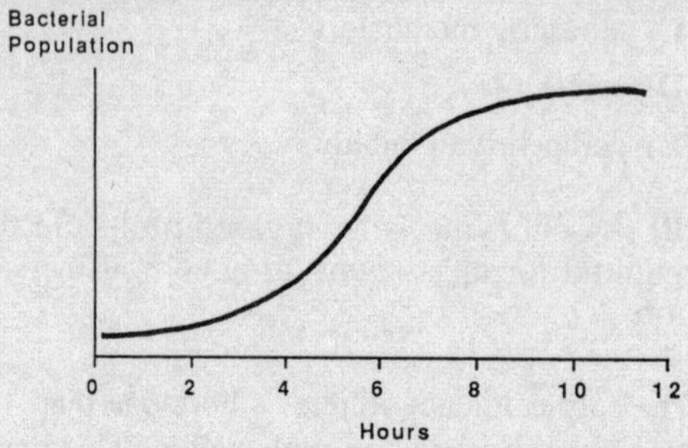

(A) Between hours 2 and 4

(B) Between hours 4 and 6

(C) Between hours 6 and 8

(D) Between hours 8 and 10

(E) Between hours 10 and 12

(B) Maximal growth acceleration occurs between the fourth and sixth hours. The diagram depicts the familiar "S-shaped" growth curve. At a low population density, the bacteria initially multiply rapidly, then reproduction slows until a steady state is reached. Growth acceleration occurs between hours 0–6, with maximal acceleration between the fourth and sixth hours. Between the sixth and tenth hours, deceleration is actually occurring. The steady state is reached between the tenth and twelfth hours.

47. In the early stages of certain diseases, pooled immunoglobulin may be administered. Often, the disease process will be significantly less severe as a result of this treatment. The pooled immunoglobulin contains antibodies that are specific for the infectious agent. This treatment is an example of

(A) active immunity

(B) passive immunity

(C) colostrum

(D) vaccination

(E) autoimmunity

(B) Passive immunity is the term used to describe the injection of pre-formed antibodies. That is, the antibodies are synthesized elsewhere (laboratory synthesis, pooled antiserum), but are given to the patient so an immediate immune response can be obtained. Active immunity occurs when an individual mounts an immune response, synthesizes antibodies, reacts to a foreign stimulus (the antigen). Active immunity occurs as result of being infected or by receiving a vaccine.

48. Which of the following is derived from the ectodermal germ layer?

(A) Mammary glands

(B) Thyroid gland

(C) Liver

(D) Eustachian tube

(E) Adrenal cortex

(A) The mammary glands are ectodermal derivatives. The thyroid gland, the liver, and the Eustachian tube are derived from endoderm. Mesodermal derivatives include the heart, the kidneys, and the adrenal cortex.

49. The first dinosaurs probably inhabited the earth during which era?

(A) Cenozoic

(B) Paleozoic

(C) Mesozoic

(D) Precambrian

(E) Silurian

(C) The first dinosaurs inhabited the earth during the Mesozoic era. The age of mammals is classified as early Cenozoic. Fish, amphibians, and reptiles each have origins tracing back to the Paleozoic era. Precambrian life consisted of primitive marine organisms. Within the Paleozoic era is the Silurian period (i.e., Silurian is a period, not an era).

50. The main reservoir of carbon for the carbon cycle is which of the following?

(A) Hydrocarbons contained in coal and oil

(B) Calcium carbonate contained in limestone

(C) Carbon contained in diamonds

(D) Carbon dioxide contained in air and dissolved in water

(E) Carbon contained in living organisms

(D) The carbon dioxide that is contained in the earth's atmosphere and that dissolved in the earth's bodies of water form the major supply of carbon for the carbon cycle.

51. Each of the following is a characteristic of mammals EXCEPT

(A) four-chambered heart

(B) homothermy

(C) only one bone in the middle ear

(D) ventral orientation of the limbs

(E) only one bone comprising the lower jaw

(C) Mammals have three bones in the middle ear, while reptiles and birds have only one bone in the middle ear.

52. Which of the following is NOT a characteristic of procaryotes?

(A) Few, if any, organelles

(B) Synthesis of protein and RNA occurs within the same compartment

(C) Contain DNA within the cytoplasm

(D) Transcription and translation are closely coupled events

(E) Occurrence of introns within the primary RNA transcript

(E) Procaryotes are typically small and mainly unicellular. Composed of a single compartment, they possess few, if any, organelles. DNA, RNA, and protein synthesis occur within this compartment, the groundwork substance of which is called the cytoplasm. Hence, transcription and translation may be both temporally and spatially related events. However, unlike eucaryotes, the RNA transcript is not composed of exons and introns. That is, the primary transcript of a procaryote does not undergo extensive modification prior to translation.

Questions 53–57

(A) Stomata
(B) Guard cells
(C) Mesophyll
(D) Companion cells
(E) Petiole

53. Regulate the exchange of gases between the leaf and the environment

(B) Guard cells are specialized epidermal cells. Two of these cells lie adjacent to one another and regulate the opening and closing of the stoma. Hence, although the actual exchange of gases occurs via the stoma, it is the guard cells that regulate this opening.

54. Stalk of a leaf

(E) The stalk of a typical dicot leaf is also called the petiole.

55. Region between the upper and lower epidermis of a leaf

(C) The region between the upper and lower epidermis is the mesophyll. This part of the leaf consists of cells densely laden with chloroplasts. Indeed, most of the photosynthesis of a plant occurs in this region.

56. Openings in the epidermis that allow transpiration to occur

(A) Stomata allow gases to be exchanged between the plant and the environment. The evaporation of water at the stoma is called transpiration.

57. Adjacent to sieve tube

(D) Companion cells are integral components of phloem. These elongate cells serve a supportive function, helping to maintain the sieve elements.

Questions 58–61

(A) Ribosome
(B) Mitochondrion
(C) Centriole
(D) Nucleolus
(E) Peroxisome

58. Membrane-bound vesicle that contains the enzyme catalase

(E) Peroxisomes are intracellular vesicles that are similar to lysosomes. All peroxisomes contain the enzyme catalase, which catalyzes the degradation of hydrogen peroxide to a less toxic molecule.

59. Possesses its own genetic material and self-replicates

(B) Mitochondria are the so-called "powerhouses" of the cell, producing the ATP necessary for cellular processes. Mitochondria also reproduce by dividing in two and contain DNA.

60. Interacts with the endoplasmic reticulum during protein synthesis

(A) Ribosomes are composed of protein and RNA. Protein synthesis is catalyzed by this complex structural unit.

61. Composed of microtubules and functions in cytoskeletal organization

(C) Centrioles are organizing centers that are composed of a cylindrical array of microtubules.

Questions 62–65

(A) Contractile vacuole
(B) Flame-cell
(C) Nephridial system
(D) Malpighian tubules
(E) Nephron

62. Excretory system of insects

(D) Malpighian tubules lie in the hemocoel of insects, where the tubules are bathed in blood. Fluid is absorbed into the tubules and water and salts are reabsorbed. Waste materials then pass into the hindgut.

63. Excretory system of the earthworm

(C) Nephridia filter the extracellular fluid of the earthworm and reclaim valuable materials.

64. Excretory organelle present in some protozoans

(A) Contractile vacuoles are responsible for maintaining water balance. These structures are present in some protozoans.

65. Functional unit of the vertebrate kidney

(E) The functional unit of the vertebrate kidney is called the nephron. The nephron consists of Bowman's capsule and a long tubule. The tubule is divided into several, well-characterized segments.

Questions 66–69

The shape and character of pea seeds produced from mating heterozygous yellow, wrinkled-shaped peas are being studied. It is known that the yellow color and the rounded shape are dominant traits, while the green color and the wrinkled shape are recessive traits. The parent seeds are dihybrids. Furthermore, it has been determined that the genes for these traits are inherited independently. The lettered answer choices below represent the expected proportions of the various first-generation offspring from this mating experiment (dihybrid cross).

(A) 1/16
(B) 3/16
(C) 4/16
(D) 9/16
(E) 12/16

66. Yellow, rounded

(D) Questions 66–69 refer to a dihybrid cross that follows simple Mendelian laws. The results of this mating can be demonstrated through the use of a Punnett square. Round (R) and yellow (Y) are dominant traits, while wrinkled (r) and green (y) are recessive traits. Thus, the parents' genotypes may be represented as RrYy. The cross is then

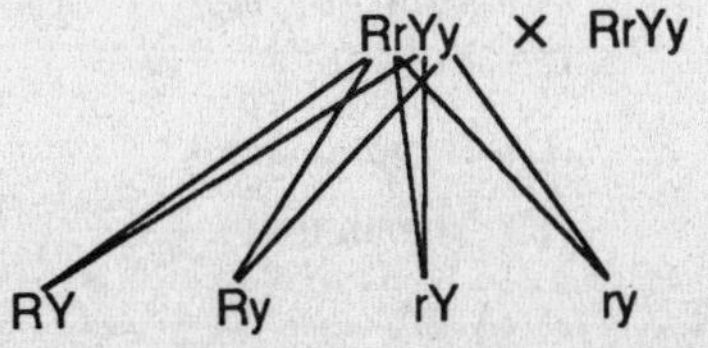

The Punnett square, then, is as illustrated:

	RY	Ry	rY	ry
RY	RRYY	RRYy	RrYY	RrYy
Ry	RRYy	RRyy	RrYy	Rryy
rY	RrYY	RrYy	rrYY	rrYy
ry	RrYy	Rryy	RrYy	rryy

Thus the combination R and Y—yellow, rounded—is present in 9/16 of the offspring. This number represents the expected proportion of offspring from the dihybrid cross that are yellow and rounded.

67. Green, wrinkled

(A) Green, wrinkled peas are characterized by the genotype rryy. Both the green color and the wrinkled shape are recessive traits. Therefore, for the recessive phenotype to be manifest, the genotype must be homozygous recessive: rryy (refer to the Punnett square provided in the answer to question 66).

68. Green, rounded

(B) Green, rounded peas are characterized by the following genotypes: RRyy and Rryy (refer to the Punnett square provided in the answer to question 66).

69. Wrinkled

(C) Wrinkled peas must have the homozygous recessive genotype: rr. The color of the pea is irrelevant (refer to the Punnett square provided in the answer to question 66).

Questions 70–72

(A) Cerebellum
(B) Olfactory bulb
(C) Medulla
(D) Hypothalamus
(E) Thalamus

70. Involved in processing odors

(B) The sense of smell is also referred to as olfaction. The olfactory bulb, located within the central nervous system, is involved in the processing of various odors.

71. Integrates sensory information from somatic receptors

(E) All somatosensory information that enters the cerebrum is relayed through the thalamus. From the thalamus, such information may be directed to appropriate cortical areas.

72. Contains centers responsible for control of blood pressure and respiration

(C) The medulla contains centers that are responsible for maintaining vital functions.

Questions 73–77

Female Reproductive System

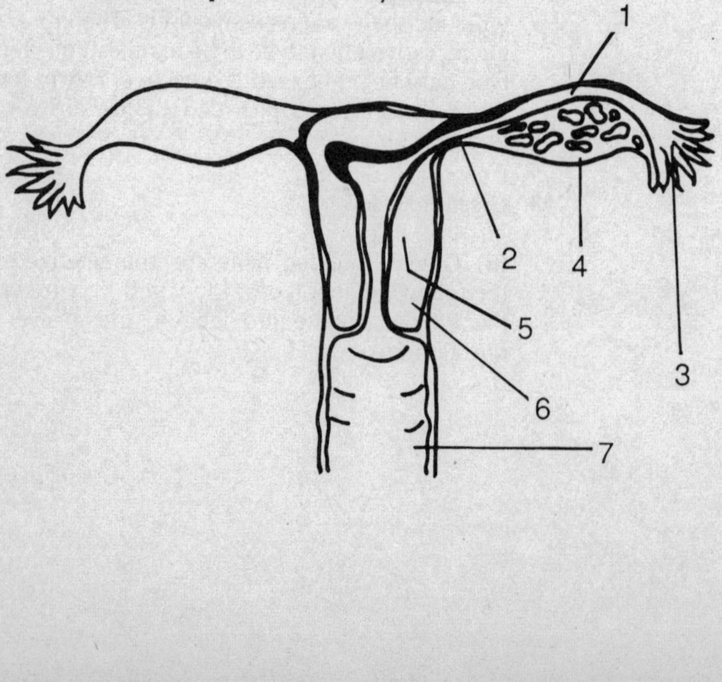

73. Fertilization normally occurs in

(A) 1
(B) 2
(C) 3
(D) 6
(E) 7

(A) Fertilization normally occurs in the ampulla of the uterine tube (1). The remainder of the labeled parts are: (2) ovarian ligament, (3) fimbriae, (4) ovary, (5) uterus, (6) cervix, and (7) vagina.

74. Implantation normally occurs in

(A) 1
(B) 4
(C) 5
(D) 6
(E) 7

(C) Implantation normally occurs in the wall of the uterus.

75. Gametes are produced in

(A) 1
(B) 2
(C) 3
(D) 4
(E) 5

(D) The ovaries have the dual functions of producing female gametes and synthesizing sex hormones.

76. Synthesis of sex hormones occurs in

(A) 3

(B) 4

(C) 5

(D) 6

(E) 7

(B) The ovary is a gland that produces eggs and sex hormones.

77. The diaphragm, a birth control device, covers

(A) 1

(B) 2

(C) 5

(D) 6

(E) 7

(D) The cervix is a muscular ring of tissue at the end of the uterus. When in position, the diaphragm covers the cervix and functions as a barrier. Thus, sperm are prevented from entering the uterus.

Questions 78–80 pertain to the electron transport chain. The reaction sequence below illustrates some of the components of the electron transport chain and the sites where ATP is generated. Also shown are various inhibitors and the steps where these chemicals exert their effects. In addition, the diagram depicts the sites of entry for several substrates of the electron transport chain.

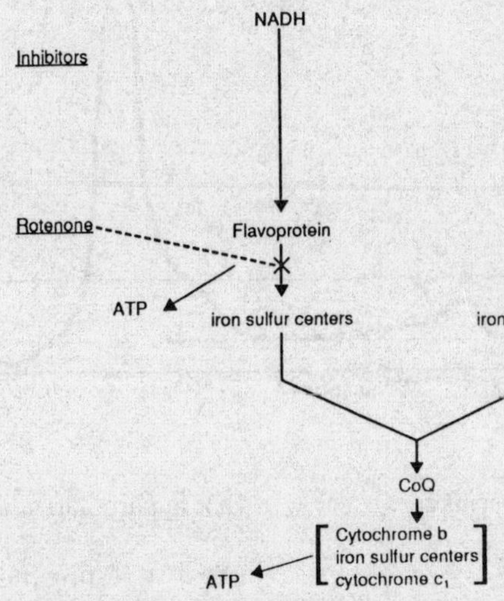

78. According to the diagram, how many ATP would succinate be expected to yield under normal circumstances?

(A) 0

(B) 1

(C) 2

(D) 3

(E) 4

(C) According to the diagram, succinate yields 2 ATP.

79. If the inhibitor rotenone is present, how many ATP would succinate be expected to yield?

(A) 0

(B) 1

(C) 2

(D) 3

(E) 4

(C) Rotenone inhibits the transfer of electrons from NADH to CoQ. Rotenone does not affect the transfer of electrons from succinate to CoQ; therefore succinate yields 2 ATP.

80. Antimycin A blocks the transfer of electrons at the site shown in the diagram. Which of the following occurs if Antimycin A is present?

(A) Electron transfer proceeds normally.

(B) Electron carriers before the inhibition site become more oxidized.

(C) Oxidation of succinate occurs completely.

(D) Electron carriers after the inhibition site become more oxidized.

(E) Succinate would yield only 1 ATP while ascorbate would yield 2 ATP.

(D) Reducing equivalents are "shuttled" down to cytochromes of the electron transport chain. If these electrons cannot pass, the carrier before the block will become more reduced. Furthermore, the carriers after the block will not receive any of the reducing equivalents and will become more oxidized.

Questions 81–84 refer to the action potential of a nerve fiber. The diagram below demonstrates the effect of several stimuli on the membrane potential of a neuron. Each triangle indicates the time at which a stimulus is applied to the nerve.

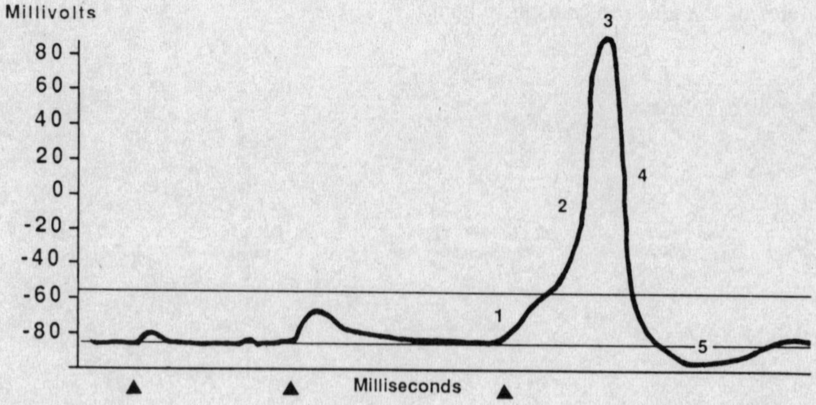

81. The interrupted line at −90 millivolts most likely represents the

(A) resting membrane potential

(B) threshold potential

(C) inhibitory potential

(D) refractory period

(E) hyperpolarization potential

(A) The resting membrane potential for the nerve fiber being studied is approximately −90 millivolts. This value signifies that the internal milieu of the cell is at −90 millivolts relative to the cell exterior.

82. The threshold potential for this nerve is most likely

(A) +80 millivolts

(B) +20 millivolts

(C) −56 millivolts

(D) −70 millivolts

(E) −90 millivolts

(C) The threshold potential for this nerve is most likely −56 millivolts. If a stimulus is of sufficient intensity to cause the cell interior to reach the threshold potential, then the nerve will "fire," and the action potential illustrated in the diagram is the result. Note the first two stimuli of the diagram raised the potential of the cell's interior to approximately −80 millivolts and −70 millivolts, respectively. However, since the threshold potential was not attained, the nerve did not fire.

83. Rapid depolarization of the membrane, as occurs in the area labeled 2, is due to which of the following?

(A) Influx of K^+ ions

(B) Efflux of Ca^{2+} ions

(C) Influx of SO_4^{2-}

(D) Efflux of ATP

(E) Influx of Na^+ ions

(E) Rapid depolarization is due to rapid influx of sodium ions (Na^+). Recall that the external environment of the cell has a high concentration of sodium ions relative to the intracellular compartment.

84. Which of the following most likely explains repolarization?

(A) $Na^+ - K^+$-ATPase ceases to function

(B) Rapid influx of Na^+ ions

(C) Rapid efflux of K^+ ions

(D) Rapid influx of Cl^- ions

(E) Rapid efflux of Cl^- ions

(C) Repolarization occurs as potassium ions (K^+) rapidly flow from the inside of the cell to the cell's exterior. In addition, sodium ions no longer flow into the cell. The Na^+-K^+-ATPase can then function to restore the cell to its normal intracellular concentration of Na^+ and K^+.

Questions 85–87

Experiments have demonstrated that DNA is a very well organized, cooperative structure. The two strands of the DNA double helix are joined by hydrogen bonds between the paired bases. Adenine and thymine are held together by two hydrogen bonds, while three hydrogen bonds will form between and join the bases cytosine and guanine. Five DNA melting curves, labeled A, B, C, D, and E, are illustrated below. The melting point of a given DNA molecule is described as being the temperature at which half the double helix is unwound. Absorption, as measured by the spectrophotometer, increases as the DNA melts. Once completely melted, the curve levels.

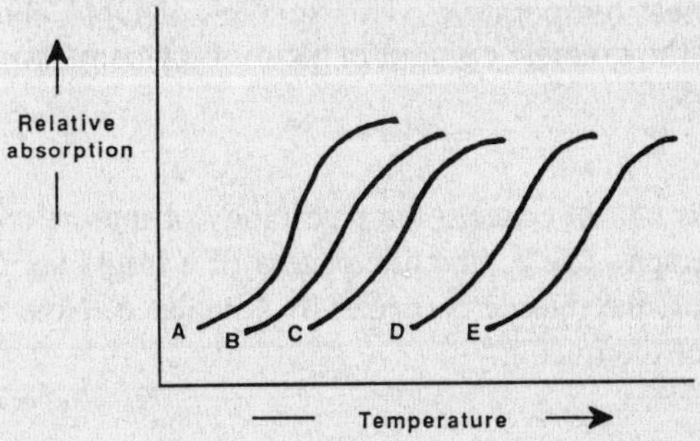

85. Which species of DNA melts at the lowest temperature?

(A) A

(B) B

(C) C

(D) D

(E) E

(A) The DNA labeled A melts at the lowest temperature.

86. Which species of DNA possesses the greatest content of adenine-thymine base pairs?

(A) A

(B) B

(C) C

(D) D

(E) E

(A) Adenine-thymine base pairs are held together by only two hydrogen bonds. Therefore, it will take less heat to disrupt adenine-thymine base pairs as compared to guanine-cytosine base pairs (contain three hydrogen bonds). Thus, the DNA labeled A, which melts at the lowest temperature, possesses the greatest content of adenine-thymine base pairs. The DNA labeled E melts at the highest temperature. This species of DNA thus has the greatest content of guanine-cytosine base pairs.

87. If a solution containing denatured DNA (assume only one species of DNA) is cooled to 25°C below its melting temperature, which of the following would be expected to occur?

(A) Phosphate groups would leave the individual bases.

(B) Annealing.

(C) Adenine-thymine base pairs would again form three intermolecular hydrogen bonds.

(D) The individual strands composing the double helices will remain isolated and irreversibly altered.

(E) Adenine will reliably base pair with guanine and with thymine.

(B) DNA will return to its normal configuration. That is, the double helix will be re-formed. This process is called annealing or re-annealing or renaturation.

Questions 88–90 concern the physiology of muscle contraction. The diagram below represents a tracing from a kymograph. The contraction pattern of a frog's leg muscle is being studied. Under appropriate experimental conditions, the muscle is repeatedly stimulated. Note the frequency of stimulation varies throughout the first portion of the tracing.

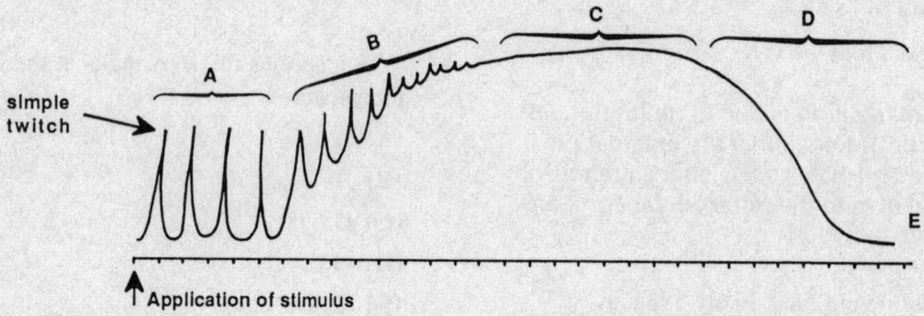

88. The portion of the kymograph labeled D probably represents which of the following?

(A) Simple twitch

(B) Tetanus

(C) Latent period

(D) Relaxation period

(E) Fatigue

(E) In part D of the kymograph tracing, muscle contraction diminishes despite repeated stimuli. This is known as fatigue. Part C of the tracing represents tetanus.

89. In part A of the kymograph, it is noted that muscle movement does not occur immediately with the application of the stimulus. Rather, there exists a finite time period between the application of the stimulus and the resultant muscle contraction. This time period is known as the

(A) simple twitch period

(B) latent period

(C) contraction period

(D) relative refractory period

(E) absolute refractory period

(B) The time period defined in the question is the latent period.

90. The energy for muscular contraction may come from each of the following EXCEPT

(A) ATP

(B) creatine phosphate

(C) glycolysis

(D) complete oxidation of glucose

(E) urea

(E) Urea is a nitrogenous waste product and does not serve as an energy source for muscular contraction. ATP, formed by glycolysis and the complete oxidation of glucose, serves as the immediate source of energy. Creatine phosphate serves to re-form ATP within the muscle by transferring the high energy phosphate group to ADP.

Questions 91–92 It has been demonstrated that hormones within plants can exert influences on plant growth. The chart below depicts the differential sensitivity of various parts of a certain plant to changing levels of plant growth regulators. These results are based on laboratory studies and have not been confirmed on plants growing freely in nature.

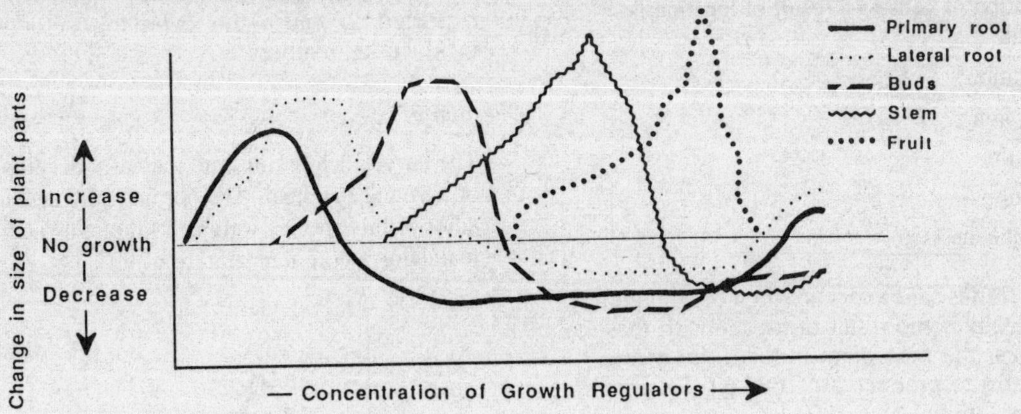

91. Which of the following will grow with the least amount of plant growth regulators relative to the other plant parts?

(A) Primary root

(B) Lateral root

(C) Buds

(D) Stem

(E) Fruit

(A) The primary root demonstrates the greatest sensitivity to low amounts of growth regulators.

92. The terminal bud of a stem is known to produce apical dominance in this plant. Which of the following best describes this condition?

(A) As the fruit of the plant grows larger, stem elongation occurs.

(B) As the fruit of the plant stops growing, stem elongation occurs.

(C) Primary root growth precedes lateral root growth.

(D) As stem elongation occurs, lateral bud growth is inhibited.

(E) As stem growth decreases, terminal bud growth increases.

(D) Apical dominance exists when the terminal bud of a stem inhibits lateral bud growth during stem elongation.

Questions 93–94

Interactions between mesoderm and its overlying epidermis can have profound effects. Several experiments using the embryonic chicken demonstrate the results of such interactions. In the first experiment, mesoderm from a feathered region of the chick is combined with ectoderm from a nonfeathered region. As a result, the ectoderm produces feathers. In a second experiment, mesoderm from a scaled area is combined with ectoderm from a feather-producing area. The result is ectoderm which produces scales.

93. Differentiation of cells as a result of location is best termed

(A) integration

(B) ingression

(C) restriction

(D) induction

(E) morphogenesis

(D) Induction is said to occur when the differentiation of cells is the result of location. In these experiments, the mesoderm induces the overlying ectoderm to produce a certain type of ectodermal derivative.

94. If ectoderm from the wing area is supplanted for the ectoderm covering leg mesoderm, which of the following is most likely to occur? Use the above experiments as a guide.

(A) Ectoderm will produce scales.

(B) Ectoderm will produce wing feathers.

(C) Ectoderm will produce leg feathers.

(D) Ectoderm will produce no feathers.

(E) Ectoderm will produce both scales and wing feathers.

(C) As outlined in the experiments, the mesoderm determines the type of growth the ectoderm will produce. Thus, the leg mesoderm would be expected to cause the overlying ectoderm to produce leg feathers.

Question 95

The curves below illustrate the early development of a young mammal. The normal fully developed adult of this species weighs 8 kilograms and maintains a core temperature of 99°F.

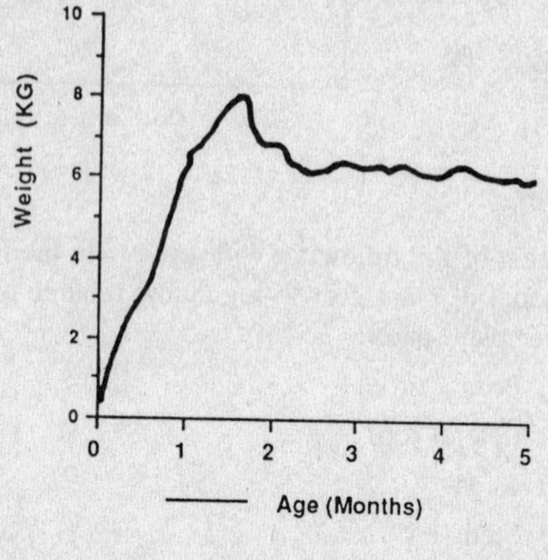

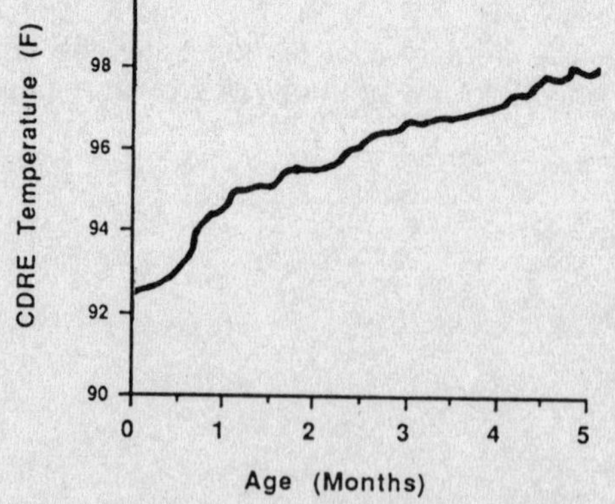

95. Based on the data presented for this animal, which of the following is a reasonable conclusion?

(A) Temperature regulation occurs as the animal's activity level increases.

(B) Weight increases linearly over the first three months of development.

(C) Maximum weight is attained after adult temperature regulation is achieved.

(D) Adult weight is attained prior to adult temperature regulation.

(E) Core temperature and body weight are inversely related over the first three months of development.

(D) Answer choice (D) represents the only reasonable conclusion that can be drawn from the data supplied. Answer choices (B), (C), and (E) are not in agreement with the data. Activity level is not discussed, so answer choice (A) cannot represent a reasonable conclusion of the data.

Chemistry Test

Lesson 10

Chemistry Test

The Chemistry Test consists of 85 multiple-choice questions. In terms of its overall level of difficulty, the test is intended for students who have had a one-year introductory course in chemistry of the sort that is included in a college preparatory curriculum.

The following table summarizes the topics tested and the approximate number of questions for each:

Topics Tested	Approximate Number of Questions
I. Descriptive Chemistry	13–14
II. Atomic Theory and Structure	11–12
III. Stoichiometry	8–9
IV. Chemical Bonding and Molecular Structure	8–9
V. Acids and Bases	7–8
VI. States of Matter	7–8
VII. Oxidation and Reduction	5–6
VIII. Laboratory Procedures	5–6
IX. Solutions	5–6
X. Equilibrium	4–5
XI. Thermodynamics	3–4
XII. Reaction Rates	1–2
TOTAL	85

Although 85 questions is a lot to answer in an hour, that is not a large number of questions when compared with the amount of information that is conveyed in a full-year course in chemistry. For this reason, not everything you learned in chemistry can be the basis for a test question. Conversely, you may encounter some questions that test areas not emphasized in your course. The outline of important concepts (below) is intended to help you refresh your memory in a general way about the concepts you learned in your chemistry course.

Questions Used in the Chemistry Test

The Chemistry Test uses several different question formats, and you should be familiar with these before you do the practice test contained in this book.

Classification Questions

This type of question uses the same set of answer choices for several items.

EXAMPLE:

Questions 1–4 refer to the following elements:

(A) Li

(B) Si

(C) K

(D) Pb

(E) O

1. Which element has the lowest first ionization energy?

2. Which element has the highest electronegativity?

3. Which element can form tetrahalides?

4. Which element has the largest atomic radius?

These four questions require knowledge about how certain properties of elements vary within the periodic table. The first question deals with the property of ionization energy. Group IA elements have the lowest first ionization energies within a given period; also, ionization energy decreases from top to bottom within a given group. Using these two statements one can determine that K (potassium) has the lowest first ionization energy.

The second question requires one to know how the property of electronegativity varies in the periodic table. Electronegativity increases from left to right in the periodic table. O, oxygen, a member of group VIA, has the highest electronegativity.

To answer the third question one must examine the valence characteristics of the elements listed. Si, silicon, which is a group IVA element, has four valence electrons that it can share with four halogen atoms to form a tetrahalide.

Question four deals with the property of atomic radius; atomic radius decreases from left to right in the periodic table but increases from top to bottom. Pb, lead, since it is so near the bottom of the table, has the largest atomic radius.

Roman Numeral Questions

For this type of question, the answer choices are always a mix of Roman numeral statements.

EXAMPLE:

In order to calculate the volume of an ideal gas given one set of conditions, one must know which of the following?

I. Pressure of the gas
II. Number of moles of the gas
III. Temperature of the gas

(A) I only
(B) I and II only
(C) I and III only
(D) II and III only
(E) I, II, and III

The correct answer to this item is (A). This question requires knowledge about the fundamental equations of ideal gases. Using the equation $PV = nRT$, one can solve for V: $V = nRT/P$. By looking up the value for the gas constant, R, one can plug in values for temperature, pressure, and moles to determine the volume of the gas.

Relationship Analysis Questions

This type of question consists of two statements. The first makes an assertion of fact while the second proposes an explanation for it. The tricky thing about this type of question is that either or even both statements may be FALSE!

Your answers to this type of question must be entered on a special section (labeled "Chemistry") in the lower left-hand corner of page 2 of your answer sheet. The oval spaces for these questions are numbered beginning with 101 and must be coded according to the following directions:

Directions: Each question on page 370 consists of two statements. Each statement in the left-hand column is referred to as I, and each statement in the right-hand column as II. For each question, determine whether I is true or false *and* whether II is true or false and fill in the corresponding T and F oval spaces on your answer sheet. *If, but only if, statement II is a correct explanation of statement I, darken the oval space labeled CE.*

EXAMPLES:

Assertions (I)		Reasons (II)
Bubbling oxygen gas through a saturated solution of $ZnCO_3$ will cause the sparingly soluble salt to precipitate	BECAUSE	the solubility product constant for this compound is proportional to $[O_2]^{3/2}$.

I II CE
Ⓣ Ⓕ Ⓣ Ⓕ ⒸⒺ

The assertion in this question deals with a saturated solution of a sparingly soluble salt. The assertion implies that $ZnCO_3$ dissolves into Zn^{+2}, C^{+4}, and $3O^{-2}$; this implication is false. $ZnCO_3$ dissolves to form one Zn^{+2} and one CO_3^{-2} so O_2 cannot function as a common ion in this situation. Likewise, the reason is also false because the solubility product constant for this compound is $K_{sp} = [Zn^{+2}]\ [CO_3^{-2}]$.

The addition of 400mL of 2M H_2SO_4 to 800mL of 1M NaOH will result in a solution with neutral pH	BECAUSE	equal numbers of equivalents of a strong acid and a strong base react to form H_2O and a neutral salt; this reaction consumes the added H^+ and OH^-.

I II CE
Ⓣ Ⓕ Ⓣ Ⓕ ⒸⒺ

The question tests one's ability to apply the concepts of concentration, normality, and titration (neutralization). The number of equivalents of acid added must equal the number of equivalents of base present in order to produce a solution with pH = 7, and the salt produced, in this case Na_2SO_4, must not contain ions that are weak acids or weak bases. Two molar H_2SO_4 is 4N with respect to $[H^+]$ while 1M KOH is 1N with respect to $[OH^-]$. Therefore, only 200mL of 2M H_2SO_4 would be required to neutralize 800mL of 1M NaOH. So the assertion is false, and the reason is true.

When a beam of alpha particles (^4_2He) is fired at high velocity against a sheet of gold foil, a few particles are scattered at large angles	BECAUSE	the alpha particles are scattered when they hit an electron because an electron is so small very few alpha particles collide with one.

I II CE
Ⓣ Ⓕ Ⓣ Ⓕ ⒸⒺ

This question refers to Rutherford's famous experiment that provided seminal knowledge about atomic structure. The assertion expresses what Rutherford did and observed. Rutherford made this observation because alpha particles that collided with the heavy, compact nuclei were scattered at large angles. Since the nucleus is very compact few alpha particles are scattered at large angles. An electron is much too small to scatter an alpha particle at a large angle.

5-Choice Completion Questions

Finally, the Chemistry Test also uses ordinary multiple-choice questions:

EXAMPLE:

$\_\_Cu(OH)_2 + \_\_N_2H_4 = \_\_Cu + \_\_N_2 + \_\_H_2O$

When 96g of N_2H_4 are consumed how many grams of H_2O are produced?

(A) 164g
(B) 180g
(C) 216g
(D) 236g
(E) 256g

(C) The first step in solving a stoichiometric problem is to balance the equation. The balanced equation is $2Cu(OH)_2 + N_2H_4 = 2Cu + N_2 + 4H_2O$. From the balanced equation we see that for every mole of N_2H_4 consumed there are 4 moles of H_2O produced. The amount of N_2H_4 consumed is 96g; the molecular weight of $N_2H_4 = 32$. Therefore, three moles of N_2H_4 are consumed. If three moles of N_2H_4 are consumed, then 12 moles of water are produced. Twelve moles of water is 216g.

EXAMPLE:

If the total kinetic energy of one mole of helium molecules at 300°K is 3.74×10^{10} ergs, then what is the total kinetic energy of two moles of oxygen molecules at 300°K? (Atomic weights: $He_2 = 4$; $O_2 = 32$)

(A) 7.84×10^{10} ergs
(B) 1.50×10^{11} ergs
(C) 6.00×10^{11} ergs
(D) 1.87×10^{10} ergs
(E) 1.00×10^{12} ergs

(A) To solve this problem one must remember that the total kinetic energy of an ideal gas depends only on the number of moles of gas present and not the molecular weight of the gas. Using the formula of kinetic energy = 3/2nRT where n equals the number of moles, one can calculate that two moles of O_2 have twice the kinetic energy of one mole of He_2 at the same temperature.

EXAMPLE:

A known volume of nitrogen takes 15 seconds to diffuse through a small pinhole under constant pressure. The same volume of an unknown gas, X, takes 30 seconds to diffuse through the pinhole under identical conditions. What is the molecular weight of gas X?

(A) 65
(B) 82
(C) 100
(D) 112
(E) 130

(D) This problem is an application of the equation:

$$\frac{time\ A}{time\ B} = \frac{\sqrt{MW_A}}{\sqrt{MW_B}}$$

Using the given information, we have:

$$\frac{time\ X}{time\ N_2} = 30\ sec./15\ sec. = 2 = \frac{\sqrt{MW_X}}{\sqrt{MW_{N2}}}$$

Squaring the equation $4 = \frac{MW_X}{28}$

$4 \cdot 28 = 112 = MW_X$

EXAMPLE:

Fifteen kcal is added to 100g of ice at −20°C. After equilibrium is reached, one would predict: (specific heat of water = 1.0kcal/kg°C; specific heat of ice = 0.5kcal/kg°C; heat of fusion of water = 80kcal/kg; heat of vaporization of water = 540kcal/kg)

(A) 0.1kg of water at 50°C

(B) 0.1kg of water at 60°C

(C) 0.1kg of water at 70°C

(D) 0.1kg of water vapor at 100°C

(E) 0.1kg of water vapor at 110°C

(B) This type of question is usually solved in the following manner:

1. .1kg of ice at −20°C → .1kg of ice at 0°C (melting temperature of ice). This requires .1kg × .5kcal/kg°C × 20°C = 1kcal and leaves 14kcal of unused heat.

2. .1kg of ice at 0°C → .1kg of water at 0°C (remember there is no temperature change during a change of state). This requires .1kg x 80kcal/kg = 8kcal and leaves 6kcal.

3. .1kg of water at 0°C → .1kg of water at ?°C

6kcal/(.1kg × 1kcal/kg°C) = 60°C.

There is enough heat to raise the temperature of the water to 60°C.

EXAMPLE:

A compound is 16% aluminum, 28% sulfur, and 56% oxygen. If the molecular weight is 342, then the molecular formula is (Atomic weights: Al = 27; S = 32; O = 16)

(A) $Al_2(SO_4)_2$

(B) $Al(SO_4)_3$

(C) $Al_3(SO_4)_2$

(D) $Al_2(SO_4)_3$

(E) $Al_2S_3O_8$

(D) The easiest way to solve this problem is to assume that there is 100g of the unknown compound:

100g of compound
= 16.0g of Al/27g/mole = .6 moles of Al

= 28.0g of S/32g/mole = .875 moles of S

= 56.0g of O/16g/mole = 3.5 moles of O

therefore the empirical formula = $Al_{.6}S_{.875}O_{3.5}$ (divide the subscripts by .6) or $AlS_{1.5}O_6$.

Empirical weight = (1 × 27) + (1.5 × 32) + (6 × 16) = 171

Molecular weight = 342

So, the molecular formula = $Al_2S_3O_{12}$ or $Al_2(SO_4)_3$.

EXAMPLE:

All of the following statements apply to ideal gases EXCEPT

(A) the motion of ideal gas molecules is random

(B) no kinetic energy is lost when gas molecules collide

(C) there are attractive and repulsive forces between gas molecules

(D) the gas molecules occupy negligible volume

(E) the total kinetic energy of an ideal gas is only a function of its temperature

(C) All of the above statements apply to ideal gases except (C). It is assumed that no attractive or repulsive forces exist between ideal gas molecules.

Chemistry Test Answer Sheet

1	A	B	C	D	E
2	A	B	C	D	E
3	A	B	C	D	E
4	A	B	C	D	E
5	A	B	C	D	E
6	A	B	C	D	E
7	A	B	C	D	E
8	A	B	C	D	E
9	A	B	C	D	E
10	A	B	C	D	E
11	A	B	C	D	E
12	A	B	C	D	E
13	A	B	C	D	E
14	A	B	C	D	E
15	A	B	C	D	E
16	A	B	C	D	E
17	A	B	C	D	E
18	A	B	C	D	E
19	A	B	C	D	E
20	A	B	C	D	E
21	A	B	C	D	E
22	A	B	C	D	E
23	A	B	C	D	E
24	A	B	C	D	E
25	A	B	C	D	E
26	A	B	C	D	E
27	A	B	C	D	E
28	A	B	C	D	E
29	A	B	C	D	E
30	A	B	C	D	E
31	A	B	C	D	E
32	A	B	C	D	E
33	A	B	C	D	E
34	A	B	C	D	E
35	A	B	C	D	E
36	A	B	C	D	E
37	A	B	C	D	E
38	A	B	C	D	E
39	A	B	C	D	E
40	A	B	C	D	E
41	A	B	C	D	E
42	A	B	C	D	E
43	A	B	C	D	E

44	A	B	C	D	E
45	A	B	C	D	E
46	A	B	C	D	E
47	A	B	C	D	E
48	A	B	C	D	E
49	A	B	C	D	E
50	A	B	C	D	E
51	A	B	C	D	E
52	A	B	C	D	E
53	A	B	C	D	E
54	A	B	C	D	E
55	A	B	C	D	E
56	A	B	C	D	E
57	A	B	C	D	E
58	A	B	C	D	E
59	A	B	C	D	E
60	A	B	C	D	E
61	A	B	C	D	E
62	A	B	C	D	E
63	A	B	C	D	E
64	A	B	C	D	E
65	A	B	C	D	E
66	A	B	C	D	E
67	A	B	C	D	E
68	A	B	C	D	E
69	A	B	C	D	E
70	A	B	C	D	E
71	A	B	C	D	E
72	A	B	C	D	E
73	A	B	C	D	E
74	A	B	C	D	E
75	A	B	C	D	E
76	A	B	C	D	E
77	A	B	C	D	E
78	A	B	C	D	E
79	A	B	C	D	E
80	A	B	C	D	E
81	A	B	C	D	E
82	A	B	C	D	E
83	A	B	C	D	E
84	A	B	C	D	E
85	A	B	C	D	E

	I		II		CE
101	T	F	T	F	CE
102	T	F	T	F	CE
103	T	F	T	F	CE
104	T	F	T	F	CE
105	T	F	T	F	CE
106	T	F	T	F	CE
107	T	F	T	F	CE
108	T	F	T	F	CE
109	T	F	T	F	CE
110	T	F	T	F	CE
111	T	F	T	F	CE
112	T	F	T	F	CE
113	T	F	T	F	CE
114	T	F	T	F	CE
115	T	F	T	F	CE

CHEMISTRY TEST

Part A

Directions: Each set of lettered answer choices below refers to the numbered questions, formulas, or statements following. Select the one lettered answer choice that best answers or fits each question, formula or statement and then darken the corresponding circle on the answer sheet. An answer choice may be used once, more than once, or not at all in a given set.

Questions 1–4

(A) Pipette

(B) Manometer

(C) Balance

(D) Calorimeter

(E) Galvanometer

Match the definitions given below with the appropriate piece of laboratory equipment.

1. Used to measure the pressure of liquids and gases
2. Used to measure small electric currents
3. Used to measure a specific volume of liquid
4. Used to measure heat

Questions 5–8

(A) Pyramidal

(B) Trigonal, planar

(C) Linear

(D) Tetrahedral

(E) Bent (V-shaped)

From the choices above, choose the shape that best describes each of the following molecules:

5. CH_4
6. AlH_3
7. CO_2
8. H_2Se

Questions 9–12

(A) CH_3COOH

(B) H_2S

(C) $C_{10}H_8$

(D) $CH_3(CH_2)_{12}COOH$

(E) H_2CO_3

Select the compound that best matches the following statements:

9. A constituent of mothballs
10. A component of vinegar
11. This compound produces the bubbles in soda
12. This compound smells like rotten eggs

Questions 13–15

(A) $BCl_3 + Cl^- = BCl_4^-$

(B) $HCN + H_2O = H_3O^+ + CN^-$

(C) $H_2O_2 + 2Br^- + 2H^+ = 2H_2O + Br_2$

(D) $2NH_3(g) = N_2(g) + 3H_2(g)$

(E) $2NaCl + CaSO_4 = Na_2SO_4 + CaCl_2$

Match the statements below with the appropriate reaction:

13. Represents a double-displacement reaction
14. Represents an oxidation-reduction reaction
15. Represents a Lewis acid-Lewis base reaction

Questions 16–19

(A) Halogens

(B) Actinides

(C) Transition metals

(D) Group IA alkali metals

(E) Noble gases

From the list above choose the group of elements that best matches the following statements:

16. Within a period these elements have the lowest electron affinity
17. This group of elements is the most inert
18. In general, this group contains the best electrical conductors
19. Within a period these elements have the largest electron affinities

GO ON TO THE NEXT PAGE

Questions 20–22

(A) 0.020 molar KOH

(B) 0.020 molar HNO_3

(C) 0.020 molar $C_6H_{12}O_6$ (glucose)

(D) 0.020 molar $Mg(OH)_2$

(E) 0.020 molar H_2SO_4

These solutions use water as the solvent.

20. Which solution has the highest concentration of H_3^+O ions?

21. Which solution has the highest pH?

22. Which solution has the lowest boiling point?

Questions 23–25 pertain to the graphs below:

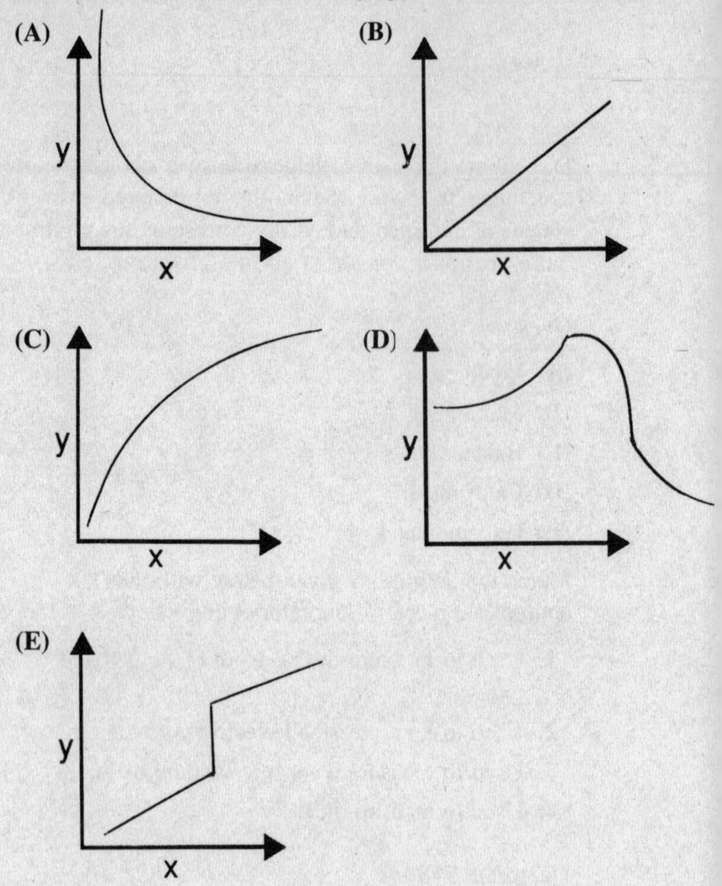

23. Which is the plot of potential energy y versus the reaction coordinate x for an exothermic reaction?

24. Which is the plot of pressure y versus volume x for an ideal gas at a constant temperature?

25. Which is the plot of the amount of the reaction product y versus time x for a first order reaction that is essentially irreversible?

GO ON TO THE NEXT PAGE

Part B

Enter your answers for this part in the special spaces that are numbered beginning with 101 in the space labeled "Chemistry" on your answer sheet.

Directions: Each question below consists of two statements. Each statement in the left-hand column is referred to as I, and each statement in the right-hand column as II. For each question, determine whether I is true or false *and* whether II is true or false and fill in the corresponding T and F oval spaces on your answer sheet. *If, but only if, statement II is a correct explanation of statement I, darken the oval space labeled CE.*

	Assertions (I)		Reasons (II)
101.	The molecule SO_2 has a net dipole	BECAUSE	oxygen has a higher electronegativity than sulfur.
102.	NO_3^- and CO_3^- are planar species	BECAUSE	each ion has three equal bonds distributed equivalently in space.
103.	The heat of fusion plus the heat of vaporization for a particular substance is not equal to the heat of sublimation	BECAUSE	ΔH_{fus}, ΔH_{vap}, and ΔH_{sub} are state functions.
104.	The alkali metals are found in their elemental state in nature	BECAUSE	they react vigorously and completely with many other elements.
105.	A catalyst increases the equilibrium of a reaction	BECAUSE	catalysts only lower the activation energy of the forward reaction.
106.	Water boils at a higher temperature on the moon	BECAUSE	the atmospheric pressure of the moon is less than that on earth.
107.	Element Z with an electronic configuration of $1s^2 2s^2 2p^5$ can be expected to form the compound MgZ_2	BECAUSE	each atom of Z needs two electrons to fill its valence shell.

GO ON TO THE NEXT PAGE

	Assertions (I)		Reasons (II)
108.	A reaction with a positive enthalpy and a negative entropy will be spontaneous	BECAUSE	the Gibbs free energy for a spontaneous reaction is negative.
109.	Sodium has a larger atomic radius than phosphorous	BECAUSE	sodium is lighter than phosphorous
110.	The f subshell contains seven orbitals	BECAUSE	the f subshell is defined by the secondary quantum number 3.
111.	The 5s orbital is filled after the 4d orbital	BECAUSE	the 5s orbital has a lower energy than the 4d orbital.
112.	Under the conditions of low pressure and high temperature, the ideal gas laws are inaccurate	BECAUSE	the deviation from the ideal gas law is due to the non-negligible volume of the molecules and the interactions between molecules
113.	In an electrolytic cell, the anode becomes positive and the cathode becomes negative	BECAUSE	anions migrate to the anode and cations migrate to the cathode.
114.	When a piece of Al is dropped into a 1M solution of $MgCl_2$, elemental Mg appears	BECAUSE	al is more readily oxidized than Mg.

Part C

Directions: Each of the following questions or incomplete statements is followed by five possible answers or completions. Select the one choice that is best in each case and then darken the corresponding circle on the answer sheet.

26. In a .1M solution of H_3PO_4 the ionic species present are (besides H_3^+O and OH^-)

(A) $H_2PO_4^-$, HPO_4^{-2}, PO_3^{-3}, PO_2^{-4}

(B) $H_2PO_2^{-3}$, $H_2PO_4^-$, PO_4^{-3}

(C) $H_2PO_4^-$, HPO_3^{-2}, PO_2^{-3}

(D) PO_3^{-4}, PO_4^{-3}, HPO_4^{-2}, $H_2PO_4^-$

(E) $H_2PO_4^-$, HPO_4^{-2}, PO_4^{-3}

27. Which of the following ions is NOT isoelectronic to a noble gas?

(A) Al^{+3}

(B) K^+

(C) Br^-

(D) Co^{+2}

(E) Ba^{+2}

GO ON TO THE NEXT PAGE

28. What volume of .3M H_2SO_4 is needed to completely neutralize 200ml of .75M KOH?

(A) 200ml

(B) 225ml

(C) 250ml

(D) 300ml

(E) 500ml

29. All of the following are true of Co EXCEPT

(A) Co has two primary oxidation states +2 and +3

(B) Co^{+3} is a weak oxidant

(C) Co can form compounds with sulfur

(D) Co can form compounds with arsenic

(E) Co metal has a bluish-white color

30. The electron configuration of Cr is (atomic number = 24)

(A) $1s^2\ 2s^2\ 2p^6\ 3s^2\ 3p^6\ 4s^2\ 4p^4$

(B) $1s^2\ 2s^2\ 2p^6\ 3s^2\ 3p^6\ 3d^6$

(C) $1s^2\ 2s^2\ 2p^6\ 3s^2\ 3p^6\ 3d^4\ 4s^2$

(D) $1s^2\ 2s^2\ 2p^6\ 3s^2\ 3p^6\ 4s^1\ 4p^5$

(E) $1s^2\ 2s^2\ 2p^6\ 3s^2\ 3p^6\ 3d^5\ 4s^1$

31. All of the following are safe laboratory practices EXCEPT

(A) never place a container of liquid on a piece of electrical equipment

(B) turn off a bunsen burner when it is not being used

(C) to dilute an acid, slowly pour water into it

(D) know where the first aid equipment is stored

(E) use toxic chemicals and solvents in a fume hood

32. A solution has a pH = 10; what is the $[OH^-]$?

(A) 1×10^{-4} M

(B) 1×10^{-10} M

(C) 1×10^{-2} M

(D) 1×10^{-6} M

(E) 1×10^{-8} M

33. The oxidation state(s) shared by each of the elements in group IV (C, Si, Ge, Sn, and Pb) is (are)

(A) +2

(B) +4

(C) +2, +4

(D) −2, +2

(E) −4, +4

34. Which of the following compounds is isoelectronic with CO?

(A) H_2

(B) Cl_2

(C) N_2

(D) CO_2

(E) NO_2

35. What is the approximate molarity of water (H_2O)?

(A) 18M

(B) 25M

(C) 55M

(D) 75M

(E) 100M

36. ${}^{14}_{6}C \rightarrow {}^{14}_{7}N^+ + e^-$ This equation is an example of which type of reaction?

(A) Alpha decay

(B) Beta decay

(C) Gamma decay

(D) Fusion

(E) Chemiluminescence

37. Which of the following molecules has the smallest dissociation energy?

(A) Li_2

(B) Na_2

(C) K_2

(D) Rb_2

(E) Cs_2

GO ON TO THE NEXT PAGE

38. All of the following molecules exist EXCEPT

(A) PCl_3
(B) PCl_5
(C) NF_3
(D) NF_5
(E) P_2I_4

39. $C_2H_5OH + 3O_2 = 2CO_2 + 3H_2O$

According to the reaction above, if 5 moles of CO_2 are produced, then which of the following is true? (MW of $C_2H_5OH = 46$)

(A) 115g of C_2H_5OH are consumed.
(B) 58g of C_2H_5OH are consumed.
(C) 192g of O_2 are consumed.
(D) 96g of O_2 are consumed.
(E) 108g of H_2O are produced.

40. $5H_2C_2O_4 + 2KMnO_4 + HCl =$
$10CO_2 + 2MnCl_2 + H_2O + 2KCl$

In the equation above, which species is the oxidant?

(A) C^{+3}
(B) C^{+4}
(C) Mn^{+7}
(D) Mn^{+2}
(E) Cl^-

41. What is the percent composition of CO_2? (Atomic weights: C = 12; O = 16)

(A) 10% C and 90% O
(B) 14% C and 86% O
(C) 18% C and 82% O
(D) 23% C and 77% O
(E) 27% C and 73% O

42. All of the following carbon isotopes are radioactive EXCEPT

(A) ${}^{10}_{6}C$
(B) ${}^{13}_{6}C$
(C) ${}^{14}_{6}C$
(D) ${}^{15}_{6}C$
(E) ${}^{16}_{6}C$

43. $8H^+ + 3CuS + 8NO^{-3} =$
$3SO_4^{-2} + 3Cu^{+2} + 8NO + 4H_2O$

(Atomic weights: CuS = 96; NO = 30)

If 200g of CuS are consumed, then approximately how many grams of NO are produced?

(A) 500g
(B) 400g
(C) 250g
(D) 200g
(E) 160g

44.

Element	Electronegativity
H	2.1
Cl	2.8
Mg	1.2
N	3.1
F	4.1

Given the electronegativities above, which of the following compounds has the bonds with the greatest polarity?

(A) HF
(B) NH_3
(C) HCl
(D) $MgCl_2$
(E) F_2

45. Approximately how many moles of potassium permanganate, $KMnO_4$, are present in 40g of this compound? (Atomic weights: K = 39; Mn = 55; O = 16)

(A) 1 mole
(B) 0.5 mole
(C) 0.25 mole
(D) 0.1 mole
(E) 0.05 mole

46. Of the following compounds, which has the highest boiling point?

(A) $CH_3—CH_3$
(B) $CH_3—CH_2OH$
(C) $CH_3—COOH$
(D) $CH_3—COH$
(E) H_2S

GO ON TO THE NEXT PAGE

47. If 500ml of a .2M NaCl solution is mixed with 200ml of a 1.6M NaCl solution and then diluted to one liter with water, what is the molarity of the resulting solution?

(A) 0.2M

(B) 0.33M

(C) 0.42M

(D) 0.54M

(E) 0.6M

48. Assign oxidation numbers to each atom in NH_4NO_2.

(A) N=4, −4; H=1; O=−2

(B) N=−3; H=1; O=3

(C) N=−1; H=1; O=−2

(D) N=3, −3; H=1; O=−2

(E) N=0; H=1; O=−2

49. A flame test of a particular element gives a persistent yellow color. This element is most likely which of the following?

(A) Pb

(B) Na

(C) Cu

(D) Sr

(E) K

50. Which of the following acids is the weakest?

(A) HF $K_A = 6.8 \times 10^{-4}$

(B) H_3PO_4 $K_A = 7.5 \times 10^{-3}$

(C) HNO_2 $K_A = 4.5 \times 10^{-4}$

(D) CH_3COOH $K_A = 1.8 \times 10^{-5}$

(E) H_2S $K_A = 1.1 \times 10^{-7}$

51. Which of the following is a monounsaturated hydrocarbon, i.e. the compound that contains one carbon-carbon double bond?

(A) C_3H_6

(B) C_2H_2

(C) C_6H_6

(D) C_5H_8

(E) C_2H_6

52. Enough Na_2SO_4 is dissolved in water at 40°C to saturate the solution. When this occurs heat is given off. All of the following statements are true EXCEPT

(A) the enthalpy change of this process is negative

(B) the boiling point of the solution is higher than that of pure water

(C) the freezing point of the solution is lower than that of pure water

(D) if the temperature of the water is lowered, then the solubility of Na_2SO_4 decreases

(E) if the temperature of the water is raised, then the solubility of Na_2SO_4 decreases

53. The equation for the solubility product constant of Ag_2CrO_4 is

(A) $Ksp = [Ag^{+2}] \cdot [CrO_4^{-2}]$

(B) $Ksp = [Ag^+]^2 \cdot [Cr^{+6}] \cdot [O_4^{-8}]$

(C) $Ksp = [Ag^+] \cdot [Cr^{+6}] \cdot [O_4^{-8}]$

(D) $Ksp = [Ag^+]^2 \cdot [CrO_4^{-2}]$

(E) $Ksp = [Ag^+]^2 \cdot [CrO_4^{-2}]^2$

68. What is the molarity of a 30%(vol/vol) solution of H_2SO_4? (Molecular weight of H_2SO_4 = 98; density of H_2SO_4 = 1.8 g/ml)

(A) 1.5M

(B) 2.0M

(C) 3.0M

(D) 4.5M

(E) 5.5M

55. Given: $Mn^{+2} + 2e^- = Mn$ $\quad \varepsilon° = -1.20V$
$Zn^{+2} + 2e^- = Zn$ $\quad \varepsilon° = -0.80V$

What is the expression for the equilibrium constant of the spontaneous oxidation-reduction reaction?

(A) $K_{eq} = .4$

(B) $K_{eq} = .8$

(C) $K_{eq} = 10^{.4/.059}$

(D) $K_{eq} = 10^{.8/.059}$

(E) $K_{eq} = 10^{-.4/.059}$

GO ON TO THE NEXT PAGE

56. The number of moles of ethane that occupies 11 liters at 27°C with a pressure of 3 atmospheres is (R = 0.082 liter-atm/mole K)

(A) $3 \times 27/0.082 \times 11$ moles

(B) $0.082 \times 11/3 \times 300$ moles

(C) $3 \times 11/0.082 \times 300$ moles

(D) $3 \times 0.082/300 \times 11$ moles

(E) $3 \times 11/0.082 \times 27$ moles

57. In qualitative analysis, Hg^{+2} can be separated from Cu^{+2} by the addition of 3M HNO_3 because

(A) $Cu(NO_3)_2$ is less soluble than $Hg(NO_3)_2$

(B) $Hg(NO_3)_2$ is less soluble than $Cu(NO_3)_2$

(C) HgS is less soluble than CuS in 3M HNO_3

(D) CuS is less soluble than HgS in 3M HNO_3

(E) Hg^{+2} is oxidized by 3M HNO_3 whereas Cu^{+2} is not

58. Assume that all the compounds in this problem have identical freezing-point depression constants (K_f). Which of the following would depress the freezing point the most when added to 1 liter of water?

(A) One mole of NaCl

(B) One-half mole of NH_4NO_2

(C) One-half mole of $MgBr_2$

(D) One mole of NH_4NO_2

(E) One mole of $CaCl_2$

59. $\_Fe(OH)_3 + \_(OH^-) + \_ClO^- = \_FeO_4^{-2} + \_Cl^- + \_H_2O$

When the equation above is balanced how many grams of H_2O are produced when 1 mole of $Fe(OH)_3$ is consumed?

(A) 18g

(B) 27g

(C) 36g

(D) 45g

(E) 54g

60. $HPO_4^{-2} + H_2O = H_3O^+ + PO_4^{-3}$

In the equation above which compounds are Brönsted bases?

(A) HPO_4^{-3} and H_2O

(B) H_2O and PO_4^{-3}

(C) H_3O^+ and H_2O

(D) HPO_4^{-2} and PO_4^{-3}

(E) H_3O^+ and PO_4^{-3}

61. 10ml of 1M H_2SO_4 is added dropwise to 100ml of .1M KOH. What is the approximate pH of the solution?

(A) 1

(B) 2

(C) 3

(D) 4

(E) 5

62. Given: $CaO + CO_2 = CaCO_3 + 40kcal/mole$

If 176g of CO_2 are consumed, then how many kcal of heat are released?

(A) 80kcal

(B) 100kcal

(C) 120kcal

(D) 140kcal

(E) 160kcal

63. The pKa of acid X is 5. The pH of a solution containing acid X and its conjugate base is 6. What is the ratio of the concentration of conjugate base to the concentration of acid? (conj. base : acid)

(A) 1:1

(B) 2:1

(C) 5:1

(D) 10:1

(E) 20:1

GO ON TO THE NEXT PAGE

64. When C_2H_6 burns completely in oxygen, which of the following are products?

I. H_2O

II. CO_2

III. Heat

(A) I, II, and III
(B) I and II only
(C) II and III only
(D) I only
(E) III only

65. Given the hypothetical reaction 2A + B = C + 3D, the equilibrium constant for this reaction is

I. directly proportional to the concentration of D cubed

II. inversely proportional to the concentration of A

III. inversely proportional to the concentration of C

(A) I, II, and III
(B) I and II only
(C) II and III only
(D) I only
(E) III only

66. Which of the following factors will initially increase the forward rate of the following exothermic reaction:

$$X \underset{\text{rev}}{\overset{\text{for}}{\rightleftharpoons}} Y + \text{heat}$$

I. Increasing the temperature

II. Increasing the concentration of X

III. Adding a catalyst

(A) I, II, and III
(B) I and II only
(C) II and III only
(D) I only
(E) III only

67. A cation with +2 charge of atomic number 56 and atomic mass 137 contains

I. 54 protons

II. 81 neutrons

III. 54 electrons

(A) I, II, and III
(B) I and II only
(C) II and III only
(D) I only
(E) III only

68. Two moles of electrons can do which of the following:

I. Reduce one mole of Ag^{+} to Ag

II. Reduce one mole of Cu^{+2} to Cu

III. Reduce 2/3 mole of Al^{+3} to Al

(A) I, II, and III
(B) I and II only
(C) II and III only
(D) I only
(E) III only

69. The ionization energy of Argon (Ar) is greater than

I. Chlorine (Cl)

II. Phosphorous (P)

III. Neon (Ne)

(A) I, II, and III
(B) I and II only
(C) II and III only
(D) I only
(E) III only

70. Selenium (Se) may be distinguished from Bromine (Br) by

I. determining the boiling point of each element

II. determining which element reacts with H under the appropriate conditions

III. determining which element reacts with oxygen under the appropriate conditions

(A) I, II, and III

(B) I and II only

(C) II and III only

(D) I only

(E) III only

71. A flask contains oxygen, nitrogen, and helium. There are 5 moles of nitrogen, 4 moles of helium, and 1 mole of oxygen. If the total pressure in the flask is 10,000 torr, then

I. the partial pressure of helium is 5000 torr

II. the partial pressure of nitrogen is 5000 torr

III. the partial pressure of oxygen is 1000 torr

(A) I, II, and III

(B) I and II only

(C) II and III only

(D) I only

(E) III only

S T O P

IF YOU FINISH BEFORE TIME IS CALLED, YOU MAY CHECK YOUR WORK ON THIS TEST ONLY. DO NOT WORK ON ANY OTHER TEST IN THIS BOOK.

Explanatory Answers

Part A

Questions 1–4

(A) Pipette
(B) Manometer
(C) Balance
(D) Calorimeter
(E) Galvanometer

Match the definitions given below with the appropriate piece of laboratory equipment.

1. Used to measure the pressure of liquids and gases

(B) A manometer measures the pressure of a gas or a liquid.

2. Used to measure small electric currents

(E) A galvanometer measures small electric currents.

3. Used to measure a specific volume of liquid

(A) A pipette accurately measures a specific volume of liquid.

4. Used to measure heat

(D) A calorimeter is used to measure the heat produced by a process.

Questions 5–8

(A) Pyramidal
(B) Trigonal, planar
(C) Linear
(D) Tetrahedral
(E) Bent (V-shaped)

From the choices above, choose the shape that best describes each of the following molecules:

5. CH_4

(D) Methane (CH_4) has four equivalent C = O bonds distributed equally in space.

6. AlH_3

(B) Aluminum trihydride has three equivalent bonds distributed equally in space.

7. CO_2

(C) Carbon dioxide has two equal C = O bonds; this molecule is linear.

8. H_2Se

(E) Hydrogen selenide is a bent molecule with a structure similar to that of H_2O because it has two pairs of non-bonding electrons.

Questions 9–12

(A) CH_3COOH
(B) H_2S
(C) $C_{10}H_8$
(D) $CH_3(CH_2)_{12}COOH$
(E) H_2CO_3

Select the compound that best matches the following statements:

9. A constituent of mothballs

(C) $C_{10}H_8$ is naphthalene, and it is found in mothballs giving them their characteristic smell.

10. A component of vinegar

(A) Acetic acid is the major acid component of vinegar.

11. This compound produces the bubbles in soda

(E) Carbonic acid decomposes into $CO_2 + H_2O$ to produce bubbles.

12. This compound smells like rotten eggs

(B) Hydrogen sulfide is produced when eggs rot, and it is responsible for the "rotten egg" smell.

Questions 13–15

(A) $BCl_3 + Cl^- = BCl_4^-$

(B) $HCN + H_2O = H_3O^+ + CN^-$

(C) $H_2O_2 + 2Br^- + 2H^+ = 2H_2O + Br_2$

(D) $2NH_3(g) = N_2(g) + 3H_2(g)$

(E) $2NaCl + CaSO_4 = Na_2SO_4 + CaCl_2$

Match the statements below with the appropriate reaction:

13. Represents a double-displacement reaction

(E) This is a double-displacement reaction: two compounds react to form two different compounds.

14. Represents an oxidation-reduction reaction

(C) In this reaction $2Br^-$ ions are oxidized to Br_2 while $2O^-$ atoms are reduced to $2O^{-2}$ atoms.

15. Represents a Lewis acid-Lewis base reaction

(A) BCl_3 is a Lewis acid, and Cl^- is a Lewis base.

Questions 16–19

(A) Halogens

(B) Actinides

(C) Transition metals

(D) Group IA alkali metals

(E) Noble gases

From the list above choose the group of elements that best matches the following statements:

16. Within a period these elements have the lowest electron affinity

(D) Group I metals have only one valence electron which they give up very easily to form a cation with a full outer shell.

17. This group of elements is the most inert

(E) The Noble gases have completely filled outer shells which are stable; therefore, they rarely react with other elements.

18. In general, this group contains the best electrical conductors

(C) Because of the ease at which electrons can flow through these elements, the best electrical conductors are metals. Those with outstanding conductivity are Cu, Ag, and Au.

19. Within a period these elements have the largest electron affinities

(A) The halogens require only one electron to fill their outer shells; since a full outer shell is stable, much binding energy can be released when halogens acquire one electron.

Questions 20–22

(A) 0.020 molar KOH

(B) 0.020 molar HNO_3

(C) 0.020 molar $C_6H_{12}O_6$ (glucose)

(D) 0.020 molar $Mg(OH)_2$

(E) 0.020 molar H_2SO_4

These solutions use water as the solvent.

20. Which solution has the highest concentration of H_3^+O ions?

(E) This problem requires that one be able to identify compounds that are acids and use the concepts of molarity and normality. By using the concept of normality, one knows that a .02M H_2SO_4 solution has a $[H_3^+O]$ = .04M while a .02M HNO_3 solution has a $[H_3^+O]$ = .02M.

21. Which solution has the highest pH?

(D) The .02M $Mg(OH)_2$ solution contains .04M OH^- ions; this is twice as much as that contained in the .02M KOH solution.

22. Which solution has the lowest boiling point?

(C) Knowledge of the colligative properties of solutions is required for this question. The solution with the lowest number of particles per liter of solvent will have the lowest boiling point elevation. All the acids and bases dissociate into two or three particles whereas glucose is a undissociating molecule.

Questions 23–25 pertain to the graphs below:

(A)

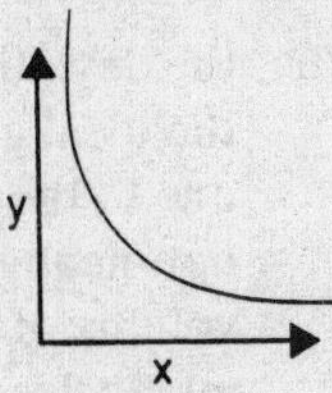

(B)

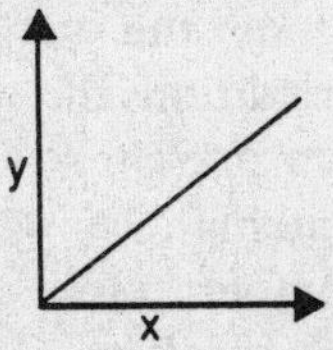

(C)

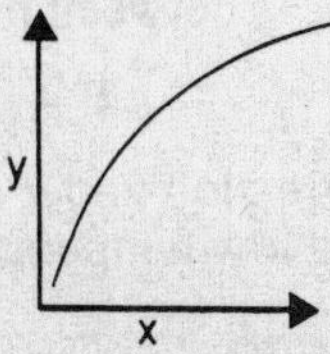

(D)

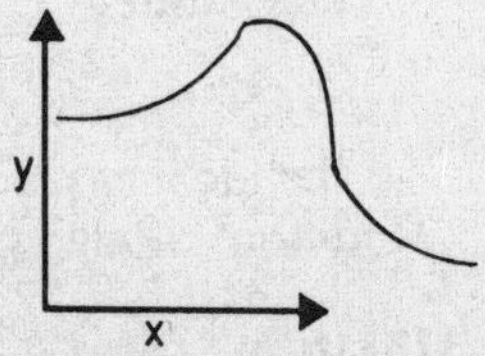

(E)

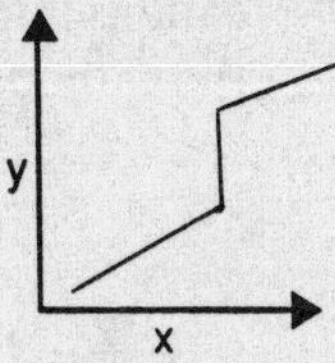

23. Which is the plot of potential energy *y* versus the reaction coordinate *x* for an exothermic reaction?

(D)

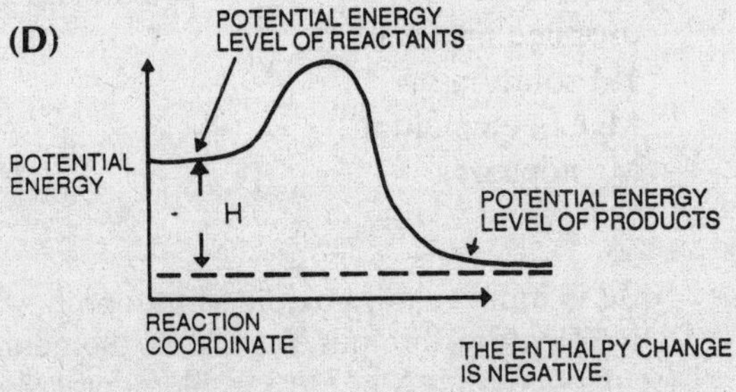

24. Which is the plot of pressure *y* versus volume *x* for an ideal gas at a constant temperature?

(A) Given that T is constant, we know that for an ideal gas $P_1 \cdot V_1 = P_2 \cdot V_2$. The curve fitting this equation is (A).

25. Which is the plot of the amount of the reaction product *y* versus time *x* for a first order reaction that is essentially irreversible?

(C) The rate equation for a first order reaction is $-dS/dt = K_1 \cdot S$ where K_1 is the first order rate constant. The solution to this rate equation is $S_t = S_o \cdot e^{-K_1 t}$ which gives the amount of substrate remaining at any time value for t. Therefore, the amount of product at time = t is $S_o - S_o \cdot e^{-K_1 t}$ and curve C fits this equation.

Part B

Assertions (I)		Reasons (II)
101. The molecule SO_2 has a net dipole	BECAUSE	oxygen has a higher electronegativity than sulfur.

T **F**

The correct reason is because the molecule is non-linear. Polar bonds are not sufficient to give a molecule a net dipole.

102. NO_3^- and CO_3^- are planar species	BECAUSE	each ion has three equal bonds distributed equivalently in space.

T **T** **CE**

Both statements are true and statement II is the correct explanation of statement I.

103. The heat of fusion plus the heat of vaporization for a particular substance is not equal to the heat of sublimation	BECAUSE	ΔH_{fus}, H_{vap}, and H_{sub} are state functions.

F **T**

$\Delta H_{fus} + \Delta H_{vap} = \Delta H_{sub}$

104. The alkali metals are found in their elemental state in nature	BECAUSE	they react vigorously and completely with many other elements.

F **T**

The alkali metals are never found in their elemental state in nature because the second statement is true.

105. A catalyst increases the equilibrium of a reaction	BECAUSE	catalysts only lower the activation energy of the forward reaction.

F **F**

Catalysts do not alter equilibrium constants. They lower the activation energy of both the forward and backward reactions.

Assertions (I)		Reasons (II)
106. Water boils at a higher temperature on the moon	BECAUSE	the atmospheric pressure of the moon is less than that on earth.
F		T

Water would boil at a lower temperature on the moon.

Assertions (I)		Reasons (II)
107. Element Z with an electronic configuration of $1s^2\,2s^2\,2p^5$ can be expected to form the compound MgZ_2	BECAUSE	each atom of Z needs two electrons to fill its valence shell.
T		F

Element Z needs only one electron to fill its outer orbital.

Assertions (I)		Reasons (II)
108. A reaction with a positive enthalpy and a negative entropy will be spontaneous	BECAUSE	the Gibbs free energy for a spontaneous reaction is negative.
F		T

A reaction with positive enthalpy and a negative entropy will always be non-spontaneous.

Assertions (I)		Reasons (II)
109. Sodium has a larger atomic radius than phosphorous	BECAUSE	sodium is lighter than phosphorous.
T		F

Phosphorous has a smaller atomic radius because the increase in nuclear charge for electrons filling the same energy level pulls the orbiting electrons closer to the nucleus.

Assertions (I)		Reasons (II)
110. The f subshell contains seven orbitals	BECAUSE	the f subshell is defined by the secondary quantum number 3.
T		T CE

Both statements are true and statement II is the correct explanation of statement I.

Assertions (I)		Reasons (II)
111. The 5s orbital is filled after the 4d orbital	BECAUSE	the 5s orbital has a lower energy than the 4d orbital.
F		T

5s is filled before 4d.

Assertions (I)		Reasons (II)
112. Under the conditions of low pressure and high temperature, the ideal gas laws are inaccurate	BECAUSE	the deviation from the ideal gas law is due to the non-negligible volume of the molecules and the interactions between molecules
F		T

The ideal gas laws need correction under conditions of high pressure and low temperature.

Assertions (I)		Reasons (II)
113. In an electrolytic cell, the anode becomes positive and the cathode becomes negative	BECAUSE	anions migrate to the anode and cations migrate to the cathode.
T		T

The anode becomes positive because it loses electrons; therefore, anions migrate toward it and vice versa for the cathode.

Assertions (I)		Reasons (II)
114. When a piece of Al is dropped into a 1M solution of $MgCl_2$, elemental Mg appears	BECAUSE	Al is more readily oxidized than Mg.
F		F

Mg is more readily oxidized (remember relative electron affinities) than Al; so elemental Al can not reduce Mg^{+2} to Mg. Elemental Mg can reduce Al^{+3}.

Part C

26. In a .1M solution of H_3PO_4 the ionic species present are (besides H_3^+O and OH^-)

(A) $H_2PO_4^-$, HPO_4^{-2}, PO_3^{-3}, PO_2^{-4}

(B) $H_2PO_2^{-3}$, $H_2PO_4^-$, PO_4^{-3}

(C) $H_2PO_4^-$, HPO_3^{-2}, PO_2^{-3}

(D) PO_3^{-4}, PO_4^{-3}, HPO_4^{-2}, $H_2PO_4^-$

(E) $H_2PO_4^-$, HPO_4^{-2}, PO_4^{-3}

(E) Phosphoric acid has three protons it can donate; therefore, it can form three anionic species.

27. Which of the following ions is NOT isoelectronic to a noble gas?

(A) Al^{+3}

(B) K^{+}

(C) Br^{-}

(D) Co^{+2}

(E) Ba^{+2}

(D) All the ions have noble gas configurations except Co^{+2}.

28. What volume of .3M H_2SO_4 is needed to completely neutralize 200ml of .75M KOH?

(A) 200ml

(B) 225ml

(C) 250ml

(D) 300ml

(E) 500ml

(C) Using the formula $V_1 \cdot N_1 = V_2 \cdot N_2$ where V = volume and N = normality, the volume of .3M H_2SO_4 required is 250ml.

29. All of the following are true of Co EXCEPT

(A) Co has two primary oxidation states +2 and +3

(B) Co^{+3} is a weak oxidant

(C) Co can form compounds with sulfur

(D) Co can form compounds with arsenic

(E) Co metal has a bluish-white color

(B) Co^{+3} is a strong oxidant: $Co^{+3} + e^{-} = Co^{+2}$ $\varepsilon° = 1.84V$.

30. The electron configuration of Cr is (atomic number = 24)

(A) $1s^2\ 2s^2\ 2p^6\ 3s^2\ 3p^6\ 4s^2\ 4p^4$

(B) $1s^2\ 2s^2\ 2p^6\ 3s^2\ 3p^6\ 3d^6$

(C) $1s^2\ 2s^2\ 2p^6\ 3s^2\ 3p^6\ 3d^4\ 4s^2$

(D) $1s^2\ 2s^2\ 2p^6\ 3s^2\ 3p^6\ 4s^1\ 4p^5$

(E) $1s^2\ 2s^2\ 2p^6\ 3s^2\ 3p^6\ 3d^5\ 4s^1$

(E) Using Hund's rule, a half-filled orbital is more stable than a full orbital. The configuration of $3d^5$ and $4s^1$ maximizes the number of half-filled orbitals. Remember that 4s is filled before 3d. Cr has no 4p electrons.

31. All of the following are safe laboratory practices EXCEPT

(A) never place a container of liquid on a piece of electrical equipment

(B) turn off a bunsen burner when it is not being used

(C) to dilute an acid, slowly pour water into it

(D) know where the first aid equipment is stored

(E) use toxic chemicals and solvents in a fume hood

(C) To dilute an acid, one slowly pours the acid into the water NOT vice versa.

32. A solution has a pH = 10; what is the $[OH^-]$?

(A) 1×10^{-4} M

(B) 1×10^{-10} M

(C) 1×10^{-2} M

(D) 1×10^{-6} M

(E) 1×10^{-8} M

(A) pH + pOH = 14 and $pOH = -\log[OH^-]$.

33. The oxidation state(s) shared by each of the elements in group IV (C, Si, Ge, Sn, and Pb) is (are)

(A) +2

(B) +4

(C) +2, +4

(D) −2, +2

(E) −4, +4

(C) The group IV elements share in common the +2 and +4 oxidation states.

34. Which of the following compounds is isoelectronic with CO?

(A) H_2

(B) Cl_2

(C) N_2

(D) CO_2

(E) NO_2

(C) Both CO and N_2 have triple bonds and the following electron dot structures:

:C⋮⋮O: :N⋮⋮N:

35. What is the approximate molarity of water (H_2O)?

(A) 18M

(B) 25M

(C) 55M

(D) 75M

(E) 100M

(C) By definition, molarity is moles of substance/liter of solution. Since 1L of H_2O weighs 1000g, we need to determine how many moles of H_2O constitute 1000g; this is 1000g/18g/mole = 55.6 moles.

36. $^{14}_{6}C \rightarrow {}^{14}_{7}N^{+} + e^{-}$ This equation is an example of which type of reaction?

(A) Alpha decay

(B) Beta decay

(C) Gamma decay

(D) Fusion

(E) Chemiluminescence

(B) A decay reaction that emits an electron or a positron is called a beta decay.

37. Which of the following molecules has the smallest dissociation energy?

(A) Li_2

(B) Na_2

(C) K_2

(D) Rb_2

(E) Cs_2

(E) Cesium has the lowest dissociation energy. The bond formed between two cesium atoms is formed by sharing 6s electrons. This bond is formed by orbitals that are far from the nucleus. A 6s bond is weaker than a bond formed by 1s, 2s, . . ., 5s electrons.

38. All of the following molecules exist EXCEPT

(A) PCl_3

(B) PCl_5

(C) NF_3

(D) NF_5

(E) P_2I_4

(D) Phosphorous can combine with the halogens to form PX_3, PX_5, or P_2I_4. Nitrogen forms only NF_3, N_2F_2, N_2F_4, and NCl_3.

39. $C_2H_5OH + 3O_2 = 2CO_2 + 3H_2O$

According to the reaction above, if 5 moles of CO_2 are produced, then which of the following is true? (MW of C_2H_5OH = 46)

(A) 115g of C_2H_5OH are consumed.

(B) 58g of C_2H_5OH are consumed.

(C) 192g of O_2 are consumed.

(D) 96g of O_2 are consumed.

(E) 108g of H_2O are produced.

(A) The equation is multiplied by 2.5. 115g of C_2H_5OH are consumed, 135g of H_2O are produced, and 240g of O_2 are consumed.

40. $5H_2C_2O_4 + 2KMnO_4 + HCl =$
$10CO_2 + 2MnCl_2 + H_2O + 2KCl$

In the equation above, which species is the oxidant?

(A) C^{+3}

(B) C^{+4}

(C) Mn^{+7}

(D) Mn^{+2}

(E) Cl^{-}

(C) An oxidant becomes reduced because it removes electrons from the atom being oxidized. Mn^{+7} is reduced to Mn^{+2} in this reaction.

41. What is the percent composition of CO_2? (Atomic weights: C = 12; O = 16)

(A) 10% C and 90% O

(B) 14% C and 86% O

(C) 18% C and 82% O

(D) 23% C and 77% O

(E) 27% C and 73% O

(E) 12/44 = .27 and 32/44 = .73

42. All of the following carbon isotopes are radioactive EXCEPT

(A) $^{10}_{6}C$

(B) $^{13}_{6}C$

(C) $^{14}_{6}C$

(D) $^{15}_{6}C$

(E) $^{16}_{6}C$

(B) For the lighter elements, stable and nonradioactive nuclei have equal numbers of protons and neutrons. In other words, the ratio of protons to neutrons is close to 1.

43. $8H^+ + 3CuS + 8NO^{-3} =$
$3SO_4^{-2} + 3Cu^{+2} + 8NO + 4H_2O$
(Atomic weights: CuS = 96; NO = 30)

If 200g of CuS are consumed, then approximately how many grams of NO are produced?

(A) 500g

(B) 400g

(C) 250g

(D) 200g

(E) 160g

(E) There are approximately two moles of CuS available to react; for every 2 moles of CuS consumed 5.3 moles of NO will be produced. 5.3moles × 30g/mole = 160g

44.

Element	Electronegativity
H	2.1
Cl	2.8
Mg	1.2
N	3.1
F	4.1

Given the electronegativities above, which of the following compounds has the bond(s) with the greatest polarity?

(A) HF

(B) NH_3

(C) HCl

(D) $MgCl_2$

(E) F_2

(A) This compound has the greatest electronegativity difference between its constituent atoms.

45. Approximately how many moles of potassium permanganate, $KMnO_4$, are present in 40g of this compound? (Atomic weights: K = 39; Mn = 55; O = 16)

(A) 1 mole

(B) 0.5 mole

(C) 0.25 mole

(D) 0.1 mole

(E) 0.05 mole

(C) The molecular weight of $KMnO_4$ is 158g/mole. 40g/158g/mole ≐ .25 mole.

46. Of the following compounds, which has the highest boiling point?

(A) $CH_3—CH_3$

(B) $CH_3—CH_2OH$

(C) $CH_3—COOH$

(D) $CH_3—COH$

(E) H_2S

(E) Remember that the greater the interactions between molecules in a liquid, the higher the boiling point. Compound A, ethane, can only form van der Waals interactions while compound C, acetic acid, can form twó polar hydrogen bonds per molecule. Also, oxygen forms more polar hydrogen bonds than sulfur.

47. If 500ml of a .2M NaCl solution is mixed with 200ml of a 1.6M NaCl solution and then diluted to one liter with water. What is the molarity of the resulting solution?

(A) 0.2M

(B) 0.33M

(C) 0.42M

(D) 0.54M

(E) 0.6M

(C) 0.2moles/liter × 0.5 liters + 1.6moles/liter × 0.2 liters = .1moles + .32moles = .42moles. Final volume = 1 liter.

48. Assign oxidation numbers to each atom in NH_4NO_2.

(A) N = 4, −4; H = 1; O = −2

(B) N = −3; H = 1; O = 3

(C) N = −1; H = 1; O = −2

(D) N = , −3; H = 1; O = −2

(E) N = 0; H = 1; O = −2

(D) The compound dissolves into $(NH_4)^+$ and $(NO_2)^-$ ions, where N = −3, H = 1, N = 3, O = −2.

49. A flame test of a particular element gives a persistent yellow color. This element is most likely which of the following?

(A) Pb

(B) Na

(C) Cu

(D) Sr

(E) K

(B) Sodium yields a persistent yellow color in a flame test.

50. Which of the following acids is the weakest?

(A) HF $K_A = 6.8 \times 10^{-4}$

(B) H_3PO_4 $K_A = 7.5 \times 10^{-3}$

(C) HNO_2 $K_A = 4.5 \times 10^{-4}$

(D) CH_3COOH $K_A = 1.8 \times 10^{-5}$

(E) H_2S $K_A = 1.1 \times 10^{-7}$

(E) The acid with the smallest dissociation constant is the weakest.

51. Which of the following is a monounsaturated hydrocarbon, i.e. the compound that contains one carbon-carbon double bond?

(A) C_3H_6

(B) C_2H_2

(C) C_6H_6

(D) C_5H_8

(E) C_2H_6

(A) A monounsaturated hydrocarbon has the general formula of C_nH_{2n}; C_3H_6 fits this formula.

52. Enough Na_2SO_4 is dissolved in water at 40°C to saturate the solution. When this occurs heat is given off. All of the following statements are true EXCEPT

(A) the enthalpy change of this process is negative

(B) the boiling point of the solution is higher than that of pure water

(C) the freezing point of the solution is lower than that of pure water

(D) if the temperature of the water is lowered, then the solubility of Na_2SO_4 decreases

(E) if the temperature of the water is raised, then the solubility of Na_2SO_4 decreases

(D) Since the solution reaction is exothermic, lowering the temperature of the water will increase the solubility of Na_2SO_4. This is an application of Le Chatlier's principle.

53. The equation for the solubility product constant of Ag_2CrO_4 is

(A) $K_{sp} = [Ag^{+2}] \cdot [CrO_4^{-2}]$

(B) $K_{sp} = [Ag^{+}]^2 \cdot [Cr^{+6}] \cdot [O_4^{-8}]$

(C) $K_{sp} = [Ag^{+}] \cdot [Cr^{+6}] \cdot [O_4^{-8}]$

(D) $K_{sp} = [Ag^{+}]^2 \cdot [CrO_4^{-2}]$

(E) $K_{sp} = [Ag^{+}]^2 \cdot [CrO_4^{-2}]^2$

(D) Solid Ag_2CrO_4 dissociates into $2Ag^+ + CrO_4^{-2}$ ions. K_{sp} is the equilibrium constant for this reaction after eliminating the $[Ag_2CrO_4]$ solid term from the denominator.

54. What is the molarity of a 30%(vol/vol) solution of H_2SO_4? (Molecular weight of $H_2SO_4 = 98$; density of $H_2SO_4 = 1.8$ g/ml)

(A) 1.5M

(B) 2.0M

(C) 3.0M

(D) 4.5M

(E) 5.5M

(E) One liter of solution contains 300ml of H_2SO_4. 300ml of H_2SO_4 weighs 540g. 540g of H_2SO_4 equal 5.5 moles.

55. Given: $Mn^{+2} + 2e^- = Mn \quad \varepsilon° = -1.20V$
$Zn^{+2} + 2e^- = Zn \quad \varepsilon° = -0.80V$

What is the expression for the equilibrium constant of the spontaneous oxidation-reduction reaction?

(A) $K_{eq} = .4$

(B) $K_{eq} = .8$

(C) $K_{eq} = 10^{.4/.059}$

(D) $K_{eq} = 10^{.8/.059}$

(E) $K_{eq} = 10^{-.4/.059}$

(D) A spontaneous oxidation-reduction reaction has a positive so the half-reactions must be combined as:

$Mn + Zn^{+2} = Zn + Mn^{+2} \; \Delta\varepsilon° = .40V$

$K_{eq} = 10^{n\varepsilon°/.059} = 10^{2 \times .4/.059} = 10^{.8/.059}$

n = number of electrons transferred per atom

56. The number of moles of ethane that occupies 11 liters at 27°C with a pressure of 3 atmospheres is (R = 0.082 liter-atm/mole K)

(A) $3 \times 27/0.082 \times 11$ moles

(B) $0.082 \times 11/3 \times 300$ moles

(C) $3 \times 11/0.082 \times 300$ moles

(D) $3 \times 0.082/300 \times 11$ moles

(E) $3 \times 11/0.082 \times 27$ moles

(C) Using PV = nRT, solve for n = PV/RT where T = 300°K.

57. In qualitative analysis, Hg^{+2} can be separated from Cu^{+2} by the addition of 3M HNO_3 because

(A) $Cu(NO_3)_2$ is less soluble than $Hg(NO_3)_2$

(B) $Hg(NO_3)_2$ is less soluble than $Cu(NO_3)_2$

(C) HgS is less soluble than CuS in 3M HNO_3

(D) CuS is less soluble than HgS in 3M HNO_3

(E) Hg^{+2} is oxidized by 3M HNO_3 whereas Cu^{+2} is not

(C) Both Hg^{+2} and Cu^{+2} belong to the acid hydrogen group. HgS is less soluble than CuS in 3M HNO_3.

58. Assume that all the compounds in this problem have identical freezing-point depression constants (K_f). Which of the following would depress the freezing point the most when added to 1 liter of water?

(A) One mole of NaCl

(B) One-half mole of NH_4NO_2

(C) One-half mole of $MgBr_2$

(D) One mole of NH_4NO_2

(E) One mole of $CaCl_2$

(E) Given the assumption, what the question is looking for is the amount of compound that will dissolve to produce the most ions. One mole of $CaCl_2$ produces three moles of ions.

59. __$Fe(OH)_3$ + __(OH^-) + __ClO^- =
__FeO_4^{-2} + __Cl^- + __H_2O

When the equation above is balanced how many grams of H_2O are produced when 1 mole of $Fe(OH)_3$ is consumed?

(A) 18g

(B) 27g

(C) 36g

(D) 45g

(E) 54g

(D) The balanced equation is: $2Fe(OH)_3 + 4(OH^-) + 3ClO^- = 2FeO_4^{-2} + 5H_2O + 3Cl^-$.

For every mole of $Fe(OH)_3$ consumed, 2.5 moles of H_2O are produced.

2.5moles × 18g/mole = 45g.

60. $HPO_4^{-2} + H_2O = H_3O^+ + PO_4^{-3}$

In the equation above which compounds are Brönsted bases?

(A) HPO_4^{-2} and H_2O

(B) H_2O and PO_4^{-3}

(C) H_3O^+ and H_2O

(D) HPO_4^{-2} and PO_4^{-3}

(E) H_3O^+ and PO_4^{-3}

(B) A Brönsted base is a proton acceptor. H_2O is the proton acceptor in the forward reaction, and PO_4^{-3} is the proton acceptor in the reverse reaction.

61. 10ml of 1M H_2SO_4 is added dropwise to 100ml of .1M KOH. What is the approximate pH of the solution?

(A) 1

(B) 2

(C) 3

(D) 4

(E) 5

(A) Since this problem involves a strong acid and strong base one can assume that they dissociate completely. The normality of H_2SO_4 is 2 and that of KOH is 1.

.01l × IM $[H^+]$ × 2 − 0.1l × .1M $[OH^-]$ = .01moles of H^+

.01moles of H^+/.11l = .091M H^+
pH = 1.04

62. Given: CaO + CO_2 = $CaCO_3$ + 40kcal/mole

If 176g of CO_2 are consumed, then how many kcal of heat are released?

(A) 80kcal

(B) 100kcal

(C) 120kcal

(D) 140kcal

(E) 160kcal

(E) If four moles of CO_2 are consumed, then 160kcal of heat are produced.

63. The pKa of acid X is 5. The pH of a solution containing acid X and its conjugate base is 6. What is the ratio of the concentration of conjugate base to the concentration of acid? (conj. base : acid)

(A) 1:1

(B) 2:1

(C) 5:1

(D) 10:1

(E) 20:1

(D) Using the Henderson-Hasselbach equation:

pH = pKa + log [conj. base]/[acid]

6 = 5 + log [conj. base]/[acid]

log[base]/[acid] = 1

[base]/[acid] = 10

64. When C_2H_6 burns completely in oxygen, which of the following are products?

I. H_2O

II. CO_2

III. Heat

(A) I, II, and III

(B) I and II only

(C) II and III only

(D) I only

(E) III only

(A) This problem deals with the combustion of ethane; the products of such a reaction are CO_2, H_2O, and heat.

65. Given the hypothetical reaction 2A + B = C + 3D, the equilibrium constant for this reaction is

I. Directly proportional to the concentration of D cubed.

II. Inversely proportional to the concentration of A.

III. Inversely proportional to the concentration of C.

(A) I, II, and III

(B) I and II only

(C) II and III only

(D) I only

(E) III only

(D) Utilizing the definition of an equilibrium constant one can write:

$K_{eq} = [C] \cdot [D]^3/[A]^2 \cdot [B]$

66. Which of the following factors will initially increase the forward rate of the following exothermic reaction:

$$X \underset{rev}{\overset{for}{\rightleftharpoons}} Y + heat$$

I. Increasing the temperature

II. Increasing the concentration of X

III. Adding a catalyst

(A) I, II, and III
(B) I and II only
(C) II and III only
(D) I only
(E) III only

(C) Increasing the temperature of an exothermic reaction favors the reverse reaction. Raising the concentration of X increases the number of collisions per unit time thereby increasing the rate of the forward reaction. A catalyst lowers the activation energy of the reaction so it increases the rate of the forward reaction.

67. A cation with +2 charge of atomic number 56 and atomic mass 137 contains

I. 54 protons

II. 81 neutrons

III. 54 electrons

(A) I, II, and III
(B) I and II only
(C) II and III only
(D) I only
(E) III only

(C) Atomic number equals the number of protons. Atomic mass equals the number of protons plus neutrons. Atomic number less the charge equals the number of electrons.

68. Two moles of electrons can do which of the following:

I. Reduce one mole of Ag^+ to Ag

II. Reduce one mole of Cu^{+2} to Cu

III. Reduce 2/3 mole of Al^{+3} to Al

(A) I, II, and III
(B) I and II only
(C) II and III only
(D) I only
(E) III only

(C) This is a straightforward stoichiometric question. Two moles of electrons can reduce two moles of Ag^+ to Ag.

69. The ionization energy of Argon (Ar) is greater than

I. Chlorine (Cl)

II. Phosphorous (P)

III. Neon (Ne)

(A) I, II, and III
(B) I and II only
(C) II and III only
(D) I only
(E) III only

(B) In general, ionization energy increases from left to right in the periodic table, and it decreases within a group from top to bottom.

70. Selenium (Se) may be distinguished from Bromine (Br) by

I. determining the boiling point of each element

II. determining which element reacts with H under the appropriate conditions

III. determining which element reacts with oxygen under the appropriate conditions

(A) I, II, and III
(B) I and II only
(C) II and III only
(D) I only
(E) III only

(D) Selenium is a solid at room temperature with a boiling point of 960°K while bromine is a liquid at room temperature with a boiling point of 331°K. Both selenium and bromine react with hydrogen and oxygen to form compounds such as HBr, H_2Se, H_2SeO_3, and BrO_2.

71. A flask contains oxygen, nitrogen, and helium. There are 5 moles of nitrogen, 4 moles of helium, and 1 mole of oxygen. If the total pressure in the flask is 10,000 torr, then

I. the partial pressure of helium is 5000 torr

II. the partial pressure of nitrogen is 5000 torr

III. the partial pressure of oxygen is 1000 torr

(A) I, II, and III

(B) I and II only

(C) II and III only

(D) I only

(E) III only

(C) The partial pressure of a liquid is equal to the mole fraction of the liquid multiplied by the total pressure. The mole fraction of nitrogen is .5, oxygen is .1, and helium is .4.

Physics Test

Lesson 11

Physics Test

The Physics Test consists of 75 multiple-choice questions. In terms of its overall level of difficulty, the test is intended for students who have had the type of one-year introductory course in physics which emphasized a college preparatory curriculum.

The following table summarizes the topics tested and the approximate number of questions for each:

Topics Tested	Approximate Number of Questions
I. Mechanics	30
A. Kinematics (e.g., linear motion, projectile motion, and circular motion)	
B. Dynamics (e.g., Newton's laws, centripetal force, and torque)	
C. Energy and Momentum (e.g., potential and kinetic energy, work, power, and conservation laws)	
D. Miscellaneous (gravity, pressure, simple harmonic motion)	
II. Electricity and Magnetism	15
A. Electrostatics (e.g., Coulomb's law and electric field and potential)	
B. Circuits (e.g., Ohm's law and simple DC current circuits with resistors and capacitors)	
C. Electromagnetism (e.g., magnetic fields and electromagnetic induction)	
III. Optics and Waves	15
A. General Properties (e.g., speed, frequency, and wavelength)	
B. Geometrical Optics (e.g., reflection, refraction, and lenses)	
C. Physical Optics (e.g., interference, polarization, and diffraction)	

Topics Tested	Approximate Number of Questions
IV. Heat, Kinetic Theory, and Thermodynamics	7 or 8
A. Thermal Properties (e.g., temperature, heat transfer, and mechanical equivalent of heat)	
B. Kinetic Theory (e.g., ideal gas law)	
C. Thermodynamics (e.g., first and second laws)	
V. Modern Concepts	7 or 8
A. Atomic (e.g., models and atomic energy levels)	
B. Nuclear (e.g., radioactivity and nuclear reactions)	
C. Relativity (mass-energy equivalence, photons, and photoelectric effect)	
TOTAL	75

Although 75 questions is a lot to answer in an hour, that is not a large number of questions when compared with the amount of information that is conveyed in a full-year course in physics. For this reason, not everything you learned in physics can be the basis for a test question. Conversely, you may encounter some questions that test areas not emphasized in your course.

The following are samples of the types of questions you will encounter on your exam:

EXAMPLE:

A radar signal having a frequency of 3,000 megahertz would have a wavelength of:

(A) 0.001 km.
(B) 0.01 km.
(C) 10 m.
(D) 0.1 m.
(E) 0.01 m.

(D) Wavelength $= \dfrac{\text{speed}}{\text{frequency}}$

3,000 megahertz = 3,000,000,000 cps

Wavelength $= \dfrac{300{,}000 \text{ km/sec}}{3{,}000{,}000{,}000 \text{ cps}}$

Wavelength = .0001 km or .1 m

All other choices are incorrect.

EXAMPLE:

Presuming there are no other outside forces, how much force is necessary to accelerate a 1-kilogram brick 1 meter per second^2?

(A) 0.1 newton
(B) 1.0 newton
(C) 10 newtons
(D) 100 newtons
(E) 1,000 newtons

(B) Using $F = ma$, $F = 1 \text{ kg} \times 1\frac{m}{\text{sec}^2}$. This, by definition, is the force of 1 newton.

EXAMPLE:

At the end of three half-lives, the amount of an 8-g sample of $^{228}_{88}Ra$ that remains undecayed is

(A) 1 g
(B) 2 g
(C) 3 g
(D) 4 g
(E) 6 g

(A) The half-life of a radioactive atom is the time required for one-half the atoms in a given sample to decay. In this sample, at the end of one half-life, 4 g of the radium will remain undecayed. At the end of two half-lives, 2 g will remain undecayed. At the end of three half-lives, only 1 g will remain undecayed.

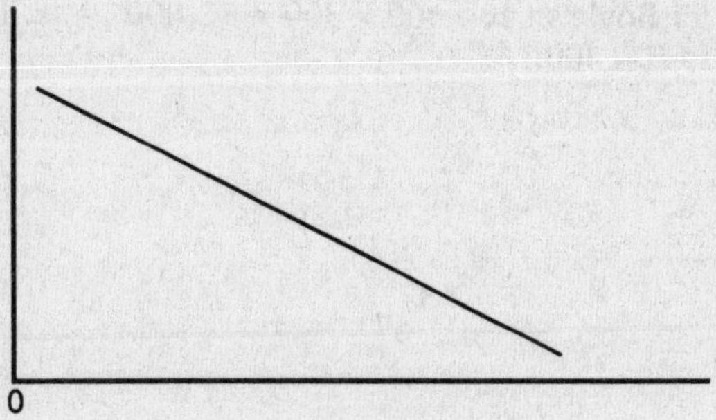

EXAMPLE:

Which of the following could this graph represent?

(A) A vibrating string at its fundamental frequency, where frequency of vibration is represented by the vertical axis and length of string by the horizontal axis
(B) The relationship between force and acceleration, where force (measured in newtons) is represented by the vertical axis and acceleration (meters per second per second) is represented by the horizontal axis
(C) The relationship between work and force, where work (measured in joules) is represented by the vertical axis and force (newtons) is represented by the horizontal axis
(D) The relationship between the energy (represented by the vertical axis) and the wavelength (represented by the horizontal axis) of light waves
(E) The relationship between distance and time of an object moving at a constant rate of speed where time is represented by the horizontal axis and distance by the vertical axis

(D) As the wavelength of a light wave increases, the amount of energy it has decreases. This shows an inversely proportional relationship as shown on the graph.

EXAMPLE:

A lamp is connected to a circuit that has a current of 0.25 amperes powered by a 4.5 V battery. The resistance in the lamp is

(A) 0.0555 ohms
(B) 1.125 ohms
(C) 1.8 ohms
(D) 18 ohms
(E) 112.5 ohms

(D) Substituting using Ohm's Law,

$$R = \frac{V}{I}$$

$$R = \frac{4.5 \text{ V}}{.25 \text{ amp.}} = 18 \text{ ohms.}$$

EXAMPLE:

A gas has a volume of 400 ml at a pressure of 300 mmHg. At a volume of 300 ml, this gas will have a pressure of

(A) 400 mmHg
(B) 500 mmHg
(C) 200 mmHg
(D) 100 mmHg
(E) 50 mmHg

(A) By the equation for Boyle's Law, 400 x 300 = 12,000 = k. By substituting, we see that $300P = 12{,}000$, so $P = 400$.

Physics Test Answer Sheet

1	Ⓐ	Ⓑ	Ⓒ	Ⓓ	Ⓔ	39	Ⓐ	Ⓑ	Ⓒ	Ⓓ	Ⓔ
2	Ⓐ	Ⓑ	Ⓒ	Ⓓ	Ⓔ	40	Ⓐ	Ⓑ	Ⓒ	Ⓓ	Ⓔ
3	Ⓐ	Ⓑ	Ⓒ	Ⓓ	Ⓔ	41	Ⓐ	Ⓑ	Ⓒ	Ⓓ	Ⓔ
4	Ⓐ	Ⓑ	Ⓒ	Ⓓ	Ⓔ	42	Ⓐ	Ⓑ	Ⓒ	Ⓓ	Ⓔ
5	Ⓐ	Ⓑ	Ⓒ	Ⓓ	Ⓔ	43	Ⓐ	Ⓑ	Ⓒ	Ⓓ	Ⓔ
6	Ⓐ	Ⓑ	Ⓒ	Ⓓ	Ⓔ	44	Ⓐ	Ⓑ	Ⓒ	Ⓓ	Ⓔ
7	Ⓐ	Ⓑ	Ⓒ	Ⓓ	Ⓔ	45	Ⓐ	Ⓑ	Ⓒ	Ⓓ	Ⓔ
8	Ⓐ	Ⓑ	Ⓒ	Ⓓ	Ⓔ	46	Ⓐ	Ⓑ	Ⓒ	Ⓓ	Ⓔ
9	Ⓐ	Ⓑ	Ⓒ	Ⓓ	Ⓔ	47	Ⓐ	Ⓑ	Ⓒ	Ⓓ	Ⓔ
10	Ⓐ	Ⓑ	Ⓒ	Ⓓ	Ⓔ	48	Ⓐ	Ⓑ	Ⓒ	Ⓓ	Ⓔ
11	Ⓐ	Ⓑ	Ⓒ	Ⓓ	Ⓔ	49	Ⓐ	Ⓑ	Ⓒ	Ⓓ	Ⓔ
12	Ⓐ	Ⓑ	Ⓒ	Ⓓ	Ⓔ	50	Ⓐ	Ⓑ	Ⓒ	Ⓓ	Ⓔ
13	Ⓐ	Ⓑ	Ⓒ	Ⓓ	Ⓔ	51	Ⓐ	Ⓑ	Ⓒ	Ⓓ	Ⓔ
14	Ⓐ	Ⓑ	Ⓒ	Ⓓ	Ⓔ	52	Ⓐ	Ⓑ	Ⓒ	Ⓓ	Ⓔ
15	Ⓐ	Ⓑ	Ⓒ	Ⓓ	Ⓔ	53	Ⓐ	Ⓑ	Ⓒ	Ⓓ	Ⓔ
16	Ⓐ	Ⓑ	Ⓒ	Ⓓ	Ⓔ	54	Ⓐ	Ⓑ	Ⓒ	Ⓓ	Ⓔ
17	Ⓐ	Ⓑ	Ⓒ	Ⓓ	Ⓔ	55	Ⓐ	Ⓑ	Ⓒ	Ⓓ	Ⓔ
18	Ⓐ	Ⓑ	Ⓒ	Ⓓ	Ⓔ	56	Ⓐ	Ⓑ	Ⓒ	Ⓓ	Ⓔ
19	Ⓐ	Ⓑ	Ⓒ	Ⓓ	Ⓔ	57	Ⓐ	Ⓑ	Ⓒ	Ⓓ	Ⓔ
20	Ⓐ	Ⓑ	Ⓒ	Ⓓ	Ⓔ	58	Ⓐ	Ⓑ	Ⓒ	Ⓓ	Ⓔ
21	Ⓐ	Ⓑ	Ⓒ	Ⓓ	Ⓔ	59	Ⓐ	Ⓑ	Ⓒ	Ⓓ	Ⓔ
22	Ⓐ	Ⓑ	Ⓒ	Ⓓ	Ⓔ	60	Ⓐ	Ⓑ	Ⓒ	Ⓓ	Ⓔ
23	Ⓐ	Ⓑ	Ⓒ	Ⓓ	Ⓔ	61	Ⓐ	Ⓑ	Ⓒ	Ⓓ	Ⓔ
24	Ⓐ	Ⓑ	Ⓒ	Ⓓ	Ⓔ	62	Ⓐ	Ⓑ	Ⓒ	Ⓓ	Ⓔ
25	Ⓐ	Ⓑ	Ⓒ	Ⓓ	Ⓔ	63	Ⓐ	Ⓑ	Ⓒ	Ⓓ	Ⓔ
26	Ⓐ	Ⓑ	Ⓒ	Ⓓ	Ⓔ	64	Ⓐ	Ⓑ	Ⓒ	Ⓓ	Ⓔ
27	Ⓐ	Ⓑ	Ⓒ	Ⓓ	Ⓔ	65	Ⓐ	Ⓑ	Ⓒ	Ⓓ	Ⓔ
28	Ⓐ	Ⓑ	Ⓒ	Ⓓ	Ⓔ	66	Ⓐ	Ⓑ	Ⓒ	Ⓓ	Ⓔ
29	Ⓐ	Ⓑ	Ⓒ	Ⓓ	Ⓔ	67	Ⓐ	Ⓑ	Ⓒ	Ⓓ	Ⓔ
30	Ⓐ	Ⓑ	Ⓒ	Ⓓ	Ⓔ	68	Ⓐ	Ⓑ	Ⓒ	Ⓓ	Ⓔ
31	Ⓐ	Ⓑ	Ⓒ	Ⓓ	Ⓔ	69	Ⓐ	Ⓑ	Ⓒ	Ⓓ	Ⓔ
32	Ⓐ	Ⓑ	Ⓒ	Ⓓ	Ⓔ	70	Ⓐ	Ⓑ	Ⓒ	Ⓓ	Ⓔ
33	Ⓐ	Ⓑ	Ⓒ	Ⓓ	Ⓔ	71	Ⓐ	Ⓑ	Ⓒ	Ⓓ	Ⓔ
34	Ⓐ	Ⓑ	Ⓒ	Ⓓ	Ⓔ	72	Ⓐ	Ⓑ	Ⓒ	Ⓓ	Ⓔ
35	Ⓐ	Ⓑ	Ⓒ	Ⓓ	Ⓔ	73	Ⓐ	Ⓑ	Ⓒ	Ⓓ	Ⓔ
36	Ⓐ	Ⓑ	Ⓒ	Ⓓ	Ⓔ	74	Ⓐ	Ⓑ	Ⓒ	Ⓓ	Ⓔ
37	Ⓐ	Ⓑ	Ⓒ	Ⓓ	Ⓔ	75	Ⓐ	Ⓑ	Ⓒ	Ⓓ	Ⓔ
38	Ⓐ	Ⓑ	Ⓒ	Ⓓ	Ⓔ						

PHYSICS TEST

Part A

Directions: Each set of lettered answer choices below refers to the numbered questions following it. Select the one lettered answer choice that best fits each question and then darken the corresponding circle on the answer sheet. An answer choice may be used once, more than once, or not at all in a given set.

Questions 1–3 relate to the following thermal properties of matter:

(A) Specific heat
(B) Heat conduction
(C) Convection
(D) Heat capacity
(E) Radiation

1. Which property involves the transfer of energy by electromagnetic waves?
2. Which term describes the transfer of heat by successive molecular collisions?
3. Which term represents the ratio of the amount of heat added to a body to the temperature change of the body?

Questions 4–5 relate to the various elements illustrated in the following schematic of an electrical circuit:

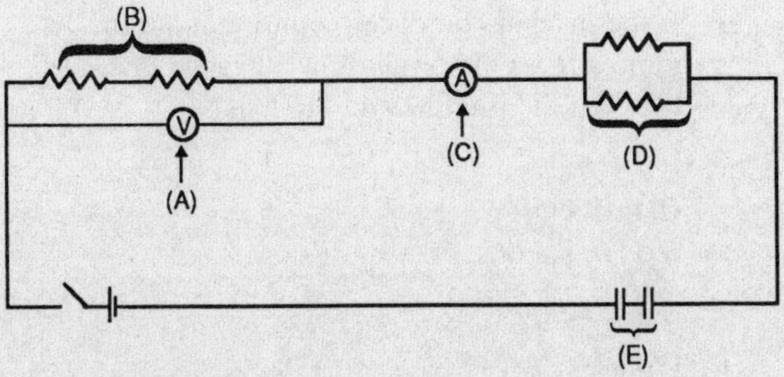

4. Which lettered choice represents resistors in series?
5. Which component measures current?

Questions 6–8 refer to an object which is undergoing simple harmonic motion. Assume dissipative forces are negligible.

(A) Period
(B) Frequency
(C) Amplitude
(D) Velocity
(E) Acceleration

6. Which term describes the maximal displacement of the object from its equilibrium position?
7. Which property of the object's motion is equal to the time necessary for the object to complete one oscillation?
8. Which property is equal to zero when the displacement of the object equals zero?

Questions 9–11 refer to the movements of five objects. The distance each object travels over a given period of time is shown in the diagram below:

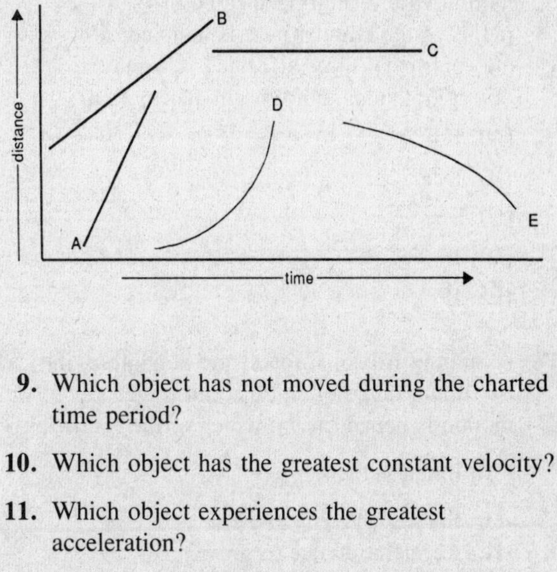

9. Which object has not moved during the charted time period?
10. Which object has the greatest constant velocity?
11. Which object experiences the greatest acceleration?

Questions 12–13 relate to physical and chemical properties of an atom:

(A) Atomic number
(B) Mass number
(C) Alpha particle
(D) Isotope
(E) Beta particle

GO ON TO THE NEXT PAGE

12. Which term represents the number of particles contained within the nucleus?

13. Which property of an atom best defines its chemical characteristics?

Questions 14–15 relate to properties of geometrical and physical optics:

(A) Diffraction
(B) Refraction
(C) Polarization
(D) Reflection
(E) Aberration

14. Which property refers to the altering of transverse waves so that vibrations are limited to one plane perpendicular to the direction of propagation?

15. Which term describes the bending of light rays as the light passes from one medium to another?

Part B

Directions: Each of the following questions or incomplete statements is followed by five possible answers or completions. Select the one choice that is best in each case and then darken the corresponding circle on the answer sheet.

16. An object is traveling in a uniform circular motion with a centripetal force of F. If the radius of the circular path is doubled, how is the centripetal force affected? Assume the object maintains uniform circular motion.
(A) 1/4F
(B) 1/2F
(C) F
(D) 2F
(E) 4F

17. Assuming frictional forces are negligible, the maximum range of an object in projectile motion is dependent on which of the following?
I. Initial velocity
II. Initial launching angle
III. Acceleration due to gravity
(A) II only
(B) III only
(C) I and II only
(D) II and III only
(E) I, II, and III

Questions 18–20

A copier machine uses a converging lens system to create copies of an original image. The converging lens may be moved, thereby altering the effective object length. The focal length of the converging lens of this machine is 10 cm.

18. If the machine produces copies that are the same size as the original, what is the distance between the original and the lens?
(A) 5 cm
(B) 10 cm
(C) 15 cm
(D) 20 cm
(E) 40 cm

19. To produce enlargements which are twice the size of the original, what would be the required distance between the original and the lens?
(A) 5 cm
(B) 10 cm
(C) 15 cm
(D) 20 cm
(E) 25 cm

GO ON TO THE NEXT PAGE

20. An image of the original is not produced. What object distance could account for this occurrence?

(A) 0.1 cm

(B) 0.5 cm

(C) 1 cm

(D) 5 cm

(E) 10 cm

21. Two liters of a gas are stored within a cylinder. The temperature of the gas is kept constant. The cylinder is then compressed so that the pressure exerted on the gas is increased from 4 atmospheres to 8 atmospheres. What volume will the gas occupy at the higher pressure?

(A) 0.5 liter

(B) 1 liter

(C) 2 liters

(D) 4 liters

(E) 16 liters

22. Which of the following is not a vector quantity?

(A) Displacement

(B) Acceleration

(C) Electric field

(D) Density

(E) Momentum

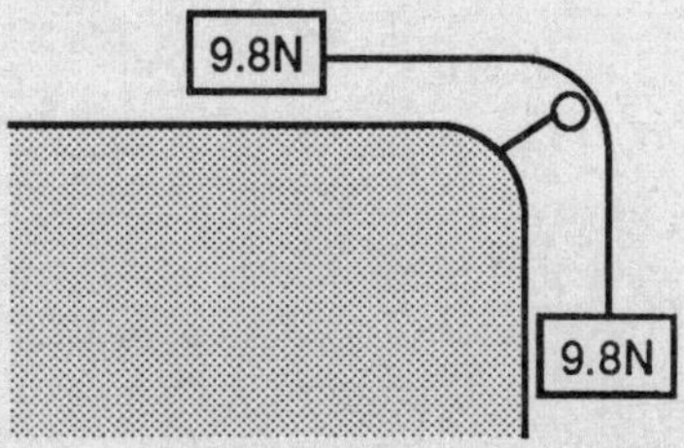

23. Two wooden blocks are connected by a massless string as illustrated above. Assuming frictionless conditions exist, what is the magnitude of the acceleration of the blocks?

(A) 0.5 m/s^2

(B) 0.9 m/s^2

(C) 1.0 m/s^2

(D) 4.9 m/s^2

(E) 9.8 m/s^2

24. The graphs below demonstrate pairs of traveling waves. If the waves in each pair are superimposed, which pair will show the greatest constructive interference?

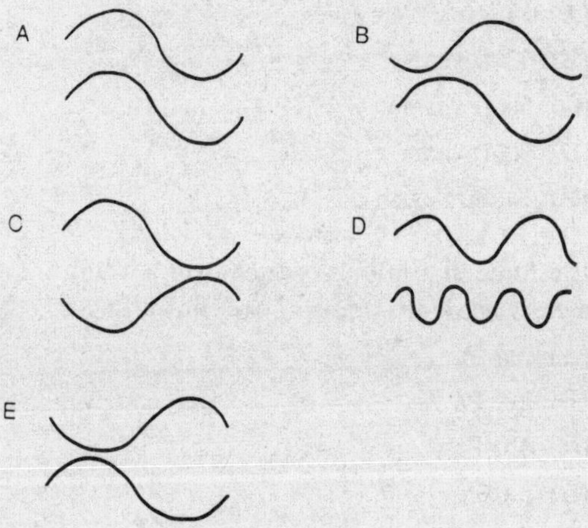

25. The lines of force near two charges equal in magnitude but opposite in sign are

(A) closer together where the electric field is weaker

(B) directed from the positive charge to the negative charge

(C) directed from the negative charge to the positive charge

(D) directed away from both the positive and negative charges

(E) farther apart where the electric field is stronger

26. The resistance of a uniform conductor is measured to be R. If the length of the conductor is halved and the cross-sectional area is doubled, what will be its new resistance?

(A) 1/8R

(B) 1/4R

(C) R

(D) 4R

(E) 8R

GO ON TO THE NEXT PAGE

27. A sample of one isotope of carbon, ^{14}C, is being studied. After a period of 28,000 years, it is determined that only 1/32 of the sample of ^{14}C remains. What is the approximate half-life of ^{14}C?

(A) 875 years

(B) 4200 years

(C) 5600 years

(D) 7000 years

(E) 14000 years

28. If a force of 10.0N is exerted over a 4.0 m^2 area, what is the pressure over this area?

(A) 0.4 Pa

(B) 2.5 Pa

(C) 4.0 Pa

(D) 5.0 Pa

(E) 40.0 Pa

29. For the circuit illustrated below, what is the potential difference across the component labeled X?

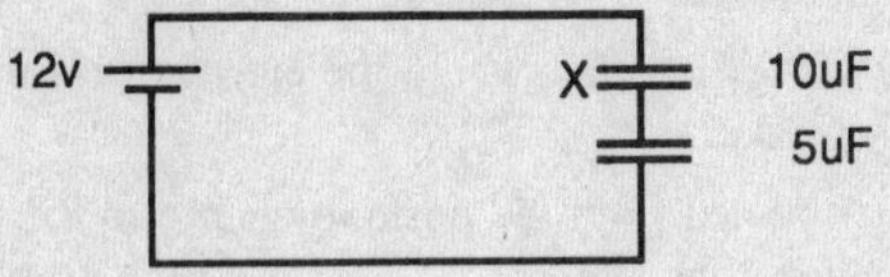

(A) 0.8 volt

(B) 1.2 volts

(C) 4.0 volts

(D) 8.0 volts

(E) 12.0 volts

30. Liquid flows through a pipe at a rate of $2m^3/s$. The cross-sectional area of the pipe is $1m^2$. Assuming laminar flow occurs, what is the approximate rate of flow if the pipe diameter is quadrupled?

(A) 0.1 m^3/s

(B) 0.5 m^3/s

(C) 2 m^3/s

(D) 8 m^3/s

(E) 32 m^3/s

31. The gravitational force between two moving spherical objects, labeled A and B, is dependent on each of the following EXCEPT

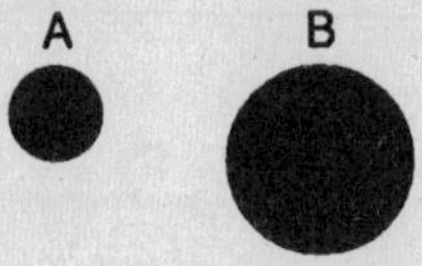

(A) mass of object A

(B) distance separating objects

(C) mass of object B

(D) velocity of objects

(E) gravitational constant

Questions 32–33 A 10kg brick is carried from ground level to the top of a 100m building. A person carrying the brick must walk 150m up a staircase to reach the top of the building. Each step is 0.2m tall. The brick is then dropped from the top of the building. Assume frictional forces are negligible.

32. How much work is done by lifting the object to the top of the building?

(A) 1000 J

(B) 1500 J

(C) 7350 J

(D) 9800 J

(E) 14700 J

33. What is the approximate kinetic energy of the object as it reaches ground level?

(A) 750 J

(B) 1500 J

(C) 4900 J

(D) 7350 J

(E) 9800 J

GO ON TO THE NEXT PAGE

34. A light illuminates a metal surface causing photoelectrons to be emitted. Which of the following most specifically accounts for the energies of the emitted electrons?

(A) Velocity of incident light
(B) Velocity of emitted electrons
(C) Size of area illuminated
(D) Frequency of incident light
(E) Mass of emitted electrons

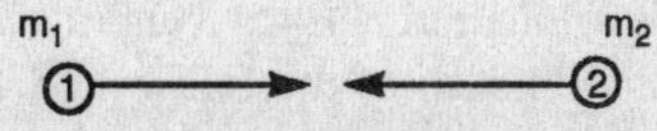

35. Two balls are rolled along a frictionless surface as illustrated above. The balls have the same mass and travel at identical speeds. If the balls meet in a completely elastic collision, each of the following conditions occurs EXCEPT:

(A) kinetic energy is conserved
(B) the mass of the system remains constant
(C) the balls will possess different magnitudes of acceleration
(D) each ball will possess the same momentum as before the collision
(E) each ball will possess the same momentum as after the collision

36. The first law of thermodynamics encompasses each of the following ideas EXCEPT:

(A) conservation of energy
(B) energy cannot be created or destroyed
(C) energy may be converted into different forms
(D) likelihood of a process occurring
(E) change in internal energy of a system equals the difference between the heat absorbed and the work done by the system

37. Which of the following always describe the image produced by a diverging lens?

I. Virtual
II. Erect
III. Smaller than object

(A) I only
(B) III only
(C) I and II only
(D) II and III only
(E) I, II, and III

38. The chart below illustrates an energy level diagram for an atom. The labeled arrows depict various transitions between energy states. Which arrow represents the transition that will emit a photon of highest frequency?

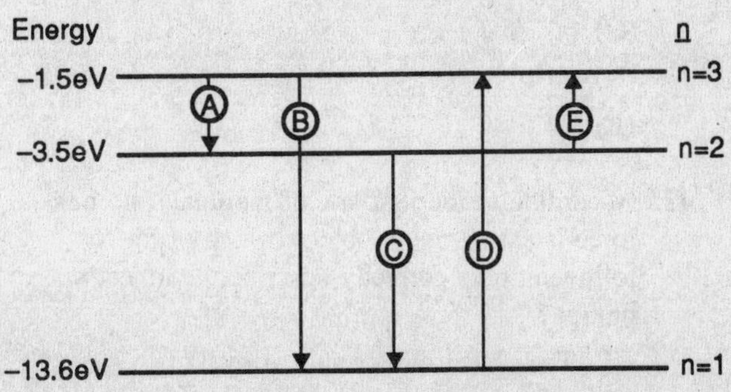

(A) A
(B) B
(C) C
(D) D
(E) E

39. A wire and a magnet are positioned or moved in a variety of ways. Which of the following will produce an electromotive force?

(A) Wire and magnet are stationary, more than 1m apart.
(B) Wire and magnet are stationary, separated by 5mm.
(C) Wire is moved parallel to stationary magnet.
(D) Magnet is moved parallel to stationary wire.
(E) Wire is moved perpendicular to magnet's lines of force.

40. A stationary horn broadcasts an emergency distress signal at a constant frequency f. A stationary observer hears the signal and then begins to recede. This observer will perceive

(A) a signal with frequency f
(B) a signal with frequency less than f
(C) a signal with frequency greater than f
(D) a signal with frequency f initially, with the frequency continually increasing
(E) a signal with frequency f initially, with the frequency continually decreasing

GO ON TO THE NEXT PAGE

41. Which of the following correctly expresses the dimensions of torque? Assume m is mass, l is length, and t is time.

(A) ml^2t^{-2}

(B) $m^2l^2t^2$

(C) $ml^{-2}t^{-2}$

(D) ml^3t^{-2}

(E) ml^2t^{-3}

42. According to the first law of motion, if no net force is acting on an object, which of the following may correctly describe the object's motion?

I. The object will remain at rest.

II. The object will continue moving at a constant velocity.

III. The object will continue moving with a constant positive acceleration.

(A) I only

(B) III only

(C) I and II only

(D) I and III only

(E) I, II, and III

43. The formation of a rainbow occurs as a result of

(A) reflection

(B) dispersion

(C) luminous intensity

(D) luminous flux

(E) polarization

44. Two point charges separated by a distance of 0.5m produce an electric force of F. If the distance between the point charges is decreased to 0.05m, the electric force would

(A) decrease by a factor of 10

(B) decrease by a factor of 100

(C) remain the same

(D) increase by a factor of 10

(E) increase by a factor of 100

45. The pascal is a unit of pressure, and is defined as one newton per square meter. The cubic meter defines the SI quantity, volume. A pascal multiplied by a cubic meter is a unit of

(A) work

(B) area

(C) power

(D) force

(E) density

46. Sound is a longitudinal wave and may be propagated in each of the following EXCEPT:

(A) steam

(B) water

(C) glass

(D) vacuum

(E) steel

GO ON TO THE NEXT PAGE

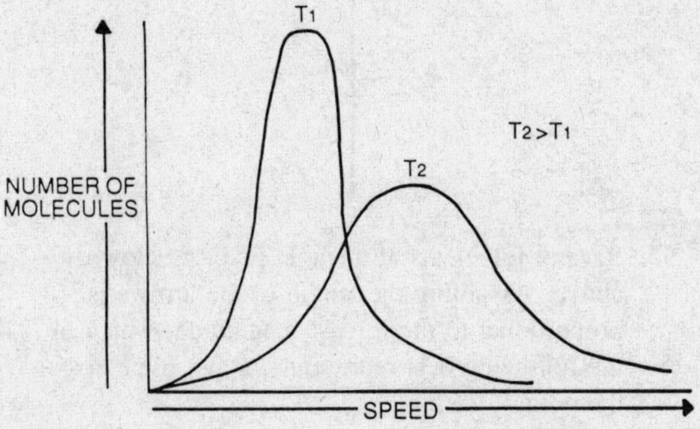

47. The graph above illustrates the distribution of molecular speeds for a pure sample at two different temperatures. The area under the curve represents the percentage of molecules at that range of speed. The same number of molecules are present at each temperature. Which of the following statements accurately reflects the data?

(A) All the molecules at the higher temperature have a greater speed than the molecules at the lower temperature.

(B) As the speeds increase the molecular size decreases.

(C) The distribution of speeds widens as the temperature decreases.

(D) As the temperature increases, the average molecular speed increases.

(E) The number of molecules at any given speed is always greater for the sample at the higher temperature.

Questions 48–49 relate to the schematic of the circuit shown below. Each labeled component provides 5 ohms resistance.

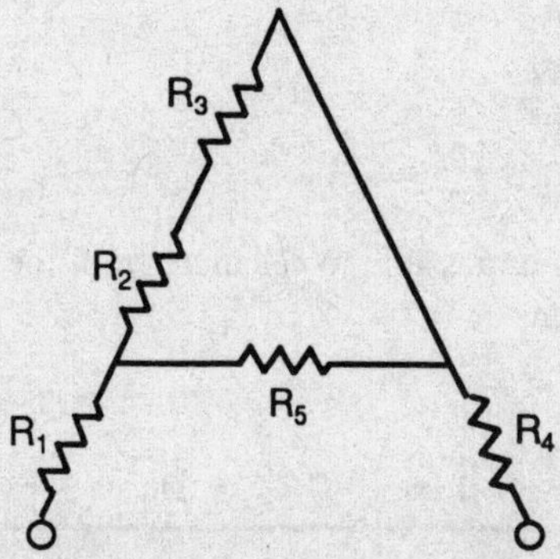

48. Which of the following illustrates a circuit equivalent to the one shown above?

(A)

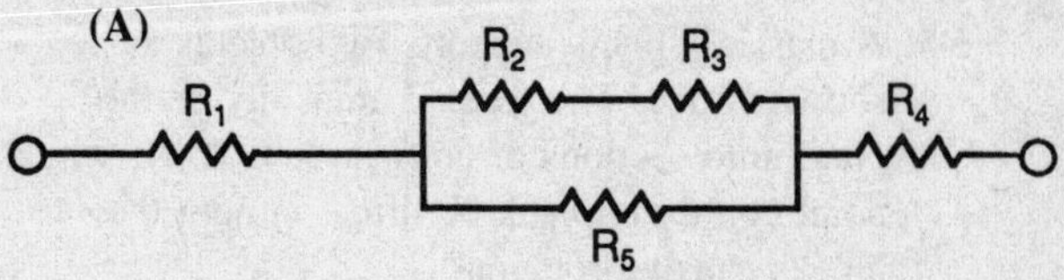

(B)

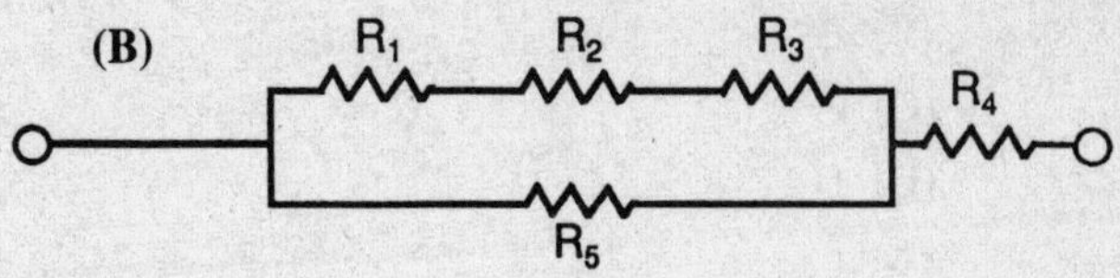

(C)

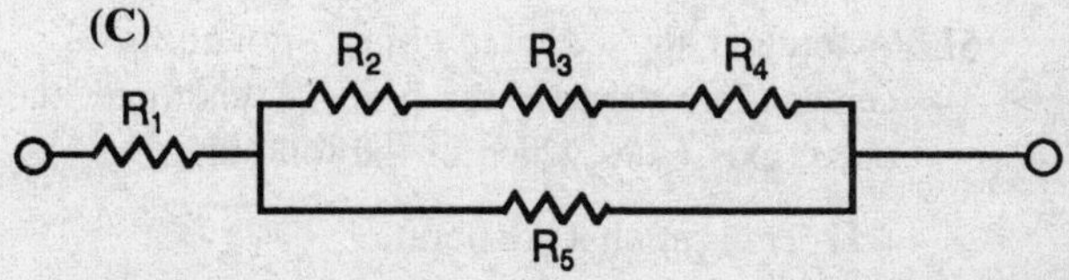

(D)

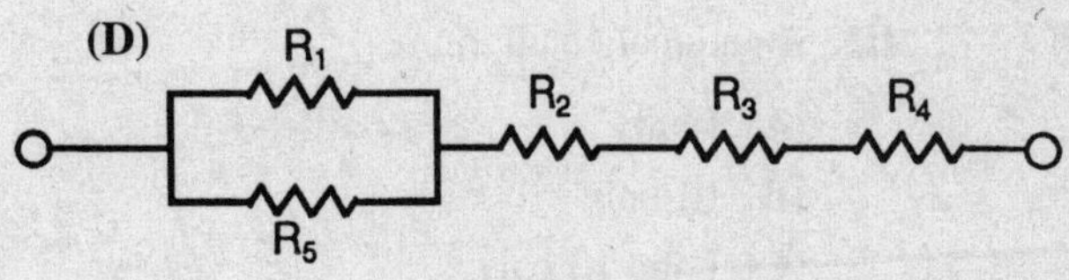

(E)

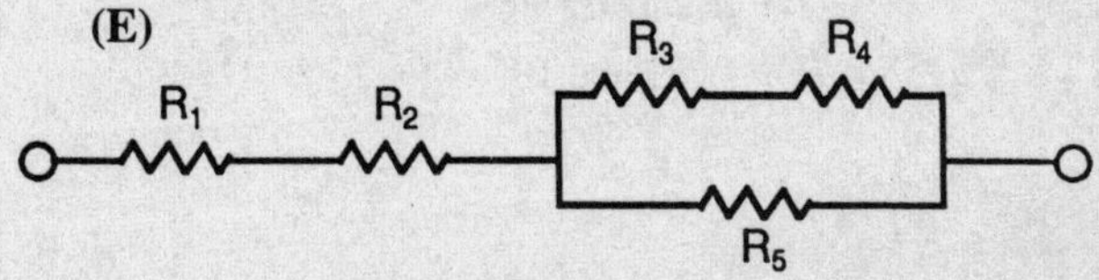

49. If the current flowing across R_4 is 2 amperes, what is the power dissipated by this component?

(A) 5 W

(B) 10 W

(C) 20 W

(D) 50 W

(E) It is impossible to calculate from the data given.

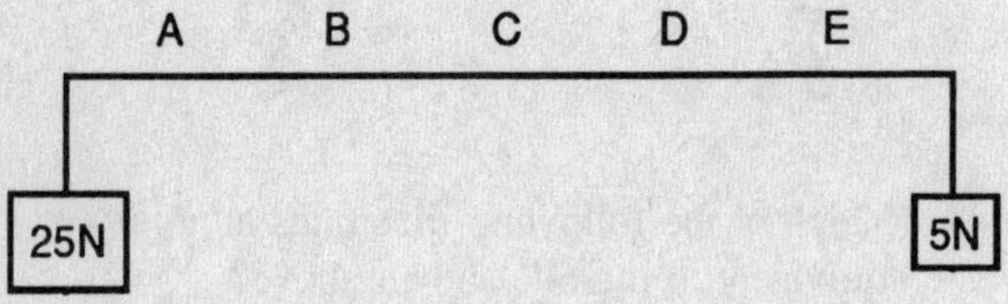

50. A massless plank supports two objects as shown above. The labeled areas divide the plank into sections of uniform length. At which point could the plank be lifted without the blocks causing rotation?

(A) A

(B) B

(C) C

(D) D

(E) E

51. A force is applied to an object through its center of gravity. On the basis of this force, the object possesses which of the following?

I. Translational acceleration

II. Rotational acceleration

III. Rotational equilibrium

(A) I only

(B) III only

(C) I and III only

(D) II and III only

(E) I, II, and III

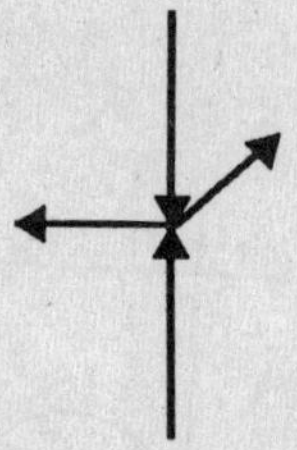

52. Several forces act at a single point as shown above. Assuming the length of the arrows is proportional to the forces' magnitude, which of the following best represents the net force at the point?

(A) 

(B) 

(C) 

(D) 

(E) 

53. Ice has a specific heat capacity of 0.5 kcal/kg°C. If 10 kcal of energy is added to 10kg of ice at −10°C, the result would be

(A) 10kg of ice at −8°C

(B) 10kg of ice at 0°C

(C) 10kg of water at 0°C

(D) 10kg of water at 1°C

(E) 10kg of water at 10°C

54. Air moving past a plane wing causes the wing to lift. Which of the following may account for such action?

(A) Air flow past the upper portion of the wing is slower than air flow past the lower portion of the wing.

(B) The pressure on the lower surface of the wing is greater than the pressure on the upper surface of the wing.

(C) Air flow past the upper and lower portions of the wing is the same.

(D) The pressure differential between the upper and lower wing surfaces is zero.

GO ON TO THE NEXT PAGE

(E) The pressure on the upper surface of the wing is slightly greater than the pressure on the lower surface of the wing.

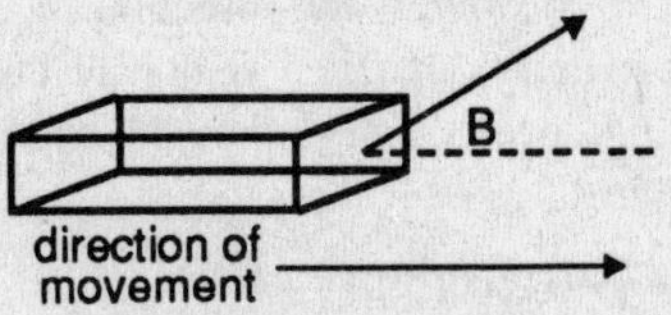

55. A crate is pulled across a floor. The force pulling the crate acts at an angle θ. Which of the following best represents a force diagram of the situation?

(A)

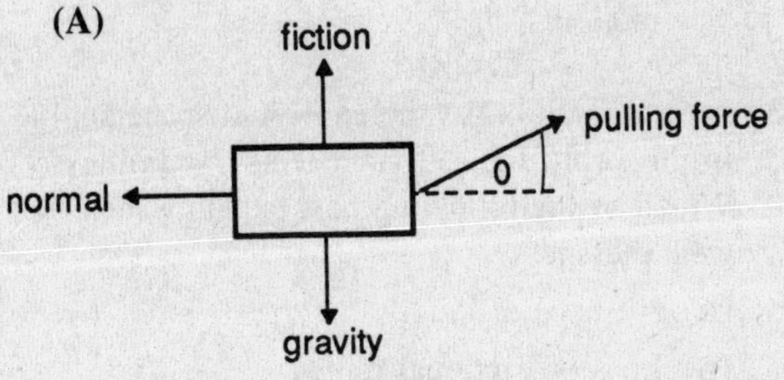

(B)

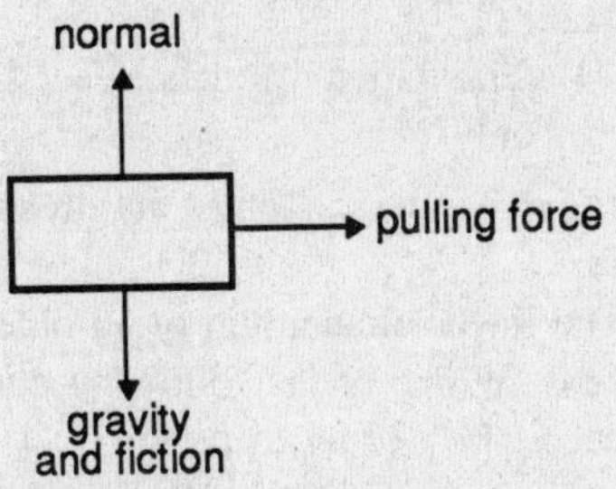

(C)

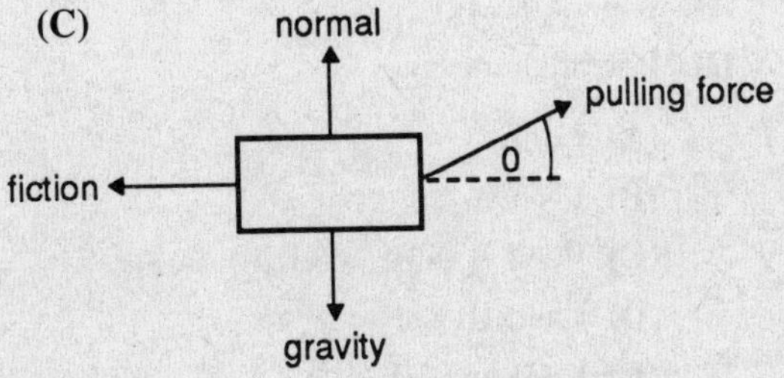

(D)

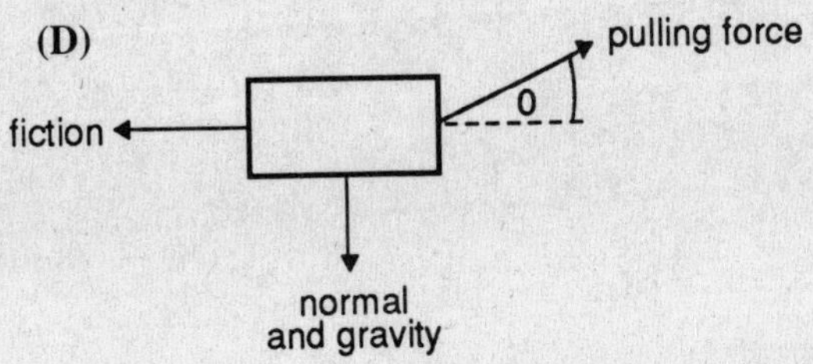

(E)

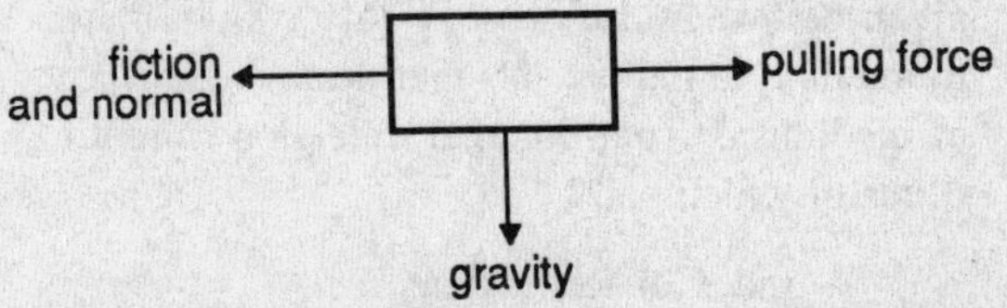

56. A certain satellite is known to have a mass of 700kg on the earth's surface. If the satellite orbits the earth at a distance of five times the earth's radius, what will be its mass?

(A) 28 kg
(B) 150 kg
(C) 350 kg
(D) 600 kg
(E) 700 kg

57. Each of the following waves travels at the speed of light EXCEPT:

(A) microwaves
(B) ultrasonic
(C) x-rays
(D) radio
(E) gamma rays

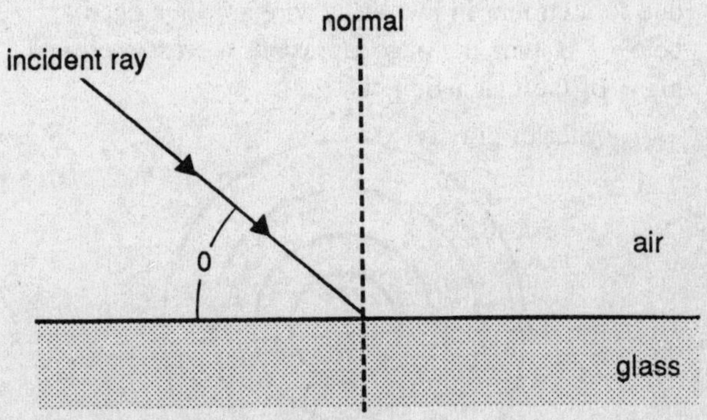

58. A light ray impinges upon the surface of a uniform piece of glass as shown above. What is the angle of reflection?

(A) 0
(B) $90° - \Theta$
(C) 90°
(D) $180° - \Theta$
(E) Cannot be determined

GO ON TO THE NEXT PAGE

59. The indices of refraction for pairs of media are given below. In each case, light rays originate in medium 1 and are incident upon the surface of medium 2. Total internal reflection cannot occur in which pair?

	Index of Refraction Medium 1	Medium 2
(A)	1.33	1.00
(B)	1.38	1.33
(C)	1.49	1.77
(D)	1.65	1.36
(E)	2.42	1.89

60. Each of the following is a characteristic of an ideal gas EXCEPT:

(A) random molecular motion occurs

(B) elastic collisions occur

(C) molecules occupy small portion of volume relative to volume occupied by gas

(D) molecules attract each other readily

(E) repulsion between molecules does not occur

Question 61–62

The concentric lines of force for a magnetic field due to a current in a straight wire are illustrated below. Assume the page represents a cross-sectional plane of the magnetic field.

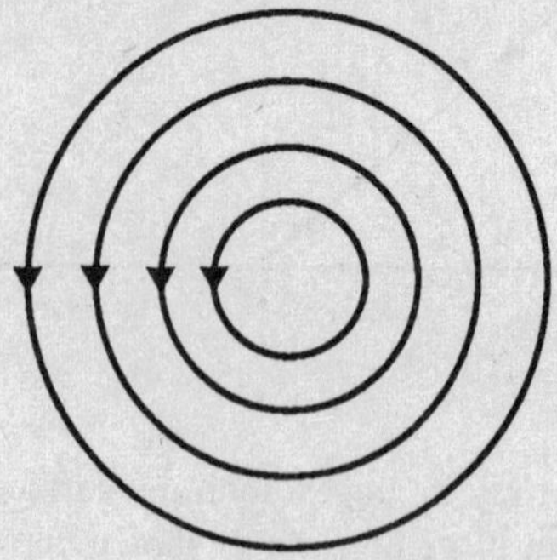

61. Which of the following most likely characterizes the direction of the current?

(A) The current flows into the page.

(B) The current flows out of the page.

(C) The current flows to the right.

(D) The current flows to the left.

(E) The current alternates; it flows into the page and then to the right.

62. Another wire is laid parallel to the first straight wire. The current flowing in the second wire is equal in magnitude to the current flowing in the first wire. However, the direction of current flow is exactly opposite. Which of the following correctly describes the force between these wires?

(A) An attractive force exists.

(B) A repulsive force exists.

(C) No force exists.

(D) Forces generated by each wire are always in the same direction.

(E) Forces violate Newton's third law of motion.

63. An astronaut orbits the earth in a space shuttle. In this orbit, the astronaut feels "weightless." Which of the following best explains such weightlessness?

(A) Absence of gravity

(B) Loss of frictional forces

(C) Astronaut and space shuttle both accelerate toward earth

(D) Gravitational forces affect space shuttle only

(E) No external forces act on space shuttle

64. The linear momentum of an object at time t is zero. Which of the following quantities is also necessarily equal to zero?

I. Velocity

II. Kinetic energy

III. Potential energy

(A) I only

(B) II only

(C) I and II only

(D) I and III only

(E) I, II, and III

65. A 10kg object is acted on by only two forces, as illustrated above. If the object's acceleration is 1 m/s^2 to the left, what is the net force on the object?

(A) 0.1N to the right

(B) 0.1N to the left

(C) 10N to the right

(D) 10N to the left

(E) 100N to the left

Questions 66–67 relate to the graph below.

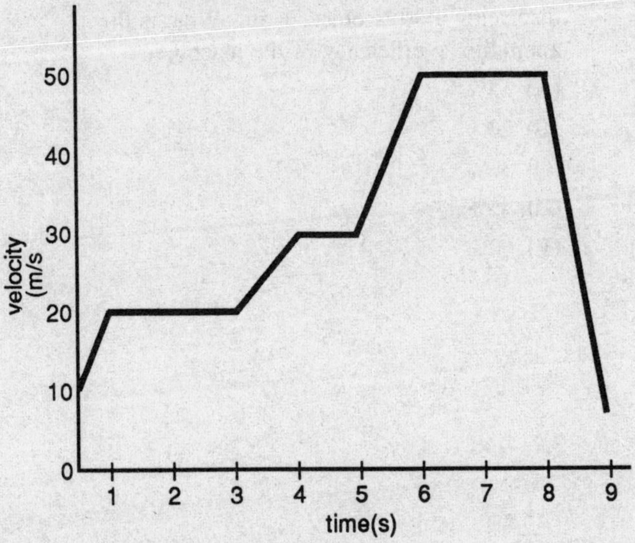

66. The approximate acceleration between the time period 4–5 seconds is

(A) 0 m/s^2

(B) 8 m/s^2

(C) 10 m/s^2

(D) 20 m/s^2

(E) 40 m/s^2

67. Which graph below best represents the time period 6–8 seconds?

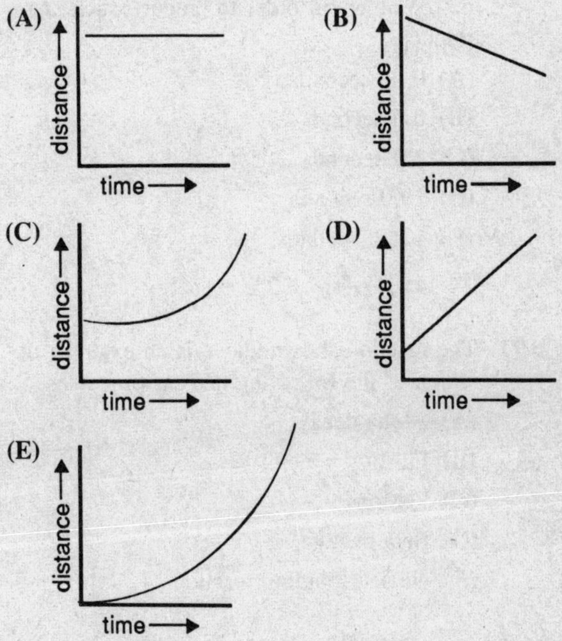

68. The objective lens of a certain microscope has a magnification of 100x, while the eyepiece magnification is 10x. The magnification of this microscope is

(A) 0.1x

(B) 110x

(C) 1000x

(D) 10000x

(E) It is impossible to calculate from the data given.

69. A charge of 5.0×10^{-9}C is in a uniform electric field of 5.0×10^4 N/C. A force of magnitude 2.0×10^{-4} is applied but is unable to move the charge against the electric field. How much work is performed on the charge?

(A) 0 J

(B) 1.0×10^{-12} J

(C) 5.0×10^{-8} J

(D) 2.5×10^{-4} J

(E) 5.0×10^{-4} J

GO ON TO THE NEXT PAGE

70. An impulse produced by a 50N force on an object is 2.5NS. How long is the force acting on the object in order to produce such an impulse?

(A) 0.05 seconds

(B) 0.5 seconds

(C) 3.0 seconds

(D) 20.0 seconds

(E) 125.0 seconds

$$4\ {}^{1}_{1}H \rightarrow {}^{4}_{2}He + 2\,{}^{0}_{1}e + \text{energy}$$

71. The reaction shown above is an example of which of the following nuclear processes?

(A) Alpha decay

(B) Fusion

(C) Fission

(D) Beta decay

(E) Nuclear binding reaction

72. A current of 2 amperes flows through a conductor with a resistance of 6 ohms. The current flows for 2 seconds. How much heat energy develops in the conductor as a result of current flow?

(A) 12 J

(B) 24 J

(C) 48 J

(D) 96 J

(E) 144 J

73. A person rotates with extended arms on a turntable. Assume dissipative forces are negligible. The person's arms are then folded and held close to his chest. Which of the following correctly describes the result of such an action?

(A) The person increases his rotational inertia.

(B) The person's angular velocity increases.

(C) The person's rotational inertia is unchanged.

(D) The person's angular velocity is unchanged.

(E) The person's angular momentum increases.

74. A pith ball electroscope possesses a certain charge. A charged glass rod is then held close to the electroscope. The pith ball moves noticeably toward the glass rod. Which of the following accounts for such an interaction?

(A) There are subtle gravitational forces between the glass rod and the pith ball.

(B) The glass rod and the pith ball each possess a net positive charge.

(C) The glass rod and the pith ball each possess a net negative charge.

(D) The glass rod and the pith ball are oppositely charged.

(E) The glass rod mass greatly exceeds the mass of the pith ball.

75. A total of 100 J of energy is supplied to a machine. The machine is then capable of displacing a 30 N object 1.5m. What is the approximate efficiency of the machine?

(A) 15%

(B) 20%

(C) 30%

(D) 45%

(E) 60%

Explanatory Answers

Questions 1–3 relate to the following thermal properties of matter:

(A) Specific heat
(B) Heat conduction
(C) Convection
(D) Heat capacity
(E) Radiation

1. Which property involves the transfer of energy by electromagnetic waves?

(E) Definition.

2. Which term describes the transfer of heat by successive molecular collisions?

(B) Definition.

3. Which term represents the ratio of the amount of heat added to a body to the temperature change of the body?

(D) Definition.

Questions 4–5 relate to the various elements illustrated in the following schematic of an electrical circuit:

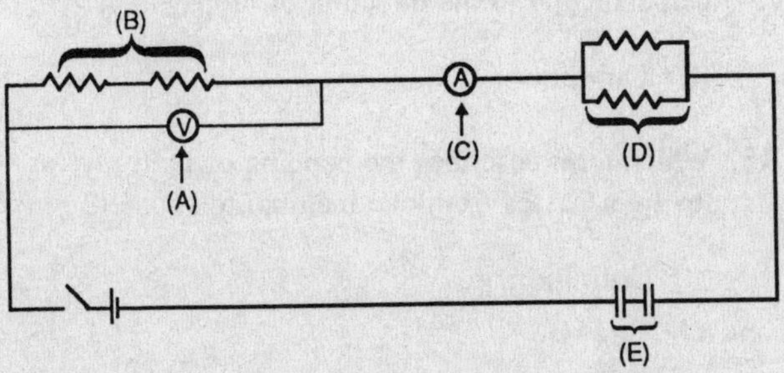

4. Which lettered choice represents resistors in series?

(B) See diagram below:

5. Which component measures current?

(C) The ammeter measures current. Recall that the unit of current is the ampere.

Questions 6–8 refer to an object which is undergoing simple harmonic motion. Assume dissipative forces are negligible.

(A) Period
(B) Frequency
(C) Amplitude
(D) Velocity
(E) Acceleration

6. Which term describes the maximal displacement of the object from its equilibrium position?

(C) Definition.

7. Which property of the object's motion is equal to the time necessary for the object to complete one oscillation?

(A) Definition.

8. Which property is equal to zero when the displacement of the object equals zero?

(E) When an object undergoing harmonic motion has a displacement of zero, it is at the equilibrium position. The restoring force will therefore be zero. If the force is zero, then the acceleration must necessarily be zero as well. Recall the relationship

$$F = ma$$
$$\text{if } F = 0$$
$$\text{then } ma = 0 \text{ and } \therefore a = 0$$

Questions 9–11 refer to the movements of five objects. The distance each object travels over a given period of time is shown in the diagram below:

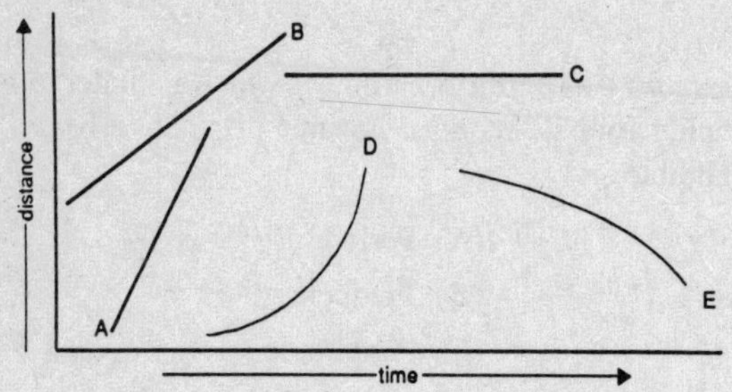

9. Which object has not moved during the charted time period?

(C) The distance value is unchanged.

10. Which object has the greatest constant velocity?

(A) Velocity is defined as the change in displacement (distance in this case) per unit time:

$$v = \frac{\Delta d}{\Delta t}$$

Hence, (A) has the greatest constant velocity as it has the greatest change in distance per unit time. Note that constant velocity is represented by a straight line in this diagram.

11. Which object experiences the greatest acceleration?

(D) Acceleration is defined as the change in velocity per unit time:

$$a = \frac{\Delta v}{\Delta t}$$

As lines A, B, and C are straight, each represents a *constant* velocity. Therefore, as acceleration is the *change* in velocity per unit time, the acceleration of A, B, and C is zero. The curvilinear representations—D and E—demonstrate positive and negative accelerations, respectively. Object D has the greatest acceleration as it possesses the greatest change in velocity per unit time.

Questions 12–13 relate to physical and chemical properties of an atom:

(A) Atomic number
(B) Mass number
(C) Alpha particle
(D) Isotope
(E) Beta particle

12. Which term represents the number of particles contained within the nucleus?

(B) Definition. The number of protons plus the number of neutrons within a given nucleus represents the mass number of the element.

13. Which property of an atom best defines its chemical characteristics?

(A) The atomic number is the defining characteristic of an atom.

Questions 14–15 relate to properties of geometrical and physical optics:

(A) Diffraction
(B) Refraction
(C) Polarization
(D) Reflection
(E) Aberration

14. Which property refers to the altering of transverse waves so that vibrations occur in one direction perpendicular to the direction of propagation?

(C) Definition.

15. Which term describes the bending of light rays as the light passes from one medium to another?

(B) Definition.

16. An object is traveling in a uniform circular motion with a centripetal force of F. If the radius of the circular path is doubled, how is the centripetal force affected? Assume the object maintains uniform circular motion.

(A) 1/4F

(B) 1/2F

(C) F

(D) 2F

(E) 4F

(B) Centripetal force is defined by the equation:

$$F = \frac{mv^2}{r} \therefore F = \frac{1}{r}$$

Therefore, force is inversely related to the radius. Consequently, if the radius of the circular path is doubled, the force will be halved.

17. Assuming frictional forces are negligible, the maximum range of an object in projectile motion is dependent on which of the following:

I. Initial velocity

II. Initial launching angle

III. Acceleration due to gravity

(A) II only

(B) III only

(C) I and II only

(D) II and III only

(E) I, II, and III

(E) As would be expected, the maximum range of an object in projectile motion is dependent on the initial velocity (v_o), the launching angle (Θ), and the acceleration due to gravity (g). The equation which defines the horizontal range is

$$\text{Range} = \frac{V_o}{g} \sin 2\Theta$$

Questions 18–20

A copier machine uses a converging lens system to create copies of an original image. The converging lens may be moved, thereby altering the effective object length. The focal length of the converging lens of this machine is 10 cm.

18. If the machine produces copies that are the same size as the original, what is the distance between the original and the lens?

(A) 5 cm

(B) 10 cm

(C) 15 cm

(D) 20 cm

(E) 40 cm

(D) A converging lens is said to possess a positive value for the focal length. The thin lens equation relates the focal length, object distance, and image distance as follows:

$$\frac{1}{O} + \frac{1}{i} = \frac{1}{f}$$

O = object distance
i = image distance
f = focal length

Another concept used in this set of problems is magnification (m):

$$m = \frac{i}{O}$$

if i = O, m = 1, image is same size as object

In this question, the copies (images) are the same size as the original. Thus, magnification equals 1, and i must equal O. The focal length is given as 10cm. Using the first equation:

$$\frac{1}{O} + \frac{1}{i} = \frac{1}{10\text{cm}}$$

and since O = i

$$\frac{1}{O} + \frac{1}{O} = \frac{1}{10\text{cm}}$$

$$\frac{2}{O} = \frac{1}{10\text{cm}}$$

$$O = (2)(10\text{cm}) = 20\text{cm}$$

19. To produce enlargements which are twice the size of the original, what would be the required distance between the original and the lens?

(A) 5 cm

(B) 10 cm

(C) 15 cm

(D) 20 cm

(E) 25 cm

(C) The images produced are twice the size of the original, so the magnification is 2:

$$m = 2 \text{ and } m = \frac{i}{O}$$

$$i = 2O$$

Substituting into the thin lens equation and solving:

$$\frac{1}{f} = \frac{1}{O} + \frac{1}{i} = \frac{1}{O} + \frac{1}{2O}$$

$$\frac{1}{10\text{cm}} = \frac{2}{2O} + \frac{1}{2O}$$

$$\frac{1}{10\text{cm}} = \frac{3}{2O}$$

$$2O = (3)(10\text{cm})$$

$$O = \frac{30\text{cm}}{2} = 15\text{cm}$$

20. An image of the original is not produced. What object distance could account for this occurrence?

(A) 0.1 cm

(B) 0.5 cm

(C) 1 cm

(D) 5 cm

(E) 10 cm

(E) No image is produced. The rays of light do not converge to form an image. The image distance then, if the light rays do not converge, can be said to be indefinite. That is, the image distance approaches infinity. If this is the case then,

$$i \to \infty \text{ then } \frac{1}{i} \to 0$$

So, if the term $\frac{1}{i}$ *approaches* zero, and

$$\frac{1}{f} = \frac{1}{i} + \frac{1}{O}$$

then

$$\frac{1}{f} - \frac{1}{O} = \frac{1}{O}$$

rearranging

$$\frac{1}{f} = \frac{1}{O} \text{ or } O = f$$

Therefore, if the object distance equals the focal length, no image is produced.

21. Two liters of a gas are stored within a cylinder. The temperature of the gas is kept constant. The cylinder is then compressed so that the pressure exerted on the gas is increased from 4 atmospheres to 8 atmospheres. What volume will the gas occupy at the higher pressure?

(A) 0.5 liter

(B) 1 liter

(C) 2 liters

(D) 4 liters

(E) 16 liters

(B) At a constant temperature, Boyle's law states:

$$P_i V_i = P_f V_f \quad \text{where} \quad \begin{aligned} P &= \text{pressure} \\ V &= \text{volume} \\ i &= \text{initial state} \\ f &= \text{final state} \end{aligned}$$

Substituting the values given:

$$(4 \text{ atm})\ (2 \text{ l}) = (8 \text{ atm})\ V_f$$

$$\left(\frac{4 \text{ atm}}{8 \text{ atm}}\right) 2\text{l} = V_f$$

$$1\text{l} = V_f$$

22. Which of the following is not a vector quantity?

(A) Displacement

(B) Acceleration

(C) Electric field

(D) Density

(E) Momentum

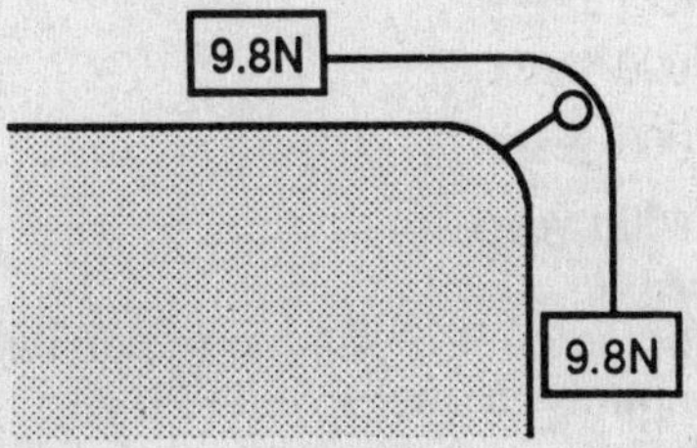

(D) Density is not a vector quantity, while each of the other choices represent a vector quantity.

23. Two wooden blocks are connected by a massless string as illustrated above. Assuming frictionless conditions exist, what is the magnitude of the acceleration of the blocks?

(A) 0.5 m/s^2

(B) 0.9 m/s^2

(C) 1.0 m/s^2

(D) 4.9 m/s^2

(E) 9.8 m/s^2

(D) The force producing the acceleration of the blocks is provided solely by the suspended block. The *mass* being accelerated however, is that due to *both* blocks. Recalling the second law of motion:

$$F = ma$$

If the weight (force) of each block is 9.8N, and the acceleration due to gravity is 9.8 m/s^2, the mass may be calculated:

$$F = ma$$

$$9.8\text{N} = m(9.8 \text{ m/s}^2)$$

$$m = \frac{9.8\text{N}}{9.8 \text{ m/s}^2}$$

$$m = 1 \text{ kg}$$

Thus, the total mass being accelerated is 2kg (two blocks), and the force is the weight of the one suspended block, 9.8N. Therefore:

$$F = ma$$

$$a = \frac{F}{m} = \frac{9.8\text{N}}{2 \text{ kg}} = 4.9 \text{ m/s}^2$$

24. The graphs below demonstrate pairs of traveling waves. If the waves in each pair are superimposed, which pair will show the greatest constructive interference?

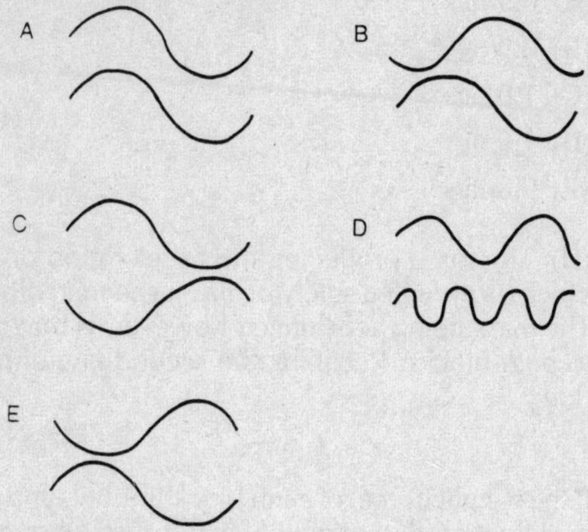

(A) The wave trains in answer choices (B), (C), (D), and (E), when superimposed result in destructive interference. That is, the sum of the individual displacements effectively cancel or lower the net amplitude. The wave train pair in answer choice (A) however, adds constructively at each point, to produce an amplitude greater than either wave does alone.

25. The lines of force near two charges equal in magnitude but opposite in sign are

(A) closer together where the electric field is weaker

(B) directed from the positive charge to the negative charge

(C) directed from the negative charge to the positive charge

(D) directed away from both the positive and negative charges

(E) farther apart where the electric field is stronger

(B) The lines of force between a positive charge and a negative charge are directed from the positive charge to the negative charge. The lines of force are also farther apart as the electric field weakens.

26. The resistance of a uniform conductor is measured to be R. If the length of the conductor is halved and the cross-sectional area is doubled, what will be its new resistance?

(A) 1/8R

(B) 1/4R

(C) R

(D) 4R

(E) 8R

(B) The resistance of a given conductor is defined by the following relationship:

$$R = P\frac{L}{A} \quad \text{where} \quad \begin{aligned} R &= \text{resistance} \\ P &= \text{resistivity} \\ L &= \text{length of conductor} \\ A &= \text{cross-sectional area of conductor} \end{aligned}$$

This relationship makes sense. The longer the conductor, the more likely a given charge will encounter resistance. Also, the smaller the conductor's cross-sectional area, the more likely a given charge will encounter resistance. The resistivity is a constant specific for each conductor. Substituting the new conditions:

$$R = p\,\frac{1/2L}{2A}$$

$$R = 1/4 \text{ (original R)}$$

27. A sample of one isotope of carbon, ^{14}C, is being studied. After a period of 28,000 years, it is determined that only 1/32 of the sample of ^{14}C remains. What is the approximate half-life of ^{14}C?

(A) 875 years

(B) 4200 years

(C) 5600 years

(D) 7000 years

(E) 14000 years

(C) The amount of sample remaining represents the amount left after five half-lives:

$$\left(\frac{1}{2}\right)^n = \frac{1}{32}$$

$$n = 5$$

The time of the half-life for this isotope is:

$$t_{1/2} = \frac{28000_y}{5} = 5600y$$

28. If a force of 10.0N is exerted over a 4.0 m^2 area, what is the pressure over this area?

(A) 0.4 Pa

(B) 2.5 Pa

(C) 4.0 Pa

(D) 5.0 Pa

(E) 40.0 Pa

(B) Pressure is the force per unit area:

$$P = \frac{F}{A}$$

Substituting and solving:

$$P = \frac{10N}{4m^2} = 2.5N/m^2 = 2.5 \text{ Pa}$$

29. For the circuit illustrated below, what is the potential difference across the component labeled X?

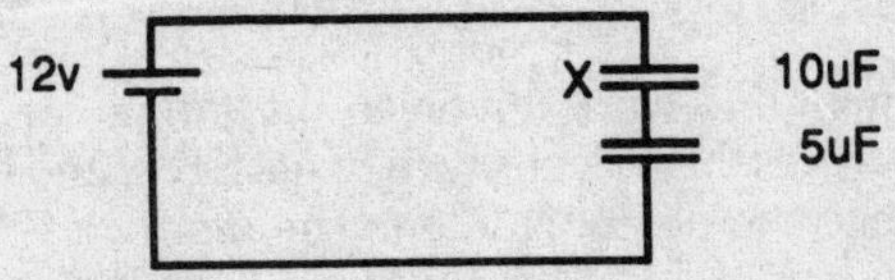

(A) 0.8 volt

(B) 1.2 volts

(C) 4.0 volts

(D) 8.0 volts

(E) 12.0 volts

(C) The potential difference across the labeled capacitor may be calculated from the relationship:

$Q = CV$ where Q = charge, C = capacitance, V = voltage (potential difference)

First, the effective capacitance of the circuit must be calculated. Then, the charge may be calculated. Finally, the potential difference across the specific component may be determined.

For capacitors in series:

$$\frac{1}{C_{eff}} = \frac{1}{C_1} + \frac{1}{C_2} = \frac{1}{10\mu F} + \frac{1}{5\mu F}$$

$$= \frac{1}{10\mu F} + \frac{2}{10\mu F}$$

$$= \frac{3}{10\mu F}$$

$$\therefore C_{eff} = \frac{10\mu F}{3} = 3.3\mu F$$

The charge on the plates:

$$Q = CV$$
$$= 3.3\mu F(12V)$$
$$= 4.0 \times 10^{-5}C$$

The potential difference across component "X":

$$V_x = \frac{Q}{C_x} = \frac{4.0 \times 10^{-5}C}{10 \times 10^{-6}F} = 4.0 \text{ volts}$$

30. Liquid flows through a pipe at a rate of $2m^3/s$. The cross-sectional area of the pipe is $1m^2$. Assuming laminar flow occurs, what is the approximate rate of flow if the pipe diameter is quadrupled?

(A) 0.1 m^3/s

(B) 0.5 m^3/s

(C) 2 m^3/s

(D) 8 m^3/s

(E) 32 m^3/s

(C) The rate of flow (R) through a pipe is defined by the following equation:

$R = vA$ where v is fluid speed and A is cross-sectional area of pipe

From the equation of continuity, it is known that the rate of flow through a system (where laminar flow exists) is constant. So

$R_i = R_f$ or $v_iA_i = v_fA_f$ where i and f denote initial and final conditions

Hence, although the velocity and area may change, the rate of flow will remain constant at 2 m^3/s.

31. The gravitational force between two moving spherical objects, labeled A and B, is dependent on each of the following EXCEPT

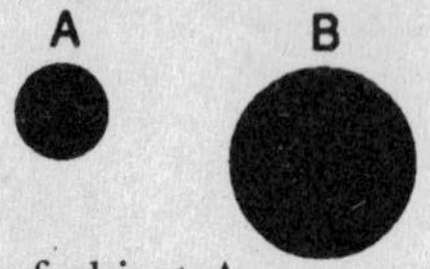

(A) mass of object A

(B) distance separating objects

(C) mass of object B

(D) velocity of objects

(E) gravitational constant

(D) The law of gravitation is expressed as follows:

$$F = G\frac{m_a m_b}{r^2}$$

where F = gravitational force, G = gravitational constant, m_a = mass of object a, m_b = mass of object b, r = the distance separating the masses

Therefore, it is demonstrated that the velocity of the objects is not a factor.

Questions 32–33

A 10kg brick is carried from ground level to the top of a 100m building. A person carrying the brick must walk 150m up a staircase to reach the top of the building. Each step is 0.2m tall. The brick is then dropped from the top of the building. Assume frictional forces are negligible.

32. How much work is done by lifting the object to the top of the building?

(A) 1000 J

(B) 1500 J

(C) 7350 J

(D) 9800 J

(E) 14700 J

(D) Work is defined as the product of the force applied and the displacement of the object in the direction of the force:

$$W = F \cdot d$$

Thus, the work involved in lifting an object involves the object's weight (its force) and the distance the object is lifted. The distance is simply the height (h) of the building. Substituting:

$$\begin{aligned} W &= F \cdot d \\ &= mgh \\ &= (10kg)(9.8m/s^2)(100m) \\ &= 9800\ J \end{aligned}$$

This value represents the object's potential energy at that height.

33. What is the approximate kinetic energy of the object as it reaches ground level?

(A) 750 J

(B) 1500 J

(C) 4900 J

(D) 7350 J

(E) 9800 J

(E) As frictional forces are negligible, the potential energy will be converted to kinetic energy. Therefore, the potential energy at the top of the building equals the kinetic energy at the bottom.

34. A light illuminates a metal surface causing photoelectrons to be emitted. Which of the following most specifically accounts for the energies of the emitted electrons?

(A) Velocity of incident light

(B) Velocity of emitted electrons

(C) Size of area illuminated

(D) Frequency of incident light

(E) Mass of emitted electrons

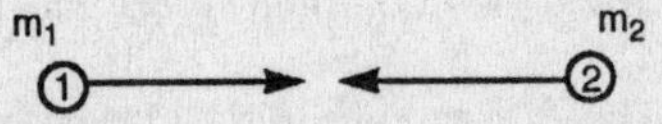

(D) Recall that energy is related to frequency by the relationship:

E = hu where h is Planck's constant
and u is frequency

Therefore, as the frequency of the incident light increases, the energy imparted to the surface will also increase.

35. Two balls are rolled along a frictionless surface as illustrated above. The balls have the same mass and travel at identical speeds. If the balls meet in a completely elastic collision, each of the following conditions occurs EXCEPT:

(A) kinetic energy is conserved

(B) the mass of the system remains constant

(C) the balls will possess different magnitudes of acceleration

(D) each ball will possess the same momentum as before the collision

(E) each ball will possess the same momentum as after the collision

(C) In a completely elastic collision, kinetic energy is conserved. Momentum (p) is defined by the expression:

$$p = mv$$

Therefore, if the mass and speed of each ball is identical:

$$m_1 v_1 = m_2 m_2$$

However, as each ball has a constant speed, the acceleration is zero for each ball.

36. The first law of thermodynamics encompasses each of the following ideas EXCEPT:

(A) conservation of energy

(B) energy cannot be created or destroyed

(C) energy may be converted into different forms

(D) likelihood of a process occurring

(E) change in internal energy of a system equals the difference between the heat absorbed and the work done by the system

(D) The first law of thermodynamics does not address the spontaneity of a given process.

37. Which of the following always describe the image produced by a diverging lens?

I. Virtual

II. Erect

III. Smaller than object

(A) I only

(B) III only

(C) I and II only

(D) II and III only

(E) I, II, and III

(E) Diverging lenses produce images with the same characteristics: virtual, erect, and smaller than the object.

38. The chart below illustrates an energy level diagram for an atom. The labeled arrows depict various transitions between energy states. Which arrow represents the transition that will emit a photon of highest frequency?

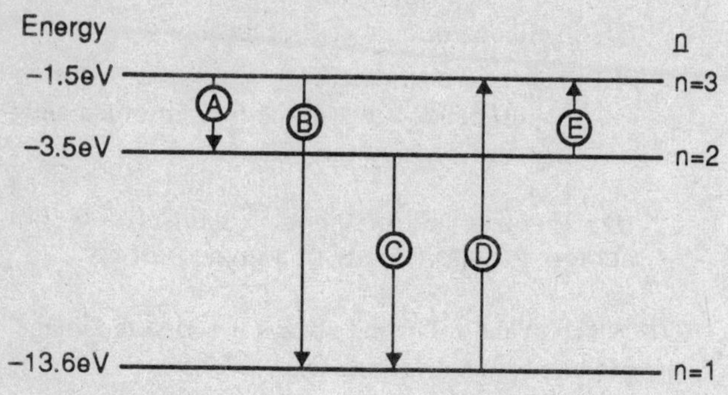

(A) A

(B) B

(C) C

(D) D

(E) E

(B) Arrow B represents a transition resulting in the *emission* of 12.1eV:

$$-1.5\text{eV} - (-13.6\text{eV}) = 12.1\text{eV}$$

Since energy and frequency are directly related, this transition will also represent a photon with the highest frequency.

39. A wire and a magnet are positioned or moved in a variety of ways. Which of the following will produce an electromotive force?

(A) Wire and magnet are stationary, more than 1m apart.

(B) Wire and magnet are stationary, separated by 5mm.

(C) Wire is moved parallel to stationary magnet.

(D) Magnet is moved parallel to stationary wire.

(E) Wire is moved perpendicular to magnet's lines of force.

(E) To produce an electromotive force the wire must cut across the lines of force of the magnetic field.

40. A stationary horn broadcasts an emergency distress signal at a constant frequency f. A stationary observer hears the signal and then begins to recede. This observer will perceive

(A) a signal with frequency f

(B) a signal with frequency less than f

(C) a signal with frequency greater than f

(D) a signal with frequency f initially, with the frequency continually increasing

(E) a signal with frequency f initially, with the frequency continually decreasing

(E) The person will initially hear a signal with frequency f. As the person moves away from the signal, the frequency will become lower. This situation illustrates the Doppler effect.

41. Which of the following correctly expresses the dimensions of torque? Assume m is mass, l is length, and t is time.

(A) ml^2t^{-2}

(B) $m^2l^2t^2$

(C) $ml^{-2}t^{-2}$

(D) ml^3t^{-2}

(E) ml^2t^{-3}

(A) Torque is defined as the product of the force and moment arm of the applied force:

$$\tau = F \cdot l$$

Force is expressed in newtons, and length in meters. The dimensions of force and length then:

$F = (\text{mass})(\text{acceleration})$ m = mass
$\tau = (m)(l/t_2)$ l = length
t = time

Therefore, the dimensions of torque:

$= (ml/t_2)(l)$
$= ml^2/t^2$ which is equivalent to ml^2t^{-2}

42. According to the first law of motion, if no net force is acting on an object, which of the following may correctly describe the object's motion?

I. The object will remain at rest.

II. The object will continue moving at a constant velocity.

III. The object will continue moving with a constant positive acceleration.

(A) I only
(B) III only
(C) I and II only
(D) I and III only
(E) I, II, and III

(C) As no net force is acting on the object, the acceleration must necessarily equal zero.

43. The formation of a rainbow occurs as a result of

(A) reflection
(B) dispersion
(C) luminous intensity
(D) luminous flux
(E) polarization

(B) A rainbow is formed by the dispersion of light. Similarly, the color spectrum produced by shining light through a prism also illustrates this principle.

44. Two point charges separated by a distance of 0.5m produce an electric force of F. If the distance between the point charges is decreased to 0.05m, the electric force would

(A) decrease by a factor of 10
(B) decrease by a factor of 100
(C) remain the same
(D) increase by a factor of 10
(E) increase by a factor of 100

(E) The force between two point charges is described by Coulomb's law:

$$F = k\frac{q_1q_2}{r^2}$$

Therefore, the force is inversely proportional to the square of the radius. As the distance separating the charges decreases by a factor of 10, the force will increase by a factor of $(10)^2$ or 100:

$$F \alpha \frac{1}{r^2}$$

$$F \alpha \frac{1}{\left(\frac{1}{10r}\right)^2} = \frac{1}{\frac{1}{100r^2}}$$

$$\therefore 100\ F \alpha \frac{1}{r^2}$$

45. The pascal is a unit of pressure, and is defined as one newton per square meter. The cubic meter defines the SI quantity, volume. A pascal multiplied by a cubic meter is a unit of

(A) work
(B) area
(C) power
(D) force
(E) density

(A) (Pressure) (Volume) = ? units

$$(Pa)\ (m^3)$$

$$\left(\frac{N}{m^2}\right)(m^3) = N \cdot m = \text{JOULE}$$

The joule is the unit of work.

46. Sound is a longitudinal wave and may be propagated in each of the following EXCEPT:

(A) steam

(B) water

(C) glass

(D) vacuum

(E) steel

(D) Sound waves require a medium for their propagation. Hence, sound waves cannot be propagated in a vacuum.

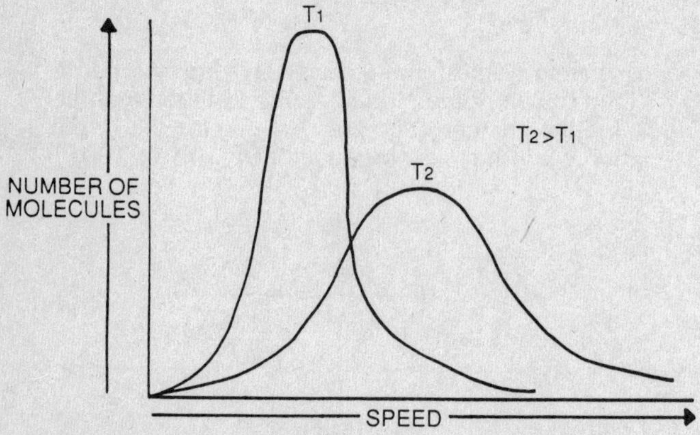

47. The graph above illustrates the distribution of molecular speeds for a pure sample at two different temperatures. The area under the curve represents the percentage of molecules at that range of speed. The same number of molecules are present at each temperature. Which of the following statements accurately reflects the data?

(A) All the molecules at the higher temperature have a greater speed than the molecules at the lower temperature.

(B) As the speeds increase the molecular size decreases.

(C) The distribution of speeds widens as the temperature decreases.

(D) As the temperature increases, the average molecular speed increases.

(E) The number of molecules at any given speed is always greater for the sample at the higher temperature.

(D) Only answer choice (D) accurately reflects the data presented.

Questions 48–49 relate to the schematic of the circuit shown below. Each labeled component provides 5 ohms resistance.

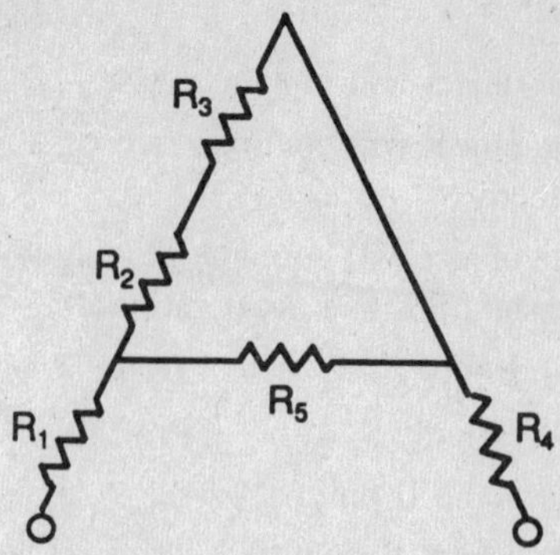

48. Which of the following illustrates a circuit equivalent to the one shown above?

(A)

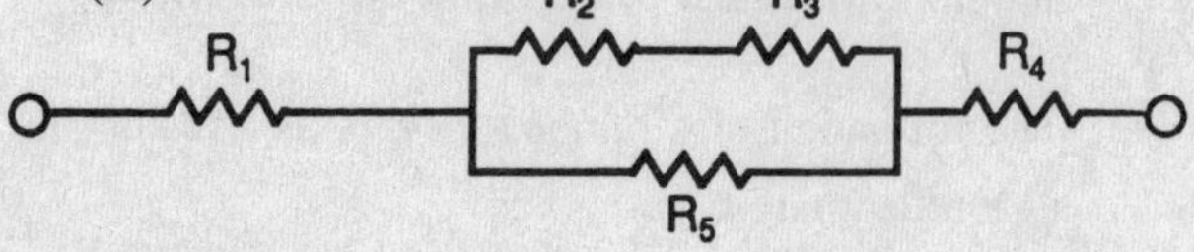

(B)

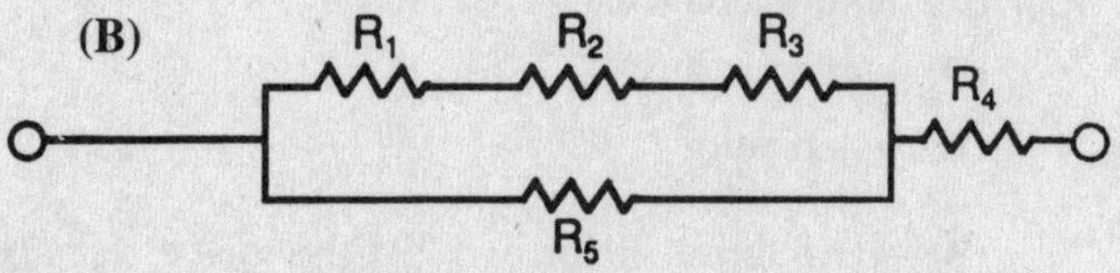

(C)

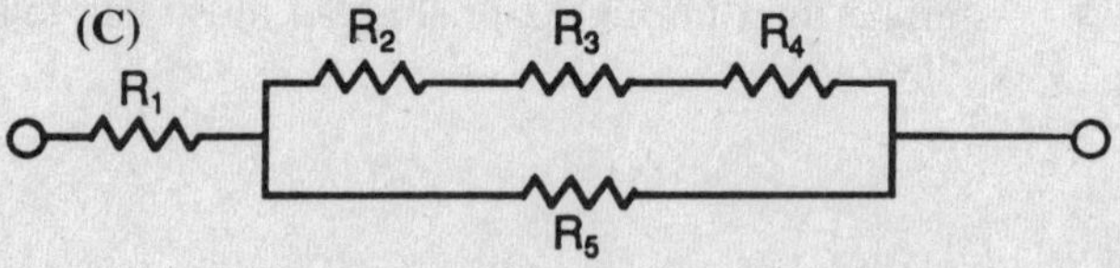

(D)

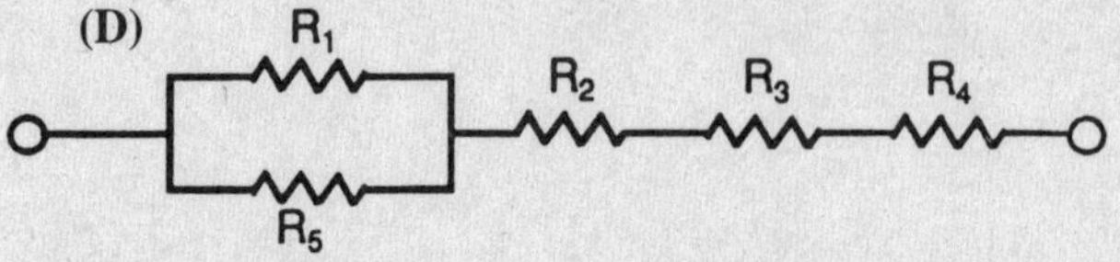

(E)

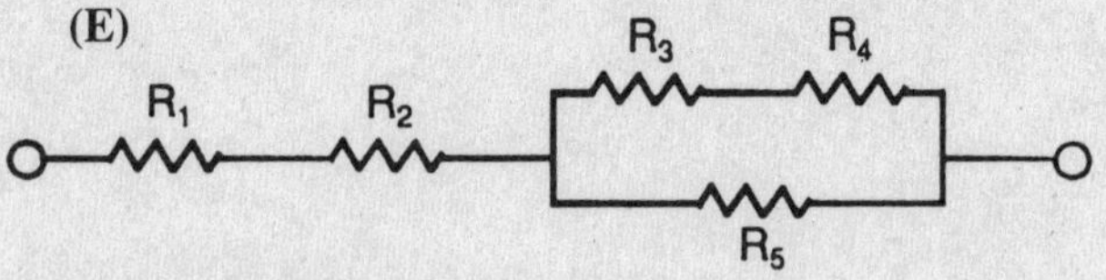

(A) The circuit illustrated in answer choice (A) is equivalent to the schematic illustrated above question 48. The other choices are not equivalent to the "A-shaped" schematic.

49. If the current flowing across R_4 is 2 amperes, what is the power dissipated by this component?

(A) 5 W

(B) 10 W

(C) 20 W

(D) 50 W

(E) It is impossible to calculate from the data given.

(C) Power is defined by the relationship

$P = i^2R$ where i is current and r is resistance

Substituting:

$$P = (2A)^2(5\Omega) = (4A^2)(5\Omega) = 20\text{ W}$$

50. A massless plank supports two objects as shown above. The labeled areas divide the plank into sections of uniform length. At which point could the plank be lifted without the blocks causing rotation?

(A) A

(B) B

(C) C

(D) D

(E) E

(A) For rotation *not* to occur, the clockwise and counterclockwise torques must be equal.

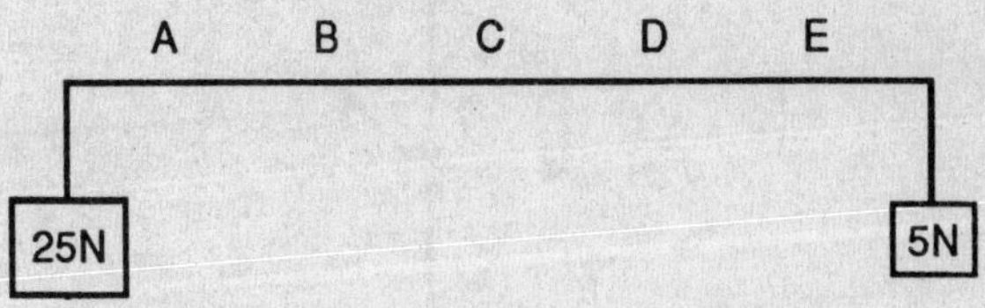

The plank is divided into six sections of equal length. If the plank is lifted at a distance *x* from one side, then the distance is 6*x* from the other side.

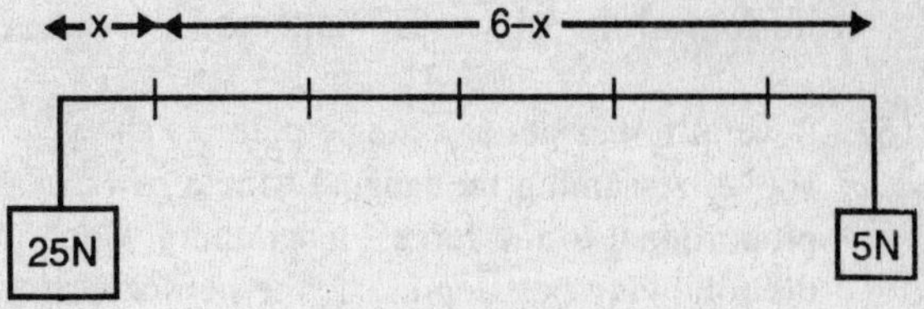

Recall the expression for torque:

$$\tau = F \cdot l$$

Setting clockwise and counterclockwise torques equal:

$$\tau_{cw} = \tau_{ccw}$$
$$(5N)(6-x) = (25N)(x)$$
$$30N - 5Nx = 25Nx$$
$$30N = 30Nx$$
$$1 = x$$

∴ The plank should be lifted at one unit length from the left side. This corresponds to (A).

51. A force is applied to an object through its center of gravity. On the basis of this force, the object possesses which of the following?

I. Translational acceleration

II. Rotational acceleration

III. Rotational equilibrium

(A) I only
(B) III only
(C) I and III only
(D) II and III only
(E) I, II, and III

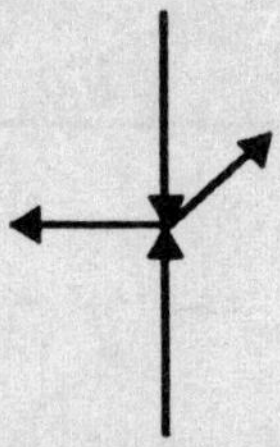

(C) The force acts through the object's center of gravity. Therefore the force will produce translational acceleration but will not cause rotational acceleration. Consequently, the rotational equilibrium of the object is unaffected.

52. Several forces act at a single point as shown above. Assuming the length of the arrows is proportional to the forces' magnitude, which of the following best represents the net force at the point?

(A) 
(B) 
(C) 
(D) 
(E) 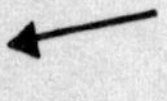

(E) Adding the vectors graphically:

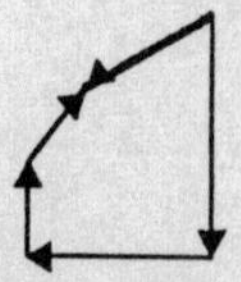

Answer choice (E) best represents the result.

53. Ice has a specific heat capacity of 0.5 kcal/kg°C. If 10 kcal of energy is added to 10kg of ice at −10°C, the result would be

(A) 10kg of ice at −8°C
(B) 10kg of ice at 0°C
(C) 10kg of water at 0°C
(D) 10kg of water at 1°C
(E) 10kg of water at 10°C

(A) The amount of heat transferred is described by the equation:

$Q = mc\Delta T$ where
q = heat transferred
m = mass
c = specific heat capacity
ΔT = temperature change

Substituting:

$$10 \text{ kcal} = (10 \text{ kg})(0.5 \text{ kcal/kg°C})\ \Delta T$$

$$\frac{10 \text{ kcal}}{5 \text{ kcal/°C}} = \Delta T$$

$$\Delta T = 2°\text{C}$$

Since the ice is initially −10°C, the result will be ice at −8°C.

54. Air moving past a plane wing causes the wing to lift. Which of the following may account for such action?

(A) Air flow past the upper portion of the wing is slower than air flow past the lower portion of the wing.

(B) The pressure on the lower surface of the wing is greater than the pressure on the upper surface of the wing.

(C) Air flow past the upper and lower portions of the wing is the same.

(D) The pressure differential between the upper and lower wing surfaces is zero.

(E) The pressure on the upper surface of the wing is slightly greater than the pressure on the lower surface of the wing.

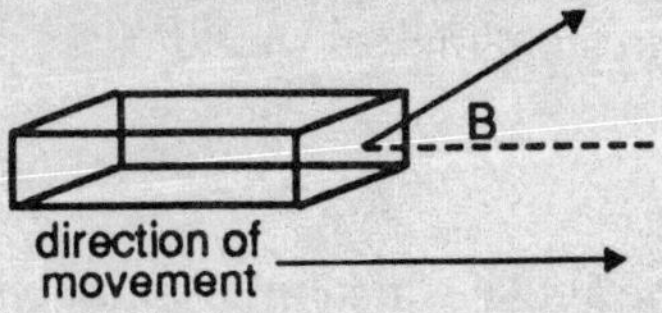

(B) This question describes an application of Bernoulli's law. In the case of an airplane wing, air moves more quickly over the top of the wing, and this causes a lower pressure over the top surface. The pressure differential leads to the "lift" of the wing.

55. A crate is pulled across a floor. The force pulling the crate acts at an angle θ. Which of the following best represents a force diagram of the situation?

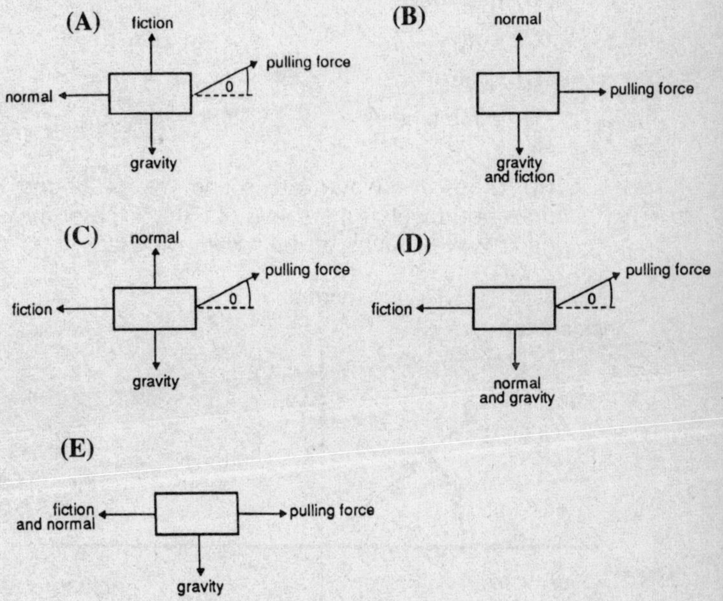

(C) Answer choice (C) best represents the force diagram under real conditions. The pulling force acts at an angle θ, friction opposes the direction of motion, gravity acts toward the center of the earth (downward), and the normal force is as illustrated.

56. A certain satellite is known to have a mass of 700kg on the earth's surface. If the satellite orbits the earth at a distance of five times the earth's radius, what will be its mass?

(A) 28 kg

(B) 150 kg

(C) 350 kg

(D) 600 kg

(E) 700 kg

(E) Mass is a measure of the amount of matter. It is independent of gravitational effects. Therefore, mass is unchanged.

57. Each of the following waves travels at the speed of light EXCEPT:

(A) microwaves

(B) ultrasonic

(C) x-rays

(D) radio

(E) gamma rays

(B) Ultrasonic waves are sound waves. Sound does not travel at the speed of light. Each of the other waves travels at the speed of light.

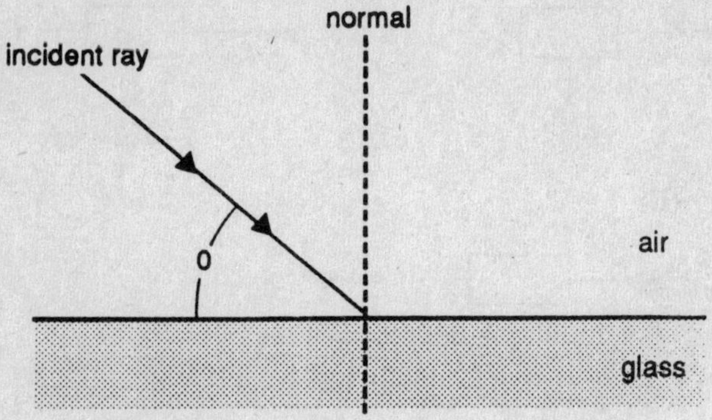

58. A light ray impinges upon the surface of a uniform piece of glass as shown above. What is the angle of reflection?

(A) 0°

(B) $90° - \Theta$

(C) 90°

(D) $180° - \Theta$

(E) Cannot be determined

(B) By definition, the angle of reflection equals the angle of incidence. The angle of incidence in this case is $90° - \theta$. Recall, the angle is measured with respect to the normal.

59. The indices of refraction for pairs of media are given below. In each case, light rays originate in medium 1 and are incident upon the surface of medium 2. Total internal reflection cannot occur in which pair?

	Index of Refraction	
	Medium 1	Medium 2
(A)	1.33	1.00
(B)	1.38	1.33
(C)	1.49	1.77
(D)	1.65	1.36
(E)	2.42	1.89

(C) Snell's law states

$$n_1 \sin \theta_1 = n_2 \sin \theta_2$$

For total internal reflection, $\theta_2 = 90°$ and the equation simplifies as $\sin 90° = 1$:

$$\frac{n_2}{n_1} = \sin \theta_1$$

From the above equation, n_2 must be less than n_1 for total internal reflection to occur. (The sine of an angle cannot exceed 1.)

60. Each of the following is a characteristic of an ideal gas EXCEPT:

(A) random molecular motion occurs

(B) elastic collisions occur

(C) molecules occupy small portion of volume relative to volume occupied by gas

(D) molecules attract each other readily

(E) repulsion between molecules does not occur

(D) For an ideal gas, it is assumed the gas molecules do not interact. That is, the molecules neither attract nor repulse each other. The remainder of the answer choices represent characteristics of an ideal gas.

Question 61–62

The concentric lines of force for a magnetic field due to a current in a straight wire are illustrated below. Assume the page represents a cross-sectional plane of the magnetic field.

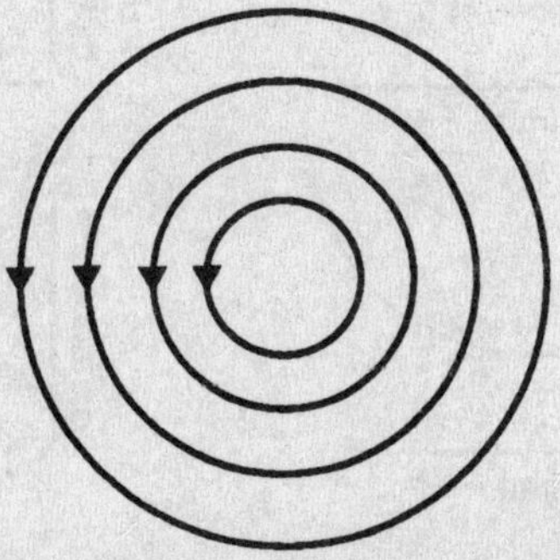

61. Which of the following most likely characterizes the direction of the current?

(A) The current flows into the page.

(B) The current flows out of the page.

(C) The current flows to the right.

(D) The current flows to the left.

(E) The current alternates; it flows into the page and then to the right.

(B) According to the right hand rule, the current will flow out of the page. Allow the fingers of the right hand to curl in the direction of the magnetic field. The extended thumb represents the direction of the current.

62. Another wire is laid parallel to the first straight wire. The current flowing in the second wire is equal in magnitude to the current flowing in the first wire. However, the direction of current flow is exactly opposite. Which of the following correctly describes the force between these wires?

(A) An attractive force exists

(B) A repulsive force exists

(C) No force exists

(D) Forces generated by each wire are always in the same direction

(E) Forces violate Newton's third law of motion

(B) The forces between parallel currents are attractive if the currents flow in the same direction. If the parallel currents flow in opposite directions, repulsive forces exist.

63. An astronaut orbits the earth in a space shuttle. In this orbit, the astronaut feels "weightless." Which of the following best explains such weightlessness?

(A) Absence of gravity

(B) Loss of frictional forces

(C) Astronaut and space shuttle both accelerate toward earth

(D) Gravitational forces affect space shuttle only

(E) No external forces act on space shuttle

(C) The astronaut, the space shuttle, and all of the shuttle contents experience the same gravitational force. Thus, everything accelerates toward the earth. Therefore, since the shuttle is accelerating toward the earth, it does not "push" back against the astronaut (like the floor of a building does to someone on earth). Thus, the astronaut feels "weightless."

64. The linear momentum of an object at time t is zero. Which of the following quantities is also necessarily equal to zero?

I. Velocity

II. Kinetic energy

III. Potential energy

(A) I only

(B) II only

(C) I and II only

(D) I and III only

(E) I, II, and III

(C) Linear momentum is defined by the expression:

$$p = mv$$

if $p = 0$, v must also $= 0$ $(m \neq 0)$

Since kinetic energy is described by the following equation:

$$K.E. = \frac{1}{2} mv^2$$

if $v = 0$, K.E. $= 0$

Potential energy, however, is independent of the object's velocity.

65. A 10kg object is acted on by only two forces, as illustrated above. If the object's acceleration is 1 m/s^2 to the left, what is the net force on the object?

(A) 0.1N to the right

(B) 0.1N to the left

(C) 10N to the right

(D) 10N to the left

(E) 100N to the left

(D) From the second law of motion:

$$F = ma$$

Since the mass and acceleration are given:

$$F = (10\ kg)\ (1 m/s^2)$$

$$F = 10N$$

The force will produce an acceleration in the direction of the force. Therefore, the net force is 10N to the left.

Questions 66–67 relate to the graph below.

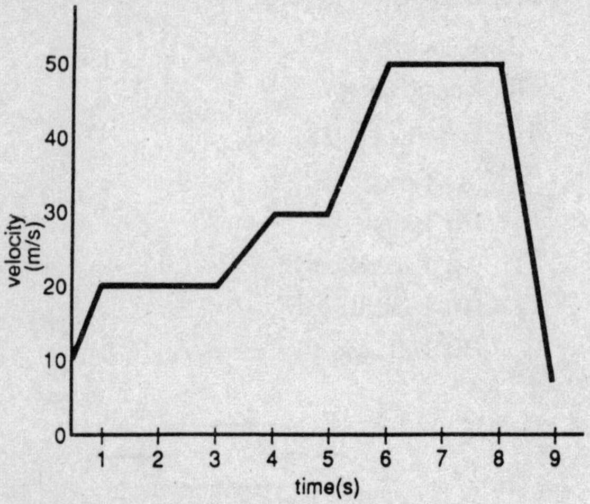

66. The approximate acceleration between the time period 4–5 seconds is

(A) 0 m/s^2

(B) 8 m/s^2

(C) 10 m/s^2

(D) 20 m/s^2

(E) 40 m/s^2

(A) Acceleration is described as the change in velocity per unit time:

$$a = \frac{\Delta v}{\Delta t}$$

In this case, the velocity is unchanged, so the acceleration is zero.

67. Which graph below best represents the time period 6–8 seconds?

(A)

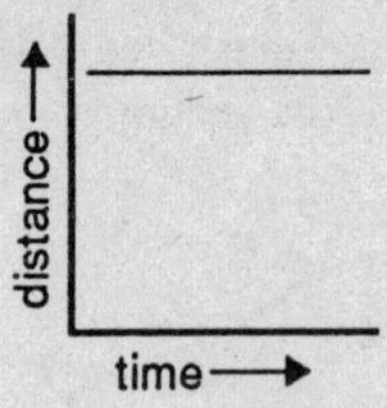

(B)

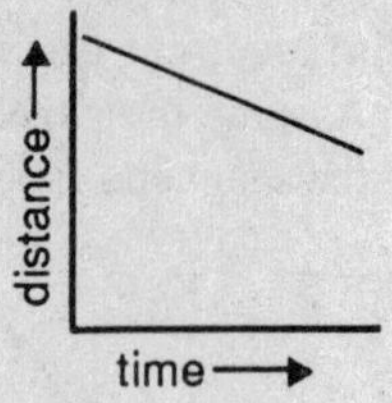

(C)

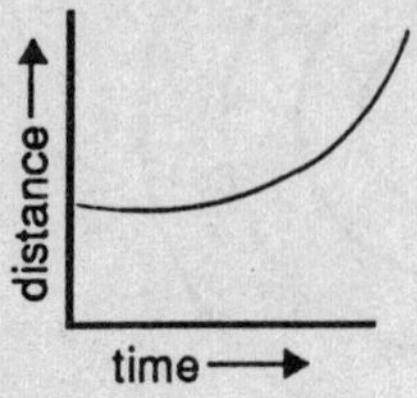

(D)

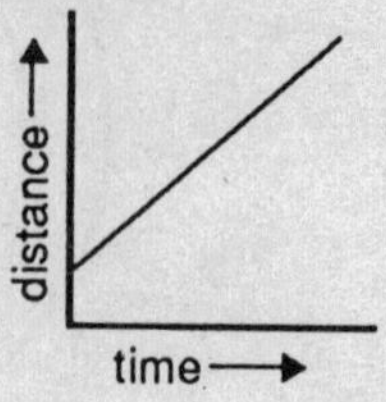

(E)

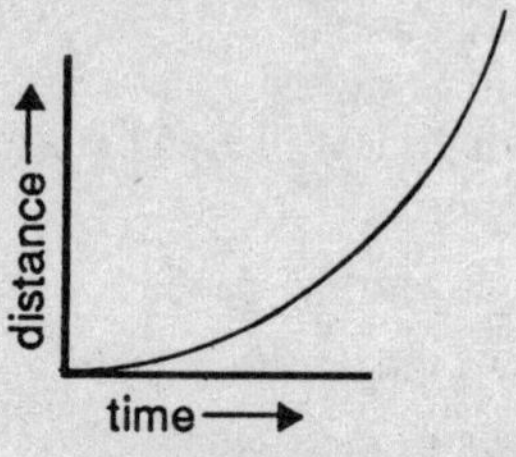

(D) In the time period 6–8 seconds, the velocity is constant. Thus, the distance covered continually increases over time. Since the velocity is uniform, the distance versus time graph will be linear with a positive slope.

68. The objective lens of a certain microscope has a magnification of 100x, while the eyepiece magnification is 10x. The magnification of this microscope is

(A) 0.1x

(B) 110x

(C) 1000x

(D) 10000x

(E) It is impossible to calculate from the data given.

(C) The total magnification of a lens system is simply the product of the magnifying powers of each lens:

$$\begin{aligned} \text{Magnification} &= m_1 \times m_2 \\ &= (100)\ (10) \\ &= 1000x \end{aligned}$$

69. A charge of 5.0×10^{-9}C is in a uniform electric field of 5.0×10^4 N/C. A force of magnitude 2.0×10^{-4} is applied but is unable to move the charge against the electric field. How much work is performed on the charge?

(A) 0 J

(B) 1.0×10^{-12} J

(C) 5.0×10^{-8} J

(D) 2.5×10^{-4} J

(E) 5.0×10^{-4} J

(A) Recall, work is the product of the applied force and the resultant displacement:

$$W = F \cdot d$$

for a charge then, $W = Eq \cdot d$

However, since no displacement occurs ($d = 0$), the work performed is zero.

70. An impulse produced by a 50N force on an object is 2.5NS. How long is the force acting on the object in order to produce such an impulse?

(A) 0.05 seconds

(B) 0.5 seconds

(C) 3.0 seconds

(D) 20.0 seconds

(E) 125.0 seconds

(A) Impulse is the product of the force and time interval that the force is applied:

$$\text{Impulse} = F\ \Delta t$$

Substituting:

$$2.5\text{NS} = (50\text{N})\ \Delta t$$

$$\Delta t = \frac{2.5\text{NS}}{50\text{N}} = 0.05\text{s}$$

$$4\ {}^1_1\text{H} \rightarrow {}^4_2\text{He} + 2\,{}^0_1\text{e} + \text{energy}$$

71. The reaction shown above is an example of which of the following nuclear processes?

(A) Alpha decay

(B) Fusion

(C) Fission

(D) Beta decay

(E) Nuclear binding reaction

(B) In the reaction given, four lighter nuclei are combined to form a nuclei with a greater mass. This is an example of fusion.

72. A current of 2 amperes flows through a conductor with a resistance of 6 ohms. The current flows for 2 seconds. How much heat energy develops in the conductor as a result of current flow?

(A) 12 J

(B) 24 J

(C) 48 J

(D) 96 J

(E) 144 J

(C) Joule's law describes the heat energy developed in a conductor:

$$W = i^2Rt$$

Substituting:

$$\begin{aligned} W &= (2\text{A})^2(6\Omega)(2\text{s}) \\ &= 48\text{ J} \end{aligned}$$

Note:

$$\begin{aligned} (\text{A} \cdot \Omega) &= \text{v} \\ (\text{A} \cdot \text{s}) &= \text{C} \\ \text{v} \cdot \text{c} &= \text{J} \end{aligned}$$

73. A person rotates with extended arms on a turntable. Assume dissipative forces are negligible. The person's arms are then folded and held close to his chest. Which of the following correctly describes the result of such an action?

(A) The person increases his rotational inertia.

(B) The person's angular velocity increases.

(C) The person's rotational inertia is unchanged.

(D) The person's angular velocity is unchanged.

(E) The person's angular momentum increases.

(B) In the absence of outside forces, angular momentum is conserved. Angular momentum = constant = (angular velocity) x (rotational inertia). Therefore, if the rotational inertia is decreased by bringing the arms close to the body, the angular velocity must increase.

74. A pith ball electroscope possesses a certain charge. A charged glass rod is then held close to the electroscope. The pith ball moves noticeably toward the glass rod. Which of the following accounts for such an interaction?

(A) There are subtle gravitational forces between the glass rod and the pith ball.

(B) The glass rod and the pith ball each possess a net positive charge.

(C) The glass rod and the pith ball each possess a net negative charge.

(D) The glass rod and the pith ball are oppositely charged.

(E) The glass rod mass greatly exceeds the mass of the pith ball.

(D) Like charges repel each other while objects of opposite charge will experience a net attractive force. Gravitational forces are much too weak to account for the observed movement.

75. A total of 100 J of energy is supplied to a machine. The machine is then capable of displacing a 30 N object 1.5m. What is the approximate efficiency of the machine?

(A) 15%

(B) 20%

(C) 30%

(D) 45%

(E) 60%

(D) The efficiency of a machine is described by the relationship:

$$\text{Efficiency} = \frac{\text{Useful work output}}{\text{Work input}}$$

The work input is given (100 J). The work output:

$$\begin{aligned} W &= F \cdot d \\ &= (30\text{N})\ (1.5\text{m}) \\ &= 45\ \text{J} \end{aligned}$$

Therefore, the efficiency is:

$$\text{Eff} = \frac{45\text{J}}{100\text{J}} = 0.45 \text{ or } 45\%$$